DRAMA
for Students

National Advisory Board

DRAMA
for Students

**Presenting Analysis, Context, and Criticism on
Commonly Studied Dramas**

Volume 22

Anne Marie Hacht,
Project Editor

Foreword by Carole L. Hamilton

THOMSON
★
™
GALE

Detroit • New York • San Francisco • San Diego • New Haven, Conn. • Waterville, Maine • London • Munich

Drama for Students, Volume 22

Project Editor
Anne Marie Hacht

Editorial
Sara Constantakis, Ira Mark Milne

Rights Acquisition and Management
Lisa Kincade, Timothy Sisler

Manufacturing
Rhonda Williams

Imaging
Lezlie Light, Mike Logusz, Kelly A. Quin

Product Design
Pamela A. E. Galbreath

Product Manager
Meggin Condino

ISBN 0-7876-8118-0
ISSN 1094-9232

Printed in the United States of America
10 9 8 7 6 5 4 3 2 1

Table of Contents

The Study of Drama

We study drama in order to learn what meaning others have made of life, to comprehend what it takes to produce a work of art, and to glean some understanding of ourselves. Drama produces in a separate, aesthetic world, a moment of being for the audience to experience, while maintaining the detachment of a reflective observer.

Drama is a representational art, a visible and audible narrative presenting virtual, fictional characters within a virtual, fictional universe. Dramatic realizations may pretend to approximate reality or else stubbornly defy, distort, and deform reality into an artistic statement. From this separate universe that is obviously not "real life" we expect a valid reflection upon reality, yet drama never is mistaken for reality—the methods of theater are integral to its form and meaning. Theater is art, and art's appeal lies in its ability both to approximate life and to depart from it. For in intruding its distorted version of life into our consciousness, art gives us a new perspective and appreciation of life and reality. Although all aesthetic experiences perform this service, theater does it most effectively by creating a separate, cohesive universe that freely acknowledges its status as an art form.

And what is the purpose of the aesthetic universe of drama? The potential answers to such a question are nearly as many and varied as there are plays written, performed, and enjoyed. Dramatic texts can be problems posed, answers asserted, or moments portrayed. Dramas (tragedies as well as comedies) may serve strictly "to ease the anguish of a torturing hour" (as stated in William Shakespeare's *A Midsummer Night's Dream*)—to divert and entertain—or aspire to move the viewer to action with social issues. Whether to entertain or to instruct, affirm or influence, pacify or shock, dramatic art wraps us in the spell of its imaginary world for the length of the work and then dispenses us back to the real world, entertained, purged, as Aristotle said, of pity and fear, and edified—or at least weary enough to sleep peacefully.

It is commonly thought that theater, being an art of performance, must be experienced—seen—in order to be appreciated fully. However, to view a production of a dramatic text is to be limited to a single interpretation of that text—all other interpretations are for the moment closed off, inaccessible. In the process of producing a play, the director, stage designer, and performers interpret and transform the script into a work of art that always departs in some measure from the author's original conception. Novelist and critic Umberto Eco, in his *The Role of the Reader: Explorations in the Semiotics of Texts* (Indiana University Press, 1979), explained, "In short, we can say that every performance offers us a complete and satisfying version of the work, but at the same time makes it incomplete for us, because it cannot simultaneously give all the other artistic solutions which the work may admit."

Thus Laurence Olivier's coldly formal and neurotic film presentation of Shakespeare's *Hamlet* (in which he played the title character as well as directed) shows marked differences from subsequent adaptations. While Olivier's Hamlet is clearly entangled in a Freudian relationship with his mother Gertrude, he would be incapable of shushing her with the impassioned kiss that Mel Gibson's mercurial Hamlet (in director Franco Zeffirelli's 1990 film) does. Although each of the performances rings true to Shakespeare's text, each is also a mutually exclusive work of art. Also important to consider are the time periods in which each of these films were produced: Olivier made his film in 1948, a time in which overt references to sexuality (especially incest) were frowned upon. Gibson and Zeffirelli made their film in a culture more relaxed and comfortable with these issues. Just as actors and directors can influence the presentation of drama, so too can the time period of the production affect what the audience will see.

A play script is an open text from which an infinity of specific realizations may be derived. Dramatic scripts that are more open to interpretive creativity (such as those of Ntozake Shange and Tomson Highway) actually require the creative improvisation of the production troupe in order to complete the text. Even the most prescriptive scripts (those of Neil Simon, Lillian Hellman, and Robert Bolt, for example), can never fully control the actualization of live performance, and circumstantial events, including the attitude and receptivity of the audience, make every performance a unique event. Thus, while it is important to view a production of a dramatic piece, if one wants to understand a drama fully it is equally important to read the original dramatic text.

The reader of a dramatic text or script is not limited by either the specific interpretation of a given production or by the unstoppable action of a moving spectacle. The reader of a dramatic text may discover the nuances of the play's language, structure, and events at their own pace. Yet studied alone, the author's blueprint for artistic pro-

duction does not tell the whole story of a play's life and significance. One also needs to assess the play's critical reviews to discover how it resonated to cultural themes at the time of its debut and how the shifting tides of cultural interest have revised its interpretation and impact on audiences. And to do this, one needs to know a little about the culture of the times which produced the play as well as the author who penned it.

Drama for Students supplies this material in a useful compendium for the student of dramatic theater. Covering a range of dramatic works that span from 442 BC to the present, this book focuses on significant theatrical works whose themes and form transcend the uncertainty of dramatic fads. These are plays that have proven to be both memorable and teachable. *Drama for Students* seeks to enhance appreciation of these dramatic texts by providing scholarly materials written with the secondary and college/university student in mind. It provides for each play a concise summary of the plot and characters as well as a detailed explanation of its themes. In addition, background material on the historical context of the play, its critical reception, and the author's life help the student to understand the work's position in the chronicle of dramatic history. For each play entry a new work of scholarly criticism is also included, as well as segments of other significant critical works for handy reference. A thorough bibliography provides a starting point for further research.

This series offers comprehensive educational resources for students of drama. *Drama for Students* is a vital book for dramatic interpretation and a valuable addition to any reference library.

Source: Eco, Umberto, *The Role of the Reader: Explorations in the Semiotics of Texts,* Indiana University Press, 1979.

Carole L. Hamilton
Author and Instructor of English at
Cary Academy, Cary, North Carolina

Introduction

Purpose of the Book

The purpose of *Drama for Students* (*DfS*) is to provide readers with a guide to understanding, enjoying, and studying dramas by giving them easy access to information about the work. Part of Gale's "For Students" literature line, *DfS* is specifically designed to meet the curricular needs of high school and undergraduate college students and their teachers, as well as the interests of general readers and researchers considering specific plays. While each volume contains entries on "classic" dramas frequently studied in classrooms, there are also entries containing hard-to-find information on contemporary plays, including works by multicultural, international, and women playwrights.

The information covered in each entry includes an introduction to the play and the work's author; a plot summary, to help readers unravel and understand the events in a drama; descriptions of important characters, including explanation of a given character's role in the drama as well as discussion about that character's relationship to other characters in the play; analysis of important themes in the drama; and an explanation of important literary techniques and movements as they are demonstrated in the play.

In addition to this material, which helps the readers analyze the play itself, students are also provided with important information on the literary and historical background informing each work. This includes a historical context essay, a box comparing the time or place the drama was written to modern Western culture, a critical essay, and excerpts from critical essays on the play. A unique feature of *DfS* is a specially commissioned critical essay on each drama, targeted toward the student reader.

To further aid the student in studying and enjoying each play, information on media adaptations is provided (if available), as well as reading suggestions for works of fiction and nonfiction on similar themes and topics. Classroom aids include ideas for research papers and lists of critical sources that provide additional material on each drama.

Selection Criteria

The titles for each volume of *DfS* were selected by surveying numerous sources on teaching literature and analyzing course curricula for various school districts. Some of the sources surveyed included: literature anthologies; *Reading Lists for College-Bound Students: The Books Most Recommended by America's Top Colleges*; textbooks on teaching dramas; a College Board survey of plays commonly studied in high schools; a National Council of Teachers of English (NCTE) survey of plays commonly studied in high schools; St. James Press's *International Dictionary of Theatre*; and Arthur Applebee's 1993 study *Literature in the Secondary School: Studies of Curriculum and Instruction in the United States*.

Input was also solicited from our advisory board, as well as from educators from various areas. From these discussions, it was determined that each volume should have a mix of "classic" dramas (those works commonly taught in literature classes) and contemporary dramas for which information is often hard to find. Because of the interest in expanding the canon of literature, an emphasis was also placed on including works by international, multicultural, and women playwrights. Our advisory board members—educational professionals—helped pare down the list for each volume. If a work was not selected for the present volume, it was often noted as a possibility for a future volume. As always, the editor welcomes suggestions for titles to be included in future volumes.

How Each Entry Is Organized

Each entry, or chapter, in *DfS* focuses on one play. Each entry heading lists the full name of the play, the author's name, and the date of the play's publication. The following elements are contained in each entry:

- **Introduction:** a brief overview of the drama which provides information about its first appearance, its literary standing, any controversies surrounding the work, and major conflicts or themes within the work.

- **Author Biography:** this section includes basic facts about the author's life, and focuses on events and times in the author's life that inspired the drama in question.

- **Plot Summary:** a description of the major events in the play. Subheads demarcate the play's various acts or scenes.

- **Characters:** an alphabetical listing of major characters in the play. Each character name is followed by a brief to an extensive description of the character's role in the play, as well as discussion of the character's actions, relationships, and possible motivation.

  Characters are listed alphabetically by last name. If a character is unnamed—for instance, the Stage Manager in *Our Town*—the character is listed as "The Stage Manager" and alphabetized as "Stage Manager." If a character's first name is the only one given, it will appear alphabetically by that name. Variant names are also included for each character. Thus, the nickname "Babe" would head the listing for a character in *Crimes of the Heart*, but below that listing would be her less-mentioned married name "Rebecca Botrelle."

- **Themes:** a thorough overview of how the major topics, themes, and issues are addressed within the play. Each theme discussed appears in a separate subhead, and is easily accessed through the boldface entries in the Subject/Theme Index.

- **Style:** this section addresses important style elements of the drama, such as setting, point of view, and narration; important literary devices used, such as imagery, foreshadowing, symbolism; and, if applicable, genres to which the work might have belonged, such as Gothicism or Romanticism. Literary terms are explained within the entry, but can also be found in the Glossary.

- **Historical Context:** this section outlines the social, political, and cultural climate *in which the author lived and the play was created.* This section may include descriptions of related historical events, pertinent aspects of daily life in the culture, and the artistic and literary sensibilities of the time in which the work was written. If the play is a historical work, information regarding the time in which the play is set is also included. Each section is broken down with helpful subheads.

- **Critical Overview:** this section provides background on the critical reputation of the play, including bannings or any other public controversies surrounding the work. For older plays, this section includes a history of how the drama was first received and how perceptions of it may have changed over the years; for more recent plays, direct quotes from early reviews may also be included.

- **Criticism:** an essay commissioned by *DfS* which specifically deals with the play and is written specifically for the student audience, as well as excerpts from previously published criticism on the work (if available).

- **Sources:** an alphabetical list of critical material used in compiling the entry, with full bibliographical information.

- **Further Reading:** an alphabetical list of other critical sources which may prove useful for the student. It includes full bibliographical information and a brief annotation.

In addition, each entry contains the following highlighted sections, set apart from the main text as sidebars:

- **Media Adaptations:** if available, a list of important film and television adaptations of the play, including source information. The list may also include such variations on the work as audio recordings, musical adaptations, and other stage interpretations.

- **Topics for Further Study:** a list of potential study questions or research topics dealing with the play. This section includes questions related to other disciplines the student may be studying, such as American history, world history, science, math, government, business, geography, economics, psychology, etc.

- **Compare and Contrast:** an "at-a-glance" comparison of the cultural and historical differences between the author's time and culture and late twentieth century or early twenty-first century Western culture. This box includes pertinent parallels between the major scientific, political, and cultural movements of the time or place the drama was written, the time or place the play was set (if a historical work), and modern Western culture. Works written after 1990 may not have this box.

- **What Do I Read Next?:** a list of works that might complement the featured play or serve as a contrast to it. This includes works by the same author and others, works of fiction and nonfiction, and works from various genres, cultures, and eras.

Other Features

DfS includes "The Study of Drama," a foreword by Carole Hamilton, an educator and author who specializes in dramatic works. This essay examines the basis for drama in societies and what drives people to study such work. The essay also discusses how *Drama for Students* can help teachers show students how to enrich their own reading/viewing experiences.

A Cumulative Author/Title Index lists the authors and titles covered in each volume of the *DfS* series.

A Cumulative Nationality/Ethnicity Index breaks down the authors and titles covered in each volume of the *DfS* series by nationality and ethnicity.

A Subject/Theme Index, specific to each volume, provides easy reference for users who may be studying a particular subject or theme rather than a single work. Significant subjects from events to broad themes are included, and the entries pointing to the specific theme discussions in each entry are indicated in **boldface**.

Each entry may include illustrations, including a photo of the author, stills from stage productions, and stills from film adaptations, if available.

Citing **Drama for Students**

When writing papers, students who quote directly from any volume of *Drama for Students* may use the following general forms. These examples are based on MLA style; teachers may request that students adhere to a different style, so the following examples may be adapted as needed.

When citing text from *DfS* that is not attributed to a particular author (i.e., the Themes, Style, Historical Context sections, etc.), the following format should be used in the bibliography section:

> *"Our Town." Drama for Students*. Eds. David Galens and Lynn Spampinato. Vol. 1. Detroit: Gale, 1998. 227–30.

When quoting the specially commissioned essay from *DfS* (usually the first piece under the "Criticism" subhead), the following format should be used:

> Fiero, John. Critical Essay on *Twilight: Los Angeles, 1992. Drama for Students*. Eds. David Galens and Lynn Spampinato. Vol. 2. Detroit: Gale, 1998. 247–49.

When quoting a journal or newspaper essay that is reprinted in a volume of *DfS*, the following form may be used:

> Rich, Frank. "Theatre: A Mamet Play, *Glengarry Glen Ross.*" *New York Theatre Critics' Review* Vol. 45, No. 4 (March 5, 1984), 5–7; excerpted and reprinted in *Drama for Students*, Vol. 2, eds. David Galens and Lynn Spampinato (Detroit: Gale, 1998), pp. 51–53.

When quoting material reprinted from a book that appears in a volume of *DfS*, the following form may be used:

> Kerr, Walter. *"The Miracle Worker,"* in *The Theatre in Spite of Itself*. Simon & Schuster, 1963. 255–57; excerpted and reprinted in *Drama for Students*, Vol. 2, eds. David Galens and Lynn Spampinato (Detroit: Gale, 1998), pp. 123–24.

We Welcome Your Suggestions

The editor of *Drama for Students* welcomes your comments and ideas. Readers who wish to suggest dramas to appear in future volumes, or who have other suggestions, are cordially invited to contact the editor. You may contact the editor via E-mail at: **ForStudentsEditors@thomson.com.** Or write to the editor at:

Editor, *Drama for Students*
Thomson Gale
27500 Drake Rd.
Farmington Hills, MI 48331-3535

Literary Chronology

1580: Thomas Middleton is born in London, England; his exact date of birth is unknown, but he was baptized on April 18.

1622: Thomas Middleton's *The Changeling* is published.

1627: Thomas Middleton dies of natural causes and is buried in Newington Butts, London, England.

1743: Hannah Cowley (Hannah Parkhouse) is born in Tiverton, Devonshire, England.

1780: Hannah Cowley's *The Belle's Stratagem* is published.

1809: Hannah Cowley dies in Devonshire, England.

1856: George Bernard Shaw is born on July 26 in Dublin, Ireland.

1874: W. (William) Somerset Maugham is born on January 25 in Paris, France.

1885: Sophie Treadwell is born on October 3 in Stockton, California.

1894: George Bernard Shaw's *Arms and the Man* is published.

1896: Antonin Artaud is born on September 4 in Marseilles, France.

1925: George Bernard Shaw is awarded the Nobel Prize for Literature.

1928: Sophie Treadwell's *Machinal* is published.

1932: W. Somerset Maugham's *For Services Rendered* is published.

1933: Michael Frayn is born on September 8 in London, England.

1935: Antonin Artaud's *The Cenci* is published.

1941: Nora Ephron is born on May 19 in New York, New York.

1948: Antonin Artaud dies of cancer.

1950: George Bernard Shaw dies on November 2 at his home in Hertfordshire, England.

1950: Anna Deavere Smith is born on September 18 in Baltimore, Maryland.

1954: Judith Thompson is born on September 20 in Montreal, Canada.

1957: Paul Rudnick is born in Piscataway, New Jersey.

1964: Suzan-Lori Parks is born in Fort Knox, Kentucky.

1965: W. Somerset Maugham dies in Nice, France.

1970: Sophie Treadwell dies on February 20.

1991: Paul Rudnick's *I Hate Hamlet* is published.

1992: Anna Deavere Smith's *Fires in the Mirror* is published.

1993: Anna Deavere Smith's *Fires in the Mirror* is a runner-up for the Pulitzer Prize in Drama.

1994: Joan Ackermann's *Off the Map* is published.

1998: Michael Frayn's *Copenhagen* is published.

2000: Moisés Kaufman's *The Laramie Project* is published.

2001: Judith Thompson's *Habitat* is published.

2001: Suzan-Lori Parks's *Topdog/Underdog* is published.

2002: Suzan-Lori Parks's *Topdog/Underdog* wins the Pulitzer Prize for Drama.

2002: Nora Ephron's *Imaginary Friends* is published.

Acknowledgments

The editors wish to thank the copyright holders of the excerpted criticism included in this volume and the permissions managers of many book and magazine publishing companies for assisting us in securing reproduction rights. We are also grateful to the staffs of the Detroit Public Library, the Library of Congress, the University of Detroit Mercy Library, Wayne State University Purdy/Kresge Library Complex, and the University of Michigan Libraries for making their resources available to us. Following is a list of the copyright holders who have granted us permission to reproduce material in this volume of *Drama for Students (DfS)*. Every effort has been made to trace copyright, but if omissions have been made, please let us know.

COPYRIGHTED MATERIALS IN *DfS*, VOLUME 22, WERE REPRODUCED FROM THE FOLLOWING PERIODICALS:

The Chronicle of Higher Education, v. 46, May 5, 2000 for "Frayn's 'Copenhagen' Plays Well, At History's Expense," by Paul Lawrence Rose. Copyright © 2000 by *The Chronicle of Higher Education*. Reproduced by permission of the author.—*Comparative Drama*, v. 35, fall–winter, 2001–2002. Copyright © 2002, by the editors of *Comparative Drama*. Reproduced by permission.—*Critical Quarterly*, v. 5, summer, 1963. Copyright © 1963 by Basil Blackwell Ltd. Reproduced by permission of Blackwell Publishing Ltd.—*The Drama Review*, v. 37, winter, 1993 for "Anna Deavere Smith: Acting as Incorporation," by Richard Schechner. Copyright © 1993 by New York University and the Massachusetts Institute of Technology. Reproduced by permission of the publisher and the author.—*English Studies*, v. 80, 1999. Copyright © 1999 Swets & Zeitlinger. Reproduced by permission.—*Interdisciplinary Science Reviews*, v. 27, autumn, 2002. Reproduced by permission.—*The Massachusetts Review*, v. 42, summer, 2001. Copyright © 2001. Reprinted by permission from *The Massachusetts Review*.—*Modern Drama*, v. 37, fall, 1994. Copyright © 1994 by the University of Toronto, Graduate Centre for Study of Drama. Reproduced by permission.—*Modern Language Quarterly*, v. 27, June, 1966. Copyright © 1966, University of Washington. All rights reserved. Used by permission of the publisher.—*The Nation*, v. 276, January 27, 2003. Copyright © 2003 by *The Nation* Magazine/The Nation Company, Inc. Reproduced by permission.— *The New Republic*, v. 207, July 6, 1992; v. 222, June 19, 2000. Copyright © 1992, 2000 by The New Republic, Inc. Both reproduced by permission of *The New Republic*.—*Newsweek*, v. 119, June 1, 1992. Copyright © 1992 Newsweek, Inc. All rights reserved. Reprinted by permission.— *The University of Mississippi Studies in English*, v. 8, 1990. Copyright © 1990 The University of Mississippi. Reproduced by permission.

COPYRIGHTED MATERIALS IN *DfS*, VOLUME 22, WERE REPRODUCED FROM THE FOLLOWING BOOKS:

Brittin, Norman A. From *Thomas Middleton*. Twayne Publishers, 1972. Copyright © 1972 by Twayne Publishers, Inc. All rights reserved.

Contributors

Bryan Aubrey: Aubrey holds a Ph.D. in English and has published many articles on English drama. Entry on *The Changeling*. Original essay on *The Changeling*.

Laura Carter: Carter is currently employed as a freelance writer. Original essays on *I Hate Hamlet* and *Imaginary Friends*.

Curt Guyette: Guyette, a longtime journalist, graduated from the University of Pittsburgh with a degree in English. Original essay on *Habitat*.

Joyce Hart: Hart is a freelance writer and author of several books. Entries on *Copenhagen* and *The Laramie Project*. Original essays on *Copenhagen* and *The Laramie Project*.

Catherine Dybiec Holm: Holm is a short story and novel author and a freelance writer. Original essay on *Topdog/Underdog*.

David Kelly: Kelly is an instructor of creative writing and literature. Entry on *I Hate Hamlet*. Original essay on *I Hate Hamlet*.

Lois Kerschen: Kerschen is a school district administrator and freelance writer. Entry on *Arms and the Man*. Original essay on *Arms and the Man*.

Anthony Martinelli: Martinelli is a Seattle-based freelance writer and editor. Entries on *The Belle's Stratagem*, *Machinal*, and *Off the Map*. Original essays on *The Belle's Stratagem*, *Machinal*, and *Off the Map*.

Wendy Perkins: Perkins is a professor of American and English literature and film. Entries on *For Services Rendered* and *Imaginary Friends*. Original essays on *For Services Rendered* and *Imaginary Friends*.

David Remy: Remy is a freelance writer in Warrington, Florida. Entry on *Topdog/Underdog*. Original essays on *I Hate Hamlet* and *Topdog/Underdog*.

Scott Trudell: Trudell is an independent scholar with a bachelor's degree in English literature. Entries on *The Cenci*, *Fires in the Mirror*, and *Habitat*. Original essays on *The Cenci*, *Fires in the Mirror*, and *Habitat*.

Carol Ullmann: Ullmann is a freelance writer and editor. Original essay on *Topdog/Underdog*.

Arms and the Man

GEORGE BERNARD
SHAW

1894

Shaw was already a celebrity arts critic and socialist lecturer when he wrote *Arms and the Man* in 1894. One of Shaw's earliest attempts at writing for the theatre, it was also his first commercial success as a playwright. Although it played for only one season at an avant-garde theatre, thanks to the financial backing of a friend, it was later produced in America in 1895. Accustomed to the melodramas of the age, however, even sophisticated audiences often did not discern the serious purpose of Shaw's play. Thus, Shaw considered it a failure.

True success did not come until 1898, when *Arms and the Man* was published as one of the "pleasant" plays in Shaw's collection called *Plays: Pleasant and Unpleasant*, and it subsequently gained popularity as a written work. Included in this collection of plays are lengthy explanatory prefaces, which note significant issues in the plays and which have been invaluable to critics. In place of brief stage directions, Shaw's plays also included lengthy instructions and descriptions. Another unique aspect of *Arms and the Man* was its use of a woman as the central character.

Set during the four-month-long Serbo-Bulgarian War that occurred between November 1885 and March 1886, this play is a satire on the foolishness of glorifying something so terrible as war, as well as a satire on the foolishness of basing your affections on idealistic notions of love. These themes brought reality and a timeless lesson to the comic stage. Consequently, once Shaw's genius was recognized, *Arms and the Man* became one of Shaw's

George Bernard Shaw Library of Congress

most popular plays and has remained a classic ever since.

AUTHOR BIOGRAPHY

Considered one of the greatest English-speaking dramatist since Shakespeare, George Bernard Shaw was born July 26, 1856, in Dublin, Ireland, and had a long and productive life. He was the only son and youngest of three children born to George Carr and Lucinda Elizabeth Gurly Shaw, who were Irish Protestant gentry. Shaw's education involved tutoring from an uncle and at a series of schools, but he quit school at fifteen to work in an estate agent's office for five years. In 1876, he went to London to join his sister and his mother, who had left Shaw's alcoholic father to pursue careers as a music teacher and opera singer.

Shaw was supported by his mother and sister as he wrote five unsuccessful novels. In 1888, he became the music critic for a newspaper, and then in 1895, he took a position as the drama critic at the *Saturday Review*, a position he held for three years. A devotee of Henrik Ibsen, he wrote *The Quintessence of Ibsenism* (1890) and modeled his own works after the individualism and the moral

and social issues that he saw in Ibsen's drama. Through his own plays, Shaw is credited with creating the "drama of ideas." Among his best-known plays are *Arms and the Man* (1894), *Saint Joan* (1923), *Man and Superman* (1905), *Major Barbara* (1905), *Candida* (1897), and *Pygmalion* (first English production in 1914; it was produced in German translation in 1913). *Pygmalion* was made into a movie, for which Shaw won an Academy Award for best screenplay in 1938. The play was later made into a musical, *My Fair Lady* (1964), with book and score by Alan Jay Lerner and music by Frederick Lowe; the musical version retained the plot, characters, and many of the lines from the original play.

In 1898, Shaw married Charlotte Francis Payne-Townshend, an Irish heiress. Their marriage lasted until her death in 1943. A vegetarian, teetotaler, and fervent socialist, Shaw championed the causes of women and the poor. He was an active member in the Fabian Society, which proposed gradual, nonrevolutionary socialist reforms in the structure of society and the economy. In 1895, with Sidney and Beatrice Webb, he helped establish the London School of Economics.

Shaw wrote numerous pamphlets and kept busy as a lecturer on issues in politics, economics, and sociology. He was also a prolific letter writer. Greatly criticized for his opposition to World War I, Shaw was eventually forgiven by the public as his predictions about the conflict came true and people started to understand the true nature of war. In 1925, he won the Nobel Prize for Literature. He died November 2, 1950, at his home in Hertfordshire, England. He left his fortune to the movement for rational spelling, the British Library, and the Royal Academy of Dramatic Art.

PLOT SUMMARY

Act 1

It is November 1885, during the Serbo-Bulgarian War. Raina Petkoff, a young Bulgarian woman, is in her bedchamber when her mother, Catherine, enters and announces there has been a battle close by and that Raina's fiancé, Major Sergius Saranoff, was the hero of a cavalry charge. The women rejoice that Sergius has proven to be as heroic as they expected, but they soon turn to securing the house because of fighting in the streets. Nonetheless, a Serbian officer gains entry through Raina's shutters. Raina decides to hide him and she denies having seen anyone when she is questioned by a Russian officer who is hunting for a man seen climbing the water pipe to Raina's balcony. Raina covers well, and the Russian leaves without noticing the pistol on Raina's bed.

When Raina hands the gun to the Serbian after the Russian leaves, the Serbian admits that the gun is not loaded because he carries chocolates in his cartridge belt instead of ammunition. He explains that he is a Swiss mercenary fighting for the Serbs because it is his profession to be a soldier and the Serbian war was close by. He adds that old, experienced soldiers carry food while only the young soldiers carry weapons. Shocked by this attitude, Raina criticizes him for being a poor soldier. He counters by describing what makes a real fool, not knowing that his version of the day's cavalry charge makes fun of her betrothed. She is incensed but agrees to let him stay once he impresses upon her the danger of going back out into the street. She tries to impress him with her family's wealth and position, saying that they have the nobility to give refuge to an enemy. He pledges her safety and advises her to tell her mother about his presence, to keep matters proper. While she is gone, he falls into a deep sleep on her bed and he cannot be roused by a shocked Catherine. Raina takes pity on him and asks that they let him sleep.

Act 2

On March 6, 1886, Raina's father, Major Paul Petkoff, comes home and announces the end of the war. Catherine is upset that the Serbians have agreed to a peace treaty, believing that her side should have a glorious victory. Major Saranoff arrives just after Petkoff makes comments indicating that Saranoff is not a talented military leader. Catherine praises Saranoff, but he announces that he is resigning from the army. Raina joins the conversation just before the discussion turns to a Swiss officer who bested the men in a horse trade and who had been, according to a friend's story, rescued by two Bulgarian ladies after a battle. Catherine and Raina pretend to be shocked by such unpatriotic behavior.

Catherine and Major Petkoff leave the two young people to have some time to alone. Raina and Sergius exchange all the silly platitudes expected of lovers about how much they missed each other and how they worship each other. However, while Raina is away to get her hat for a walk, Sergius flirts with the maid, Louka, whom he has apparently chased in the past. Louka protests his behavior and reveals that there is someone for whom Raina has real feelings, not the fake ones she puts on for Segius. Sergius becomes angry and insults Louka, although he is confused about his own feelings.

Sergius goes to help Petkoff with some final military business. In his absence, Catherine tells Raina that Petkoff has asked for the coat they gave the enemy soldier when he left. Just then, the Swiss officer, Captain Bluntschli, arrives to return the coat. The women try but fail to hurry him away before Petkoff and Sergius see him. Bluntschli offers to help them with the logistics of their troop movements, and Petkoff invites him to stay, much to the discomfort of the ladies.

Act 3

Bluntschli is busy drawing up orders, and Saranoff signs them as everyone else is lounging in the library. Petkoff complains that he would be more comfortable in his old coat, but he cannot find it. Now that Bluntschli has returned it, Catherine insists that the coat is in the blue closet, where she placed it since the last time her husband looked. When the servant finds the coat in the appropriate closet, Petkoff dismisses the incident as a foible of old age.

When Saranoff and Petkoff go out to deliver orders to the couriers, Raina has a chance to talk with Bluntschli alone, and she lets him know that his story about his evening in her room made it through camp rumors all the way to her father and her fiancé. After bantering about honor and lies, Raina reveals that she had slipped her portrait and a note into her father's old coat when she gave it to Bluntschli. Unfortunately, Bluntschli never discovered it, and they realize that it could still be in the pocket. A messenger arrives with telegrams that tell Bluntschli that his father has died and that he must attend to the family business.

Louka and the manservant, Nicola, have an exchange about Louka's ambitions and about the role of servants. Nicola realizes that it might be more to his advantage to let Louka marry Saranoff and to then become their servant. Later, Saranoff and Louka argue about whether Saranoff is afraid to express his love for Louka, and she reveals that Raina has fallen for Bluntschli. Saranoff challenges Bluntschli to a duel, but when Raina charges that she saw Saranoff with Louka, he backs off. Raina then stirs Saranoff's emotions by telling him that Louka is engaged to Nicola.

Petkoff enters, complaining that his coat had to be repaired. When Raina helps Petkoff put on the coat, she pulls the incriminating photo from the pocket and tosses it to Bluntschli, not knowing that her father has already seen the photo. When Petkoff does not find the photo in his pocket, the questioning begins about the photo's inscription to a "Chocolate Cream Soldier," and an avalanche of truthful revelations from all parties begins. Nicola wisely denies being engaged to Louka so she can marry Saranoff. As Catherine protests the dishonor to Raina, Louka injects that Raina would not have married Saranoff anyway because of Bluntschli. The Swiss captain is hesitant to declare himself in love until he learns that Raina is twenty-three years old, and is not the teenager he thought she was. Confident then that she is old enough to know her feelings, Bluntschli asks for Raina's hand in marriage. Again, Catherine protests because she thinks Bluntschli cannot provide for her daughter appropriately, so he tells them of his great wealth. Raina puts up a token protest about being sold to the highest bidder, but Bluntschli reminds her that she fell in love with him before she knew he had any rank or money. She capitulates, and the play ends with everyone happy.

CHARACTERS

Captain Bluntschli

Bluntschli is a realist who believes in adapting to a situation in order to survive. A professional soldier, he knows that he is only a tool and he has no illusions about war and the practical actions one must take to win battles and stay alive. His most famous feature is that he keeps chocolates in his cartridge belt rather than bullets. His common sense appeals to Sergius, who is in awe of Bluntschli's ability to figure out troop movements. This influence helps Sergius make the decision to be honest about Louka and to change his life.

When Bluntschli takes refuge in Raina's bedroom, he starts a chain of events that changes his life and the lives of all those associated with the Petkoff family. Despite his pragmatism, Bluntschli has a romantic side, illustrated by such actions as: he ran off to be a soldier rather than go into his father's business; he climbs a balcony to escape rather than drop into a cellar; and he himself returns the borrowed coat rather than shipping it, because he wants to see Raina. He has always known that total pragmatism can be as unrealistic as overblown idealism and he has tried to maintain a balance. However, over the course of the play, this balance flip-flops as he changes from a soldier who looks askance at love, to a man who is leaving the army to get married and to take care of his father's

MEDIA ADAPTATIONS

- A film version of *Arms and the Man*, adapted by Shaw and produced by John Maxwell, was created for British International Pictures in 1932.

business. Thus, the man who changed Raina's and Sergius's lives has also had his own life transformed.

Louka

An ambitious and sometimes spiteful maid who is desperate to rise above her station, Louka is attracted to Major Sergius Saranoff, and he to her. However, Sergius is engaged to Raina, and he is gentry while Louka is just a servant. Louka shames Sergius about the hypocrisy of his behavior. She tries to break up his relationship with Raina when Captain Bluntschli returns, knowing that Bluntschli is the enemy soldier who hid in Raina's bedroom. Louka is herself supposedly engaged to another servant, Nicola, who advises her to accept her place in life, but she rejects his downcast philosophy and eventually wins her man and a new life.

Nicola

A wily servant, Nicola covers for Raina and Catherine's intrigues. He believes that class division is an indisputable system, and he advises Louka to accept her place. He found Louka, taught her how to be a proper servant, and plans to marry her, but he comes to see how Louka's marriage to Sergius would create an advantage for both Louka and for himself. Thus, he changes his story about his engagement to Louka, and he promotes Louka's ambitions. Ultimately, Nicola wants to run his own business, so he will do whatever it takes to stay in favor with potential patrons, while taking advantage of opportunities to earn extra capital for special services.

Catherine Petkoff

Raina's mother and the wife of Major Paul Petkoff, Catherine is a nouveau-riche social climber. Crudely ignorant and snooty, Catherine is Shaw's voice for the stereotypical expectations of romanticized love and war. Catherine is disappointed when the war ends in a peace treaty, because she wanted a glorious victory over a soundly defeated enemy. Although she allows Bluntschli to hide in her home and she helps to keep him secret, she thinks Sergius Saranoff is the ideal handsome hero her daughter must marry for an appropriate match. She declares Bluntschli unsuitable until she finds out how rich he is, and then she quickly changes her mind.

Major Paul Petkoff

Raina's father and Catherine's husband, Major Petkoff is an amiable, unpolished buffoon who craves rank and has somehow stumbled into wealth. His rank was given to him for being the richest Bulgarian, but he has no military skills. His purpose in the play is almost that of a prop. It is his old coat that is lent to Bluntschli and which then gives Bluntschli the excuse to come back to see Raina. It is Petkoff who discovers the incriminating photo in his coat pocket that leads to the revelation of the truth and to the resolution of the story.

Raina Petkoff

The central character in the play, Raina learns to discard her foolish ideals about love in exchange for real love. Raina is central because Catherine and Paul Petkoff are her parents, Sergius is her fiancé, Louka and Nicola are her family's servants, and Bluntschli is her dream soldier. The play starts in her bedroom, where we learn what a dreamy romantic she is about love and war, before the enemy soldier comes through her window and begins to shatter her fairy-tale illusions with his realism.

Shaw was known for creating lively, willful, and articulate female characters. He also often included a youthful character in his plays, one who could express a childish approach to life. Raina fits both these descriptions. She is unworldly and sometimes acts like a spoiled child to get her way. Catherine points out that Raina always times her entrances to get the most attention. Nonetheless, Raina is intelligent. She probably wouldn't have fallen for Bluntschli if she had not been open to his arguments and if she were not smart enough to see the differences in qualities between Bluntschli and Saranoff. She is also honest enough with herself to realize that she is not truly in love with Saranoff, but was just playing a role to meet social expectations. Raina has enough bravery and compassion to aid an enemy soldier in need, and she is courageous and adventurous enough to take a risk with Bluntschli and to start a new life.

Major Sergius Saranoff

Major Saranoff is Raina's fiancé, and he is a shining example of Raina and her mother's romanticized image of a hero. He is almost quixotic in his attempt to live up to this image, especially in battle, for it is hopeless to try to embody a myth. Thus, Shaw uses this character to show that these romanticized ideals were probably nonsense all along. Sergius is often referred to as the Byronic hero or as the Hamlet of this play because he has an underlying despair about life. He clings to his idealized image of himself because he is afraid to find out who he really is. He knows that he is a different person with Raina than he is with Louka, and Louka has pointed out his hypocritical behaviors to him. Sergius realizes that there must be more to himself than the idealized soldier the young ladies worship, but of the other selves that he has observed in himself he says: "One of them is a hero, another a buffoon, another a humbug, another perhaps a bit of a blackguard." He is disconcerted by the feeling that "everything I think is mocked by everything I do." In losing Raina and declaring his love for Louka, Sergius is freed to be himself and to discover his own values.

THEMES

Romanticism of War

In line after line, Shaw satirizes the romantic notions about war that glorify a grisly business. If not for the comic dialogue, the audience would more easily recognize that they are being presented with a soldier who has escaped from a horrific battle after three days of being under fire. He is exhausted, starving, and being pursued. Such is the experience of a real soldier. Late in the play, Shaw throws in a gruesome report on the death of the man who told Bluntschli's secret about staying in Raina's bedroom; there is nothing comic or heroic about being shot in the hip and then burned to death. When Raina expresses horror at such a death, Sergius adds, "And how ridiculous! Oh, war! War! The dream of patriots and heroes! A fraud, Bluntschli, a hollow sham." This kind of description caused Shaw's critics to accuse him of baseness, of trying to destroy the heroic concept. That a soldier would prefer food to cartridges in his belt was considered ludicrous by critics, but in the introduction to *Plays: Pleasant and Unpleasant*, Shaw was reported to have said that all he had to do was introduce any doubters to the first six real

TOPICS FOR FURTHER STUDY

- Shaw greatly admired the artist and socialist William Morris. Write a brief biography that identifies Morris and his legacy.

- The title of *Arms and the Man* comes from the opening line of Virgil's epic poem "The Aeneid." Write a summary of this poem and contrast its message to that of Shaw's play.

- Shaw identified himself as a socialist and he helped to organize the Fabian Society. What is the Fabian Society, what were its goals, and what were some of the works that Shaw wrote while a Fabian?

- *Arms and the Man* was set during a war in the Balkans between the Bulgarians and the Serbians. The Serbians were recently again involved in a war that resulted in international intervention. Trace and report on the history of the various Balkan conflicts from the late 1800s to the present day, including the Serbian involvement in the start of World War I.

- Shaw is credited with initiating the "theater of ideas." What does this term mean? How were Shaw's plays different from most theater during the Victorian era and what was Shaw's impact on the theater world?

---

soldiers they came across, and his stage soldier would prove authentic.

It is also noteworthy that Catherine is dissatisfied with a peace treaty because, in her unrealistic vision of glorious war, there is supposed to be a crushing rout of the enemy followed by celebrations of a heroic victory. Shaw's message here is that there can be peaceful alternatives to perpetual fighting. He was dedicated throughout his life to curbing violence, especially that of wars, and *Arms and the Man* was one of the vehicles he used to plead his case.

Romanticism of Love

Shaw was a master flirt and he enjoyed the playful farce of romantic intrigues. But he recognized that playing a game differed from serious love, and he tried to convey as much in *Arms and the Man*, which is subtitled "An Anti-Romantic Comedy." In the play, Raina and Sergius have paired themselves for all the wrong reasons: because their social status requires a mate from the same social level; and because Sergius plays the role of the type of hero that Raina has been taught to admire, and Raina plays the role that Sergius expects from a woman of her station. The problem is that neither is portraying his/her real self, so their love is based on outward appearances, not on the

true person beneath the facade. They are both acting out a romance according to their idealized standards for courtship rather than according to their innermost feelings. Just as the cheerleader is expected to fall for the star quarterback, Raina has fallen for her brave army officer who looks handsome in his uniform. When Bluntschli and Louka force Raina and Sergius to examine their true feelings, Raina and Sergius discover that they have the courage and desire to follow their hearts instead of seeking to meet social expectations.

Class Discrimination

As a socialist, Shaw believed in the equality of all people and he abhorred discrimination based on gender or social class. These beliefs are evident in the relationships portrayed in *Arms and the Man*. Shaw allows a maid to succeed in her ambitions to better herself by marrying Sergius, an officer and a gentleman. This match also means that Sergius has developed the courage to free himself from the expectations of his class and instead marry the woman he loves. The silliness of Catherine's character is used to show the illogical nature of class snobbery, as she clearly makes divisions between her family and the servants, even though, or perhaps because, the Petkoffs themselves have only recently climbed the social ladder. The play also

---

attacks divisions of rank, as Captain Bluntschli has leadership abilities that the superior-ranking officers, Majors Petkoff and Saranoff, do not have, illustrating the fact that ability has little to do with rank. Ability also has little to do with class, as exemplified by the character of Nicola, who is declared the ablest, and certainly the wiliest, character in the play.

Idealism versus Realism

Arms and the Man illustrates the conflict between idealism and realism. The romantic ideal of war as a glorious opportunity for a man to display courage and honor is dispelled when Sergius admits that his heroic cavalry charge that won the battle was the wrong thing to do. His notable action does not get him his promotion and Sergius learns that "Soldiering, my dear madam, is the coward's art of attacking mercilessly when you are strong, and keeping out of harm's way when you are weak."

Sergius and Raina must face the fact that their ideals about love are false. Fortunately, both of them are actually released by this knowledge to pursue their true loves. But first, Sergius goes through a period of despair in which he questions whether life is futile if the ideals by which he has set his standards of conduct fail to hold up when exposed to reality. This question is an underlying current throughout the play. Shaw gives a happy resolution, but it is a serious question that most people must face in life.

Much is made of Bluntschli's realism—i.e., keeping chocolates instead of ammunition in his cartridge belt, showing contempt for sentimentality, and reacting in a practical manner to his father's death. However, Nicola is the consummate realist in the play. Nicola's message is: adapt, exploit, survive. Bluntschli proves to have a romantic side, after all, and thus is the most balanced character in the play in that he seems to know when to temper his romanticism with realism and when to stick to his ideals.

STYLE

Ruritanian Romance

Although already established as a model for romances prior to the publication of Anthony Hope's popular 1894 novel *The Prisoner of Zenda*, Ruritanian romance takes its name from the imaginary country of Ruritania found in Hope's book.

This type of story generally includes intrigue, adventure, sword fights, and star-crossed lovers, ingredients that are all found in *Arms and the Man*. However, Shaw ultimately attacks this genre by exaggerating the absurdities of the plot and by transforming the typically cookie-cutter characters into people facing reality. He thus inverts the conventions of melodrama and inserts critical commentary into the cleverly funny lines of his play. There is the threat of a sword fight that never comes to fruition, since Bluntschli is too sensible to accept Saranoff's challenge—which illustrates Shaw's belief that dueling is stupid. Romance also plays a big role in *Arms and the Man*, but, again, Shaw turns the tables by having the heroine and her fiancé abandon their idealized relationship, which would have been prized in a Ruritanian romance, for a more realistic and truer love.

Comedy

One standard trait of comedic plays—often used by Shakespeare and also used by Shaw in *Arms and the Man*—is the use of an ending in which all the confusions of the play are resolved, and every romantic figure winds up with his or her ideal partner. The gimmicks in *Arms and the Man* of the lost coat and the incriminating inscription on the hidden photograph are also ploys that are typical of comedy. The gimmicks serve as catalysts to spark the humorous confusion, and work as objects around which the plot turns. In Shaw's hands, however, comedy is serious business disguised by farce. Always an innovator, Shaw introduced moral instruction into comedic plays, rather than taking the conventional route of writing essays or lectures to communicate his views.

Redefining Romance and Heroism

Shaw does not simply dismiss Raina's idealism in favor of Bluntschli's pragmatism. He replaces her shallow ideals with more worthy ones. By the end of the play, Raina understands that a man like Bluntschli is more of a real hero than Sergius. The audience also discovers that Bluntschli's practical nature is not without romance because he has come back to see Raina rather than sending the coat back by courier. In fact, he admits to Sergius that he "climbed the balcony of this house when a man of sense would have dived into the nearest cellar." Together, Raina, Bluntschli, and Sergius attain a new realism that sees love and heroism as they really should be, according to Shaw. Thus Shaw does not reject romance and heroism, but rather brings his characters to an

COMPARE & CONTRAST

- **1890s:** After centuries of rule by the Ottoman Turks, in 1878, northern Bulgaria becomes autonomous, and a united Bulgaria gains its independence in 1908.

  Today: A German ally in both world wars, Bulgaria falls to Soviet domination during World War II and remains under its control until 1990. Upon signing of the European Constitution in 2004, Bulgaria is de facto considered a full-fledged member of the European Union. Bulgaria also joins NATO in 2004.

- **1890s:** After becoming an autonomous principality in 1829, Serbia is recognized in 1878 as an independent country. In 1882, the ruling prince, Milan Obrenovi, is proclaimed king.

  Obrenovi establishes a liberal constitution, but his son Alexander, who rules from 1889 to 1903, rejects it, evoking hostility in Serbia until he is assassinated in 1903.

  Today: From 1992 to 2002, Serbia and Montenegro are joined as the country of Yugoslavia. After 2002, the two states are in a loose federation, and a referendum in each republic concerning full independence is to be held in 2006.

- **1890s:** *Arms and the Man* is in limited production and is not appreciated until its publication several years later.

  Today: *Arms and the Man* is produced around the world and is one of Shaw's most popular plays.

---

understanding of a higher definition of these values. That is, the course of the play has worked to maneuver the characters and the audience into a new position and thus redefine romance and heroism according to the light of realism.

HISTORICAL CONTEXT

Victorian Rule

Queen Victoria, the longest-reigning monarch in British history, was born in 1819 and ruled from 1837–1901. She was married in 1840 to her cousin, Prince Albert, and it was he who insisted on the straitlaced behavior and strict decorum that have become known as Victorian values. They had nine children, whose marriages and prodigy entangled most of the thrones of Europe, including grandchildren Emperor William II of Germany and Empress Alexandra, wife of Nicholas II of Russia. Prince Albert died in 1861 and Victoria largely withdrew from public life, thus damaging her popularity and the political clout she had previously wielded.

When Benjamin Disraeli became prime minister in 1874, he flattered Victoria into resuming some involvement in public affairs, and she regained admiration as well as the title of Empress of India. Disraeli worked for social reform while promoting the growth of the British Empire. In contrast to Disraeli, Victoria greatly disliked William E. Gladstone, who served as prime minister four times between 1868 and 1894. Considered a great statesman, Gladstone championed tax reforms, an end to colonial expansion, and Irish home rule.

Relative prosperity existed in the late 1800s in England, although there were some years of high unemployment. Agricultural production was at its height. The Crimean War (1854–1856) had been a disaster for England, but otherwise the empire spread prosperously around the globe to include Canada, Australia, India, and large sections of Africa, as well as various Asian and West Indies islands and ports. It is estimated that at one point, one-fourth of the world's population lived under British rule. Consequently, British influence was dominant around the world in this time period and this legacy has had lasting effects into the twentieth and twenty-first centuries.

Victorian Society

During the second half of the nineteenth century, the family was considered to be the focal point of society. The term "Victorian" is now associated with an inflexible set of manners and prudishness. In truth, the morality of the times was based on a heroic idealism and an honorable work ethic. Character and duty were the watchwords of the times. Class divisions continued, but individual advancement within a class was encouraged. As in many societies, there was a Victorian underworld in which prostitution thrived. It was this conflicting social situation in such morally high-minded times that led Shaw to write his play *Mrs. Warren's Profession*, a comedy about a prim young lady's discovery that her mother is the owner of a series of brothels. This play was refused a license by the ministry until 1905 because of its unseemly subject.

Victorian Literature

Victorian literature throughout the nineteenth century was noted for its humor. Charles Dickens, William Thackeray, and Lewis Carroll were among the many British writers who were successful with comic fiction. Early Victorian theatre was characterized by artificial plots, shallow romantic characters, and melodrama, and played to largely uneducated audiences. By midcentury, Dion Boucicault and Tom Taylor had gained popularity with their comedic plays, in which it was fashionable to play upon the titillation of stories about "fallen" women. Besides farces, many plays of the time were intrigues with complicated and ludicrous plots.

Realistic drama got a start in the 1860s work of T. W. Robertson, but it was not until the 1890s that the most prominent dramatists, Sir A. W. Pinero and H. A. Jones, tried to follow suit. However, neither Pinero nor Jones was able to fully break away from the usual fare expected by theatergoers. Nonetheless, the influence of Henrik Ibsen caused Pinero to join in the movement to write serious "problem" plays, such as his *Second Mrs. Tanqueray* (1893). Ibsen, an enormously influential Norwegian critic and playwright, attacked social norms and hypocrisies. His plays focus on real human concerns and portray characters of depth who are trying to make sense of their lives. Ibsen believed that drama can honestly and meaningfully deal with social problems. In 1891, J. T. Grein organized the Independent Theatre to present plays by Ibsen; it was this theatre that staged Shaw's first plays, which were heavily influenced by Ibsen. In 1895, Oscar Wilde brought further innovation to comedy with one of the greatest English plays, *The Importance of Being Earnest*.

CRITICAL OVERVIEW

Although Shaw's drama was not generally appreciated or understood in his early years as a playwright, he was eventually recognized for his genius and is now considered one of the most important British playwrights of modern times, second only to Shakespeare in the history of British theater. This change of opinion developed over time as a result of changes in social attitudes and a general maturing of the theater. Once Shaw's first collection of plays appeared in print, people had the time while reading to unearth the riches of his works. The influence of Ibsen on drama changed the usual fare fed to theatergoers, educating them about the role of drama in telling stories that could instruct and could portray real people and their emotions. These changes made audiences more receptive to the innovations and themes that Shaw conveyed in his plays.

In the 1890s, however, while critics found Shaw's dialogue amusing, they found his work difficult to classify. Early critics misinterpreted his characters, finding them inhuman, and concluded that Shaw had a heartless approach to life. Shaw's attack on the phony idealism associated with war caused him to be accused of trying to destroy the concept of heroism. When Shaw included in *Arms and the Man* a soldier who carried chocolates rather than bullets, along with descriptions of a bungled cavalry charge and a grisly death, critics accused Shaw of looking only at the baser side of life.

Shaw has had a myriad of books and articles written about him. The following is a brief review of what some of the most eminent critics have said about Shaw's work as a whole, and about *Arms and the Man* in particular. These reviews are a reflection of the general opinion expressed by those who have studied his works.

One of Shaw's biographers was the famous British novelist, essayist, and religious writer, Gilbert K. Chesterton. Although Chesterton disagreed with Shaw on most social policies, he understood Shaw's dramatic method. Chesterton writes that Shaw "resolved to build a play not on pathos, but on bathos," the reverse of common practice at the time. In other words, Shaw did not follow the melodramatic convention of appealing to pity or sympathy; instead, he exaggerated the pathos and made abrupt changes from a lofty to an ordinary style. Chesterton adds that in *Arms and the Man*, "there was a savage sincerity," a "strong satire in the idea."

Serbians read a list of the dead and wounded during the Serbo-Bulgarian war in 1885 © Hulton-Deutsch
Collection/Corbis

The world-renowned Argentine writer Jorge Luis Borges—commenting on the commonplace criticism of Shaw's early plays, which said that Shaw was attempting to destroy the heroic concept—responds that such criticism "did not understand that the heroic was completely independent from the romantic and was embodied in Captain Bluntschli of *Arms and the Man*, not in Sergius Saranoff." Borges adds that the body of "Shaw's work . . . leaves an aftertaste of liberation."

German playwright and critic Bertolt Brecht notes of Shaw: "Probably all of his characters, in all of their traits, are the result of Shaw's delight in upsetting our habitual prejudices." Certainly this practice is evidenced in the class prejudices depicted by the Petkoffs against their servants and against their enemies in *Arms and the Man*. Shaw was known to take some radical positions in his lifetime, but he never resorted to any sort of terrorism other than satire. According to Brecht, "[Shaw's] terror is an unusual one, and he employs an unusual weapon—that of humor."

Shaw considered *Arms and the Man* to be a failure when it was first staged, because so few people realized his true message or intent. Within ten years, however, lack of understanding was seldom a problem among his readers and audiences who

had grown to understand Shaw and his dramatic realism. Critic Arthur Bingham Walkley, a contemporary of Shaw's, is quoted by Barbara M. Fisher in *George Bernard Shaw* as writing: "In the form of a droll, fantastic farce, [*Arms and the Man*] presents us with a criticism of conduct, a theory of life." H. W. Nevinson, writing in 1929 for the *New Leader*, sums up Shaw's drama by noting that Shaw's "plays have laid bare the falsities and hypocrisies and boastful pretensions of our . . . time. I can think of no modern prophet who has swept away so much accepted rubbish and cleared the air of so much cant."

CRITICISM

Lois Kerschen

Kerschen is a school district administrator and freelance writer. In this essay, Kerschen examines the elements of the play that convey Shaw's socialist feelings about class structures and stereotypes.

Although the dominant themes of *Arms and the Man* are the foolishness of romanticized love and of glorified war, there is another theme concerning social classes. Shaw was one of the key figures in the establishment of the Fabian Society, a middle-class socialist group that believed reform should come through the gradual education of the people and through changes in intellectual and political life, not through revolution. One of the reforms sought by the Fabian Society was the establishment of equality, legally and socially, for all people. There-fore, in *Arms and the Man*, as with the stereotypes that Shaw targets concerning heroes and the con-ventions of romance, he also takes aim at the stereo-types and false tenets of class.

Shaw greatly admired the Norwegian play-wright Henrik Ibsen. According to the *Norton Anthology of British Literature*, Shaw preferred Ib-sen's plays that "attacked middle-class conven-tionality and hypocrisy rather than those which probed more subtly and poetically into deeper as-pects of experience." Indeed, it is this convention-ality and hypocrisy that Shaw targets in *Arms and the Man*. For one thing, Shaw makes fun of the high-class pretensions of the Petkoff family. In the stage directions to Act 1, Shaw describes Raina's bedroom as "half rich Bulgarian and half cheap Viennese." He describes Catherine as "a very splen-did specimen of the wife of a mountain farmer, but is determined to be a Viennese lady, and to that end wears a fashionable tea gown on all occasions."

When Raina informs Bluntschli that he is in the house of Petkoff, "the richest and best known [family] in our country," she expects him to be im-pressed. She brags that her father holds the high-est command of any Bulgarian in the Russian army, but it is only the rank of major, which does not say much for the Bulgarians. Raina also brags that hers is the only private house in Bulgaria that has two rows of windows and a flight of stairs to go up and down by. When Bluntschli feigns being impressed, she adds that they have the only library in Bulgaria. She condescendingly tells Bluntschli that he has shown great ignorance, but the audience recognizes that Raina is the one who is pathetically ignorant. She advises Bluntschli that she tells him all these things so that he will know he is not in the house of ignorant country folk. As proof, she declares that she goes to the opera in Bucharest every year and has spent a month in Vienna. Bluntschli says, "I saw at once that you knew the world" when what he is seeing is that she is very unworldly. Bertolt Brecht wrote in 1959 in his article "Ovation for Show" in *Modern Drama* that Shaw insisted "on the prerogative of every man to act decently, logi-cally, and with a sense of humor" and that a per-son was obligated to behave this way "even in the

> SHAW ARGUED THAT WOMEN SHOULD NOT FALL FOR SOCIETY'S DICTUM THAT THEY BE SELF-SACRIFICING, BUT SHOULD INSTEAD TAKE CARE OF THEMSELVES FIRST SO THAT THEY COULD THEN BE IN A POSITION TO HELP OTHERS."

face of opposition." Apparently, Shaw gave this at-tribute to Bluntschli.

Shaw further shows the vulgarity of the Petkoffs when Raina explains that "Bulgarians of really good standing—people in OUR position—wash their hands nearly every day." Raina thinks that simply washing hands is a sign of a gentleman, not knowing that her primitive lifestyle sets her standards low. In Act 2, Major Petkoff blames his wife's chronic sore throat on washing her neck every day. His lecture on the foolishness of fre-quent bathing is a further sign from Shaw that we are dealing with people who have only recently barely risen above the great unwashed masses. Throwing in the comments about washing being the fault of the English whose climate makes them so dirty is a playful barb at Shaw's own audience.

The repeated reference to their library once again shows that the Petkoffs think that all they need to be gentry is to have a room called the li-brary. Putting a bell in it just heightens the ludi-crousness of their pretensions. When Petkoff asks why they cannot just shout for their servants, Catherine replies that she has learned that civilized people never shout for their servants. He counters that he has learned that civilized people do not hang their laundry out to dry where other people can see it. Catherine finds that concept absurd and declares that really refined people do not notice such things, as if she knew. Obviously, neither of them have any idea what refinement is, especially if they have only recently begun learning proper habits.

Bertolt Brecht, in his essay "Ovation for Show," wrote that "Probably all of [Shaw's] char-acters, in all their traits, are the result of Shaw's

WHAT DO I READ NEXT?

- Shaw wrote *The Intelligent Woman's Guide to Socialism and Capitalism* (1927) as a political primer for women, who had just gained suffrage in Britain. Available in a 1984 reprint edition from Transaction Publishers, this book strongly advocates socialism as the best economic solution.

- Shaw's *Complete Plays with Prefaces* (1962), published by Dodd Mead, is a collection of all of Shaw's dramatic works, including the famous prefaces that are so valuable to the study of Shaw and his messages.

- Shaw wrote *The Quintessence of Ibsenism* (1890) as a tribute to the great Norwegian playwright and critic Henrik Ibsen, whose

philosophy about the power of literature to instruct inspired Shaw's career. This book was reprinted in 1994 by Dover Publications.

- Henrik Ibsen greatly influenced Shaw and other dramatists of his age. A collection of Ibsen's plays can be found in *Henrik Ibsen: The Complete Major Prose Plays* (1988), published by Plume Books.

- Oscar Wilde is another of Britain's greatest playwrights. Wilde's *The Importance of Being Earnest*, first produced in 1895, is arguably his best work and perhaps the most famous comedy of manners in theater history. Numerous editions are available, including a Dover Edition from 1990.

---

delight in upsetting our habitual prejudices." For example, Saranoff assumes that Bluntschli is bourgeois because Bluntschli's father is a hotel and livery keeper. He has jumped to the wrong conclusion because Bluntschli is too humble to brag about his father's holdings. Louka challenges Saranoff's prejudices when she says, "It is so hard to know what a gentleman considers right" after Saranoff jumps back and forth between familiarity with her and putting a barrier between them because he is supposedly a gentleman and she only a maid. In one minute, Louka is worth chasing; in another, she is "an abominable little clod of common clay, with the soul of a servant." But Louka retorts that it does not matter what she is because she has now found out that he is made of the same clay. Shaw is, of course, making the point that virtue and baseness are not the properties of any one class but that we are all human.

Louka is resentful of a society that tries to restrict her to a certain "place." The audience can tell that Louka is better suited to being a mistress than a maid. Nicola tries to convince her that a rigid structure of classes is part of the natural order of things, and that people are more content when they accept their place and stop torturing themselves

with useless aspirations. Louka replies disdainfully that Nicola has "the soul of a servant." He may have capitulated to social restrictions, but she will not. In *The Quintessence of Ibsenism*, Shaw argued that women should not fall for society's dictum that they be self-sacrificing, but should instead take care of themselves first so that they could then be in a position to help others. Louka is an example of a woman following this advice.

In Act 3, the audience is finally shown the famous "library" and learn that, in truth, it contains only a few books. Once again, Shaw is making fun of the Petkoffs' attempt at upward mobility. In a conversation between Sergius and Louka, Louka asks if poor men are any less brave than rich men. He replies, "Not a bit." However, he qualifies his answer by adding that they are just as brave in battle, but cower before officers. Shaw's voice is heard as Sergius concludes: "Oh, give me the man who will defy to the death any power on earth or in heaven that sets itself up against his own will and conscience: he alone is the brave man." Louka challenges his definition of true courage. She says that servants do not have the liberty to express their own wills, to show bravery. If she were an empress, though, she would show courage by marrying the man she loved, even if he were far below her in station. She accuses Sergius of not having that kind of courage, and he claims that he does but he loves Raina. Of course, Louka is setting him up to be without excuses for marrying her once he learns that Raina loves Bluntschi, and Shaw has successfully set forth a debate about class and courage for his audience to ponder.

Class distinctions become all muddled at the end of the play, and barriers are broken, as Shaw hoped they would be in real life. Nicola becomes a servant to a servant, or is it a compatriot, when he declares that Louka has "a soul above her station; and I have been no more than her confidential servant." Then Sergius becomes engaged to Louka, so the class barrier between them comes down. In a further blow for equality, Louka addresses Raina by her first name. Raina and her mother are indignant at the liberty a mere servant has taken, but Louka says, "I have a right to call her Raina: she calls me Louka." It seemed logical to Shaw, and he hoped his audience would see the sense of this peer treatment. The final jab at snobbery is taken when Catherine objects to Raina marrying Bluntschli until she finds out that he is rich. Then he becomes instantly acceptable. The hypocrisy of basing marriage on money instead of love could not have been lost on the audience.

Arthur St. John Adcock, a British poet, novelist, and journalist, understood why Shaw took his moral and socialist preaching to theatre audiences rather than to a lecture podium: "it would bear the more fruit because it fell upon their minds like a pleasant and enlivening dew and not like a destroying thunderstorm." He added: "I doubt whether any man has attacked more social evils and respectable shibboleths, or had a profounder, more far-reaching influence on his own time." Ultimately, Shaw was an optimist. He could present social reform in a comedy because he found humor in the human situation. He knew it was better to laugh than cry, and he truly believed that good sense and justice would prevail. He would not have bothered to present his ideas if he did not think that people were capable of reasoning their value. For that faith in their innate goodness and intelligence, Shaw's audiences have rewarded him with a lasting reputation as one of the greatest playwrights of all time.

Source: Lois Kerschen, Critical Essay on *Arms and the Man*, in *Drama for Students*, Thomson Gale, 2006.

A. M. Gibbs

In the following essay, Gibbs examines Shaw's balancing of the satire of romantic conventions

> WITH THIS REVELATION, SHAW TRANSFERS THE AURA NORMALLY ASSOCIATED WITH THE BROODING BYRONIC HERO IN NINETEENTH-CENTURY LITERATURE TO A QUITE DIFFERENT CHARACTER TYPE. THE PLAIN-SPEAKER BECOMES THE MAN OF MYSTERY."

with a less conventional romantic narrative in Arms and the Man.

> THE MAN: Ive no ammunition. What use are cartridges in battle? I always carry chocolate instead; and I finished the last cake of that hours ago.
>
> RAINA: [*outraged in her most cherished ideals of manhood*] Chocolate! Do you stuff your pockets with sweets—like a schoolboy—even in the field?
> (*Arms and the Man*)

Much of the laughter in *Arms and the Man* arises from the steady deflation of romantic ideas of love and war. Yet it is a misreading of the play to see it as simply an anti-romantic and anti-heroic work. In production, a fine balance of tones needs to be achieved in order to preserve the integrity and meaning of the play. In some words of advice to producers of the play, Shaw wrote of its essential tonal qualities as follows:

> unless the general effect of the play is thoroughly genial and good-humored, it will be unbearably disagreeable. The slightest touch of malicious denigrement or cynicism is fatal. If the audience thinks it is being asked to laugh at human nature, it will not laugh. If it thinks it is being made to laugh at insincere romantic conventions which are an insult to human nature, it will laugh very heartily. The fate of the play depends wholly on the clearness of this distinction.

For all its Falstaffian perspectives on military valour, the play does not denigrate courage as a human virtue. And within the context of its satirical treatment of 'insincere romantic conventions' a compensating romantic narrative of a less conventional kind is developed.

The two principal, and related, subjects of satire in the play are: the glorification of war, and the so-called Higher Love which is supposed both to stimulate military valour and in turn to be stimulated by it. One dramatic form to which the work is related is the military adventure play, a form which has a long history in England, going back to the Love and Honour drama of the seventeenth century. But nearer at hand as an influence upon the more romantic aspects of the play was a source revealed in the text itself when Raina refers Bluntschli to a scene in *Ernani,* Verdi's opera based on the historical play *Hernani* by Victor Hugo:

> I thought you might have remembered the great scene where Ernani, flying from his foes just as you are tonight, takes refuge in the castle of his bitterest enemy, an old Castilian noble. The noble refuses to give him up. His guest is sacred to him.

In the love plot of *Ernani,* the union of the lovers, Elvira and the aristocratic outlaw Ernani, is threatened in two ways. Ernani has a rival in the form of his enemy, Don Carlo, who is the historical Charles V; but at the same time Elvira is about to be reluctantly united in marriage to a relative (the 'old Castilian noble' referred to in *Arms and the Man*) Don Ruy Gomez de Silva. Ernani, having become involved in a conspiracy against Carlo's life, is captured and pardoned, and the way is temporarily clear for him to marry Elvira. But as the two are about to enter their nuptial chamber they are arrested by the jealous Silva. The opera, as distinct from Victor Hugo's play which ends happily, concludes in a *liebestod* with Ernani committing suicide and Elvira, declaring eternal love, falling dead upon his body.

In the more romantic aspects of its dramatic structure, *Arms and the Man* bears some clear traces of the plot motifs in *Ernani:* the concealment of the fleeing enemy, the point of honour by which the claims of hospitality outweigh enmity, the dramatic discovery of the fugitive's identity and even the alignment of forces which threaten the possibility of marriage between Bluntschli and Raina. (Sergius and Petkoff perform similar functions in this respect to Don Carlo and Don Ruy.)

The characters in Shaw's play translate readily in one's mind into operatic types: Sergius is explicitly described by Bluntschli as being 'like an operatic tenor', and the other personae in the play, from Major Petkoff (basso profundo) to Louka (second soprano), also bear a strong resemblance to stock characters in opera. Raina is an expert on the subject of opera—it is a means of asserting the civilization of the Petkoffs and of Bulgaria—and her

imagination is obviously shaped to a considerable extent by operatic conventions. In *Ernani* Shaw would have found presented in sharp outline the stereotypes of exalted love and heroism which are satirised in his play. The opera begins with a chorus of rebels singing the praises of their life of warfare:

> This life, O how joyful!
> With hilt, blade and rifle,
> Our true friends thro' all.

Elvira's thoughts are never far from death when she is speaking of her love for Ernani and the elevated mood of their love relations (typified in such things as the duet 'Ah, morir potessi' in Act II and the dialogue between the two before Don Ruy's entry in Act IV) remains unbroken throughout.

Shaw's satirical treatment of the conventions of romantic opera has some affinities with the methods of early Gilbertian comedy. In Gilbert's *The Palace of Truth* (1870)—a play reminiscent in various ways of *A Midsummer Night's Dream*—the court of King Phanor is transferred to an enchanted palace in which the magic powers compel all the characters to say exactly what is in their minds about one another. Characters are reversed and love partners changed. Poetical compliment turns to plain speaking, and vice versa. A prince tells his adored mistress that she is 'comparatively plain'. A coquette makes advances to several gentlemen whilst demurely explaining her tactics as she proceeds. A normally boorish courtier explains archly that his manners were an affectation designed to

> . . . prove, perchance, a not unwelcome foil
> To Zoram's mockery of cultured taste,
> And Chrysal's chronic insincerity!

The comedy in Gilbert's later play *Engaged* (1877), depends on much the same sources of laughter, in candid revelations of prosaic fact and frankly appetitive motives beneath the postures of romance. When writing the scene in Act II of *Arms and the Man* in which Sergius, having rapturously farewelled Raina in accents of the 'higher love', suddenly has his attention caught by the distinctly attractive maid with whom he then proceeds to flirt, Shaw must surely have remembered the scene in *Engaged* where Gilbert puts Cheviot (left similarly alone on the stage) through the same paces:

> CHEVIOT: . . . Dismiss from my thoughts the only woman I ever loved! Have no more to say to the tree upon which the fruit of my heart is growing! No, Belvawney, I cannot cut off my tree as if it were gas or water. I do not treat women like that. Some men do, but I don't. I am not that sort of man. I respect women; I love women. They are good; they are pure; they are beautiful; at least, many of them are.

[*Enter MAGGIE from cottage: he is much fascinated*]
This one, for example, is very beautiful indeed!

As Dan H. Laurence in his edition of Shaw's letters points out, William Archer had already communicated his views of *Arms and the Man* to Shaw before writing the review in which he declared that in the second act 'we find ourselves in Mr Gilbert's Palace of Truth', and described the play as 'a fantastic, psychological extravaganza, in which drama, farce, and Gilbertian irony keep flashing past the bewildered eye'. Shaw, in one of his most illuminating commentaries on his own work, pointed out the vital distinctions between his and Gilbert's comedy:

> I must really clear that Gilbert notion out of your head [he wrote to Archer] before you disgrace yourself over Arms and The Man. You have a perfect rag shop of old ideas in your head which prevent your getting a step ahead.

> Gilbert is simply a paradoxically humorous cynic. He accepts the conventional ideals implicitly, but observes that people do not really live up to them. This he regards as a failure on their part at which he mocks bitterly. This position is precisely that of Sergius in the play, who, when disilluded [*sic*], declares that life is a farce. It is a perfectly barren position: nothing comes of it but cynicism, pessimism, and irony.

> I do not accept the conventional ideals. To them I oppose in the play the practical life and morals of the efficient, realistic man, unaffectedly ready to face what risks must be faced, considerate but not chivalrous, patient and practical, and I . . . represent the woman as instinctively falling in love with all this even whilst all her notions of fine-mannishness are being outraged. . . . It is this positive element in my philosophy that makes Arms and The Man a perfectly genuine play about real people, with a happy ending and hope and life in it, instead of a thing like [Gilbert's] *Engaged* which is nothing but a sneer at people for not being what Sergius and Raina play at being before they find one another out.

The 'mechanical topsyturvyism' of early Gilbertian comedy leads, in Shaw's view, only to a comically cynical view of human nature and human ideals. In contrast, Shaw's comedy does not simply negate romance. Rather, what he achieves in the play is a rejuvenation of a typical romance structure, by attaching to well-tried dramatic situations an unconventional set of values and affirmations. Instead of the romance of conventional fiction, it offers the romance of reality, of the discovery of true feeling beneath the social equipment superficial and assumed feeling. It is in terms such as these that the relations between Raina and Bluntschli are developed in the play, their romantic intimacy increasing as her romantic attitudes are progressively discarded:

BLUNTSCHLI: . . . When you strike that noble attitude and speak in that thrilling voice, I admire you; but I find it impossible to believe a single word you say . . .

RAINA: [*wonderingly*] Do you know, you are the first man I ever met who did not take me seriously?

BLUNTSCHLI: You mean, dont you, that I am the first man that has ever taken you quite seriously?

RAINA: Yes: I suppose I do mean that. [*Cosily, quite at her ease with him*] How strange it is to be talked to in such a way!

The candid, friendly and amiable person that such moments in the play discover in Raina is consistent with the image of the human being who, to her mother's annoyance, times to perfection her pretty entrances by listening for cues 'off-stage'. But it is a quite different persona from the actress who poses regally for Sergius and who becomes caught up in the rhetoric and fantasies of the Higher Love. In the process of un-masking the postures of the Higher Love, the play shows us not an emptiness beneath, but the possibilities of deeper and more meaningful forms of intimacy.

In some respects, the alternative romance which develops between Raina and Bluntschli follows fairly conventional lines. The amatory possibilities of their relations are already established in Act I, in Raina's moments of maternal solicitousness for her fugitive guest, and, conclusively, in the penultimate line of Act I, spoken as she surveys the un-wakeable and potentially compromising figure on her bed: 'the poor darling is worn out. Let him sleep.' Feelings other than those expressed in the present dialogue on stage are conveyed by the report of Raina's sending a photograph of herself to Bluntschli with the inscription 'Raina, to her Chocolate Cream Soldier: a Souvenir'. It is noteworthy, too, that Bluntschli is allowed the democratic or republican equivalent of aristocratic rank, when he is revealed to be the owner of a large chain of hotels. In writing the play, Shaw judged to a nicety the degree to which conventions could be altered, and the degree to which they had to be allowed to run their course.

Bluntschli does much more in the play than represent the practical life and morals of the efficient, realistic man. This describes a leading aspect of his character; but it does not convey the mobility of wit and sharpness of insight which he is given in the dialogue. And it is not a contradiction but a natural development of the image we have formed of him earlier when he says in Act III that he is a man of 'an incurably romantic disposition':

> I ran away from home twice when I was a boy. I went into the army instead of into my father's business.

I climbed the balcony of this house when a man of sense would have dived into the nearest cellar. I came sneaking back here to have another look at the young lady when any other man of my age would have sent the coat back—

With this revelation, Shaw transfers the aura normally associated with the brooding Byronic hero in nineteenth-century literature to a quite different character type. The plain-speaker becomes the man of mystery. Shaw underlined this with a happy revision of the last line of the play. In the MS draft, the play ended on a comparatively weak line, with Sergius saying of the departed Bluntschli 'What a man! What a man!' The play as published ends with a line suggesting more sharply the way in which ordinariness attains extraordinary dimensions in Bluntschli, as well as providing a satirical comment on his machine-like efficiency—'What a man! Is he a man!'

The concept underlying the characterisation of Bluntschli, of the visionary pragmatist or romantic realist is traceable to Carlyle, whom Shaw mentions in connection with *Arms and the Man* in the Preface to *Three Plays for Puritans.* The idea of such a synthesis of forces exercised a considerable influence on Shaw's imagination in the early period of his dramatic career, the portraits of Caesar and Undershaft being further explorations of it. Shaw's comments on Carlyle's conception of the 'true hero of history' throw light on the treatment of Bluntschli, Sergius and the idea of the hero in *Arms and the Man:*

> Carlyle, with his vein of peasant inspiration, apprehended the sort of greatness that places the true hero of history so far beyond the mere *preux chevalier,* whose fanatical personal honor, gallantry, and self-sacrifice, are founded on a passion for death born of inability to bear the weight of a life that will not grant ideal conditions to the liver. This one ray of perception became Carlyle's whole stock-in-trade; and it sufficed to make a literary master of him. In due time, when Mommsen is an old man, and Carlyle dead, come I, and dramatize the by-this-time familiar distinction in Arms and the Man, with its comedic conflict between the knightly Bulgarian and the Mommsenite Swiss captain. Whereupon a great many playgoers who have not yet read Cervantes, much less Mommsen and Carlyle, raise a shriek of concern for their knightly ideal as if nobody had ever questioned its sufficiency since the middle ages.

It is principally through Bluntschli that the play's critical view of romantic notions about military valour and the *preux chevalier* is expressed. Catherine Petkoff's excited reverie early in Act I about the cavalry charge in which Sergius was involved—'Cant you see it, Raina: our gallant splendid Bulgarians with their swords and eyes flashing, thundering down like an avalanche and scattering the wretched Serbs and their dandified Austrian officers like chaff'—provides the foil for Bluntschli's later, grimly prosaic account of what happens in cavalry charges:

> It's like slinging a handful of peas against a window pane: first one comes; then two or three close behind him; and then all the rest in a lump. . . . You can tell the young ones by their wildness and their slashing. The old ones come bunched up under the number one guard: they know that theyre mere projectiles, and that it's no use trying to fight. The wounds are mostly broken knees, from the horses cannoning together.

In the midst of discussion of the play's complicated relations of love in Act III, a sharply graphic reminder of the horror of the war in the background is provided in Bluntschli's report of the death of his friend: 'Burnt alive. . . . Shot in the hip in a wood-yard. Couldnt drag himself out. Your fellows' shells set the timber on fire and burnt him, with half a dozen other poor devils in the same predicament.'

Like Bluntschli, Sergius is not a uni-dimensional character. But the mobility Sergius displays takes the form of vacillation between intransigent or extreme postures. Shaw rings various changes on Cunninghame Graham's celebrated remark in Parliament, 'I never withdraw', as the keynote of Sergius's character. Whichever of the 'half dozen Sergiuses who keep popping in and out of [his] handsome figure' tends to do so in the shape of a rigid pose. Sergius can find no middle ground between views of life as romance and views of it as empty farce: 'Raina: our romance is shattered. Life's a farce.' Apart from its recollections of Cunninghame Graham, Sergius's character is an amalgam of various nineteenth-century literary ideals. In Act I, in an ironic speech which prepares the audience for her later self-discoveries in the play, Raina confesses to her mother that 'it came into my head just as he [Sergius] was holding me in his arms and looking into my eyes, that perhaps we only had our heroic ideas because we are so fond of reading Byron and Pushkin, and because we were so delighted with the opera that season at Bucharest'. In the stage direction before Sergius's first entry in the play, Shaw identifies his sensibility with *what the advent of nineteenth century thought first produced in England: to wit, Byronism*. Byronism, in the account which follows, is seen as a mixture of sensitive, ironic intelligence, scorn at the failure of people (including the Byronic individual himself) to live up to ideals, cynicism, and a *'mysterious moodiness'* such as that of Childe Harold. Shaw has this figure defeated in both love and, in terms of strategic skill, war, by a character who has more in common with Sidney Webb than with Childe Harold.

Yet Shaw is careful not to make Sergius merely an object of ridicule in the play. Like Raina, Sergius has engaging flashes of candour, as when he tells Louka that the Higher Love is a 'very fatiguing thing to keep up for any length of time'. And Shaw gives him a fine moment of moral victory over Bluntschli in the final scene of the play when it is revealed that the latter has all along been thinking of the twenty-three-year old Raina as a girl of seventeen:

> SERGIUS: [*with grim enjoyment of his rival's discomfiture*] Bluntschli: my one last belief is gone. Your sagacity is a fraud, like everything else. You have less sense than even I!

Occasionally Sergius appears as a more knowing person than Bluntschli; and his spirited, virile character is not always presented in an unfavourable or ridiculous light.

The comedy of *Arms and the Man* is not completely devoid of political overtones, even though this is a comparatively minor aspect of the play. In the final scene of the play, Shaw gently underlines the fact that Bluntschli is a 'good Republican' and a 'free citizen'. Louka's engagement with Sergius constitutes some challenge to the rigidities of the class system in Bulgaria, though we feel that her most likely course after marriage would be to become herself a bastion of upper-class power. But in her Act III scene with Sergius, she has turned the play's preoccupation with courage very clearly in a new direction. She describes as schoolboyish Sergius's notion of the brave man as one who will 'defy to the death any power on earth or in heaven that sets itself up against his own will and conscience', and substitutes her own definition of 'true courage' as a willingness to become *déclassé* for love: 'if you felt the beginnings of love for me you would not let it grow. You would not dare: you would marry a rich man's daughter because you would be afraid of what other people would say of you.' She is not, of course, a disinterested pleader. But her spirited rejection of servanthood, set off as it is by Nicola's docile but adroit submission to it, is one feature of the play which extends its revolutionary thrust beyond the spheres of love and honour.

The unions which are foreshadowed at the end of the play hardly lend themselves to close analysis in political terms. But an ending in which the hussar marries a maidservant, and the well-bred young lady a hotel keeper, has more than a slight air of calculated indecorousness. Through the distancing perspective of Shaw's toyland Bulgaria, an English Victorian audience could no doubt afford to smile at the discovery of man alive and woman alive beneath the inhibiting conventions of a military caste system, and views of love and war based on romantic opera.

Source: A. M. Gibbs, "Romance and Anti-Romance in *Arms and the Man*," in *The Art and Mind of Shaw*, Macmillan Press, 1983, pp. 69–79.

Charles A. Berst

In the following essay, Berst discusses the "complexities and ambivalences" often overlooked by audiences in Shaw's work, specifically the "mixture of the romantic and prosaic" in Arms and the Man.

The tightly knit humor of incident and character in *Arms and the Man* has tended to obscure the more inclusive range of Shaw's artistic achievement in the play. At the first performance, the audience reacted with uproarious laughter; it would seem that the play had been a triumph, but Shaw was seeking something more. Afterwards, in a letter to Henry Arthur Jones, he remarked:

> I had the curious experience of witnessing an apparently insane success, with the actors and actresses almost losing their heads with the intoxication of laugh after laugh, and of going before the curtain to tremendous applause, the only person in the theatre who knew that the whole affair was a ghastly failure.

Apparently someone in the audience was in sympathy with Shaw's at least half-sincere reservations. When he appeared at the end of the performance, there was a solitary boo from the gallery, which called forth Shaw's famous response: "My friend, I quite agree with you—but what are we two against so many?" In this first play to follow his three unsuccessful "Unpleasant Plays," Shaw was no doubt experiencing one of his first tastes of popularity based on an appreciation for his humor, a popularity which sublimated his more serious concerns. In an attempt to educate audiences away from the sentimentalism and shallow naturalism of nineteenth-century drama, he sought a mode of social analysis, criticism, and satire. But from his awareness that "Unpleasant Plays" annihilated themselves through lack of a willing audience and from his own natural disposition to comedy, he turned to humor as a vehicle for thought. Audiences, however, were prone to take the humor and leave behind the thought, along with everything peripheral to it.

"ILLUSIONS ABOUT WAR,
GENTILITY, AND LOVE ARE
ULTIMATELY GIVEN THEIR TRUE
PERSPECTIVE THROUGH PROSAIC
AWARENESS, BUT AT THE SAME
TIME SHAW REVEALS WITH
ARTISTIC SENSITIVITY THAT SUCH
AWARENESS IS MOST VITALLY
ATTACHED TO LIFE WHEN IT IS
COMBINED WITH THE INCENTIVE
POWER OF ROMANCE."

Shaw later found it necessary to plead that *Arms and the Man* was "a classic comedy and not an opera-bouffe without the music." It was not a *Chocolate Soldier.* His concern over the problem is evidenced in his commentary on the character of Sergius. Realizing that this role was likely to be overplayed and hence misinterpreted, he sought, in vain, to have Richard Mansfield play Sergius instead of Bluntschli in the American production. The danger was that the genuine subtlety and seriousness of Sergius, which render him truly high comedy and effect the most interesting contrast with Bluntschli, would be lost in an *opera bouffe* interpretation. Shaw remarks:

> The whole difficulty was created by the fact that my Bulgarian hero, quite as much as Helmer in *A Doll's House,* was a hero shown from the modern woman's point of view. I complicated the psychology by making him catch glimpse after glimpse of his own aspect and conduct from this point of view himself, as all men are beginning to do more or less now, the result, of course, being the most horrible dubiety on his part as to whether he was really a brave and chivalrous gentleman, or a humbug and a moral coward. His actions, equally of course, were hopelessly irreconcilable with either theory. Need I add that if the straightforward Helmer, a very honest and ordinary middle-class man misled by false ideals of womanhood, bewildered the public, and was finally set down as a selfish cad by all the Helmers in the audience, *à fortiori* my introspective Bulgarian never had a chance, and was dismissed, with but moderately spontaneous laughter, as a swaggering impostor of the species for which contemporary slang has invented the term "bounder"?

Notably, Shaw was seeking to portray not a bounder, but a "comedic Hamlet" awakening to a tentative consciousness of his own absurdity and tortured by it. As such, Sergius is sensitive and reasonably complex, neither brave nor cowardly, neither a gentleman nor a humbug, but a hollow soul seeking the meaning of life on the periphery of experience. He is comic in his uncertainty and childishness, but it is the comedy of the incongruity between a soul flying with noble impulses on the one hand and exploring itself dubiously on the other, the comedy of disparity between ideals and actions rather than the comedy of a bizarre, overstuffed character-type. Shaw felt that this distinction was lost in the laughter of his audience.

The critical consensus about *Arms and the Man* is epitomized in Archibald Henderson's comment that "the play has for its dramatic essence the collision of romantic illusion with prosaic reality." This calls forth a rather simple formula, generally equating Raina and Sergius with romantic illusion and Bluntschli with prosaic reality. A close look at the play, however, shows that this formula is too generalized and too simple. Shaw's artistic accomplishment is in fact highly subtle, complex, and philosophically challenging, creating at its best a high comedy which is a synthesis of both tragicomic sensitivity and penetrating social perception.

Rather than contrasting the fantastic with the prosaic, or portraying an evolution in Raina's vision from the romantic to the realistic, the play expresses the interlocking relationship and mutual dependence of romanticism and realism. Through the three major characters, it reveals the double standard of the human mind which is genuinely thrilled with absurd heroics, yet at the same time reserves a realistic level of awareness regarding its own self-deception. It involves Coleridge's willing suspension of disbelief, translated into life. As usual in Shaw, simple absolutes are undercut by multifaceted qualifications and second thoughts. The play is thus a revelation of the psychology of romanticism, exploring its coexistence with, rather than its distance or dissociation from, reality. Such an inclusive, nonabsolutist approach is the essence of Shavianism. Shaw expresses his principle clearly in the Preface to this play:

> But the obvious conflicts of unmistakeable good with unmistakeable evil can only supply the crude drama of villain and hero, in which some absolute point of view is taken, and the dissentients are treated by the dramatist as enemies to be piously glorified or indignantly vilified. In such cheap wares I do not deal.

Although by comedic and philosophic nature Shaw had a disposition to cut through illusion to reality, he was too good a dramatist to serve them up as distinct alternatives. Especially in *Arms and the Man,* through the interaction of character, temperament, and event, he achieves a subtle fusion of the fantastic and the prosaic which gives texture and depth to the surface elements of a comic situation.

Raina Petkoff would be too much a fool for dramatic credibility were it not for a leavening of skepticism with which Shaw provides her as early as the opening lines of Act I. Her mother recounts the success of the cavalry charge led by Sergius; her words are given a mock-heroic ring which swings the moment into absurdity: "Cant you see it, Raina: our gallant splendid Bulgarians with their swords and eyes flashing, thundering down like an avalanche and scattering the wretched Serbs and their dandified Austrian officers like chaff." Raina echoes her mother's enthusiasm, but not without a constant counterpoint of negation in terms of her former doubts: she had kept Sergius waiting a year before consenting to a betrothal, because Byron and Pushkin and the opera at Bucharest were too much like dreams. Now it would seem that a brave new world has opened before her.

But the artificiality of such a moment of enthusiasm cannot last long without being confronted with facts of life, and Shaw confronts it immediately with the inglorious sequel to glorious cavalry charges, the cruel pursuit and slaughter of fugitives. Within ten minutes the vision of the battle degenerates from the noble abstraction of a heroic victory to the reality of a tattered, dirty, bloody, exhausted fugitive standing starkly incongruous in the lady's bedroom. The prosaic human element is thus brought into immediate juxtaposition with the romantic heroic element, causing the latter to vaporize in its insubstantiality. The sequence of the total act deftly turns from the unreal romance of an absent hero's operatic victory, to the imminent danger of a pursued fugitive, and finally to a more real, "prosaic" romance of compassion and maternal affection.

Danger is the catalyst through which Raina's vague romantic dreams become a romance of life. Ironically, it is Aristotle's tragic components, pity and fear, which bring her into immediate psychological sympathy with Bluntschli. She conceals him partly out of romance, but more basically out off compassion for him and fear of the brutal bloodshed which will undoubtedly ensue if she does not. His obvious weakness and exhaustion, his childlike taste for chocolate, and his frightening admission that the slightest provocation will make him cry awake in her the spontaneous womanly instinct of maternal affection. The psychology of her emotion is not unlike Candida's for Morell, though Raina has the awe and innocence of a younger woman. She can be temporarily indignant at Bluntschli's laughter about Sergius as Don Quixote, but his laughter reflects her own earlier doubts, now enforced by the greater reality of the present. All that is instinctive, vital, and maternal in Raina confronts her romantic dreams of Sergius in this first act, and though she may not immediately recognize it, her servant Louka realizes whom she will marry. Already Shaw has brought his two antagonists, romance and reality, onto the battlefield, and there is no doubt as to which wins out. The question of victory is too inconsequential to occupy the serious attention of the play: what is interesting is the nature of the battle and its ability to reveal fully the strengths, weaknesses, and similarities of the contending qualities.

As Act I portrays the prosaic viewpoint of Bluntschli, Act II allows free play to the romantic world of Raina and Sergius, a world which meets restrictions and difficulties even in its simplest contacts with life. That the romantic disposition simply cannot sustain the burden of a normal existence is surely no new insight on Shaw's part, but what is valuable and effective here is his stark objectification of its difficulties, revealing how a basic folly in one's outlook toward life ramifies itself into dozens of little follies which incapacitate normal action and end in boredom and fatigue. Since her romantic love is no instinctive part of her, Raina must stage-manage it. "She always appears at the right moment," says her father. "Yes," says her mother, "she listens for it." The entrance on cue, the noble air, and the spying out of the window on Sergius, which Louka suspects, are all contrivances to support an artificial pattern. "Higher love" in a young lady of twenty-three is an adolescent hangover; it obviously tires Sergius very quickly—he turns to Louka for relief—while Raina herself is not slow to indicate her own rebellion: "I always feel a longing to do or say something dreadful to him—to shock his propriety—to scandalize the five senses out of him." This is one step beyond her previous skepticism: this is clear irreverence, indicating that the natural focus of a realistic perspective in her has undercut the foolishness all along.

By Act III, Raina is merely clinging to the vestiges of her heroic romance with Sergius. Her remark, "My relation to him is the one really beautiful and noble part of my life," is as false in her own mind as is her subsequent assertion that she has lied only twice in her life. This is obviously play-acting, and though she still may have some illusions about Sergius, she certainly has few about the fraudulence of her own pretensions. When Bluntschli comments that he finds it impossible to believe a single word she says, she collapses from the heroic into the familiar: "How did you find me out?" She flatters herself that no one else has penetrated her façade, whereas Shaw has made it abundantly clear elsewhere that Louka, her mother, and her father all see through her. Only she and Sergius are fooled by her dream world, and even they cannot keep up with its demands. Recognizing the truth about herself, Raina can recognize the truth about Sergius as well; and when she discerns his flirtation with Louka, she tears him into little pieces of humiliation, laughing at herself at last in complete purgation, guessing Bluntschli's state of mind: "I daresay you think us a couple of grown-up babies, dont you?" In Act I she had concealed Bluntschli partly in the spirit of the romance of the situation, but more basically out of compassion and maternal affection, the two qualities of romance and reality being joined. This joining is never present in her relationship with Sergius, a relationship she instinctively mistrusts, but it reappears in Act III, along with the realization that Bluntschli takes her as a woman, not as a tinsel goddess. Hence, Raina's role may generally be an evolution from romance to reality, but it is by no means uncrossed by contradictory currents. She undergoes an education under the influence of Bluntschli, but it involves an awakening of her latent impulses and insights more than an alteration of her basic disposition.

The character of Bluntschli reverses the order of the romance-reality evolution. In Act I, he appears to be the antithesis of a romantic hero. He introduces, with a shock of contrast, the grisly proximity of war. His uniform is torn and splattered with mud and blood. He is prepared to fight to the death only because he knows that, if caught, he will either be slaughtered like a pig or taken into the street for vengeful amusement. Stuffing himself with chocolate and tending to cry and sleep, he is more like a helpless child than a man. What there is of the man seems hopelessly antiheroic—his fear of death, his laughter at Sergius, and his description of a cavalry charge in terms of a handful of peas thrown at a window pane. In exhaustion, the prosaic soldier is almost schizophrenic: in his coolness, professionalism, and laughter, he is the subtle cynic of warfare, yet at odds with this cynicism are the tastes and incapacities of a child. The final effect is to remove war from noble abstractions through the humanizing element of one who has no

illusions about it and who is, in fact, a walking negation of it.

Bluntschli's character shifts and grows in Act II by verbal report. The prosaic and professionally pragmatic approach to war is deftly contrasted with the ineffectuality of romantic amateurs. Petkoff and Sergius reveal him as the highly experienced and competent captain who had the clear sight to advise Sergius to resign, had the best of them in a horse-soldier barter, and managed a miraculous escape while enjoying the favors of a Bulgarian lady. Sergius disparages Bluntschli's competence in terms which reveal his own incapacity—the Swiss captain is a commercial traveler in uniform, a bourgeois. Several quick strokes render a remarkable class distinction. The gentleman is helpless in the hands of the tradesman; a consummate soldier and bourgeois can make a child of a gentleman. A basic social change of the nineteenth century is clarified briefly in passing—the genteel classes, adhering to their codes, are linked to custom and illusion. Their decline is inherent in the inefficiency of these illusions, which are taken full advantage of by the *bourgeoisie,* whose values and actions are based on practical experience and skills. Thus Sergius has only scorn to compensate for the fact that he was bested in the practical barter of war by a commercial traveler. This is a child's scorn, half-suppressing an uneasy sense of admiration for one whose ability is manifestly superior. Bluntschli's image thus evolves from one of ragged, inglorious defeat to one of keen military know-how and cunning—half-romantic in his prosaic genius, as compared to his bumbling Bulgarian foes.

It is a paradox that, as Bluntschli's bourgeois, shopkeeping abilities become more apparent, he grows in pseudoromantic stature. In Act III, he operates almost like a highly competent machine, first in disposing of the Bulgarian regiments, then in his facetious choice of a machine gun as his weapon for the proposed duel with Sergius. Sergius at last refuses to duel with him because "Youve no magnetism: youre not a man: youre a machine." Yet Bluntschli is not a representative of Henri Bergson's automaton—one who is funny because he loses contact with the vital flow of life and becomes machinelike. Rather, efficiency and humdrum are clearly means to an end for him and involve the most flexible mental contact with the realities of life. His very prosaicness, cutting through the automatism of convention and pretense, gives him the true freedom of action which is at the heart of all that is serious in life. When Raina collapses from her imperious acting, she remarks: "Do you know, you are the first man I ever met who did not take me seriously?" He responds very truthfully: "You mean, dont you, that I am the first man that has ever taken you quite seriously?" This genuine seriousness is the key to Bluntschli's humor. He has the true Shavian perspective of amusement at anything which is intrinsically false or absurd, from his own desperate plight in Act I to Raina's pretensions and her cat-and-mouse fight with Sergius in Act III. To the somber or romantic mind, the little melodramas of life are bloated with importance; to the truly serious mind, a sense of their comedy reduces them to proper proportions.

Thus in Act III it is Bluntschli who has that combination of prosaicness and imagination which is necessary to solve the problem of the disposal of the Bulgarian cavalry; it is Sergius who is the machine, rubber-stamping the orders which come from Bluntschli's practical mind. The romantic image of Sergius deteriorates, not only in itself, but especially by contact and contrast with the efficiency of the Swiss captain. Bluntschli's ability and cool common sense tend to assume a romantic aura: he grows in stature as some of the elements of a superman begin to radiate from him, the man who has the natural genius to succeed where others fail. The crowning union of romance with the prosaic temperament occurs when Bluntschli admits to "an incurably romantic disposition." Romantically he ran away from home as a boy, romantically he joined the army, romantically he climbed Raina's balcony instead of seeking her cellar, and romantically he has returned. It is clear at last that his relationship with Raina has all along been more truly romantic than Sergius'. The point, however, is scarcely made before the Shavian brilliance juxtaposes it with Bluntschli's compromising misjudgment of Raina's age, followed by his prosaic proposal and the magnificently bourgeois attraction and encumbrance of a chain of Swiss hotels. The romantic and the prosaic end in a magician's shuffle, and Sergius' final exclamation and question—"What a man! Is he a man?"—come too fast for the ambiguous reflection that in his romance Bluntschli is quite human, while in his prosaicness he is to some degree the Superman.

One critic interprets Bluntschli as a debased Falstaff, playing opposite Sergius' debased Hal and therefore making an ironic comment on the shallow alternatives offered to nineteenth-century man. But the facts and tone of the play bely this ingenious comparison and conclusion. Sergius is more a Hotspur than a Hal. He finally offers no true alternative to Bluntschli, because Bluntschli is

concurrently humanized and exalted with the qualities of both Falstaff and Hal. And if, in the general emphasis of the action, Bluntschli progresses from an image of reality to one of romance, Raina evolves in the opposite direction, from romance to reality, the two characters creating an aesthetic tension in their development and interaction which reveals multifold aspects of both qualities. Both qualities, of course, have actually existed in each character from the beginning, but for dramatic effectiveness the most forceful indications of this do not come until late in the development of the play.

In the character of Sergius, Shaw reveals a third element in the relationship of romance and reality—that of tortured self-consciousness, the tragedy and comedy of a man caught in bewilderment between his noble impulses and the ignominiousness of life. Even before Sergius appears, the daring heroism of his cavalry charge is pulverized by prosaic fact. First, it is brought into question by the essentially mock-heroic tone of Catherine Petkoff's description and by Raina's extravagant, foolish reaction. Then, it is utterly demolished by Bluntschli's humorous perspective which typifies the entire action as the folly and ignorance of an operatic tenor or a Don Quixote, who in this case survived only by a bit of uncanny luck. G. K. Chesterton asserts that sentimentalism is necessary because it is one of the very practical incentives behind action. Shaw would generally agree, but he indicates that this is a dangerous truth in warfare, where sentimentalism often leads to annihilation. When Sergius appears in Act II, he is uncomfortably trying to avoid this fact by retreating inside a new romanticism, that of Byronic cynicism. As would be expected of Shaw, Sergius is no mere romantic clown, which would be an easy duck to shoot down. Rather, he has "the physical hardihood, the high spirit, and the susceptible imagination of an untamed mountaineer chieftain." He is aware of the disparity between his own romantic disposition and the dull facts of the world. Heroic charges are out of place in the prosaicism of modern warfare, where soldiering is a coward's art of attacking when strong and retreating when weak. What he fails to see is that the disparity invalidates his romanticism—rather, he would have it invalidating reality. His outlook is distorted by confusion and cynicism resulting from the irony of his position: he remains a major because he won a battle in the wrong way, while others are promoted for losing battles in the right way. For consolation, he turns to Byronic disillusionment and scorn, a romantic pose much more interesting and complex than that of a mere war hero.

The "higher love" is another aspect of the search for Truth above reality; but as war has an ingredient of cowardice, love has an ingredient of biology, and nineteenth-century idealism lacked the medieval *savoir faire* that allowed Chrétien de Troyes to depict Launcelot genuflecting before Guenevere's bed, which he had just familiarly occupied. The strain of higher love necessitates a release for the lower, but the romanticism of Sergius as a late Victorian, albeit a Bulgarian, is not sophisticated enough to combine them in the same person. So he grabs Louka, and in doing so, he merely adds to the doubts which nurture his schizophrenic split between illusion and reality. Like Hamlet, he is acutely aware of his many-sided personality, which is a romantic estimate of himself, but also true to life. Is he hero, buffoon, humbug, blackguard, or coward? Certainly he is all of these. But one thing he definitely is not: he is not a noble lover. The strain of higher love is too great because it has no meaningful contact with the true personalities of either Raina or Sergius. Since higher love involves the mere acting of a foreign role, it cannot be maintained with prolonged consistency. Bergson points out that the essence of the true self is a continuity flowing through time. Sheer physical drives render a continuity of higher love impossible: Sergius is subject to lust on the one hand, Raina to her maternal-womanly instincts on the other. Shaw passes off his observation with the candor of a piquant smile.

Just as Bluntschli's sense of humor gives him a considerable depth of seriousness, Sergius' intense seriousness makes him comical. His heroic propensities and subsequent doubts render him both a comic machine and tragicomic introvert, and it is a revelation of Shaw's skill that both elements deterministically converge, bringing Sergius to his fate. His tragicomic introspection in Act III, carrying over the self-analytical strain of the previous act, is highly active and varied. It is a soul-searching which, though seemingly at odds with romanticism, is highly romantic in its Byronism. First, he questions the concept of authority—who is *he* to give orders to the soldiers? Next, he goes to the very heart of his predicament: "Mockery! mockery everywhere! everything I think is mocked by everything I do." At last, he is convinced by Louka that true courage exists in such things as defying the whole world in order to marry the person you love, no matter how far beneath you that person may be. Louka takes advantage of his image of himself and traps him intellectually. He agrees that if he touches her again, he will wed her.

Concurrently, the mechanical aspect of his nature guides his action. The stubbornness of the self-assured hero asserts itself first in Act II. When Catherine Petkoff suggests that he withdraw his resignation, he folds his arms and exclaims: "I never withdraw." This mechanical pattern repeats itself in Act III. As an officer, he mechanically signs Bluntschli's orders; as a gentleman, he mechanically challenges Bluntschli to duel; and finally, after he has refused to withdraw or apologize in a number of situations, he at last touches Louka—and she dares him to keep his word: "You can withdraw if you like." To which, quite consistently, the conditioned man replies: "Withdraw! Never!" The trap has been sprung, introspectively consistent, according to the code of a gentleman's word, mechanically perfect, penetratingly comic. Significantly, this is the point of truth for Sergius, equally as realistic and illuminating as that for Bluntschli and Raina.

In Act III, the horror and ludicrousness of war are brought into graphic focus through Bluntschli's account of his friend who was wounded and burned alive in a wood yard, and the true instincts of love are revealed in Raina's love for Bluntschli, active and vital, beneath her feigned love for Sergius. The truth converges upon Sergius, and although his reaction is strongly tinged with Byronic despair, he is caught in the essence of reality which propels him toward Louka. He can now with an honest mind legalize his normal biological drives toward a pretty wench, and at the same time he can fulfill his sense of courage in doing so. It is romantic in its prosaicness. Sergius is a notable advancement over the gull of Jonsonian and Restoration comedy: he is both duped and dupes himself into a lowly marriage, but in doing so he is being true to his genuine nature, and he finds himself in spite of himself.

The characters most in touch with reality are the two servants, Louka and Nicola. It is a necessity of their class that, though they may have romantic daydreams, these dreams should always be in touch with potentially profitable facts. Here again Shaw draws a telling contrast, differentiating between the strictly prosaic temperament and the prosaic temperament with romantic ambition. Nicola is the absolute realist; in his clarity of insight is etched the predicament of an entire social class. He remarks to Louka: "Child: you dont know the power such high people have over the like of you and me when we try to rise out of our poverty against them." His eyes are open to his dependence on the wealthy classes, and within this framework he operates with complete efficiency and cleverness, getting all he can out of it, planning to set up a shop in Sophia with the Petkoffs as his principal customers. In his pursuit of economic security, he even forgoes marriage to Louka, since as Sergius' bride she will be a good customer rather than an expensive wife. Such clearheadedness attracts the admiration of Bluntschli, who remarks: "Never mind whether it's heroism or baseness. Nicola's the ablest man Ive met in Bulgaria. I'll make him manager of a hotel if he can speak French and German." Nicola is the prosaic ideal, and Bluntschli's prosaic side is naturally keenly attracted to him. Yet what makes Bluntschli rounded and human is that he also has a strong motivating romantic temperament. Lacking this balance, Nicola is more base than heroic. He would make an excellent hotel manager. There is something mundane, lifeless, and dehumanizing in this prosaic perspective. For a servant—or a hotel manager—its end is clever servility.

In contrast, Louka combines clear prosaic vision with imagination, ambition, and romance, and succeeds thereby in rising above servility. Between Nicola and Louka there is a Pygmalion-Galatea relationship foreshadowing Higgins and Eliza. Nicola has taught her not to overuse make-up like common Bulgarian girls, and to be clean and dainty like a lady. But, like Higgins, he has created a monster beyond his control—he has made a real woman out of a servant. His advice promotes social stratification: "The way to get on as a lady is the same as the way to get on as a servant: youve got to know your place." To Louka, this is but "cold-blooded wisdom," and one may anticipate Eliza's words: "the difference between a lady and a flower girl is not how she behaves, but how she's treated." As Nicola introduces in a natural fashion a didactic element regarding the social and economic dependence of the servant class, Louka brings into question the superstructure of gentility. She sees clearly that Nicola has the soul of a servant and that the effect of such souls is to reinforce class distinctions. But she views such distinctions as not very flattering to the social elite. The moral laxity of the upper classes tends to put her on a par with them. This feeds her natural ambition. Thus she can say familiarly to Sergius: "Gentlefolk are all alike: you making love to me behind Miss Raina's back; and she doing the same behind yours." She has the insight all along that Raina will marry Bluntschli if she has the chance. Obviously, biological drives are more basic than "higher love," and this fact encourages Louka's hope of climbing above her class to marry Sergius. In his abandoning higher love and in her marrying for social advancement, there is a sexual and economic honesty which is in accord with

the play's denouement. As with Raina and Bluntschli, the fairy-tale romance of the general situation is undergirded by natural and prosaic impulses.

The mixture of the romantic and the prosaic which Shaw achieves in his characters he carries further into a contrast between the characters and the events and setting. In Act I, the pervasive prosaicness of Bluntschli is in contrast with the romantic setting of a lady's bedroom and with the melodramatic events of a heroic cavalry charge, a strange man at the window, and Raina's daring concealment of him. In Act II, the romantic, Byronic Sergius is in contrast with the laundry on the fruit bushes and the after-breakfast atmosphere. The servants are quarreling, an ignominious peace has been established—it is a time for flirting with the servant girl, disposing of troops, and telling vulgar stories about the war. Act III offers a fusion of the prosaic and the romantic, with troop dispersion, the plotting of servants, flirting, the domestic comedy of Petkoff's coat, and practical concerns over eligibility in betrothal, all offering a constant counterpoint to the threat of a duel over a lady, the development of romantic love between the two couples, and the romance of a double marriage in the offing. By constantly juxtaposing the prosaic and romantic in such ways, Shaw achieves a maximum reflection of their many facets and interrelationships. His ideas on the matter, which are more an intuitive grasp of multifold ironic interplays between romance and reality than straightline logical conclusions, are thus given full expression and pertinence in a dramatic situation.

The play develops three major themes. First, there is the satire on war, its heroics represented by Sergius, its prosaicness by Bluntschli. This brings into focus both the nature of the individual soldier and the tactics and psychology of warfare. Second, there is the satire on the nature of the genteel classes, on what comprises a lady, a gentleman, and a servant. Third, there is an exploration of the spectrum of human disposition which ranges from the romantic to the prosaic, the two elements being not just opposites, but, paradoxically, capable of appearing in life as shadings of each other. All the characters serve an illuminating function in this area. The themes run concurrently, coalescing at last in Act III in terms of paradox.

The war theme is brought to a head in Bluntschli's recounting of his wounded friend being burned alive in a wood yard. Raina exclaims on its horror, Sergius remarks on its ridiculousness. In fact, it is both, just as Sergius' charge was both brave and ridiculous and Bluntschli's preference for chocolates over ammunition involves both realism and foolhardiness. The tragedy and humor of war tend to coexist. The theme satirizing the genteel classes is brought to a conclusion in the betrothal of Sergius and Louka. The common concept that a gentleman is a gentleman only if he behaves like one is subjected to the inquiry—but what does a gentleman behave like? By seeking consistently to maintain genteel love with Raina in Act II, Sergius is both noble and idiotic; by sticking to his gentlemanly code of honor regarding Louka in Act III, he is both honorable and ridiculous. To descend below one's class is to be both courageous and self-indulgent; to climb the social ladder is to be both ingenious and conceited. The theme regarding the romantic and prosaic in life quickly destroys the simple abstraction of "higher love" in Act II, and in Act III achieves a more nearly lifelike resolution in ambivalence. Prosaic Louka marries romantic Sergius, romantic Raina marries prosaic Bluntschli. Yet, in her social elevation, Louka attains romance, and in following his biological instincts, Sergius capitulates to prosaic impulse. In the same vein, Raina pursues her natural maternal-sexual drives, and Bluntschli culminates his romantic act of climbing to a lady's balcony with the romantic conclusion of marrying the lady.

The ending of the play consequently involves a fusion of disparate elements, from prosaic fact to romance, resolving themselves on a pragmatic biological level and evoking from all the characters concerned a higher degree of honesty and self-awareness than they had possessed at the beginning. It was Shaw's hope as artist and philosopher that some of this heightened awareness would rub off on his audiences. But in making his art popular, he made his point obscure. The increase in perception he sought tended to be drowned in laughter. Further, his ideas are less subject to strict analysis than to intuition; consequently, the deceptively easy single-line approach, which asserts that "Shaw says this" or "Shaw says that," simply is not accurate, since it fails to grasp the complexities and ambivalences of Shaw's artistic thought and method. Yet it is these complexities and ambivalences that give depth and subtlety to his art. In *Arms and the Man* he wishes to reveal the blindness of the romantic element in life more than he desires to satirize romantic characters. All life is a mixture of the romantic and the prosaic; what is important is that the prosaic temperament properly assimilate and control the romantic element. Life simply cannot support sustained romance. By its very dreamlike nature, romance must be essentially

discontinuous, and hence out of touch with what Bergson called "the fluid continuity of the real." Illusions about war, gentility, and love are ultimately given their true perspective through prosaic awareness, but at the same time Shaw reveals with artistic sensitivity that such awareness is most vitally attached to life when it is combined with the incentive power of romance.

Source: Charles A. Berst, "Romance and Reality in *Arms and the Man*," in *Modern Language Quarterly*, Vol. XXVII, No. 2, June 1966, pp. 197–211.

Michael Quinn

In the following essay, Quinn examines the distance between Shaw's stated intentions in Arms and the Man *and what the play actually achieves.*

One of the difficulties with Shaw is that too often, like Mistress Quickly, "a man does not know where to have" him. Largely on the basis of his own noisy claims, he still retains much of the prestige of a 'great thinker', standing, in somewhat heretical and clownish garb, at the end of the line of what John Holloway has called 'Victorian sages', a latter-day Carlyle whose aim also was "to make his readers see life and the world over again, see it with a more searching or perhaps a more subtle and sensitive gaze". But, as Holloway insists and demonstrates at length from the works of his selected sages, "everything depends on their interpretation in detail", without which one cannot be sure of the "exact meaning" of the sages's message. In the case of Shaw the difficulty is greatly increased by a common confusion, deliberately encouraged by the author himself, between the polemical pamphleteer, whose favourite form was the preface, and the successful dramatist. That there is a confusion and that it hinders an adequate assessment of Shaw as a dramatist needs, I think, to be emphasized. It is surely not accidental that none of Holloway's sages presented his message mainly in dramatic form, for drama resists more strongly than any other medium the intrusion of new ideas. As Arthur Miller wrote in the Preface to his *Collected Plays,*

> Where no doubt exists in the heart of the people a play cannot create doubt; where no desire to believe exists, a play cannot create belief.

Shaw was fully aware of this difficulty, recognizing, with his views, "how impossible it was for (him) to write fiction that should delight the public". But he pinned his hopes on the fact that

> It is quite possible for a piece to enjoy the most sensational success on the basis of a complete

misunderstanding of its philosophy: indeed, it is not too much to say that it is only by a capacity for succeeding in spite of its philosophy that a dramatic work of serious poetic import can become popular.
(Preface to *Plays Unpleasant.*)

If one could be sure that no one took Shaw's prefaces seriously, this might be laughed off as a pleasant enough piece of witty nonsense; but often the prefaces are taken very seriously indeed and in this particular case I am not at all sure that this comment does not reflect an odd disjunction in Shaw's own mind between form and content.

That Shaw was essentially a comic dramatist hardly needs stressing today. The surprising popularity of *Saint Joan,* on the stage, in the study, and perhaps most of all recently in the classroom, may have masked the fact for a time, but latterly there have been critics who have dared to suggest that even Shaw's 'tragic masterpiece' should properly be regarded as a comedy. But what kind of comedy did he write? It was all very well for him to compare himself to Molière and remind us "that my business as a classic writer of comedies is 'to chasten morals with ridicule' . . ." Comedy, however, cannot easily free itself from its age; not only does it assume the presence of an audience to laugh at its jokes but it requires the agreement of the audience as to what is or is not funny or delightful. And the kind of comedy at which Shaw apparently aimed faced special difficulties in England, where classical comedy has always had a hard row to hoe, the possibilities of the form having been seriously damaged, perhaps even ruined, at the outset of its career by the genius of the predominantly romantic Shakespeare. Jonson made a brave attempt to shape a native classical comedy for the English stage and the special conditions of the Restoration theatre permitted another somewhat idiosyncratic but impressive experiment; but sentiment seems to have too deep roots in the English temperament to be cauterized by the pure comic spirit and keeps reviving, like bindweed, to strangle its enemy. Shaw did not, I think, contribute much to a revival of classical comedy in English, yet his efforts to work out a comic form that would serve his special purposes may throw some light on the nature of the problem facing any serious comic dramatist in this country. His struggle is perhaps clearest at the very beginning of his dramatic career, when his statements of intention are most explicit and his plays show more obviously the influences against which he was fighting; and *Arms and the Man* may serve as a convenient text, since it was not only his first popular success but has retained its place in

IF A POINT OF VIEW IS TO BE ATTACKED SERIOUSLY, IT MUST BE SERIOUSLY DEFENDED: OTHERWISE, THERE IS NO DRAMA, ONLY A MASSACRE. THE NATURE OF 'IDEALISM' IS NEVER DEFINED WITH ANY PRECISION AND THE EXPOSURE IS PRESENTED ONLY THROUGH A SIMPLE OPPOSITION OF 'IDEALIST' AND 'REALIST'."

the repertory and for many stands as a typical Shaw play.

The English theatre in the 1890's was in a state of transition; that is, it seems to have been changing in a rather more radical and self-conscious way than is normal even for the theatre. In the prefaces to *Plays Unpleasant* and *Plays Pleasant* Shaw himself has given us a lively and no doubt biased account of the battle being fought between the 'theatricality' of the Irving school and the 'drama of ideas', a battle in which Shaw played a leading part both as critic and playwright. He wanted to make the drama 'serious', suitable for "persons of serious and intellectual interests", by writing plays that forced "the spectator to face unpleasant facts" and so dealt "sincerely with humanity". *Arms and the Man,* first produced in 1894, was undoubtedly conceived as a home-made bomb for use by the *sansculottes* and, despite its 'pleasantness', its explicit aim was to introduce to the English stage in an English form the attack on 'Idealism' which Shaw believed to be the quintessence of Ibsenism. This 'idealism', "only a flattering name for romance in politics and morals", was seen as a serious menace, for it shed "fictitious glory on robbery, starvation, disease, crime, drink, war, cruelty, cupidity, and all the other commonplaces of civilization . . ." Moreover, Shaw's preface seems to imply that his attack will not only reveal the dangers of 'idealism' but will suggest a positive remedy.

To me the tragedy and comedy of life lie in the consequences, sometimes terrible, sometimes ludicrous, of our persistent attempts to found our institutions on the ideals suggested to our imaginations by our half-satisfied passions instead of on a genuinely scientific natural history.

Already implicit in this passage is Shaw's optimistic belief in a purposive cosmic energy, the Life Force, with which men must co-operative, but such co-operation is seriously hindered by 'idealism' and 'romance'; the echoes of Carlyle and of the whole nineteenth-century faith in progress mark this as firmly Victorian. Yet the central accusation remains serious and of interest to us: that 'Idealism' masks the real issues of the day and allows people to tolerate complacently what should be intolerable injustices and sufferings and that love and war are two areas of human experience where this pernicious evasiveness operates most dangerously. In *Arms and the Man* he attacked both at once.

What seems quite clear from the outset is the *Arms and the Man* does not, in any worthwhile sense, fulfil Shaw's stated intention. If a point of view is to be attacked seriously, it must be seriously defended: otherwise, there is no drama, only a massacre. The nature of 'idealism' is never defined with any precision and the exposure is presented only through a simple opposition of 'idealist' and 'realist'. Raina, as idealist, hopes

> that the world is really a glorious world for women who can see its glory and men who can act its romance,

and the key idealist image is of Sergius leading the charge against the Austrian guns. The realist, on the other hand, (and it is surely significant that it is Sergius, not Bluntschli, who speaks), defines soldiering as

> the coward's art of attacking mercilessly when you are strong, and keeping our of harm's way when you are weak. . . . Get your enemy at a disadvantage; and never, on any account, fight him on equal terms.

The two points of view are set against each other without ever mingling, so that there is no need to elaborate the distinction with any subtlety nor is there any pressure on the spectator to think the matter through to its ultimate consequences. If the dangers of idealism in war were to be exposed seriously, one might have expected some use of particular detail of the kind likely to evoke a strong value-judgement; but the most horrific is the brief account by Bluntschli of the wounded man who was burnt alive in the woodyard. And even the few telling images are quickly robbed of their moral effectiveness by the phlegmatism of Bluntschli or the maudlin generalisations of Sergius. The two viewpoints are, as I say, juxtaposed without intermingling; the resolution on the level of ideas is

achieved by the revelation that in fact there never has been any opposition at all. The characters in *Arms and the Man* are not spokesmen for contrasting ideas as in Shaw's later plays but are all flakes of much the same kind; none of them believes in the idealism that is being attacked, with the possible exception of Louka, with whom we are clearly intended to sympathize. When the masks are stripped off, they all agree with Bluntschli on the value of being practical, despite its "crawling baseness".

This lack of a real opposition in the play may be traced further to an essentially superficial attitude to the motivation of characters in the play. When Shakespeare wrote his most bitter consideration of the menace of false ideals in love and war, he traced the public folly of military idealism back to the private vice of unrestrained passion: "all the argument is a cuckold and a whore".

> Then everything includes itself in power,
> Power into will, will into appetite,
> And appetite, an universal wolf,
> So doubly seconded with will and power,
> Must make perforce an universal prey,
> And last eat up himself.
>
> (*Troilus & Cressida.* I. iii. 119–124)

Such treatment makes the accusation more general and more inescapable in that it roots it in human nature, while the language of appetite allows Shakespeare to convey the pressures behind 'idealism' with a fierce immediacy. Shaw, in his preface, suggested a similar relation in his reference to "our half-satisfied passions", but in the play itself love is a mere game, as innocent of passion as crocquet. All we have on the level of motivation is the stripping off of masks, and the revelation that Raina is moved more by womanly pity than by romantic ideals, Sergius more by a pretty face and a pert resistance, while Bluntschli's motivation remains a mystery to the end. Of course we accept, for the sake of the play, that the characters think they believe in these ideals by there is no suggestion, nor any encouragement to consider, why they adopt such a mode of thinking; and that surely is the important question for an attack on idealism. *Arms and the Man* is not satire, nor does it 'chasten morals with ridicule', nor is it serious in the sense that Shaw protested that his plays were to be.

That *Arms and the Man* does not prove to be a 'serious' comedy in the neo-classical tradition is, as one would expect, primarily a matter of form. Yet this is something of a surprise as Shaw himself was very much aware of the problem of form; his dramatic criticism in the 1890's contains many attacks on the current popularity of the 'well-made play', which he saw as the formal expression of the innate triviality of the contemporary theatre. In his additions to *The Quintessence of Ibsenism* he outlined what he believed to be the fundamental pattern of the *pièce bien faite:* exposition, situation, unravelling. This made for an essentially artificial image of life, presenting to the spectator an unjustified hope that the problems of life could be resolved by a variety of contrivances from a hitherto concealed birthmark to a hitherto unsuspected goodness of heart in the villain. Instead, Shaw advocated a pattern that he maintained he found in Ibsen, a pattern in which the unravelling was replaced by 'discussion', the whole point of the 'discussion' being that it involved a facing of the truth with intellectual honesty in place of the contrived evasion of it in the *pièce bien faite*. It remains an open question whether Shaw ever achieved this ideal pattern in any of his plays; certainly, in *Arms and the Man,* there is very little that can reasonably be called 'discussion' and what there is is certainly not confined to a climactic revelation in the last act. Indeed, considering his own frequent assertions of how unorthodox were his ideas, there is a remarkable absence of any sense of the dramatist struggling to adapt the form of his play to the needs of a new kind of expression; in sharp contrast to the plays of Ibsen and Strindberg, the dominent impression is of a play dominated and controlled from the start by a well-established theatrical convention.

In structure *Arms and the Man* adheres fairly closely to the principles of the *pièce bien faite* as defined by Shaw himself. The first act presents a blatantly romantic situation that calls forth all the responses and expectations normally associated with Anthony Hope's Ruritania, responses that, despite the preposterously romantic trappings, still retain their appeal, and expectations that are by no means left unsatisfied. There is nothing essentially objectionable in this anachronistic kind of costume drama; it has been used by modern dramatists—Claudel, Maxwell Anderson, Christopher Fry, and even John Whiting—as a convenient device for distancing the action, but in almost every instance there is a pressure towards symbolic interpretations that is wholly absent in Shaw. Moreover, the action of Shaw's play moves unerringly along the lines laid down by the well-made play: the romantic expectation looks forward to a resolution of the differences between Raina and Bluntschli so that the hopes raised by Raina's "poor darling" at the end of Act I may be fulfilled. Romance does not require the heroine to marry her first choice, so

that the collapse of the engagement between Raina and Sergius is in no sense a deflation of the audience's romantic expectations. The second act presents entanglements not unworthy of a competent bedroom farce and the third act resolves these complications by means of a 'discovery'—that Bluntschli thought Raina was only 17—that is more difficult to grasp and hardly more credible than the best concealed strawberry birthmark or the longest-lost letter of revelation. I would suggest then that the play's driving force is directed not towards the exposure of vice or folly, or the chastening of morals with ridicule, but towards a happy ending in the medieval and Shakespearean manner, an ending which, as in so many of Shaw's plays, allows the girl to have both the man and the money. And I find little evidence of any controlling satiric intention which would make of this happy ending an ironic comment.

The gap between Shaw's professed intention and what in fact he achieved is evidence of the perennial problem of the theatre. Shaw was always a practical man and, in the Preface to *Plays Pleasant,* he shows that he was only too well aware that the battle for the London stage had to be fought not on a polite academic jousting-ground but in the glaring light of economic realities. The audience at the Royal Court in the Barker-Vedrenne period may have had "a lecture-going, sermon-loving appearance", but certainly in the 1890's any manager who offered a mere lecture or sermon to his audience was in danger of paying heavily for his presumption. The majority of playgoers had to be deceived into entering the theatrical chapel of Ibsen and Shaw and drugged into listening to their sermons; only then did they acquire a taste for that particular kind of entertainment. Shaw insisted at the beginning of his career as a dramatist that "I have always cast my plays in the ordinary practical comic form in use at all the theatres", and at the very end he still maintained that, in matters of "the incidents, plot, construction, and general professional and technical qualities" of a play, he was "a very old-fashioned playwright"; throughout he seems to have believed that he could persuade an audience to accept new ideas by presenting them in old forms. But the form makes the play; the new wine may not burst the old bottles, but it is unlikely to taste like new wine.

Arms and the Man is a very good play of its kind, but it is not the kind of play one might have expected from Shaw's preface. Far from being a satiric comedy, it belongs in the great tradition of English artificial comedy; like Wilde's *The*

Importance of Being Earnest, it takes up the form of the "well-made play" and treats the matter with witty intelligence, so that sentiment is kept firmly in check. Indeed, the virtues of *Arms and the Man* spring largely from those very qualities that tend to make it ineffective as a chastener of morals. For instance, the characters may be provided with little in the way of credible motivation and are not even spokesmen for ideas as in Shaw's unpleasant plays; but they are vividly sketched in strictly theatrical terms, drawing on numerous well-established stage conventions, so that Bluntschli, Sergius, Raina and Petkoff are more likely to stick in the memory than Sartorius, Mr. Warren or even Lickcheese. The comedy in *Arms and the Man* depends essentially on the consistency of the world presented. There is really no outsider in the play, no voice to point a sickening moral in the manner of sentimental comedy nor a chastening gibe as in satire; Bluntschli triumphs, not because he is different from the other characters but simply because he is better at their own game. All of them live, to a greater or lesser extent, in their own world of professed romance and real practicality and we delight in the incongruity: "the bravest of the brave" converted to a "poor devil pulling at his horse", "the higher love" proving in practice a "very fatiguing thing to keep up for any length of time", and so on. Man is not really heroic; he is not even consistent, for he cannot for long hold sentiment and behaviour together. This is matter for high comedy and it is well handled; but it has little to do with satire, chastening morals with ridicule, or with the menacing idealism defined by Shaw in his preface.

Source: Michael Quinn, "Form and Intention: A Negative View of *Arms and the Man*," in *Critical Quarterly*, Vol. 5, No. 2, Summer 1963, pp. 148–54.

SOURCES

Adcock, Arthur St. John, "George Bernard Shaw," in LitFinder.com, Ross Publishing, Inc., 2005.

"Bernard Shaw," in *The Norton Anthology of English Literature*, 5th ed., edited by M. H. Abrams, Vol. 2, W. W. Norton, 1986, pp. 1759–62.

Borges, Jorge Luis, "For Bernard Shaw," in *Other Inquisitions, 1937–1952*, by Jorge Luis Borges, translated by Ruth L. C. Simms, University of Texas Press, 1964, pp. 163–66.

Brecht, Bertolt, "Ovation for Shaw," translated by Gerhard H. W. Zuther, in *Modern Drama*, Vol. 2, No. 2, September 1959, pp. 184–87.

Chesterton, G. K., *George Bernard Shaw*, John Lane, 1909, pp. 118–20.

Fisher, Barbara M., "Fanny's First Play: A Critical Potboiler?" in *George Bernard Shaw*, edited by Harold Bloom, Chelsea House Publishers, 1987, p. 252.

Nevinson, H. W., "George Bernard Shaw," in *New Leader*, August 23, 1929.

Shaw, George Bernard, *Arms and the Man*, in *Plays: Pleasant and Unpleasant*, H. S. Stone, 1898.

FURTHER READING

Booth, Michael Richard, and Joel H. Kaplan, *The Edwardian Theatre: Essays on Performance and the Stage*, Cambridge University Press, 1996.
    An overview of the Edwardian entertainment industry, this book is a collection of essays that cover cultural studies and the inner workings of the theatre in this age.

Davis, Tracy C., *George Bernard Shaw and the Socialist Theatre*, Praeger, 1994.
    This book traces the theatrical and political influences on Shaw and discusses his economic practices and theories as they relate to his work in the theatre.

Henderson, Archibald, *George Bernard Shaw: Man of the Century*, Appleton-Century-Crofts, 1956.
    Henderson was Shaw's official biographer and knew the playwright for 47 years. This book, edited by Shaw himself, is a comprehensive examination of Shaw's life and work, including his correspondence.

Innes, Christopher, *The Cambridge Companion to George Bernard Shaw*, Cambridge University Press, 1998.
    This popular and comprehensive guide to all things Shaw includes essays by leading scholars on a wide variety of topics.

Jackson, Russell, *Victorian Theatre: The Theatre in Its Time*, New Amsterdam Books, 1990.
    A sourcebook about the Victorian stage containing articles, letters of actors and managers, memoirs, contracts, and more, this book provides a detailed look at the world of Victorian theatre.

Jenkins, Anthony, *The Making of Victorian Drama*, Cambridge University Press, 1991.
    Jenkins examines seven playwrights, including Shaw, who contributed to the theatre of ideas and who helped to gain respectability for the theatre. Jenkins also looks at the social and political context in which these playwrights worked.

The Belle's Stratagem

HANNAH COWLEY

1780

Hannah Cowley's *The Belle's Stratagem* was first produced in 1780 and is considered her most famous play. It is a lighthearted comedy about manners and courtship, set in the fashionable society of late-eighteenth-century London. Scholars often note that Cowley's style in *The Belle's Stratagem* is suggestive of her predecessors. Even the title of this play pays homage to one such Augustan playwright, George Farquhar, and his play *The Beaux's Stratagem*.

Many of the stories from the Restoration and Augustan playwrights juxtapose two storylines; *The Belle's Stratagem* is no different. The two plot-lines are Letitia Hardy's ingenious scheme to entrap and win the heart of her arranged husband, Doricourt, and the marital problems of the insanely jealous Sir George Touchwood and his wife, the sheltered and beautiful Lady Frances. Both plots focus on men learning to respect women; however, there is added depth to this story, as it is also layered with questions about identity and feminism. The role of the masquerade as a metaphor for the many masks women must wear within society becomes an important element in both plotlines. The two juxtaposed stories meet with a crescendo at the masquerade ball, creating a bewildering parody of fashionable society, marriage, and the role of women in the eighteenth century.

AUTHOR BIOGRAPHY

Hannah Cowley is one of the foremost playwrights of the late eighteenth century. Often underrecognized,

Hannah Cowley   Mary Evans Picture Library

possibly because of her gender, her skill for writing fluid dialogue and developing spirited, unforgettable comic characters places her in a category with her better-known, male contemporaries.

Cowley was born Hannah Parkhouse in 1743 in Tiverton, Devonshire, England. Her father Philip Parkhouse, a bookseller with extensive schooling, provided Cowley with an impressive and rare education for a young eighteenth-century woman. As a result, Cowley was well versed in many subjects.

In 1772, Hannah married Thomas Cowley, son of another bookseller, who worked in several jobs, including as a theatre critic. In 1776, she decided to try her hand at writing for the stage to supplement the couple's income. She submitted her first finished play, which she penned in only a few weeks' time, to David Garrick, a theatre manager and actor. Surprising to everyone, including Cowley herself, her debut work *The Runaway* was produced on February 15, 1776, at Drury Lane, and was well received by critics and the public alike.

After Garrick's retirement later in 1776, Cowley initially had difficultly getting new plays staged. In a bizarre twist, another woman playwright, Hannah More, staged several plays that bore an uncanny resemblance to one of Cowley's as-yet-unproduced plays, leading some, including

Cowley herself, to accuse More of plagiarism; the dispute, however, was never resolved.

In 1780, Cowley's luck began to turn. Her play *The Belle's Stratagem* premiered on February 22, 1780, and was a great success. *The School of Eloquence* (April 3, 1780) was equally successful, but *The World As It Goes* (February 24, 1781) essentially bombed. This failure led to another, and, thus, in search of steadier income for the family, Thomas Cowley departed for India in 1783 to work for the East India Company, leaving behind Cowley and the couple's children.

Thomas Cowley never returned to England; he died in India in 1797. Hannah, however, began to prosper in her playwriting, producing at least seven plays between 1783 and 1794. As her popularity grew, she attempted writing poetry, but found it far less lucrative than her work for the stage. In 1789, she suffered personal tragedy when her eldest daughter died, followed in death the next year by Philip Parkhouse, Cowley's father.

Cowley's popularity as a writer began to wane in the late 1790s and early 1800s. She decided to return to her hometown in Devonshire, where she remained until her death in 1809. She continued to write in her final years, undertaking a revision of her earlier works to make them more palatable for the conservative audiences of the early nineteenth century. *The Works of Hannah Cowley* (1813), published after her death, contains these revised, or watered-down, versions of her plays, and, as such, has been largely ignored by twentieth- and twenty-first-century scholars. To get a true feel for Cowley's writing, readers should seek out the publications of her original plays.

PLOT SUMMARY

Act 1

The Belle's Stratagem opens at Lincoln's Inn, where Saville is looking for his good friend, Doricourt, who has recently returned from travels. While waiting, Saville talks with a townsman, Courtall, about the plentiful unmarried women throughout town. They also discuss how the unwed women are extremely eager to marry because so many young men are away fighting the Americans in the Revolutionary War. Saville tells Courtall that Doricourt is to marry Letitia Hardy. Courtall is excited that Doricourt is to be wed, because Doricourt is a heavily courted young man. His marriage will free the minds of many women for other men.

Later, at Doricourt's, Crowquill, the author of a local gossip column, attempts to pry scandalous information from Doricourt's porter. It is to no avail as, according to the porter, Doricourt is free of such trifle. Saville arrives, still looking for Doricourt, and eventually he is taken to see his friend's apartment by a Frenchman employed by Doricourt.

At the apartment, Doricourt and Saville discuss servants. Doricourt employs French and German servants because he believes they are less intelligent and, thus, more loyal. Saville disagrees, and the two men change topics, discussing instead marriage and women of the world. Doricourt explains that he finds Letitia Hardy attractive, but he believes her soul is lacking fire and lust. Doricourt speaks of the beautiful women of France and Italy, while expressing his indifference for British women. Again, Saville disagrees. The two men end the conversation agreeing that British men do, in fact, make the best friends, companions, and business partners.

Meanwhile, at an apartment owned by the Hardy's, Flutter, Villers, and Mrs. Racket discuss the upcoming marriage between Doricourt and Letitia. Eventually their conversation shifts to the marital problems between Sir George Touchwood and his wife, Lady Frances. Mrs. Racket finds Touchwood to be an excessively jealous brute. Villers and Flutter believe Mrs. Racket is being a bit too dramatic. Flutter tells a wildly embellished story, whereupon Villers says, "I never believe one tenth part of what you say," exposing Flutter as an extravagant gossip.

Letitia makes her first appearance and complains that Doricourt expressed indifference for her at their first meeting. She is disappointed, but Mrs. Racket reminds her that Doricourt has courted and been courted all throughout Europe and that the young Letitia should not expect much from him at first. Hardy, Letitia's father, enters the room and professes that Doricourt loves his daughter. Letitia begs to differ and sets in motion a plan to truly win Doricourt's heart. She plans to first make Doricourt hate her, then to transform his hate into passionate love, because, Letitia believes, " 'tis much easier to convert a sentiment into its opposite than to transform indifference into tender passion."

Act 2

At Sir George Touchwood's house, Mrs. Racket and Miss Ogle confront Sir George about his jealousy, claiming that he is oppressive and that

his beliefs in marriage are a century and a half old. Lady Frances remains quiet until Flutter reveals that Sir George released her favorite bullfinch, out of jealousy for the bird. Lady Frances becomes upset, and for the first time leaves her husband's side to go about town with Mrs. Racket and Miss Ogle. The three women visit an auction house owned by Silvertongue. While there, Courtall spies Lady Frances and begins to lust after her.

Act 3

Back at Hardy's, Letitia has set her plan into action. When Doricourt arrives for dinner, Letitia acts like a fool, making brash, unintelligent comments; insulting Doricourt's expression; and alluding to the fact that she is not a virgin. Letitia's plan nearly backfires when Doricourt decides to leave London immediately. Mrs. Racket, knowing of Letitia's plan, begs him to stay the night and to attend the masquerade ball. Although upset with Letitia, Doricourt agrees to attend the ball.

After meeting Lady Frances, Courtall sets his own plan into action, although, unlike Letitia's plan, his is not for love. Courtall tells Saville that he plans to seduce Lady Frances at the masquerade ball by posing as her husband. Courtall sends his servant, Dick, to discover what type of costume Sir George will be wearing. This spiteful, immoral plan enrages Saville and he feels compelled to foil Courtall's plan. Saville leaves Courtall's apartment and catches up to Dick. Saville tells Dick that if he brings the information back to him, without telling Courtall of his plan, then Saville will provide him with extra pay. Dick is excited to comply, and Saville sets his own counterplan into motion.

Back at the Touchwood's, Sir George is lamenting that he and his wife are disunited. Villers tells Sir George that Lady Frances missed him desperately during her day on the town with Mrs. Racket and Miss Ogle. Lady Frances returns and is sad. She missed her husband. The two embrace and Lady Frances tells Sir George that she never wants to be anywhere but by his side. The couple decide to attend the masquerade ball together.

Act 4

At the masquerade, the three plans—Letitia's, Courtall's and Saville's—come into play. Letitia arrives alone dressed in a costume that conceals her identity. She spies Doricourt and dances gracefully in front of him. He is immediately smitten, but Letitia floats away. She soon returns, this time singing beautifully. Again, Doricourt pines for her attention, begging to see her face. Letitia talks to

Doricourt, but refuses his advances. Doricourt is full of love and passion; he follows Letitia, showering her with compliments. Finally he grabs her and explains that he believes fate has ordained that she should be his wife. She agrees, but tells him he must wait until tomorrow. She then leaves the masquerade. Doricourt is dizzied by his experience and when Flutter asks about his mood, he points to Letitia and exclaims that he is in love. Flutter, forever the liar and embellisher, professes that the woman Doricourt is smitten with is married. Doricourt is devastated. Hardy sees this exchange and tries to explain that the woman is not married and that, in fact, it was Letitia. Doricourt does not believe Hardy, and he leaves the masquerade.

Meanwhile, Saville has arrived with an amorous young woman named Kitty Willis. Saville is dressed identically to Sir George, and Kitty Willis is dressed identically to Lady Frances. Saville, knowing that Courtall plans to seduce Lady Frances under the guise of being Sir George, has enacted an elaborate plan to trick Courtall into believing that Kitty Willis is Lady Frances. When Sir George and Lady Frances arrive, Saville whisks Lady Frances away, explaining that there is danger at the ball. Courtall arrives and sees Saville sitting with Kitty Willis, but he mistakenly believes it is Sir George sitting with Lady Frances. When Saville leaves, Willis is sitting alone. Courtall swoops in and pretends to be Sir George. He tells Willis that they must leave and the two depart. Unbeknownst to Courtall, he is leaving with Willis, instead of Lady Frances.

Courtall takes Willis back to his apartment. Saville, Flutter, and others barge into Courtall's apartment before Courtall can unmask Willis. Courtall claims he has the delightful Lady Frances in his bedchamber. As he announces this, Willis comes prancing out, revealing herself to everyone. Courtall is humiliated. Everyone laughs, and Courtall states he must immediately leave London for Paris.

Act 5

After the masquerade, Doricourt is distraught that the woman of his dreams is married. Saville tries to console him, but Doricourt is depressed that he must marry Letitia. He decides to fake insanity and he enlists Saville's help. Saville reluctantly agrees to tell the Hardys that Doricourt was poisoned at the masquerade and that it has caused him to go insane. Mrs. Racket is saddened to hear this and explains to Saville that the woman Doricourt was swooned by was, indeed, Letitia. Relieved, Saville immediately reveals Doricourt's ruse.

Angered that Doricourt would create such a lie, Mrs. Racket demands that Saville bring Doricourt to the Hardy's, madness and all. Saville, again, reluctantly agrees, and keeps the secret from his friend. Doricourt arrives, acting insane, and Mrs. Racket immediately calls his bluff. Doricourt explains that he fell in love with a different woman at the masquerade and cannot bear the thought of marrying Letitia. Suddenly, the woman from the masquerade enters the room and reveals herself as Letitia. She explains that she concocted her stratagem to entice Doricourt to love her. She tells Doricourt that she is willing to be any type of wife he desires, but he is so smitten that he begs her to be nothing but herself. Everyone rejoices and the celebration of their marriage begins.

CHARACTERS

Courtall

Courtall is a womanizer and could possibly even be called a misogynist. His name indicates a character with no discrimination, a man who pursues all women for the sport of it. In the opening scene he talks with Saville about Doricourt. Saville reveals that Doricourt is to be married and this makes Courtall happy because Doricourt is very sought after by the ladies. In fact, Courtall explains that Doricourt's marriage is next best only to his death with regards to increasing Courtall's chances with women. Courtall resurfaces later at an auction house and looks lecherously at Lady Frances Touchwood. Lady Frances is a sheltered woman and is taken aback by Courtall's leers. At the auction house, Courtall begins his lustful pursuit of Lady Frances. With the help of a servant, Courtall decides to dress in a costume that matches Sir George Touchwood—Lady Frances's husband—with the hopes of tricking Lady Frances and seducing her. His plan is foiled by Saville's disgust with Courtall and his secret longing for the pure, unspoiled Lady Frances.

Crowquill

Crowquill is the author of the local gossip column. His name is a type of quill used as a writing instrument. He divulges information about travels, rumors about families, speculations about relationships, and other gossip and scandals through the local paper. Crowquill tries to extract information about Doricourt from the Porter by paying him a small fee.

Dick

Dick is one of Courtall's servants. Courtall asks Dick to discreetly discover what Sir George Touchwood will be wearing to the masquerade. Courtall has bad intentions and ultimately wants to trick Sir George's wife and seduce her. Later, Saville catches up to Dick, telling the servant that he'll double Courtall's fee if, upon his discovery of Sir George's costume, the servant also tells Saville, but keeps their exchange a secret. Saville, knowing of Courtall's deceptive plan to seduce Lady Frances, wants to save Lady Frances from Courtall's lecherous behavior. Dick agrees and delivers the information to both Courtall and Saville, but keeps Saville's inquiry from Courtall.

Doricourt

Doricourt is a handsome, wealthy, sought-after single man. His name comes from the term *d'or* meaning golden, hence he is the *golden courtship*, i.e. the man all women seek. In an age when many young men are off fighting a war against the American colonies, young men are in high demand—especially men like Doricourt. He is well traveled, intelligent, and amusing. Also, it has been arranged that Doricourt will marry Letitia Hardy, daughter of a wealthy man. However, upon meeting Letitia, Doricourt is not terribly impressed with the young lady. It is not that he finds her unappealing; he is simply indifferent to her. Doricourt is not bothered by the prospect of marrying a woman that he is indifferent to because he can roam freely, travel, and cavort with various women. However, this becomes a much larger issue for Letitia. Given her intelligence, Letitia knows that a marriage built upon a foundation of indifference results in misery for a wife. Thus, she enacts and elaborate plan to ignite Doricourt's heart, making him lust after her with all of his being. Her plan involves changing Doricourt's feelings first from indifference to disgust, then from disgust to love, because she believes "'tis much easier to convert a sentiment into its opposite than to transform indifference into tender passion." Amazingly, she near-flawlessly completes her plan and it appears that Letitia and Doricourt will have a long, happy life together as husband and wife.

Mrs. Fagg

Mrs. Fagg is a puffer and employee of Silvertongue. Puffers are hired to inflate the prices of objects at auctions either by bidding for them to run up the price or by extolling them in the presence of would-be buyers. Mrs. Fagg is dreary, exhausted woman, plagued with fatigue and worn down by her hard work for meager pay puffing for Silvertongue.

Flutter

Flutter is renowned for his constant embellishment of stories. His name means to make an ostentatious display and to create perpetual meaningless chatter. Needless to say, Flutter lives up to his name. He defends himself stating that he never lies, but believes that the common stories of the world aren't worth talking about without a bit of added imagination. Flutter causes much trouble throughout the play with his incessantly lying and non-stop gossip. In one such instance, he upsets Lady Frances Touchwood and enrages Sir George Touchwood when he reveals to Lady Frances that her husband released her favorite pet bullfinch out of jealousy for the bird. Although the story is true, it was only a rumor and Flutter felt compelled to tell the seedy story and stir up unrest in the marriage. In another scene, Letitia Hardy has concealed her true identity at the masquerade and has successfully entrapped Doricourt's heart. He is smitten with the unnamed, masked woman. Flutter approaches Doricourt and questions why he is so a-twitter. Doricourt points to Letitia, explains that the woman has stolen his heart, and asks Flutter if he knows of the woman. Flutter, never to be caught without an answer, states that Letitia is, in fact, a married woman. He tells Doricourt to get over his obsession and that his only hope is an affair. Doricourt is devastated and Flutter's lie almost destroys Letitia's plans. Essentially, Flutter's role is to embellish stories, disrupting relationships, plans, and emotions.

Hardy

Hardy is Letitia's wealthy father. As his name implies, he is physically robust. Hardy is apparently a good businessman, but he lacks any connection to the activities of the heart. He is confused by Letitia's unrest with the prospects of marrying Doricourt, citing that her feelings of his indifference are ridiculous. Hardy believes that marriages always start from this point and they move forward. It is apparent that he sees Letitia as too much of a thinker, caught up in emotions and things in her head, e.g. her need for love over stability. Nonetheless, Hardy loves his daughter and supports her needs. At the masquerade, when Doricourt falls madly for the masked Letitia, only to fall into despair when Flutter explains that the woman is a married, Hardy attempts to clear up the misunderstanding. He tells Doricourt that Flutter is mistaken and that the masked woman is indeed Letitia.

Doricourt does not believe Hardy and leaves in a huff. With this, Hardy is willing to carry out Letitia's plans, pretending to be deathly ill, finalizing the last stage of his daughter's elaborate plan to win Doricourt's heart.

Letitia Hardy

Letitia Hardy is an intelligent, independent, attractive single woman. Her father, Hardy, is wealthy and caring. Letitia is also remarkably courageous and daring. She is an example of feminism in an era when such an idea was virtually undiscovered. Upon her initial meeting with her prospective husband—Doricourt—Letitia is shy and unmoved by the man. He responds to her behavior with indifference. Unsatisfied with the status quo life of being married to an indifferent husband, Letitia decides that she would rather have Doricourt hate her than feel little for her. However, showing her understanding of eighteenth-century society and a desire to live within it, Letitia concocts and elaborate plan to show Doricourt her true self, believing that her physical and intellectual beauty will win his heart. First, Letitia decides she must change Doricourt's feeling from indifference to hate, believing it is easier to change someone's feelings from hate to love, than from indifference to love. When Letitia and Doricourt are scheduled to meet for dinner she does not attend, but arrives late, behaving unpolished, amorously, and unintelligently. Doricourt finds her repulsive. Then when they meet under at the masquerade under disguise, Letitia unleashes her amazing talents, creative wit, poetic mind, and seductive beauty. Doricourt is unknowingly redirected and finds the unnamed, masked woman incredibly appealing, seductively intelligent, and wonderfully beautiful. Although her plan is nearly thrown of track by the meddling Flutter, she is able to keep it together. With the help of Mrs. Racket, Miss Ogle, her father and others, Letitia successful turns the table on Doricourt and traditional eighteenth-century courtship, igniting her marriage with unheard of desire, lust and passion.

Mask

Mask is a puffer and employee of Silvertongue. Puffers are hired to inflate the prices of objects at auctions either by bidding for them to run up the price or by extolling them in the presence of would-be buyers. Mask, as his name implies, makes his living through impersonation. Unlike the other puffer, Mrs. Fagg, Mask has not yet been fatigued by Silvertongue.

Miss Ogle

Miss Ogle is a friend of Mrs. Racket. Both women are keen on the workings of eighteenth-century social life and the roles of women. In a way, they are quite progressive. Although they are singled or widowed (Mrs. Racket), they move about town and work hard to convince other, younger women to live more freely. In particular, Miss Ogle finds Sir George Touchwood to be an example of male oppression. She scolds Sir George, telling him that his ideas of marriage and relationships are a century and a half dead and that he treats his wife, Lady Frances, with disrespect. Miss Ogle and Mrs. Racket insist that Lady Frances accompany them about town to auctions, forcing Sir George to comply. The two women leave with Lady Frances and take her about town where she is lustfully followed by the lecherous Courtall.

Porter

Crowquill tries desperately to extract information for Porter in an early scene. Porter ends up pocketing Crowquill's money, explaining that Doricourt is free of scandals, gossip and other such trifle that might usually appear in Crowquill's column.

Mrs. Racket

Mrs. Racket, as her name implies, is a boisterous woman with an active, busy social life. She is a widow, but often talks of her desire to someday marry Villers. She, like her good friend Miss Ogle, is a progressive woman, eager to spread the word to younger women to live more freely. In particular, Mrs. Racket finds Sir George Touchwood to be a brute and an oppressive husband. Sir George explains that he likes his wife by his side and that he did not marry a woman of society because they lack morality. Mrs. Racket becomes upset with Sir George. She explains that a true fine lady of society has a liberal mind and is sought after for her abilities in conversation and her polite nature. Mrs. Racket and Miss Ogle insist that Lady Frances accompany them about town to auctions, forcing Sir George to comply. The two women leave with Lady Frances and take her about town where she is lustfully followed by the lecherous Courtall. In addition, Mrs. Racket helps Letitia understand society's expectations of a woman's role in courtship. Mrs. Racket is very blunt and curt. She reminds Letitia that the finest women from all across Europe have been courting Doricourt and that his indifference should be expected. However, she supports Letitia's desire to build a relationship upon love, not indifference. With Mrs. Racket's help and the support of others, Letitia is able to win Doricourt's heart.

Saville

Saville is a quiet, kind, caring man and good friend of Doricourt. His name is often believed to be a combination of *savoir* which means "to know" and *ville*, which means town. As to be expected by his nomenclature, Saville seems to have a very keen understanding of what happens throughout the town. He is not a gossip like Flutter and he uses his knowledge only at crucial moments. Most impressively, Saville is able to counteract and defuse Courtall's lecherous plan to seduce the pure Lady Frances Touchwood. With remarkable networking and a crisp, deductive intellect, Saville not only stops Courtall's plan, he also turns the table and humiliates the despicable man. In a strange twist, the ever-jealous Sir George Touchwood cannot bear to know that another man, Saville, saved his wife from seduction. However, Sir George believes that if Saville were his brother, then such an action would, in fact, be acceptable. Sir George decides that Saville must marry his sister in order to preserve his marriage with Lady Frances. Saville also uses his knowledge to save Letitia's plan. After Letitia won Doricourt's heart from behind her mask, Flutter nearly spoiled her plans by stating that the masked Letitia was a married woman. Doricourt entrusts Saville with his feelings, stating that he cannot marry Letitia when he knows that a woman of such magnificence exists. In order to escape his marriage to Letitia, Doricourt plots to fake insanity, stating that an Italian woman at the masquerade drugged him, destroying his mind. Saville complies for his friend's sake, only to later learn that, once again, Flutter was lying about the masked woman. When Letitia and Mrs. Racket reveal their plan to Saville, he, in turn, reveals Doricourt's insane rouse, allowing Letitia's plan to be completed. Without Saville's knowledge of the town, many unfortunate events would have been carried out and many lives would have been hurt.

Silvertongue

Silvertongue is the owner of the auction house and employer of Mrs. Fagg and Mask. As his name implies he is sweet spoken, eloquent, and, although he does not pay his employees well, he is a successful auctioneer.

Lady Frances Touchwood

Lady Frances Touchwood is the beautiful wife of the amazingly jealous Sir George Touchwood.

Her character is not particularly deep, but serves mostly to polarize Letitia Hardy. Where Letitia acts with intelligence, wit, and individuality, Lady Frances is defined by the presence of her husband. She is not a society woman, meaning Sir George selected her to be his husband because she would not be a woman about town. He desired a wife that would always be by his side, never wander, and have little inclination for parties, auctions, or any event outside of the home or away from her husband. Lady Frances met all these criteria up until Flutter exposed Sir George's jealousy of even her favorite bullfinch, which he release from its cage because he could not bear to witness his wife love anything but himself. Oddly, Lady Frances's one day away from Sir George resulted in the Courtall's lecherous pursuit. This unfortunate turn of events immediately cauterized Lady Frances's new inclination to become a society woman.

Sir George Touchwood

Sir George Touchwood is the brutish, unattractive husband of the sheltered, beautiful Lady Frances Touchwood. His name means a woody substance that easily catches fire, like tinder, and as his name implies, it takes very little to ignite Sir George into fiery jealousy. Sir George, aware of his own insane jealousy, selected a sheltered wife from the outskirts of society to limit his jealous explosions. Lady Frances met his qualifications, but his dedication to keep her behind closed doors baffles his friends and infuriates progressive women like Miss Ogle and Mrs. Racket.

Villers

Villers is a sophisticated man about town. He knows much about everyone in town, but is quiet and keeps to himself. People often confide in him and he is honest with his response to questions. Mrs. Racket states that if she were to ever remarry it would be to Villers. Although his role in the play is minimal, he helps complete Letitia's plan.

Kitty Willis

Kitty Willis is a loose, amorous woman who plays an essential role in Saville's plan to save Lady Frances Touchwood from Courtall's lecherous plans. She dresses up exactly like Lady Frances and when Courtall approaches, pretending to be Sir George Touchwood, Kitty Willis leaves with Courtall. Courtall believes that Willis is Lady Frances. However, he is also under the impression that the woman he is leaving with believes him to be Sir George. Courtall then takes the masked Kitty

TOPICS FOR FURTHER STUDY

- Letitia's plot to win Doricourt's heart is creative and inventive; however, in many respects, she took a long road to achieve what could have been done if she had only revealed her true self upon their initial meeting. Explore this situation and try to come up with three examples, either personally or historically, where an event would have ended up with the same results through a more direct route.

- Hannah Cowley is often thought of as an early feminist in that she explored oppression in a male-dominated society. Looking back through history, who are other key figures and what are other key moments in the rise of women's liberation? Prepare a report that documents your findings.

- A group of artists called the Guerrilla Girls has worked to uncover injustices in the history of women and art. It has been speculated that some male artists acting as mentors for female artists may have taken their female understudies' works and sold them as their own. Research men like David Garrick or Richard Sheridan, men who managed theatre and encouraged female playwrights. Do scandals surround either man? Do you believe there is any chance that they may have stolen ideas from female playwrights? Why or why not?

- The marriage between Sir George Touchwood and Lady Frances is comparably different than the marriage between Letitia Hardy and Doricourt. In fact, Miss Ogle states that Sir George's idea of marriage died a century and a half prior. With this in mind, how has the idea of marriage changed in the United States over the last 150 years? Discuss how the roles of men and of women have changed, and how homosexuality is redefining marriage.

Willis back to his apartment with plans of seduction. Saville, Flutter and others arrive, knowing that Courtall believes Kitty Willis is Lady Frances, burst in, and catch Courtall in the act of seducing not the beautiful, pure, married Lady Frances, but a sluttish, loose tramp. Kitty Willis loves the plot and plays along until the bitter end and she final reveals herself when the men burst into Courtall's apartment. Courtall is devastated and immensely embarrassed. He exits the room stating that me must escape to Paris.

THEMES

Marriage and Courtship

Marriage and courtship are the primary themes of *The Belle's Stratagem*. Courtship is used to construct the foundation for marriage. However, it is apparent that regardless of the quality of courtship or the extent of love, an eighteenth-century marriage will proceed—unless, of course, a future spouse falls ill or dies. In the case of Letitia and Doricourt, their union is considered arranged and inevitable, even though the two feel indifference toward one another. Doricourt has little trouble accepting this type of arranged marriage for the sake of family and money, because, as an attractive man in the late 1700s, he will have little trouble finding passionate, sexual relationships with mistresses once he is married. However, Letitia feels differently. It is expected that Letitia will remain loyal to her husband and steadfast to her commitment of marriage, a prospect that seems very difficult and unpleasant to imagine if she marries a man who feels little for her. Her life would become fairly meaningless if she were to marry a man who did not love her; her freedoms would be limited and her sense of joy and love would be extinguished. Knowing this, Letitia decides to take her future into her own hands, turning conventional eighteenth-century courtship on its head.

Juxtaposed against Letitia's situation is the situation of Lady Frances Touchwood, kept wife of Sir George Touchwood. Sir George's intense, fiery jealousy has completely limited Lady Frances's exposure to the world and to other people. He contains her like a jewel that he allows to shimmer only for his eyes. Their courtship was short and it was understood that Sir George wanted a wife who would love him and him alone. He has no room in his jealous heart for her friends, for children, or even for pets.

Letitia refuses to become a wife about town living a loveless marriage, or a kept, sheltered wife, isolated from the world. She would rather abandon the institution of marriage and live alone, true to herself, than to live a lifetime of lies. However, she is also aware she cannot walk away from an arranged marriage. Instead, she makes Doricourt hate her, hoping to turn his disgust into passion. This is an ingenious plot because, if Doricourt hates her and she is unable to turn his heart, then he will leave her and she will not be seen as a woman who abandoned marriage. In fact, Doricourt is willing to go so far as to fake insanity in order to avoid marrying Letitia, before he realizes that she is the mystery woman from the ball. In the end, her paradoxical approach to courtship does, in fact, win Doricourt's heart, and it appears that the two will share a good, equitable, passionate marriage.

Jealousy

Jealousy plays a remarkable role in the play, almost destroying a marriage. If not for Sir George's jealousy, he would never have let go his wife's favorite pet, a bullfinch. When Flutter reveals to Lady Frances that Sir George freed the bird out of insane jealousy, Lady Frances is angry with Sir George. Her anger, fueled by his jealousy, compels Lady Frances to go with Mrs. Racket and Miss Ogle without her husband for the first time. Her trek sparks Courtall's lecherous desires, and, if not for Saville's counterplan, it is quite possible that Courtall would have seduced Lady Frances and destroyed the Touchwood's marriage.

Feminism and Identity

Feminism and identity are crucial to the construction of the play. Letitia's plan that turns traditional, eighteenth-century courtship on its head is an incredibly stark and feminist movement. It empowers Letitia, placing her in the role of guiding and dictating the courtship. However, in order for her plan to work, she must hide her true identity. Upon first meeting Doricourt, she is indifferent because he is a stranger. Her indifference is reflected by her future husband, which sets the stage for a weak, impassionate marriage. Knowing this, Letitia

concocts a plan and dons a new identity at the ball. At this second rendezvous, Letitia pretends to be dim and amorous, turning Doricourt's emotions from indifference to disgust. At their third encounter, Letitia disguises her physically identity and uses her true charm, beauty, and intelligence to turn Doricourt's emotions to love and passion. At their fourth encounter, Letitia finally reveals herself, stepping out from behind her physical and mental masks to expose her true identity. This revelation is both uplifting and disheartening. It is uplifting because Doricourt sees her true beauty, both physically and mentally, and he falls madly in love, begging Letitia to be forever herself. However, it is disheartening because she had to compromise her identity and manipulate a male-dominated system to gain Doricourt's attention.

STYLE

Conflict and Tension

The Belle's Stratagem relies heavily on conflict to create tension between characters and to raise anxiety in the viewer. Conflict in a play is the issue to be resolved in the story. In this play, conflict arises repeatedly in different arenas, creating great tension. Letitia's, Courtall's, and Saville's constant planning leave countless opportunities for their plans to be disrupted. For example, Flutter disrupts Letitia's plan, and it looks as if the couple that have finally fallen in love may never marry. Also, it looks as if Courtall may be successful at seducing Lady Frances unless Saville's remarkably complex plan is not completed. At any moment, this conflict could unravel, leaving Courtall to either seduce the lovely Lady Frances or to walk away from his immoral pursuit unscathed. All of these conflicts create substantial tension, enrapturing the audience or reader.

The Role of the Heroine in Eighteenth-Century Comedic Drama

Given Cowley's era, the role of Letitia as a heroine is remarkably progressive. Not only does Cowley create a wildly successfully comedy, but she delivers a feminist message under the guise of humor. Letitia is the most intelligent, courageous character in the play. Without her daring prowess and desire to live a good life married to a loving husband, Letitia would not be a heroine. In fact, she would become a victim of a male-dominated, oppressive society. Her determination and creativity are essential to the plot development and intrigue

<h1>COMPARE
&
CONTRAST</h1>

- **1780s:** The United States Constitution is codified as the supreme law of the United States of America.

  Today: The United States Constitution is the oldest written national constitution still in force.

- **1780s:** The American Revolutionary war comes to a conclusion, resulting in an America free from British rule.

  Today: The United States of America and Britain are allies. The leaders of both countries frequently work together on international projects.

- **1780s:** Benedict Arnold commits treason, changing sides to fight against the Americans. He cites his love of his country, Britain, as the driving force that causes him to turn against his American friends.

  Today: The term "Benedict Arnold" is still synonymous with traitor. Oddly, though, many Americans continue to follow and support his dogmatic principle of undying, unwavering loyalty to one's country.

that Cowley creates within the conflicts of the play. In a brash way, Cowley herself becomes a heroine through her writing, by delivering her feminist message in a palatable, comedic format. If it were direct or overly dramatic, her message may have never been produced, let alone cherished and applauded.

HISTORICAL CONTEXT

American Revolutionary War

On April 19, 1775, the night after the ride of Paul Revere, the infamous "shot heard round the world" rang out, signifying the start of the American Revolution. Over the next eighteen months, the American militia grew substantially, capturing British forts and creating a navy. In addition to military advances, many American writers, such as Thomas Paine, began an intellectual assault on King George III. In May 1776, King Louis XVI of France committed one million dollars in arms and munitions to the Americans, whereupon Spain also promised support. Soon thereafter, a massive British war fleet arrived in New York Harbor, with over 40,000 soldiers and sailors. On July 4, 1776, the thirteen American states declared independence from England.

The enormous number of British troops was nearly too much for the American armed forces, but keen planning and a series of small victories led to an unlikely American victory in the war. The struggle for independence then spread abroad, as British vessels fired on French ships and the two nations declared war on each other. Spain entered this war as France's ally in 1779, and soon thereafter, Britain declared war on the Dutch, who had been trading with France. Britain's overextended armed forces were not only battling the Americans, French, Spanish, and Dutch, they were also fighting in the Mediterranean, Africa, India, and the West Indies. Although war raged on, the American Revolution officially ended April 11, 1783, when the new American Congress declared an end to the Revolutionary War.

The Effects of War on Eighteenth-Century British Women

The American Revolutionary War and its effect on British women is touched on in *The Belle's Stratagem*. In 1780, when the play first ran in England, the number of marriageable men was palpably diminished. In order to fight the many battles in which the British were engaged and still have reserves to defend their own borders from invasion, the bulk of young British men were

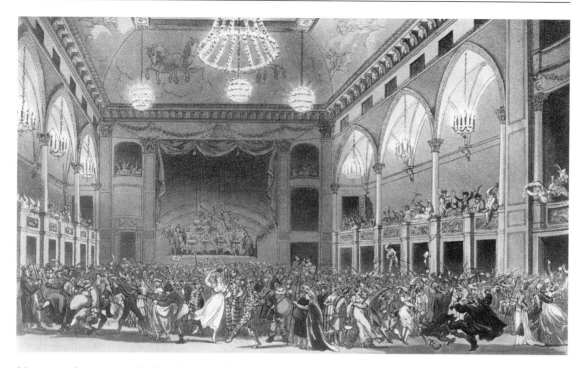

Masquerade party at the Pantheon in London, 1809 © Historical Picture Archive/Corbis

recruited for the armed forces. In fact, in the play, Courtall even goes so far as to state, "The ladies are going to petition for a bill that, during the war, every man may be allowed two wives." The majority of young, single men were off at war far and wide across the globe, defending England's interests.

With so much competition for available men, the rules of courtship underwent a temporary shift. Instead of men eagerly pursuing women, many women were struggling to catch the eye of a few men. The majority of the men who did not go to battle were extremely wealthy; their families' financial standing and their ability to ship their sons off on travel adventures enabled many of these men to escape mandatory service. Thus, the men who were left in England were often the upper echelon of the fashionable society—the most sought after men in all of England. Although this change in courtship due to the lack of men may have been a worrisome burden for many women, the lack of men may have helped fuel a brief, but prolific explosion for creative, intelligent women. It can be argued that a lack of male writers forced people to consider female playwrights like Hannah Cowley, giving women a chance to show their writing

prowess and giving a voice to the unheard masses of British women writ large.

CRITICAL OVERVIEW

Although *The Belle's Stratagem* premiered over two hundred years ago, there is still little written about Cowley or about other eighteenth-century female dramatists. It is remarkable that one of the first, formidable female playwrights of the English language has not received greater attention. However, it does speak to the oppression women endured during the male-dominated centuries that followed Cowley's premiere. During the eighteenth century, women playwrights received little exposure, often having to funnel their writing through theatres dominated by men. It is often believed that much writing by women dramatists was lost or has been wrongly attributed to men. Plays like *The Belle's Stratagem*, however, would not have been claimed by a man because of its powerful female protagonist. As Jean Gagen states in the *University of Mississippi Studies in English*, "[Cowley's] most celebrated characters are undoubtedly her witty young heroines, who are often the prime manipulators and intriguers in her plays, which usually center on courtship and marriage."

Although Cowley made no attempt to disturb or reform the status quo of eighteenth-century courtship, she was an independent, resourceful feminist. Without disrupting the place of men—a surefire way to impede working in theatre—Cowley instead focused on making a statement about women's abilities, rights, and intelligence. She selected comedy to delivery her progressive message. If she would have selected another device to express her opinion, there is a chance her voice would not have been heard.

CRITICISM

Anthony Martinelli

Martinelli is a Seattle-based freelance writer and editor. In this essay, Martinelli examines how physical and mental masquerades change the rules of courtship, successively freeing and damning eighteenth-century women.

In *The Belle's Stratagem*, Hannah Cowley constructs, at face value, a lighthearted comedy about manners, courtship, and marriage in fashionable society in late-eighteenth-century London. The play pays homage to a play by one of Cowley's favorite playwrights, George Farquhar, titled *The Beaux's Stratagem*. However, as in many of Cowley's works, her protagonist is a heroine and, although the play is a comedy, Cowley has much to say about male-dominated, eighteenth-century society. As if to foreshadow the underlying message of her play, *The Belle's Stratagem* wears a mask resembling Farquhar's play, bending not only the play's title but its content. In her play, Cowley shrouds Letitia Hardy behind three masks—indifference, vulgarity, and costume—to upend eighteenth-century courtship, exposing the oppressive nature of marriage in a male-dominated society.

In the early scenes of the play, it is revealed that Letitia Hardy is to marry Doricourt and that the two have recently met for the first time. During their first meeting, Letitia is not moved by Doricourt. She is an intelligent woman and she is not easily motivated by the standard cultural norm that she is forced to obey, namely that her marriage is arranged and that she must marry Doricourt. Since she has little motivation or feeling for Doricourt, both because they do not know each other and

because she does not approve of the rules of marriage, she presents herself behind a veil of indifference to her future husband. Doricourt feels her indifference and explains to his friend Saville that Letitia is "a fine girl, as far as mere flesh and blood goes," but that she lacks "spirit! Fire! *L'air enjoué* [a certain aura of playfulness or sprightliness]! That something, that nothing, which everybody feels, and which nobody can describe." Unfortunately, Letitia's first mask leaves Doricourt unfulfilled.

The real tragedy of Letitia's first mask is that she truly possesses everything that Doricourt so desires in a wife. Letitia is courageous, daring, intelligent, and beautiful. She is well spoken and thoughtful. She is not deceptive or immoral. Yet, the rules of courtship force her to draw up a shroud between herself and her future husband, one that covers her impeccable beauty. More so, her decision to veil herself disrupts the courtship but does not remove her from its grasp. Thus, Letitia finds herself still locked into her arranged marriage, which is beginning on a foundation of mutual indifference, damning her to a loveless future.

However, being a daring, creative woman, Letitia does not succumb to her position. She discusses with Mrs. Racket her own indifference toward Doricourt and his indifference toward her. Racket, an older but progressive-thinking widow, tells Letitia,

> Can you expect a man, who has courted and been courted by half the fine women in Europe, to feel like a girl from a boarding-school? He is the prettiest fellow you have seen, and . . . he has seen a million of pretty women.

Racket is not being rude but realistic. She knows that men are not smitten by looks and looks alone, especially those who are as affluent and well traveled as Doricourt. Racket does not intend to discourage Letitia, but she hopes that the young girl will at least approach her future husband with an air of realism. Letitia, forever a strong woman, states, "I will touch his heart, or never be his wife" and then she sets into motion an amazingly elaborate plan to win Doricourt's heart.

In order to change Doricourt's feelings, Letitia decides that she must first turn his indifference to hatred because she believes, "'tis much easier to convert a sentiment into its opposite than to transform indifference into tender passion." With Racket's warning that her belief may be a "good philosophy" but a "bad maxim," Letitia heads off behind her first mask of indifference to begin making her second mask of vulgarity. Erin Isikoff writes in *Look Who's Laughing: Gender and*

Comedy, "through the agency of a mask, of a false identity, Cowley reconciles respectability and accomplishment. Masks, then, not only mediate identity but also manage to protect it, so that a woman in disguise can plot with gentility." As Isikoff eloquently states, Letitia is still in a position to reveal her amazing qualities. Doricourt has seen nothing of Letitia's true qualities, other than her physical beauty. With this in mind, Letitia is empowered to use her veiled position to her advantage, mindful, of course, that her plan could backfire. Nonetheless, Letitia would rather not marry than concede her life to a loveless marriage.

Before Letitia dons her vulgar mask, she tries to anger Doricourt by not attending a scheduled dinner. When Doricourt expresses no concern of his missing future bride, Letitia decides that she is left with no option. At their next meeting, Letitia is awkward, amorous, and sluttish. She makes rude comments about Doricourt's appearance and even alludes to the idea that she may not be a virgin. Doricourt is remarkably surprised and disgusted with his future bride, proclaiming, "Surely this cannot be Miss Hardy!" All the while, Letitia continues to deal her hand toward hate, and all the while, Doricourt takes each card. Eventually, Letitia's father can no longer stand her banter, because he knows she is not such a woman, and he removes her from the room. Exasperated, Doricourt tells Racket that he cannot marry such a woman and explains that he will be leaving London immediately. Luckily for Letitia, Racket knows of Letitia's plans and begs Doricourt to at least stay through the night to attend the masquerade, and he agrees. With this, Letitia's plan is both working—i.e., Doricourt's indifference has been transformed into hatred—and nearly foiled, because he almost left before seeing her true identity.

With the bait set, Letitia only has to arrive at the masquerade in a costume that conceals her physical self. Her final mask is the only tangible one she dons. Wearing her costume, Letitia arrives at the masquerade alone, first approaching Doricourt with a stunning dance. He is immediately smitten, but Letitia runs off, eager to tantalize him with her other offerings. She returns again, this time with a beautiful song, which only continues to enrapture Doricourt. Yet again she leaves. At their next interaction, Doricourt grabs Letitia. He is drunkenly charmed and demands to know her name, stating, "Fate has ordained you mine." With this, Letitia has hit her mark. Doricourt has fallen madly in love with the true Letitia, although she is still hidden away behind her costume. With this,

> WITH THIS, THE PARADOX OF HER STRATAGEM BECOMES APPARENT. ALTHOUGH LETITIA HAS TRICKED DORICOURT INTO LOVING HER TRUE IDENTITY, SHE STILL FINDS HERSELF TRAPPED IN THE INESCAPABLE CONUNDRUM THAT IS EIGHTEENTH-CENTURY COURTSHIP."

the paradox of her stratagem becomes apparent. Although Letitia has tricked Doricourt into loving her true identity, she still finds herself trapped in the inescapable conundrum that is eighteenth-century courtship. Even at the bitter end, after she reveals herself to Doricourt, she damns her position stating, "You see I *can* be anything. Choose then my character; your taste shall fix it." With this, all of Letitia's actions have done nothing but force her to create an elaborate scheme that could have easily been prevented had she simply shown her true colors at their first meeting. Hence, whether she won Doricourt's heart upon their first meeting or later, Letitia is still oppressed by her role in the male-dominated society through her willingness to be anything for her husband. Plus, her inability to step outside of the constrictions of eighteenth-century decorum does nothing but lock her into her role, no matter how creative her plan may have been.

Here, though, arises an incredibly important aspect of Cowley's work and Letitia's plan. Although, as Isikoff smartly states, "[Letitia's] revolutionary stratagem, while it steals from Doricourt the energy of their courtship, [it] does not challenge its existence." However, given the time period during which Cowley was writing *The Belle's Stratagem*, even a brief examination of the rules and oppressive nature of courtship and marriage was a daring feat. It is damning that a woman of Letitia's intelligence would be left with no option other than to don various masks and trick the fool into becoming her husband. Yet, it is empowering that she can use her wit and guile to circumvent traditional rules of courtship and change the course of her life by

WHAT DO I READ NEXT?

- *The Innocent Mistress*, written by Mary Pix in 1697, is another remarkable eighteenth-century work by a woman. It is a comedy of intrigue that comments on love and courtship and the evils of marriages based on money.

- *The Busybody*, written by Susanna Centlivre in 1709, is a noteworthy play by another eighteenth-century female dramatist. It is a conventionally structured comedy that comments on the inadequacies of marriage as an answer to women's problems.

- *The Times*, written by Elizabeth Griffith in 1779, is a subtle, physical-comedy play by an eighteenth-century female dramatist who was a direct contemporary of Hannah Cowley.

- *The Runaway*, written in 1776 by Hannah Cowley, represents Cowley's first substantial success as a playwright. It is a fresh, high-spirited comedy that was influenced, possibly even controlled, by David Garrick, who was an avid supporter of female dramatists in the late eighteenth-century.

- *Early Women Dramatists, 1500–1800*, by Margarete Rubik, provides a good overview of the role women dramatists played from the Renaissance through the end of the eighteenth century. Included are sections devoted to specific playwrights and analyses of the most significant plays of the time.

---

turning her loveless future into one of passion. Nonetheless, all of the strength of Letitia's plot is lost based on its origin. To be moved to reject a system—as Letitia does when she wears her first mask of indifference—and then look diligently to find a way to reenter the system—as Letitia does when she enacts and completes her plot—does not at all free Letitia from society's restrictions. Essentially, Crowley uses Letitia to expose the problematic oppression of women in late-eighteenth-century England, but she offers very little detail with regard to how it can be changed.

Source: Anthony Martinelli, Critical Essay on *The Belle's Stratagem*, in *Drama for Students*, Thomson Gale, 2006.

Elizabeth Kowaleski Wallace

In the following essay, Wallace describes how Cowley endorses a "cosmopolitan" and "performance-based theory of identity" in The Belle's Stratagem *and how that allows for social liberation.*

In act 3 of Hannah Cowley's 1780 comedy *The Belle's Stratagem*, the character Hardy contemplates the choice of a costume for an upcoming masquerade:

Let me see.—What shall my dress be? A Great Mogul? No.—A Grenadier? No;—no, that I foresee, would make a laugh. Hang me, if I don't send to my little Quick, and borrow his Jew Isaac's dress:—I know the Dog likes a glass of good wine; so I'll give him a bottle of my Forty-eight, and he shall teach me. Aye, that's it—I'll be the Cunning Little Isaac! If they complain of my want of wit, I'll tell 'em the cursed Duenna wears the breeches and has spoiled my part. (3.1, p. 40)

The humor of this scene relies on a metatheatrical in-joke: Hardy was originally played by the versatile actor John Quick (1748–1831), who had played not only the role of Isaac Mendoza in Sheridan's *The Duenna* (1775) but also Tony Lumpkin in a 1773 production of *She Stoops to Conquer*. Cowley counts on her audience to recognize the transparency of Hardy's announcement: Quick both calls attention to the idiosyncrasies of his previous role and reminds us that he only plays at being Hardy here. This metatheatrical moment is consistent with Cowley's attempt to foreground performance throughout her comedy as she encourages her audience to recognize a Shakespearean paradox: if human subjectivity is defined by constant role-playing, then only on the stage do people really appear as what they are. The actor is the only truly sincere being since her performance is the explicit demonstration of ever-shifting human potential.

And so in act 4, Quick plays Hardy playing the Jew Isaac Mendoza, whom the audience (and presumably the characters also, for they seem to have seen *The Duenna* as well) recognize not as an actual Jew—nor even as a representation of an actual Jew—but as a specific dramatic rendering of Jewish identity. Hardy enters into an altercation with another masker, who taunts him with racial slurs: "Why, thou little testy Israelite! Back to Duke's Place; and preach your tribe into a subscription for the good of the land on whose milk and honey ye fatten.—Where are your Joshuas and your Gideons, aye? What! all dwindled into Stockbrokers, Pedlars, and Rag Men?" Putting his fingers to his head, Hardy replies: "No, not all. Some of us turn Christians, and by degrees grow into all the privileges of Englishmen! In the second generation we are Patriots, Rebels, Courtiers, and Husbands" (4.1, p. 50). This is certainly an interesting response, one that could be played in a number of different ways. Is the playwright condemning or condoning the process by which Mendoza's ethnic origins are erased? Is a Jew who has turned Christian still a Jew who only masquerades as what he is not? Does he therefore only perform the role of Patriot, Rebel, Courtier, or Husband, thereby covering, hiding, or disguising what was originally stamped upon his character? Or, is Cowley here endorsing the idea that the Jew turned Christian leaves behind his origins and that he successfully adopts a new English identity?

On the one hand, as a play, *The Belle's Stratagem* evinces an awareness of the destabilizing effects of performance as well as the anxiety this destabilization can produce. As the character Sir George Touchwood complains, society has become "one universal masquerade, all disguised in the same habits and manners" (2.1, p. 27). He is unsettled because he can no longer recognize distinction of character or class of female. Indeed, the masquerade scene in act 4 introduces us to a variety of poseurs—shady characters who exploit appearances to get what they want. Miss Flutter claims she can tell the histories of half the people at the event: "In the next apartment," she alleges, "there's a whole family, who, to my knowledge, have lived on Water-Cresses this month, to make a figure here to-night—; but to make up for that, they'll cram their pockets with cold Ducks and Chickens, for a Carnival to-morrow" (4.1, p. 52).

"INSTEAD, THIS PLAY PROMOTES THE IDEA THAT THE ROLE CAN BECOME THE DEFINING MARK OF WHO YOU ARE, AND THAT AUTHENTICITY IS ACHIEVED NOT IN 'BEING WHO YOU REALLY ARE' BUT IN PLAYING YOUR ROLE TO ITS FULLEST EXTENT."

Yet, on the other hand, Hardy's speech as Mendoza could be said to be a gesture toward an early modern cosmopolitanism, an atmosphere that is reinforced elsewhere in the play. Cowley's imagery is permeated by references to eighteenth-century globe-trotting. Cosmopolitanism is further enforced by the fact that so many characters in this play are in movement. We watch them as they shift geographic location (from country to city), as they travel (to the continent and back), as they traverse the length of the metropolis, and visit tourist sites, auction houses, masquerades, and other diversions. All of this movement brings an open feeling to the text, but it also unlocks the theme of identity: many characters in this play are depicted as fluid, capable like Quick/Hardy of assuming more than one face. Thus, we can hypothesize that Quick interjected a Shylock-like moment of pathos into the scene as textual evidence suggests the author's endorsement of Hardy-as-Mendoza's pronounced fluidity. Cowley seems to lean toward the notion that identity (and even ethnic identity) need not be stamped irretrievably and essentially on the soul. Instead, this play promotes the idea that the role can become the defining mark of who you are, and that authenticity is achieved not in "being who you really are" but in playing your role to its fullest extent.

What makes *The Belle's Stratagem* most remarkable as a play, then, is its endorsement of a theatrical cosmopolitanism that forms the basis of a potentially progressive nationalism, one in which individuals are free to make themselves—as British women and men—what they will. Choosing the category of the "inauthentic" over the apparently authentic, the performance of an identity over a native character, Cowley champions the experience of those like Jews—or, as we will see, more centrally, women—who stand to gain much from a performance-based theory of human identity. For her, cosmopolitanism affords the opportunity for a social performance with liberating potential.

Furthermore, Cowley's comedy capitalizes on the inherent connection between theatricality and "traveling culture," a historical coupling with a long tradition. Theatrical culture, from the commedia del l'arte to the opera, has always been characteristically mobile, moving across both national and local borders. Not only dramatic texts, stage effects, theatrical styles but also actors themselves traditionally travel and thus resist in their movements strict efforts to police an indigenous art. In her discussion of cosmopolitanism and the stage, Una Chaudhuri argues that the theater functions "as a laboratory for observing the new dynamics of identity formation, and for testing the identities" generated in transit and translation. This function stems from an important similarity in the protocols of theater making and cosmopolitanism. Both cultural projects are rooted in a doubleness. While theater "produces and reproduces something that is prior to it (the script)," diasporic experience—like that of the Jew in eighteenth-century London—can be said to reproduce an originary experience that lies elsewhere. "The theater is a space of creative reinscription," writes Chaudhuri, "a space where meaning, like deterriorialized identity, is not merely made, but *re* made, negotiated out of silence, stasis, and incomprehension." For theorists of both performance and diasporic studies, the question of exactly what is "reproduced" on the stage and in a diasporic setting is open for debate: What is the status of the script/originary experience? To what extent can these be said to exist unproblematically at all?

Throughout the eighteenth century, the status of both the script and the originary experience was hotly contested: while theater critics and theorists debated the relationship of the "real" and true in human experience to what was represented on the stage, political essayists discussed the relationship of native origins to national identity. For an example of the first discussion, we need only turn to Jeremy Collier's polemical attack on the nature of the theater, an attack that launched a voluminous debate that continued well into the eighteenth century (and, for that matter, still continues today). Collier maintains that, prior to the dramatic effect of the theater, "[t]he Lines of Virtue and Vice are

struck out by Nature in very legible distinctions; they tend to a different Point, and these are the Native appearances of Good and Evil: And they that endeavor to blot the Distinction, or rub out the Colours, or change the Marks, are extremely to blame." In other words, theatricality is sinister precisely because it distorts what would otherwise be perfectly clear—the "native" nature of good and evil. His choice of the word "native" links the debate over the distorting effect of stage to the distorting effect of cosmopolitanism, for cosmopolitanism is also said to distort "native" identities that would otherwise remain perfectly legible. To put on an act—as a Briton who is really a Jew, for example—is to unsettle not only the "native" categories of right and wrong but also the categories necessary to an indigenous identity.

Stepping back from the long eighteenth century, we find that Collier's comments inaugurate an age that was deeply divided in its response to theatricality. For most of the eighteenth century, a passionate love for the theater coexisted with powerful attempts to contain certain kinds of performance. A large and active theatergoing population continued to thrive despite a series of efforts—ranging from the Licensing Act of 1737 to Pope's satirical attack on theater impresario Colley Cibber in the 1742 *Dunciad*—to curb broadly based, popular forms of theatrical spectacle. In Hogarth's print *Southwark Fair* (1733/34), for example, a range of entertainments, from a contortionist to a tightrope walker, from a peepshow to a tiny puppet show, suggests not only the proliferation of theatrical shows but also a middle-rank moralistic response to the licentiousness, salaciousness, and even criminality associated with such shows. Hogarth devotes a large portion of his print to the "legitimate" theater, represented to the left of the print by a collapsing stage. In this scene, Cibber and Bullock, among others, tumble to the ground, while the show cloth above the calamitous scene tells the story of the theatrical in-fighting that brought about such ruin. Clearly Hogarth finds much to satirize and critique in the broad range of eighteenth-century theatrical practices, and he crowds them altogether in a way that makes them practically indistinguishable. Yet, the richness of detail—the very energy that goes into representing the lurid and illicit—arguably undercuts the explicit morality of the print. The eye is drawn to the very thing it supposedly learns to reject; the very point of the print is to entertain the viewer vicariously through access to a range of performances that are cast in a morally dubious light. The emphasis falls less on "the danger of performance" and more on everything that happens when performance is both literally and metaphorically unlicensed.

But the concern with licensing theater—that is, controlling both its content and its effect—is only one expression of a persistent eighteenth-century anxiety over uncontrolled performance. Whether that performance occurred in an unlicensed theater, in a drawing room, at the gambling table, or simply on the streets, it provoked an equally didactic response. In the pages of the *Tatler* and the *Spectator* and elsewhere, an ascendant middle-rank sensibility increasingly insists upon the adaptation of a nontheatrical, deep, and "authentic" character, one that eschews showy behaviors, gestures, or postures in favor of an abiding sensibility. Richard Steele, for example, extols the virtues of the "new" man whose "outward Garb is but the emblem of his Mind, it is genteel, plain, and unaffected; he knows that Gold and Embroidery can add nothing to the Opinion which all have of his Merit. . . . He is still the principal Figure in the Room." For Steele, true masculinity resides in a refusal to egregiously *act* the part of a man, as sartorial restraint is but a signal for a whole new kind of manhood. As Erin Mackie explains, "from the bourgeois point of view . . . good taste emphasizes modesty, restraint, and practicality, and decorum in distinction to bad (aristocratic) taste corrupted by ideologically retrogressive qualities of personal ostentation, irrational excess, arbitrary election, and libertine abandon." In keeping with this insistence on the absence of show, any kind of obviously dramatic behavior indicates the *inauthentic* self. That even the most sincere among us must at one time or another necessarily play a role is an irony lost on the polemicists. I have written elsewhere about the special pressures exerted on the stage by an antiperformance discourse: how does one celebrate the virtues of deep and authentic nonperformative identity in a performative setting? How does one act the part of someone who is not acting?

By 1817, Jane Austen takes full advantage of the notion that theatricality and inauthenticity are inextricably linked in *Mansfield Park,* as Henry Crawford's superior acting skills make him immediately suspect. But Crawford is additionally suspect for his cosmopolitanism. In this novel in particular, Austen counts on her audience to recognize the implicit connection between those who travel, refusing the pull of local attachments, and those who fail to achieve moral depth. Throughout most of the eighteenth century, the binary opposition between the local or the parochial and the not

local or the cosmopolitan coincides neatly with the division between the "authentic" and the "inauthentic," categories which in turn are aligned with native "innocence" and foreign "corruption." Pope gives us one example of this coincidence in book 4 of *The Dunciad* where the traditional grand European tour serves only to lead a young English gentleman away from the virtues of his indigenous culture. Far from enlightening the young scholar, contact with Europe only corrupts him:

> Intrepid then, o'er seas and lands he flew:
> Europe he saw, and Europe saw him too.
> . . . [H]e sauntered Europe round,
> And gathered ev'ry Vice on Christian ground;
> Saw ev'ry Court, heard ev'ry King declare
> His royal Sense, of Op'ras or the Fair;
> The Stews and Palace equally explor'd,
> Intrigu'd with glory, and with spirit whor'd;
> Try'd all *hors-d'oeuvres,* all *liqueurs* defined,
> Judicious drank, and greatly-daring din'd;
> Dropt the dull lumber of the Latin store,
> Spoil'd his own language, and acquir'd no more.

To complete his attack on Continental corruption, Pope refers by name to the locally situated Sir Henry Jansen, Charles Fleetwood, and Colley Cibber, all managers of Drury Lane:

> See now, half-cur'd, and perfectly well-bred,
> With nothing but a Solo in his head;
> As much Estate, and Principle, and Wit,
> As Jansen, Fleetwood, Cibber shall think fit.

The last couplet explicitly links the licentious pleasures of European travel, an especially dissipated kind of cosmopolitanism, with theatrical production. It suggests that both the theater and European contact—perhaps precisely because the stage is so responsive to European trends—are a source of corruption. Both lead the innocent away from a truer form of culture, and both result in a less authentic English identity. The only solution is, apparently, to stay home—and away from the kind theater that Jansen, Fleetwood, and Cibber represent.

By the end of the century, the virtues of staying close to home were similarly apparent to Hannah More, who accordingly abandoned her own career as a playwright to return to her native Bristol. In an essay entitled "Moral Sketches of Prevailing Opinions and Manners, Foreign and Domestic," More urges her readers to celebrate their insularity: "In making our country an island, Divine Providence seems to have made a provision for our happiness as well as our security. As that circumstance has protected us from the sword, it should also protect us from the manners of our foreign neighbors. The more she labours to resume them, the more she will lose of her independent character. . . . The British character, we hope, will always retain its indigenous flavour." For More as for Pope, national integrity can only occur where the danger of the foreign has been kept at bay. "We will not say that [Britain] may acquire a superiority over other nations—of that she has long been in possession," writes More, "—No; we must not try her by her comparative, but by her positive merit: not by placing her in juxta-position with other countries, but with the possibilities of her own excellence."

However, in *The Belle's Stratagem,* just as Cowley uses the theater to interrogate the relationship between inauthentic and authentic identity, between performed and "true" subjectivity, so too does she undo the opposition between cosmopolitanism and insular parochialism. In this play, cosmopolitanism is the precondition for a certain kind of provincialism. Or, to put it another way, in this play cosmopolitanism facilitates the definition of indigenous "Englishness," which provides for an enhanced sense of the local. To take one example, the character Doricourt claims that his continental travels have sharpened his understanding of the English character. He declares what he knows from experience: "Englishmen make the best Soldiers, Citizens, Artizans, and Philosophers; but the very worst Footmen" (1.3, pp. 7–8). He describes travel abroad as the opportunity to study Italian music or to appreciate French fashion and ornament. After finishing the Grand Tour, he opines, "we return to England, and find the nation intent on the most important objects; Polity, Commerce, War, with all the Liberal Arts, employ her sons; the latent sparks glow afresh within our bosoms; the sweet follies of the Continent imperceptibly slide away, while Senators, Statesmen, Patriots and Heroes, emerge from the virtu of Italy, and the frippery of France" (1.3, p. 8). Here, continental pleasures are not simply discounted as foreign dissipations; instead they are formative experiences that can be brought home where they can ignite the passions that make for better Britons. England enthusiastically consumes foreign culture by appropriating and transforming what is best abroad. Doricourt speaks not for a phobic drawing of boundaries but for a more complicated relationship, one wherein Britain would be impoverished by absence of a foreign culture that is decidedly "lesser," yet also constitutive of Englishness. A cosmopolitan experience makes Britain more, not less, British than it was.

In a similar fashion, Letitia Hardy, in disguise at the masquerade in order to win Doricourt's affection, calls on a full range of global images to articulate the depth of her passion. In answer to the question "what if you loved your husband, and he were worthy of your love," she enthuses that she would be anything and all. She would "live with him in the eye of fashion, or in the shade of retirement—change my country, my sex—feast with him in an Esquimaux hut, or a Persian pavilion—join him in the victorious war-dance on the borders of Lake Ontario, or sleep to the soft breathings of the flute in the cinnamon groves of Ceylon—dig with him in the mines of Golconda, or enter the dangerous precincts of the Mogul's Seraglio—cheat him of his wishes, and overturn his empire to restore the Husband of my Heart to the blessings of Liberty and Love" (4.1, p. 59).

This terrestrial sweep alludes to the outposts of the expanding empire—Northwest Territories, Persia, North America, Ceylon, India, the mysterious "East." But Letitia's speech also suggests that imperial expansion is the natural backdrop for a decidedly English love. Her last statement, analogizing the wars of love and imperial struggle, arguably neutralizes the violence of imperial expansion. But it also suggests that English domesticity comes into clearest relief when seen against a global backdrop. Here what is local and particular—the love of an English girl for an English boy—can be expressed only through the terms of an non-English geography.

If a dramatic discourse like Letitia's speaks to the lure of globalism, antiperformance discourse characteristically insists on the pleasures of staying at home, often associating a life on the town with the dereliction of domestic duty. This insistence has special meaning for women, who bear the burden for domesticity and are particularly instructed to avoid opportunities for performance of any kind. In an often-cited passage from Hannah More, parents are counseled to teach their daughters that "this world is not a stage for the display of superficial or even of shining talent, but for the strict and sober exercise of fortitude, temperance, meekness, faith, diligence, and self-denial." Yet, ironically More resorts to the language of the stage to define woman's "true" role, as she writes of woman's "due performance of which Christian graces, angels will be spectators, and God the judge." This irony aside, throughout More's writings the world of balls, fashionable assemblies, theaters, and card tables is to be shunned in favor of quiet domesticity, a relative invisibility within the confines of the home. At the same time, most types of motion—the quick turn from one activity to the next, or the too eager gravitation toward a social pleasure or dissipation—increasingly mark the problematic female subject.

In *The Belle's Stratagem*, as if to answer Hannah More and those promoting female provincialism, Cowley positions the character of Lady Frances Touchwood between two characters, her husband, Sir George, and Lady Racket. Where will Lady Frances be safer—at home in the country, isolated from the public eye and under her husband's protection, or at loose in the city and under the tuition of the Fine Lady? Yet Cowley stacks the deck against Sir George: he is represented as so pathologically jealous that he released his wife's favorite bullfinch because he was jealous of the kisses she gave it (1.3, p. 12). Sir George, proselytizing against an urban life for women, finds in the lifestyle of the Fine Lady everything that is inimical to proper womanhood—mobility, antidomestic sentiment, dissipated social performance. He complains that the Fine Lady "is seen everywhere but in her own house. She sleeps at home, but she lives all over the town. In her mind, every sentiment gives place to the Lust of Conquest, and the vanity of being particular. The feelings of a Wife, and Mother, are lost in the whirl of dissipation. If she continues virtuous, 'tis by chance—and if she preserves her Husband from ruin; 'tis by her dexterity at the Card-Table!" (1.1, p. 25). According to Sir George, a Fine Lady is too visible: she fails to stay with the walls of her husband's house and hence resists in her movement the prescribed roles of wife and mother. Female gambling only exacerbates the sense that women can operate beyond patriarchal control. Yet Sir George seems to assume that the "real" woman who opposes the Fine Lady is not only housebound but largely invisible. Her roles are presumably not "performed" but rather innate, even "authentic."

Sir George further equates an absence of performance with the kind of transparency among the ranks of women that previously assured stable social relations: "Heaven and earth! with whom can a man trust his wife, in the present state of society? Formerly there were distinctions of character amongst ye: every class of females had its particular description; Grandmothers were pious, Aunts discreet, Old Maids censorious! but now aunts, grandmothers, girls, and maiden gentlewomen, are all the same creature;—a wrinkle more or less is the sole difference between ye" (2.1, p. 26). For Sir George, then, society ought to be a structured hierarchy where human beings discover their "natural" roles and where women in particular find their places predetermined by gender, rank, and age. However, in his eagerness to assign women their natural places, he misses the idea (now a feminist commonplace) that femininity itself is inevitably another kind of masquerade, with wife and mother as two of the most exacting social roles for women. Indeed, he accuses Mrs. Racket herself of refusing her "natural role" as a widow: "[Y]our air should be sedate, your dress grace, your deportment matronly, and in all things an example to the young women growing up around you" (2.1, p. 26).

To answer Sir George, Cowley creates in Mrs. Racket a rare type—an outspoken, fashionable woman who is neither dissipated nor devious. This character offers an unusual late-century defense of cosmopolitanism and especially of the opportunities it affords for women. According to Mrs. Racket, a "Fine Lady" is someone who takes full advantage of a diverse and thriving social scene. She is someone "for whom Nature has done much, and Education more; she has Taste, Elegance, Spirit, Understanding. In her manner she is free, in her morals nice. Her behaviour is undistinguishingly polite to her Husband, and all mankind; her sentiments are for their hours of retirement. In a word, a Fine Lady is the life of conversation, the spirit of society, the joy of the public!—Pleasures follow her where ever she appears, and the kindest wishes attend her slumbers" (1.1, p. 25). Unlike Hannah More, Mrs. Racket defends a cosmopolitan setting as the appropriate backdrop for a vibrant female intellect. Though her character is not above reproach, she does exude an exciting energy, and she does articulate well the stakes of urban immersion for women.

As the plot unfolds, Lady Frances finds herself drawn into a series of exciting but potentially dangerous social situations. In particular, stalking her at the masquerade in act 4, Courtall plans to trick her into an affair by disguising himself as her husband. The plot is foiled by Saville, who substitutes a courtesan named Kitty Willis for Lady Frances. In rendering Lady Frances as a character who can be brought to the brink of destruction yet ultimately be preserved, Cowley makes her point: a deep sense of domestic responsibility occurs not where a woman has been isolated from the forces of corruption but where she is free to fall. Only by participating in the social masquerade does Lady Frances inure herself to its dangers. Moreover, paradoxically true female virtue is only possible where libertine threat looms large. Saville delivers this moral and further insists that Sir George must allow for his wife's performance as it serves a useful social purpose: "Lady Frances was born to be the ornament of Courts. She is sufficiently alarmed, not to wander beyond the reach of her Protector;—and, from the British Court, the most tenderly anxious Husband could not wish to banish his Wife" (4.5, p. 77). The relative freedom Saville urges for Lady Frances—the liberty to attend public assemblies and functions—is not quite the full range of movement given to Mrs. Racket. Still, it is clear that public performance serves here not to undermine female character but to facilitate and enhance its representation.

And this point is nowhere clearer than in the play's primary plot, that concerning Doricourt and Letitia Hardy. With his appetite whetted by foreign travel, Doricourt initially sees little that attracts him to Letitia. He finds previous parental provisions for their marriage chafing—until Letitia performs the role that convinces him he cannot live without her. Cowley borrows and improves upon Goldsmith, who in turn only foregrounds a more widely acknowledged paradox: no one is ever so much herself as when she deliberately acts what she is not. In this case, Letitia veils herself mysteriously and finds a range of opportunities in her disguise. We have already seen how her costume widens the scope of her vocabulary. No longer bound by the language of modest domesticity, she opens up and, against the backdrop of the masquerade, becomes the charming and alluring creature of Doricourt's dreams.

In her groundbreaking work on English masquerade, Terry Castle writes that customarily eighteenth-century "masqueraders did not dress as themselves, nor did they dress as people like themselves. . . . [O]ne was obliged to appear, in some sense, as one's opposite. . . . The conceptual gap separating true and false selves was ideally an abyss." Yet Cowley's use of the masquerade not only contradicts this assertion but also exposes the stable binary understanding of human identity on which this statement depends: to say that one went to the masquerade as one's opposite is to imply that someone knew precisely who she or he was. In Cowley's comedy we see how the "true" self is nothing more than a provisional category; the mask neither covers an "authentic" identity nor reveals the "opposite" of the truth since the categories of a "true" and "false" identity collapse into one another. For Cowley, the masquerade enables the presentation of the "truth." As we have seen with Hardy, not only is John Quick his other role, but he also is John Quick. Similarly, at the masquerade, Hardy's daughter Letitia is utterly charming in her disguise: she is sophisticated, witty, and exciting. More importantly, she is what she really is, if only English decorum had not scripted for her a more modest and less demonstrative role.

The theme of Letitia's true identity is resolved in act 5. Just when Doricourt believes that he is inextricably bound to marry Letitia Hardy—a woman he does not love—the mysterious masquerader—in fact Letitia Hardy covered by a mask—returns to him. Cowley's imagery shifts from masking to veiling, partly to echo the Alcestis story, to which act 5 alludes, but partly also to reintroduce the theme of what it means to perform a specifically English version of womanhood. As she presents herself to Doricourt in her true identity, Letitia refers simultaneously to her nation's "veiling" of female subjectivity and to a reserve that was naturally her own. Doricourt's initial dislike of her English maidenhood led her to reject what had been imposed on her: "The timidity of the English character threw a veil over me, you could not penetrate," she explains. "You have forced me to emerge in some measure from my natural reserve, and throw off the veil that hid me." Claiming that she can be anything her mate desires, she asks him, "shall I be an *English* wife?—or, breaking from the bonds of Nature and Education, step forth to the world in all the captivating glare of foreign manners?" (5.4, p. 81).

The curious alignment of "Nature and Education" suggests that the playwright wants it both ways here: the modesty so common to English womanhood is indigenous and put upon, just as Letitia's reserve was natural and imposed. These concepts appear paradoxical, even contradictory, until we remember the dramatic context in which the lines are delivered: we as the audience have been watching an actress who has been simulating both a modest reserve and a captivating flair. The question of what is "natural" in English womanhood evaporates when the discussion is framed by a proscenium arch: for what is truly natural in a performance that only imitates a "natural" inclination that is supposedly beyond art? Thus Cowley may allow her actress to claim an "indigenous" or authentic grounding for English womanhood, but in the end that supposedly authentic grounding comes alive best in performance.

However, what about the destabilizing effect of making Letitia's "natural" reserve an effect of performance? After all, like Kate Hardcastle in *She Stoops to Conquer,* Letitia is mistaken for a woman of easy virtue: at the end of act 4, rumor convinces Doricourt that she is the kept woman of Lord George Jennet. This rumor can be construed as a simple comic misunderstanding—or as a potentially uncanny doubling, since the audience might well have expected the actress (Frances Younge in the original production) to have been, in point of fact, of somewhat questionable character. In a similar fashion, the morally impeccable Lady Frances (Mrs. Hartley) is easily doubled by Kitty Willis, suggesting once again that the lady and the whore—like the lady and the actress—are distinguished only by the roles they act.

The instability introduced by Letitia's playing appears to have especially affected Mrs. Inchbald when she wrote the introduction to an 1806 publication of the play: "The incident, from which the play takes its title, is, perhaps, the least pleasing, and the least probable, of any amongst the whole; still, this stratagem, as the foundation of a multiplicity of many others, far better conceived and executed, has claim to the toleration of the reader, and will generally obtain admiration from the auditor, by the skill of the actress who imitates a simpleton." Inchbald's comment epitomizes the position of those who find moral stability in the refusal to play, yet who find pleasure in the very nature of performance. In particular, she appears appalled by the idea that Letitia used the art of the masquerade to win her lover: "Who does not scorn that romantic passion, which is inflamed to the highest ardour, by a few hours with a woman whose face is concealed?" She further implies that Letitia is—and always was—quite simply the woman beneath her mask. Rejecting the complex dialectic between Letitia's "assumed" and "real" identities, Inchbald claims instead to locate the pleasure of the scene in the moment of Letitia's unveiling: "And yet, who does not here have sympathies with the lover, and feel a strong agitation, when Letitia, going to take off her mask, exclaims in a tremulous voice—'This is the most awful moment of my life'?" To privilege this remark over others may clear Letitia from the charge of duplicity, but it also deprives the scene of its theatrical richness, a richness that depends precisely on a metatheatrical awareness. Inchbald seeks to rescue a play which seems curiously attractive to her despite its clearly unacceptable pro-performance message. It is little wonder, then, that her edition omits the final epilogue, which, as we will see, explicitly engages the audience on the question of its own performance.

By the time we reach act 5, Cowley has made her point clear: in this play, human identity is fulfilled not in the consistent refusal to perform but in the recognition that all social interaction is necessarily an act. The epilogue taunts those who insist on thinking themselves beyond acting their parts. First, female audience members are reminded that the most natural female face is already a mask:

What Lady Bab, or Grace,
E'er won a woman—in her natural face?

Mistake me not—French red, or blanching creams,
I stoop not to—for those are hackney'd themes;
The arts I means are harder to detect,
Easier to put on, and worn to more effect;—
And thus—
Do pride and Envy, with their horrid lines,
Destroy th' Effect of Nature's sweet designs?
The mask of sweetness is at once applied,
And gentlest manners ornament the Bride.

More chilling is the role-playing that covers up the violence of paternal tyranny:

And you, my gentle Sirs wear Vizors too:
And here I'll strip you, and expose to view
Your hidden features—First I point at you.
That well-stuff'd waistcoat, and that ruddy cheek;
That ample forehead, and that skin so sleek,
Point out good-nature, and gen'rous heart—
Tyrant! stand forth, and, conscious own thy part:
Thy wife, thy children, tremble in thy eye;
And peace is vanquished when the Father's nigh.

While the Shakespearean allusions are unmistakable here, Cowley's tone is significantly darker than the Bard's, and it is worth asking how the stakes of performance are different for her. Why does she feel compelled to defend the actor as the only "authentic" individual in the playhouse?

Sure 'tis enchantment! See, from ev'ry side
The Masks fall off! In charity I hide
The monstrous features rushing to my view—
Fear not, there, Grand-Papa—nor you—nor you:
For should I show your features to each other,
Not one amongst ye'd know his Friend or Brother,
'Tis plain, then, all the world, from Youth to Age,
Appear in Masks—here, only on the Stage,
You see us as we are: here trust your eyes;
Our wish to please, admits of no disguise.

For Cowley, only the play can rescue humanity from its own savage potential, for the play has the virtue of veiling *and* unveiling its citizens. The play demands not that we be who we absolutely and essentially are, but rather that we admit that human beings are slippery, multifaceted individuals who engage in a range of self-defining behaviors. In this way, Cowley endorses masking as movement or as the free play of identity that refuses to fix character as only this or that. Quite simply, she celebrates the pleasure, power, and truth of play.

However, in the end, Cowley's performance-based theory of human subjectivity is equally important for what it implies about not just individual but also national identity. Returning full circle to the Jew Issac Mendoza, we recognize that Cowley's play locates national identity not in terms of place, or essentialized "native" character, but in terms of fluidity, self-invention, and self-awareness. Moreover, *The Belle's Stratagem* implies that nationhood itself is formed through play. A nation is comprised of individuals, men and women alike, who have freely made themselves as national subjects, and the native citizen has no patriotic advantage in this making.

Under early modern vagrancy laws, actors were problematic subjects partially because they—like the cosmopolitans Rob Wilson discovers in the writings of early modern philosophers—appeared to be "rootless and mobile, avowedly universal, uncommitted and detached." However if (as Wilson also argues) the "world citizen" can be also characterized as "enlightened and mobile, all but freed from particularized prejudices, fixed ties, and narrow local/national boundaries," then the actor becomes an appropriate figurehead for a progressive nationalism. In his very mobility, the actor embodies openness to plurality. He practices a tolerance of multiplicity and difference. In this way, he becomes the nation's most promising citizen. But those of us who are not actors can also learn an important lesson from Cowley's play. To accept and promulgate a performance-based definition of national character leads away from static and bounded definitions of *nation* as a territory, definitions that are far too often based on an essentialist understanding of Englishness. Like certain kinds of cosmopolitanism, a performance-based theory of identity such as that endorsed by Cowley in *The Belle's Stratagem* also "undermines the 'naturalness' of ethnic absolutisms, whether articulated at the nation-state, tribal, or minority levels." In the moment when an English actor plays a Englishman who plays a Jew, the concept of *nation* is temporarily expanded: England becomes a creative space of possibility and play—not a bounded space for the static policing of identity but a platform where imagined nationhood is meaningfully staged.

Source: Elizabeth Kowaleski Wallace, "Theatricality and Cosmopolitanism in Hannah Cowley's *The Belle's Stratagem*," in *Comparative Drama*, Vol. 35, No. 3–4, Fall–Winter 2002, pp. 415–31.

Erin Isikoff

In the following essay, Isikoff examines, within the context of eighteenth-century values, Cowley's use of the contrasting "tropes of modesty and of masquerade" in The Belle's Strategem.

Hannah Cowley's comedy, *The Belle's Strategem* (1780), recounts Letitia Hardy's successful attempt to win the affections of her fiancé, Doricourt, with a strategy of varied personas. Letitia orchestrates her own romance by acting out alternate female identities and thereby tricking

Doricourt into his role of the faithful hero. Hidden behind different female facades, Letitia experiments with the possible allures inherent in vulgarity, wit, and propriety. Thus, the play calls for a critical examination of its constructions of female identity and a careful evaluation of the ideals of behavior and self that are sanctioned for the heroine as either proper or powerful. Indeed, an analysis of Letitia's encounters with her intended constructs a dichotomy between the eighteenth-century tropes of modesty and of masquerade, the two sorts of veils that obscure our heroine and engender her successes and failures.

Modesty and masquerade can be understood as two versions of the same practise, two methods that disguise the nature of a woman's true identity and feelings. However, eighteenth-century commentators viewed the matter differently, considering the former as a respectable (unsexual) and essential female uniform and the latter as a degrading (sexual) and dangerous garb. *The Belle's Strategem* suggest that both a modest demeanor and a masquerade costume are types of trappings to be put on and off as the occasion suits, but it leaves open the question of which is the better strategy for Letitia and for any woman intent on charming. It is not immediately clear which type of mask empowers Letitia and which veil cages her within delimiting social norms. Nor is it obvious how the ending of the comedy, as usual a happy marriage, mediates between the two. As modesty is both a sort of masquerade and its counteragent, its joyous triumph at the finale needs clarification.

Cowley's play reads as a comic meditation on not only the pleasures but also the limitations of disguise for a heroine intent on her own plot, intent on plotting. Letitia's strategems easily triumph over the selfish fop who is its object until the two are joined in marriage and the fool becomes the husband. Indeed, *BS* figures the female discourse of desire as a masked discourse, both in the sense that Letitia reveals her love for Doricourt only when her identity is hidden and also as the play effectively veils its advocacy of female empowerment with a reestablishment at its closure of patriarchal proscriptions against female activity. This masked discourse signals an author reliant herself on strategies of indirection, strategies that are masked. The true nature of Cowley's positions is hidden; the play evaluates virtue and vice inconsistently and obscures its morality. Cowley, like Letitia, plots and, like Letitia, she plots in disguise.

The text of the play insists on the link between Cowley and Letitia. Significantly, Letitia's various identities rely not only on facial disguise, but also on the mask of language. It is precisely Letitia's varied conversational personas (like Cowley's comic talent) that earn our notice and our interest. Through vulgar, witty, and proper language, Letitia also writes a comedy for herself. In addition, the prologue and the epilogue to *BS* address the issue of masquerade and by so doing construct parallels between author and heroine. Cowley presents herself anonymously, veils herself, and her mask too is a sort of emancipation from the perils of public performance. The resumption of patriarchal values that concludes the work comments not only on Letitia's presumption, but on Cowley's own masquerade and her plot of female empowerment in and through disguise.

The prologue to *BS* invokes the image of the masquerade as theater. Behind the curtain, "trainbearers to tragic queens" mingle with "Harlequin, and Punch, and Banquo's ghost," so that "all this night perform a grand review." However, this description of assorted costumes effectively unmasks the male players who will perform Cowley's work; Cowley's first maneuver of *BS* is to deny the theater's power of masquerade in a play that presents a heroine's attempts to conceal identity. Does this demystification of the theater foreshadow the necessary failure of Letitia's masquerade plot? The prologue then levies a curse on Hannah Cowley, "To *damn* this author—but oh! save her play." To counteract, perhaps, her insistence on unmasking, the prologue speaks in favor of a plot of mystery and drama, in favor of masquerade, in favor of the belle's (Letitia's) stategem of disguise. Thus Cowley institutes in the prologue a dialogue about the possibilities of masquerade, so that the drama begins with its moral debate already underway. This debate is established as both contentious and firmly undecided. At the moment when the prologue most vehemently declaims against Cowley it also conceals her identity so that the defamation of demystification enacts another transformative mask, that of anonymity. "Tis thus we're serv'd, when saucy women write—. . . When lady writers crowd our Covent stage!".

The prologue raises the issue of masquerade in order both to thematize it and to denote Cowley, along with Letitia, as a masquerading subject. Both author and heroine are engaged in the debate about the propriety of false or anonymous identities. Both are also potentially guilty of the impropriety, the "sauciness," of plotting ("writing"). Cowley implicates Letitia and herself in these unresolved debates, thus enmeshing them both in strategems

> " BY FOCUSING INSTEAD ON THE GOOD HUSBAND AND THE PROMISE OF A COMPANIONATE MARRIAGE, COWLEY DISGUISES THE PREEMINENCE SHE ATTACHES TO REBELLIOUS MASQUERADING."

necessarily accommodating, necessarily indirect. By writing a self-damning prologue, Cowley promises her audience a performance that contradicts its own mastery and a heroine both damned and saved. Letitia and Cowley both may be accused of indelicacy, but from their unseemly disguises emerge comic, delightful plots.

It seems likely that Cowley took the issue of masquerade, its propriety and impropriety, seriously. An important dramatist of the late eighteenth century, Cowley put on plays with David Garrick, R. B. Sheridan, George Coleman, and Thomas Harris, London's most prominent contemporary producers. *BS* itself, her fourth piece, had a twenty-eight-night run in 1780 and earned Cowley over 500 pounds. However, Cowley published many of her poems under a pseudonym, "Anna Matilda." Authorship and decorum are sometimes at odds, but through the agency of a mask, of a false identity, Cowley reconciles respectability and accomplishment. Masks, then, not only mediate identity but also manage to protect it, so that a woman in disguise can plot with gentility.

Letitia's masquerade plot and the various identities it engenders register this debate between disguise and propriety. Cowley allows the adventures of a young girl to attest to the arguments for and against masquerade and modesty. It is Letitia who concocts the plot of the *BS,* telling her father Mr. Hardy, "a plan has struck me, if you will not oppose it, which flatters me with brilliant success." The rather intellectual plan, which is opposed by Mrs. Rackett as "good philosophy," but "a bad maxim", is even in Letitia's own estimation, "a little paradoxical." It centers on its own "brilliancy," for it exploits Lady Brilliant's masquerade, which all the play's characters plan to attend. Letitia, determined to reverse Doricourt's unfavorable reception of her charms at their first meeting, contends that "as he does not like me enough, I want him to like me still less, and will at our next interview endeavor to heighten his indifference into dislike." She further explains, "'tis much easier to convert a sentiment into its opposite, than to transform indifference into tender passion." Specifically, Letitia, perceiving that her modest demeanor has veiled her talents and left her loved one uninterested, imagines alternate personalities in which to appear to more or less advantage. By this method, Doricourt will be tricked out of his indifference, an indifference he might never take the trouble to evaluate of his own accord. Because "Men are all dissemblers, flatterers, deceivers!", Letitia schemes to seduce with lies.

Letitia's intentions shape the comedy, which only ends with the success of her plot and its revelation to Doricourt. And Cowley reserves for Letitia all the energy and activity of the play. When Letitia remarks of her plot, "I have the strongest confidence in it. I am inspired with unusual spirits, and on this hazard willingly stake my chance for happiness. I am impatient to begin my measures", it is apparent that the issues at stake for the heroine yoke the comic to the dramatic. Letitia responds to romantic crisis with vigor and invention, with high seriousness, because it seems that her guardians are no guarantors of her happiness. Mrs. Rackett, her chaperone, answers Letitia's fears and schemes with nonchalance: "I can't stay now to consider it. I am going to call on the Ogles, and then to lady Frances Touchwood's, and then to an action, and then—I don't know where." Her father, Mr. Hardy, is both too ignorant and too indolent to bother about his daughter's welfare: "Well 'tis an odd thing—I can't understand it,—but I foresee Letty will have her way, and so I shan't give myself the trouble to dispute it." Thus Letitia monopolizes our attention with good reason. When Letitia recruits all the "spirit or invention in woman", she claims a lion's share of Cowley's dramatic power as well.

Mr. Hardy, patriarchy's representative, brings his assumptions about proper venues for female invention to bear on Letitia's dilemma, encouraging her to win Doricourt's affection by resorting to all the powers of her toilette. But Doricourt has no objection to Letitia's physical attractions, no criticism of her "complexion, shape, and features." He judges her "a fine girl, as far as mere flesh and blood goes." Mr. Hardy seems unaware of the issues truly at stake in the match, and hence unable to ensure its completion. Significantly, Letitia's command of language, her art, empowers her in the very transaction about which the play concerns

itself and yet in which she is otherwise disempowered, her marriage. The agreement made years ago between Mr. Hardy and Doricourt's father renders Letitia passive in this most important occasion; Letitia's witty transformation ensures her own active participation in the disposal of her body and her property. By masquerading Letitia enters the patriarchal discourses of economics and law. Ironically, patriarchy's contractual negotiations could not come off sucessfully without her help.

For Doricourt, Letitia lacks "spirit! fire! l'air enjoue! that something, that nothing, which every body feels, and which nobody can describe, in the resistless charmers of Italy and France." Thus her masquerade plot is particlarly well suited to win over a man enamored of nameless effects and mysterious charms. Doricourt, bored already with his fiancée now that the "hour of expectation is past", is ripe for a trap which entices with variety and paradox. Indeed, the more usual strategies of increasing romantic interest are shown not to work in Doricourt's case; when Letitia absents herself from dinner in order, perhaps, to peak his interest by thwarting his expectations of her company, Mrs. Rackett reports the failure of such an attempt. Letitia asks if her absence was "a severe mortification to him", but her chaperone reponds in the negative: "I can't absolutely swear it spoiled his appetite; he ate as if he was hungry, and drank his wine as though he liked it" Letitia learns from this mistaken strategem and plans something more "rash and complex, her first transformation into that which he cannot but despise a vulgar coquette.

Letitia's first mask relies primarily on language to evoke the indelicacy and insipidity of the false persona. Here, Letitia does not literally cover her face, but rather changes her speech (and mimics unseemly behavior) to establish an alternate identity. Ironically, Letitia's artificial vulgarity suggests Doricourt's feminine ideal, in whom, "A mind, a soul, a polished art is seen. Although Letitia uses linguistic wiles to pervert that ideal, already the play privileges Letitia's masquerade plot for its ingenuous approximation of Doricourt's desires and its consequent devaluation of them.

Letitia's first masquerade, as a "vulgar soul", illustrates exactly the qualities that Doricourt despises, and thus relies on reversal in its triumph over him. First Letitia exaggerates and mocks the modesty which f— Doricourt "wants . . . zest, it wants poignancy", by hiding behind Mr. Rackett and peeping at Doricourt through her fingers. Then she begins a recitation whose pettiness, rudeness, and coquetry are enough to turn his heart to "marble." Doricourt responds to Letitia's image of low breeding just as she might wish him to; his indifference "'tis advanced thirty-two degrees towards hatred." It may be, of course, that Letitia's linguistic vision of indecorum is only a "literary" depiction—but even if this is so, her representation is immediately readable to Doricourt because he too is removed enough from the actuality of immodest behavior to be aware only of his own upper-class assumptions surrounding it, the same assumptions upon which Letitia has constructed her pastiche.

In the eighteenth century, the age of the dictionary and of the stabilization of spelling and grammar, polite and proper conversation marked gentility. The mechanics of cultured speech identified the educated upper class and the lack thereof pointed to a more humble social position. Letitia chooses her vulgar words carefully so that they break a number of the neoclassical rules of language usage. Her mask relies on colloquialism, solecism, and archaism—categories of lower-class linguistic error which Carey McIntosh has identified. Letitia relishes her colloquialisms, substituting adjectives for adverbs ["I can talk as fast as any body"], attaching prefixes to verbs ["When papa was a hunting, he used to come a suitoring"], making unclear pronoun references ["I was daunted before my father, and the lawyer, and all them"], relying on clichés ["I wasn't born in a wood to be scared by an owl"], continually asserting authority for her statements ["Sure I may say"], and signaling the direction and intention of her discourse with repetitions and verbal commas ["laws," "why," "you know," "I used to say"]. And she does not neglect to pepper her discourse with solecisms, disorderly and imprecise usages of grammar and diction which create ambiguities and inaccuracies. Letitia constructs sentences notably unparallel ["he's as slow in speech as aunt Margery when she's reading Thomas Aquinas—and stands gaping like mumchance"], for example, and is often vague ["I have read it in a book"]. Lastly, she is guilty of archaism, of speaking in an old-fashioned (seventeenth-century) style, when she heavily labels her antitheses ["Sure I may say what I please before I am married, if I can't afterwards"] and when she uses the relative pronoun "that" incorrectly ["Laws, don't snub me before my husband— that is to be"]. McIntosh's categories aside, Letitia's colorful expressions ["Oh, lud," "flimflams," "ifags"], her blatant references to courtship ["D'ye think a body does not know how to talk to a sweetheart?"], her unbridled laughter ["He, he,

he!"], and her shameless boasts ["cousin, you may tell the gentleman what a genus {sic} I have"] pointedly identify her as vulgar and ill-bred. This first persona, by inverting the normal relationship between language and identity, allows Letitia to use social assumptions to her own purposes.

Although Letitia schemes for the hand of a man of whom patriarchy approves, her strategies of deception and inversion blatantly contradict notions of morality and seemliness. Letitia's first masquerade links her with all of the ignorance and ugliness that she portrays. Letitia's new personality temporarily endangers her social position; although her disingenuous masquerade plot does not threaten her sense of self-worth, in Doricourt's eyes it strips her of her dignity and value. Letitia's first bold maneuver, taken alone, might deprive her of her lover's respect and, ultimately, his hand. As Doricourt tells Mrs. Rackett: "Doricourt's wife must be incapable of improvement—but it must be, because she's got beyond it." However, Letitia's plot calls for both the subversion of her own honor, and for a reversal of Doricourt's own expectations and opinions. Now that he despises Letitia Hardy, he must be forced into a passion, and his object can only be Letitia if her face is masked instead of her wisdom.

In the second installment of her masquerade romance, Letitia adopts not only an alternate persona, that of the witty charmer, but also an alternate physical identity, that of masked grace. This transformation takes place at Lady Brilliant's masquerade ball where Letitia takes advantage of the opportunity for disguise. However, the success of Letitia's first mask, her cleverly imitated vulgar speech, points to the ease with which the heroine adopts another persona and to the suspicion that every character trait, both undesirable and desirable, that she evinces may be only a disguise. Now Letitia tries to be witty or modest enough to change Doricourt's hatred into passion; to some extent Cowley must also intend these more seemly behaviors to appear as those of convenience.

The inappropriate immodesty of Letitia's first persona pales in comparison with the assertiveness and daring with which Letitia enacts her second identity at a masquerade proper. The masquerade, in eighteenth-century England, was tainted by associations of at least exoticism, and often sexual, intellectual, and even moral chaos. The masquerade allowed all its participants to disguise themselves with other identities; its enjoyment stemmed from the liberation that accompanied such a loss of position in the social hierarchy. Masked, a man might insult his neighbor, or even his superior. A woman in disguise might boldly flirt with a man to whom she had never been introduced. Such a spectacle of collective disorder necessarily evoked powerful responses. Some participants delighted in impersonation and the colorful mix of characters that lent a surreal air to the event. Others bemoaned the contortion of reality and absence of decorum therein. Critics repeatedly inveighed against the licentious antics which a masked ball occasioned, from jostling to dancing to embracing. The masquerade facilitated "improper" assignations of all sorts; adultery, prostitution, and homosexuality all profited from its particular freedoms.

As always, the repercussions of masquerade libertinage were felt mostly by the women who succumbed to the temptations of its emancipations. The *Weekly Journal* of April 18, 1724 warned: "Fishes are caught with Hooks, Birds are ensnar'd with Nets, but Virgins with Masquerades." How significant then that *BS* dramatizes the tale of a virgin who masquerades to ensnare a suitor and not the more usual narrative of a virgin seduced by a masked villain! Indeed, Cowley's comedy does formulate the latter story, but only as a counterpoint to Letitia's plot. The Touchwood subplot describes Courtall's evil scheme against female virtue, in the person of Lady Frances Touchwood, but his intentions are frustrated by the Wise (Savvy) Man of the Town (Ville), Saville.

The masquerade, with all its pleasures and dangers, permits the impermissible, and thus is essentially an imaginative moment par excellence. As Terry Castle has noted, it is throughout eighteenth-century literature a powerful plot catalyst, facilitating flirtations, liasons, abductions, heroics and the like. Cowley's play is no exception in its reliance on the masquerade's dramatic power. The prologue introduces the theme and in Act I, scene ii Doricourt tells Saville, his confidante, that he intends to accompany the Hardy's to Lady Brilliant's. No other event vies for the theatrical interest that is concentrated in Act IV, scene i, the masquerade scene. All Cowley's characters share in its energies; in fact, they all attend! Lady Frances Touchwood's idealized view of the spectacle indicates its enticements: "Delightful. The days of enchantment are restor'd; the columns glow with saphires and rubies, emperors and fairies, beauties and dwarfs, meet me at every step." But Saville cautions her about its concomitant evils: "lady! there are dangers abroad—Beware!". As it did in the prologue, *BS* continues to engage in a debate about the

masquerade, and in this debate it invests the majority of its intensity.

Cowley heightens the importance of Lady Brilliant's masked ball by hinting that the whole society of the comedy operates, on a larger level, as just such a festival of disguise. Cowley suggests that Act IV, scene i is no aberration—but rather the most obvious manifestation of evil inclinations that are permanently sustained, albeit hidden. Instead of painting the masquerade as society's designated receptacle for the improper desires which it cannot expunge, Cowley compares everyday polite behavior with disguise, deceit, and vulgarity. Courtall lies to his "unpresentable" country cousins, so that he will not have to introduce them into society as his relations. Doricourt's foreign manner of dress excites the whole *ton* into a fervor of fashionable affectation. Sir George Touchwood, having sworn himself an enemy to British women of fashion, marries one and earns Doricourt's scorn, "Why, thou art a downright, matrimonial Quixote." Flutter, in his own flighty way the consummate man about town, identifies the system of values that underpin the social world. Flutter says: "A fair tug, by Jupiter—between duty and pleasure!—Pleasure beats and off we go. Io triumphe!". It is Sir George who most clearly denominates what Cowley means us to see: "And what is the society of which you boast?—a mere chaos, in which all distinction of rank is lost in a ridiculous affectation of ease. In the same select party, you will often find the wife of a bishop and a sharper, of an earl and a fiddler. In short, 'tis one universal masquerade, all disguised in the same habits and manners." Sir George blames the masquerade society on the wives, on the women, whose pernicious desires inculcate the destruction of the social hierarchy and the salubrious order which stemmed from it. As Cowley masks herself in anonymity to protect herself from the particular audacity of female authorship, and creates a heroine who plots a masquerade romance, the connection between women and masks seems to be sustained as a truth in *BS;* to what extent the masquerade and women are to be castigated for society's evils, however, is less clear.

Only at the masquerade proper can Letitia hone her "polished art"; while the vulgar speech patterns of her first charade successfully alienates Doricourt's already weak sense of attachment to his fiancée ["Though she has not inspir'd me with violent passion, my honour secures her felicity."], it is the masking of the face which permits the enactment of the more difficult proposition of producing a passion. Terry Castle notes that costume in general was thought to prompt sexual transgression, but that "it was the mask in particular, that indispensable element of masquerade disguise that was thought most powerfully aphrodisiacal—for wearer and beholder alike. . . . Anonymity, actual or stylized, relaxed the safeguards of virtue [and . . . masked individuals were seen as fetishistically exciting."] The masquerade as a whole was a spectacle of disorderly sensuality, the perfect setting for Letitia's flirtation; her disguise in particular ensured that any of Doricourt's attentions to her would be erotically charged. Indeed, throughout Act IV, scene i Letitia refuses Doricourt's insistent pleas that she remove her mask, urging: "Beware of imprudent curiosity; it lost Paradise." To appease Doricourt's desire for knowlege would be to satiate his desire for anything else. The mystery of her countenance stimulates his interest and aids in the incitement of ardor.

The masquerade licensed both of Letitia's required devices, mystery and wit. The *Weekly Journal* of February 15, 1718, in a glowing description of one of the first masked assemblies to take place in Haymarket, noted: "There is an absolute Freedom of Speech, without the least Offence given thereby." Not all observers agreed that the unbounded raillery left the rules of decorum unviolated. Critics anxiously denounced the indulgence of rude, familiar, or loud speech and the prevalence of unabashed and promiscuous flirtation. Ironically, this unregulated intercourse facilitated Letitia's carefully disciplined witty discourse with Doricourt. Letitia's control over her speech is as absolute in her public guise of the charming incognita as it is in her private portrayal of a foolish coquette. There reigns in her masquerades a method to her madness, a regulation of her hold disguises.

Indeed, the masquerade itself was an organized inversion, founded on the principles of reversal and paradox. As Castle expresses it, "the controlling figure was the antithesis." Letitia's strategy of inversion (turning indifference to hatred to passion) and varied disguises is a distillation of the properties of the masquerade and a concise manifestation of it. As a vulgar miss in the drawing room, she introduced low, ill manners where only high breeding should be; as a precise wit at the orgiastic masked ball, she introduces high-society decorum where only indecent liberties are taken. And, to find paradoxes within paradoxes, just as Letitia personifies the rebellious perversions of the masquerade, with all the improper emancipations that it promised women, she also thereby personifies the mystery and diversity of the woman who Doricourt imagines as ideal, the

woman of "spirit! fire! l'air enjoue! that something, that nothing, which every body feels, and which nobody can describe." Doricourt follows Letitia's masked figure throughout the rooms of the assembly, entranced by her "spirit", her "air bewitching", her "Delightful wildness!", and, of course, the continual frustration of his desire to unmask her. Doricourt finally exclaims his intensely felt passion: "Fate has ordained you mine . . . I never met with a woman so perfectly to my taste; and I won't believe it formed you so, on purpose to tantalize me." Just when Letitia's self-creations liberate her from anyone's preconceptions of female identity and womanly methods of charming, her second mask tallies exactly with Doricourt's vision of female perfection. Thus, her revolutionary stratagem, while it steals from Doricourt the energy of their courtship, does not challenge its existence. Letitia wears masks only to guarantee that someday she might appear before an adoring husband without one. Still, she revels in her success, "This moment is worth a whole existence!".

It seems that only at the masquerade, the site of especially female imprudence, can Letitia win the man patriarchy has chosen for her as a prudent choice. So Letitia's plot is ironically premised both upon female desire and female complacence, both upon rebellion and dutifulness. Letitia, the "enchantress who can go to masquerades, and sing, and dance, and talk a man out of his wits!", puts her second successful charade in the service of patriarchal ideology. Letitia's excursion to Lady Brilliant's renders her both the ideal (redeemer) and fallen (redeemed) woman of the text; Letitia's masquerade plot seduces Doricourt's false prejudices and yet ensures Letitia's own transformation from independent heroine to good wife. It is the specific discourse of the second mask which records Letitia's disempowerment. The wit with which she entices Doricourt subtly yet efficiently displaces her control over the masquerade scene and over her suitor.

The language she chooses to engage his interest is as consciously part of high culture as the vulgar discourse of her first persona was consciously part of the low. It is best denoted as the "courtly-genteel", a discourse passed down from the *amour courtois* tradition founded in Provençe in the late eleventh century. Courtly-genteel language retained, in the eighteenth century, its links to privilege and culture and was used by the upper classes to add grace and refinement to their speech. Specifically, its themes of "dependency, courtship, petition, dedication, honor, unsalaried service, friendship, and prayer" denoted polish and discrimination. Its archetypes, the knight errant and the lady love for whom he lives and dies, represented the union of desire and purity, passion and honor, and thus suggested ideal models of romantic behavior. How unusual and determined, then, must Letitia's courtly-genteel romance be at a masquerade where speech otherwise floundered in its own emancipated coarseness.

Letitia wins Doricourt's admiration at the masquerade by exploiting the concerns of the courtly-genteel and by choosing words which signaled courtly taste. "Your mistress will be angry", she teases Doricourt when he flirts with her, invoking the medieval language of courtship. Later, Letitia insists on her personal honor: "At present be content to know that I am a woman of family and fortune." Letitia's genteel strategy impresses her lover as "most charming", as full of "vivacity—wit—elegance", so that he believes her "a woman of brilliant understanding!". After the masked ball, Doricourt admits that he "loved her, died for her—without knowing her." Letitia's second mask of language also triumphs; Letitia's linguistic disguise successfully plots another manipulation of Doricourt, the metamorphosis of his hatred into passion.

Certainly, Letitia's genteel wit constructs romantic relationships between women and men that emphasize the ascendancy of the female. She tells an anonymous masker, vying for her attention: "Charity! If you mean my prayers, heaven grant thee wit, pilgrim." To toy with him further, she asks him (!) for a dance, "*Dare* you dance?" (italics mine). To Doricourt, she is aloof and superior, in marked contrast to her vulgar coquetting. At Lady Brilliant's, Letitia even evinces a distrust of love talk, chastising Doricourt, "You grow too free." In her second charade, through the courtly-genteel discourse, Letitia attempts to establish a barrier between Doricourt and his desires and to challenge, in order to tame, his passion with her own repulse. "My name has a spell in it", she rebuffs him. "As you value knowing me, stir not a step. If I am followed, you never see me more. Adieu", she commands, orchestrating their relationship according to her own plot. At their first meeting, she felt, with mortification: "at the same moment his slave, and an object of perfect indifference to him!". Now she can reverse the rhetoric, configuring Doricourt's slavery with equanimity. For Letitia, courtly-genteel conversation offers a ready-made language (female superiority, centrality, purity) with which to assert her own power over her lover so that his expressions of devotion cannot deviate from the prescribed path of her intentions.

However, Letitia's use of the courtly-genteel discourse, her second mask, hinders the straightforward success of her masquerade plot because her understanding of the nature of courtliness, with its veneration of women, does not encompass its underlying hierarchy, the subservience of the feminine ideal to the knight of action who is nominally her defender. In other words, Letitia's invocation of genteel speech exposes her not only to Doricourt's passionate submission but also to his threatening passion. Indeed, Letitia errs in employing a genteel discourse in a setting expressly un-genteel; her insistence upon polished conduct where all rules of behavior are thwarted is decidedly inopportune. Paradoxically, the strength of Letitia's masquerade plot diminishes at the point of its conceptual origination. Letitia's power relies upon masks, upon false identities, and upon the freedom from feminine propriety which they bring, but her ability, while masked, to control Doricourt decreases when he too perceives himself emancipated from the constrictions of decorum.

Indeed, in the masquerade scene, the most fervent practitioners of the courtly-genteel conversation turn out to be men with suspect designs. The anonymous masker repeatedly petitions Letitia for her attentions: "Charity, fair lady! Charity for a poor pilgrim"; "Will you grant me no favour?"; "I dare do anything you command". And Doricourt swamps her with avowals of courtship and dedication: "you, the most charming being in the world, awaken me to admiration. Did you come from the stars?"; "By heavens! I never was charmed till now"; "Married! the chains of matrimony are too heavy and vulgar for such a spirit as yours. The flowery wreaths of Cupid are the only bands you should wear"; "An angel!". But these declarations soon exhibit their nature. The confessions of passion and service mask (and only lightly) other intentions, less focused on Letitia's power over men and more on their power over her.

Letitia's second mask of wit betrays her plot of independent assertion by encouraging a response which would again entrap her in situations not of her own making. Doricourt endeavors to kiss her against her will. "[Y]our chin would tempt me to kiss it, if I did not see a pouting, red lip above it, that demands—(*Going to kiss*)", he exclaims. He twice grabs her indelicately, once crying "oh, to catch thee, and hold thee for ever in this little cage! [*Attempting to clasp her*]". This prompts Letitia's cool response, "Hold, sir," but Doricourt, unwilling to be deferred, insists, "Tis in vain to assume airs of coldness—Fate has ordained you mine."

And rudely clutching her another time, he implies that her own flirtation, her own use of the courtly-genteel discourse, encourages his coarse actions: "What! you will have a little gentle force?". Clearly, men and women refer to the courtly tradition with differing expectations. Men expect that it licenses a bodily passion and women imagine that it encourages a passionate dedication that transcends the physical. But the conjunction between the genteel sallies and the location of conversation, the masquerade, privileges the knight over the lady; even Doricourt, ironically named "the knight of the woful [sic] countenance" by Sir George Touchwood, intimidates Letitia, the *play's* heroine, at her own game.

The masquerade, then, is a problematic festival of freedom for women and the masquerade plot an encumbered method of comedy. Letitia's romance dares Doricourt's rude freedoms, dares lesser indignities such as sexual favors in a quest for greater dignities such as a husband's love and a happy marriage finale. But only to the extent that Letitia ultimately succeeds in winning Doricourt's love will the risk she takes, throwing away an indifferent respect in exchange for hatred and disrespect, be justified. Letitia might have been expected to inculcate his conversion by placing "trust to the good old maxim,—Marry first, and love will follow." But because Letitia insists that "never to be his wife will afflict me less than to be his wife, and not be beloved", she plots an unseemly romance which embraces freedoms of behavior and speech and threatens to self-destruct into tragedy. Yet, her experience at Lady Brilliant's must have functioned as some sort of rude awakening; immediately afterwards, Letitia's plot undergoes a striking change.

When Letitia returns from her second encounter with Doricourt, she seems to have realized that her plot has endangered her self-sufficiency, has threatened her independence. Forced to endure insults, while without patriarchal protection, she now turns over her strategy to those of her father's household who would oversee it. Her father, good naturedly inept, admits his lack of influence over Doricourt: "when I went up to him, . . . out of downright good nature, to explain things—my gentleman whips round upon his heel, and snapp'd one as short if I had been a beggar woman with six children, and he overseer of the parish." Still, he cannot stand idly by as Letitia manages her own future and after "thinking of plots to plague Doricourt . . . they drove one another out of my head so quick, that I was as giddy as a goose, and could make nothing of them", he thoughtlessly offers a rather

casual acquaintance control over Letitia's destiny. This man, one Mr. Villers, the Man of the Town (Ville), has played only a minor comedic role in the play thus far, and his usurpation of Letitia's plot and her enthusiastic acceptance of his presumption reveal just how jarring and unpleasant the masquerade must have been to a heroine capable of delicate feelings.

By turning over her strategy to a man of the *ton,* Letitia ensures her own recuperation as a worthy wife, and a modest woman. At their first meeting, this modesty prompted Doricourt's indifference, and Letitia's bold impersonations of characters with which to actively engage his interest, both unfavorable and favorable. But after a sexually charged encounter that left her discomfited, Letitia wants to resume the persona of a proper lady so that she might transform Doricourt's indelicate passion into respectful love. Letitia encourages patriarchal regulation so that her plot can no longer detour outside the boundaries of propriety and threaten to leave her a social outcast. Letitia resorts to proper, modest femininity in the service of the happy ending; we might say she turns her plot over to patriarchy in the service of comedy.

Mr. Villers, acting as patriarchy's representative in the absence of any ability in Mr. Hardy, jumps at the chance to organize a young woman's romance merely for his own aggrandizement. He directs Mr. Hardy to feign mortal illness in order to force Doricourt to marry the vulgar Miss Hardy however much he may pine for the incognita with whom he has had an improper liason. The levity with which he treats his scheme contrasts sharply with the high seriousness that Letitia evinced as she plotted to secure her own happiness. "Nothing so easy", he promises, "I have it all here; [*Pointing to his Forehead*]." And though he claims, "I'll answer for the plot", he then heads for Parliament, inviting Mr. Hardy who, if the new plot is to work, cannot be seen in public. This contradiction is noted by the least insightful character of the comedy, Mr. Hardy himself, but Mr. Villers laughs off his mistake.

But Letitia, however Villers discounts the importance of their maneuvers, continues to view events with gravity. Viller's plot, an odd concoction of events usually held as sacred, death and marriage, impresses Letitia with its finality. Usually concise and determined, she wavers, "Oh, heavens!—I—'Tis so exceeding sudden, that really." Already, Letitia has ceased to be the heroine of the play, and the center of its action and energy. Cowley begins to write Letitia as indecisive and fearful, patriarchy's heroine, not *BS*'s. Viller's strategy of inversion, for Letitia and Doricourt to be "married in jest", now appears to Letitia as an "odd idea", and although she agrees to "venture it", she clearly is suspicious of the central trope of masquerade which has been the basis of her own plots against Doricourt. It is Villers who enables her continued participation in the charade, walking her through the necessary steps, "You go and put off your conquering dress, and get all your awkward airs ready."

Doricourt, like Letitia, also registers dissatisfaction with the masquerade and the blatant sexuality of his encounter with the masked charmer. Indeed, Act V, scene ii, with its insistence on the suffering Letitia's scheme causes Doricourt, and on the power she now wields over him through the absolute success of her first two machinations, reads as rather disjunctive with Letitia's abdication that has gone before. However, because her masked strategy permits Doricourt both to love her with respect and to desire her without it, it seems to him "Oh, insufferable?". Doricourt, like Letitia, cannot hear that the purity of their relationship, a relationship for which they have the highest hopes, be tainted with improper sexuality. He too wants to erase the indelicate associations that surround his mystery lover: "The sentiment I have conceived for the witch is so unaccountable, that, in that line [a possible assignation], I cannot bear her idea." Doricourt, like Letitia, no longer believes in the trope of masquerade, in his principles of spirit, fire, and playfulness. He disparages the "mystery in her manner", as illicit, and goes so far as to speak in favor of a "woman of honour" as a wife worthy of adoration. Now Doricourt also begins to hope for a comic resolution to his difficulties.

And although this comedy now discredits masquerade as Letitia constructed it, it does not discount the possibility of a patriarchal orchestration of the same. All the peripheral male characters somehow emerge as central to the final comic charade. Villers plots a false death and a marriage founded on deceit, and in a parallel subplot Saville disguises himself in order to protect Lady Frances Touchwood from the perverse desires of Courtall. Doricourt himself pretends to be mad. Indeed, once Villers' scheme gets underway it enlists Saville's aid in entrapping Doricourt. It is really Saville who manages Doricourt, who pushes and pulls him about with language, so that he agrees to "act the lunatic in the dying man's chamber." And, importantly, Saville manages Letitia's last masked appearance: "*Enter* LETITIA, *masked, led by* SAVILLE." Under Saville's aegis, her final disguise renders her a

victim, no longer able to use mystery and language to put herself at an advantage over Doricourt, and to make herself master of the situation. Viller's plot demands that Letitia despairingly cry out her powerlessness: "I believed him, gave him up my virgin heart—and now!—Ungrateful sex!". In addition, Letitia's last charade again subjects her to pernicious speculation about her honor and to consequent disrespect, forcing her to explicitly, "in this company", defend herself by asserting that "my heart, my honour, my name unspotted as hers you have married; my birth equal to your own, my fortune large." Viller's strategy thereby reminds her of the dangers for women inherent in the masquerade and the necessity of giving up control of her own romance. *BS* devolves into the comic tale of men (Villers, Saville, Doricourt, Hardy) deceiving one another during contractual negotiations surrounding a society marriage.

What differentiates Letitia's masquerade from that of Villers and Saville, that of polite society (Ville)? Letitia's own strategems, for all that they empowered her, did not challenge the intentions of Mr. Hardy and the property patriarchal negotiations to dispose of her future. Letitia's schemed only to convert Doricourt to a willing and passionate husband, not to thwart her father's plans for her match. Since the patriarchal plot shares its end with Letitia's, and even appropriates most of her means, it must really be a strategy to repress female desire and the plot of its self-fulfilment. The target of the patriarchal scheme enacted in Act V is not Doricourt's self-determination in marriage, but Letitia's. Her masquerades have to be contained so that heroines do not learn to invoke principles of inversion and paradox. Her false identities, vulgar and witty, have to be recuperated as devices of polite society, approved and disciplined. Villers' masquerade plot allows Letitia to appear in both her disguises once more, but these representations of her inventions prove her a pawn of plot not its master. Letitia's final evocation of other female personas, under the auspices of patriarchy, stifles the rebellion of her masquerade plot, annulling its emancipatory quality.

Masquerade and modesty are now indistinct tropes for the heroine whose reintegration into patriarchy requires a well-harnessed charade. Letitia's readoption of a modest demeanor at the end of the comedy suggests the interchangeable nature of modesty and other more subversive female personas such as vulgarity and witty forwardness. At Lady Brilliant's, Letitia hinted at the ease with which one changes one's identity for the love and acceptance of a man: "I'd be anything—and all!—grave, gay, capricious—the soul of whim, the spirit of variety—live with him in the eye of fashion, or in the shade of retirement—change my country, my sex." Letitia, pointing to the ease with which she might transform herself into the most proper or the most perverse of women, is not highlighting the invention and poetry of the female mind, but rather proposing her own insignificance; without a man she represents a blank, a cipher. In the final scene of the play, she attempts to explain: "The timidity of the English character threw a veil over me you could not penetrate. You have forced me to emerge in some measure from my natural reserve, and to throw off the veil that hid me. . . . You see I can be any thing: choose then my character—you shall fix it." Letitia claims that modesty, "timidity," is itself a screen over a woman's true self; thus, she leaves to Doricourt's discretion the choice among wifely possibilities, between modesty and something else again.

As *BS* is a comedy, Doricourt does not complain that his "charming, charming creature!" cannot lay claim to her "natural reserve" without our suspicion that she embraces it out of convenience; in fact, he closes the play by remarking that her "innate modesty" is a "sacred veil", without noticing the paradox, the contradiction between an inherent quality and a chosen one. Thus, although Letitia dreads the "awful moment" when "the slight action of taking off my mask stamps me the most blest, or miserable of women", Doricourt's blindness to the difference and to the similarity between modesty and masquerade smooths over the crisis. Doricourt's conversion from a "strange perversion of taste" to "the grace of modesty" is weak and incomplete. The patriarchal plot to discipline Letitia for her interchangeable adoption of good and evil personas deconstructs at the end of the text when Letitia marries a man who cannot fathom her infractions against propriety.

Doricourt's conversion to the ideal of the "sacred veil" challenges the patriarchal prohibition against female self-creation and is in fact a conversion to Letitia's masquerade plot. This feminization of the anti-hero resuscitates Cowley's feminist subtext and reinscribes subversive value upon the marriage of Letitia and her beloved. Without Doricourt's positive evaluation of Letitia's stratagem, it would be much more problematic that Cowley privileges the patriarchal masquerade plot and permits it to oversee the marriage of Doricourt and Letitia. Perhaps in order for Cowley to safely dramatize (to mask) the story of a woman who writes her own romantic comedy, she needed to discipline the heroine in several ways, wresting from her the controls of her strategems, marrying her off under duress, and reinscribing her within the confines of modesty and propriety. Cowley mediates the plot of female desire so as to mask its arrangement of a woman's life history and the liberating possibilities it promises to those intent on directing their own life stories.

By focusing instead on the Good Husband and the promise of a companionate marriage, Cowley disguises the preeminence she attaches to rebellious masquerading. She subsumes her representation of Letitia's triumphant desire by yoking it to a proper marriage; *BS* functions as another text which "legitimize[s] romantic passion *within* approved social bonds", another eighteenth-century text which reintegrates antisocial passion into comic ending. At the masquerade Letitia seduced Doricourt with visions of a "Persian pavilion," and a "mogul's seraglio", but this indelicate speech, unsuitable to a virgin and thereby punishable, portrayed sensuality as a wife's domain. The conclusion of the play (Doricourt's equation between feminine seemliness and masquerade liberties) suggests that Letitia will have the opportunity to experience sexual adventure with a husband who appreciates her eroticism. Hence Cowley's own masquerade demanded the comic form. In order to represent alternate, rebellious femininities, and some of them empowering, Cowley needed to write within a form which promised social reintegration and rehabilitation.

The ideal compensation which Cowley permits her heroine presumably points to the author's own evaluation of modesty as itself a fiction, no better than other fictions, especially those one might choose to write. Modesty, itself a performance, cannot damn other performances of female possibility, especially those that celebrate their illusory nature, in other words, masquerades. Perhaps, then, Cowley entrusts the epilogue of the text (a defense of masks) to Letitia in order to reassign the trope of masquerade to women, to ultimately return it to its most legitimate employers. Letitia's epilogue wrests the "arts" of disguise away from patriarchy: "And you, my gentle sirs, wear vizors too, But I'll unmask you, and expose to view Your hidden features." In the place of the theatrical players (also male) of the prologue, she unmasks the "Tyrant," and the other "monstrous features", of the men in the audience, men who hypocritically conceal their true natures from each other. Letitia reserves for women the positive qualities of concealment—and defends the "mask of softness . . . at once applied, And gentlest manners decorate the bride!". She speaks in favor of masked strategies of lovemaking like her own. Thus when Letitia closes the comedy by appearing to speak for all the players, it seems clear that she speaks for a woman's right to orchestrate her own fate, her own way of achieving shared ends: "Our wish to please cannot be mere disguise!". And she speaks for Cowley's desire to write a comedy of female participation in the significant events that make up a woman's life. Cowley glosses over the possibility that a heroine or a woman writer might not desire "to please" the patriarchy, but to do something totally different, something that might be untenable within an ideal pattern of compensations, untenable within comedy. Patriarchy subsists on disguise, Letitia's epilogue reports: "'Tis plain, in real life, from youth to age, All wear their masks." But *BS* suggests that if a daughter of patriarchy were to exploit these normative means to a radical end, the means itself would become radicalized and the comedic license permitted to Letitia and Cowley herself would be revoked.

Source: Erin Isikoff, "Masquerade, Modesty, and Comedy in Hannah Cowley's *The Belle's Strategem*," in *Look Who's Laughing: Gender and Comedy*, edited by Gail Finney, Gordon and Breach, 1994, pp. 99–118.

Jean Gagen

In the following essay, Gagen analyzes Cowley's comedies, including The Belle's Strategem, *remarking on how Cowley's heroines are "independent and resourceful."*

Hannah Cowley, who lived from 1743 to 1809, is just beginning to receive some of the notice and appreciation as a playwright which she deserves. A recent critic who refers to Cowley as the finest woman playwright since Aphra Behn perhaps overstates Cowley's merits. Certainly Susanna Centlivre's achievement as a playwright earlier in the century has been much more widely recognized than Cowley's. Nevertheless, Hannah Cowley's plays deserve a place of honor in the roll call of eighteenth century playwrights. In fact, as early as 1782, the reviewer of *The Belle's Stratagem* in *The Critical Review* asserted that this play was the "best dramatic production of a female pen . . . since the days of Centlivre, to whom Mrs. Cowley is at least equal in fable and character, and far superior in easy dialogue and purity of diction" (vol. 53, p. 314). The reason for the neglect of Cowley's plays in this century is not easy to understand. But the appearance in 1979 of the two volume edition of her plays edited by Frederick Link now makes her dramas much more readily accessible than formerly.

Mrs. Cowley wrote thirteen plays—two of them tragedies—but her reputation rests on her comedies. The way in which she began writing for the stage has often been repeated. While attending a theatrical performance with her husband, she remarked, "Why I could write as well myself!" She took her husband's laughter as a challenge, and the next day she began to write a play that she eventually called *The Runaway*. She finished it quickly and sent it to Garrick to read; he encouraged her and suggested revisions. In 1776 Garrick presented the play at Drury Lane, where it met with more success than she dreamed possible. In fact, a reviewer for *The Critical Review* marveled at the skill which this "untutored genius" displayed (vol. 41, p. 239). Cowley continued to write for the stage for eighteen years, and many of her comedies were popular successes with long runs and frequent revivals.

Her characters are often stereotypes drawn from Restoration and earlier eighteenth century comedy, but at her best she is able to give them freshness and vitality. Although she was much more deeply influenced than Centlivre by the emphasis on moral reformation in drama, Cowley's desire to write plays free of moral offense did not stifle her sense of humor. Her plays are full of laughter and wit. Not only did she have unusual skill in the handling of dialogue but she was also capable of portraying well a wide variety of types of characters. Her most celebrated characters are undoubtedly her witty young heroines, who are often the prime manipulators and intriguers in her plays, which usually center on courtship and marriage.

Cowley was not primarily a reformer or disturber of the status quo. She was not a feminist in any militant way. Yet in the independence, resourcefulness, and daring of her witty heroines, Cowley is surely making a statement about women, their capabilities, and their rights. She defined comedy as "a picture of life—a record of passing manners—a mirror to reflect to succeeding times the characters and follies of the present." One of the follies on which she often focused was the failure to respect and cultivate the minds of women and to give them more control over their lives, especially in the choice of a husband. She ridicules men who have patronizing attitudes towards women and who undervalue them and their abilities. Moreover, the agents of her ridicule are women of wit and ingenuity who are capable of manipulating and deceiving these men and gaining from them or in spite of them what they wish to have.

In *Who's the Dupe* (1779), a short farce which became one of Cowley's most popular dramatic productions, Cowley satirizes what she refers to in a perfatory note as "the disgusting vulgarity in an upstart citizen." In the prologue, moreover, she remarks that since learned men and writers have often satirized the "petty foibles" and faults of women and exposed their "whims and vanity," she as a woman asks leave to laugh at these same learned men, whose sarcastic pens have spared neither "Matron Maid or Bride." And this is precisely what Cowley has done in this broadly amusing farce.

Old Doiley, the vulgar "upstart citizen," wealthy but ignorantly enamoured of "Larning," is the chief butt of Cowley's satire. Old Doiley is determined to have a son-in-law who is "Larned" and has chosen the pedant Gradus from Oxford to be his daughter Elizabeth's husband. Elizabeth, however, dupes both her father and Gradus and wins for her husband the man Granger whom she loves. She engineers the ruse by means of which Gradus is discredited as a learned man in her father's eyes, while Granger, who has never seen the inside of a university, entrances Old Doiley so thoroughly with his display of bogus learning that Doiley offers to leave him every farthing of his fortune if he will only marry Elizabeth.

The humor of this situation is made all the more pointed by the fact that when Old Doiley and Gradus are talking together shortly after Gradus' arrival, Old Doiley complains of the money wasted on educating girls in such matters as French and dancing, "Jography" and "Stronomy," while Gradus eagerly seconds these opinions and extols those "immortal periods" when women could neither read nor write. Both men underestimate the wit of women and deservedly fall victim to the stratagems which Elizabeth devises in order to escape marriage with Gradus. Gradus, of course, is a familiar comic figure—the pedant who may know a great deal about what is in books, particularly ancient books, but who knows almost nothing about life in the real world, including women.

When Old Doiley repudiates Gradus in favor of Granger, Gradus knows that he has been duped and that the oration by means of which Granger has enraptured Old Doiley is only high-sounding, polysyllabic gibberish without a word of Greek in it. But Doiley, declaring himself the happiest man alive, remains in blissful ignorance of how completely he has been duped. In fact, he patronizingly urges Gradus to trot back to Oxford for further study so that he can learn the difference between Greek and English.

> HER WITTY HEROINES ALL LOOK FORWARD TO MARRIAGE, BUT THEY DEMAND A MARRIAGE BASED ON LOVE AND MUTUAL RESPECT AND TRUST, AND THEY EXPECT TO HAVE THE DECIDING VOTE IN THE SELECTION OF THEIR HUSBANDS."

Letitia Hardy in *The Belle's Strategem* (1782), Cowley's most popular comedy, faces a situation very different from that which confronted Elizabeth Doiley. Letitia was contracted in marriage to Doricourt when both of them were children. But until the time for their marriage was approaching, neither had seen each other for years. Unfortunately for Letitia, Doricourt is not impressed by Letitia's reputation as a beauty. "Why, she's *only* a fine girl: complexion, shape and feature; nothing more . . . she should have spirit! fire! *l'air enjoué!* that something, that nothing, which everybody feels, and which nobody can describe, in the resistless charmers of Italy and France" (I.iii.9). Despite this lack of enthusiasm for Letitia, Doricourt is nevertheless determined to do the honorable thing and marry her. Letitia, however, is deeply troubled over Doricourt's apparent indifference to her because she is more attracted to him than ever before. But she has no intention either of marrying a man who does not love her or of letting this handsome man she adores escape without a struggle.

She tells her father that she has a plan to win Doricourt's love, although this plan may seem a bit paradoxical. She intends to heighten Doricourt's indifference to actual dislike because she believes that "'tis much easier to convert a sentiment into its opposite, than to transform indifference into tender passion" (I.iv.18). Her plot, quite simply, is to appear before Doricourt as a simpleton, loud, garrulous, crude, and completely lacking in refinement. Doricourt is so thoroughly repelled by her that he wants to set off for Bath that very night. But a friend who is privy to Letitia's plot persuades him to stay one night more and attend the masquerade.

At the masquerade, Doricourt notices how *divinely* a masked beauty dances. Soon he learns how bewitching as well as beautiful she is, how spirited and wild. Soon he is madly in love with this beautiful unknown, who, of course, is Letitia. Letitia continues to tease Doricourt and to refuse to show him her face. She also makes it quite clear that she will never be snared unless Hymen spreads the net to catch her.

On the advice of a friend, Letitia agrees to torment Doricourt further by seeing if he will promise to marry her even when he thinks she is a simpleton. Poor Doricourt is thus trapped, so to speak, into doing what he considers honorable—that is, marry a revolting simpleton.

Shortly after the wedding, Letitia, now disguised as the unknown beauty of the masquerade, enters and pretends to be deeply distressed over Doricourt's marriage. She claims that Doricourt's professions of love won her "Virgin heart," and that her honor is as spotless as that of the girl he has married. Her birth is also equal to his and her fortune large. Then she leaves Doricourt desperate with misery and wretchedness. Later, however, after a few more complications in the plot, Doricourt learns the identity of the masked lady and the tricks played on him. But he is overjoyed to find himself married to the witty and beautiful Letitia, who, because she has the "delicate timidity" of the English character, threw a veil over her charms. But now that he knows her better, he insists that no woman in France or Italy or even in the entire world could surpass her in delightfulness. Letitia's stratagem has worked. Her wavering, reluctant fiancé is now an ardent lover, and one supposes he will be an ardent husband too.

A Bold Stroke for a Husband (1783), set in Madrid, deals not with one woman but with two women who take bold strokes for husbands. In one case, Victoria, a deserted wife, regains her husband Don Carlos, who has succumbed to Laura, an unscrupulous fortune hunter; Don Carlos, in an alcoholic stupor, has even deeded to Laura the estate that came to him through his wife Victoria. In the other plot, Olivia repels two unwelcome suitors selected by her father and wins for her husband a man she truly loves. In these interwoven plots, women are the prime manipulators; they are the brains and boldness behind the strokes that gain them their husbands. In comparison with these women, the men are relatively weak and passive, and, in the case of Don Carlos, grossly culpable and foolish also.

Victoria has to overcome her repugnance for the role she feels compelled to play. But she is determined not merely to win back her husband, whom she still loves, but also the property, without which she and her children will be financially ruined. Disguised as a young man named Florio, she easily wins the love of the fickle Laura, who promptly discards Don Carlos, though she keeps the deed to the property he has given her.

Eventually Don Carlos appreciates the goodness of his wife and is half mad with remorse over his treatment of her and with fury over Laura's perfidy. In a rage he decides that he will kill this new paramour Florio. When he bursts in on Laura and Florio ready to plunge his sword into the bosom of his "blooming rival," Florio doffs his hat and reveals "himself" as Victoria, who now urges him to plunge the sword into her bosom since she has already been stabbed far more deeply by the anguish of betrayed love.

This is too much for Don Carlos, and we are simply told that "he sinks." Then Victoria rushes to him begging forgiveness for her too severe reproaches and assuring him that he is as dear as ever to her. When Carlos protests that she knows not what she does, for he has made her a beggar, she joyfully informs him of another bold stroke by means of which she has regained the estate he had deeded to Laura. She has engaged a friend to impersonate her uncle Don Sancho. He has convinced Laura that the deed Carlos had given her was invalid because Don Sancho himself was the owner of this property. In a rage, Laura tore up the deed. Now, realizing that she has been tricked out of this estate, Laura stalks out in a fury, vowing revenge, while Carlos turns to his "charming wife," full of gratitude and love.

Olivia's stratagems to free herself from the suitors chosen for her by her father and to win Julio instead are equally successful and much more light-hearted. She has repelled her music-loving suitor by claiming that the Jew's harp is her favorite instrument. She has driven another suitor away by posing convincingly as a shrew. She has also sought out Julio, met him at the Prado, and won his love while veiled and her identity unknown. Only after a number of amusing complications does she reveal her identity and accept him as her future husband. Thus the play ends with the restoration of a marriage and with an imminent marriage, both brought about by the bold strokes of two strong, ingenious, and daring women.

In *More Ways than One* (1786) another strong-minded and delightfully witty heroine appears in the person of Miss Archer. Beautiful, wealthy, and sophisticated, she has a well-cultivated mind, the experience of traveling in Europe, and the reputation for rejecting scores of adoring suitors. Though she is under the guardianship of a wealthy and avaricious old man Evergreen, she is not in the least threatened by him in any way. Evergreen apparently has no control over her fortune and makes no attempt to arrange a marriage for her. In fact, he is eager to get rid of her. Annoyed by her impudence and independence, he tells her to go ahead and marry one of her suitors—she has his consent. But she tartly replies that she wants the consent of a much more important personage—herself. In the meantime, she is not yet ready to give up the right to make conquests. But when the time comes to "retire from the scene of action," she promises to pick out the most constant of her adorers, to "go gravely with him to church," then "drive soberly to the seat of his ancestors" and thereafter become a dutiful wife, studying family receipts and making wine. She ends her sarcastic picture of her future married life by claiming that when the sixteen year old girl Arabella whom Evergreen is planning to marry has become a "young widow," she will invite her and her new husband to drink to Evergreen's memory in a cup of "cowslip" of her own brewing (I, i, p. 6).

When Evergreen in a rage orders Miss Archer to seek new lodgings immediately, she cheerfully refuses and continues to twit her "own dear, sweet guardian" who in marrying a sweet young wife is going to become a "sweet simpleton, at the sweet age of sixty" (p. 7).

Evergreen's prospective young bride is under the guardianship of her uncle Feelove, who is not only an avaricious but a ruthlessly incompetent physician. Moreover, he has subjected her to a repressive upbringing which has left her ignorant, naive, and utterly unable to help herself out of the predicament Feelove has placed her in by arranging for her to marry Evergreen. Raised in the country by two spinsters who taught her only such household arts as sewing and "making seed-cake, and stewing codlings," she cannot read or write, has never heard of "Point or Brussels," and her only card game is "beggar my neighbour." Arabella knows so little about the ways of the world that she supposes she has to marry the old man Feelove has chosen for her. Feelove never allows her to stir from his home, and Evergreen intends to continue this kind of incarceration in his own home. But Arabella finds a sympathetic friend and mentor in Miss Archer. To Evergreen's face she vows that no matter how stringently Evergreen tries to protect his young bride from the dangers of young men and the infections of fashionable life, she herself will teach this "pretty young cherub" to captivate the whole town and to acquire a greater desire for laces, feathers, diamonds, and fops than can be satisfied in six years. But what Miss Archer actually does for Arabella is much more important. She helps her to escape marriage to Evergreen and to marry instead young Bellair, who had fallen so desperately in love with Arabella that he had feigned an illness in order to gain entrée into Feelove's home and be nursed by Arabella. Although Cowley avoids any suggestion of lasciviousness on the part of either Bellair or Arabella, the tears of pity Arabella feels for the supposedly dying Bellair are symptoms of her quite natural attraction to him. Her childlike frankness in expressing her distaste for Evergreen and her preference for Bellair is the source of several pleasant comic scenes.

When Bellair finally seizes an opportunity to declare his love to Arabella and to assure her that she need not marry the old man whom she detests, Arabella is delighted and astonished and more than willing to flee from Feelove's house with Bellair. Unfortunately, not knowing the identity of Arabella's prospective husband, Bellair takes her to Evergreen's home thinking that this "grave gentleman" will provide a sanctuary for her until Bellair can arrange the elopement. Cowley makes good comic use of Bellair's mistake and Evergreen's glee over it. But through the help of Miss Archer, all is still not lost.

When she learns that Evergreen has already hired a coach to whisk Arabella off to an unknown destination to protect her from Bellair, Miss Archer acts quickly. Evergreen has already enveloped Arabella in a large white riding cape and hood in preparation for her drive. But in the few moments that he is absent, Miss Archer bribes the foppish knight from the country, Sir Marvel Mushroom, who has fortunately appeared at just the right moment, to conceal himself in the riding cape and hood while she and Arabella jump into Marvel's waiting carriage. Miss Archer then directs the driver to take Arabella to a lodging for safekeeping.

Eventually everyone concerned with Arabella's future ends up at this lodging, where Bellair wins Feelove's consent to marry Arabella and both Feelove and Evergreen, though they angrily wrangle with each other, have to accept the fact that they have both been outwitted and outmaneuvered. Once again a resourceful and clever young woman has frustrated the attempt to force a young woman into a repulsive marriage as if she were a mere pawn in a financial negotiation.

During her efforts on behalf of Arabella, Miss Archer has been carrying on a rather tempestuous courtship of her own, marked by many misunderstandings. By the time Arabella's happiness is sealed, Miss Archer and Mr. Carlton, who are well suited to each other, are also looking forward to marriage.

Again in *School for Greybeards* (1786) a young girl Viola, who is about to be hustled into a marriage to a man she does not love, is spared this fate through the help of a forceful and fearless young woman—in this case, her young mother-in-law Seraphina, who has recently married Viola's father Don Alexis. Don Alexis has already realized that he has made an ass of himself in marrying a mere girl, for he now knows from experience that it is easier "to spin cables out of cobwebs . . . than to manage a young rantipole wife" (I, p. 11). Seraphina often reminds us of Sheridan's Lady Teazle as she playfully torments her husband by her many pointed references to his age. She admits that she loves to sit on her balcony while "All the impudent young face-hunters in Lisbon" fall prostrate before her, "adoring, and deifying" her. In fact, she insists that she will enjoy admiration until she becomes "old, shrivell'd" and "grey-pated" as Don Alexis is now (II, pp. 18–19).

When Alexis threatens to block up all the windows and nail shut the doors to secure his honor, she retorts that if he cannot find better security than these devices, he'll be one of the herd of cuckholds. The best security for *his* honor, she tells him, is *her* honor: "It is due to my own feelings to be chaste—I don't condescend to think of you in the affair. The respect I bear myself, makes me necessarily preserve my purity—but if I am suspected, watch'd, and haunted, I know not but such torment may weary me out of principles, which I have hitherto cherish'd as my life" (II, p. 19).

Although marriage to Seraphina has taught Don Alexis that youth and age do not mix well in matrimony, the importance of love between the partners still escapes his rather dense mind. When his friend Don Gasper remarks that his son Don Octavio is sufficiently attracted to Alexis' daughter Viola to be willing to marry her, Don Alexis snaps at the suggestion. It apparently never occurs to him to consult Viola herself about her feelings.

Viola happens to be deeply in love with Don Sebastian and has no interest whatsoever in Don Octavio. Fortunately, when Octavio comes to woo Viola, he mistakes Seraphina for Viola and proceeds to woo her in all the trite, conventional ways, which provide her with a great deal of ironic amusement. Because she enjoys his mistake, she does not undeceive him. Then she suddenly realizes that she can use this mistake to help Viola escape from her father's house and meet and marry Don Sebastian. Seraphina as Viola convinces Octavio that she despises the sober, quiet prudence of a courtship which is approved by her father. Only if her father opposes the marriage and she will have to face all sorts of "blissful" difficulties, such as scaling ladders to elope and being pursued, will she believe that Octavio really loves her. Of course, all this very clearly reminds us of Sheridan's Lydia Languish.

Don Octavio unsuspectingly accepts all these conditions and persuades Alexis that they must plot against this "dear little madcap." Don Alexis accordingly *orders* Viola to see Octavio no more. In fact, Don Alexis is vastly amused by what he thinks is a clever ploy to secure Viola's marriage to Octavio while she imagines that she is eloping without her father's consent. Of course, it is Seraphina (still playing the part of Viola) who climbs down the ladder from Don Alexis' house, though she has stipulated that she has a friend who must accompany her. That friend is Viola who, once out of her father's house, meets and marries Don Sebastian. Thus, once again, men—both Don Alexis and Don Octavio—who regard women as property to be disposed of in marriage without any regard for their own inclinations—are outmaneuvered and made ridiculous by the sex which they patronizingly brand as the weaker sex.

Cowley apparently thought of marriage as the normal and desirable goal for women. Her witty heroines all look forward to marriage, but they demand a marriage based on love and mutual respect and trust, and they expect to have the deciding vote in the selection of their husbands. Cowley glorifies these women who are independent and resourceful, intelligent and well educated without becoming pedantic, and completely undeterred by the authority that men attempt to impose on them in the choice of their mates. Instead of weeping or arguing against the injustice of tyrannical fathers or guardians, they often devise very complicated stratagems by means of which they outwit would-be tyrants and win for husbands the men they love. Sometimes they also exercise their wit and ingenuity in rescuing some of the weaker members of their sex from the unwelcome marriages which domineering parents or guardians try to force on them. These courageous ladies have insight and initiative. They can think for themselves, make their own decisions, and act with intelligence and daring. They are Cowley's "new women."

Source: Jean Gagen, "The Weaker Sex: Hannah Cowley's Treatment of Men in Her Comedies of Courtship and Marriage," in the *University of Mississippi Studies in English*, Vol. VIII, 1990, pp. 107–16.

SOURCES

Cowley, Hannah, *The Belle's Stratagem*, in *Eighteenth-Century Women Dramatists*, edited by Melinda C. Finberg, Oxford University Press, 2001.

Gagen, Jean, "The Weaker Sex: Hannah Cowley's Treatment of Men in Her Comedies of Courtship and Marriage," in *University of Mississippi Studies in English*, Vol. 8, 1990, p. 108.

Isikoff, Erin, "Masquerade, Modesty, and Comedy in Hannah Cowley's *The Belle's Stratagem*," in *Look Who's Laughing: Gender and Comedy*, edited by Gail Finney, Gordon and Breach, 1994, pp. 101, 108.

FURTHER READING

Canfield, J. Douglas, and Maja-Lisa von Sneidern, eds., *The Broadview Anthology of Restoration and Early Eighteenth Century Drama*, concise ed., Broadview, 2003.
    Composed of twenty-one plays, this anthology concentrates on Restoration drama and revolution drama with various subgenres. Each play contains extensive annotation and important historical information.

Gagen, Jean, "Hannah Cowley," in *Restoration and Eighteenth Century Dramatists*, 3d ed., edited by Paula R. Backscheider, Gale Research, 1989.
    Gagen gives a brief yet thorough synopsis of Hannah Cowley's life and work. Information about Cowley is scarce; thus Gagen's short biography is an excellent resource.

Garrick, David, *Diary of David Garrick*, Ayer Press, 1928.
    David Garrick, an eighteenth-century actor and theatre manager, was known for his openness to dramatic newcomers, especially women.

Woodfield, Ian, *Opera and Drama in Eighteenth-Century London: The King's Theatre, Garrick, and the Business of Performance*, Cambridge University Press, 2001.
    This book explores the cultural and commercial life of opera in late-eighteenth-century London. It includes a rare examination of the role of women in opera management.

The Cenci

ANTONIN ARTAUD

1935

Les Cenci (The Cenci) is Artaud's only known play based on the guidelines of the Theatre of Cruelty. The play relates Artaud's version of the story of the late-sixteenth-century Roman nobleman, Francesco Cenci, and his daughter Beatrice. Written in a style meant to overwhelm the audience's moral preconceptions, *The Cenci* dramatizes the torture that the cruel Count Cenci invoked upon his family; the family's plot to have him murdered; and the family's torture and execution by Catholic authorities. On stage, *The Cenci* involves a spectacle of light and sound. Artaud directed and starred as Cenci in the original production of the play in 1935. The play shocks the audience not only because of its cruelty, violence, incest, and rape, but because its characters seem to speak strangely and artificially. This is because the theory behind the play, which is influenced by the surrealist movement and by Balinese dance theatre, calls for the characters to represent universal forces instead of realistic individuals.

AUTHOR BIOGRAPHY

Antonin Artaud is a French writer, actor, and intellectual figure as well known for his supposed madness and troubled genius as for his prolific output of writings, plays, films, and drawings. Although he suffered from mental illness and spent a great deal of his life in sanitariums, he is far more

T h e   C e n c i

respected for his artistic and intellectual innovations than for his biographical mystique.

Born September 4, 1896, in Marseilles, France, to a Catholic family, Antonin Artaud was raised mainly by his mother, his grandmothers, and his governess, because his father, a shipfitter, was frequently away on business. Artaud contracted a severe case of meningitis at age four, and as a result he suffered throughout the rest of his life from neuralgia, a condition characterized by sharp and intense pains in nerve centers. At age seventeen, he became depressed, destroyed the manuscripts of his early work, and withdrew from school. In 1915, he was sent to a sanatorium near Marseilles.

Artaud spent a short amount of time in the army in 1916, but was quickly discharged. He spent the next four years living in various sanitariums, reading and drawing. In 1920, he expressed a desire to live and write in Paris, and his parents referred him to a leading psychotherapist named Edouard Toulouse, who was also the editor of a literary magazine called *Demain*, which published some of Artaud's work. Artaud began to work as a theatre and film actor in 1922, and in 1923, he published his first book of poetry, *Tric trac du ciel* (Backgammon of Heaven). He wrote a variety of prose works throughout his acting career, and he became a leading figure in the surrealist movement, until he was expulsed from it in 1926. Meanwhile, he began a sexual relationship with a Romanian actress named Génica Athanasiou, but due to an addiction to opiates and other drugs he had developed, the relationship ended in 1927.

From 1927 through the early 1930s, Artaud concentrated on translating his theoretical work for the film industry, writing a variety of scripts while continuing to act. He attempted to launch a theatre company, Théâtre Alfred Jarry, with several friends, and composed two books characterized by extreme violence. In the early 1930s, Artaud began to write the essays that would be included in *The Theatre and Its Double* (1938), which criticizes the Western theatre conventions of the day and characterizes what came to be known as Theatre of Cruelty. Perhaps Artaud's most groundbreaking innovation, Theatre of Cruelty combines elaborate lighting, props, and magic tricks with violent themes that included rape, murder, and torture. It was intended to shock the audience and force them to confront the seamier side of life. Artaud's play *The Cenci*, first performed in 1935, is his best-known work that follows these conventions.

Artaud drifted around to various hotels in Paris, and in 1936, he made three trips to Mexico

Antonin Artaud © Hulton Getty/Liaison Agency

to study the Tarahumara Indian tribe and to explore his interest in primitivism. In August 1937, in a state of worsening psychosis, he traveled to Ireland. In September that same year, he was expelled from Ireland, restrained, and placed in a French asylum. Artaud spent the duration of World War II in various asylums, undergoing a complex religious conversion. In 1943, he was put through several courses of electroshock therapy. Afterward, he began to write prodigious amounts of material, much of which remains incomprehensible to most readers, including rewrites of classical Western texts; ambitious philosophical theory; autobiographical tales; and fantastical, often violent, narratives. He was released from Rodez Asylum in 1946, and he died of cancer in 1948.

PLOT SUMMARY

Act 1

The Cenci begins with Cardinal Camillo talking with the powerful Count Cenci about a murder in which Cenci is implicated. Camillo threatens to publicly proclaim the crime unless Cenci gives a third of his possessions to the Pope, but Cenci refuses, jeers at the Church, and stresses his desire to "practice evil." When Camillo leaves, Cenci expands on his desires, suggesting that he wants to kill his wife and two of his sons, as well as rape his daughter Beatrice.

In the next scene, Beatrice is with her lover Orsino in a moonlit garden in the Cenci palace. Beatrice laments that her father is keeping them apart, but when Orsino vows to overcome all obstacles for their love, Beatrice tells him that their love is doomed because of her duty to her family. She then expresses her loathing for her father and departs for dinner.

At the dinner, Cenci frightens his guests by telling them that two of his "rebellious" sons have been killed and that he wishes his entire family doom and destruction. Beatrice begs the guests not to leave, and Cenci threatens to kill anyone's offspring who says anything about what has happened at dinner. Cenci orders everyone away except Beatrice, whom he approaches and tells that he knows the "charm" to make her "meek and tame." Beatrice flees and Cenci says that now she cannot escape him.

Act 2

The second act begins with Lucretia telling Bernardo that she loves him, at which time Beatrice enters and asks for help in escaping from Cenci. Beatrice describes how Cenci is torturing her and her brother. Cenci enters and seizes Beatrice by the arm, but Lucretia steps between them and Bernardo drags his sister out of the room. Cenci tells his wife that his family is a wound, that they have "corrupted everything," and that they are plotting against him. Lucretia protests, but Cenci tells her he is taking the family to a silent fortress.

In act 2, scene 2, Camillo attempts to persuade Giacomo Cenci to plot against his father, but Giacomo retorts with criticism of the Church. Camillo then urges him to listen to Orsino, who reveals to the audience that he has abandoned his hopes to marry Beatrice and that he desires to see the Cenci family destroyed. Orsino describes Cenci's tyranny to Giacomo and persuades him to plot a scheme against the count.

Act 3

Act 3 begins with Beatrice rushing onstage to tell Lucretia that her father has raped her. Lucretia attempts to return her to her senses, and Beatrice describes a recurring dream from her childhood in which she is lying naked and hungry in a room until a wild animal appears and chases her through the cellars. Lucretia says that the dream signifies that "no one can escape his fate," and she appeals to Orsino for help when he enters with Giacomo. Orsino suggests that

they appeal to secular justice, or justice outside of papal authority, but Beatrice says that she can believe only in the justice that she chooses. Orsino suggests that Giacomo publicly denounce his father and that they employ two mute assassins to kill Cenci.

In the next scene, Orsino, Giacomo, and the assassins wait outside the fortress for Cenci and his family to cross the bridge. When the family appears, the assassins descend upon Cenci and fire two pistol shots, but they fail to kill him.

Act 4

The final act opens with Cenci ordering Lucretia to find Beatrice. Cenci withdraws, and Beatrice sends the assassins into his room with daggers. They come out and mime to Beatrice that they have failed. She calls them cowards, sending them back in again. After Cenci's death cry is heard, the assassins return to Beatrice, who gives them money and gold.

After Bernardo warns that soldiers are coming, Camillo enters telling them that he represents the Pope. When he asks to see Cenci, Lucretia and Beatrice tell him that the count is sleeping, but Camillo says that he must wake Cenci so that Cenci can be confronted with grave charges against him. After Camillo finds Cenci dead, he has his guards arrest the family. Lucretia blurts out that she is the only one with keys to Cenci's apartment, and Camillo questions Beatrice about her relationship with her father. The guards remove Bernardo from his sister, and he punches at them, screaming.

The next scene is inside a papal prison in which Beatrice is attached to a torture wheel. Bernardo laments their fate and Beatrice tells him not to despair. Camillo enters and tells Beatrice to confess, and Lucretia urges her to repent. Giacomo agrees, telling her that Orsino has escaped in disguise, and Camillo hands her a death warrant to sign. Beatrice compares the Pope's cruelty to her father's, and Camillo tells her that she is already condemned. After Camillo makes her sign the death warrant, Beatrice tells him never to mention the name of God to her again. Camillo tells Bernardo that his life is spared, and Beatrice and Lucretia alternate segments of a speech about morality, religion, destiny, and their impending deaths.

CHARACTERS

Andrea

Andrea is Cenci's servant.

Assassins

The two mute assassins employed to kill Cenci make two unsuccessful attempts before murdering the count. Orsini, who describes them as "brutish, dull-witted scoundrels who would kill a man as unthinkingly as we might tear a piece of paper in two." The reason the assassins fail twice in their attempted murder of Cenci seems to be a combination of incompetence and cowardice rather than any feelings of guilt or conscience. After Camillo catches them, they provide written confessions condemning themselves to execution.

Banquet Guests

Beatrice describes the guests at Cenci's dinner table in act 1, scene 3 as "all the chief nobility of Rome." They become increasingly horrified and afraid as the situation worsens; they ignore Beatrice's plea to protect her; and they leave as soon as Cenci bids them to do so. Prince Colonna, the only character besides Camillo who makes an attempt to face up to Cenci, is among the guests.

Camillo

A cardinal close to the Pope, Camillo is a shrewd and pragmatic figure who admits that the Catholic Church is rooted in cynicism. Although he does not have any fervent moral or religious convictions and does not believe in God, he is a figure of moral and religious authority in the play. He bargains with Cenci over his land and his criminal deeds; he nearly stands up to Cenci at dinner; he persuades Giacomo to plot against his father; and he investigates Cenci's murder, presiding over the execution of Lucretia, Beatrice, and Giacomo. Orsino calls him a "spoiled priest," and ultimately he is revealed to be a hypocrite, since he is willing to cover up a murder for a price and to urge a son to murder his father, but he is unwilling to have any mercy on Beatrice or the rest of the Cenci family for their complicity in Cenci's murder. Camillo's character can be seen to represent the corruption and power of the Catholic Church.

Beatrice Cenci

Beatrice is Cenci's daughter, and the play centers on her torture, rape, and execution. Because her father reduces her to desperate circumstances, she abandons her relationship with Orsino and places her duty to her family as her top priority. She refuses to trust secular or religious justice to deal with her cruel father, and this decision is justified by the fact that the religious and civil figures of power at Cenci's banquet fail to protect her in any way.

Beatrice therefore conspires to have her father assassinated, and for this she is imprisoned and executed. She never comes to feel guilt or regret and she never repents for her actions, which is why Camillo has her tortured before she is executed.

One of Beatrice's defining characteristics is her sense of spirituality, which Orsino calls "intolerable mysticism." She is able to anticipate future events, based on her understanding of her father's character but also based on what appears to be a kind of psychic foreknowledge. Beatrice's attitude toward religion changes and evolves throughout the play; at first she is convinced that God would not allow Cenci's crimes to happen, but she comes to rebel against all kinds of authority, including God, since she tells Camillo never to mention God's name to her again.

Beatrice considers her duty to her family her most important value, but it later becomes clear that this is somewhat at odds with her rejection of tyrannical authority figures such as her father. By the end of the play, after her recognition that no one, including herself, has chosen between good and evil, Beatrice says that she fears that she has ended by resembling her father. This idea is particularly intriguing given that she appears to be so virtuous while Cenci appears to be so evil, and it reinforces the sense of moral upheaval in the play.

Bernardo Cenci

Bernardo is Cenci's youngest son, whom Cenci calls womanish and plans to leave alive so that he can bemoan the rest of his family. He is extremely close to Beatrice and attempts to protect and defend her as far as he is able. When he is taken away from his sister by Camillo's guards after Cenci's death, he reacts violently, screaming, "They have sacrificed my soul," and in prison, he kisses Beatrice and clings to her desperately. Despite the fact that Bernardo is involved in the murder plot, Camillo spares his life because he is too young. When he hears that he will survive, Bernardo despairs that he must live when the "flame which lit [his] life," or Beatrice, is about to die.

Count Cenci

Cenci is the villain of the play, intent on torturing and destroying his family. He continually desires to be shocking and cruel, and his mission in life is to commit evil crimes. He glories in the deaths of two of his sons, terrifies the guests at his banquet, antagonizes Lucretia, harasses Bernardo, disinherits Giacomo, and rapes Beatrice. Although he is powerful and well connected, he does not seem to have any friends or allies, and he believes that his family is plotting against him even before they begin the plot to assassinate him. He is murdered on the third attempt by the assassins who Orsino has located for the family.

A master at horrifying others, Cenci seems to feel alive only when he is engaging in a form of cruelty. Although the reasons behind this cruelty remain somewhat unclear, he stresses that his impulses stretch to the root of his soul and character. He is not religious, but he believes that he is a force of destiny and nature, an ultimate figure of authority, power, and subjugation.

To understand Cenci's character, it is important to remember that Artaud's convention in *The Cenci* is that characters say whatever they feel, and often go beyond what they would realistically realize about themselves. Therefore, the vividness and extremity of Cenci's cruelty, as he expresses it in language, is intended to be a reflection of his true nature more so than it is intended to reproduce a realistic character's speech. Cenci is a bitter and vicious old father figure, and it is likely that he is a representation of the essential nature of paternal, civil, and financial authority. If this is the case, he shows no remorse and no restraint, because he embodies a power structure and a moral system that Artuad considers fundamentally tyrannical, arbitrary, and unjust.

Giacomo Cenci

One of Cenci's older sons, Giacomo is involved in the plot to murder his father. He is angry at his father because the count has disinherited him, and he agrees to plot against Cenci after he hears that his father is torturing Beatrice and Lucretia. During his conversation with Camillo, Giacomo reveals his distaste for the Catholic Church and for what he calls its faithless cynicism, but he heeds the cardinal's advice to plot against Cenci. Convinced by Orsino, he goes along with the scheme despite a comment at the end of act 3 that reveals his disillusionment with Beatrice's notion of personal justice: "Family, gold, justice: I despise them all."

Lucretia Cenci

Lucretia is Cenci's somewhat-timid second wife. She loves Cenci's children despite the fact that she is not their biological mother, and she tries to calm Cenci and maintain peace in the household. While comforting Bernardo, she reveals that she has suffered in her life and is a sensitive woman. She is a devout Christian throughout the play, often referring to God and making the sign of the cross. Unlike Beatrice, she does not seem to anticipate Cenci's evil actions, although she does come to recognize the full extent of his cruelty and she participates in the plot to kill him. She foolishly confirms Camillo's suspicions about the family's involvement in Cenci's murder by saying that she alone has the keys to his apartment and that no one could have entered without her knowledge. This contributes to her imprisonment and execution.

Prince Colonna
See Banquet Guests

Orsino

Beatrice's lover at the beginning of the play, Orsino was ordained as a priest but is willing to break his vows out of love for her. After Beatrice informs him that her duty to her family takes precedence over their love, and after he is shocked by Cenci's actions, Orsino turns against the family and does what he can to help them destroy each other. In act 2, scene 2, Orsino describes Beatrice as brooding in an "intolerable mysticism," referring in part to her foresight of the horrific events of the play, and he proposes that Giacomo defy the law and act against Cenci's tyranny. His motive, as he reveals in this scene, is simply to see the family ruined, and toward this end, he provides two mute assassins to allow Beatrice and the others to have Cenci killed. In Percy Bysshe Shelley's version of the story, Orsino plots to have Cenci killed so that he can win and marry Beatrice, but in Artaud's version, Orsino seems interested only in the destruction of the entire family. After Cenci's death, Orsino manages to escape, disguised as a charcoal seller, and at the end of the play he is presumably still fleeing from the Pope's soldiers.

THEMES

Morality and Religion

One of the intriguing and potentially confusing aspects of Artaud's play is its treatment of religion and morality. It is important to recognize that *The Cenci* is largely absent of religious and moral values in the sense that they control the actions of the characters. Some characters, such as Beatrice and Lucretia, believe in God and cling to a conventionally moralistic view of the world, but their basic moral values and religious convictions begin to erode once they are exposed to the full extent of Cenci's tyranny. Artaud is concerned with the

TOPICS FOR FURTHER STUDY

- Discuss *The Cenci* in terms of the emotional response of its audience. In what ways is the play shocking? How do you think Artaud intended his audience to react to the play? How does he go about inspiring this response? In what ways does he succeed, and in what ways does he fail? Describe your reaction to the play, paying particular attention to how it shocked or disturbed you, and compare it with the reaction of your peers.

- There are many myths and idealizations about Artaud's life. Research his biography, including his early life and his long battle with mental illness, and compare fact with fiction. How and why were the myths about Artaud developed? How did Artaud's health impact his artistic career? How was he perceived by his contemporaries and how has he been perceived by subsequent generations?

- Read Artaud's famous book *The Theatre and Its Double* and research the Theatre of Cruelty that Artaud establishes in this work. What do you think of this theory? In what ways could *The*

Cenci be considered an example of the Theatre of Cruelty? In what ways does it differ from the theory? How did Artaud's prominence as a theorist affect his work and how has it affected the response to his work?

- Research the history of the real Cenci family. What is known about Francesco Cenci's personality and the personality of his daughter Beatrice? Why and how did they become famous? What were the conditions of sixteenth-century Rome? How is the history reflected accurately and how is it falsified or embellished in Artaud's play?

- Research the theatrical elements of Artaud's original production of *The Cenci*. What did the set look like? What did he use to make the sounds? How did his emphasis on gesture, light, and sound come to fruition? Describe the experience of the performance and what it would have been like in the original audience. Discuss why you think audiences and critics, in general, originally had such an adverse reaction to the play.

---

eruption of fundamental, amoral forces in the play, in accordance with his philosophy about the Theatre of Cruelty and its guidelines for shocking the audience and capturing its imagination.

In a sense, therefore, the play portrays the Catholic Church less as a faith-based organization than as an institution of cynical and amoral power. This is why neither Camillo nor the Pope is particularly concerned with God or with divine justice. Similarly, the moral beliefs of characters such as Cenci or even Beatrice are not organized into a wider philosophy, but are expressions of the most fundamental aspects of their characters and the natural forces behind them. Cenci, Beatrice, and Orsino have no interest in civil justice, and they all decide to take matters into their own hands. Even the representatives of civil authority, the guests at Cenci's dinner banquet, are unconcerned with saving Beatrice or punishing Cenci; like Camillo, they

seem to care only about saving themselves and increasing their own power.

The amoral and irreligious atmosphere of the play allows Artaud to more fully explore the basic and natural elements of human ethics and theology. In a sense, Artaud is able to reveal the true nature of his characters by putting aside their social and personal value systems, and in another sense, he is able to examine the nonhuman, or superhuman, forces that he sees in the world, since the characters of *The Cenci* are intended to represent natural forces more than realistic individuals. However, Artaud may also be suggesting that Christianity and Western moral philosophy lack truth and conviction, which is why they have no place in his play.

Tyranny and Authority

The central action in *The Cenci* is found in the cruel actions of authority figures. Artaud examines the fundamental nature of power, particularly the power of the father, as it is unleashed on its subjects and as they respond to it. The conflict between Cenci and his family is the chief example of this theme; the count's entire life is based on torturing his family, and the events of the play follow the family's violent reaction to this behavior. Camillo, and by extension the Pope and the Catholic Church, are also important examples of authoritative power. Artaud broadens his exploration of the themes of authority, tyranny, and rebellion by examining the struggle between the Church and Cenci, as well as the Church's imposition of its moral sentence over Cenci's family.

Authority is always cruel, tyrannical, and unjust in this play, and Artaud seems to be suggesting that these characteristics are inevitable in any institution of power. As discussed above, the characters of *The Cenci* are not bound by conventional morality, and figures of power, such as Cenci, go to extremes that do not seem possible or comprehensible for a real person. However, Cenci stresses early in the play that his desire for annihilation comes from his fundamental nature, as if it is inevitable in the idea of authority and he has merely decided to suppress it no longer. Perhaps this is why Orsino, with his treachery against Beatrice, and Camillo, with his cynical and hypocritical cruelty, are capable of slightly more realistic versions of treachery; the play may be an effort to bring to light the cruelty that is fundamental to all power. This reading of the play would also help explain Beatrice's assertion in the play's final line that she has ended by resembling her father; her imposition of power by having her father assassinated is similar to the tyrannical violence and cruelty that Cenci inflicted upon her.

STYLE

Myth and the Superhuman

Although it may not appear to be much like what is commonly thought of as myth, *The Cenci* is intended to follow the tradition of ancient Greek and Roman mythology. Artaud's play does not provide an explanation or a justification of a natural event, such as why there are seasons or rainbows, but it does attempt to make insights into the fundamental aspects of nature, humanity, and existence. It can therefore be considered a myth in the sense that it identifies natural, universal forces such as cruelty and rebellion, and dramatizes their effects on a particular situation.

Like a Greek myth, Artaud's play includes characters that can be considered superhuman, or at least nonhuman in the sense that they do not have entirely realistic personalities and do not express themselves in ordinary language. Instead, Artaud's characters act as though powerful and fundamental forces are working through them, and they often speak in a hyperconscious manner that reveals what is at the base of their desires. Artaud believed that this format was an important aspect of the Theatre of Cruelty, allowing the characters to express their true feelings and desires much more fully than is possible in normal human speech. Thus, for example, Cenci refers to the "myth" of himself and says unreservedly that he must allow the evil at the root of his soul to manifest itself. Although it is implausible that a real person would act or speak in this way, Artaud's characterization of Cenci in these terms allows the character to more fully express the pure and universal force of tyranny.

Gesture, Light, and Sound

Artaud believed that his stage directions about gesture, light, and sound were as critical as the dialogue in *The Cenci* because the all-sensory experience of the audience is of chief importance in the Theatre of Cruelty. It is therefore important to pay close attention to these directions in an analysis of the play's style. For example, when Beatrice and Cenci interact physically or exchange a glance, it raises the stakes of the situation and is as important in the development of their relationship as an entire speech. Other sounds, images, and dances, such as the armor-clad men moving slowly "like the figures on the face of the great clock of Strasbourg Cathedral," enhance the atmosphere of the scene, while at the same time determining its meaning and context. Perhaps the most important reason that Artaud uses elaborate and flashy gestures, light, and sound in his play, however, is to overwhelm the audience and shock it out of its preconceptions.

HISTORICAL CONTEXT

French Culture in the 1920s and 1930s

French literary and artistic culture went through dramatic and marked changes in the early twentieth century. Inspired by drastic and even cataclysmic events such as World War I, writers and artists entered new modes and broke ties with the past. A number of movements and philosophies were

COMPARE
&
CONTRAST

- **1590s:** The Roman Catholic Church operates under the ordinates established at the Council of Trent. It is one of the most influential bodies in Europe and regains much of the power that it was in danger of losing during the Protestant Reformation.

  1930s: Still working under essentially the same theological bases established at the Council of Trent, the Catholic Church is a powerful international organization, but it has much less direct political influence than it did in the sixteenth century.

  Today: The Catholic Church continues to wield considerable influence across the globe and finds a growing membership in third-world countries.

- **1590s:** Rome is again a prosperous and cosmopolitan city, having recovered from its sacking by Emperor Charles V in 1527.

  1930s: Benito Mussolini's fascist government is centered in Rome, and he drastically rebuilds the city, damaging much of its architectural heritage.

  Today: Still the capitol of Italy and the base of the Catholic Church, Rome is a unique and cosmopolitan city.

- **1590s:** European theatre is considerably less prominent than it was during the Renaissance period, particularly in cities such as Rome and Paris where the Catholic Church determines what is morally acceptable.

  1930s: The European theatre is undergoing major and important changes, particularly in Paris, as new theories about drama gain influence.

  Today: Theatre remains an important part of European artistic and intellectual life, although, as in the United States, cinema draws larger crowds and is responsible for the most popular artistic innovations.

founded in the postwar years, including Dadaism. An artistic movement based on irrationality, cynicism, and the rejection of conventional aesthetics, Dadaism lost its impetus by the beginning of the 1930s. Many former Dadaists became involved in the surrealist movement, which was led by the influential poet and literary critic André Breton. Surrealism dismissed rationality and incorporated elements of fantasy and the supernatural into art, literature, and drama, in order to construct a positive and absolute reality, or a superreality.

By the early 1920s, Artaud had become a prominent figure in the surrealist movement, contributing vigorously to the debate about what constituted the surrealist way of thinking. In 1926, however, he was expelled from the movement, ostensibly as a result of his attempt to launch a commercial theatre, at a time when Breton's surrealist movement had recently become explicitly communist. An equally, or perhaps more important, reason for Artaud's expulsion may have been that

Artaud's work was always somewhat more violent, alienated, and negativistic than that of Breton and the other central figures.

Artaud never reconciled with the surrealists, and between 1927 and 1931, he experimented with varying theories and philosophies, becoming more involved in the cinema and the theatre. In 1931, he saw a performance of Balinese dance theatre—a form of theatre in which gesture is extremely important to the expression of supernatural and philosophical themes. This experience inspired Artaud to develop the Theatre of Cruelty, which provides the theoretical foundation for *The Cenci* and is described in a series of Artaud's articles from the early 1930s that later were published collectively as *The Theatre and Its Double*.

Late-Sixteenth-Century Rome and the Cenci Family

The storyline of Artaud's play is based in part on the powerful Roman nobleman, Francesco

Portrait of Beatrice Cenci, by Guido Reni, c. 1662 © Araldo de Luca/Corbis

Cenci, and his family. Cenci was known for his cruelty, particularly toward his twelve children, and after a violent quarrel in 1595, he locked Beatrice Cenci and her stepmother in a remote castle between Rome and Naples. Beatrice tried unsuccessfully to escape; began a relationship with the keeper of the castle; and eventually conspired with her lover, her stepmother, and two of her brothers to murder Cenci. When the plotters were discovered, all of them confessed under torture and were condemned to death by a papal court. Their story became famous and has been the subject of plays, paintings, and prose.

All of these events took place during what is known as the counterreformation movement, a response by the Roman Catholic Church to the Protestant Reformation and to the liberal ideas of humanism. Revolutionary ideas about religion and morality spread rapidly through Europe in the early sixteenth century, and the Catholic Church began to organize a number of efforts to reassert its dominance. Implemented chiefly by the Council of Trent (1545–1563) and popes through the early seventeenth century, proponents of the counterreformation spread conservative ideas; combated Protestantism; and burnt heretics at the stake. Rome itself, which was and is the home of the Catholic

Church, was a prosperous city at the end of the sixteenth century, although its nobility was often in conflict with papal authority over legal rights and ownership.

CRITICAL OVERVIEW

Although Artaud was periodically in vogue with various artistic and intellectual groups, he was never widely accepted or understood during his lifetime. *The Cenci* was one of his great disappointments, attacked and reviled by the critical community. As Naomi Greene writes in her book *Antonin Artaud: Poet without Words*, "The critical reviews were harsh, with the notable exception of Pierre Jean Jouve, who believed that *Les Cenci* had greatly affected its audience." Produced five years after the failure of Artaud's theatre company Théâtre Alfred Jarry, *The Cenci* closed after just seventeen performances, and its harsh reviews helped to drive Artaud from the theatre for the rest of his life.

Since Artaud's death in 1948, *The Cenci* has become increasingly well regarded among critics. It is his only play to espouse the philosophy of the Theatre of Cruelty, which he established in his most famous work, *The Theatre and Its Double*. By the 1960s, the critical community generally viewed *The Cenci* as a work of major importance in the development of modern drama. Critics, such as Martin Esslin in his study *Antonin Artaud: The Man and His Work*, helped to reestablish Artaud's reputation and place *The Cenci* into the context of his overall life and career, while critics such as Jacques Derrida have discussed how Artaud's work relates to later developments in poststructuralist theory.

CRITICISM

Scott Trudell

Trudell is an independent scholar with a bachelor's degree in English literature. In the following essay, Trudell discusses how the overwhelming sensory experience of The Cenci *challenges its audience's moral convictions.*

The Cenci is clearly intended to be a shocking play. Artaud chooses a horrific story for his subject and, unlike Percy Bysshe Shelley in his version of the story, includes no condemnation of the immorality of the characters. In fact, Artaud emphasizes that

Beatrice, Camillo, Orsino, and the other characters are much more similar to Cenci than they first appear, since none of them are bound by any system of moral rules. In accordance with Artaud's theory of the Theatre of Cruelty, they are like universal forces acting on the basis of fundamental convictions and desires, and they pay no heed to any moral or religious guidelines. The play creates an atmosphere in which morals do not exist, partly in order to dismiss the distracting human constructs of ethics and religion so it is possible to examine more closely the basic realities of the world.

The Cenci does not sidestep a moral debate, however; it challenges its audiences' morals very directly and asks them to reevaluate their assumptions about what, for example, cruelty, evil, innocence, and goodness actually are. Artaud criticizes and attacks the moral codes of a variety of institutions and personalities, including the Catholic Church, civil authority, rebellious and self-righteous youth, and bitter lovers. In fact, his play implicitly condemns as absurd all forms of moral conventionality. The audience of *The Cenci* is left with a sense that ethical systems are simply arbitrary rules based on the whims of those in power. With a variety of techniques fashioned to overwhelm his audience and force them to look at the roots of the convictions that they take for granted, Artaud suggests that human ethics is a fundamentally unjustified endeavor with no basis in universal truth.

One of the most important methods by which Artaud establishes this view is his unique and innovative dramatic style, rooted in his theory of the Theatre of Cruelty. *The Cenci* may be a difficult play to enjoy or appreciate because at first it seems rather unrealistic, with characters speaking lines that make them sound very little like actual people and acting in extremes implausible for ordinary people. The intention of Artaud's play, however, is not just to be real, but hyper-real, or super-real—to go beyond what is normally considered reality by transcending the ordinary and the realistic. Artaud was a firm believer in the idea that the theatre should not be weighed down by the constraints of everyday reality, and he worked hard to create a raw and extreme world that is not fantastical or artificial at all.

The Theatre of Cruelty brings this super-reality to the audience is its call for extreme and brutal dramatic action. The evils and horrors that occur in the play are larger than life; they are outside the normal realm of human experience and yet, like the events of an ancient Greek tragedy, they are meant

> *THE CENCI* ATTEMPTS TO SHOCK AUDIENCES OUT OF THEIR ETHICAL COMPLACENCY, SOMETHING THAT ARTAUD DISDAINED AND DESPISED, BY OVERWHELMING THEM WITH THE PRIMEVAL AND BRUTAL AMORALITY OF THE WORLD."

to display the roots of human psychology. This is why Cenci self-consciously characterizes his evil plots as an intrusion into real life, as if he realizes that he a character in a play and is stating his intention to break this barrier. Cenci states:

> The great difference between the villainies committed in real life and the villainies acted out on the stage is that in real life we do more and say less, while in the theater we talk endlessly and accomplish very little. Well, I shall restore the balance, and I shall restore it at the expense of real life.

This quote emphasizes that Artaud will go to great lengths to come closer to reality than is possible in more conventional forms of drama. In his article "What the tragedy *The Cenci* at the Folies-Wagram will be about," reprinted in the 1970 Grove Press edition of the play, Artaud describes his style as a response to the tendency of his era "to forget to wake up." Artaud writes: "I have attempted to give a jolt to this hypnotic sleep by direct physical means. Which is why everything in my play turns, and why each character has his particular *cry*." This hypnotic sleep, Artaud implies, is a moral and ethical sleep, since earlier in the article he refers to the "pettifogging [insignificant quibbling] human distinctions between good and evil" and he contrasts this moral pettiness with the "fabulous amorality" of the ancient Greek and Roman gods. *The Cenci* attempts to shock audiences out of their ethical complacency, something that Artaud disdained and despised, by overwhelming them with the primeval and brutal amorality of the world.

Artaud accomplishes this goal not just by dramatizing an extreme and violent plot, but by stressing the amorality of all of his characters. Cenci is the most extreme character in pursuing his personal and

WHAT DO I READ NEXT?

- *The Cenci* (1819), Percy Bysshe Shelley's dramatization of the tragic fate of the Cenci family, is a masterful romantic play in blank verse, which influenced Artaud's version of the story.

- André Breton's 1924 *Manifeste du surrealisme* (Surrealist Manifesto) is the seminal work on the surrealist movement, of which Artaud was a key member until he was expelled in 1926.

- *Heliogabale; ou, l'anarchiste couronne* (Heliogabalus; or, The Anarchist Crowned) is Artaud's 1934 historical novel about the violent Roman emperor Heliogabalus. Some critics maintain that it exemplifies the ideals of the Theatre of Cruelty more fully than does *The Cenci*.

- Samuel Beckett's fascinating play *Waiting for Godot* (1953), which seems to have no dramatic conflict or plot, is perhaps the most famous example of the Theatre of the Absurd, a dramatic movement that was influenced by Artaud's Theatre of Cruelty.

---

amoral will, but as the play progresses it becomes clear that all of the major characters allow their basic, fundamental desires to overcome conventional moral rules. This is why Beatrice has no interest in prosecuting Cenci under civil law; why she utters the key phrase, "From now on I can believe only in the justice I myself shall choose"; and why in the final lines of the play she reveals that "I fear that death may teach me that I have ended by resembling him." It is also why Orsino can suddenly shift from loving Beatrice to desiring to destroy her and her family, and it is why Camillo, a cardinal very close to the Pope, can say that he does not believe in God. These are characters defined not by social, religious, or ethical codes, but by basic, amoral impulses.

Cenci is the only character, however, with the possible exception of Camillo, who is completely amoral throughout the play and who experiences no profound change in his attitude toward morality. Characters such as Beatrice and Lucretia go through a process of disillusionment and evolution before they abandon their previous ideas of morality and justice and resort to basic amoral impulses to govern their actions. Lucretia's struggle is one of purposeful self-deception, by which she refuses to believe that Cenci is as cruel as evidence has proven him to be. Like Beatrice, she believes in the religious morality of God's justice; both of them frequently invoke God's name and ask for God's

help at the beginning of the play, as when Beatrice says to Cenci at the banquet, "No one can defy God's justice with impunity." Their faith begins to erode as the amorality of the world becomes clearer and clearer, however, and by the end of the play, Beatrice tells Camillo, "Let no one ever dare mention the name of God to me again."

Artaud intends for the audience to go through a similar religious disillusionment and to identify with Beatrice as a forthright character with whom they can share the journey to an acknowledgement of the fact that the world is Godless and amoral. She makes an effective protagonist because, unlike her father, she clearly has good reason to turn away from the conventional religious moral code. Thus she is a useful tool for expressing Artaud's amoral vision of the world, and she helps to add a dimension of atheism and anti-Catholic sentiment to the play.

Also important in this regard are the character of Camillo and Artaud's direct references to the Catholic Church. Beginning with the first scene of the play, when Camillo attempts to blackmail Cenci, Artaud attacks the Church as a faithless and hypocritical institution without substance or meaning. Camillo and the Pope have no moral or theological basis for their judgments; they care only about preserving and expanding their power and influence in a cynical and practical manner. This is an important and marked change from Shelley's

Balinese dancers in the dance-drama Barong   © Wolfgang Kaehler/Corbis

drama, in which Camillo's character has great sympathy for Beatrice and vehemently argues her case before the Pope. In Artaud's version, Beatrice is completely abandoned by both civil and religious authority, as well as by her lover, and is left to suffer in a world where no benevolent morality exists.

Artaud's final touch in imposing his amoral worldview on the audience, and shaking them out of their ethical sleep so that they understand the meaninglessness of their moral systems, is the overwhelming confluence of sound, light, and movement that Artaud calls for in an authentic production of *The Cenci*. Artaud hoped that this shocking atmosphere would make the audience participate in the play through their nerves; he wanted to involve and implicate them in its events so that they would go through a similar moral breakdown as that of Beatrice. The style of the play is affronting enough to parallel Beatrice's violation by her father, which ultimately and ironically succeeds in convincing her of Cenci's worldview. Like Beatrice, the audience is intended to reject God and morality because Artaud, who played the role of Cenci in the original production, is violating them in a physical and oppressive manner. This agenda may make *The Cenci* difficult to appreciate or enjoy, but it forces its viewer to absorb Artaud's

dark glimpse of the amoral reality at the root of the world.

Source: Scott Trudell, Critical Essay on *The Cenci*, in *Drama for Students*, Thomson Gale, 2006.

SOURCES

Artaud, Antonin, "What the Tragedy *The Cenci* at the Folies-Wagram Will Be About," in *The Cenci*, by Antonin Artaud, translated by Simon Watson-Taylor, Grove Press, 1970, pp. x–xii; originally published in *Le Figaro*, May 5, 1935.

———, *The Cenci*, translated by Simon Watson-Taylor, Calder & Boyars, 1969.

Greene, Naomi, *Antonin Artaud: Poet without Words*, Simon and Schuster, 1970, pp. 38–39.

FURTHER READING

Brustein, Robert, "Antonin Artaud and Jean Genet: The Theatre of Cruelty," in *The Theatre of Revolt: An Approach to Modern Drama*, Atlantic Little, Brown, 1964, pp. 361–412.

Brustein disucsses Artaud's seminal work *The Theatre and Its Double*, which provides the philosophical and theoretical groundwork behind *The Cenci*.

Plunka, Gene A., ed., *Antonin Artaud and the Modern Theatre*, Fairleigh Dickinson University Press, 1994.

Plunka provides insight into Artaud's life and theories, then explores how Artaud's work relates to a variety of other twentieth-century dramatists.

Savarese, Nicola, "Antonin Artaud Sees Balinese Theatre at the Paris Colonial Exposition," in *TDR: The Drama Review*, Vol. 45, No. 3, pp. 51–77.

Savarese describes the Balinese dance theatre performed in Paris in 1931 and discusses Artaud's reaction to it. The performance was crucial to inspiring Artaud to establish his theory of the Theatre of Cruelty and to write *The Cenci*.

Sellin, Eric, *The Dramatic Concepts of Antonin Artaud*, University of Chicago Press, 1975.

After a brief sketch of Artaud's life, Sellin provides an explanation of Artaud's dramatic theory and influences, discussing at length the visual and auditory spectacle that Artaud developed in the original version of *The Cenci*.

The Changeling

THOMAS MIDDLETON AND WILLIAM ROWLEY

1622

The Changeling, by English dramatists Thomas Middleton and William Rowley, was first performed at London's Phoenix Theatre in 1622, during the period known as the Jacobean age. The play was first printed in London in 1652 or 1653. A dark story of lust, murder, and adultery, with a comic subplot set in a lunatic asylum, *The Changeling* was a popular play in its own day, but then fell into neglect. The last performance before modern times was in 1668. Interest in the play renewed in the twentieth century, and since 1930, there have been numerous successful productions in Britain and the United States.

The Changeling is considered to be Middleton's finest tragedy. It was common at the time for dramatists to collaborate, and Middleton and Rowley collaborated on five plays over a period of five years. For *The Changeling*, scholars believe that Rowley wrote the first and last scenes and the subplot, while Middleton was responsible for the main plot and the characterization of the major characters.

The Changeling takes its title from the fact that several characters go through changes that make them unrecognizable from what they formerly were or appeared to be—such is the power of love and lust.

AUTHOR BIOGRAPHY

Thomas Middleton was born in 1580 in London, England; his exact date of birth is unknown, but he

was baptized on April 18. His father was a prosperous bricklayer who died when Middleton was five. Middleton attended grammar school and in 1598 he matriculated at Queen's College, Oxford, where he studied from 1598 to 1601. There are no records indicating whether he ever received a degree.

Middleton married Magdalen Marbeck in 1602, and returned to London the following year. By this time, he was writing plays for the prominent theatre manager, Philip Henslowe. His earliest surviving independent play is *Blurt, Master Constable* (1602). From 1602 to 1607, he penned many plays for boy's companies, especially the Boys of St. Paul's. Many of these plays were citizen comedies (also called city comedies), which were set in London, featured mostly lower- and middle-class characters, were moral in tone, and which glorified the city of London. Examples of some popular Middleton citizen comedies are *Michaelmas Term* (c. 1606), *A Trick to Catch the Old One* (c. 1605), and *A Chaste Maid in Cheapside* (1611), which is probably Middleton's most widely read play today. Middleton also wrote tragedies, including *The Revenger's Tragedy* (1607)—although the authorship of this play is sometimes questioned—and *A Yorkshire Tragedy* (1608).

It appears that from 1608 to 1610, Middleton struggled to make a living and may have been in debt. Between 1615 and 1617, he wrote *A Fair Quarrel*, marking his first collaboration with actor and playwright William Rowley. He collaborated on works with other playwrights of the time as well, including Thomas Dekker, Michael Drayton, Anthony Munday, John Webster, and possibly even William Shakespeare.

By this time, Middleton had become well known as a dramatist and he began to prosper. He was hired on many occasions to write and produce City of London pageants, and in 1620, he was appointed city chronicler, a position he retained until his death. With the income he continued to receive from his plays, he became moderately well-to-do. He wrote for the King's Men, the Prince's Men, and for Lady Elizabeth's Men.

The two plays that are generally considered his masterpieces in the genre of tragedy were written late in his career. These were *Women Beware Women* (c. 1625), his last know play, and *The Changeling*, written in collaboration with Rowley and performed in 1622.

In 1624, Middleton's play *Game at Chess* was a theatrical sensation at the Globe Theatre. It dealt with the English dislike of Spanish influence at the English court, and the English suspicion of Catholics. The play was the first to be performed for nine consecutive days, and it would have continued even longer had it not been suppressed by the authorities for its anti-Spanish content.

Middleton died of natural causes, and was buried July 4, 1627, in Newington Butts, London. He is often ranked by contemporary scholars behind only Ben Jonson and William Shakespeare in the ranks of Elizabethan and Jacobean dramatists.

PLOT SUMMARY

Act 1

When *The Changeling* begins, Alsemero has fallen in love with Beatrice, whom he has just met in a church. He intends to cancel his voyage from Alicant, Spain, to Malta, and marry her. When he tells Beatrice of his love, she regrets that five days ago she was promised in marriage to Alonzo de Piracquo.

De Flores enters the scene; he is the servant of Vermandero, Beatrice's father. Beatrice despises De Flores, but he is in love with her and persists in seeing her at every opportunity. When her father enters, Beatrice asks him to invite Alsemero to his castle. Vermandero agrees when he discovers that Alsemero's deceased father was an old friend of his.

The second scene introduces the subplot. Alibius, an old doctor who is in charge of a lunatic asylum, confides in his servant Lollio that he is worried his young wife Isabella may seek affection elsewhere. He asks Lollio to keep watch on her while he is away and to prevent visitors to the madhouse from seeing her. Pedro and Antonio enter; Antonio is dressed to look like a fool, and Pedro pays Alibius to admit him to the asylum.

Act 2

Beatrice has decided she wants to marry Alsemero. De Flores enters, still using every excuse to see Beatrice, even though she insults him. He tells her that Alonzo has arrived with his brother Tomazo. After De Flores exits, Beatrice, repelled by De Flores, says she will get her father to dismiss him.

Vermandero, Alonzo, and Tomazo enter. While Beatrice and Vermandero talk, Tomazo tells his brother that Beatrice did not seem pleased to see him. Alonzo dismisses the remark. After Vermandero informs Alonzo that Beatrice has requested a three-day postponement of their wedding, Tomazo repeats his misgivings. He tells Alonzo not to marry Beatrice because she is in love with someone else. Alonzo refuses to listen.

In the second scene, Beatrice confesses her love to Alsemero. He wants to challenge Alonzo to a duel, but Beatrice fears this will only make the problem worse. She has already decided on a course of action. When she sees De Flores, she speaks kindly to him and promises him some medicine that will cure his bad skin. He is delighted at her apparent change of heart. She tells him she is being forced to marry a man she hates, and De Flores realizes she wants him to murder Alonzo. She gives him money and he readily agrees to perform the deed. Beatrice says she expects him to leave the country after the murder; she is pleased that she can get rid of De Flores and Alonzo at the same time. De Flores, however, sees this as an opportunity to possess Beatrice sexually.

Act 3

While De Flores is showing Alonzo around the castle, De Flores stabs him to death. Unable to remove a ring from Alonzo's finger, he cuts off the finger instead.

Meanwhile, in the madhouse, Lollio introduces Isabella to Franciscus, who is only pretending to be mad, and to Antonio, who is only pretending to be a fool. Both men wish to gain access to Isabella. After Lollio exits, Antonio reveals his true self and declares his love for Isabella, but she is not impressed. Antonio persists, and Lollio overhears his words of love. After he escorts Antonio out, Lollio makes a pass at Isabella. She tells him that if he does not stop, she will get Antonio to cut his throat. Alibius enters and informs them they must get some madmen and fools to put on a dance to entertain the guests at the wedding of Beatrice and Alonzo.

De Flores reports to Beatrice that he has murdered Alonzo. He shows her the dead man's finger, which horrifies Beatrice. The ring was a gift from her, at her father's request. She tells De Flores to keep the ring, which is worth three hundred ducats. When this does not please him, she gives him three thousand golden florins. De Flores explains that he did not commit murder for financial reward, but Beatrice does not understand what he is trying to tell her. She offers to double the sum, but when he scorns at that, she asks him to get out of the country and to write to her, naming his own price. He replies that if he leaves, she must too, since they are bound together in guilt. He tries to

MEDIA ADAPTATIONS

- *The Changeling* was adapted for film in Great Britain in 1998. The film was directed by Marcus Thompson and starred Ian Dury, Billy Connolly, and Colm O'Maonlai.

kiss her and reveals how desperately he wants to make love to her. She tries to reject him, but he reminds her of her guilt. She tries to impress on him the difference in their social class, but he claims that her evil act has made them equals. He says that if she does not do what he wants, he will inform on her. She makes one last effort to offer him money, but again he refuses. She begins to see the terrible consequences of her actions.

Act 4

Beatrice has yielded to De Flores's sexual demands, and has also married Alsemero. Alone in the afternoon, she realizes she cannot offer herself to her new husband, because he will know she is not a virgin. In Alsemero's medicine cabinet, she finds a book that prescribes a potion designed to show if a woman is a virgin. She tries it out on Diaphanta, on whom it has the required effect: she gapes, sneezes, and then laughs. Beatrice arranges for her to go to Alsemero's bed that night, in the pitch darkness, and pretend to be Beatrice.

Vermandero issues warrants for the arrest of Antonio and Franciscus, since he believes they are responsible for the murder of Alonzo. Tomazo enters, seeking revenge for his brother's death. He challenges Alsemero to a duel, and Jasperino reports to Alsemaro that he and Diaphanta have overheard suspicious conversations between De Flores and Beatrice. Puzzled, Alsemero gives Beatrice the virginity test, which Beatrice, knowing how to react, passes with flying colors.

Isabella shows Lollio a letter that Franciscus has written to her, confessing his love for her. Lollio teaches Antonio the dance that is to be performed at the wedding. Isabella enters, disguised as a madwoman and ready to flirt with Antonio, but

Antonio speaks roughly to her, and she rejects him. Lollio then falsely informs Antonio that Isabella really is in love with him. The two men agree to conspire against Franciscus. But then Lollio tells Franciscus that Isabella is in love with him, and encourages him to beat up Antonio when the evening revels end.

Act 5

Beatrice is angry with Diaphanta because it is two o'clock in the morning and the maid still has not returned. De Flores sets fire to Diaphanta's chamber, hoping she will run home and die in the fire. Beatrice starts to love him because he takes care of her interests. The plan works; Diaphanta is burnt to death.

Tomazo, still seeking revenge but not knowing on whom to take it, encounters De Flores and strikes him in anger. De Flores does not hit back since he feels the pangs of conscience. Vermandero informs Tomazo that he has arrested Antonio and Franciscus for the murder; their behavior in disguising themselves looked so suspicious.

Alsemero accuses Beatrice of adultery. She confesses that she employed De Flores to murder Alonzo, but explains that she did it out of love for Alsemero. Alsemero confronts De Flores with Beatrice's confession. Then Vermandero, who believes he has caught the murderers, enters, and Alsemero brings forth the guilty pair. De Flores has fatally wounded Beatrice and has also stabbed himself. Beatrice confesses she sent Diaphanta in her place to the bedroom, and De Flores admits his guilt. He stabs himself again and dies; Beatrice dies also, leaving Vermandero, Tomazo, and Alsemero to reflect on the fact that justice has been done.

CHARACTERS

Alibius

Alibius is a jealous old doctor who is in charge of a private lunatic asylum. He is married to Isabella, a woman much younger than himself, and he is worried that when he is away another man may usurp his position. He therefore instructs his servant Lollio to prevent any of the visitors to the asylum, who may include young nobleman who come to gawk at the inmates, from seeing Isabella.

Alsemero

Alsemero is a nobleman from Valencia who falls in love with Beatrice. He immediately postpones his voyage to Malta to declare his love for her. Alsemero is an honorable man. When he finds out that Beatrice is betrothed to Alonzo but would sooner marry him, Alsemero, he wants to challenge Alonzo to a duel. But Beatrice refuses to allow this. When Jasperino informs him that he and Diaphanta have overheard suspicious conversations between De Flores and Beatrice, Alsemero gives her a potion that is supposed to reveal whether a woman is a virgin. Not a jealous man by nature, he does not want to think ill of his new bride and is relieved when she passes the test. When Beatrice is finally forced into confessing her crime to him, he is horrified and rejects her utterly.

Antonio

Antonio is the changeling, the counterfeit fool. He is a member of Vermandero's staff, but he gets permission to leave for a while, pretending that he is going on a trip to Bramata. In truth, he wants to gain access to Isabella, so he pretends to be a fool and is admitted to the lunatic asylum. After a while he casts his disguise aside and declares his love for Isabella. Unfortunately for Antonio (as well as for Franciscus), he happens to enter the asylum on the same day that Alonzo is murdered. When this fact transpires, Vermandero arrests him for murder. He is only spared the gallows when the truth comes out in the final scene.

Beatrice

Beatrice, also called Joanna, is the young, beautiful daughter of Vermandero. But behind her beauty lies an immature, selfish, cruel and cunning nature. When the plays begins, she is engaged to marry Alonzo, and it appears that she has some affection for him. But as soon as Alsemero declares his love for her, she switches her affections to the new man. Not wanting to be thwarted in her desires, and without a thought for the possible consequences, she employs De Flores, a man whom she loathes and despises, to murder Alonzo. But she completely misjudges De Flores. She thinks she can pay him for his services and get him to leave the country; instead, he demands sex from her. She is forced to submit to him, since he makes her realize that they are partners in crime and she cannot escape from him. But this creates another problem for her. Although she is now free to marry Alsemero, she cannot allow him to detect on their wedding night that she is not a virgin, so she employs Diaphanta to go to Alsemero's bed in her place. De Flores then efficiently disposes of Diaphanta in a house fire, before the truth can come out, and Beatrice decides that she is now in love with him.

Her crimes catch up with her when Jasperino overhears incriminating conversations between her and De Flores and reports them to Alsemero. When challenged by her husband, she confesses her role in the murder, but omits the substitution of Diaphanta in the marriage bed. After being rejected by her husband, she is stabbed by De Flores. Wounded, she is shamed in front of her father, and finally admits the full truth to Alsemero just before she dies.

De Flores

De Flores is a servant of Vermandero, Beatrice's father. He has an ugly appearance, particularly the skin on his face. De Flores is known to most people as an honest man, and Vermandero thinks highly of him. But in fact De Flores has no ethical sense at all, and his besetting sin is his sexual obsession with Beatrice. He invents any little excuse to go and see her, even though she loathes him and insults him. He is ready to endure such humiliations simply to have a glimpse of her. De Flores is more experienced and worldly-wise than Beatrice, and when she hints to him that she would like to see Alonzo murdered, he at once sees how he can use the opportunity to blackmail her into sexual submission. After he has killed Alonzo, he ignores Beatrice's attempts to buy him off, insisting that he will only be satisfied by his sexual enjoyment of her. Having outwitted and outmaneuvered her, he has his desire. Then, when Beatrice is threatened by the fact that Diaphanta has not returned from Alsemero's bed, it is De Flores who thinks up a scheme to save her. De Flores is so efficient in planning and acting upon it that Beatrice convinces herself that he is a man worth loving, because he takes such good care of her. Although De Flores does have some moments when his conscience troubles him, when his crimes are discovered, he remains defiant. He kills himself and Beatrice so they can be together in hell.

Diaphanta

Diaphanta is Beatrice's maid who flirts with Jasperino. At Beatrice's request, she takes Beatrice's place in Alsemero's bed on the wedding night. Beatrice thinks Diaphanta is a little too eager to accept the assignment and wonders whether she really is a virgin. But she is satisfied when she gives Diaphanta the test for virginity prescribed in a medical book, and the maid passes it. But Diaphanta apparently enjoys her love-making with Alsemero since she fails to return at midnight, as she had promised. When the first streaks of dawn appear in the sky, De Flores sets fire to Diaphanta's chamber, to lure her home. When the alarm is sounded about the fire, Diaphanta rushes back to her chambers, where she meets her death in the flames, just as De Flores had intended.

Franciscus

Franciscus is an employee of Vermandero who gets a leave of absence. He uses it to disguise himself as a madman and enter the lunatic asylum, where his purpose is to declare his love for Isabella. For a while he acts like a madman, but then sends Isabella a love letter, which unfortunately for him is intercepted by Lollio. Franciscus is arrested along with Antonio on suspicion of the murder of Alonzo, and would have been hanged had the truth not come out.

Isabella

Isabella is the young wife of Alibius. She is attractive to men and her old husband fears that her affections may stray. Confined to a room where she may only meet the inmates of the lunatic asylum rather than the visitors, she finds herself subject to the unwanted romantic attentions of Antonio and Franciscus. She also has to fend off an attempted seduction by Lollio. Isabella's common sense and good judgment are contrasted with Beatrice's complete lack of those qualities.

Jasperino

Jasperino is Alsemero's friend. He expresses surprise at Alsemero's sudden change of plans after he falls in love with Beatrice, and decides that he will entertain himself by seducing Diaphanta, who seems more than willing to be seduced. Jasperino later reports to Alsemero that he and Diaphanta have overheard incriminating conversation between De Flores and Beatrice.

Lollio

Lollio is Alibius's servant. Alibius charges him with ensuring that none of the visitors to the lunatic asylum are allowed to see Isabella. Lollio, who wants to seduce Isabella himself, readily agrees. He introduces Franciscus and then Antonio to Isabella, not realizing that they are only pretending to be madman and fool, respectively. When Lollio tries to kiss Isabella, she rebuffs him severely, telling him that if he does not stop, she will get Antonio to cut his throat. Lollio then tries to set Antonio and Franciscus against each other by telling each man separately that Isabella is in love with them.

Pedro

Pedro is Antonio's friend who takes him to the lunatic asylum.

Alonzo de Piracquo

Alonzo de Piracquo is a nobleman who when the play begins is engaged to marry Beatrice. Beatrice's father thinks very highly of him and is pleased that he is going to he his son-in-law. But Beatrice quickly loses interest in Alonzo when she meets Alsemero. Alonzo's brother Tomazo warns him not to marry Beatrice but he does not listen. He is murdered by De Flores as De Flores shows him around Vermandero's castle.

Tomazo de Piracquo

Tomazo de Piracquo is Alonzo's brother. He sees that Beatrice does not love Alonzo, and advises him not to marry her. After the murder of Alonzo, Tomazo comes to Vermandero's castle, seeking revenge, but he does not know the identity of the murderer. At first he is courteous to De Flores, thinking him an honest man (Act 4, scene 1), but later (Act 5, scene 2) takes an instinctive dislike to him and strikes him. At the end of the play he is satisfied that justice has been done.

Vermandero

Vermandero is Beatrice's father. He occupies a high position in Alicant society, since he lives in a castle and is attended by servants and has other employees. He is an old friend of Alsemero's late father, so is well-disposed to Alsemero. He is a good-hearted man, hospitable and honorable who is forced in the final scene of the play to watch in dismay as the evil acts are revealed and his own daughter is killed.

THEMES

Reason and Passion

This tragedy is propelled by a conflict between reason and passion, in which passion rules. In dealing with sexual desire, the central characters fail to use proper judgment. Lust overwhelms all other considerations. In the case of Beatrice, there is considerable irony in the explanations she offers herself for her changing emotions. She falls in love with Alsemero immediately, but convinces herself that she is making a reasoned choice. She justifies her desertion of Alonzo by telling herself that when she fell for him, she was being led astray by appearances and she lacked judgment. She even warns Alsemero of the need to test an emotion such as love, by the use of reason. But she gives a clue to her state of mind when she admits in act 1 to a

"giddy turning" in her affections as she turns from Alonzo to Alsemero. This does not sound like the state of mind that accompanies reasoned judgment. In fact, Beatrice is deceiving herself, justifying her fickleness by claiming it is something else. She even convinces herself that Alsemero is a man of sound judgment, because she approves of his choice of Jasperino as a friend: "It is a sign he makes his choice with judgement," she says. She extrapolates from that she too, in choosing a man of judgment, is exercising a similar virtue: "Methinks I love now with the eyes of judgement, / And see the way to merit." The truth, however, is that Beatrice is living in a state of self-delusion, which she never questions. When it comes to her dealings with De Flores, for example, it never occurs to her that De Flores wants from her something other than money. She fails to assess his character correctly.

Alonzo is another character who blinds himself to reality, owing to romantic or sexual desire. In act 2, scene 1, he fails to notice that Beatrice does not greet him with any warmth and shows no interest in him at all. He rejects Tomazo's warning simply because he cannot bear to hear any ill spoken of Beatrice, even though the evidence of her coolness toward him is obvious to his brother. Tomazo is one of the few characters in the play who retains his good judgment (since he is not affected by love or passion), and he speaks a truth that the play will ultimately reveal: "Why, here is love's tame madness: thus a man / Quickly steals into his vexation." He means that it is madness to fail to perceive an ugly truth due to feelings of love, because it will quickly lead to distress. In Alonzo's case, it leads to more than that—it leads directly to his death.

Diaphanta also suffers the fatal consequences of letting passion override judgment. On Beatrice's wedding night, she enjoys Alsemero's embraces too much and fails to return at the appointed hour. She dies in a fire as a result.

De Flores is yet another character in whom lust annihilates judgment. Unlike Beatrice, he does not fool himself into believing something other than the truth. He knows that Beatrice loathes him, and yet he keeps going back to see her, whenever the opportunity presents itself, and he endures her abuse. He knows that from a rational point of view, his actions make no sense. But he also knows that he lusts after Beatrice with such passion that nothing else is of any significance. He admits that he "cannot choose but love her," and that "I can as well be hanged as refrain from seeing her." De

TOPICS FOR FURTHER STUDY

- Some critics have argued that Beatrice is unconsciously attracted to De Flores from the beginning. Is there any evidence from the play to support such a notion? What might she find attractive in De Flores?

- Dramas often feature characters who act as foils for other characters; they set one another off, offering the audience a study in contrasts. In what sense is Isabella a foil for Beatrice? Is Alsemero a foil for De Flores?

- In their collaboration, Middleton wrote most of the main plot, while Rowley wrote the comic subplot. What evidence can be produced to show the closeness of their collaboration? In other words, how are the two plots related, in terms of themes and language?

- Research and describe the main features of the Elizabethan and Jacobean playhouses. What was the physical structure of the theaters, i.e., what did they look like? In what sense was the audience more involved in the action than a modern audience might be? How were plays staged? What social class of people attended the plays?

Flores has gone beyond the point where he can exercise judgment; he is in the grip of lust and it will not let him go.

Once the characters have fallen under the spell of love or passion or lust, the crimes that follow seem inevitable.

Appearance versus Reality

There is a contrast between appearance and reality. Beatrice looks outwardly fine, but her beautiful appearance masks a selfish, ruthless, violent nature. During the play, she goes through a series of inner transformations that make her quite different from how she initially appears. Early on, betrothed to Alonzo, she is in love with Alsemero; later, in the dumb show that begins act 4, scene 1, she appears as a modest, virtuous bride in a solemn wedding procession, while the reality is that she is an accomplice in murder and has already been unfaithful to her husband. By passing the virginity test, she appears to be a virgin when she is not. She is also soon to create adulterers out of her maid and her unknowing husband; then finally, she will change affections once more, from her husband to De Flores. This makes Beatrice one of the "changelings" of the play's title.

The deception of Alsemero, who thinks he is making love to his bride when in fact his lover is Diaphanta, adds another layer to the appearance versus reality theme. This theme is also part of the comic subplot, which comments on the main plot. Antonio (who is described in the *dramatis personae* as the changeling) pretends to be a fool, and Franciscus pretends to be mad. Their appearances are quite contrary to the reality, although in a sense they too, like Beatrice, Alsemero, and De Flores, are mad for love, since they go to such absurd lengths to access to Isabella.

The theme of appearance versus reality also extends to Lollio who (like De Flores) appears to be the loyal servant of his master, but in fact is plotting to have Isabella for himself. Isabella provides a twist to the appearance-reality theme. Alibius suspects that she is virtuous only on the surface and that she will be tempted to gain sexual satisfaction elsewhere; he thinks there may be a dichotomy between the way she appears and who she really is. In that, however, he is mistaken. Although Isabella is not beyond using playful sexual innuendo with Lollio and Antonio, she is what she appears to be: a virtuous wife.

STYLE

Imagery

There are many images of eyes and references to sight, many of which are used with unconscious irony by Beatrice, who points out that the eye can deceive when it comes to reaching reliable judgments about love and character. In act 1, scene 1, she says to Alsemero:

> Our eyes are sentinels unto our judgements,
> And should give certain judgement what they see;
> But they are rash sometimes, and tell us wonders
> Of common things, which when our judgments find,
> They can then check the eyes, and call them blind.

Beatrice says of her quickly forgotten love for Alonzo, "Sure, mine eyes were mistaken," and she contrasts the superficiality of the eyes with what she calls the "eye of judgment" and "intellectual eyesight." The irony is that Beatrice is never more blind than when she thinks she is seeing with the eyes of judgment.

Images of sickness, poison, and blood reinforce the themes of the play. In the first scene, Alsemero, dismissing any idea that he is unwell, says, "Unless there be some hidden malady / Within me that I understand not." He does not know it yet, but the love he has just conceived for Beatrice will act as a sickness, a poison to him. Beatrice regards De Flores as like a "deadly poison," and says that he is to her a "basilisk" (a mythical reptile whose glance was said to be fatal). When the poison introduced by Beatrice and De Flores has done its work, Jasperino refers to the situation as an "ulcer" that is "full of corruption." An image of sickness is also used by De Flores, who refers to his lust for Beatrice as a "mad qualm" (a qualm is an illness).

Images of sickness are balanced by references to healing. Beatrice offers to make a medicine to cure De Flores's skin; Jasperino informs Diaphanta that he can be cured of the madness he jokingly claims to suffer from by sexual intercourse with her. Alibius, who is a doctor, claims to be able to cure both madmen and fools. The irony is that he cannot; the inmates are kept in line with whips, not cured by medicine. There is no medicine that can cure the sickness that afflicts Beatrice and De Flores, which also infects the characters around them.

Images of blood convey both lust and murder. Jasperino says he has the "maddest blood i' th' town," by which he means the most lustful. De Flores uses the word in the same sense when, after realizing he has a workable plan to possess Beatrice's body, he exclaims: "O my blood! / Methinks I feel her in mine arms already." But De Flores's use of the word is also linked to his knowledge that he must shed blood (by murder) in order to satisfy his blood (his lust). After he has killed Alonzo, he seeks to collect from Beatrice what his lust

demands, and he uses the word blood to mean murder: "A woman dipped in blood, and talk of modesty?" The blood image recurs later, when Alsemero tells his daughter that she should have gone "a thousand leagues" in order to avoid "This dangerous bridge of blood!"

Finally, Beatrice herself takes up the image of blood but she links it not to lust or murder but to the medical practice of blood-letting to cure a patient. This connects the image of blood with the references in the play to healing. In act 5, scene 3, Beatrice says to her father:

> I am that of your blood was taken from you
> For your better health. Look no more upon't,
> But cast it to the ground regardlessly;
> Let the common sewer take it from distinction.

HISTORICAL CONTEXT

Jacobean Drama

Jacobean drama in England covers the period from 1603 to 1625, coinciding with the reign of King James I. The Jacobean professional theatre has been described by David Farley-Hills in *Jacobean Drama* as "the most brilliant and dynamic the world has seen." The dominant figure during the first part of the Jacobean period was William Shakespeare (1564–1616). Although many of Shakespeare's plays were written during the reign of Elizabeth I, some of his greatest works appeared in the first decade of the Jacobean age, including the tragedies of *Othello*, *King Lear*, *Macbeth*, and *Antony and Cleopatra*, and the romances *Pericles*, *Cymbeline*, *The Winter's Tale*, and *The Tempest*. During this decade, Shakespeare's preeminence was challenged by other dramatists, including Ben Jonson (1572–1637), George Chapman (c. 1560–1634), John Marston (c. 1575 or 1576–1634), Middleton, John Webster (c. 1580–c. 1625), and John Fletcher (1579–1625).

The Jacobean theatre enjoyed the rich legacy bequeathed by the Elizabethan age: a public used to attending plays and to paying for the privilege; a number of permanent theatres, both large and small; and a system that enabled those involved in writing and putting on plays to gain some financial reward from doing so. The largest theatres were open-air buildings such as the Globe, which could accommodate an audience of several thousand. The Globe was made famous as the theatre where Shakespeare's plays were first performed. Other large theatres in London were the Fortune, the Curtain, and the Hope. There were also smaller, covered

COMPARE
&
CONTRAST

- **Jacobean Age:** In 1623, the first folio edition of Shakespeare is published. It contains thirty-six plays, eighteen of which are published for the first time. Over 1,000 copies are printed.

  Today: There are 228 surviving copies of Shakespeare's first folio, over one-third of which are owned by the Folger Shakespeare Library in Washington, D.C. In 2003, Oxford University's Oriel College sells its copy of the first folio to philanthropist Sir Paul Getty.

- **Jacobean Age:** Great Britain in the reign of James I is an emerging European power. Largely Protestant, its great rival is Catholic Spain, and there is mutual suspicion between the two countries.

  Today: Religion is no longer a divisive factor in relations between European nations. Spain and Britain are democratic nations, and both are members of the European Union.

- **Jacobean Age:** In 1605, a group of Catholics smuggles thirty-six barrels of gunpowder into the vault of parliament. King James is addressing parliament when a man named Guy Fawkes is apprehended as he is about to ignite the fuse. This attempt to wipe out the entire government of Britain becomes known as the Gunpowder Plot. Fawkes is hanged in 1606.

  Today: On November 5 every year, England commemorates the foiling of the Gunpowder Plot. The event is called Guy Fawkes Night or Bonfire Night. Huge bonfires are lit, fireworks are set off, and effigies representing Guy Fawkes are tossed on the bonfire.

---

theatres, such as Paul's and Blackfriars. Paul's had room for an audience of only about a hundred; the capacity of Blackfriars was about seven hundred.

The Phoenix, the theatre where *The Changeling* premiered, was a small private theatre on Drury Lane. Built in 1609 to stage cockfights, and thus originally called the Cockpit, the building was converted to a theatre in 1616. After being badly damaged in a riot in 1617, it was rebuilt and named the Phoenix.

Enclosed theatres were more expensive than open-air theatres like the Globe, and therefore the enclosed theatres attracted wealthier audiences. The open-air theatres attracted a much wider cross-section of London society, from artisans to gentry. The genius of the Elizabethan and Jacobean dramatists lay in their abilities to write plays that could please both the serious, educated public as well as patrons who merely wanted a robust, easily digested form of entertainment.

Treatment of Madness

In sixteenth and seventeenth century England, there were no effective treatments for mental illness. In London, the insane were confined to Bedlam Hospital, and for a fee, visitors were admitted to the hospital to gawk at the antics of the patients. People regarded such a visit much as a modern person might regard a trip to the zoo. Thomas Dekker's play *The Honest Whore* (1604) has a scene in which a duke and his companions visit Bedlam for entertainment. This practice is the source of Alibius's fear in *The Changeling* that aristocratic visitors to his madhouse may catch the eye of his young wife Isabella.

Patients in Bedlam were sometimes kept naked and in chains. Discipline appears to have been harsh, as is shown in *The Changeling*, in which Lollio keeps a whip handy to control the patients. As a Londoner, Middleton may well have observed such practices on a visit to Bedlam. That such treatment of the insane was not unusual can be gleaned from Shakespeare's play *As You Like It* (1599 or 1600), in which the heroine Rosalind remarks lightheartedly, "Love is merely a madness, and I tell you, deserves as well a dark house and a whip as madmen do." In Shakespeare's *Twelfth Night*, when Malvolio is falsely declared to be mad, he is bound

Alicante, Spain © Jonathan Blair/Corbis

and confined to a dark room, where he is tormented by the fool, Feste. For Elizabethan and Jacobean audiences, insanity appears to have been a topic from which much amusement could be derived.

CRITICAL OVERVIEW

Middleton was a popular playwright in his own day, but not long after his death, his works were neglected and were largely forgotten. In the nineteenth century, Middleton's work was revived, although his plays were often considered too coarse and vulgar by moralistic Victorian critics. Twentieth century scholars and critics put aside such scruples and established Middleton's best work as superior to any of his contemporaries, barring William Shakespeare and Ben Jonson.

The Changeling is usually considered Middleton's greatest tragedy. In the opinion of T. S. Eliot, in his essay on "Thomas Middleton" in *Selected Essays*, *The Changeling* stands out as the greatest tragedy of its time, with the exception of Shakespeare's tragedies. For Samuel Schoenbaum in *Middleton's Tragedies*, "Nowhere else in Middleton are action and dialogue, character and theme blended together into such powerful

harmony." Critics have frequently praised the characterization of Beatrice and De Flores. The scene between these characters in act 3 (scene 4) is often singled out for comment. J. R. Mulrayne in *Thomas Middleton* calls this scene "one of the most powerful encounters between two antagonistic yet similar personalities in the whole range of theatre," a judgment with which others concur.

Critics also note the effectiveness of the playwriting collaboration between Middleton, who wrote the tragic parts of the play, and Rowley, who wrote the comic subplot. George Walton Williams, for example, points out how the two plots are related, "structurally, tonally, thematically, and metaphorically with a subtlety and effectiveness that lets them speak as one on the unifying concept of transformation, or the condition of being a changeling."

CRITICISM

Bryan Aubrey

Aubrey holds a Ph.D. in English and has published many articles on English drama. In this essay, Aubrey analyzes Middleton's characterizations of Beatrice and De Flores.

The principal interest in *The Changeling* lies in the two central characters, Beatrice and De Flores. De Flores is a study in sexual obsession. He is a ruthless character who is also efficient and knowledgeable about the ways of the world. He was born a gentleman but fell on hard times. Other than his reference to his "hard fate," the details of his past life are never specified, but he surely resents his situation as a servant to Vermandero. The ugliness of his appearance is emphasized, but like another famous villain—Iago in Shakespeare's *Othello*—he is perceived by others as "honest." He allows his inner life and motivations to be seen by the outside world, which gives him an advantage, since no one suspects him of wrongdoing. Once he has conceived a sexual desire for Beatrice, a woman who, as the daughter of his employer, he can never in the normal course of events expect to have, he allows his lust to completely dominate his thoughts and actions. De Flores is a slave to his obsessive desire, seeking out any moment he can to be in Beatrice's presence, even though she expresses her loathing for him to his face. Masochistically, De Flores will endure any humiliation as long as it allows him to gaze on the object of his obsession. He continues to act in this way, in spite of an awareness that he is making a fool of himself ("Why, am I not an ass to devise ways / Thus to be railed at?"). It seems that with every rejection, his desire grows stronger. Like a stalker, he observes his prey and bides his time.

De Flores holds a great advantage over Beatrice because he is more experienced in the world than she is. When he realizes that she wants to get rid of Alonzo, his mind works fast. He knows this gives him an opportunity to possess her, and he acts with single-minded daring. He is utterly confident of the success of his plan. Unlike Beatrice, he knows who he is dealing with. Her inexperience and naïveté are no match for his cunning and foresight. It is not an equal contest.

One way that De Flores reveals himself is through his language. His speech is awash with sexual puns (he is not the only character in the play to exhibit this quality). For example, when he picks up the glove Beatrice has dropped, his words have an obscene double meaning:

Now I know
She had rather wear my pelt tanned in a pair
Of dancing pumps than I should thrust my fingers
Into her sockets here.

The last line has the connotation of sexual penetration by the man of the woman.

APPARENTLY UNTROUBLED BY CONSCIENCE, BEATRICE ONLY CONFESSES HER GUILT WHEN SHE IS CORNERED AND DEFEATED. AND AT FIRST SHE CONFESSES ONLY TO WHAT ALSEMERO ALREADY KNOWS."

When Beatrice flatters De Flores because she is about to employ him to commit murder, and says his hard face shows "service, resolution, manhood, / If cause were of employment," De Flores responds with words that are full of sexual innuendo, although these double meanings are not recognized by Beatrice.

'Twould be soon seen,
If e'er your ladyship had cause to use it.
I would but wish the honour of a service
So happy that it mounts to.

"Use," "service," and "mounts" all have sexual connotations in De Flores's mind, as Christopher Ricks has pointed out in his essay, "The Moral and Poetic Structure of *The Changeling*," which appears in *Essays in Criticism*. Ricks also points out that in this scene, Beatrice misses De Flores's meaning every time; she simply does not understand how his mind works. This cross-talking is also apparent in act 4, scene 3, the powerful scene in which De Flores brings the severed finger, the evidence of the murder, to Beatrice. This is his "service" to her, which must in his mind be rewarded with "service," that is, sexual intercourse.

Like anyone in the grip of a deep obsession, De Flores cares for nothing except the achievement of his desire. This is why he can so truthfully say to Beatrice that unless she allows him to possess her, he will confess everything to the authorities. He will risk everything, even his life, in pursuit of his goal. And unlike Beatrice, De Flores shows no repentance at the end of the play when their joint deeds are unmasked. His words to Alsemero, even when he is wounded by his own hand and about to give himself the fatal blow, are not of contrition but of cruel triumph and defiance: "I coupled with your mate / At barley-break. Now we are left in hell."

WHAT DO I READ NEXT?

- Middleton's *A Chaste Maid in Cheapside* (1611) is often considered Middleton's finest comedy. It is a skillfully plotted, cynical drama about the seamier side of life in London, as unscrupulous characters seek money, marriage, and sex. The title is a joke, since Cheapside was a notorious location in London frequented by prostitutes.

- William Shakespeare's dark comedy *Measure for Measure* (1604) has some similarities with *The Changeling*. Like De Flores, Shakespeare's character Angelo allows his sexual obsession with a woman to lead him into sinful actions. The play also features the plot device known as the "bed trick," in which a man is tricked into making love to a woman who is not the woman

he thinks she is. Shakespeare's play, however, ends in forgiveness rather than death.

- *Volpone* (first performed 1606) is one of Ben Jonson's great comic plays. It satirizes hypocrisy, greed, and self-deception, which are all unmasked in the end. Some of the characters resemble predatory birds such as the crow, vulture, and raven. Volpone is likened to a fox.

- *The Shakespearean Stage, 1574–1642* (2d ed., 1980), by Andrew Gurr, is a concise guide to the Elizabethan and Jacobean theatre world. There are chapters on the companies, the actors, the playhouses, the audience, and how the plays were staged.

These few moments of sexual conquest represent for De Flores the fulfillment of his entire life; nothing else gave him comparable enjoyment:

> I thank life for nothing
> But that pleasure; it was so sweet to me
> That I have drunk up all, left none behind
> For any man to pledge me.

So much for De Flores—man at his worst, a character any audience can love to hate. But what of Beatrice? Why does this catastrophe overtake her? Young and beautiful, with suitors at her feet, she should have been on the threshold of a happy life. Una Ellis-Fermor, in her book, *Jacobean Drama: An Interpretation*, describes Beatrice as a "spoilt child," and it is easy to see the aptness of the phrase. Beatrice is used to getting what she wants and does not like to be thwarted in her desires. But she is very inexperienced, does not understand the nature of men, and has no developed moral awareness. Part of her problem is her misplaced self-confidence; she does not know her own ignorance. On first meeting with Alsemero, when he declares that he is in love with her, she is bold enough to give him a little piece of advice about how the eyes can deceive, and judgment should be made with the reasoning mind. This is advice that she is singularly unqualified to give, since she is

led astray by first impressions just as much as Alsemero is. Beatrice is a young woman with a great capacity for self-delusion. She makes one bad decision after another, and yet thinks she is being very astute. When she first has the idea of getting De Flores to kill Alonzo, for example, she draws on the philosophical idea that even the ugliest thing in creation is good for some purpose. Ellis-Fermor comments that Beatrice is here like a "clever child who has learnt a rule from a book." When De Flores enters, Ellis-Fermor states, Beatrice is

> still a child playing with a complicated machine of whose mechanism or capacities she knows nothing, concerned only to release the catch that will start it working and delighted when, in accordance with the text-book's instructions, it begins to move.

The moment of truth for Beatrice arrives in act 3, scene 4, in which De Flores reports that he has done the deed she required of him—Alonzo is dead. Beatrice's first response is one of joy; she is so happy she weeps. But then De Flores shows her the proof—the dead man's finger with the ring on it, and Beatrice recoils in horror. "Bless me! What hast thou done?" she exclaims. It is as if for the first time she realizes what has actually happened, that a real, flesh-and-blood man has been murdered. The sight of the ring, which was a gift her father made her send Alonzo, adds to her distress because it connects the murder with something directly associated with her.

The remainder of the scene constitutes a very rude awakening for Beatrice. At first she thinks it is just a matter of money that will make De Flores, who has now become an extreme inconvenience to her, disappear. When the truth begins to dawn on her, she thinks it impossible that anyone could be so wicked and cruel as to make Alonzo's death "the murderer of my honour!" But De Flores's hard and irrefutable logic holds a mirror up to her own nature and shows her that actions have real consequences that cannot be escaped. She realizes that "Murder . . . is followed by more sins." However, this does not make her repent. She is determined to brazen it out and pose as Alsemero's virgin bride. Deceit, adultery, and death (that of Diaphanta) soon follow.

Apparently untroubled by conscience, Beatrice only confesses her guilt when she is cornered and defeated. And at first she confesses only to what Alsemero already knows. Even then she tries to minimize her guilt, claiming that the murder was done for Alsemero's sake. She reveals the full truth, including the "bed trick" involving Diaphanta, and begs for forgiveness, only when she knows that her death is upon her. Even at the last, she blames De Flores for her downfall. Several times in the play she likens him to a serpent, and tells Alsemero in the final scene that she "stroked a serpent." This puts in mind the biblical myth of Eve, who was tempted by Satan in the form of a serpent. Beatrice seems to think of herself as the innocent one overcome by a creature with evil intent, whereas in fact she bears at least equal responsibility for what happened. Beatrice pays a high price for her immaturity and lack of moral awareness, but the dramatist leaves the audience in no doubt that she deserves her fate.

Source: Bryan Aubrey, Critical Essay on *The Changeling*, in *Drama for Students*, Thomson Gale, 2006.

Joost Daalder
and Antony Telford Moore

In the following essay, Daalder and Moore discuss the dramatic tension inherent in the dual nature of Beatrice's reaction to De Flores and in Alsemero's sexual development.

One of the most striking occurrences in the early scenes of Middleton and Rowley's *The Changeling* is Beatrice's extraordinarily vehement reaction to her father's servant, De Flores. Let us briefly consider what leads up to her first attack on him.

" BEATRICE AND ALSEMERO THINK, WRONGLY, OF LOVE AND LOATHING AS TWO QUITE DISTINCT FEELINGS. THE DRAMATISTS, HOWEVER, DRAW ATTENTION TO THE CONNECTION BETWEEN THE TWO. . . ."

Alsemero has already fallen in love with Beatrice when the play starts, and he cancels his planned trip to Malta as a result. Beatrice, more unusually, thinks of him as 'the man was meant me' (I.i.84) even though only five days before she had agreed to become betrothed to Alonzo de Piracquo. Alsemero and Beatrice are presented as besotted with each other when we first see them together in I.i, and Alsemero's friend Jasperino decides he might as well forget about further travel and instead try to seduce Beatrice's waiting-woman Diaphanta. It is at this sexually charged moment that De Flores enters.

De Flores addresses Beatrice with 'Lady, your father—', obviously intending to say more, but is immediately interrrupted by Beatrice with the words 'Is in health I hope' (I.i.91). From De Flores's aside a little later (99–106) it seems clear that he tries to get physically close to Beatrice as often as he can, but when we hear Beatrice's 'Is in health I hope' we do not, as an audience, know anything other than that De Flores appears to be offering perfectly reasonable information to Beatrice about her father, Vermandero. Beatrice's interrruption seems rude and quite beside the point. De Flores answers with 'Your eye shall instantly instruct you lady./ He's coming hitherward' (93–4).

This answer does not need to be interpreted as indicating anything negative about. De Flores. He may, in effect, be saying: 'He is indeed in fine condition, as you yourself can verify when he comes here in a moment—in fact, I was trying to tell you of his imminent arrival'. There is no evidence that Vermandero actually instructed De Flores to announce his coming, but the audience may readily see the servant as helpful, both to Vermandero and Beatrice, in doing so. Yet Beatrice reacts with

What need then
Your duteous preface? I had rather
He had come unexpected: you must stall
A good presence with unnecessary blabbing,
And how welcome for your part you are
I'm sure you know. (94–9)

The predominant point of Beatrice's speech appears to be that she wants to make it abundantly plain to De Flores that his presence is *not* welcome to her; indeed, she implies that he should know as much by now.

What is not clear is just why he is so unwelcome. Later, Beatrice repeatedly blames his face. A theatre audience can see from De Flores's first entrance that his face is marred by a skin condition, something which leads Beatrice to refer to him as a 'standing toad-pool' in II.i.58. When, towards the end of the play, Beatrice admits explicitly, though only to herself, that she loves him, she still expresses distaste for his face: 'His face loathes one, / But look upon his care, who would not love him?' (V.i.70–1). There are indications, however, that it is not just the physical ugliness of De Flores's face which puts her off. De Flores, who often proves himself to be an excellent analyst, says that she 'At no hand can abide the sight of me, / As if danger or ill luck hung in my looks' (II.i.35–6), which Beatrice appears to confirm in an aside a little later: 'This ominous, ill-faced fellow more disturbs me / Than all my other passions' (II.i.53–4).

It is thus tempting to explain Beatrice's revulsion as caused by De Flores's face, and not just by her distaste for the skin condition but, beyond that, by a sense on her part that somehow his loathsome face spells disaster to her. And so, the course of events in the play makes clear, it does. It is not, of course, as though he would have harmed her in any case: we know that she herself sets the tragic events in motion by hiring him as an assassin. But this does not mean that her fear of him is unjustified. As she puts it in one of her last speeches: 'My loathing / Was prophet to the rest, but ne'er believed' (V.iii.156–7). Despite her use of the passive voice, as though *someone else* should have believed her loathing (a locution which is so expressive of her divided nature), we can for ourselves acknowledge that *she* should have acted on her misgivings. This remains so even if we see her loathing as partly caused by an unconscious realization on her part that what she reacts to in De Flores is not only his own evil but some sort of representation, or mirror, of her own.

We can be sure that it is not just his face which she hates. If that were the case, De Flores's reaction to her 'how welcome for your part you are / I'm sure you know' (I.i.98–9) would make little sense. He says in an aside:

Will't never mend, this scorn,
One side nor other? Must I be enjoined
To follow still whilst she flies from me? Well,
Fates, do your worst; I'll please myself with sight
Of her, at all opportunities,
If but to spite her anger. I know she had
Rather see me dead than living—and yet
She knows no cause for't but a peevish will.
    (99–106)

In line 100, 'One side nor other' is a very interesting phrase. Daalder comments in his edition: 'on the one side or the other (probably: because either she stops scorning me or I stop creating that attitude in her)'. There is more to be said. 'One side nor other' suggests an extraordinarily close connection between De Flores and Beatrice. De Flores goes on to expand on the idea of an inextricable link when he says: 'Must I be enjoined / To follow still whilst she flies from me?' (100–1). Superficially, this looks like a simple description of De Flores's own compulsion, but the phrase implies something more. In 'To follow still whilst she flies', *whilst* hints that the following and the fleeing are mutually dependent actions; and *still* gives a picture of the following and fleeing continuing interminably. Perhaps *enjoined,* too, in the previous line, develops an expectation of some powerful bond between Beatrice and De Flores. Within the bounds of the sentence, then, the future lovers are seen to be joined intrinsically, caught forever in a process of reaction and counter-reaction. As well, De Flores's sense that Beatrice's scorn may never mend 'One side nor other' may imply that her apparent loathing of him has part of its cause on her side, i.e. in her mind or nature. He appears to realize, even if not quite articulately, that her scorn is in part 'internal,' within Beatrice—is something which it is not in his power to remove, no matter what he does.

Yet De Flores's discernment extends beyond even this. He seems to recognize, or at least sense, that Beatrice's problem is that she loathes him without knowing why. He says: 'I know she had / Rather see me dead than living—and yet / She knows no cause for't but a peevish will' (104–6). Daalder's gloss on line 106 is solely concerned with Beatrice's 'peevish' will—as though, if only we can grasp the exact meanings and implications of that difficult adjective, we may also discover just what inspires Beatrice's loathing. Yet, however important the word 'peevish' is here, what is ultimately more interesting and significant is that De Flores says 'She *knows* no cause for't but a peevish will' (our emphasis). Curiously, De Flores almost speaks as though he is Beatrice's father-confessor or psychiatrist—as though she has told him what, in her conscious mind, motivates her to loathe him, even though what she 'knows' does not provide an adequate explanation. There seems a hint here (present in the language used by the dramatists even if not necessarily intended by De Flores) that there is another reason, which Beatrice does *not* know. There is, apparently, an obscure—perhaps unconscious—reason, why, at least on the surface, Beatrice detests De Flores. We are not yet made aware what that reason may be, but we *are* made aware that it exists. 'She *knows* no cause for't' sounds a small alarm bell, alerts our suspicions about Beatrice, and directs our attention to the evidently important question of what the heroine of this play does and does not know. Beatrice, De Flores asserts, does not *know* what moves her to hate him (other than a 'peevish will'), but that she does display hatred towards him is beyond doubt, and there *is* a reason for it, even if she is ignorant of its nature.

The notion that there is a reason for Beatrice's seeming hatred which remains unknown to the woman herself also steers the audience toward the possibility that all is not what it seems: that perhaps Beatrice does not entirely hate De Flores, and that somehow her lack of knowledge of her motivation makes her hatred less than complete. Even Alsemero is obviously surprised by her strange outburst in lines 94–9, saying: 'You seemed displeased, lady, on the sudden' (107).

The evidence so far does not allow an onlooker or reader to come to the firm conclusion that Beatrice's visible, conscious loathing is in some way, or to some extent, a manifestation of unconscious love. Nevertheless, even Beatrice herself is puzzled by her vehement conscious reaction to De Flores, as her next speech to Alsemero makes plain:

Your pardon, sir; 'tis my infirmity
Nor can I other reason render you
Than his or hers, or some particular thing
They must abandon as a deadly poison
Which to a thousand other tastes were wholesome.
Such to mine eyes is that same fellow there,
The same that report speaks of, the basilisk.
    (108–14)

Beatrice's explanation that her displeasure is—or is due to—her 'infirmity' (108) points in the direction of something seemingly quite different from what she asserts in her later, oft-repeated claims, viz.

that it is just De Flores's face which she hates. Here, she confesses that she cannot give Alsemero any reason for her loathing other than some ill-defined sense that to her De Flores is like a 'deadly poison' (111), even though to others his presence might be 'wholesome' (112). Although there is a reference to the effect of De Flores's face in her mention of 'the basilisk' (l14), the most significant thing in this speech is her conscious admission that De Flores's impact on her is mysterious, and perhaps to be explained as merely evidence of an 'infirmity'.

A complacent spectator or reader might at this point go along with Beatrice's conscious thought process, and conclude that her reaction to De Flores is simply the result of an irrational aversion. A more thoughtful person would, nevertheless, wonder why it is that *she* is so strongly affected by him even if others are not: later, we find unambiguous proof that her conscious loathing is closely bound up with unconscious desire, although we never discover why Diaphanta, for example, is not fascinated by De Flores. On the surface, Beatrice's unusual dislike of De Flores seems a little like an allergy. That is how it is seen by Arthur L. Little in a recent discussion, and that is how Alsemero sees it too. The rather innocent Alsemero's view is that there is nothing abnormal about Beatrice's reaction:

This is a frequent frailty in our nature.
There's scarce a man amongst a thousand found
But hath his imperfection: one distastes
The scent of roses, which to infinites
Most pleasing is, and odoriferous;
One oil, the enemy of poison;
Another wine, the cheerer of the heart
And lively refresher of the countenance.
Indeed this fault, if so it be, is general:
There's scarce a thing but is both loved and
    loathed.
Myself, I must confess, have the same frailty.
    (115–125)

Beatrice then asks:

And what might be your poison, sir? I am bold with you.

To which Alsemero replies:

What might be your desire perhaps: a cherry. (126–7)

Little takes it that De Flores leaves the scene after line 106 (which does not actually happen: he is still on stage at I.i.223, when Beatrice drops her glove), after which

the conversation between Beatrice and Alsemero changes into the subject of health and illness, and Beatrice speaks of DeFlores as her 'infirmity' and 'deadly poison' [108, 111]. And once Alsemero pontificates on the commonness of man and woman's allergic imperfections [115–25], admitting to his own allergic reactions to cherries [127], he and Beatrice betray their entanglement in physical sexuality. Their dispositions are seemingly the same: both are allergic to sexual things. The sexual nature of Beatrice's allergy to DeFlores is scripted into DeFlores's name which refers either to 'defloration' or more pointedly to 'deflowerer'. Alsemero focuses his sexual infirmity on cherries. His allergy to sexuality is further accentuated by his choosing aphrodisiac objects, when he casually and extemporaneously tries to name some of the allergic imperfections found in the population more generally [117–22]. His sexual subtext is The Song of Songs: 'O that you would kiss me with the kisses of your mouth! For your love is better than wine, your anointing oils are fragrant, your name is oil poured out; / therefore the maidens love you' and 'I am a rose of Sharon, a lily of the valleys. / As a lily among brambles so is my love among maidens' (1.1–2, 2.1–2). The Song (as subtext or intertext) betrays the sexual underpinnings of the conversation here between Beatrice and Alsemero.

Little produces a great deal of value here . . . but we believe that his material can be put to more effective and precise use than he has yet done. In our view, the dramatists have a far more sophisticated understanding of what Beatrice and Alsemero say than the speakers themselves. Beatrice does seem to have some vague sense that De Flores is like a poison to her, but rather than relating this to anything specific within him or her, she reflects that she is, to use Little's language, merely 'allergic' to De Flores. He is, for some obscure reason, a 'deadly poison' (111) to *her,* but might well be 'wholesome' (112) to a thousand other tastes. Alsemero elaborates on this idea. There is nothing peculiar about being allergic to something, he assures her: some people are allergic to e.g. roses, which are most pleasing to others, and so on. He himself, it turns out, is allergic to cherries.

Little's reference to The Song of Songs seems to us apposite. We are doubtful that the naive Alsemero himself can be supposed to have that in mind when referring to roses, oil, and wine. Like Little, however, we do think that these objects are not only allergenic to some (though not to others), but are also, at the same time, 'aphrodisiac objects'; the dramatists presumably use the language of The Song of Songs to establish that association in our— the audience's—minds. In hearing Alsemero's speech, a Renaissance audience would have recalled The Song of Songs more readily than a modern one. For that matter, spectators of the period could have thought of roses, oil, and wine as sexual even without any recollection of The Song of Songs. Gordon Williams, in his extensive dictionary of sexual language, shows in great detail that to a Renaissance audience a rose quite commonly

signified something sexual, as (1) 'the flower of sexuality', (2) an image for 'maidenhead', and (3) an image for 'whore'. 'Oil', he demonstrates, was often used for 'semen' or 'vaginal emission'. Wine was frequently alluded to as an aphrodisiac. To us, it seems that the dramatists present *Alsemero* as speaking about allergies, while *the audience* is meant to become aware of sexual implications in his speech. There is a profound reason for this. The dramatists are less interested in using Alsemero to make unintended sexual jokes than in making us aware of the fact that he is *unconsciously* speaking about aphrodisiac objects. The ironic discrepancy between what he is consciously thinking about and what he unconsciously reveals reaches its most telling manifestation when he says that what is his poison is exactly what might be Beatrice's desire: 'a cherry' (127). In the note on line 127 in his edition, Daalder designated the cherry as "sexy". . . . Gordon Williams lists 'cherry' as an image for 'sexual organ'. His examples make plain that it could be thought of as male or female. It could also refer, he says, to a woman's nipple.

But why is an audience entitled to think of words like 'roses', 'oil', 'wine', and 'cherry' as alluding to sexual matters here? We suggest that this is a matter of dramatic context, the scene being so constructed that sex is never far from the audience's mind. At the beginning of the play, in his very first speech (I.i.1–12), Alsemero already thought of Beatrice as Eve, the centuries-old archetypal temptress. Not much later we see him greeting Beatrice with a kiss. Jasperino remarks on the apparent change in his sexually-naive friend:

> How now! the laws of the Medes are changed, sure!
> Salute a woman? He kisses too. Wonderful! Where learnt
> he this? And does it perfectly too; in my conscience, he
> ne'er rehearsed it before. (I.i.57–60)

Such touches make us aware that Alsemero is going through a process of sexual development which involves profound and even baffling change ('the laws of the Medes' were supposedly immutable; cf. Daniel 6:8), in a way which is only partly conscious. He is sexually inexperienced, and afraid of sex, but also drawn to it. At the same time he is powerfully attracted to Beatrice. Jasperino, for his part, is sexually aroused by Diaphanta (I.i.89–91). De Flores, too, soon after he enters, reveals his sense that he is forced to follow Beatrice while she tries to avoid him. We can see the intensity of his sexual feeling for her well before his name is first mentioned in line 224, when Vermandero urges De Flores to pick up the glove which Beatrice has dropped.

It is at that later point that a spectator or reader is likely to begin entertaining serious intellectual suspicions that Beatrice has an unconscious sexual interest in De Flores. But Beatrice's initial reaction to him and her subsequent conversation with Alsemero already reveal more than has commonly been assumed. When Alsemero pontificates (to use Little's expression) on people's allergies, in response to Beatrice's expressed distaste for De Flores, we know he is doing this as someone attracted to her. Similarly, we know that Beatrice's strong reaction to De Flores does not merely spring from some vague 'infirmity' (108), as she avers. We are aware that De Flores is sexually drawn to her, and even at the most innocuous level it is natural for us to wonder if her loathing for him is connected with that fact. At first most of us probably think of her as finding him physically off-putting, and as not 'welcome' (98), because she does not like his sexually-based attentions. But this also means that we quite readily come to think of the language as sexually charged. It is thus not fanciful to think of Alsemero's images of roses etc. as sexual, so long as we realize that this does not mean that Alsemero *himself* is drawing attention to their sexual nature. On the contrary, the dramatists are doing this, and by implication calling attention to Alsemero's naivety. When Alsemero says that his 'poison' is a 'cherry' what matters is not so much that we try to identify very precisely just what sexual sense that word has but that we acknowledge that, in addition to its literal sense, it does have sexual connotations, and that *Alsemero is not aware of that second, sexual sense.*

In short, then, Alsemero thinks he is simply talking about a stone fruit, but in the sexually charged context of this scene, the dramatists imply, we are to see his concern with cherries as an unconscious preoccupation with sex (indeed, it would be not too inaccurate to gloss 'cherry' here as 'sex'). The further implication is that what most people find attractive is something which Alsemero has not yet come to terms with, something he as yet unconsciously resists. His unconscious difficulty with sex seems to be 'translated', so to speak, into a conscious dislike of the stone fruit that he *thinks* he is talking about. It is not that he is not consciously attracted to Beatrice; we have seen that he is. But the whole process of sexual initiation frightens him—in ways that are not wholly within the compass of his conscious mind.

The same buried anxiety seems to underlie the words with which he opens the play:

'Twas in the temple where I first beheld her,
And now again the same. What omen yet
Follows of that? (I.i.1–3)

Later, when Alsemero discovers Beatrice's evil, he says: ''Twas in my fears at first' (V.iii.76). We might think that he means there that *she* (i.e. the evil which he intuitively senses in her) frightened him, and that sense is not excluded, but Alsemero himself speaks of the potent impact of 'blood and beauty' which sparked off his mistaken devotion for her (V.iii.74). With hindsight, he feels that he should have listened to the intuitive voice which told him that a sexual liaison with her would harm him.

The most important line in Alsemero's speech about allergies is, we believe, 'There's scarce a thing but is both loved and loathed', which is tellingly followed by 'Myself, I must confess, have the same frailty' (I.i.124–5). From Alsemero's point of view, these lines perhaps mean: 'There is hardly anything which does not have the property of inspiring love in some people, yet, in those who are allergic to it, it may cause the opposite effect, namely loathing. I must confess that I, too, have my allergy to a particular thing'. But 'There's scarce a thing but is both loved and loathed' can have quite a different sense which, unbeknownst to Alsemero, is in fact the more revealing one, viz. 'There's scarce a thing which cannot be loved and loathed by the same person'. The frailty which Alsemero confesses to having is no doubt in that case to be taken, by the audience, as referring to his *unconscious* 'allergy' to sex, symbolized by the cherry which he loathes. Yet at a *conscious* level he loves sex: Jasperino has informed us not long before that Alsemero was kissing Beatrice 'perfectly' (I.i.59) by way of greeting, and he does not show himself sexually inhibited on his wedding night.

Alsemero also raises the possibility that a cherry may at the same time be Beatrice's 'desire' (127). This suggests (though he does not intend it to) that what *he* unconsciously loathes, i.e. sex, is what *she* unconsciously desires. And that reading of course fits the situation very exactly. Consciously, Alsemero displays sexual love towards Beatrice while unconsciously he is afraid of her, or at least of her sexual impact. With Beatrice's feelings for De Flores matters are the other way round. Again, sex is 'both loved and loathed'. She loathes De Flores at a conscious level, as her speeches in this scene have made very plain. But unconsciously she desires her cherry. Consciously, she says in response to Alsemero:

> I am no enemy to any creature
> My memory has but yon gentleman. (128–9)

In other words, on the surface De Flores is her 'poison'. She consciously resists his impact, but unconsciously she is drawn to him as though to a 'cherry'. The strength of his appeal is the greater precisely because it *is* unconscious: in Freudian terms, she 'represses' it, but it cannot go away, and overwhelms her with the more force. As she does not understand its nature, it continues to harm her even after she and De Flores embark on a sexual relationship. Her misunderstanding of her feelings for him is all too pathetically plain quite late in the play when she says of De Flores: 'His face loathes one, / But look upon his care, who would not love him?' (V.i.70–1). The idea that she loves him because of his 'care' seems like a pure rationalization.

'There's scarce a thing but is both loved and loathed'. That ringing, alliterative phrase, 'loved and loathed', touches on the familiar notion that love and hate are intimately related and even interchangeable. Beatrice and Alsemero think, wrongly, of love and loathing as two quite distinct feelings. The dramatists, however, draw attention to the connection between the two, and delineate that connection as something that we moderns would describe in Freudian terms: while the one feeling is in the conscious mind, its connected opposite is in the unconscious. And it is the resulting tension which so much of the play presents and explores with rare power and insight.

Source: Joost Daalder and Antony Telford Moore, "There's Scarce a Thing But Is Both Loved and Loathed': *The Changeling*," in *English Studies*, Vol. 80, No. 6, December 1999, pp. 499–508.

Lisa Hopkins

In the following essay, Hopkins explores the "dynamics of gender and power relations" in The Changeling.

When Beatrice-Joanna opens the closet of her new husband, Alsemero, she is appalled to discover that it contains a pregnancy test. She immediately plans her strategy for outwitting him:

> None of that water comes into my belly:
> I'll know you from a hundred. I could break you
>   now,
> Or turn you into milk, and so beguile
> The master of the mystery, but I'll look to you.

These lines perform a swift and probing exposure of the dynamics of gender and power relations in *The Changeling*. Alsemero presumably imagines that his scientific experiments will offer him full access to the hidden secrets of women's bodies. In terms of Renaissance fears about female sexuality, this would surely represent a powerfully attractive fantasy to the audience of the play. All the men in this play seek, as Cristina Malcolmson among others has shown, to exercise a highly repressive control over the actions of women; but while men like Alibius must suffer in a constant state of uncertainty about their wives' chastity, Alsemero believes himself to have to hand the infallible means of prying into the last secret of women and, consequently, exercising over them a control that is utterly unchallengeable. Ironically, he secretes the mechanism of this ostensible tool of control in his "closet," traditionally, as evidenced by the titles of such cookery books as *A Closet for Ladies and Gentlewomen* and *The Good Huswifes Closet,* a space demarcated for the exclusive use of women, and one, moreover, associated with the domestic skill of food preparation, to which Alsemero's own "concoctions" are thus paralleled, his invasion of the feminine space of the closet and his parody of the female-dominated process of cooking tellingly imaging his intended probing of the elusive internal secrets of the female body.

Beatrice's discovery of the closet, however, strikes a fundamental blow at the position of superiority into which Alsemero is confident that he has maneuvered himself. It is one of the scene's most telling structural ironies that before her discovery of the actual *means* of Alsemero's bid for omniscience, Beatrice was already firmly convinced that he *was* omniscient:

> Never was bride so fearfully distressed.
> The more I think upon th'ensuing night,
> And whom I am to cope with in embraces—
> One who's ennobled both in blood and mind,
> So clear in understanding (that's my plague now),
> Before whose judgement will my fault appear
> Like malefactors' crimes before tribunals
> (There is no hiding on't)—the more I dive
> Into my own distress.
>
> (4.2.1–10)

Beatrice's faith in Alsemero's "understanding" and "judgement" is absolute, leading her to subscribe to the myth that a man can detect the presence or absence of a hymen. But it is not in these physical terms that she envisages the processes of her detection: her language instead clusters round the metaphorical, the nonspecific, and the abstract—"ennobled," "clear in understanding," "judgement," "fault," "malefactors' crimes." Mechanics and specifics have no place here; within the transparency of the soliloquy, where Beatrice-Joanna's own mental processes are laid bare to us, she herself imagines a transparent world, where a phenomenology of "clarity" and "appearance" lays bare all crime to a detached surveillance. There is no personal dynamic encoded within her talk of "whom," "one who's ennobled," and "tribunals"; she figures instead an impersonal authority manifested in an appraising eye. She offers no theory of the mechanism of disclosure; although she is a daughter of the citadel, within which are "secrets" (1.1.164), it seems that she cannot, here, conceive of any process by which secrecy may be maintained.

All this changes when she herself performs precisely the act of laying bare that she imaginatively attributes to others, and when, in so doing, she becomes aware of the particular structures conditioning the epistemotogical power-relations that have been previously mystified for her. The rifling of Alsemero's closet becomes a means whereby she can read, preemptively, his own reading of her. Rather than relying on the innate and impersonal "judgement" with which she had so Foucauldianly credited him, Alsemero's superior knowledge and power need in fact to be maintained by the most artificial of helps. Moreover, the tools of his mastery are not exclusive to him. Much is made in this play of exclusivity of possession, particularly in Alibius's obsessive attitude to Isabella; what we see here is precisely that, as in the case of Alonzo de Piracquo's ringed finger, demarcators perceived as essential to the maintenance of male identity can with the greatest of ease be transferred to others, whom they empower. Once she has understood this, Beatrice-Joanna can indeed proceed to "beguile / The master of the mystery" (4.1.37–38).

The means by which she does so are telling, for she has learned her lesson well. Her words chart a complete transformation from the abstractions that had earlier characterized her figuring of the processes of knowledge acquisition; she begins instead to pay precise attention to detail, having now understood that it is the medium of information transfer that conditions the message. The pregnancy test consists of "two spoonfuls of the white water in glass C." To forestall it, Beatrice-Joanna decides that she has essentially two options: "I could break you now, / Or turn you into milk" (4.1.36–37). The idea of turning the water into milk is presumably suggested to her by the fact that the water is white, but it is, in the context, in its turn suggestive of other aspects of the situation, and in particular the fundamental association of milk with pregnancy. The presence of milk in the breasts is at once often one

of the early signs of pregnancy and also provided a standard test to which a woman suspected of having recently given birth could be subjected. Beatrice-Joanna's mention of milk in this connection, then, represents a deliberate subversion of the processes of gynecological inspection designed to ensure male control of female sexuality. She will deprive the master of the mystery by a mystery of her own, the inscrutable processes of pregnancy and lactation, and the female body will successfully mystify the scrutiny of the male eye. Interestingly, Cristina Malcolmson's account of the play links its fear of Spanish infiltration in general with a particular fear of a particular woman, the Spanish Infanta, as a mother, or at least as the mother of the future king of England: relating the play to the Puritan opposition to the proposed marriage of Prince Charles to the Infanta, she points out that "the marriage negotiations largely focused on the number of Catholics that would be associated with the nursery, and the number of years that the prince would be under his mother's influence."

Ironically, of course, this particular plan of evasion is never put into action, for Beatrice-Joanna herself does not yet know whether or not she is pregnant, and so whether or not this is necessary; moreover, the rapidity of the play's narrative momentum means that even at the time of her death, the state of her womb will remain a mystery to herself and the audience alike. But what she discovers next makes the pregnancy test redundant:

> Ha! That which is next is ten times worse;
> "How to know whether a woman be a maid or not."
> If that should be applied, what would become of me?
>
> (4.1.39–41)

Here at least Beatrice-Joanna is sure of the truth, and she knows that Alsemero must not know it. This test, unlike the pregnancy one, comes equipped with a full scientific pedigree—"the author Antonius Mizaldus" (4.1.44–45)—but, as Middleton surely knew and as Shakespeare certainly indicated in Hamlet's warnings to the players, the intentions of the *author* are always vulnerable to those of the *actor*. Beatrice-Joanna can frustrate Alsemero's processes of inquisition here too, but this time it will be through performance.

The notion of performance is one that often figures prominently in Middleton's tragic dramaturgy. *The Revenger's Tragedy* and *Women Beware Women* both culminate in elaborately ironic masques of death that, in the latter case at least, are pointedly at odds with the representational aesthetics prevalent in the bulk of the play: the "realist" setting of the widow's house forms an unlikely preparation for the spectacular court finale, with its mesh of tightly interlocking plot and counterplot, while in *The Revenger's Tragedy* the theatricalization of the closing scene stylizes and attenuates the force of the moral point. In *The Changeling,* performance becomes openly equated with the immoral mendacity castigated by Puritan opposition to theater when Beatrice-Joanna first vicariously rehearses and then personally enacts a staging of virginity—in itself, ironically, a state guaranteed precisely by an *absence* of performance—which completely deceives her audience, Alsemero.

The performance of virginity here would, to a Jacobean audience, undoubtedly have been strongly reminiscent of the allegedly similar method employed in the divorce case of Frances Howard, daughter of the earl of Suffolk, and her first husband, Robert Devereux, second earl of Essex (son of Queen Elizabeth's favorite). Middleton's reworking of the story of Frances Howard both here and in his play *The Witch* has often been remarked; I want to focus particularly, though, on his use not only of specific motifs and actions but on the processes of dramatization that he both employs and represents in relation to the Howard divorce case. (As the later trial of Frances and her second husband had revealed, the events surrounding the divorce had themselves been conceived of by those involved as highly theatrical in character, with correspondence using code names for the principal participants and with the Lieutenant of the Tower referring to Frances's lover as "so great an actor in this sta[g]e.") Frances Howard's campaign to have her marriage annulled had in itself involved careful presenting and indeed staging of the evidence. Her initial petition was very anxious to represent her as frustrated by the impotence of her husband only because she wished to "be made a mother," rather than because of any specifically sexual desires; when it came to establishing her virginity, she set up an elaborate scene in which a heavily veiled woman who was widely believed to be a substitute was examined, as Diaphanta fears to be, by a female jury. Performing the self continued to feature strongly in Frances Howard's behavior when two years after her annulment had been granted and she had been married for a second time to Robert Carr, earl of Somerset, she was tried for the murder of Carr's friend, Sir Thomas Overbury. Decoratively dressed and weeping prettily, she succeeded in winning hearts at her trial in the most unpromising of circumstances: Lady Anne Clifford commented in her diary that "my Lady Somerset was arraigned & condemned at Westminster hall where she confessed her fault and asked the King's Mercy, & was much pitied by all beholders." The king spared her life and indeed released her from the Tower shortly before Middleton and Rowley wrote their play.

That Diaphanta's reference to a female jury and the staging of the virginity test clearly allude to the Frances Howard story has, then, been established. There are, however, two other references to the history of Frances Howard in the play that both relate closely to the performative element of Beatrice-Joanna's response to the discovery of the virginity test. The first time that we see Beatrice-Joanna and De Flores together, she drops a glove, which De Flores retrieves for her. She rejects the returned glove angrily:

Mischief on your officious forwardness!
Who bade you stoop? They touch my hand no
     more:
There, for t'other's sake I part with this—
(*Takes off and throws down the other glove*)
Take 'em and draw off thine own skin with 'em.
                                                    (1.1.225–28)

The episode, apparently Middleton's invention, seems to rework an occasion when Frances Howard, who may well have been angling to catch the attention of Prince Henry, is said to have dropped a glove, which the prince declined to take up on the crudely pointed grounds that it had been "stretcht by another." The prince's use of sexual symbolism here is certainly similar to De Flores's suggestive delight at the thought that he "should thrust my fingers / Into her sockets here" (1.1.231–32); moreover, there is, arguably, a possible parallel with the celebrated episode of the countess of Salisbury's garter, and a telling contrast between the lubricity of the Jacobean interpretations and the pure-mindedness of Edward

III's famous dictum "Honi soit qui mal y pense." In Middleton's retelling, though, the roles of the participants are dramatically reversed to make the Frances Howard figure not the recipient but the inflicter of the insult. If we see this as an allusion to Prince Henry, in short, we must recognize that Beatrice-Joanna has here too beguiled the master of the mystery by using his own weapons against him.

The other occasion in which the past of the real Frances Howard becomes reworked in that of the fictional Beatrice-Joanna seems not to have been previously noticed, but is even more pointedly, and literally, dramatic. Immediately before his defloration of Beatrice-Joanna, De Flores comments:

> 'Las, how the turtle pants! Thou'lt love anon
> What thou so fear'st and faint'st to venture on.
> (3.4.169–70)

Here he echoes very closely the Epithalamion of *Hymenaei,* the masque written by Jonson for Frances Howard's first marriage, to the earl of Essex:

> Shrink not, soft virgin, you will love
> Anon what you so fear to prove.

Middleton is very likely to have been aware of Jonson's wedding poetry for Frances Howard, because he himself had been the author of the now lost *Masque of Cupid,* performed as part of the celebrations of Frances Howard's second marriage, to the earl of Somerset. Jonson too was involved once more: his *A Challenge at Tilt* and *The Irish Masque* formed part of the entertainment. Since *A Challenge at Tilt* was spoken by two Cupids, there may well have been enough thematic overlap between this and Middleton's Cupid-based masque to necessitate at least some degree of cooperation in ensuring programmatic continuity. Moreover, the passage in *Hymenaei* in which Truth and Opinion debate the relative merits of marriage and virginity may be seen as ironically paralleled in the exchange between the wife and supposed virgin, Beatrice-Joanna, and the maid, Diaphanta, who is so anxious to be rid of her virginity.

David Lindley has recently speculated at some length on the poets' feelings at discovering that they had, in effect, been inveigled into composing epithalamia for a wedding based on a web of deceit and murder. In Jonson's case, his situation may well have been particularly uncomfortable, since he had provided offerings for both the Countess's marriages; he would therefore surely have been struck even at the time of the second wedding by some element at least of incongruity in this second feting of a ritual that had proved so ill-fated the first

time round. Nevertheless, Lindley has argued strongly that the writers of praise poems for the second marriage need not necessarily have had to grit their teeth quite so much as we, with the benefit of hindsight, might imagine:

> a lack of scrupulousness about the precise awareness that poets like Donne might be supposed to have had can fatally colour everything that follows. Since almost all critics also assume that an adulterous relationship between the couple was public knowledge in 1613, they are compelled to the position that the poets must have chosen to shut their ears and avert their moral gaze in order to praise Frances Howard. Since most critics have an investment in the defence of their authors' integrity they then search for the criticism that must, somehow, be present in the texts.

He argues that the wedding was arranged in such haste that practical considerations would probably have been more pressing than ideological ones, particularly in the case of Middleton himself, "if Chamberlain's assertion that they only had 'fowre dayes warning' be credited. It must have been an 'off-the-peg' piece, and can scarcely have had much verbal material—one reason perhaps, why it has not survived." Nevertheless, when the poets later came to hear all the sordid details of the Overbury murder, and to see that the Countess's demeanor in the witness stand apparently excused her from the penalties applied to her subordinates and assistants, they may well have felt that their services had been procured under false pretences, and that Frances Howard had, indeed, beguiled the masters of their mystery.

Middleton's rewriting of her story certainly seems to take a revenge on her, and, moreover, a peculiarly literary one. When Alsemero finally perceives her falsehood, he offers, at the same time, an ironic recognition of the cleverness with which she has deceived him: "You read me well enough. I am not well" (5.3.16). Beatrice at first attempts to face it out, and discovering that Alsermero suspects that Diaphanta was implicated, demands "Is your witness dead then?" (5.3.57) (interestingly, the Countess of Somerset's sorcerer, Simon Forman, had died before her case came to trial, but his name was nevertheless much used in the evidence against her, after searches of his house and interrogations of his widow). Finally, she attempts to clear herself by admitting what she clearly sees as the less damaging part of the truth: she confesses the murder of Piracquo, but continues to deny adultery, revealing the extent to which she has internalized her society's ideological fetishization of female chastity at the apparent expense of all else. In reply, Alsemero imprisons her, fittingly enough, in the very closet that she has violated; by the time she emerges from it, she is mortally wounded, and makes, finally, a full and free confession.

In this, she differs strikingly from the attitudes of many other Jacobean stage villains. Iago refuses explanation to the last:

> Demand me nothing; what you know, you know:
> From this time forth I never will speak word.

Hieronimo in *The Spanish Tragedy,* despite having been already quite forthcoming, goes to the lengths of biting out his own tongue rather than provide further information, though what else remains him for him to tell is unclear; Vittoria in *The White Devil* offers splendid defiance to the tribunal of her accusers. Beatrice-Joanna, however, adopts a position of unmitigated repentance and self-abnegation, and, in what was presumably a pointed contrast with the behavior of the Countess of Someset, regards herself as unworthy of any mercy. Just as the outset of her closet scene soliloquy saw her fully interpellated into a position of ideological subjugation in which her image of herself was as a helpless and transparent prey of a culture of ceaseless surveillance, so she has now come again to internalize her husband's, her father's, and ever her lover's assumptions about her own status as whore and villainess. The brief moment of freedom in which *her* preemptive reading of *him* had rendered her opaque has been lost; she has resumed her designated position as the objectified other of demonization. Middleton, in short, has, by his staging of Beatrice-Joanna, returned the mystery to the master, reversing the perceived injustice of the Countess of Somerset's pardon by insisting on the full exaction of the processes of the law on her dramatic representative. Beatrice-Joanna and Frances Howard may each have been able to produce a substitute to beguile the master of the mystery of their own virginity tests, but Middleton regains the upper hand by his own dramatic substitution of the publicly chastised Beatrice-Joanna for the recently released Countess.

In doing so, the weapons he deploys against the figure of Frances Howard are derived precisely from the same species of theatricality as animated her own performances of herself (whether vicarious or personal) as virgin and as penitent. Had his *Masque of Cupid* survived, it would be fascinating to see whether he drew on its motifs, but the close parallel with the Jonson Epithalamion certainly suggests a reappropriation of dramatic material that had been previously "misused" in the service of the Howard/Somerset wedding. In many ways,

The Changeling is in fact careful to present itself as a reworking of other plays. Cristina Malcolmson has remarked on its many affiliations with *Twelfth Night* (itself perhaps staged as a part of the celebration of a wedding), and Joost Daalder points to Vermandero's echoing of *Doctor Faustus* when he says of Hell, "We are all there; it circumscribes [us] here." Even more pointedly, *The Changeling* recasts many motifs and moments found in Middleton's own *Hengist, King of Kent,* written two or three years earlier. Both plays are lavish in the use of the dumb show; both revolve round a licentious woman (Beatrice-Joanna, Roxena) believed to be virtuous, and a chaste one (Isabella, Castiza) mistreated by an unworthy husband; the role taken by Horsus, secret lover of Roxena, in planning villainies is not dissimilar to that of De Flores. Moreover, *Hengist* too has an overriding concern with chastity. The play opens in the reign of a king, Constantius, who has (most unusually for a male character in Jacobean drama) vowed perpetual chastity because of his strongly Catholic religious beliefs, and who persuades Castiza, the woman he is forced to marry, to take a similar resolve. Much is made of the religious angle—at one point Constantius wishes to fast because it is the eve of St. Agatha (1.2.216–20), and Vortiger resists the incoming Saxons on the grounds that "y'are strangers in religion Cheifly" (2.3.34). At one point, chastity is associated both with Catholicism and with the image of the closet:

> *Hers.* Faire is shee and most fortunate may shee
>   bee
> But in maide lost for ever, my desire
> Hath beene ye Close Confusion of that name
> A treasure tis, able to make more theeues
> Then Cabinetts set open to entice . . .
> . . .
> *Heng.* Mary pray help my memory if I should
>   (2.3.160–68)

To prevent the detection of this loss of her chastity, Roxena spontaneously offers herself for an onstage virginity test: when Horsus falls down with grief at hearing that Vortiger desires her, she declares:

> Oh tis his Epilepsie, I know it well,
> I holp him once in Germany, Comst agen?
> A virgins right hand stroakt upon his heart
> Giues him ease streight But tmust be a pure virgin
> Or ells it brings no Comfort
>   (2.3.249–53)

At first Horsus threatens to shame her by refusing to cooperate; eventually, however, she persuades him that she has a plan, and he is duly "cured." Throughout this scene, it is Roxena who takes the lead, as is emphasized in the parodic visual image of the man, instead of the woman, "falling backwards." (There is also further ironic play on this motif when Castiza, who has been raped by her husband in disguise, refuses to swear onstage that she is chaste.) When Middleton reworks this scene in *The Changeling,* the comparison with *Hengist* works to ensure that although Beatrice too may seem, as Roxena was, in control, our awareness of the metatheatrical ancestry of the episode serves to stress that, however much greater her knowledge may be than that of Alsemero, she is merely a puppet of the omniscient author.

In making this play so pointedly and consistently a re-presentation of events and speeches already alternatively presented, then, Middleton is doubly able to offer a reformation of homosocial bonding after disruption by threatening women, not only in the father-son and brother-brother relationship sealed between Alsemero and Vermandero and Alsemero and Tomazo over the dead body of Beatrice-Joanna, but also in the links that bind Middleton and Rowley themselves with Marlowe, Shakespeare, and Jonson in a controlled demonstration of mastery over the mysteries of performance that women's efforts at fallacious self-staging had attempted to beguile. Metatheatricality is thus made the crucial tool for the undermining of Beatrice-Joanna's own too-potent theatricality.

For the puritan in Middleton, the idea of performance securing and enacting its own punishment must have been an appealingly ironic one. His characteristic tragic strategy is indeed to involve his characters in fantastically complex self-staging situations in which their deaths are ironically brought about in ways that frustrate their performance intentions, as with the double masque of revengers at the end of *The Revenger's Tragedy* or the plotting and counterplotting of the closing scene of *Women Beware Women.* In each of these instances, those who attempt to wrest control of the script are brutally punished by the workings of a deeper plot of whose existence they have no inkling: the revenger's tragedy is in one sense at least precisely the revenge of the dramatist, and of metatheatrical conventions invisible to the intratheatrical character. The falsity that in Puritan ideology inheres in all acting is aptly countered by an aesthetic that punishes precisely the performative nature of the theatrical self, while at the same time ironically heightening the theatrical pleasure of the *audience* by its sophisticated self-referentiality. *The Changeling,* with its extravagantly theatrical deployment of a Webster-like antimasque of madmen and of the

consciously archaic form of the dumb show, partakes here of the same aesthetic of self-reflexivity as characterizes Middleton's habitual use of tragic form, and makes his reinscription of Beatrice-Joanna into the cultural norms she has challenged so much the more overt an act of deployment of the most privileged forms of that culture. Ultimately, then, it is the mastery who retains the mystery.

Source: Lisa Hopkins, "Beguiling the Master of the Mystery: Form and Power in *The Changeling,*" in *Medieval and Renaissance Drama in England,* Vol. 9, edited by John Pitcher, Associated University Presses, 1997, pp. 149–61.

Norman A. Brittin

In the following essay excerpt, Brittin comments on sources for The Changeling *and Middleton's collaboration with Rowley and places the play within the context of Middleton's tragedies.*

The greatest dramatic achievement of Middleton and Rowley, *The Changeling,* a tragedy licensed for acting on May 7, 1622, has its sources in new works that the authors had read not long before composing their play. The most important source is *The Triumphs of Gods Revenge against the Crying and Execrable Sinne of Willful and Premeditated Murther* by John Reynolds, a collection of exceedingly moralistic stories published after June 7, 1621. Reynolds tells his stories clumsily, for he is intent only on communicating the moral that murder cannot be hidden but that it will always be revealed and God's justice eventually accomplished. The authors recognized possibilities for a tragedy in History IV of Reynolds's Book I, a heavy-handed account of love, murder, and adultery in Spain which provides the framework for the main plot. To this story was welded material from Leonard Digges's *Gerardo the Unfortunate Spaniard,* a translation of a Spanish romance licensed for printing March 11, 1622. *The Changeling* also has a subplot, for which no exact source has been identified although a part resembles the pursuit of Rebecca Purge by two gallants in Middleton's early *The Family of Love.*

One imagines that Middleton and Rowley planned carefully in the spring of 1622 how to put dramatic life into their tragedy and that they then composed it in a fever of inspiration that finally resulted in this brilliant climax of their collaboration. The play was first acted by the Lady Elizabeth's Men at the *Phoenix;* and it received the honor on January 4, 1624, of a court performance. It was popular until the closing of the theaters in 1642, and it was revived after the Restoration. Audiences

> IN BOTH OF MIDDLETON'S
> GREAT TRAGEDIES, THE
> BLINDNESS OF THE PROTAGONISTS
> IS THE SALIENT THEME. THE
> GOOD CHARACTERS ARE BLIND TO
> EVIL; THE BAD CHARACTERS,
> BLIND TO GOOD; AND ALL OF
> THEM STUMBLE INTO FATAL
> SITUATIONS."

especially enjoyed the comic figure of the Changeling (Antonio) in the subplot.

The Changeling is a product of close collaboration; whichever author was holding the pen, the effects in all parts were carefully devised. Nevertheless, the study of the internal evidence in the text reveals a clear division of the shares of the two authors. Rowley wrote acts I; III.iii; IV.iii; and V.iii. Middleton wrote acts II; III.i,ii,iv; IV.i,ii; and V.i,ii. Middleton handled most of the main plot; Rowley, practically all of the subplot. But Rowley opened the play with the main plot and brought both plots to a close in the last scene. This division of the writing is evidenced by differences of verbal habits, of versification, and of characterization. Middleton's fancy for the interjection "Push," for certain abstract terms, and for potent irony; his interest in such character types as the heroine and villain of the main plot; and his flexible blank verse with many feminine endings—all stand in contrast to Rowley's liking for puns, his use of a latinized vocabulary, his clumsy blank verse, and his interest in creating humorous clown characters such as Lollio and Antonio of the subplot.

As the play opens, Alsemero, a young Valencian, delays his departure from Alicant for Malta because he has fallen in love for the first time in his life. He is infatuated with a beautiful girl he has seen in the church—a meeting place he regards as a good omen. She is Beatrice-Joanna, daughter of Vermandero, commander of the castle. After a kiss or two, a little gallantry, and some love talk, she regrets that Alsemero has appeared too late—only five days after her father has contracted her to

Alonzo de Piracquo. Alsemero is invited to visit Vermandero's castle. Brushing aside his daughter's demurrer over marrying within a week, her father relishes the thought of having Piracquo for son-in-law: "I'll want/My will else." Her aside reveals her willful nature: "I shall want mine if you do it" (I.i.222–23).

In addition to the sudden, blazing love which has caused Beatrice to change her mind, the first scene reveals that she loathes "as a deadly poison" (I.i.114) an ugly gentleman who serves her father, De Flores. De Flores, who cannot keep away from Beatrice, is possessed by the thought of possessing her. When she drops a glove, she throws the other one down rather than take the first from De Flores. The authors stress greatly her antipathy to De Flores, who in the source is simply a young gallant. With the gloves in his hand—a lady's favor given with bitter disdain—De Flores muses:

> Here's a favour come with a mischief now! I know
> She had rather wear my pelt tann'd in a pair
> Of dancing pumps, than I should thrust my fingers
> Into her sockets here: I know she hates me,
> Yet cannot choose but love her: no matter:
> If but to vex her, I will haunt her still;
> Though I get nothing else, I'll have my will.
>   (I.i.235–40)

So Vermandero's will is for Beatrice to marry Piracquo, whereas her will is set on having Alsemero, and De Flores wills to have her himself. Also during the scene (in preparation for later plot needs) Alsemero's traveling companion Jasperino courts Beatrice's woman Diaphanta.

Alonzo de Piracquo willfully ignores the warning or his brother Tomazo that Beatrice appears not to love him. Ironically, under the circumstances, Alonzo feels a complacent "security": he cannot think that Beatrice even knows the meaning of inconstancy, "much less the use and practice" (II.i.148). He would like to marry her at once, but he agrees to a three-day postponement of the wedding.

Middleton retains from the source Beatrice's secret meeting with Alsemero and the kissing and embracing of the lovers. According to Reynolds, Beatrice tells Alsemero that "before *Piracquo* be in another world, there is no hope for *Alsemero* to injoy her for his wife in this" one. "Passion and affection blinding his judgment, and beautie triumphing and giving a law to his Conscience," Alsemero says that "hee will shortly send him a Challenge, and fight with him . . ." But the girl does not want Alsemero to hazard his life. The situation is the same in the play: Beatrice fears to lose

Alsemero by the sword or by the law; but "Blood-guiltiness becomes a fouler visage . . ." (II.ii.40).

At this point in the play (the incident is not in the source), she thinks of the sinister ugliness of De Flores. De Flores himself has said that she treats him "as if danger or ill luck hung in my looks" (II.i.36). She feels harm and danger coming toward her every time she sees him. His presence exasperates her, infuriates her—until she suddenly changes her manner, having decided to buy at "so good a market" (II.ii.42). This change is the more ironic because, not long before, she had abased him and thought of wheedling her father into dismissing him.

Middleton greatly speeds up Reynolds' leisurely narrative, for De Flores appears immediately after Alsemero's departure. He has spied on their meeting, hoping that, if Beatrice should prove false with Alsemero, her defection with himself will be more likely. (He has much the spirit of Horsus in *The Mayor of Queenborough*.) When Beatrice, making a show of interest in him, promises to treat his loath-some pimples and even touches his face with her own hand, he is enraptured. He soon learns that she needs the service of a resolute man to kill Alonzo. All the while he is thinking of her body: Middleton has him parody her words with coarse innuendos on "creation," "makes me man," "service," "mounts," and "act" (II.ii.92–133). When De Flores understands that she desires Alonzo's death, he knows at once that he will gain his reward, his desire: "it will be precious; the thought ravishes!" (II.ii.133)

Middleton's irony is pervasive. Beatrice, willing to pay well and assuming that De Flores will leave the country, blinds herself to realities; her complacency produces strong dramatic irony as she congratulates herself that she will be rid "Of two inveterate loathings at one time . . ." (II.ii.147). Middleton condenses the action by having Alonzo request De Flores to show him the fortifications of the castle. As they traverse the passages and vaults, they talk of the wonders of the fort; and De Flores' speeches drip of irony: "All this is nothing; you shall see anon/A place you little dream on" (III.ii.1–2). Then De Flores treacherously kills him and cuts off a finger to get a diamond ring that will prove he has done the job.

Beatrice, meanwhile, commends herself for judgment and wisdom: "I've got him [Alsemero] now the liberty of the house;/So wisdom, by degrees, works out her freedom . . ." (III.iv.12–13). Dramatic irony soon reveals how fatuous the girl is; she is not working out her freedom but her bondage; and her "wisdom" is truly folly. She perceives her

true situation during her conversation with De Flores, who immediately enters to report. Their interview is one of the greatest scenes in all drama.

Tears of joy spring to her eyes when she hears the favorable news, but she recoils when she sees Alonzo's finger: "Bless me, what hast thou *done?*" (III.iv.29). In one respect, Beatrice resembles Lady Macbeth: she has not visualized the act of murder. Murder was a way out of trouble that a clever person could arrange; she did not *see* it with eyes of realization. To De Flores her qualm seems absurd—to shudder at a finger when she has effected a murder. Scoffingly, he places the two acts in a more reasonable perspective: "I cut his heart-strings:/A greedy hand thrust in a dish at court,/In a mistake hath had as much as *this*" (III.iv.31–33 [italics added in this paragraph]).

The callousness of De Flores gives her the first hint that she is in a dirty business. The diamond on Alonzo's finger is now a token of successful murder; but it had been a love token: "'Tis the first token my father made me send him" (III.iv.34). She presents it to her agent in murder as a tip; with some pride, she assures him it is worth nearly three hundred ducats. Yet she does not intend it as the payment for his services. What began as polite fencing over his recompense quickly turns into a doubly baffling debate that disillusions each of them. Beatrice believes she is being generous in offering "three thousand golden florens;/I have not meanly thought upon thy merit" (III.iv.62–63). He has hinted that his merit is such that he scorns wages; now he is angered as he realizes that she has seen him only as a servant; and her use of "merit," contrasted to his, can be only an insult. De Flores reminds her that money cannot buy a clean conscience. He has told himself that the murder is "but light and cheap/For the sweet recompense . . ." (III.iv.19–20). Nevertheless, though he stresses conscience as overshadowing any fee and thus impresses Beatrice, he cannot escape feeling guilty; for he is stung by conscience several times in the play.

Beatrice has simply not understood what line his hints have taken; she is puzzled, alarmed, fearful: "I'd fain be rid of him. [*Aside*]/I'll double the sum, sir" (III.iv.74–75). Since the offer doubles his displeasure, she urges him to take flight—"And if thou be'st so modest not to name/The sum that will content thee, paper blushes not,/Send thy demand in writing, it shall follow thee . . ." (III.iv.79–81). It is dreadfully ironic for her to use the word "modest." He argues that he will not go without her, that as partners in guilt they belong together, and that she should kiss him "with a zeal"—grant him the intimacy that her seductive behavior in the hiring scene had hinted at. There is additional irony in the term "forgetful" when she warns him that he is forgetting not only his place but also the risk that familiarity will expose them to. He insists that she is being forgetful, reminding her of her indebtedness: "I have eas'd you/Of your trouble, think on it; I am in pain,/And must be eas'd of you ..." (III.iv.99–100). This statement brings her to half-realization of what her accomplice desires but she attempts to thrust the recognition away, feeling his desire too great an affront to be borne: "I would not hear so much offence again/For such another deed"—upon which, he reminds her that "the last is not yet paid for ..." (III.iv.106–7).

Then he tells her exactly what he expects. Her horror is such that still she does not fully understand her situation:

Why, 'tis impossible thou canst be so wicked,
Or shelter such a cunning cruelty,
To make his death the murderer of my honour!
Thy language is so bold and vicious,
I cannot see which way I can forgive it
With any modesty. (III.iv.121–126)

"'Tis impossible ... I cannot see ..." Her lack of realization, her blindness, produces the most cutting irony. For De Flores gives her the wonderful retort: "Push, you forget yourself;/A woman dipp'd in blood, and talk of modesty!" With this repetition of "forget" and "modesty" Middleton achieves a tremendous irony of anticlimax.

Beatrice now regrets the hasty decision that led her to conspire with De Flores, and her feeling is expressed in one of Middleton's most telling metaphors: "O misery of sin! would I had been bound/Perpetually unto my living hate/In that Piracquo, than to hear these words!" She seeks refuge, however, in the conventions of the social system: "Think but upon the distance that creation/Set 'twixt thy blood and mine, and keep thee there" (III.iv.131–32). Her "there" means away, at a distance, apart; but De Flores finds a new position for "there": "Look but into your conscience, read me there." They are equals in conscience, for she is no more than what murder has made her: "settle you/In what the act has made you; you're no more now .../You are the deed's creature ..." (III.iv.132–37).

His next statement brings home to her the new truth of her condition: "peace and innocency has turn'd you out/And made you one with me." So she has been turned morally out of doors, to be an outlaw, a criminal—for she is basically a wild creature, an outlaw—and one dependent on others' favors; in fact, she is dependent on his favors and his will. He had earlier asserted that he would have his will.

Her "foul villain!" is echoed mockingly by his "fair murderess" (III.iv.141–42). He taunts her with changing her affection—"a kind of whoredom in the heart; and he's chang'd now/To bring thy second on. ..." Here is more irony; for Alonzo is certainly changed. De Flores issues his ultimatum: unless she surrenders to him, she will never enjoy Alsemero: "I'll confess all; my life I rate at nothing" (III.iv.150). Her reply "De Flores!" is a fine touch revealing her deflation! It prepares for her counterproposal, which she states while kneeling and weeping: all the wealth she possesses. Now she has been stripped of all pretension, she voices her thrilling appeal: "Let me go poor unto my bed with honour,/And I am rich in all things!" De Flores puts her to silence; he values his pleasure above "the wealth of all Valencia." Then comes the ultimate blow that forces surrender: "Can you weep Fate from its determin'd purpose?/So soon may you weep me" (III.iv.162–63).

De Flores had knelt to her earlier, begging her to let him be of service, and now she has knelt to him, imploring mercy. Her fate she sees as vengeance for the murder, and she fears she has been cursed from conception to "engender with a viper first" (III.iv.166). As they leave, De Flores voices their epithalamium: "thou'lt love anon/What thou so fear'st and faint'st to venture on" (III.iv.170–71). This scene, with its magnificent dramatic poetry, some of which T. S. Eliot placed on a par with that of Shakespeare or Sophocles, is the highest point of Middleton's tragic dramas.

Act IV opens with a dumb show (one is reminded again of *The Mayor of Queenborough*) which quickly pantomimes concern over Piracquo's disappearance, Vermandero's choosing of Alsemero as husband for his daughter, and the wedding of Beatrice and Alsemero. As De Flores smiles at the way events have developed, Alonzo's ghost appears to him, showing the hand which lacks one finger. The appearance of the ghost is a reminder to De Flores' conscience and a projection of his secret thoughts; for De Flores cannot get away from the *deed* of murder. When he is greeted as a friend of Alonzo's by Tomazo de Piracquo, he says in an aside: "Methinks I'm now again a-killing on him,/He brings it so fresh to me"; and "His company even overlays my conscience" (IV.ii.45–46, 57). Tomazo ironically thinks him honest and helpful: "He'll bring it out in time, I'm assured on't" (IV.ii.59), but he later feels infected by the presence of De Flores and strikes him. De Flores cannot strike back, being inhibited by his sense of guilt; and he also acknowledges the rightness of Tomazo's subtle instinct. Just before De Flores and Beatrice perpetrate their second murder, the ghost again appears, causing alarm and fear in Beatrice and making De Flores speak of "a mist of conscience" (V.i.60). Middleton thus enforces upon his audience the moral order of the world.

Beatrice is now married to the man she desires; but, confronting her wedding night, she fears that Alsemero may discover the truth about her, because her husband, she says, is "So clear in understanding, . . ./Before whose judgment will my fault appear/Like malefactors' crimes before tribunals . . ." (IV.i.6–8). She is right to fear; for, as Miss Bradbrook indicates, Alsemero's "will does not overpower his judgment." Finding that Alsemero has a book with a description of a virginity test and suspecting that he will give it to her, she memorizes certain responses to ensure her passing it. But to make doubly sure, she bribes her woman Diaphanta, who passes the test satisfactorily, to take her place in the bridal bed. When Jasperino tells Alsemero that he and Diaphanta have heard Beatrice and De Flores talking intimately, suspicion leads him to give his bride the virginity test, which, of course, Beatrice passes.

Diaphanta has agreed to leave Alsemero's bed by midnight, but pleasure keeps her there. Her unreliability is fatal; Beatrice quickly resolves upon her death, and forty lines later De Flores has independently decided to kill her (V.i.5–7, 45–47). The action thus bears out Beatrice's statement: "Murder, I see, is followed by more sins" (III.iv.164). To carry out his plan, De Flores sets fire to the house. There is some element of spectacle here though not so considerable as in *Mayor*. More important for the theme of the play, Beatrice says: "I'm forc'd to love thee now,/'Cause thou provid'st so carefully for my honour" (V.i.47–48). All during the fire episode, in fact, she is emphasizing her love for the ugly De Flores. The irony of De Flores's remark about Diaphanta, "O poor virginity,/Thou has paid dearly for't" (V.i.103–4) is outdone by Beatrice's brazen insistence that her lover be rewarded for his service.

One must suppose that some time elapses between the wedding night and the final scene; but the authors hurry straight on to have Jasperino place Alsemero where he can observe that his wife and De Flores have had a meeting. In the source, Alsemero, having inexplicably become intensely jealous, taxes Beatrice with infidelity, whereupon she tells him that De Flores committed murder at her request so she could be married to Alsemero. Alsemero raises no issue regarding the murder. After her confession, Beatrice no longer troubles to conceal her scandalous behavior with De Flores, and her jealous husband surprises them together.

In *The Changeling,* Alsemero thinks that Beatrice's loathing of De Flores only masks her true feeling and that her modesty only masks her sensuality. When he throws in her face her "tender reconcilement" (V.iii.50) with De Flores and accuses her of adultery, she declares that she is no adultress but a "cruel murderess" (V. iii.66). She explains the circumstances and bids him: "Forget not, sir,/It for your sake was done" (V.iii.78–79).

Beatrice remains blind; she does not know her husband. Although Alsemero volunteered to challenge Piracquo, he is not the man to connive at her greater crime even though it was done for his sake. He is appalled at the situation he is in. De Flores corroborates Beatrice's confession and her husband's suspicion of her infidelity. "O cunning devils!" cries Alsemero. "How should blind men know you from fair-fac'd saints?" (V.iii.109–10) But the eyes of the blind are opened, and infamous truths lie visible. When her father calls to her, Beatrice responds:

O, come not near me, sir, I shall defile you!
I am that of your blood was taken from you
For your better health; look no more upon't,
But cast it to the ground regardlessly,
Let the common sewer take it from distinction.
                                        (V.iii.152–56)

Upon De Flores, she says, hung her fate. She realizes now her fatal likeness to him which for so long had made her repel him: "She instinctively feared in him that which was latent in her." She sees herself as that De Flores-evil, that defilement to others which Tomazo has sensed in De Flores as a poison and infection.

The subplot of *The Changeling* involves a January-and-May couple, old Doctor Alibius and his young wife Isabella. He is proprietor of a sanatorium for fools and madmen, where, being very jealous of his wife, he has her locked up during his absences by his man Lollio. She resents this treatment, and one might expect her to retaliate upon her husband by having her "will" and cuckolding him. She is given this opportunity by two men of the household of Vermandero, who wear disguises—Antonio as a tool and Franciscus as a madman—to gain entry to Alibius' establishment to seduce his wife. Besides this pair, Lollio also insists upon having a share of her favors should she slip. But she does not.

Isabella's situation is roughly similar to Beatrice's; the authors of the tragedy evidently desired to parallel the main plot with their subplot. Miss Bradbrook developed the idea that the subplot "acts as a kind of parallel or reflection in a different mode: their relationship is precisely that of masque and antimasque. . . ." "Antimasque" is an appropriate term to use for the grotesque comedy of Rowley's subplot; for, set on lower social level, it involves characters pretending idiocy and madness yet suffering from the madness of love which induces crime in the main plot. Although Isabella is surrounded by real and pretending madmen, she keeps sane.

The theme of appearance and reality is touched on when she disguises as a madwoman and is not recognized by her would-be lover. Various links of imagery between the two plots have been noted by commentators. The title, too, is meant to link both plots. As Holzknecht has pointed out, there is more than one changeling in the play: Antonio pretends to be a changeling, in the sense of halfwit; Beatrice is also a changeling, in the sense of a fickle person; and Diaphanta is a changeling, in the sense of a person secretly exchanged for another.

The two plots are drawn together in the last two scenes. In the rapid dénouement, the deaths of the guilty pair produce the automatic satisfaction of Tomazo's vengeance. There remain an explicit commentary on the theme of changes—Alsemero's statement (V.iii.199–206) being paralleled by those of Antonio, Franciscus, and Isabella—and, with Alsemero's resolve to be a son to Vermandero, the assurance of a return to the moral order.

In both of Middleton's great tragedies, the blindness of the protagonists is the salient theme. The good characters are blind to evil; the bad characters, blind to good; and all of them stumble into fatal situations. Both Bianca and Beatrice make discoveries about themselves, but their insight amounts to supersophistication; they become hardened and boldened, not softened and abashed; depraved, not penitent. Middleton has no illusions about sin and no help for those who embrace it. He watches their dreadful, inevitable decline and fail with merciless eyes.

Source: Norman A. Brittin, "Tragedies," in *Thomas Middleton*, Twayne Publishers, 1972, pp. 132–42.

SOURCES

Eliot, T. S., "Thomas Middleton," in *Selected Essays*, Faber, 1958, pp. 161–70.

Ellis-Fermor, Una, *Jacobean Drama: An Interpretation*, 4th ed., Vintage Books, 1961, pp. 144–49.

Farley-Hills, David, *Jacobean Drama: A Critical Study of the Professional Drama, 1600–1625*, Macmillan Press, 1988, p. 1.

Middleton, Thomas, and William Rowley, *The Changeling*, edited by Joost Daalder, A. C. Black/W. W. Norton, 1990.

Mulrayne, J. R., *Thomas Middleton*, Longman, 1979, pp. 36–45.

Ricks, Christopher, "The Moral and Poetic Structure of *The Changeling*," in *Essays in Criticism*, Vol. X, No. 3, July 1960, pp. 290–306.

Schoenbaum, Samuel, *Middleton's Tragedies: A Critical Study*, Columbia University Press, 1955, pp. 132–49.

Shakespeare, William, *As You Like It*, edited by Agnes Latham, Methuen, 1975, p. 78.

Williams, George Walton, "Introduction," in *The Changeling*, University of Nebraska Press, 1966, pp. ix–xxiv.

FURTHER READING

Bromham, A. A., and Zara Bruzzi, *"The Changeling" and the Years of Crisis, 1619–1624: A Hieroglyph of Britain*, Pinter Publishers, 1990.
    This work examines the relationship between *The Changeling* and the politics of the early seventeenth century. The play's authors see it as a warning to England against marital and political alliance with Spain.

Chakravorty, Swapan, *Society and Politics in the Plays of Thomas Middleton*, Clarendon Press, 1996, pp. 145–65.
    This chapter discusses sex, desire, power, and politics in *The Changeling*. De Flores has learned how to turn the rules of chivalry and courtly love against the rulers.

Farr, Dorothy M., *Thomas Middleton and the Drama of Realism: A Study of Some Representative Plays*, Oliver & Boyd, 1973, pp. 50–71.
    Farr analyzes the acuteness of Middleton's psychological insight, seeing the characters as victims of their capacity for evasion and self-delusion. She also discusses imagery, irony, and the relationship between the main plot and the subplot.

Holmes, David M., *The Art of Thomas Middleton: A Critical Study*, Clarendon Press, 1970, pp. 172–84.
    Holmes discusses the characterizations and relationships in the play. Beatrice and Alsemero are infatuated with each other. Beatrice is tragically ignorant of the nature of real love, and her ignorance makes her vulnerable.

Copenhagen

MICHAEL FRAYN
1998

Copenhagen, winner of the 2000 Tony Award for best play, attempts to answer the question that has been on the minds of many quantum physicists and historians from World War II: What actually took place in a secret meeting between Niels Bohr, who is considered the father of quantum physics, and Werner Heisenberg, who was working on, but failed to create, the atomic bomb for Nazi Germany? The meeting took place in 1941. Heisenberg had been a student of Bohr's. The two scientists had collaborated and brought forth the basic tenets that would become the foundation of quantum physics. Heisenberg was a German; Bohr was a Jew who was residing in Copenhagen, Denmark. The meeting took place while Denmark was occupied by the Nazis. Bohr's house was wiretapped, so when Heisenberg appeared at Bohr's doorstep, the two men took a walk so that no one could record their conversation. All that was publicly known was that after the meeting, Bohr would have nothing to do with Heisenberg.

The play does not provide a clear answer to the question of what took place during that meeting. It does, however, provide a lot of background information about these two powerful thinkers and the struggles they must have encountered in their attempt to honor their friendship during extremely turbulent, even life-threatening, circumstances. Both scientists were capable of figuring out how to create an atomic bomb. Bohr would eventually help the U.S. forces and he was instrumental in the creation of the atomic bombs that were dropped on the

Michael Frayn Photo by Brad Rickerby. © Reuters NewMedia Inc./Corbis

Japanese cities of Hiroshima and Nagasaki. But what happened to Heisenberg? Did he deliberately confound the Nazi efforts to create a similar weapon? Or did he attempt to create it but fail? Frayn leaves these overarching questions for the audience to ponder.

Margrethe Bohr is another character in this play. She was, in real life, an intelligent woman and a supporter of her husband. Although she did not have a science education like her husband, she typed all his research papers and was a strong sounding board for his theories. In the play, it is to Margrethe that the two men direct their discussion. They attempt, for her sake (and the sake of any nonscientific audience members), to translate their technological information into a language that everyone can understand. Margrethe also acts as a mediator and as a truth monitor. She makes the men look deeper into their actions, and insists that they shun personal emotion and get to the root of what is really going on between them.

Copenhagen opened on May 28, 1998, in London, at the Cottesloe Theatre. Two years later, it made its U. S. premiere at New York's Royale Theatre, on March 23, 2000. Since then, it has traveled around the world, receiving overwhelmingly high praise as a dramatic piece.

AUTHOR BIOGRAPHY

Frayn was born September 8, 1933, in London. His mother died when he was twelve, whereupon his father transferred him from an exclusive private school to a public school for financial reasons. He was later educated at Emmanuel College, Cambridge, where he studied philosophy. By age twenty-four, he was working at the British newspaper, the *Guardian*, as a reporter and columnist, and then moved to the London *Observer*. He is a prolific writer, mostly known as a playwright and novelist, who has more than a dozen novels and twenty-plus plays to his name. He has also written numerous scripts for television and film, and has translated many of Anton Chekhov's plays from Russian into English.

Since the 1960s, Frayn has won many awards for his work, including, to name just a few: the Somerset Maugham Award for *The Tin Men* (1965); the London *Evening Standard* Best Comedy of the Year Award, and the Society of West End Theatre Award for best comedy of the year for *Noises Off* (1982); the Antoinette Perry Award for best play and the Tony Award for best play for *Copenhagen* (2000); the Society of West End Theatre Award for best play of the year, Laurence Olivier Award for best play, *Plays and Players* Award for best new play, and New York Drama Critics' Circle Award for best new foreign play, all for *Benefactors*; and the Commonwealth Writers Prize and the Whitbread Award for best novel for *Spies* (2002). His film *First and Last* (1990) won an international Emmy Award.

According to writer and critic Blake Morrison, who is quoted in a Sarah Lyall article in the *New York Times*: "There are two sides to [Frayn]. . . . On the one hand he has a real taste for farce, but he's also a very serious-minded man, with an almost dry academic temperament." Although he is still a successful comedy writer, Frayn's subject matter has become more serious as he has aged. Larissa MacFarquhar, writing in the *New Yorker*, observes: "Frayn has reverted to older philosophical questions . . . [such as] What is a good life? What is forgivable? What is happiness?"

Frayn was married to Gillian Palmer, a psychotherapist, for thirty years, and the couple had three children together; they divorced in 1989. Seven years later, Frayn married Claire Tomalin, an author. He lives in London and continues to write. His play *Democracy* premiered in London in 2003 and in New York City in 2004. His play *Copenhagen* was adapted to film in 2002 by BBC-TV.

PLOT SUMMARY

Act 1

Copenhagen is set in one small space for the entirety of the play. The first act begins in the same way that the second act ends—with a discussion of what took place during a visit between Niels Bohr and Werner Heisenberg in 1941. During the course of the play, the characters, from the afterlife, thrash out the details of this meeting, looking back and trying to grasp the feelings, the setting, and the circumstances that led up to the meeting, as well as what took place while the two scientists took a short walk outside of Bohr's home that fateful day.

The first act provides background details. Nazi Germany was occupying Denmark, where the Bohrs lived. Niels Bohr, Denmark's most revered scientist, was half Jewish, and his life was threatened by the occupation. Heisenberg was a high-ranking physicist in Nazi Germany. Both men had the knowledge of how to create a nuclear bomb. They were once cohorts but now stood on opposite sides of the war.

Frayn offer details about the relationship between Niels and Heisenberg. Niels, Margrethe, and Heisenberg discuss how Heisenberg, as a graduate student, came to study with Niels, who was considered the father of quantum physics. Heisenberg, for his own credit, would go on to create the basics of quantum mechanics. The men discuss the discoveries that each of them had come up with. They also discuss the more personal relationship between them, one that was described, at one point, as like father and son.

As the men reminisce, Margrethe keeps reminding her husband that Heisenberg was working with the Nazis and was therefore their enemy. Heisenberg does not totally deny this, although he does hint that, despite Heisenberg being German, he did all he could do to make sure that the Bohrs remained safe from the Nazis. Heisenberg was not completely safe himself during the war. He was constantly watched, had been considered a suspicious person, and was interrogated by the Nazis more than once. Heisenberg was called a "white Jew" by the Nazis because he taught Einstein's relativity theory—what the Nazis referred to as "Jewish physics." Heisenberg recalls having been hesitant to talk to Bohr during their infamous meeting, knowing that Bohr's house had been wiretapped.

Heisenberg could have gone to the United States to teach, as many German physicists had done. But he wanted to stay in his homeland. He wanted to remain there, wait out the war, and help to rebuild the scientific community in Germany after the war.

The Bohrs, in the meantime, talk about their concern about Heisenberg's visit. They did not want their fellow citizens to think they were collaborating with the Nazis. Before Heisenberg arrived at their home that night, Margrethe had cautioned Niels to stick to physics and not talk about politics.

Margrethe and Niels try to figure out why Heisenberg would want to visit them. The topic of fission finds its way into their talk. Niels had been working on fission for three years. He did not think that Heisenberg had done any work in that area. But Margrethe counters that everyone else was working on it, why not Heisenberg? He has been working on a weapon for Germany based on nuclear fission, Margrethe suggests. Niels does not believe so. According to calculations at that time, this advancement in weaponry was many years in the future. It was a complicated procedure that would take not only time but an almost incomprehensible wealth of resources. But the husband and wife continue to discuss nuclear fission, giving the audience background information on the history of the development of this inquiry into the splitting of the atom and its potential implications.

Then the three characters switch the time reference, slipping back to 1941 and playing out the scene of that meeting. They greet one another awkwardly. Many years have passed since they have seen each other. Many things have happened that have separated them. They begin their conversation by bringing up shared memories, those of skiing and vacationing together. Interspersed in their memories is a discussion of fission, as each scientist tries to feel the other one out, wondering where they are in their research. But the different politics, that of Nazism and the occupation of Denmark, as well as the Holocaust, keep interfering with the free flow of their conversation.

The three characters continue to discuss a mix of quantum physics—using metaphors of skiing to help explain the science—and personal tragedies, like the loss each family has felt upon the death of one son each. Then the two men go for their famous walk. While they walk, Margrethe fills in more personal details about the men's relationship. Upon returning from their walk, Niels's abruptness toward Heisenberg makes Margrethe suspect that whatever Heisenberg has said has deeply upset Niels. After Heisenberg leaves, Niels keeps repeating that

MEDIA ADAPTATIONS

- In 2002, PBS, in association with the British Broadcasting Company (BBC), produced a DVD of *Copenhagen*, starring Stephen Rea as Bohr, Daniel Craig as Heisenberg, and Francesca Annis as Margrethe.

Heisenberg cannot be right. When Margrethe asks what Niels is talking about, Niels goes into an explanation of what happens in a nuclear reaction.

Heisenberg, once again in the setting of the afterlife, returns to the discussion. The audience is provided with the beliefs that were held in the 1940s concerning why it would be so hard to create a nuclear bomb. The act ends with the men searching their memories in an attempt to figure out what was actually said at their meeting and why Heisenberg had come to visit. Their memories conflict on certain details, so no clear conclusion is reached.

Act 2

In act 2, the men exchange memories of what it was like when they first met, how they used to walk together to help them think, and how they inspired one another's creative thought processes. They also talk about the effect their discoveries had on the world at large. They mention the names of other scientists in their field and how their theories of complementarity and uncertainty—and the "whole Copenhagen Interpretation"—came about. Margrethe suggests, as the men recount the development of their relationship, that maybe that is why Heisenberg came to Copenhagen in 1941. Maybe he wanted to get back to those earlier days when the relationship between Heisenberg and Niels was stronger and more productive. But immediately after positing this suggestion, Margrethe withdraws it. She reminds the men that they did not create their theories together. "You didn't do any of those things together," she tells them. Then she recalls how, even though they spent a lot of time together, they actually did their best work when they were apart.

At this point, the men turn to their metaphors for quantum physics and the difficulties in the

evolving foundation of the science. There were contradictions and quarrels among the leading physicists as to how to proceed and how to calculate the data they were conceiving. Even Heisenberg and Niels fought. "You were the Pope and the Holy Office and the Inquisition all rolled into one!" Heisenberg tells Niels, referring to the fact that Niels tended to have the last word in the development of quantum physics at that time. Niels's word was revered in the sciences. But both Niels and Heisenberg were puzzled by the way quantum physics worked. The actions of a detached electron do not always follow the path that Heisenberg's mathematical structure suggested it should. "It was a fascinating paradox," Niels says.

In the end, Niels points out, after their three years of collaborative research and hypotheses, the two men changed the world. "Not to exaggerate," Niels says, "but we turned the world inside out!"

As the second act closes, the three characters return, once again, to the meeting in 1941. They discuss all the pressures they were feeling at the time. The conversation returns to the atomic bomb. Niels reminds Heisenberg that the reason Heisenberg was not able to create the bomb was that he forgot to work out a mathematical equation. Heisenberg, Niels suggests, made an assumption that turned out to be false. The solving of the mathematical equation would have showed Heisenberg his error, Niels claims. Meanwhile, Margrethe catches comments the men make that are not quite the truth. She digs deeper into what they are saying and makes them admit their personal reasons behind some of their decisions. She especially confronts Heisenberg, who tries to claim that he suffered during that time, that he was a victim. "On your hands and knees?" Margrethe says. "It's my dear, good, kind husband who's on his hands and knees! Literally." She is referring to the fact that Niels ultimately had to be smuggled out of Denmark to Sweden before the Nazis came to take him away to a concentration camp. He moved from Sweden to England, and eventually to the United States. Heisenberg then confesses that he was involved in Niels's successful escape to Sweden. He was the one who had sent word that the Nazis were coming for Niels.

The play closes on a philosophical note. The three characters remind one another that they, at the end of their lives, will turn to dust, as will their children. No more decisions will have to be made, Niels says, because at some point there may be "no more uncertainty, because there's no more knowledge." Then Heisenberg reminds everyone that there is still uncertainty. This is a reference not only to science but also to the fact that no one knows for sure what actually happened at that now famous 1941 meeting.

CHARACTERS

Margrethe Bohr

Margrethe Bohr is the wife of Niels. In real life, she was very close to her husband and very much aware of the details of his work as well as his challenges, both work-related and personal. Margrethe and Niels were a close-knit team; therefore, her participation in the discussions of this play are very significant. She provides a more objective view when the men's discussion becomes bogged down. She also offers a different perspective when the men come to a blockage either in memory or in tone. She chides both men from time to time, pointing out their recall errors. For instance, she reminds them that they accomplished their best work while they were separated, not while they were together. Margrethe also acts as an interpreter for the audience as well as a medium or substitute for the audience. The men remind one another that they must talk in plain language so that Margrethe can understand their concepts. This is done so the audience will not be overwhelmed by scientific jargon.

Niels Bohr

Niels Bohr, in real life, was considered the father of quantum physics. He was at one time a teacher or mentor to Heisenberg. He is older than Heisenberg, who considers Bohr a father figure. Niels was in real life distraught after the meeting with Heisenberg, and in the play he cannot exactly remember what happened on that 1941 night. He remembers that he was upset but he cannot completely put his finger on the reason. He knows it had something to do with fission and thinks he was concerned that Heisenberg might be trying to create a bomb for Nazi Germany. Niels was the theoretician. He imagined concepts that Heisenberg would then take and create practical models from. Niels's warmth for Heisenberg is apparent, despite his concern of what Heisenberg might have created.

Werner Heisenberg

Werner Heisenberg was a German who may or may not have worked for the Nazis. This possibility is very difficult for the Bohrs to deal with, despite the fact that they once considered Heisenberg

as a son. Heisenberg, in the play, seems to come to the Bohr's house to either rationalize his involvement in the war or to ask for forgiveness for any hardships the Bohr's have suffered. However, he does this reluctantly. In the process, he also mentions the hardships that he too suffered. He even goes so far as to remind Bohr that it was Bohr who actually influenced the creation of the atomic bomb and not himself. Heisenberg was a student of Bohr's at one time, and that relationship is still apparent, even many years later. Heisenberg honors Bohr, even though he often kids him about being slow. Heisenberg, as portrayed in this play, appears to miss the close relationship that he once had with Bohr.

THEMES

Morality in a Time of War

What is the role of the scientist in a time of war? Frayn appears to ask this question in *Copenhagen*. Is it the scientist's duty to use the results of the most recent and significant research to help to protect his or her homeland, even if it means the destruction of thousands of lives? Or does a scientist have a moral obligation to use his research to improve life on this planet? Who made the better decision between Bohr and Heisenberg? Was it Bohr, when he helped create the atom bomb, thus saving the world from several cruel dictators, despite the cost to Japan? Or did Heisenberg make a better moral decision, if in fact he did thwart the creation of an atomic bomb and thus disallowed the Nazis the upper hand in World War II? Can one even talk in terms of morality when the discussion of war is raised? Or do all morals go out the window in times of dire circumstances such as a war? These are some of the questions that Frayn raises in his play. And even though these questions are not answered, morality in a time of war is one of the main themes underlying Frayn's play.

Friendship

Another underlying theme of this play is that of friendship, or more specifically, how the social and political circumstances surrounding two people can strain their relationship. No one will ever know for sure how politics interfered with the relationship between the real Heisenberg and Bohr, but Frayn attempts to demonstrate that, even in times of war, fragments of friendship remained intact between the two men, at least on a fictional

TOPICS FOR FURTHER STUDY

- Research the later years of such physicists as J. Robert Oppenheimer, Enrico Fermi, Niels Bohr, and Werner Heisenberg. How did these men react to their part in the creation of nuclear weapons and the destruction that was caused by the bombs? Did their lives change because of the bombs? Were they more militant or less so? What activities did they later become involved in that might determine how they felt?

- Read biographies of Bohr and Heisenberg and then read the letters that Niels Bohr wrote to Heisenberg but never sent (published online at http://werner-heisenberg.unh.edu) and create your own dialogue between these men as they comment on their meeting, their involvement in the development of the atomic bomb, and their concepts of morality during wartime.

- Read the Geneva Convention rules of war. Then write a paper discussing the various tenets laid out by this document. Do you think the rules of war are moral? Do they go far enough? Would you add more rules? Be specific as to the laws you would discard or reinforce.

- Pretend you are a scientist some time in the future. Imagine that you have created a scientific breakthrough. How would it help people? How could it harm people? What would be the moral questions that you would have to ask yourself as you considered going public with the results of your research?

---

basis. Despite their contradictory political beliefs, their oppositional positions on either side of a brutal war, and possibly a conflict in their concepts of how scientists should use new discoveries to create destructive weapons, readers come away from Frayn's play with a sense that the deep-seated friendship between Heisenberg and Bohr was not completely eradicated. For example, Heisenberg confesses that he was behind the successful attempts at hiding and ultimately saving Bohr from the Nazis when they came looking for him in Denmark. Frayn also tries to show the depths of the men's relationship by describing it as a father-and-son connection, implying that, no matter what hindrances might be placed between the men, there was no denying that they would be forever linked. The men, according to Frayn, thought alike and promoted and complemented one another's creative and scientific thoughts.

Uncertainty

Uncertainty is one of the concepts behind quantum physics, but it is not only in reference to quantum physics that Frayn uses this theme. There is, of course, the uncertainty of what actually happened between Bohr and Heisenberg during their meeting in 1941. That is one of the main focal points of the story. But uncertainty does not end with this unanswered question. It really only begins there. There is the uncertainty in life itself. Heisenberg discusses some of his wartime experiences; and Bohr talks about the death of his son. As long as there are things to learn and discover, there will be uncertainty, as Frayn relates to his audience at the close of the play.

Power of Science

Bohr's and Heisenberg's discoveries in quantum physics might truly have, as Bohr states in the play, turned the world inside out. Not only did science change but also the view of reality itself was changed with the men's discoveries and theories, which put the men in prominent positions. Their knowledge was coveted by the heads of state of several nations; and both Bohr and Heisenberg became pivotal figures in world politics.

Through Frayn's play, the reader grasps the significance of this political power, as well as the responsibility behind it. Frayn helps the reader realize the tremendous burden that falls on the shoulders of geniuses such as Heisenberg and Bohr—people whose intelligence allows them to create paradigm shifts in the way people all over the world think and perceive existence.

Fate

One of the more subtle themes of this play is fate. Consider the world, Frayn seems to be saying, if Heisenberg had created the atomic bomb and given it to the Nazis. What would the world be like if that had happened? As fate would have it, no matter what the reason that Heisenberg did not create the bomb—whether intentionally or by error—the explosion of the atomic bomb ended the war and eventually led to the supremacy of military power in the United States. If fate had also dictated that Bohr was killed while trying to flee Denmark to escape the Nazis, or if Bohr had been captured by the Nazis, the United States might not have been able to produce an atomic bomb. There is also the possibility that if Heisenberg and Bohr had not been brought together by fate in the first place, quantum physics may never have been imagined.

STYLE

Setting

Frayn's play takes place in the afterlife, as three characters reminisce about, and try to sort through, particularly interesting details of their lives. By placing these characters in the afterlife, Frayn has the freedom to allow speculation and reflection. The characters are able to come together and focus on their relationships, how they unfolded, what they entailed, and how they affected not only one another and their families but the world at large. In the afterlife, the characters are free to question one another's actions and motives; they can challenge one another's beliefs and memories; and they can look back more objectively, since their human egos no longer exist. The threats that existed during their lifetimes no longer concern them. They are able to see the consequences of their actions, which adds more weight to their decisions, and they can afford to be philosophical about the passions that drove their lives, without the psychological burdens that might have blinded them while they were still alive.

Talking Heads

There are no props involved in this play except for three chairs. The main focus is on the three

characters and their accounts of the Copenhagen meeting between Heisenberg and Bohr, their discoveries, and their relationships. There is also little action other than the characters sitting and standing or varying their positions as they concentrate on one another. The heart of the play is a long, detailed discussion. No one leaves the stage but rather wanders off to the side if not included in the present conversation.

Since the play involves historic figures and a complicated branch of science, the characters must relay a wealth of information about themselves and their scientific discoveries to an audience that might know next to nothing about the lives of the characters and their impact on society. In order to do this, the characters bring up personal stories from their past, they use metaphors, and they provide everyday examples that illuminate some of the principles of quantum physics.

Conflict

The conflict in Frayn's play can be seen as a search for truth. There are three people involved in this play and each of them has their own version of what happened during that 1941 meeting. Each character offers an opinion of that night and an opinion of the effects that their relationships had on each other. Although the premise of the play is the search for the truth, the reader comes away wondering if there is one truth that all three characters would agree on. Each character's interpretation varies slightly from the others, possibly providing a germ of truth to the whole, but parts of each version conflict with the other character's versions.

For example, there is the question about Heisenberg's loyalties. Was he sympathetic with the Nazis? And if so, how deeply? The search for the truth of this question has deep implications, especially since Bohr was Jewish. Then there is the question of whether Heisenberg was working on the atomic bomb. Did Bohr believe this to be true? And if so, is that why he went to the United States to help that nation produce the atomic bomb first? Would Bohr have done that if he did not believe that Heisenberg would have done it first for Germany? There is also the conflict that is implied in each man's decision to become involved in the production of such a catastrophic weapon.

Balance of Forces

Although there is conflict in this play—among the characters as well as within each character—there is also a balance of forces. Bohr and Heisenberg, in other words, are equally matched. Both men have exceptional intelligence. They both worked toward a similar goal in science. They helped one another and were both equally capable of understanding and applying fission. Their discussion and arguments are equally believable. Another example of this balance is the male characters' attempts to keep their discussions on an even keel with Margrethe, who in many ways represents the reader. They keep their language in lay terms so that the science they discuss can be easily understood. This brings the reader into the discussion, thus keeping the balance even. The play would be senseless to most spectators and readers if the male characters became lost in an esoteric dialogue about quantum physics.

HISTORICAL CONTEXT

Werner Heisenberg

Heisenberg was born in 1901 in Würzburg, Germany, and as an adult he was the head of Nazi Germany's nuclear energy program. In school, he majored in physics and by the time he entered graduate school, at the University of Munich, it was widely accepted that the quantum theory as created by Niels Bohr was faulty. Heisenberg took it upon himself to figure out the quantum mechanics that would correct it. Toward this goal, in 1925, he created matrix mechanics. Two years later, he came to a conclusion that would be called the Uncertainty Principle, which states: the more precisely a position is determined, the less precisely the momentum is known in that instant, and vice versa. This was and still is a major principle of quantum physics. It was in that same year, 1927, that Heisenberg worked with Bohr in Copenhagen to create what would be called the Copenhagen Interpretation, which became the underlying interpretation of quantum mechanics.

At the end of World War II, Heisenberg, along with several other German scientists, was imprisoned and sent to England. He was later released and returned to Germany, where he continued in his role as teacher at the Max Planck Institute for Physics and Astrophysics. He was awarded the Nobel Prize in physics in 1932, for his discovery of allotropic forms of hydrogen.

Heisenberg was also a distinguished classical pianist. He was married to Elisabeth Schumacher, and the couple had seven children. He died in 1976.

Niels Bohr

Bohr was born in 1885 in Copenhagen. He received his doctorate in physics at Copenhagen University in 1911. Upon graduation, he worked on the problem of the structure of the atom. Eventually he created a new model of the atom and its electrons, which included the idea of quanta. His model helped physics move forward, despite inaccuracies that were later discovered in his theory. His concept was, however, finally proved to be correct.

In 1922, Bohr received the Nobel Prize in physics. He continued his research after winning the prize and created the theory of complementarity, which suggested that an electron might be both particle and wave. During the war, Bohr sheltered many Jewish scientists who escaped from Germany's Nazi regime. It was Bohr who leaked the information to the United States government that Germany was trying to build an atomic bomb. He and his family had to secretly leave Denmark and flee to Sweden, to escape the Nazis. He later spent time in the United States and was involved in the Manhattan Project at Los Alamos. He later had second thoughts about the bomb and, in 1955, created the Atoms for Peace Conference in Geneva.

Bohr spent most of his life in Denmark, where he was a professor at the University of Copenhagen. In 1920, he founded the Institute for Theoretical Physics and remained the Institute's director until his death. He married Margrethe Nørlund upon graduating from college, and the couple had six sons, one of whom was also a Nobel Prize winner. He died from a stroke in 1962.

The Manhattan Project and the Bomb

As rumors began circulating, around 1939, that the Germans were developing an atomic bomb, the United States government realized it must begin its own program. General Leslie Groves, a member of the Army Corps of Engineers, headed this plan, which was later termed the Manhattan Project.

There were several significant research programs going on simultaneously in the United States at that time, but it was at the University of Chicago, where scientists were studying atomic theory, that the first controlled nuclear reaction occurred on December 2, 1942. This portion of the program was managed by physicist Enrico Fermi, who had immigrated to the United States from Italy.

The next problem that scientists had to solve was the creation of the fuel for an atomic bomb. This undertaking occurred at a facility called Oak Ridge, located in Tennessee. The task was to separate the nuclear fuel U-235 from U-238, natural uranium. In the state of Washington, the Hanford Engineer Works produced plutonium.

J. Robert Oppenheimer was assigned the task of identifying the most qualified scientists and engineers to work on the Manhattan Project. He would go on to direct the facilities at Los Alamos, New Mexico. It was at Los Alamos that a group of scientists from all over the world would create the bombs. The plant in Tennessee eventually produced the fuel, U-235, which was taken to Los Alamos and used in the bomb referred to as Little Boy. The plutonium from Hanford was used in the bomb that was called Fat Man.

Little Boy was dropped on the city of Hiroshima, Japan. Over 66,000 people were immediately killed, and another 69,000 were injured. With the effects of radioactivity, it was estimated in 1945 that a total of at least 140,000 people died due to the dropping of Little Boy. Three days after the first bomb was dropped, the bomb called Fat Man exploded over Nagasaki, Japan. It has been estimated that at least another 70,000 people were killed by this explosion.

The Bohr-Heisenberg Meeting

Germany had conquered most of Europe and was threatening to take over Russia when Heisenberg traveled to Denmark to visit with his old teacher and former collaborator. The Danish physicist was living in the so-called Residence of Honor in Copenhagen, a palatial home reserved for the most distinguished scientist in Denmark. In turn, Bohr often entertained visiting scientists from other countries, so it was not unusual for Bohr to receive Heisenberg as a guest, despite the tension that had developed in their relationship due to the hostile Nazi occupation of Denmark.

In spring 1941, Heisenberg had discovered the possibility of a chain-reaction that might occur in the splitting of the atom, the power of which he realized could be used to create a nuclear bomb. Later that year, he accepted an invitation to speak at a conference in Denmark, thus giving him a chance to meet with Bohr. They met sometime in the middle of September. There were no records kept at the meeting, but in 1956, fifteen years after the meeting, a journalist, Robert Jungk, wrote a book about the meeting, which was translated into English two years later as *Brighter than a Thousand Suns*. The book contained part of a letter that Heisenberg had written to Jungk, explaining the meeting Heisenberg had with Bohr.

Upon reading Jungk's book, Bohr drafted several letters addressed to Heisenberg. However, he never sent these letters and never had the letters published. After Bohr's death, Margrethe sealed these letters with other personal papers of her husband's. Until recently, the only published account from the Bohr family related to that meeting was contained in an article written in 1964 by Aage Bohr called *The War Years and the Prospects Raised by the Atomic Weapons*.

Another book, *Heisenberg's War* (1993) by Thomas Powers, was published about this topic. Powers's book inspired the ideas contained in Frayn's *Copenhagen*. In 2002, the remaining members of the Bohr family decided to end the speculation concerning the infamous meeting, and they opened the unpublished letters that Bohr had written. Copies of these documents can be found at http://www.nbi.dk/NBA/papers/introduction.htm. At http://werner-heisenberg.unh.edu/ readers can find copies of responses from the Heisenberg family.

CRITICAL OVERVIEW

Copenhagen has won praise from audiences and critics alike, as well as several prestigious awards. It also has gained the attention of academics. Jonothan Logan writes in *American Scientist* that, although he found the play to be "quick, clever and artfully plotted," he is concerned about Frayn's alteration of the historical facts and his rearrangement of "the moral landscape the real Bohr and Heisenberg inhabited." Logan contends that Frayn's reliance on Thomas Powers's book *Heisenberg's War* for the content of his play was faulty because the Powers book was flawed and thus "won little respect from historians."

Another scholar, Paul Lawrence Rose, writing for the *Chronicle of Higher Education*, begins his article: "Scholars are never satisfied when they see their specialized subjects turn fodder for stage, screen, or novels." Rose is a specialist on Heisenberg and he praises Frayn for developing "through his often electric dialogue a synergy on stage that has made the play a success." Rose even goes so far as to state that there has not been another play that "has achieved the brilliance of *Copenhagen* in rendering the technical discussion of scientific ideas dramatically convincing and, at the same time, accessible to scientists and non-scientists alike." But Rose has problems with Frayn's depictions of the characters. In particular, he questions Frayn's depiction of Heisenberg: "Was Heisenberg really the character depicted so

Physicist Niels Bohr © Corbis

sympathetically on stage? Was his attitude toward Nazism really so ambivalent, or so justifiable, as Frayn variously suggests?"

Despite the controversy of historical fact versus Frayn's dramatic presentation, there is hardly anyone who has criticized the artistic value and presentation of the play. *Washington Post* reviewer Nelson Pressley concludes that *Copenhagen* is "as ingenious as advertised." Pressley even comments that, despite arguments against Frayn's "fairly sympathetic view of Heisenberg," the play is still a worthy creation:

> Frayn entertains so many possibilities in this play, and is so direct about the stakes . . . that it's hard to imagine *Copenhagen* being invalidated by anything short of a complete transcript of the meeting [between Bohr and Heisenberg].

Jules Becker, in the Worcester, Massachusetts *Telegram and Gazette*, suggests that if nothing else, Frayn's play should excite the audience, inspiring them to go back to the textbooks and dig into history a little deeper to come to their own conclusions about the real-life counterparts of the characters depicted in the play. Becker observes: "*Copenhagen* may not ultimately explain whether Heisenberg visited Bohr to help the Nazis or to stymie their effort. Yet it does make a cogent argument for understanding the scientists along with

their science and the importance of a science-friendly public."

Seattle Times reviewer Misha Berson calls *Copenhagen* a "brilliant, demanding play." Jack Kroll in *Newsweek* writes: "Frayn creates riveting suspense and, without dumbing down the dialogue, makes the discussion of matters like quantum physics and matrix mathematics seem like revelations of character." And *Washington Post* writer Peter Marks points out: "Good writing has a way of relaxing the spirit in much the manner that a session in the hot tub releases the tension in one's neck and back, and Michael Frayn, author of the Tony-winning play, is in this regard a stress-relief wizard."

The questions that circle around the real-life Bohr-Heisenberg meeting may never be answered either in history or in drama, but Frayn's attempt in *Copenhagen* continues to inspire discussion. Whether it answers any questions, and indeed whether it is historically factual, is immaterial to many audience members and critics alike, including Julia M. Klein, who writes in the *Chronicle of Higher Education*: "All the letter writers, so intent on being right, are busy pounding a metaphorical mattress with a hammer. They haven't noticed that readers long ago started rolling their eyes."

CRITICISM

Joyce Hart

Hart is a freelance writer and author of several books. In this essay, Hart focuses this essay on the various roles that the character Margrethe portrays in Frayn's work.

There are three characters in Michael Frayn's award-winning play *Copenhagen*, and the main focus of the play is on only two of them, Niels Bohr and Werner Heisenberg. This leaves the third character, Margrethe Bohr, in a very special position, one that changes depending on the needs of the play. In her various roles, Margrethe sometimes acts as the moderator of the discussions between Bohr and Heisenberg. At other times she plays out her role as wife and protector of Bohr. In different situations, Margrethe is representative of the general audience, someone in need of explanations in order to become more deeply involved in the dialogue. And in yet different settings, she is provides details for the audience's sake. In studying Margrethe's role, readers can get a better grasp on how Frayn smoothed out the flow of his play, a work that might otherwise have come across as a dry dialogue between two intelligent men whose esoteric language might not have been translatable to a general audience. Margrethe's role also offered Frayn a chance to add drama, background information, and interest to the otherwise scientific discussion.

It is Margrethe who opens the play with the question: "But why?" And it is this question that drives the play. Everyone wants to know why Heisenberg decided to come to the Bohr's house that night in 1941, while the city of Copenhagen was occupied by the Nazis. Why take the risk? What were Heisenberg's motives? And ultimately, what did that meeting accomplish? The actors are portraying three people who have already died, and yet, Margrethe states, these questions still linger like ghosts. As the opening dialogue between Margrethe and her husband continues, Margrethe fills in the background information that sets the tone of the play. She mentions the war, the occupation, and the fact that in Germany's eyes, she and her husband are the enemy. And although by the end of the play no one is wiser as to what occurred during Bohr's and Heisenberg's meeting, Margrethe provides the first clue in the play concerning the consequences or outcomes of these two scientists coming together on that night: "I've never seen you as angry with anyone as you were with Heisenberg that night," Margrethe offers. She also mentions that after that meeting, the friendship between the two men ended. So within just a few sentences, Margrethe has taken the audience back to that night, with all its tension and apprehension, preparing the audience for the discussion between the two scientists, which is yet to begin.

In the next section, Margrethe acts as a counterpoint to Bohr's memories of Heisenberg. Every time Bohr mentions something nice that he remembers, Margrethe contradicts him. This provides the audience with a fuller picture, a more colorful portrayal of Heisenberg. Bohr thinks of Heisenberg as a part of the family, for example, while Margrethe says there was something alien about Heisenberg. And when Bohr uses positive adjectives to describe Heisenberg, such as quick, eager, and bright, Margrethe turns these compliments toward the negative, stating that Heisenberg was too quick, too eager, and too bright. However, even Margrethe softens a little later in the play and upgrades the way the men themselves describe their relationship. They refer to it as a business association, whereas Margrethe likens their connection to that of father and son. But no matter if she is

THE CHARACTER OF MARGRETHE MAY PLAY A SUPPORTIVE ROLE, BUT IT COULD EASILY BE PROCLAIMED THAT SHE IS WHAT HOLDS THE PLAY TOGETHER."

condoning Heisenberg or praising him, her comments add complexities to the plot. Was Heisenberg a good man? Did he have moral perceptions? Or was he manipulative and exploitive? These questions are never clearly answered, but through Margrethe's role, a deeper intrigue is added to the play by her provision of questions and contradictions. These are not easy concepts, Margrethe seems to imply. There are no simple solutions.

As the play progresses, Margrethe returns to the role of information gatherer. She talks about the men's work and about politics. She also acts as historian, providing a more accurate recall of the 1941 meeting. She seems clearer than the men about the details of that meeting, demonstrating, possibly, a more objective vision, but also giving the play a further deepening of complexities. She offers details concerning why Heisenberg was in Copenhagen at that time. He was attending a meeting, of course, but Margrethe adds the fact that the organization that sponsored this meeting was known for spreading "Nazi propaganda." This places Heisenberg in a more precarious position. The Nazi's were exterminating Jews. And Bohr was part Jewish. This makes the audience question whether Heisenberg was a friend or a foe. Bohr states: "Heisenberg is a friend." But back in her role as contrarian, Margrethe counters: "Heisenberg is a German." And she fears Heisenberg's visit will make her countrymen think the Bohrs are collaborating with Heisenberg. So not only is Margrethe questioning the politics of Heisenberg, she is also demonstrating for the audience's benefit, the depth of fear and the possible retribution this visit could have caused. In other words, this is not just a meeting between two friends, an old teacher and his student. It is not just simple curiosity that drives the question "Why did

WHAT DO I READ NEXT?

- *A Landing on the Sun: A Novel* (2003) is representative of Frayn's novel writing. This book presents a mystery about Brian Jessel, a member of Great Britain's cabinet office, whose death is somewhat suspicious.

- For a funnier side of Frayn, try reading his play *Noises Off* (1982), a sexual farce that is actually two plays in one: the first of which is acted out on stage, and the second of which follows the disastrous events that occur backstage immediately following the presentation onstage, as bumbling actors and stagehands stumble through the production.

- *An Experiment with an Air Pump* (1998), a play by Shelagh Stephenson, is set in two different time periods, 1799 and 1999. The focus of the first time period is on scientist Joseph Fenwick, who struggles with a mix of his own ambitions and desires for progress with his moral beliefs. In the second time period in the late twentieth century, his counterpart, a female genetic researcher, does the same. Many philosophical and social issues are discussed in this play.

- *Proof* (2001) won the Pulitzer Prize for drama for its author, David Auburn. This play is centered on math and science, but only obliquely. It really explores love, relationships, genius, and madness.

Heisenberg come and what did the two men discuss?" No, there is much more drama going on here. And it is Margrethe's role to emphasize and to clarify this.

In the middle of the first act, Margrethe's role changes a bit. She takes on an air of comedic relief. The men are deep in a discussion of quantum physics, mentioning the infamous Schrodinger's cat, which, according to theory, is both dead and alive at the same time, as long as neither condition is verified. Margrethe interjects at this point, "Poor beast," which provides the audience with a chance to catch its breath. The concepts of quantum physics are very lofty and require mental effort to comprehend. Margrethe's comment allows the audience to laugh, to relax. A little later, when Heisenberg again returns to physics, he comments that "the particle has met itself again, the cat's dead." To this, Margrethe says, "And you're alive." This comment might also arouse a giggle from the audience, but it is a double-edged sword. It sounds funny, coming immediately after Heisenberg's statement, but her comment also links back to an earlier discussion about why Heisenberg is still teaching physics in Germany, when most other physicists have already left the country. Margrethe's statement that Heisenberg is still alive is a subtle reference that she believes he is in an alliance with

the Nazis. A few lines later, Margrethe returns more definitely to the side of comedy, when Bohr references how many times a theory of his had to be changed. Each time her husband mentions a change, Margrethe brings the discussion back to the audience by remarking on how many times she had to retype Bohr's paper. She again breaks the monotony of scientific dialogue, bringing the common person in the audience something easier to think about, something everyone can relate to—the tedious work that is involved in even the loftiest concepts.

Close to the end of act 1, Bohr mentions that he and Heisenberg must talk in a language that is clear to Margrethe. He says they must use "plain language." But what is interesting is that Margrethe also has a request of sorts. She does not ask them to speak in plain language, but rather she asks that they look inside and speak the truth. She mentions the fact that Heisenberg used to refer to her husband as the Pope. This is not, according to Margrethe, because Heisenberg thinks of Bohr as a "spiritual father" as he proclaims, but because he wants "absolution." She suggests that the reason that Heisenberg came to see Bohr was to be forgiven for what he was about to do—help create the atomic bomb for the Nazis. And once she points this out, the conversation between Bohr and

Heisenberg becomes more enlivened. The men drop the scientific details and begin to speak of feelings and the morality of war. Margrethe now has taken on the role of the truth detective. She is quiet for a long time as the men hash out their mutual roles in the development of atomic weaponry. And as they do this, Margrethe is listening. When the men reach a certain point just shy of a conclusion, she spurs them forward. She corrects their perceptions and prods them in a more honest direction. And out comes the truth (at least the dramatic truth if not the real truth). Thus through Margrethe, the play feels as if it has come to some sort of conclusion, despite the fact that there are still many questions left unanswered.

In act 2, Margrethe again focuses on truth-gathering as she sums up the closest thing to a reason that the play offers for Heisenberg's visit to Copenhagen. Whether this is factual truth or truth according to the playwright, it is Margrethe who mouths it. After a long dialogue between the characters about the accomplishments of both Bohr and Heisenberg, Margrethe faces Heisenberg with some interesting information. She states a catalog of events, such as Heisenberg's published paper on the uncertainty theory, which ensures him teaching positions at prestigious educational institutions. She references how young he was. "The youngest full professor in Germany," Bohr says, reinforcing Margrethe's comment. Margrethe states this fact of Heisenberg's youth to build up Heisenberg, to put his accomplishments in front of the audience. But her real motive is not to make Heisenberg a hero. She has another idea completely. She is back in her contrarian's role. Just as soon as she has poured over his credits, she slams the door in his face. "You came to show yourself off to us," Margrethe says, claiming this as the only true reason for Heisenberg's visit. "You've come to show us how well you've done in life." And in the play, at least, Heisenberg confesses this is true. Margrethe has further bared the truth. And as she says, her perceiving the truth leads others to admit to more truth. "A chain reaction. You tell one painful truth and it leads to two more." Here her character cleverly uses atomic reaction as a metaphor.

And so, through her various roles, Margrethe adds depth, comic relief, a search for honesty, and a possible conclusion. Her character, although not in the spotlight, is what binds the other characters with the audience and keeps the play lively and on track. Without the character of Margrethe, Frayn would not have had a vehicle through which to add dramatic effect. Using Margrethe in this way, Frayn

can allow his two scientist characters to renew memories, discuss physics, and question their moral decisions without constantly pausing to explain themselves. The character of Margrethe may play a supportive role, but it could easily be proclaimed that she is what holds the play together.

Source: Joyce Hart, Critical Essay on *Copenhagen*, in *Drama for Students*, Thomson Gale, 2006.

Klaus Hentschel

In the following essay, Hentschel examines the "historical polyphony"—that is, the multiple views presented as all being equally plausible—in Copenhagen *and its possible effects on "public expectations . . . of historical writing."*

Michael Frayn's play *Copenhagen,* which premiered in 1998, has attracted much attention and is certainly one of the most intriguing plays taking its inspiration from the history of science. This paper analyses one of its central characteristics, namely what I have termed 'historical polyphony'. Instead of advocating one amongst a multitude of widely differing reconstructions of what 'really' happened at a meeting between Bohr and Heisenberg in occupied Copenhagen in September 1941, Frayn's piece enacts three somewhat plausible versions one after another. This break with tenets of classical dramaturgy such as the 'uniqueness' and 'separability' of the stage characters parallels strange features of the quantum world. It might also lead to a wider appreciation of a new level of historiography in which documents (such as the recently released draft letters by Bohr to Heisenberg) are neither 'authorities' nor 'witnesses' but simply traces of past processes whose reconstruction and contextualisation is the task of the historian.

In September 1941, eighteen months after German troops had invaded Denmark, two German physicists travelled to Copenhagen. Officially, Werner Heisenberg and Carl Friedrich von Weizsacker were to attend a conference on astrophysics arranged by the Deutsches Wissenschaftliches Institut in the occupied Danish capital, an institution created mainly for purposes of cultural propaganda and boycotted by most of the local scholars and scientists. But actually the main reason for the visit was that Heisenberg wanted to speak with Niels Bohr, his long time mentor during the exciting period of development of quantum mechanics and its philosophical interpretation in the mid 1920s. What precisely Heisenberg wanted to discuss with Bohr, and what exactly happened during their brief meeting has been a matter of dispute ever since.

"FRAYN SKILFULLY USES
THE DEGREES OF FREEDOM
REMAINING AFTER SUCH A
CONSCIENTIOUS CHECK AGAINST
THE FACTS. HE PERCEPTIVELY
IDENTIFIES THE DIFFERENT
HISTORICALLY POSSIBLE ACTIONS
WITHIN THIS ZONE, DELIMITED
BY THE UNCONTROVERSIAL
SOURCES."

The accounts given by their colleagues and relatives, some of whom were informed soon after the meeting, as well as by the famous physicists themselves, and later by various journalists, historians, and scientists, diverge radically. Some have claimed that Heisenberg was on a spy mission to find out what Bohr and the allied scientists knew about the prospects and technicalities of building an atomic bomb—remember that in 1941 it was still far from clear whether that was feasible at all, and that a year later the German Heereswaffenamt pegged all related nuclear weapon developments down to lower priority status as unlikely to deliver before the end of the war. Others insist quite on the contrary that Heisenberg tried to persuade Bohr to join him in stymying any serious efforts on either side to develop each a terrible weapon while a world war was still raging and a dangerous demagogue ruling Germany. Yet others think that Heisenberg was just looking for advice from his father figure or for moral absolution for his actions and sufferings in Germany at the time. Proponents of the first and second versions such as Paul Rose and Thomas Powers have criticised each others' accounts tooth and nail, and as the controversy has progressed, it has become clear that a harmonising synthesis of such widely differing accounts is not only difficult to achieve but unlikely ever to occur.

When in the middle of the 1990s the successful playwright Michael Frayn came across Thomas Powers' book on 'Heisenberg's war', he was fascinated by the topic. Powers' version is one of the most journalistic accounts, turning it into a story about the unsung hero Heisenberg, who had intentionally deceived German authorities by miscalculating the critical mass and delaying the German project to the point that it was shifted to the back burner. Rather than taking over Powers' sensationalistic interpretation of the story, however, or spicing it up for reasons of dramatic effect, Frayn took the unusual step of researching the historical episode extensively, coming across competing and conflicting accounts of Heisenberg's role in Nazi Germany and, time and again, of this same meeting with Bohr in 1941. The resulting play, *Copenhagen,* was previewed in the Cottesloe auditorium of the Royal National Theatre in London on 21 May 1998, and opened a week later, to be followed by various other productions throughout the world. I think it is fair to say that it rapidly became one of the most well known and hotly debated plays featuring a theme from the history of science, comparable only with Brecht's *Galileo,* or Kipphardt's *Oppenheimer.*

If I may be so bold as to boil down a script full of wit, superb dialogue, and cleverly interspersed gems of popularisation of the intricacies of quantum mechanics, the play's main strategy is to enact not one but various versions of the meeting, reflecting but not mirroring the multiple perspectives on it just mentioned. They are played out one after another as three different possibilities for what might really have happened, what the historical actors could have said, and what their motives and thoughts may have been. Right at the beginning, the central question 'Why did he come? What was he trying to tell you?' is posed and answered with a disillusioned 'He explained over and over again. Each time he explained, it became more obscure'. The audience's expectation of a coherent plot with a clear beginning and a clear end, a linear structure, and perhaps a moral at the end, is not fulfilled. Each new round shakes the definition which the last one has created, each strives to be the definitive scenario, but in vain. Frayn's piece plays out possibilities, potentia in the Aristotelian sense, which Heisenberg had linked to the interpretation of the psi function in some of his later writings on the philosophy of quantum mechanics. Instead of advocating any one of the three actual versions in the two acts of which *Copenhagen* is composed, Frayn construes a play of potentia, i.e. 'something in the middle between the idea of an event and the actual event, a strange kind of physical reality just in the middle between possibility and reality'. Elsewhere I have called this 'historical polyphony'.

In search of a precedent for such a well balanced polyphony of different versions, one could perhaps think of Akiro Kurosawa's 1950 film *Rashomon,* or of Sartre's Flaubert biography (1971/72), but as far as I know Frayn's play is the first to produce such a multivocality in a theme taken from history of science.

How have historians of science reacted to the piece? Well, members of this rare species, to which the present author also belongs, have a reputation for chronic nitpicking, and we certainly do find plenty of that in their commentaries on *Copenhagen.* In an attempt to break away from this disposition, I will try here not to pontificate about the many points that ought to have been included in Michael Frayn's piece for the sake of better historical contextualisation. For the playwright has quite consciously made use of his poetic license. His Bohr speaks too articulately and unhaltingly, Margrethe is uncharacteristically belligerent, etc. I do concede that it is somewhat easier for me to take the high ground than for several of the other commentators, whose versions of the meeting between Heisenberg and Bohr in 1941 are already indelibly imprinted in the annals of our discipline. More lies behind this common predilection for correcting dates and facts and filling in contextual background information than simple defence of one's own reconstruction. To this day, history of science is widely expected to record or seek out the one and only truth, to tell us 'what really happened' as the German historian Leopold von Renke demanded in the heyday of the nineteenth century historicist movement.

Michael Frayn's play is a successful attempt at shaking off this mindset and leaving room for more than one interpretation. Two individuals looking through a kaleidoscope at a single object are unlikely to give exactly the same description of what they see, even if they take same viewing position. Similarly, any two historians of science familiar with the rather meagre end even contradictory sources available are hardly more likely to arrive at identical reconstructions of precisely what happened during that portentous meeting between the two leading physicists. By this I am not, by any means, advocating some sort of arbitrariness, whether it comes under the guise of postmodernism or simply out of laziness. Every version must be in conformity with the accepted facts, which are mutually supported by different sources. Frayn skilfully uses the degrees of freedom remaining after such a conscientious check against the facts. He perceptively identifies the different historically possible actions within this zone, delimited by the uncontroversial sources.

By doing so Frayn simultaneously violates more than one axiom of traditional drama which also holds in various texts in the history of science. I would like to refer to these axioms as 'uniqueness' and 'separability', in conscious analogy to the opposition between classical and quantum mechanics.

As regards uniqueness: In classical physics every state of a system is assigned a descriptive function that enables one (in principle) to make definite predictions about any measurements taken within this system. At a given point in time, a classical particle has a specific energy, mass, charge, acceleration, etc., which, in principle, can be determined as precisely as you want. Analogously, traditional biographies describe their heroes in such a way that no doubt remains about their qualities, motives, and actions. The classical biographer has his figure completely in hand; he whittles away at it until none of the remaining contours conflict with his design. Any jutting corners or sharp edges are smoothed away or simply concealed. The new element of quantum mechanical systems is, very briefly put, the necessity of introducing a general function to describe, not a specific state, but a whole set of possible states that all obey the known boundary conditions of the system. Before the system is measured, it cannot be stated with certainty which of these states is realised, only how probable each of them is. Frayn's two main characters are the theatrical equivalent of this. They 'play out' different possibilities of how their dialogue might have proceeded, not synchronously, but sequentially as the piece progresses. Their 'state function' is, quantum mechanically speaking, not a pure state but a superposition. Each 'observation' by the audience of the series of staged processes leads to a collapse of the complex wave function and thus to one of the many possibilities being 'played out to the end'. For instance, in the middle of the second act when Heisenberg opens the front door of the Carlsberg villa once again:

> Bohr: He stands on the doorstep blinking in the sudden flood of light from the house. Until this instant his thoughts have been everywhere and nowhere, like unobserved particles, through all the slits in the diffraction grating simultaneously. Now they have to be observed and specified.

> Heisenberg: And at once the clear purposes inside my head lose all definite shape. The light falls on them and they scatter.

It is not just indeterminacy triggered by our incomplete knowledge, as uninvolved observers of the event, about the true motives and states of the actors, but that the characters themselves don't know their own purposes and states:

> Bohr: . . . there's someone missing from the room. He sees me. He sees Margrethe. He doesn't see himself. Heisenberg: Two thousand million people in the world, and the one who has to decide their fate is the only one who's always hidden from me.

Confronted with only insufficiently 'measured'— i.e. documented—events, historians too are often only able to weigh conflicting reconstructions of them against each other and sound out their probabilities. Likewise, at the end of the performance, Frayn's audience is not able to do more than assign a higher or lower probability to the various versions of the conversation (each person judging according to his or her own preferences, knowledge of the subject, predisposition, etc.). Unique determinability is lost. But instead of lamenting this loss, we must learn how to deal constructively with inherent probabilism. It also leads us away from the tendency towards black and white depictions of past decades. With respect to the Nazi era and its crimes, for example, the prevailing pest-war trend was to hunt down (a few) culprits and use them as scapegoats while apologising for (many) supposedly innocent bystanders. Historical reality, however, takes place in the complex grey area in between these two extremes, in which categorical verdicts (guilty/not guilty) do not hold.

As regards separability: In classical physics it is basically always possible to treat systems which are spatially far enough away from each other as separate entities, because the propagation of forces and interactions is limited by the speed of light. In quantum mechanics, however, sometimes even such remote systems remain interrelated, because interactions that occurred in their prehistories have led to correlations of certain properties. Thus arise, among other things, the mysterious EPR correlations and other strange effects only comprehensible in quantum mechanics. Frayn's dialogues illustrate this collapse of classical separability by subtly entangling the characters as the action unfolds. In each scene the dialogue partners have an explicitly stated 'initial state' (for example Bohr's determination not to invite Heisenberg to accompany him on a walk, or Heisenberg's plans for opening the conversation and guiding it). But instead of simply 'developing' these mutual intentions and following the course of the 'interaction' to its outcome, the state itself actually changes as a result of the interaction (Bohr sets out on a walk after all; Heisenberg constantly loses his train of thought, etc.).

Already in the first act, for instance, we the audience observe destructive interferences leading to uncomfortable pauses and a constantly threatening breakdown in communication. But we also observe constructive interferences that revitalise memories of the good old days when they were still congenial coworkers. In either case, though, the development remains uncertain, unpredictable (even Margrethe's firm assumption that, once started, the walk would last two to three hours does not materialise).

Aside from its fascinating multiperspectival exegesis of this meeting, Frayn's play has more to offer. It invites analogous treatment of other such cases: a polyphonic composition of conflicting voices about, say, Robert Oppenheimer's motivations to build the atomic bomb, or Max Planck's role in the Third Reich, or the fundamentally disparate public images of the life and work of Albert Einstein. In the history of science there are isolated efforts along these lines, for example Geoffrey Cantor's analysis of the reception of Michael Faraday. But few historians of science have the courage to relinquish the fictitiously tidy integrity of their characters, which in extreme cases has led to some fiddling with the facts. Isaac Newton, for instance, was frequently purged' of his alchemistic studies because they could not be made to conform with the image the nineteenth century had of proper science. David Nye's antibiography of Thomas Edison is one rare attempt to sketch at once more than one version of his hero. It evokes such contradictory images as Edison the Victorian husband, the eccentric scientist, amateur tinkerer, elegant magician, and secretive alchemist. But such biographical experiments remain islands lost in a sea of streamlined figures, not to mention standard autobiographies with their intolerably starched self-portraits. And this, even though—or perhaps because?—biographies are the most popular form of literature on the book market. Will the public forever demand literary constructions of closed lifelines, tracing their courses from cradle to hearse? I would like to hope that a piece like Frayn's *Copenhagen* might change general expectations by offering a taste of the fascinating variety of ways of reading history with its irreducible ambiguities.

Frequently, the reception of the piece points in the opposite direction, though. Many seem to assume that the historical polyphony is merely an unfortunate consequence of an atypically serious lack of good sources. Correspondingly, there is a widespread hope that one day clarity may eventually be achieved, once and for all, after new sources come to light: let's say a tape recording of Bohr about this conversation, still stored away in a safe at the Niels Bohr Institute; or let's assume, for the sake of argument, that recordings by Heisenberg that had hitherto been withheld were finally made public and accessible. Would this not finally clear up the issue? The historian of science Gerald Holton seems to share this hope. In a July 2000 contribution to the debate about *Copenhagen* he told his readers about a draft letter by Bohr to Heisenberg which Bohr's son Aage had found in Jungk's book. According to Holton, we must simply 'remain with half knowledge' until the release of this letter before a final verdict can be reached, suggesting we would then gain 'full knowledge' about 'what really happened'.

The recent release of all written materials in Bohr's hand (including the abovementioned draft letter) was a good test case for this contention. It was triggered by an international conference devoted to Frayn's play held in September 2001, in Copenhagen, during which many possible perspectives both on the Bohr-Heisenberg meeting and on Frayn's piece were raised. While the meeting was still under way, the Bohr family decided to release all of Bohr's various draft letters to Heisenberg, which had been kept in the archives of the Niels Bohr Institute, thus preempting their scheduled release in 2012, fifty years after Niels Bohr's death. The family apparently felt the pressure to clear the mist enveloping this material. I don't think it is unfair to assume that the hidden agenda behind this was to decide the case, of course in favour of Bohr's version. Heisenberg's family promptly reciprocated, also putting some material on the web, with the clear intention of defending their famous relative.

But soon after the Bohr material had been put on the web (both in the original languages and in English translation), it became clear that no major revision of what we already knew was in the offing. The various letters and unsent drafts written between 1957 and 1962 mostly confirmed what was already known from earlier accounts by Bohr's son Aage and various members of his institute. What these letters do show is the difficulty Bohr had in broaching the subject, and in finding the right tone. They also shed new light on the role of Carl Friedrich von Weizsacker, who had accompanied Heisenberg on that famous visit to Copenhagen in 1941, and whose remarks about why German victory seemed to be unavoidable must have left deep traces in the minds of his shocked Danish colleagues. But in other respects these documents raise more questions than they answer, for instance about the location of the famous conversation between Bohr and Heisenberg. Whereas all previously known sources had pointed to either Bohr's home or a park behind his institute, Bohr here referred to his office, a highly unlikely place for such a delicate topic as German nuclear research, particularly given both Heinseberg's and Bohr's suspicions that they were under surveillance by the Gestapo. Was this just a slip of the pen, or a minor mistake? How much was Bohr's memory of the meeting, nearly two decades later, affected by what he had heard from others about Heisenberg's attitudes and actions during the Nazi period, including the apologetic version which had just then been published in Robert Jungk's book *Brighter than a thousand suns?* After all, this publication from 1956, spreading the since persistent myth of Heisenberg and other German physicists, purported footdragging in the German Uranium Project in order to deprive Hitler of the atomic bomb, had prompted the first set of these draft letters." How much was Bohr able to keep out issues of the day, such as the need for international collaboration? Both physicists acted as policymakers for their respective countries after the Second World War, and were equally aware of its importance. As historians and journalists know only too well from oral history, such subliminal lapses of memory occur frequently in interviews recorded years after the event. Interestingly, Bohr himself addresses this point in one of the draft letters:

> I remember quite definitely the course of these conversations. . . . It is obvious that during the course of the war such a wise person as yourself must gradually lose faith in a German victory and end with the conviction of defeat, and I can therefore understand that perhaps at the end you may no longer have recalled what you had thought and what you had said during the first years of the war.

But any conceivable slip of the memory naturally only applied to Heisenberg's reminiscences. Bohr had perfect confidence in his own. This cocksureness is typical of eye witness accounts, without, however, guaranteeing their accuracy. Don't misunderstand me. I do not automatically want to call into doubt his testimony, which may be absolutely correct. But we simply can't know for sure. As even the members of the Niels Bohr Archive point out in their introductory remarks, Bohr's statements in these letters cannot be taken at face value. Telling as they are for the historical situation in which they were written (1956/57), they are neither unbiased testimony about what happened in September 1941, nor sufficient for the full refutation of Heisenberg's version even if everything stated in them were true. Nor do the interesting points raised by the Heisenberg family on their webpage about his moral dilemmas refute Bohr's version, either.

What this episode tells us is quite contrary to what the relatives on either side might have intended. Any such material written long after the event, even by one of the main actors, is bound to lead to disappointment, because each time we will only have gained one more version, one more perspective of the kaleidoscope, one more voice in a polyphonic chorus. As authoritative as each source may be in its own right, it would remain a party, burdened with its own interests and its own context, its own temporal and spatial locality.

The historical polyphony of Frayn's piece actually tells us about much more than just the irresolvable ambiguity of this singular case. It contains a general lesson about the value of historical documents. To get to this deeper level of historiography, a distinction between three 'hermeneutic stances' introduced by the social historian Adrian Wilson to define practical attitudes towards historical material and its possible uses is helpful. Even though each of these stances carries deep epistemological assumptions, they need not be explicit (and in fact often aren't), which does nothing to diminish their active role in the respective historical accounts.

According to the first, and oldest, hermenuetic stance, documents from the past are simply authorities. One preserves them, assembles them, if necessary rediscovers them, or at least reconstructs them if the originals are irretrievably lost. This is the spirit in which, for instance, scholars in the Renaissance studied texts from antiquity—as preserved windows into the glorious past which just needed to be dusted off, restored, and perhaps reconstructed from surviving bits and pieces or translated. The presumption coming with this first stance is that of transparency of sources. They are perceived as direct records, 'voices of the past', speaking for themselves, as it were. The task of the historian is then limited to a sort of extraction of information from these authorities, a 'scissors and paste' history (as R. G. Collingwood termed it), a gigantic assemblage of selected facts from a large heap of remaining 'data'.

Historians became conscious of certain basic problems with this first approach surprisingly late. They noticed that their 'data' were full of hidden assumptions and hidden agendas, that they were far from neutral accounts of what had happened. Some documents were intentionally misleading, others

were in fact forgeries, not always of recent origin but sometimes stemming from the very era under study, perhaps created to mislead enemy nations, neighbouring cities, or merely the tax authorities. The method of source criticism was invented (sometimes also called 'critical history', 'historical criticism', or the 'critique of documents') and during the nineteenth and early twentieth centuries developed into quite a sophisticated set of powerful tools by which, for instance, a shockingly high percentage of all surviving documents from the Middle Ages were proven to have been forged or tampered with. But rather than the assumptions of the first stance being negated, they were only modified, subjugated. Henceforth, documents were treated as witnesses, who sometimes tell the truth, often intend to do so, but sometimes do not. The task of the historian now was remodelled as finding out who had lied and who told the truth, of separating reliable, uncorrupted sources from the questionable ones, of wiping off the thin layer of dust and mischief that might have found their way into them. The windows into the past were still thought to be there, just a little tinted, blurry, and somewhat more limited in their purview. It had become harder to hear the voices of the past, but it was still conceived as possible, after a searching interrogation by the critical historian who attentively assessed his sources, very much like a judge in court questioning witnesses in order to determine their credibility. The goal of historians, according to this second stance, still is to restore a 'clean' record of the past, based on those pieces which had passed muster in this scrupulous criticism of sources.

In the third and, historically speaking, last hermeneutic stance, documents have lost their status as authorities or witnesses but are simply taken for what they are, namely effects or traces of past processes. The first question then raised by the historian has to be by whom and for what purpose they were made, and through which channels they have come down to us today. Our case shows that this investigation of the genesis of documents is by no means a superfluous sidetrack, but a quintessential part of the historian's task. Many of the documents quoted pro and con Heisenberg's and Bohr's versions stem not from the time of the meeting, but from fifteen or more years later. A corollary of this third stance is a loss of historical immediacy: we lose the illusion of being able to jump back in time. But then we have to bear in mind that this always was an illusion, tempting as it might have been, given the sense of authenticity evoked by some of the more 'vivid' or 'authoritative' sources.

Scientists at U.N. International Atomic Energy Conference exhibit; Dr. W. Heisenberg second from right © Bettmann/Corbis

It is to this third hermeneutic stance of historiography that we are led by Frayn's play. Had it just been a conventional piece with one coherent plot followed through from beginning to end, we would have remained on the second level, with the actors as more or less convincing advocates of their historical counterparts. It would fall to the audience to judge who was most convincing, Bohr, Heisenberg, or Margrethe. Now, with three conflicting versions of the meeting played out in succession, this simple coordination between drama and reality is broken. Precisely like the historian facing mutually contradictory, and on top of it all, grossly incomplete documentary evidence, the audience too is confronted with irreconcilable versions whose polyphony is not muted (at least in the better performances). In no other theatre piece that I know are such solid bridges thrown across the deep gulfs normally separating the worlds of science, history, and theatre. Whether we can expect any change in public expectations with regard to the definitiveness of historical writing remains to be seen, but in any case it has occasioned a most fruitful discussion between dramatists, actors, historians, and scientists.

Source: Klaus Hentschel, "What History of Science Can Learn from Michael Frayn's *Copenhagen*," in *Interdisciplinary*

Science Reviews, Vol. 27, No. 3, Autumn 2002, pp. 211–16.

Robert L. King

In the following review-essay, King discusses staging in Copenhagen, *particularly how lighting and blocking are used to ambiguous effects.*

Early reviewers appreciated the staging of Michael Frayn's *Copenhagen* as a dramatic rendering of its theoretical physics. The play's lighting and blocking display human interactions as parallels to the waves and particles of matter, simultaneously interdependent and isolated. The first time I saw the play, the circles of light in and through which its three characters move struck me as welcome illustrations of how bodies in space have clear and shifting positions simultaneously, by turns fully visible, stationary, in motion, or in partial light. In conventional staging, where characters stand determines what they see and how they are seen by others, the audience included. We expect directors to block characters' movements to illuminate a playwright's vision, and spare properties often direct an audience's attention to the play of words. So, straining to focus on pools of light, and expecting, mistakenly, scientific exposition, I gave into jet lag for a dozing moment. But soon my head was snapped erect by the realization that beneath the simplicity of the staging and of much of the dialogue, Frayn was presenting, not clarity, but how muddled our ways of knowing inevitably are and how foolish our attempts to apply abstract "truths" to human affairs. Even in the pursuit of pure scientific knowledge, our affections and affectations, our prejudices and preconceptions, intrude.

Two of *Copenhagen*'s three characters, Niels Bohr and Werner Heisenberg, in fact made revolutionary discoveries in physical theory; they did so in competitive cooperation, but mutual respect and friendship never fully suppressed their conflicting egos, as the third character, Margrethe Bohr, testifies. In a program note—all one needs to follow the play's discussion of physics—Heisenberg's uncertainty principle is summarized: "The more accurately you know a particle's position, the less accurately you know its velocity, and vice versa." Or, in its human application: One form of accurate knowledge creates doubt about another. Bohr further complicated the theory with his principle of complimentary; in the words Frayn gives him: "Particles are things, complete in themselves. Waves are disturbances in something else." As a consequence, we must choose one of the two ways

of seeing, but "as soon as we do we can't know everything about them." So the two insights, crucial to making the atomic bomb, are revolutionary discoveries that end in paradox, an often mysterious, discomforting form of knowledge that Frayn extends to his portrayals of character:

HEISENBERG [to Bohr]: We can't completely understand your behaviour without seeing it both ways at once, and that's impossible, because the two ways are mutually incompatible.

How we know each other, then, makes full human understanding impossible, and like *Copenhagen*'s discusssions of physical theory, imperfect character relationships are suggested by the play's staging. The technical achievement of the production has, however, diverted attention from a greater artistic one, for *Copenhagen* takes the play of ideas well beyond the theoretical limits set by Shaw and Brecht, the two modern playwrights clearly committed to the principle that drama provoke its audience to rational thought as preclude to a new social awareness or action. Unlike the thesis play which directs an enlightened conclusion or pits conflicting positions against one another, *Copenhagen* presents, as only a drama can, the intellectual excitement and emotional burden of uncertain or incomplete knowledge, and it does so without taking moral refuge in an indeterminacy with no practical consequences.

Shaw was explicit about his own purpose: "My plays are built to induce . . . intellectual interest." He admired Ibsen and Strindberg for their "attack[s] all along the front of refined society," and he endorsed the "problem" play for its "remorseless logic and iron framework of fact." To Brecht, the theorist of alienation, Shaw practiced what he praised: "The reason why Shaw's own dramatic works dwarf those of his contemporaries is that they so unhesitatingly appealed to reason." Shaw's "Quintessence of Ibsenism" elevates his didactic commitment to the level of a formal theory in which the "unraveling in the third [act]" of a "well-made play" is replaced by a "discussion and its development." Shaw discovered this "technical novelty" empirically; even today, the climactic discussion of *A Doll's House* remains the prime example of his new dramatic form. The discussion that Shaw admires does not tie up the loose ends of a plot to the audience's satisfaction; instead, it settles a question in dispute and so has the decisiveness of a formal debate. It is climactic because all that can be said has been said, and the audience is left to choose one of two positions, one of which is obviously preferable. In its dialogue as well as its form, Ibsen's last act also exemplifies techniques of debate in which Nora controls the discussion and directs its resolution. Like a disputant, Nora distinguishes her opponent's meanings: when Torvald says "loved," she replies, "You never loved me. You've thought it fun to be in love with me"; when he calls her "incompetent," she turns his word back upon him, "I must learn to be competent." When Torvald asserts as a fact that "no one gives up honor for love," Nora responds with a strategy taught to Renaissance men, the direct denial: "Millions of women have done just that." Her slamming the door puts a triumphant exclamation point to her victory as debater. The discussion has a clear winner, a resolution similar to the intellectual satisfaction an audience gets when plot complications are resolved. Likewise, although Brecht claims that his dramatic form frees the audience to "think for itself," his political lessons come through with unmistakable clarity. At the end of *Copenhagen,* however, the character who most strongly wants the others to understand him is resigned, as the audience must be, to accept an inconclusive ending, one which leaves ideas in play, jostling against one another, mutually uninforming.

Frayn's imagined conversations take place after the deaths of *Copenhagen*'s three characters. The premise frees him to create arguments that the German physicist, Werner Heisenberg, might have used to justify his Nazi-sponsored research to his early mentor, Niels Bohr, in meetings that took place in 1941 and 1947. Heisenberg did in fact go to Copenhagen early in the war and returned after it, both times to talk to Bohr. Beyond that, the record of what they actually said is blank; historians rely, reasonably enough, on circumstantial evidence to argue contrary conclusions: that Heisenberg willingly tried to develop the atomic bomb for Hitler or that he deliberately obstructed efforts to make one; that he was indifferent to the destruction of Jews or that he went to Copenhagen to save Bohr and thousands of others. Frayn seems to be offering a resolution of such opposing positions when he attributes a debater's proposition to Heisenberg as he drives to recover a certain account of his conversation with Bohr: "I chose my words very carefully. I simply asked you if as a physicist one had the moral right to work on the practical exploitation of atomic energy." But Bohr's reply prevents a Shavian discussion or a Brechtian lesson: "I don't recall." In Frayn's view, answering that question Yes or No would only comfort us with smug certainty imposed from an impersonal

"FRAYN WAS PRESENTING, NOT CLARITY, BUT HOW MUDDLED OUR WAYS OF KNOWING INEVITABLY ARE AND HOW FOOLISH OUR ATTEMPTS TO APPLY ABSTRACT 'TRUTHS' TO HUMAN AFFAIRS."

historical distance. A better proposition, one that would be a witty paradox in other hands, comes in the play's opening minutes when Heisenberg alludes to his theoretical achievement as physicist: "Everyone understands uncertainty." He quickly qualifies that absolute ("Or thinks he does") and in a sharp antithesis locates abstract knowledge in its confused human context: "No one understands my trip to Copenhagen."

In the play's structure, theoretical physics is subordinated to character; what we think we know is only one part of what makes us human. Frayn delays his most complete explanation of the uncertainty principle until well into the second of *Copenhagen*'s two acts when Heisenberg, in one of many artful lines that ambiguously combine the idiomatic and the esoteric, says, "That's when I did uncertainty." He talks about taking a walk and realizes that if he could be seen through a distant telescope, he would appear as a series of "glimpses" to the spectator, not as someone on a continuous path. This insight told him that fellow scientists view "what we see in a cloud chamber," not as a fixed reality observable for and in itself but as something conditioned by their point of view and by their laboratory techniques. Whenever we observe—the unstated analogy to the theatre audience is a constant—we introduce "some new element into the situation" which allows us to measure its effects but which also makes that measurement less than absolutely accurate. Bohr confirms this point in his summary of Einstein: "Measurement . . . is not an impersonal event that occurs with impartial universality. It's a human act, carried out from a specific point of view in time and space, from one particular viewpoint of a possible observer." This comment also comes late in the play, long after Bohr has advocated logical calculation as a step toward deciding whether to welcome Heisenberg to his home; early in Act I, he meets his wife's objection to the visit with, "Let's add up the arguments on either side in a reasonably scientific way." His first reason, though, is based on ethos not logos, "Heisenberg is a friend," and it argues for the priority of human values over scientific ones in weighing arguments.

Throughout *Copenhagen*, scientific problems and procedures are silently subordinated to questions of character and motivation even as the dialogue recounts the physicists' thinking in precise detail. An audience need not follow discussion of isotopes and neutrons, of U-238 and U-235, to appreciate Frayn's point about the worth of certain ideas in an uncertain world. Theoretical abstractions and laboratory experiments, once proved to work, can no more be isolated from their effects than physics can be removed from politics, for as Heisenberg says of the latter pair, "The two are sometimes painfully difficult to keep apart." As dramatic and thematic preliminary to such observations, Frayn has the men recount their first meeting when Heisenberg, a "cheeky young pup" as Bohr remembers him, publicly questions the mathematics in the older man's lecture. Although Heisenberg was not only cheeky but correct, the men became friends, the human relation more important than the mathematics. Later, when Bohr wonders if he could have "miscalculated" absorption rates of neutrons in their first conversation, each of the three characters in close sequence asks what "exactly" was said. To come to terms with the past they want an exact historical record, a way of knowing as comforting in its way as mathematical certainty but more of a false fire because it relies on memory which, even in the pursuit of truth, has a capacity to deceive. Frayn himself creates a drama based on the recollections of his three characters, but he cautions his audience on memory's reliability when Margrethe corrects her husband's recollection, and he defends himself by calling memory "a curious sort of diary."

In contrast, Heisenberg's faith in mathematical certainty can be absolute. He recalls being excited by a vision of "a world of pure mathematical structures," and disputing with Bohr, he declares, "What something means is what it means in mathematics." But when Frayn obliges him to account for the Bohrs' working partnership, Heisenberg must qualify his pure belief; "Mathematics becomes very odd when you apply it to people. One plus one can add up to so many different sums,"

and his voice then trails off. Logic offers no firmer ground for clear resolutions; the steps to its conclusions are taken by flawed human beings. Both Bohr and Heisenberg warn and are warned against "jump[ing] to conclusions" about each other. Although Heisenberg's theory "lays waste to the idea of causality" as a physical force, prejudice as a moral and social cause had profound practical effects for the Nazi atomic project. Heisenberg says that the men who "should have been making their calculations for us" were in England, and Margrethe gives the reason, "Because they were Jews." Hitler saw the Jewish scientists as less than human, their science too relativistic, so he lost the men who did the calculations necessary to solve the diffusion equation. Heisenberg's reaction to Margrethe, completely in character, compresses uncertainty and certainty with unconscious irony: "There's something almost mathematically elegant about that." In many lines like these, *Copenhagen* argues, outside of logic, that human concerns-the very stuff of much drama-inform all our actions and that the formal structures of our thinking are inevitably qualified in practice by uncertain "somethings" and "almosts."

Countering Heisenberg's drive for certainty, Bohr can delight in paradox, the trope that turns in on itself and, so, leaves ideas in suspension, unresolved, perhaps mysterious. In a subtle undercurrent, Frayn introduces paradox and its natural partner, ambiguity, in simple language; they are his stylistic renderings of a uncertain certainty. Besides the early "Everyone understands uncertainty," we get a critique of the play's dialogue: "Each time he explained, it became more obscure." A pun on "chilly" questions the bond between the men: "A little chilly tonight, perhaps for strolling." Margrethe speaks of "the questions that haunt us still," and the last word can be either adjective or abverb—both meaningful in context. Recalling the Bohrs' lost children, Heisenberg sees them both as "simultaneously alive and dead in our memories," an observation that applies to the characters themselves in the dramatic exchanges Frayn creates. Like them, a responsive theatre audience lives in paradoxical time with present and past alive and dead simultaneously, and what Heisenberg says later applies to them as well, "All we possess is the present, and the present endlessly dissolves into the past." These insights belie Heisenberg's judgment on the pleasure Bohr takes in scientific mysteries:

HEISENBERG: You actually loved the paradoxes, that's your problem. You revelled in the contradictions.

BOHR: Yes, and you've never been able to understand the suggestiveness of paradox and contradiction.

That's your problem. You live and breathe paradox
and contradiction, but you can no more see the beauty
of them than the fish can see the beauty of water.

From the first word of *Copenhagen,* Frayn locates the audience in the ambiguous space between
Heisenberg certainty and Bohr suggestiveness;
we are teased into thought without following
Brechtian signposts or Shavian deductions. The
first word, "But," is the conjuction that doesn't
quite connect, that qualifies what comes before.
Not only does silence precede it, Margrethe also
wants to know a reason: "But why?" The last words
of the play are similarly unsettling—sentence fragments delivered by Heisenberg, the character who
most strongly wants to be understood but who can
conclude only to "that final core of uncertainty at
the heart of things." Early critics could disagree
whether Nora did the right thing precisely because
A Doll's House so openly argues to a dramatized
conclusion. Her worthy may be debated after the
curtain goes down, but Ibsen closes the door on his
case as forcefully as she slams it on her marriage.
Mother Courage's wagon may go around in stage
circles, but Brecht directs the audience to follow
his straightforward thinking about war and survival. No such quasi-logical finality resolves the
human ambiguities and theoretical paradoxes in
Copenhagen. Had Frayn put Heisenberg's last
words in axiomatic form—Be certain of
uncertainty—the assertion would teach us only to
be guarded in thought and action.

This final stasis is a satisfying ending to a non-
linear play that relies almost exclusively on the dramatic present, an immediate present that subsumes
stage presence, the historical present and the past
all at once. The three characters remain in view
throughout; when Bohr and Heisenberg go for a
walk, they circle the edges of the playing space,
bare except for a few straight chairs and Margrethe.
Imagined as dead by the playwright, the three can
examine their motives before and after the speeches
they recreate, and Margrethe can speak directly to
us from an apparently dispassionate point of view.
Her first words echo Bohr's second line in the play,
"Now we're all dead and gone." The men have yet
to meet at the point, but Frayn's staging has put
Heisenberg before us as a way of insisting on the
theatrical present through his repeated "Now":
"The more I've explained the deeper the uncertainty has become. Well, I shall be happy to make
one more attempt. Now we're all dead and gone.
Now no one can be hurt, now no one can be betrayed." Characters and their ethos, Heisenberg
suggests, can be abstracted from the circumstances

of historical time, and a truth may emerge. Frayn's
staging seems to collaborate with Heisenberg: a
minimal use of props, pools of light from above,
and bland period costumes. The paucity of stage
effects, those circumstances that can direct an audience to judge, narrows and sharpens *Copenhagen*'s focus. Beyond the words of its resurrected
characters, the play offers no theatrical signs to
convey sure meaning—no symbolic seagulls, no
vulgar Paycock furniture. As a result, the immediate present acquires a dominance even as the characters reconsider their versions of the past.

Much as Frayn summons the past into that
present, he finds the significant in the transient and
the essential in the accidental. What Heisenberg
says of social contacts opposes the permanent ("essential") and the fleeting ("circumstances") and
ironically modifies them with antithetical quali-
fiers: "Essential perhaps, in certain circumstances."
What we try to fix as permanent truth is similarly
qualified by our angle of vision as spectators, for
Frayn has situated the theatregoer in a position
analogous to the physicist's. Not only must we
choose how to listen—to lines and speeches either
as convincing in themselves or as parts of dialogue
(as waves or particles)—but we must also evaluate
the characters' speeches as choices made under a
major constraint. Early in the play, Margrethe acknowledges the historical and dramatic pressures
that prevent full disclosures: "What can any of us
say in the present circumstances?" Ordinarily, stage
entrances make characters "present" and give
promise of something to come, an action to unfold
plot or dialogue to develop relationships. In a departure from the norm, Heisenberg does not enter
a scene without first appearing on stage, and his
entrances, such as they are, circle back to the constant "Now" of his opening speech. This formal
pattern of recurrence undermines any expectations
of chronological or logical progression that the audience might have. The "Here" in "Here I am"
refers to the actor's place on stage and to several
distinct places which—absent scenery—must be
imagined both by actor and audience. Heisenberg
speaks the line to himself as he walks toward the
Bohr house, and yet again, "But now here I am,"
much later in dialogue with Bohr who, positioning
himself to recreate a conversation, resigns himself
to follow Heisenberg's prompting, "Very well.
Here I am walking very slowly." At three important times, Heisenberg prefaces his entrance to the
house with "I crunch over the familiar gravel"—
near the beginning and end of Act I and near the
end of the play. The lines signaling these returns

sound like creative variations on Brecht's rehearsal prompts:

> Three aids ... may help to alienate the actions and remarks of the characters being portrayed:
>
> 1) Transposition into the third person.
>
> 2) Transposition into the past.
>
> 3) Speaking the stage directions outloud.

Speaking in the first person, as actual performance dictates, and in the present tense, Frayn's characters retain their immediacy and gain emotional distance at the same time. Like the repeated 11 crunch, the men's greeting—a version of hundreds of conventional entrances—is reenacted at the close of the first act:

> HEISENBERG: My dear Bohr!
>
> BOHR: Come in, come in . . .

These textual and thematic returns are realized theatrically in the characters' movements and gestures, and the pattern argues subtly about our ability to know. For, although the three characters have applied singular talents and intelligence to understand themselves and each other, their discussions, explanations, reconstructions and reminiscences do not make connected sense of the past. At best, they "glimpse" discrete points in a loop, but to their credit they labor hard to make their circular journey and finally they learn to cherish the moment that they glimpse. Journeying with them, the audience is led to evaluate modes of thinking from the privileged position of intellectual voyeurs and at the same time to fill out the empty space imaginatively.

Copenhagen, like many other plays, stands squarely in the tradition dominated by *Waiting for Godot.* Its minimal setting and its non-linear form connect Frayn to Beckett, while the questions that Heisenberg and Bohr raise have profound political and social implications. They are heirs of Didi and Gogo, but they do not play roles to pass the empty time; rather, along with Margrethe, they play them as reenactments of actual events, as present recreations of discussions and of their historical contexts. At times, the Brecht and Beckett traditions merge, as in one passage when the characters resemble actors in rehearsal trying to get inside their roles. Since the roles are the selves they would study, however, the playacting teaches a form of objectivity:

> MARGRETHE: I watch the two smiles in the room . . .
>
> BOHR: I glance at Margrethe . . .
>
> HEISENBERG: I look at the two of them looking at me . . .
>
> BOHR: I look at him looking at me . . .

Their limited self-awareness authorizes interpretations of the others' acting; Bohr, addressing the audience, uses language that calls attention to Heisenberg's practiced delivery and, so, to his sincerity: "With careful casualness he begins to ask the questions he's prepared." And Heisenberg, in turn, cues a response to Bohr: "He gazes at me, horrified." A few lines later, Bohr tries to engage the historical past with a form of theatrical improvisation: "Let's suppose for a moment that instead I remember the paternal role I'm supposed to play. Let's see what happens if I stop, and control my anger, and turn to him. And ask him why." Watch them watching themselves closely, Frayn seems to advise, and see how proper sight can lead to insight for the audiences as well as the characters. So, we learn with Margrethe that the past, laden with emotional weight, resists rounded, causally finished accounts: "What I see isn't a story! It's confusion and rage and jealousy and tears." We sympathize with Bohr, his memory burdened by the loss of children and his role in developing the Bomb: "Before we can glimpse who or what we are, we're gone and laid to dust." At the very end, we are aligned with Heisenberg who wanted mathematical certainty but must, too, be content—richly content at that—with fragments:

> In the meanwhile, in this most precious meanwhile, there it is. . . . Our children and our children's children. Preserved, just possibly, by that one short moment in Copenhagen. By some event that will never quite be located or defined. By that final core of uncertainty at the heart of things.

Copenhagen also entertains the weighty questions of man's place in the universe, of ultimate responsibility for unintended consequences and of evil. Frayn roots these and other moral abstractions in flawed human beings; the imperfect truths they earn survive their social and theatrical roles. And, for me, Frayn's truths survive performance, for the second time I saw *Copenhagen,* having read the text and knowing what to expect, I left the theatre shaking my head at the wisdom of the play's inconclusiveness. If it has a Shavian lesson, it's something like Relish the Moment, always remembering that we can never really know if we got the moment right.

Source: Robert L. King, "The Play of Uncertain Ideas," in *Massachusetts Review*, Vol. 42, No. 2, Summer 2001, pp. 165–76.

Paul Lawrence Rose

In the following review-essay, Rose discusses the multiple perspectives included in Copenhagen *and their effects on the audience and science historians.*

Scholars are never satisfied when they see their specialized subjects turn fodder for stage, screen, or novels. The adaptor, like the translator, is by definition something of a traitor to his topic. There are so many pitfalls awaiting the artistic magus. He can get an essential personality wrong, as Peter Shaffer may have done with his hyperactive Mozart in *Amadeus,* or worse, with his Salieri, whom the playwright slanders as a murderer. Or he may get the facts of a historical situation wrong, as Rolf Hochhuth allegedly did in recounting Pius XII's nonreaction to the Holocaust in the 1963 play *The Representative.*

In such cases, specialists inevitably carp, and at conferences and in faculty-club chatter, they attempt to recapture the dignity of precision by the renewed staking out of violated scholarly turf. But can that sacred turf ever be fully reclaimed once its invasion has been so publicly observed and, worst of all, when the disreputable artistic distortion of fact has been rapturously received by the laity as an improvement on the arid original? Scholarly exactitude may command its tens of admirers, but poetic license hath its tens of thousands.

These gloomy thoughts of a pedantic specialist on Werner Heisenberg are prompted by the arrival on Broadway of what is being hailed as the play of the year, Michael Frayn's *Copenhagen,* which opened in April at the Royale Theater. The drama revolves around the notorious encounter, in September 1941 in Copenhagen, between Heisenberg, Nazi Germany's brightest star in physics, and his old mentor and friend, Niels Bohr, then a partly Jewish citizen of Nazi-occupied Denmark, and later, at Los Alamos, N.M., a key mind behind the creation of a nuclear-fission bomb. The play is an intermittently fascinating jeu d'esprit that flutters around the uncertain nature of knowledge—both personal and scientific. With just three characters—Heisenberg, Bohr, and Bohr's wife, Margrethe—Frayn develops through his often electric dialogue a synergy on stage that has made the play a success at London's Royal National Theatre and ensured its production not only in New York, but in France, Germany, and Denmark, as well as prompting conferences in London, in New York, in Amiens, at Dartmouth College, and in Copenhagen itself.

What explains all this commotion? Of course, physicists are so pleased to see any reasonably interesting picture on stage of their often hermetic lives that they have flocked to the play, but then physicists are hardly a large enough contingent to regularly fill a theater. The trendy issue of the "two cultures," however, ensures that any serious attempt at bridging the

THE *COPENHAGEN* EXPERIENCE CARRIES THE AUDIENCE ALONG HEADILY ON A SCIENTIFIC ROLLER COASTER. FORGET ABOUT UNDERSTANDING JUST LOOK AT THE VIEWS!"

gap between scientists and nonscientists will appeal to our academic consciences; this year, the University of Pennsylvania had the bright idea of making Copenhagen required reading for all freshmen.

The play cleverly exploits parallels between the questioning by humanistic postmodernists of historical facts and the questioning by constructivists of scientific facts. To oversimplify considerably, constructivists might consider particle physics to be fanciful belief system molded by social and cultural factors, with no more underlying truth than alchemy. That's a notion that may hold some appeal for select scholars of the history of science.

Would it be cynical to suggest, however, that it has equal charm for the lion's share of viewers, who might find it reassuring to learn that the science they know so little about might just be pie in the sky anyway? If all is unknowable, then does it matter that I got a D on all those problem sets in organic chemistry and became an investment banker?

Nor should one omit the work's sheer theatricality, talky as it may be. As it flits dizzyingly from philosophy to physics to politics to personality to history, there's no time for the audience to get a real grip on any of the crucial points at issue. At intermission, viewers happily recall how they didn't quite understand this or that bit, but how brilliant it all seems.

What's wrong with that? The intellectual vertigo induced by Frayn's quicksilver writing may be intended to capture some of the intellectual excitement inherent in the discoveries of science, and of life. But the price we pay for the dramatic thrill Frayn has concocted—the sacrifice of historical and scientific truth—is simply too great. The *Copenhagen* experience carries the audience along headily on a scientific roller coaster. Forget about understanding just look at the views!

Copenhagen is a kind *Rashomon*—like treatment of a central historical episode, but one refracted through a postmodernist lens and complicated by philosophical ideas derived (a little too glibly) from the quantum mechanics pioneered by Heisenberg and Bohr—such oftmisunderstood, if oft-cited, concepts as Heisenberg's uncertainly principle and Bohr's complementary principle. The limits of knowledge, of knowledge of others, of oneself, of the external world of politics and mortality; the plasticity of memory; the impossibility of arriving at definitive moral judgments—this is the heady stuff of *Copenhagen*. The 20th century has seen at least two remarkable plays that drew their inspiration from the world of science—Bertolt Brecht's *Life of Galileo* and Friedrich Durrenmatt's *The Physicists*—but none has achieved the brilliance of *Copenhagen* in rendering the technical discussion of scientific ideas dramatically convincing and, at the same time, accessible to scientists and nonscientists alike.

But even the play's admirers may have felt a certain unease. Was Heisenberg really the character depicted so sympathetically on stage? Was his attitude toward Nazism really so ambivalent, or so justifiable, as Frayn variously suggests? Did the meeting really take the former rather forms—that Frayn depicts? On a more general level, must our historical knowledge of people and events inevitably be as foggy as Frayn paints it?

If we can come nearer the historical truth of the meeting than Frayn's uncertainty principle allows, then the glittering decor of *Copenhagen* may turn out, indeed, to be constructed on false historical foundations that undermine its whole intellectual edifice. And here pipes up the aggrieved author, who has devoted two chapters of his recent book to analyzing the Copenhagen visit from both its scientific and moral standpoints. For the central facts of the visit are really not in doubt, even if some people like Frayn refuse to face them.

Frayn, of course, might object that facts, here, are irrelevant. After all, he affects to be an entertainer rather than a historian (although in his printed postscript, he likes to play the historian). The play is certainly full of entertaining anecdotes and mannerisms. It's a pity, though, that Frayn's eye for the picturesque didn't select such gems as Heisenberg's barging in on a dismayed Einstein after the war, or Heisenberg's sickening postwar meeting with the physicist Max Born that degenerated into an anti-Semitic tirade and ended with Heisenberg's spitting at his former teacher. Or, while at Copenhagen, his

enthusing to colleagues there about the current Nazi conquest of Europe.

Moreover, historians have been able to discover a few things about Heisenberg's visit that undermine Frayn's claims of unknowability. We know, for a start, that Heisenberg went there on an intelligence mission triggered by a Swedish press report that the Allies were working on a bomb. Heisenberg's intimate friend was the physicist Carl-Friedrich von Weizsacker (who in recent years has finally conceded that in 1939 and 1940 he was willingly working to produce a bomb for Hitler). Alarmed by the Swedish report, Weizsacker discussed the bomb race with his father, Ernst, a senior official in the German Foreign Office later convicted at Nuremberg of war crimes. Soon after the father-son discussion, a mission to Copenhagen by Heisenberg and Carl Friedrich was swiftly approved at the highest levels of the Nazi government. The general purpose was to discover if Heisenberg had missed some broad principle necessary to a nuclear-weapons program and to discern if Bohr knew anything about the Allied bomb effort.

At one point during his visit with Bohr, Heisenberg made a crude drawing of a gigantic reactor-bomb, a drawing that reflected an erroneous line of research that his assistants had been pursuing and that was also discussed in an official German report a few months later. Both men would have concluded that such a weapon was a far-fetched idea. Without doubt, Heisenberg also wished to have Bohr confirm that the critical mass of uranium 235 required for a true atomic bomb would be on the order of tons, thus ruling out any possibility of its being built. There was no difficulty in Bohr's agreeing with that since, until 1943, when he was informed of the Allied work, Bohr genuinely believed, like Heisenberg, that a bomb was impossible because of that presumed critical mass. That was why Bohr remained reasonably unalarmed on a scientific level by Heisenberg's conversation. It was the moral situation—Heisenberg's working on a bomb for Hitler and pumping Bohr for information—that revulsed him.

Frayn perverts the moral significance of the meeting as well as distorting and suppressing its scientific and political agenda. Frayn instead sees it as emblematic of what is for him the central moral paradox of modernity: Was the saintly Bohr, who helped develop the Allies' nuclear weapons, actually morally inferior to Heisenberg, the acolyte of Nazism, who failed for whatever reason to make a bomb? Put this way, Heisenberg would undoubtedly have been delighted with Frayn's presentation of a case he himself implied but was afraid to make publicly. The bogus moralizing that Heisenberg did dare to utter openly is alluded to in the play: "Does one as a physicist have the moral right to work on the practical exploitation of atomic energy?" Or, as he put it after the war: "[Do] physicists have the moral right to work on atomic problems during wartime?"

Those generalized, vague questions were typical Heisenberg evasions. The real moral issue that Heisenberg should have faced was the very specific one of whether German physicists should have worked-as they didon a bomb for Hitler. For Bohr—who was openly worried about the race toward nuclear fission and, even in late 1943, urged transnational consideration of such a bomb's consequences—the question that confronted him after his arrival in the West was a different one. Was the Nazi evil so great as to justify working on a bomb that would defeat Hitler? The larger issue that confronted Bohr—whether anyone should work on a bomb for any government—was an ethical quandary that the Allies didn't have the luxury of pondering during the emergency of the war, but that became pressing in 1945 and after. It was that more-general question that Heisenberg craftily made the central issue of his wartime work, but that was only after the war, when the moral battlefield had changed.

What influences have led Frayn to shun the fairly straightforward historical and moral facts of the Heisenberg story, in favor of his own peculiar interpretation? Curiously, despite his essential premise of historical uncertainty, Frayn does indeed purport to give an accurate impression of the history of Heisenberg and his involvement in the German atomic project, particularly of his visit to Copenhagen. But as Frayn admits in a lengthy postscript to the painted text, that impression is based largely on *Heisenberg's War,* a popular 1993 book by the journalist Thomas Powers, whose ignorance of German and physics enabled him to happily fantasize about Heisenberg as a secret resister who knew exactly how to make a bomb, but effectively sabotaged the project by delay or intentional mistakes. Heisenberg, in Powers's view, also became associated with the rescue of the Danish Jews and the July Plot against Hitler. In real life, Heisenberg, like his friend Weizsacker and Weizsacker pere, disapproved of the plot as an act of treason and never justified it even after the war. Frayn, however, advances a notion that was suggested by Ernst von Weizsacker and Heisenberg, and bought by Powers—that the Weizsacker circle clandestinely resisted Hitler and was connected to a German official who tipped off the Danes to the impending deportation of Danish Jews. Ernst von Weizsacker's judges at Nuremberg didn't buy that argument, and nothing found in the historical record since has lent the scenario any more credibility. Powers's quaintly romantic view, as he has conceded, has not found any takers among serious historians. Indeed, there really is no longer any doubt about either Heisenberg's loyalty to the Third Reich or his scientific misunderstanding of an atomic bomb.

Recent research has established the facts of Heisenberg's allegiance to the Reich. Consider his negotiations with Heinrich Himmler to obtain a chair at the University of Munich and Heisenberg's insistence that he be allowed to publish an article in the ss's scientific journal to vindicate, he said, his "honor." Note his visits to occupied Krakow, Holland, and Copenhagen, and his crass comments to his former friends in those places about how marvelous the Nazi conquest of Europe was. Mark his wistful remarks in Switzerland in 1944 about how the war was lost, but "how beautiful it would have been if only we had won," and his truly amazing assertion to Jewish acquaintances in England and America after the war that, if only the Nazis had been given 50 years, everything would have settled down nicely.

The evidence is consistent in showing Heisenberg to have been a brilliant but weak man, whose shallow moral character allowed him to be easily corrupted by his nationalist German sympathies into colluding with Nazism. His ability to rationalize instantly, whatever the circumstances, any path of conduct stood him in good stead after the war, when he concocted his various "versions" of what had happened at Copenhagen and, indeed, of his entire career as scientific chief of the Nazi atomic-bomb project.

As to the scientific aspect, Heisenberg's misconceptions about the nature of an atomic bomb have in the last few years been exposed once and for all by the release and publication of the Farm Hall transcriptstaped conversations of German scientists interned at Farm Hall, England, at the time of Hiroshima—as well as by the availability of the nearly 400 secret wartime reports of the German project of which Heisenberg was the scientific chief. Those sources unequivocally reveal just how crude and wrong-headed Heisenberg's approach was to the theory of the bomb. Although he understood that the bomb would have to use a fast-neutron reaction in nearly pure uranium 235, he misconceived the formula and equation that would have yielded the correct critical mass of uranium on the order of tens of kilograms. Instead, he concluded through false reasoning in 1940 that tons would be required. That scientific error blinded him for the remainder of the war. (He also erred in conceiving of an alternative kind of messy, small-scale of bomb that essentially would have been an exploding reactor—the idea that he discussed with Bohr in 1941.)

It was only after the news of Hiroshima that Heisenberg finally went back to the drawing board and, within a week, concluded that, after all, only kilograms of uranium were needed. Had he realized that in 1940, the German project would certainly have gone into high gear, and perhaps even succeeded.

Frayn refuses to comprehend, or perhaps acknowledge, Heisenberg's scientific misunderstandings. The play does portray Heisenberg as squirming a bit when conceding that on the evening of Hiroshima, he had told Otto Hahn and others that a ton of uranium would be needed for a bomb. But then Frayn allows Heisenberg to explain this away in a manner clearly believable to the author and endorsed in the play's postscript, where Frayn decides, after all, that he will play the role of historian.

Confusingly, Frayn allows Heisenberg to argue that: (a) he had never calculated the critical mass, but was going on a generally accepted intuitive view of a large bomb mass, and (b) he did the detailed calculation using diffusion theory only for a seminar given at Farm Hall on August 14, 1945. Frayn doesn't appear to notice (though some in his audiences have) that even if one were to believe that version of events, it undermines the play's notion of Heisenberg as a saboteur of Hitler's bomb-making effort.

At any rate, Frayn's version is blatantly wrong in one crucial respect. Heisenberg had indeed made an earlier, erroneous calculation, in 1940, yielding a mass of tons, and it is that calculation (based on a random-walk analysis) that Heisenberg explained repeatedly, and in detail, at Farm Hall on August 6, 7, and 9. However, the analysis of the critical mass in the August 14 seminar is quite differently, and correctly, conceived. In the days between August 9 and 14, Heisenberg had desperately gone back to first principles and rethought the whole critical-mass problem.

Frayn trickily alludes in a very vague way to the 1939–40 calculation of tons of uranium in Act I, perhaps expecting his audience to forget that, when the critical mass of tons is raised dramatically at the climax of Act II, it has been arrived at by calculation, not conjured out of thin air. Frayn's sleight of hand camouflages the fact that, at Farm Hall in the first days after Hiroshima, Heisenberg still fervently believed in the technical correctness of his early calculation.

The bottom line is that Heisenberg, like Weizsacker, had been working hard in 1939–40 to make a bomb for Hitler, but—scientifically speaking—was barking up the wrong tree.

Frayn has evidently fallen for some of the more absurd moral justifications by the Axis scientists for their serving the Nazi regime. Those excuses included Heisenberg's sanctimonious comment in 1948 that "I have learned something that my Western friends do not yet completely wish to admit—that in such times almost no one can avoid committing crimes or supporting them through inaction, be he on the German, Russian or Anglo-Saxon side." That self serving statement allowed Heisenberg to pose at least as Bohr's moral equal, perhaps even his superior, and it is a notion that drifts noxiously in and out of *Copenhagen.*

It is simply monstrous to draw or imply a moral symmetry between Bohr and his disciple. Niels Bohr was a man of the most intense moral awareness, whose integrity has been universally recognized. If he became involved in the Los Alamos bomb project after his narrowing escape from Denmark, in 1943, it was only after his serious ethical misgivings about such a weapon had been overcome by consideration of the immediate evil presented by Nazism. To put a character of Bohr's moral stature on anywhere near the same plane as a superficial, rationalizing sophist like Heisenberg suggests an incomplete knowledge not only of the historical facts, but of human character. Heisenberg never accepted moral responsibility for his role either in the Nazi state or in the Nazi atomic-bomb project.

It was that evasion that drove Heisenberg to invent the Copenhagen version that Frayn obviously prefers. Yet this version was—in the words of Heisenberg's sympathetic British minder, Ronald Fraser, during a second visit to Copenhagen after the war—"a typical Heisenberg fabrication. . . . He rationalizes that quickly that the stories become for him the truth. . . . Pitiful, in a man of his mental stature."

"Now no one can be hurt, and no one betrayed," purrs Heisenberg in the play. But the memory of Bohr has been hurt, and Heisenberg's true history betrayed. And Heisenberg is left approvingly with the last treacherous—and banal—words in the play about "some event that will never quite be located or defined ... that final core of uncertainty at the heart of things."

The elegiac and exhausted ending of the play is where the accumulation of distortions and mistakes finally turns into something altogether more distasteful. It has the appearances of a Lear-like transcendence of the destructive futility of human striving. We are with three characters, all passion spent, but with Heisenberg having the unanswered final say. He is granted a wrenching speech lamenting the death of his poor "dishonored Germany," which audiences receive as a moving testimony.

It is a spurious absolution, for Heisenberg himself was one of those who made that dishonoring possible through his selfish compromises with the Nazi regime irony to which Frayn seems oblivious. Frayn's irony, instead, is applied to a vicious denigration of Bohr, "the good man," who emerges by the end as a self absorbed prig, in different to the births and welfare of his own children, who contributed to the deaths of tens of thousands through his work on the Allied bomb.

Bohr is not the only one who turns out to be an unintentional villain. The Allies are in general, and the Jews, too; after all, as Frayn's play points out—in a moment that stuns a New York audience—the true inventors of the bomb, Otto Frisch and Rudolf Peierls, were Jews. Everyone, then, is seen to be guilty, and so everyone is blameless. There is no difference between the Gestapo and British intelligence. The British bombing of Dresden and Berlin is as bad as Hitler's Blitz on British and Polish civilians. Churchill and Roosevelt are amoral power-wielders, just like Hitler (another Heisenberg glibness), and so on.

It all makes one wonder what the Second World War was fought for. Was it just another dreadful mistake like its precursor? Was appeasement, after all, the right policy, as a few radical British historians have argued?

When I first read *Copenhagen,* I found its elan disarming. But the generally uncritical reception in the last two years and the prospect of more of the same in New York have aroused, no doubt unworthily, a more puritanical feeling. Thanks to the play's chic postmodernism as well as the complexity of its ideas, the subtle revisionism of *Copenhagen* has been received with a respect denied to such cruder revisionisms as that of David Irving's Holocaust denial. Revisionism it is, nonetheless, and *Copenhagen* is more destructive

than Irving's self evidently ridiculous assertions—more destructive of the integrity of art, of science, and of history.

Source: Paul Lawrence Rose, "Frayn's *Copenhagen* Plays Well, At History's Expense," in *Chronicle of Higher Education*, Vol. 46, No. 35, May 5, 2000, pp. B4–6.

SOURCES

Becker, Jules, "*Copenhagen*: A Magical Blend of Physics and Dramatic Events," in *Telegram and Gazette* (Worcester, Massachusetts), May 11, 2002, p. A6.

Berson, Misha, "Frayn's *Copenhagen* Is Intensely Engaging," in *Seattle Times*, October 2, 2002, p. F1.

Frayn, Michael, *Copenhagen*, Methuen, 1998.

Klein, Julia M., "When Plays Touch on History, What Is Truth?" in *Chronicle of Higher Education*, Vol. 47, No. 38, June 1, 2001, p. 19.

Kroll, Jack, "An Atomic Encounter," in *Newsweek*, Vol. 135, No. 17, April 24, 2000, p. 73.

Logan, Jonothan, "A Strange New Quantum Ethics," in *American Scientist*, Vol. 88, No. 4, July–August 2000, pp. 356–59.

Lyall, Sarah, "Ambiguity Fires a Novelist and Playwright," in *New York Times*, October 25, 1999, p. E1.

MacFarquhar, Larissa, "A Dry Soul Is Best," in *New Yorker*, Vol. 80, No. 32, October 25, 2004, p. 64.

Marks, Peter, "The Physics of Ambiguity, Acutely Observed in *Copenhagen*," in *Washington Post*, July 13, 2004, p. C1.

Pressley, Nelson, "*Copenhagen*: High-Fission Drama," in *Washington Post*, March 1, 2002, p. C1.

Rose, Paul Lawrence, "Frayn's *Copenhagen* Plays Well, at History's Expense," in *Chronicle of Higher Education*, Vol. 46, No. 35, May 2000, pp. B4–B6.

FURTHER READING

Cassidy, David C., *Uncertainty: The Life and Science of Werner Heisenberg*, W. H. Freeman, 1993.
  Cassidy looks at the life and times of Heisenberg as well as at the influences that affected him. A history of quantum mechanics is woven through the story as Heisenberg struggles through trials of exploration.

Frayn, Michael, and David Burke, *The Copenhagen Papers: An Intrigue*, Picador, 2003.
  This book has little to do with Frayn's play. Rather it is based on an interesting development that occurred while the play was in production. It is a dialogue of sorts that occurred between Frayn and Burke (an actor who portrayed Niels Bohr in Frayn's play). It is sometimes funny and always fascinating as the reader witnesses a witty exchange of ideas.

Groueff, Stephane, *Manhattan Project: The Untold Story of the Making of the Atomic Bomb*, Little Brown, 1967.

This book details the U.S. project of bringing together the most brilliant scientists of the 1940s in an attempt to be the first country to create the ultimate weapon of destruction.

Hey, Tony, and Patrick Walters, *The New Quantum Universe*, Cambridge University Press, 2d ed., 2003.

Hey and Walters treat the historic moments of discovery in quantum mechanics as well as its applications in the future. This book is accessible for general readers. Such futuristic topics as the nanotechnology revolution, quantum cryptography, computing, and teleportation are also discussed.

Murdoch, D. R., *Niels Bohr's Philosophy of Physics*, Cambridge University Press, 1989.

In this book, Murdoch explores the background of Niels Bohr's discoveries in physics—in particular, the differences between Bohr's concepts and those of Einstein's are examined, with a special emphasis on Bohr's theory of complementarity.

Fires in the Mirror

ANNA DEAVERE SMITH

1992

In 1991, in the Crown Heights section of Brooklyn, New York, a member of the Lubavitch branch of Hasidic Judaism lost control of his car, jumped the curb, and killed a seven-year-old black child. This incident and the circumstances surrounding it led to a period of extremely high tension between the black community and the Jewish community in Crown Heights, including riots and the murder of the Lubavitcher Jew, Yankel Rosenbaum. As these events were unfolding, Anna Deavere Smith began a series of interviews with many of those involved in the conflict as well as those who were able to make key insights into its nature, its causes, and its results. In her play *Fires in the Mirror*, first produced in New York City in 1992, Smith distills these interviews into monologues by twenty-six different characters, each of whom provides an important and differing view on the situation in Crown Heights.

When Smith performs her play, she acts in the role of each interviewee, embodying his/her voice and movements, and expressing his/her message and personality. These perspectives combine to form a profound explanation of the conflicts between the different Crown Heights communities. Smith examines many of the historical causes of the situation, many of the racial theories that help to explain it, and a broad variety of opinions on the events and people involved, in order to come closer to the truth about what happened and why. Her play, which is the thirteenth part of her unique project *On the Road: A Search for the American Character* combines journalism and drama in order to examine not just the

Anna Deavere Smith © Andrew DeMattos/Corbis

racial tension and violence in Crown Heights, but much broader themes, including racial, religious, gender, and class identity, and the historical conflict between these communities in the United States.

AUTHOR BIOGRAPHY

Smith was born September 18, 1950, in Baltimore, Maryland. The daughter of an elementary school principal and a coffee merchant, she was the oldest of five children. Smith attended Beaver College, outside of Philadelphia, from 1967 to 1971, and after graduating she became interested in the Black Power movement, moving to San Francisco, in part to participate in social and political agitation. While living in San Francisco, she began to take classes at the American Conservatory Theatre, where she earned an MFA in 1976, and then she moved to New York City to work as an actor. Smith then began a professorial career teaching at universities, including Yale, New York University, and Carnegie Mellon. She also began a unique, long-term project called *On the Road: A Search for American Character*, made up of a series of plays that combine journalism with dramatic performance.

Smith's first play/documentary for *On the Road* was produced in Berkeley, California, in

1983. She went on to write and perform two additional plays in the 1980s, but it was her play *Fires in the Mirror* (1992) that rocketed her into the spotlight. In 1993, *Fires in the Mirror* was published in book form, was a runner-up for a Pulitzer Prize, and was televised by PBS as part of the "American Playhouse" series. She has since written and performed four additional plays, including *Twilight: Los Angeles 1992* (1993), which won an Obie Award and was nominated for a Tony Award.

Smith has also acted in television shows, including *The West Wing*, and movies, including *The American President* (1995). She was awarded a prestigious "genius grant" from the MacArthur Foundation in 1996, and in 1998, in association with the Ford Foundation, she founded the Institute on the Arts and Civic Dialogue at Harvard (now at New York University) to address socially and politically conscious art. Smith continues to write, act, teach, and perform. She has taught at Stanford University, is a tenured professor at Tisch School of the Arts at New York University, and is an affiliated faculty member at New York University School of Law.

PLOT SUMMARY

Identity

The opening section of *Fires in the Mirror* is called "Identity." In its first scene "The Desert," Ntozake Shange discusses identity in terms of feeling a part of, yet separate from, one's surroundings. In the next scene, an anonymous Lubavitcher woman tells the story of a black child coming into her house on Shabbas, the Jewish holy day, to switch off their radio. "101 Dalmations" is George C. Wolfe's perspective on his racial identity, in which he argues that blackness exists independently of whiteness.

Mirrors, Hair, Race, and Rhythm

The second section, "Mirrors," contains only one scene, in which Aaron M. Bernstein discusses how mirrors are associated with distortion both in literature and in science. Physicists make telescopes with mirrors as large as possible in order to minimize the "circle of confusion."

The next section, "Hair," begins with a scene in which an anonymous black girl talks about how Hispanic and black teenagers in her Crown Heights junior high school think about race and act according to their racial identities. In "Me and

James's Thing," the Reverend Al Sharpton explains that he straightens his hair (a practice that developed in the 1950s to simulate "white" hair) because he once promised the soul music star James Brown that he would always wear it this way. Next, Rivkah Siegal discusses the common Lubavitch practice of wearing a wig.

Angela Davis is the speaker in the only scene in the section "Race." She considers how the place of blacks and women in U.S. society has changed since the 1960s, and then goes on to discuss the concept of race more generally. In the "Rhythm" section, Monique "Big Mo" Matthews discusses rap, particularly the attitude toward women in hip-hop culture.

Seven Verses

The first speaker in "Seven Verses" is Professor Leonard Jeffries, who describes his involvement in *Roots*, the classic book and then television series about the slave trade. Letty Cottin Pogrebin argues in the next scene that blacks attack Jews because Jews are the only racial group that listens to them and views them as full human beings. Minister Conrad Mohammed then outlines his view of the terrible historical suffering by blacks at the hands of whites, stressing that blacks, and not Jews, are God's chosen people.

In the scene "Isaac," Letty Cottin Pogrebin reads a story about her mother's cousin, who participated in Nazi gassing in order to survive the Holocaust. Robert Sherman then contends that the English language is insufficient for describing and understanding race relations.

Crown Heights, Brooklyn, August 1991

The final section of the play begins with Rabbi Joseph Spielman, who gives his versions of the accident that killed Gavin Cato and of the stabbing of Yankel Rosenbaum, stressing that the black community lied about the events in order to start anti-Semitic riots. Reverend Canon Doctor Heron Sam then describes his opposing view of the two events, full of resentment that the Lubavitcher Grand Rebbe's entourage was reckless and unconcerned about having killed Gavin Cato. In "Wa Wa Wa," an anonymous young man from Crown Heights describes what he saw of the accident, maintaining that the police never arrest Jews or give blacks justice. Michael S. Miller then argues that the black community in Crown Heights is extremely anti-Semitic.

MEDIA ADAPTATIONS

- *Fires in the Mirror* was adapted and filmed for television in 1993, as part of the "American Playhouse Series" on PBS. It starred Smith, was directed by George C. Wolfe, and was produced by Cherie Fortis.

In "Knew How to Use Certain Words," Henry Rice explains his role in the events. While he was trying to stop blacks from instigating violence, he was hit and handcuffed by the police and, after he was released, threatened by a young black man. Norman Rosenbaum gives a speech about the injustice of his brother's stabbing. In the next scene, "16 Hours Difference," Rosenbaum describes his reaction at the time he heard about his brother's murder.

In "Bad Boy," an anonymous young man contends that the sixteen-year-old blamed for Yankel Rosenbaum's murder is an athlete and therefore would not have killed anyone. Sonny Carson then describes his connection with the black youth community and his motivation for leading them in activism against the white power structure.

Rabbi Shea Hecht argues that integration is not the solution to race relations, and he interprets the Lubavitcher Grand Rebbe's comment that all are one people. In "Rain," Reverend Al Sharpton discusses why he went to Israel to pursue legal action against the driver who killed Gavin Cato. Richard Green then speaks of the rage of black youths in Crown Heights and the lack of role models for black youths.

In "The Coup," Roslyn Malamud contends that the blacks involved in the rioting were not her neighbors, and she blames the police department and the leaders of the black community for letting things get out of control. Reuven Ostrov describes how Jews get scared because there are Jew haters everywhere. Finally, Carmel Cato describes his trauma at seeing his son die and expresses his resentment of powerful Jews.

CHARACTERS

Anonymous Girl

The anonymous girl of "Look in the Mirror" is a "Junior high school black girl of Haitian descent" who lives near Crown Heights. She discusses who follows and copies whom in junior high school, making insights about the racial attitudes that develop during adolescence.

Anonymous Lubavitcher Woman

The anonymous Lubavitcher woman in the second scene of the play is a mother and preschool teacher in her mid-thirties. She appears slightly flustered by the religious restrictions that dictate what Hasidic Jews can and cannot do on Shabbas, but she laughs about the situation in which a black boy turns off their radio for them.

Anonymous Young Man #1

"A very handsome Carribbean American man with dreadlocks," the anonymous young man of the scene "Wa Wa Wa" insists that the police unjustly favor Jews over blacks. He was on the street when Yosef Lifsh's car ran over Gavin Cato, and he believes that Lifsh was drunk. When no one wants to do anything to stop Lifsh from getting away, the young man starts to cry. He believes that there will never be any justice because the words of black people "don't have no meanin'" in Crown Heights.

Anonymous Young Man #2

An African American man in his late teens or early twenties, the anonymous young man from the scene "Bad Boy" insists that young black men are either athletes, rappers, or robbers and killers, but not more than one of these things. For this reason, he argues, the sixteen-year-old athlete accused of killing Yankel Rosenbaum is innocent.

Aaron M. Bernstein

A physicist at the Massachusetts Institute of Technology, Aaron Bernstein is a man in his fifties who wears a shirt with a pen guard. He describes how physicists create telescopes in order to minimize the "circle of confusion" caused by mirrors that are not "perfectly spherical or perfectly / parabolic."

Sonny Carson

An activist and agitator, Sonny Carson is involved in the Crown Heights riots. He does not "advocate any coming together and healing of / America," but wants to make up for past injustices by protesting, and instigating violence. Commenting that "Jews come second to the police / when it comes to feelings of dislike among Black folks," he cites his close connection to the youth of Crown Heights and his ability to mobilize them into activism that will last all summer.

Carmel Cato

Gavin Cato's father, Mr. Cato is a deeply traumatized man with a "pronounced West Indian accent." Originally from Guyana, Mr. Cato describes his son's death and his own reaction afterward in the final scene of the play. He explains that what is "devastating" him is that there is no justice because Jews are "runnin' the whole show." He then claims, however, that there is no way the Jews can "overpower" him since he is "special," having been a breech birth (born feet first).

Angela Davis

Davis is the activist and intellectual whose scene "Rope" discusses the need for a new way of viewing race relations. She became involved in philosophy and activism while studying in the United States and Europe during the 1960s. In 1970, she was placed on the FBI Most Wanted List and was imprisoned on homicide and kidnapping charges, of which she was acquitted in 1972. Since then, she has had a successful and prominent career as a scholar and activist, writing about issues such as race theory, and working to achieve prison reform, racial equality, and women's rights. As her scene in *Fires in the Mirror* reveals, Davis is a sophisticated historian and philosopher as well as a practical thinker about community and community relations. At the time of her scene in the play, she is a professor in the History of Consciousness Department at the University of California, Santa Cruz.

Richard Green

Green is a community activist who speaks about the rage that young blacks feel and about their lack of role models and guidance. He stresses that leaders of the black community, such as Al Sharpton, do not control the youths actually carrying out the riots, and that the youths' rage builds up and cannot be contained. Implicitly defending the young black people who used phrases like "Heil Hitler" in the riots, he argues that they do not even know who Hitler was, and that the only black leader they know is Malcolm X. Green is the director of the Crown Heights Youth Collective and the codirector of a black-Hasidic basketball team that developed after the riots. His main role during the period of racial tension was to attempt to end the violence.

Rabbi Shea Hecht

A Lubavitcher rabbi and spokesperson, Rabbi Hecht talks about community relations in his scene "Ovens." Dismissing the idea that religious groups should try to understand each other, he says they need only to have mutual respect based on their unique needs. He does not acknowledge that it is difficult for a community of people to have respect for another community's unique needs unless they understand what these needs are.

Leonard Jeffries

Jeffries is a controversial intellectual figure who speaks in the play about his work with Alex Haley on the famous book and television series *Roots*. After enjoying marked success in his private education, Jeffries worked and studied in Europe and Africa and then took a position as professor of African American studies at the City University of New York. By this time, he had developed a profound interest in working as an advocate for black social advancement, and he had begun to espouse some of his key theories about race and race relations. He began to come under criticism for his views that there are biological and psychological differences between blacks and whites, and that wealthy European Jews played an important role in running the slave trade. A *New York Times* editorial in 1990 denounced Jeffries as an incompetent educator and a conspiratorial theorist, and between 1992 and 1994 Jeffries fought a legal battle with the City University of New York over his chairmanship of the African American Studies Department. His scene in Smith's play questions whether he is an anti-Semite; explores his personal history and his view of himself; and plays with the notion of losing and discovering African roots.

Roslyn Malamud

A Lubavitcher resident of Crown Heights, Ms. Malamud blames black community leaders for instigating the riots and blames the police for letting them get out of control. She is shocked and horrified by the riots, and seeks to blame the series of events on individuals and policies rather than community groups or any kind of entrenched racial tension. She claims that her black neighbors want exactly what she wants out of life, although she admits that she does not know them.

Monique "Big Mo" Matthews

A rapper from Los Angeles, Mo is a skilled poet and a socially conscious political thinker. In the preface to Mo's scene, Smith writes, "Mo's everyday speech was as theatrical as Latifah's performance speech," referring to the famous rap artist and actor Queen Latifah. Mo feels a great deal of anger at black male rappers who demean women and who have a double standard about promiscuity, and she expresses these sentiments in her music and in conversation. Mo has ties to feminism because of what she calls her "female assertin,'" and she believes that rap music is a powerful tool of expression that is essentially rhythm and poetry.

Michael S. Miller

Executive director at the Jewish Community Relations Council, Mr. Miller points out that "words of comfort / were offered to the family of Gavin Cato" from Lubavitcher Jews, yet no one from the black community offered condolences to the family of Yankel Rosenbaum. He argues that "There is no boundary / to anti-Judaism" among blacks.

Letty Cottin Pogrebin

Well known Jewish American writer and founding editor of *Ms.* magazine, Letty Cottin Pogrebin appears in two scenes. Smith describes her as "Direct, passionate, confident, lots of volume," and it is also apparent from Pogrebin's lines that she is self-confident and eloquent. In "Near Enough to Reach," Pogrebin speculates that the tension and violence between blacks and Jews is due to the fact that Jews are close to blacks and take them seriously enough to address them in their rage. In "Isaac," she is reluctant at first to share a Holocaust story because she worries that they are becoming dulled through overuse, but she goes on to read about the horrific experience of her other's cousin.

Henry Rice

A resident of Crown Heights, Mr. Rice was involved in the riots, first as a skeptic of those preaching peace, and then as a preacher of peace. He was hit by the police and handcuffed, then threatened by a young black man with a handgun. "Good-natured, handsome, healthy," he describes the anger between police and blacks, and the violence on both sides.

Norman Rosenbaum

Yankel Rosenbaum's brother, Norman Rosenbaum is a barrister from Australia who is angry and upset about his brother's death. He speaks out passionately in his first scene that there should be justice for his brother's murderers, and in his second scene, he describes his reaction to the news that Yankel had been killed.

Reverend Canon Doctor Heron Sam

The pastor of St. Mark's Church in Crown Heights, Reverend Sam gives his version of the events in Crown Heights. Finding fault with a number of the Lubavitcher Grand Rebbe's habits and activities, he claims that Yosef Lifsh ran the red light and that the Jews did not care about the fatally injured Gavin Cato. He says, "These Lubavitcher people / are really very, / uh, enigmatic people. / They move so easily between / simplicity and sophistication," a comment that gets to the root of his feelings toward Lubavitchers as a group.

Ntozake Shange

A "playwright, poet, novelist," Ntozake Shange is a profound abstract thinker. In the opening scene of the play, she considers what "identity" is and how people are different from their surroundings.

Reverend Al Sharpton

A politician, minister, and activist famous for his advocacy of black civil rights, Sharpton is one of the key black community leaders involved in the Crown Heights events. Sharpton grew up in Brooklyn and was ordained as a Pentecostal minister in 1963. In addition to working as a manager in the music industry with singers including James Brown, Sharpton began a career in community activism. He rose to a prominent role in the black community in 1986, after he organized protests in Howard Beach, where a black man had been chased into the street by a white mob and then killed by a car. A year later, Sharpton became closely involved with the case of Tawana Bradley, a fifteen-year-old black girl who claimed she had been raped by five or six white men, one of whom had a police badge. Inquiries later suggested that Bradley had been lying, but this did not seriously damage Sharpton's career as an activist.

At Gavin Cato's funeral in 1991, Sharpton spoke out against racism by Hasidic Jews and helped to mobilize large protests in Crown Heights. He then flew to Israel personally to serve legal papers to Yosef Lifsh, the bodyguard who ran over Gavin Cato. In the play, Sharpton speaks in two scenes. In the first scene, he discusses why he wears his hair straight, in a style associated with whites, explaining that it is because of a promise he made to James Brown and that it is not a "reaction to Whites," although it is not entirely clear that this is true. In his other scene, "Rain," he describes and defends his role in the events following Gavin Cato's death, which he calls a *complete* outrage."

Robert Sherman

Sherman is the director of the mayor of New York's "Increase the Peace Corps," a youth organization promoting nonviolence. He "smiles frequently," and he is "upbeat, impassioned . . . Full. Lots of volume, clear enunciation, teeth, and tongue very involved in his speech." While trying to define and explain the racial situation in Crown Heights, he becomes frustrated with the English-language vocabulary about race and he stresses that the language's inadequacy in expressing ideas about race "is a reflection / of our unwillingness / to deal with it honestly."

Rivkah Siegal

"A very pretty Lubavitcher woman, with clear eyes and a direct gaze," Rivkah Siegal is a graphic designer. Wigs have long been a "big issue" for her, in part because she feels like they are "fake" and she is "kind of fooling the world" when she wears one.

Rabbi Joseph Spielman

A Lubavitcher rabbi and a spokesperson in the Lubavitch community, Rabbi Spielman maintains that Jews share no blame whatsoever in the Crown Heights racial riots. Wearing a black fedora, black jacket, and reading glasses, he is interviewed in his home. Rabbi Spielman's one-sided explanation of the accident and the events that followed reveal that he is unable or unwilling to view the situation from the perspective of members of the black community. He also engages in racial stereotypes of blacks, commenting that they were drinking beer on the sidewalks and that a black person stole a Lubavitcher Jew's cellular phone.

George C. Wolfe

George Wolfe is the producing director of the New York Shakespeare Festival, for which *Fires in the Mirror* was written. After constantly being treated as a "special special creature" in his private black grade school, he remembers being treated as though he were insignificant when he ventured outside of the black community. His words become slightly muddled when he attempts to explain how his blackness is unique and independent of whiteness.

THEMES

Racially Motivated Anger and Violence

The central theme of *Fires in the Mirror* is the racially motivated anger and violence in Crown

TOPICS FOR FURTHER STUDY

- Research Gavin Cato's death and the events that followed, as they were related in the press. Examine newspaper stories in the *New York Times* and the *Wall Street Journal* as well as accounts of the situation in magazines and in newspapers such as the *New York Post*. How would you describe the general perspective of each publication that you view? How does it compare it to the perspectives of some of the characters in Smith's play? How do you think your view of the events would be different if you had not seen Smith's play, but had only encountered the situation in the media?

- Consider the stylistic elements of Smith's unique form of drama, and research the larger scope of *On the Road: A Search for American Character*, her project that combines journalism and theatre. Discuss why you think Smith has chosen to use words verbatim from her interviews, why she uses so many short scenes, why she has chosen to act as each of the characters herself, and why she places the monologues into poetic verse. Describe Smith's place in the journalistic community and in the contemporary dramatic scene.

- Choose a well-known figure, such as Angela Davis, the Reverend Al Sharpton, or Letty Cottin Pogrebin, and research that person's real life and career. What is your subject's place in twentieth-century race relations? How and why was s/he a key figure in the Crown Heights events? How does his/her public perception compare to his/her portrayal in Smith's play?

- Smith is a versatile journalist, playwright, and performer who is able to excel at all three roles and gain a close connection to her material. Follow her documentary-play process by interviewing three or four people on a topic of your choice, transforming these interviews into brief theatrical scenes, and performing your scenes for an audience. Then evaluate your work. How was this format helpful for exploring your issue? How was it difficult or unhelpful? Describe what you learned about your topic and how this method helped you do so.

Heights, Brooklyn, in the early 1990s. From the many perspectives in Smith's play, the reader is able to piece together a representative variety of emotions that blacks and Lubavitcher Jews felt toward each other. The play also provides many contradictory descriptions of the violence that resulted from these emotions, which helps flesh out the truth of the historical events.

Smith explores the historical background behind what happened in Crown Heights by highlighting possible explanations and theories behind the relations between blacks and Hasidic Jews in Brooklyn. She includes perspectives on black history and Jewish history, particularly slavery and the Holocaust, and she explores different perceptions of black and Jewish relations with the police, the government, and the white majority in the United States. Acknowledging the diverse and multifarious causes behind the anger and violence in Crown Heights, Smith highlights the views of black and Lubavitcher leaders and spokespeople as well as anonymous members of each group. Her play seeks an explanation of the conflict but does not necessarily imply that any one viewpoint about it is completely accurate.

Inter-Community Relations

Fires in the Mirror is thematically ambitious in the sense that it does not confine itself to Brooklyn but uses the situation in Crown Heights to provide more general insights about race relations. The characters consistently provide their perspectives on whether racial harmony is possible in the United States, and many discuss how to go about achieving this goal. Not all characters desire peace, however; some continue to seek retribution for past and current crimes. Sonny Carson, for example, looks to redress racial injustice by working as an agitator. In expressing views about race in the United States and abroad, Smith draws from many key philosophies about race relations and refers to important figures in the history of race relations, including Malcolm X, Alex Haley, and Adolph Hitler.

Smith broadens her focus further by including commentary on gender and class relations, such as Monique "Big Mo" Matthews's scene about sexism in the hip-hop community, and in the variety of scenes that make reference to the economic disparities between the Lubavitch and black communities. Angela Davis, like Robert Sherman and other characters, encourages the reader to think outside the traditional understanding of race, which she describes as obsolete and inadequate for understanding how communities of people interact. Theories such as these are tested in real contexts, particularly during the final section, in which characters forcefully articulate their understandings of community and community relations because emotions are running so high.

Identity

Throughout *Fires in the Mirror*, Smith considers how people construct their notions of selfhood, particularly how they see themselves in relation to their community and race. From anonymous young men and women, to well-known leaders like Al Sharpton, to middle-aged Lubavitcher housewives, characters reveal a struggle to establish their personal identities and to negotiate how they fit into their religious and racial communities. In George C. Wolfe's scene, for example, in which Mr. Wolfe becomes somewhat muddled, insisting that his blackness is independent from another person's whiteness, Smith suggests that a person's racial identity may depend on his/her relationship with other races as well as with the way that they view their own race. Mr. Wolfe argues that his racial identity exists independently of other racial identities, but Smith implies that it may in fact be more complex than this.

History

Smith is a historian, in the sense that her goal is to gather a multiplicity of perspectives in order to focus on the truth of the past. By displaying the many sides of the issue, she delves into the root causes of the situation in Crown Heights and she attempts to communicate what really occurred. At the same time, however, Smith is also interested in theories of historical understanding. Her play acknowledges

the complexity of the situation and the difficulty of ever ascertaining exactly what is at the root of it all, implying that history is not objective, but that all people, including historians, form their understandings of past events based on their racial attitudes, emotions, and attachments. Smith may even be suggesting that there is something deeply unknowable about history, which is why she refuses to take any objective stance on the situation in Crown Heights.

STYLE

Journalistic Drama

Smith's unique style of drama combines theatre with journalism in order to bring to life and examine real social and political events. Each scene is drawn verbatim from an interview that Smith has held with the character, although Smith has arranged the subject's words according to her authorial purposes. She captures the essence of the characters she interviews, distilling their thoughts into a brief scene that provides a separate and coherent perspective on a particular situation or idea.

Poetic Verse

One of the key tools in Smith's artistic process is to render the words in poetic verse; this allows her to arrange each character's words in an aesthetically beautiful form, and to emphasize certain words and phrases that she finds important and that express the rhythm of the interviewee's speech. Smith also includes pauses, breaks indicated by dashes, and nonsensical noises like "um" to capture a sense of character and real speech. Then, in a one-woman show, Smith actually embodies the people she has interviewed: dressing like them, using their words, and moving using their gestures. This creative form of journalistic drama, which Smith developed herself, allows her as writer and actor to vividly express the people involved in the themes and events of her subject. It gives her a great deal of authority over the subject matter, and draws the audience into a variety of real perspectives on a real-life situation.

Diverse Perspectives

Fires in the Mirror contains twenty-nine different scenes, involving twenty-six different characters. The characters in these scenes vary widely in their opinions about the themes of the play, based on their backgrounds, personalities, politics, and ties to the situation. Smith uses so many opposing voices because, when taken as a whole, they create a profounder impression of what really happened in Crown Heights than a single perspective would, even if this single perspective were supposedly unbiased.

HISTORICAL CONTEXT

Crown Heights is a neighborhood in Brooklyn, New York, with a black majority, largely from the West Indies, and a Hasidic Jewish minority, making up about 10 percent of the population. The neighborhood includes a large number of undocumented black immigrants, and it is the worldwide capital of the Chabad-Lubavitch branch of Hasidic Judaism. Also known simply as Lubavitch, which means "city of brotherly love" in Russian, this sect is composed of adherents to the strict teachings and customs of Orthodox Judaism. At the time of the riots, the Lubavitcher Grand Rebbe, or spiritual leader, was Rabbi Menachem Mendel Schneerson, who many Lubavitcher Jews considered to be the Jewish Messiah. Tensions between Jews and blacks in the Crown Heights neighborhood had been running high because of the perception among Lubavitchers that there was a great deal of black anti-Semitism, and because of the perception among blacks that there was a great deal of white racism and that Lubavitchers enjoyed preferential treatment from the police.

On August 19, 1991, a car driven by Grand Rebbe Schneerson's bodyguard, Yosef Lifsh, ran a red light, was hit by another car, and jumped a curb onto the sidewalk where Lifsh ran over a seven-year-old black child named Gavin Cato. A private Hasidic-run ambulance appeared on the scene to evacuate the driver, possibly on orders from a police officer, but left Gavin Cato to wait for the New York City ambulance. Cato died a few hours later, and members of the black community began to react with violence against Lubavitcher Jews and the police. That evening, a group of young black men stabbed and killed a Hasidic scholar from Australia named Yankel Rosenbaum. Sixteen-year-old Lemrick Nelson Jr. was arrested in connection with the murder.

Rioting by both black and Lubavitcher groups continued throughout the next day, and Yosef Lifsh departed from the United States for Israel. Although twenty police officers were injured, the police were somewhat restrained in their response, partly because of sensitivity at the time due to the recent brutal beating of Rodney King by police officers in Los Angeles, which was caught on videotape and broadcast throughout the nation. The Reverend Al Sharpton demanded Yosef Lifsh's arrest and he led protests through Crown Heights. New York City mayor David Dinkins visited Crown Heights to urge peace, but was silenced by insults and by objects thrown at him. The rioting died down by August 23, but tensions between blacks and Lubavitchers remained high.

On September 17, the day of the Jewish holiday Yom Kippur, after a Brooklyn grand jury refused to indict Yosef Lifsh, Al Sharpton flew to Israel to notify Lifsh of a civil suit against him. Proceedings against Lemrick Nelson Jr., accused of killing Yankel Rosenbaum, continued throughout the year and into the next fall, when he was acquitted of all charges. Hasidic Jews rallied outside Lubavitch headquarters that evening, October 29, 1992. The next day New York governor Mario Cuomo ordered a state review of the case. The Lubavitcher community filed a lawsuit against Dinkins and his administration, criticizing their mishandling of the riots, and Dinkins's unpopularity among Jews was a major factor in his loss to Rudolph Giuliani in the 1993 mayoral elections.

CRITICAL OVERVIEW

Fires in the Mirror was Smith's major breakthrough. The play was a runner-up for the Pulitzer Prize, and the critical reaction to it was overwhelmingly positive. Robert Brustein, for example, writes in his *New Republic* article "Awards vs. Achievements" that Smith's play is one of "the most interesting works being produced in New York." Brustein describes the play's commentary about race, and stresses that it vividly expresses emotions such as grief and rage "with an eloquent, dispassionate voice."

Reviews of the play tend to focus on the accuracy and efficacy of its political commentary, and it has become known as a superb historical document about race relations in the United States. Richard Schechner, however, was among those who discussed Smith's stylistic prowess as a writer and performer. In an article in *TDR: The Drama Review*, Schechner praises Smith's acting skills, writing that "Smith composed *Fires in the Mirror* as a ritual shaman might investigate and heal a diseased or possessed patient," in order to absorb her characters and portray them skillfully.

After PBS produced an adapted version of the play for television in 1993, broadening the

Members of the Jewish Defence League and leaders of the African American community debate after four nights of riots in Crown Heights, Brooklyn, New York © J. A. Giordano/Corbis Saba

influence of the work, positive reviews began to appear in periodicals with wide circulations. A *Time* critic, for example, calls the television production of the play "riveting." Exposure such as this, as well as the success of her play *Twilight: Los Angeles 1992* helped launch Smith's acting career in television and film.

CRITICISM

Scott Trudell

Trudell is an independent scholar with a bachelor's degree in English literature. In the following essay, Trudell examines the theme of identity in Fires in the Mirror *and how it relates to the racially motivated violence in Crown Heights.*

The main subject of Smith's commentary in *Fires in the Mirror* is the specific historical event of the 1991 racial tension and violence in Crown Heights, Brooklyn. Each character provides a unique perspective about how feelings such as rage, hatred, misunderstanding, and resentment were formed in individuals, and how they eventually manifested themselves in a massive community conflict. Smith

is able to penetrate the nature and meaning of this conflict so provocatively, however, only by exploring the key broader issues at its roots, particularly how people develop and understand their religious, ethnic, cultural, sexual, and class identities.

Identity is a definitive issue in *Fires in the Mirror*; it preoccupies characters, including the Reverend Al Sharpton, "Big Mo" Matthews, Rivkah Siegal, and several of the anonymous black and Lubavitcher men and women. It is the subject of the first section, it is important to the extended title of the play (*Fires in the Mirror: Crown Heights, Brooklyn and Other Identities*), and it is vital to Smith's subtle authorial commentary on race relations. An examination, therefore, of how Smith treats the concept of identity and how the characters understand their identities in relation to their own and other communities will reveal what lessons can be learned, in Smith's opinion, from the situation in Crown Heights.

"Identity" is the first word in the play, after Ntozake Shange's introductory "Hummmm." Shange sees identity as an interplay between being a "part of [one's] surroundings" and "becom[ing] separate from them." As an example, she describes how a person who has been in the desert incorporates the desert into his/her identity but is still "not the desert." This notion of identity seems to pose more questions than it actually answers, but it is important because it begins to acknowledge the complexities inherent in forming a distinct racial identity.

George C. Wolfe's description of his "blackness" is similarly unclear. He breaks off, pauses, and becomes muddled when he tries to state that he is "not—going—to place myself / (*Pause.*) / in relationship to your whiteness," and when he attempts to establish the self-sufficiency of his blackness: "My blackness does not resis—ex—re—/ *exist* in relationship to your whiteness. . . . it does not exist in relationship to—/ it *exists* / it exists." His hesitancy and the sense that he is trying to convince himself of the truth of what he is saying throws doubt over the independence of his black identity. On the contrary, his scene seems to imply that racial identity is locked into a sense of self that is very much dependent on what self is not, or on what self perceives as the other or opposite of oneself.

Early on in the play, therefore, Smith throws into doubt the idea that identity is a unique series of individual traits that do not change based on one's surroundings or relationships to other people. Instead, identity can be formed and altered by a neighborhood such as Crown Heights; this is why the subtitle of Smith's play, "Crown Heights, Brooklyn and Other Identities," suggests that Crown Heights is an identity in itself and that a resident of the neighborhood incorporates their geographical area into their sense of self. Add to this the idea that characters understand their race only in relation to other races and the result is a notion of identity that is very much dependent on how one views one's surroundings and one's neighbors as well as oneself.

The ensuing scenes continue to provide insights into what identity actually is and how people develop a racial self-consciousness. Angela Davis, for example, stresses that race is a flexible and even arbitrary construction, in her scene "Rope." Arguing that the traditional concept of race is an outmoded notion constructed by European colonists attempting to conquer and colonize the world, she stresses that Europeans divided the populations of the earth into "firm biological, uh, / communities" in order to divide and dominate others. This European concept of racial identity is meaningful only through a differentiation from other races. Davis argues that it is vital to move beyond a historical notion of race in order not to be "caught up in this cycle / of genocidal / violence,"

> " THE ENFLAMED, RAGING
> IDENTITY THAT BLACKS AND JEWS
> FROM CROWN HEIGHTS SEE WHEN
> THEY LOOK IN THE MIRROR
> IS SMITH'S MOST IMPORTANT
> METAPHOR FOR THE IDENTITY
> CRISIS AT THE ROOT
> OF THE VIOLENCE IN
> THE NEIGHBORHOOD."

and that it is important to make connections and associations with other communities.

Most of the characters in Smith's play, however, understand race as a firm biological category in which a person's identity is determined by his/her relationship to other racial groups. Community leaders such as Rabbi Shea Hecht insist that there should be no attempt for black and Jewish groups to understand each other, while Minister Conrad Mohammed argues that the Jews have stolen the identity of blacks and are "masquerading in our garment" by pretending to be God's chosen people. These are extreme views, but normal citizens—such as the anonymous teenage girl in "Look in the Mirror" who sees her class as strictly divided into black, Hispanic, and white groups, or the anonymous young man in the scene "Wa Wa Wa," who groups Lubavitcher Jews with the police—seem to acknowledge no common cultural or geographical identity between races. Even Roslyn Malamud, who argues that blacks want "exactly / what I want out of life," says that she does not know any blacks and is unable to mix with them socially because of their differences.

This firm and separate understanding of racial identity leads, as Davis says, to "genocidal / violence" because people who subscribe to it thrust everything that is negative and different from them onto another racial group. The "rage" that Richard Green describes, and which Davis would suggest comes from centuries of racial oppression, "has to be vented" somehow, and since blacks see their identity as completely separate from the Lubavitcher

WHAT DO I READ NEXT?

- Alex Haley's famous novel *Roots* (1976), which was adapted into a popular television series by ABC in 1977, dramatizes the life of Kunta Kinte, a black slave kidnapped and taken on the brutal passage from Africa to the United States. The book emphasizes that Kunta never lost his pride and connection to his African heritage.

- *Angela Davis: An Autobiography* (1974) is Davis's compelling account of her early career as an activist, including her imprisonment between 1970 and 1972.

- *Twilight: Los Angeles 1992* (1993), Smith's next play in her journalistic drama project, focuses on the 1992 civil unrest in Los Angeles following the acquittal of the four police officers who were caught on videotape beating Rodney King. It uses the same format as *Fires in the Mirror* and has received wide critical acclaim, including an Obie Award.

- *Race Matters* (1993), cultural theorist Cornel West's best-known work, provides eight essays that assign equal blame to blacks, whites, liberals, and conservatives for their roles in the poor state of race relations in the United States.

---

identity, they are able to direct all of their anger at Lubavitcher Jews. Green states that young black agitators are "not angry at the Lubavitcher community," but their rage takes this form anyway, despite the fact that Lubavitcher Jews are also a minority group who encounter discrimination and disdain in the United States.

Letty Cottin Pogrebin offers an explanation of this confusing set of circumstances in her scene "Near Enough to Reach." Discussing how Jews came to be scapegoats for the discrimination and oppression directed against blacks, Pogrebin points out that "Only *Jews* listen, / only *Jews* take Blacks seriously, / only *Jews* view Blacks as full human beings that you / should *address* / in their rage." Her comments emphasize that blacks and Jews share a certain affinity because of the historic discrimination against their races by non-Jewish whites.

Most characters however, Jewish and black, do not feel any kind of Crown Heights solidarity, and see themselves as entirely separate racial groups according to the traditional European concept. Jewish characters such as Rabbi Joseph Spielman, Michael Miller, and Reuven Ostrov do not acknowledge any community ties with blacks and identify black anti-Semitism with historic anti-Jewish massacres in Germany and Russia. Meanwhile, black characters, including Leonard Jeffries, Sonny Carson, Minister Conrad Mohammed, the anonymous young man

from "Wa Wa Wa," and the Reverend Al Sharpton, tend either to group Jews together with dominant non-Jewish white culture or to blame Jews specifically for the oppression of blacks.

A close reading of the section "Mirrors" and the implication of the title *Fires in the Mirror* helps to reveal Smith's commentary on how black and Jewish perceptions of their own identities make it possible for them to blame each other for the historic oppression of their racial groups and to direct all of their contempt and rage about racial injustice at each other. On the surface, the kinds of mirrors to which the section "Mirrors" and the play's title refer are telescope mirrors, which provide an amplified view of an external object. If this were the case, the title *Fires in the Mirror* would refer to an image of the riots from the perspective of an outside observer, as though each character was a mirror within the telescope and the play itself was the telescope. The many diverse perspectives are attempts to reduce, in Professor Aaron M. Bernstein's words, the "circle of confusion" at the center of the racial tension.

The more common meaning of a mirror, however, is also crucial to Smith's subtext about identity and self-reflection. As Professor Bernstein stresses, a "simple mirror is just a flat / reflecting / substance," although "the notion of distortion also goes back into literature." Therefore, in addition to referring to a tool like a telescope that allows outside observers to view the racial violence of 1991, the title *Fires in the Mirror* suggests that the characters of the play, and possibly the audience as well, view themselves and their identities as a fire that is reflected, and possibly distorted, in a mirror.

The enflamed, raging identity that blacks and Jews from Crown Heights see when they look in the mirror is Smith's most important metaphor for the identity crisis at the root of the violence in the neighborhood. Smith implies that a central motif of the play, searching for an image of an individual's identity, is comparable to seeing in a mirror a burning flame that consumes any notion of the complex, interrelated, historically aware conception of what identity really is. Without an understanding of the complex interrelations of their identities and their common bonds, racial groups in close proximity, such as the blacks and Jews in Crown Heights, are able to focus all of their rage and anger on each other, and violence inevitably follows.

Source: Scott Trudell, Critical Essay on *Fires in the Mirror*, in *Drama for Students*, Thomson Gale, 2006.

Richard Schechner

In the following essay, Schechner discusses Smith's technique in Fires in the Mirror *and her overall performance art.*

A woman faces the camera, her voice nasal and New York. Roz Malamud speaks with the kind of accent that sounds "Jewish." "I wish I could [. . .] go on television. I wanna scream to the whole world. [. . .] I don't love my neighbors, I don't know my black neighbors." A few minutes later television time, Carmel Cato, from the same Crown Heights, Brooklyn, neighborhood as Malamud, but a world away, his voice roundly "black" in its tones, talks through tears about how a car slammed into his daughter, Angela, and his seven-year-old son, Gavin, killing him. "Angela she was on the ground but she was trying to move. Gavin was still. They was trying to pound him. I was trying to explain it was my kid!"

The two people—plus many others: men and women, professors and street people, blacks, Jews, rabbis, reverends, lawyers, and politicians—are enacted by Anna Deavere Smith, an African American performer of immense abilities. My concern here will not be with the events in Brooklyn in 1991 and 1992, nor with the "black-white race thing" that continues to torture America, but with Smith's artwork. I want to investigate how Smith does what she does in *Fires in the Mirror*.

In conventional acting a performer develops a character by reading a play text written before rehearsals begin, improvising situations based on the dramatic situation depicted in the play, and slowly coming to understand the external social situation and the internal emotional state of the character— Hamlet, Hedda Gabler, whoever. The character is a complex fiction created collectively by the actor, the playwright, the director, the scenographer, the costumer, and the musician. The whole team works together to create onstage a believable, if temporary, social world.

Smith works differently. She does not "act" the people you see and listen to in *Fires in the Mirror*. She "incorporates" them. Her way of working is less like that of a conventional Euro-American actor and more like that of African, Native American, and Asian ritualists. Smith works by means of deep mimesis, a process opposite to that of "pretend." To incorporate means to be possessed by, to open oneself up thoroughly and deeply to another being.

Smith composed *Fires in the Mirror* as a ritual shaman might investigate and heal a diseased or possessed patient. Like a ritualist, Smith consulted the people most closely involved, opening to their intimacy, spending lots of time with them face-to-face. Using both the most contemporary techniques of tape recording and the oldest technique of close looking and listening, Smith went far beyond "interviewing" the participants in the Crown Heights drama. Her text was not a preexisting literary drama but other human beings. Smith composed *Fires in the Mirror* by confronting in person those most deeply involved—both the famous and the ordinary.

Meeting people face-to-face made it possible for Smith to move like them, sound like them, and allow what they were to enter her own body. This is a dangerous process, a form of shamanism. Some shamans exorcise demons by transforming themselves into the various being—good, bad, dangerous, benign, helpful, destructive. The events of August 1991 revealed that Crown Heights was possessed: by anger, racism, fear, and much misunderstanding. The deaths of Gavin Cato and Yankel Rosenabum stirred up hatreds. And yet, even in their rage, fear, confusion, and partisanship, people of every persuasion and at every level of education and sophistication opened up to Smith. Why?

Because she—like a great shaman—earned the respect of those she talked with by giving them her respect, her focused attention. People are sensitive to such deep listening. Even as a fine painter looks with a penetrating vision, so Smith looks and listens with uncanny empathy. Empathy goes beyond sympathy. Empathy is the ability to allow the other in, to feel what the other is feeling. Smith absorbs the gestures, the tone of voice, the look, the intensity, the moment-by-moment details of a conversation.

But in so doing, she does not destroy the others or parody them. Nor does she lose herself. A shaman who loses herself cannot help others to attain understanding. As spectators we are not fooled into thinking we are really seeing Al Sharpton, Angela Davis, Norman Rosenbaum, or any of the others. Smith's shamanic invocation is her ability to bring into existence the wondrous "doubling" that marks great performances. This doubling is the simultaneous presence of performer and performed. Because of this doubling Smith's audiences—consciously perharps, unconsciously certainly—learn to "let the other in," to accomplish in their own way what Smith so masterfully achieves.

Source: Richard Schechner, "Anna Deavere Smith: Acting as Incorporation," in the *Drama Review*, Vol. 37, No. 4, Winter 1993, pp. 63–64.

Robert Brustein

In the following review-essay, Brustein describes the varied characters Smith develops and portrays around the Crown Heights riots in Fires in the Mirror, *praising Smith's collection of "all these tensions into an overpowering conclusion."*

The 1992 Tony Awards ceremonies confirmed once again that the heart and blood, if not the brains, of the Broadway theater is the musical. This magnetic force field is not only expected every night of the year to draw thousands of out-of-towners to the island of Manhattan. It has also been charged with the added burden of keeping millions of television viewers glued to their screens every spring for an evening of awards. As a result, the great bulk of Tony prime time is invariably devoted to extended excerpts, complete with sets and costumes, from all of the nominated musicals, making them the main focus of the event, the source of the most tumultuous applause. To further persuade Nielsen-baked couch potatoes that theater can be as popular as cable TV or network sitcoms, the presenters are almost invariably movie and television stars, some of whom may have actually once acted on stage.

It is true that a number of Tonys also go to straight plays, but compared with the riotous fervor reserved for musical offerings such awards generally seem like an obligation. They are also

something of an embarrassment, considering how few serious plays actually open on Broadway each season. (This year's award went to Brian Friel's *Dancing at Lughnasa*—perhaps Tony voters thought it was a play about a hoofer.) Glenn Close, functioning as hostess for the event, even felt obliged to remind the glittering Minskoff audience that "many of the most famous musicals came from plays." On Broadway, Shakespeare is sanctioned for providing the inspiration for *Kiss Me Kate* and Shaw for contributing the book to *My Fair Lady*.

Close, wearing a variety of shimmering gowns for the occasion, including a blue-and-green number that made her look as if seaweed were growing up her arms, was a Tony winner herself (for a part in *Death and the Maiden*). Her acceptance speech credited Amnesty International with helping to foster a world community "where cruelty and abuse don't exist anymore"; she helped to foster some of her own with the zinger of the evening, a paraphrase of Herb Gardner to the effect that "there is life after Mr. and Mrs. Rich" (neither The *New York Times* critic nor his theater columnist wife, Alex Witchel, showed much appreciation for her performance). Close nevertheless seemed to share Witchel's weakness for Hollywood hunks, whinnying like a mare over Alec Baldwin (and perhaps inflaming feminists further by introducing Michael Douglas as "my fatal attraction").

The Tony event had its occasional entertainments, few of them rehearsed: Carol Channing squinting like a snow owl in the giant black-rimmed glasses she used to read the teleprompter, Liza Minnelli (who sloshes her sibilants) being forced to speak the name of a choreographer with three esses in it, William Finn giving two largely incoherent acceptance speeches for *Falsettos,* Vincent Gardenia extolling the virtues of Dancing at Lasagna (a title nobody could pronounce), Faith Prince commending "the unsustained love" of her husband, the camera's way of catching virtually all of the nominees applauding themselves when their names were mentioned. It was the usual display of egotism, ecstasy, and entropy. But for reasons I'm still trying to understand, I couldn't work up my usual quotient of rage over the ceremony. Perhaps the Tonys have gotten too predictable for sustained indignation.

Although many performers displayed red ribbons symbolizing their sympathy for aids victims, there was more implied concern over that problematic patient, the ailing city of New York, which inspired a variety of pep talks both from presenters and winners. Significantly, three of the four nominated musicals were set in the city, and the fourth—*Jelly's Last Jam*—had New York scenes. Everybody's favorite show, obviously, was that nostalgic paean to a more innocent Manhattan, *Guys and Dolls,* excluded from Best Musical because it wasn't new. (It won for Best Revival.) Through reasoning that escapes me, *Crazy for You* collected the prize, despite the fact that its Gershwin score was almost sixty years old.

But nothing about the Tonys makes much sense. It's not just that the judges are self-interested theater people voting their opinions and prejudices, or that the prizes are so clearly designed to boost box office, or that internecine competition is incompatible with a creative process based on difference. By recognizing only shows produced within a fourteen block area, the Tonys manage to exclude from consideration (except for a single award to a resident theater—this year the Goodman) about 99 percent of the nation's theatrical activity. This includes the most interesting works being produced in New York.

Among these is *Fires in the Mirror,* a one-woman evening conceived, written, and performed by Anna Deavere Smith at the Joseph Papp Public Theater. Creating monologues out of interviews with twenty-six diverse characters, most of them fiercely antagonistic to each other, Deavere has accomplished the remarkable feat of capturing opinions and personalities in a way that goes beyond impersonation. Even more remarkable, she has dealt with one of the most incendiary events of our time—the confrontation of blacks and Jews following the accidental death of Gavin Cato in Crown Heights and the retaliatory murder of an innocent bystander, Yankel Rosenbaum—in a manner that is thorough, compassionate, and equitable to both sides.

Smith is associate professor of drama at Stanford and a Bunting Fellow at Harvard. She is also a sensitive sociologist, and a gifted actress and mimic. Donning a variety of hats, caps, yarmulkes, cloaks, and accents, she manages to move easily among a large number of people from vastly different backgrounds and temperaments. And although the Crown Heights incident is the detonating cap, it is by no means the only explosive subject in the show. *Fires in the Mirror* is part of a series to be called *On the Road: A Search for American Character.* The title suggests her ambition to bring to the stage a wide spectrum of contemporary types, both celebrated and obscure.

FIRES IN THE MIRROR DRAMATIZES THOSE EMOTIONS, AND TEMPERS THEM, WITH AN ELOQUENT, DISPASSIONATE VOICE."

The first half of the evening is devoted to some of those who make up the American character, with Smith speaking in their (mostly Brooklyn) voices: the playwright Ntozake Shange expounding on the nature of the desert with a kind of stoned imperturbability; Gittel Lazerson, a preschool teacher, talking in high nasal tones about how she has to get a black kid to turn off the radio on Shabbus; the playwright-director George C. Wolfe describing how he could be treated as an extraordinary child and a "nigger" at the same time; and an anonymous 13-year-old girl reflecting on how black people are really into hair styles. As if to confirm this, the Rev. Al Sharpton materializes to claim that he copied his own coiffure from James Brown ("the father I never had"), while a Lubavitcher woman named Rikvah Siegel tells of the five wigs she must wear as a woman among Hasids.

Reflecting on race, Angela Davis surprises us by saying she now believes that "race is an increasingly obsolete way to construct community," while a female rapper named "Big Mo" takes after her male counterparts for failing to understand rhythm and poetry. One character who offers no surprises is Leonard Jeffries (Smith collapses into a chair and dons a green African kepi to play him). He boasts about how he was hired by Alex Haley to keep *Roots* honest, and then says he was betrayed when Haley went off to make a series on Jewish history. Jeffries claims to have been tired when he made his infamous anti-Semitic speech in Albany, yet displays his usual paranoia in charging Arthur Schlesinger Jr. with suggesting that "this is the one to kill" just because the historian devoted a full page to him in *The Disuniting of America.* Nation of Islam Minister Conrad Muhammed (Smith in a red bow tie) affirms that the Jewish Holocaust was nothing compared with 200 million people killed on slave ships over a 300-year period. Not only do African Americans win Muhammed's prize for competitive suffering, but "we are the chosen . . . the Jews are masquerading in our garments." Letty Cottin Pogrebin reflects on how if you want a head-line, "you have to attack the Jews," though "only Jews regard blacks as full human beings."

The Crown Heights section collects all these tensions into an overpowering conclusion. Through the use of Wendall K. Harrington and Emmanuelle Krebs's graphic projections, a series of photographs captures the contorted world of violence, accident, grief, and revenge. Rabbi Joseph Spielman sadly de-scribes how, though Gavin Cato was killed through no malicious intent, angry blacks began running through the streets, shouting for Jewish blood. The anger was fired by rumors that a Jewish ambulance wouldn't help the child and by charges that "they" never get arrested. One anonymous black man sees significance in the fact that the blue-and-white col-ors of New York police cars and Israeli flags are the same. Michael Miller of the Jewish Community Relations Council, while expressing sympathy for the dead child, agonizes, "But 'Heil Hitler' from blacks? 'You better warm up the ovens again' from blacks?"

The incendiaries stoke these fires. Smug and self-satisfied, Sonny Carson warns of another "long hot summer," and Sharpton, flying to Israel in a media-savvy effort to arrest the driver of the car that struck Cato, announces, "If you piss in my face I'm gonna call it piss, I'm not gonna call it rain." A sharp-tongued Brooklyn yenta attired in a span-gled woolen sweater asks, "This famous Reverend Al Sharpton, which I'd like to know, who ordained him?" She adds that black people have nothing to do with their time, "so somebody says, 'Do you want to riot?' "

People on both sides of this conflict can claim to be victims of injustice and prejudice, but the scariest thing about the incident, aside from the ab-sence of leadership and appalling mismanagement by the city, was the tinderbox nature of the com-munity, a condition magnified in Los Angeles. In both riots, the condition can be ascribed to hope-lessness and lack of opportunity. One anonymous black boy tells us that there are only two choices for kids like him, to be a d.j. or a "Bad Boy," and with disc jockeys in short demand, the Bad Boys form the armies of the rampage. The most har-rowing words, though, belong to the survivors of the dead. Norman Rosenbaum shouts at Yankel Rosenbaum's funeral, "My brother's blood cries out to you from the ground." And Carmel Cato, an exhausted Caribbean, tells of how the death of his

child was "like an atomic bomb." The simile is apt in describing his grief and rage, not to mention the grief and rage expressed throughout the country in these inflamed times. *Fires in the Mirror* drama-tizes those emotions, and tempers them, with an eloquent, dispassionate voice.

Source: Robert Brustein, "Awards vs. Achievements," in *New Republic*, Vol. 207, No. 2, July 6, 1992, pp. 28–30.

J. Kroll

In the following review, Kroll praises Smith's "fierce honesty" in Fires in the Mirror *and her art, and provides background on her artistic method.*

"I am large, I contain multitudes," said Walt Whitman. He should have seen Anna Deavere Smith, who becomes the 26 characters in her ex-traordinary one-person show, *Fires in the Mirror.* In 90 minutes Smith, a 41-year-old actress, drama-tist and Stanford University professor, creates a dy-namic human collage depicting the racial riots in Crown Heights, Brooklyn, that took place last sum-mer, when 7-year-old Gavin Cato was killed by a car driven by a Hasidic man. This led to angry out-bursts by African-Americans against Jews and the retaliatory killing of a Hasidic scholar, Yankel Rosenbaum. Watching the electrifying Smith at the Joseph Papp Public Theater in New York (until June 28) is like seeing these events in a series of lightning bolts that illuminate the protagonists at their quintessential moments. The result is a rivet-ing work that captures the tensions of racial, class and cultural conflict in what is hardly a melting pot but a boiling caldron.

"I'm trying to tell the story from various points of view and to find things the media didn't," says Smith with excessive modesty. With her vivid face, laser-beam eyes, strong, supple voice, a few props and swift changes in dress, Smith leaps into each character. Using verbatim dialogue from her own interviews, Smith "embodies," in her word, Hasidic rabbis, black ministers, Jewish housewives, street kids, a woman rapper. A leather-jacketed Smith nails the brainy glamour of black radical Angela Davis, who calls for new ways of coming together or else "we will be caught up in this cycle of geno-cidal violence."

Smith captures the tragic absurdity of that cy-cle. The accident that killed Gavin Cato becomes a Brooklyn "Rashomon" as it's described from the angles of Jews and blacks. A black youth attacks the police for protecting the Jewish driver. Invent-ing a startling conspiracy theory, he points out that the Israeli flag and a police car both have the same colors-blue and white. Rabbi Joseph Spielman says that a Jewish passenger was calling the police on a car phone when a black youth stole the phone from his hand. Rosenbaum's brother Norman cries out: "My brother was killed . . . for no other reason than he was a Jew!" Black activist Sonny Carson says: "I'm not going to advocate any coming together and healing of America and all that shit. No way!"

Culture collision: Smith even finds humor in the collision of exotically different cultures. Gittell Lazerson tells how her baby flipped on the radio during the Sabbath, when Orthodox Jews can't turn on appliances. She had to go find a black kid to turn it off: "He probably thought, 'And people say Jewish people are really smart, and they don't know how to turn off their radios'." Such homely details contrast with the anger of Nation of Islam Minister Conrad Muhammad, who compares five years of the Holocaust with 300 years of black slavery.

As these voices collide, you can't help wondering where Smith herself stands in the kind of conflict she's dramatizing.

"I'm not Afrocentric in a typical way," she says. "An Afrocentric person would never do this piece. My voice is in the juxtaposition of other voices. It's in the choices that I make." Her fierce honesty in those choices almost convinces you that there's still objective truth in a violently polarized time. The oldest of five children in a Baltimore family, Smith went to Beaver College, a small women's school (now coed) near Philadelphia. Her interest in language led her to the American Conservatory Theater in San Francisco. In 1976 she came to New York where she "pounded the pavement," getting small parts in soap operas. She taught at NYU, Yale and Carnegie Mellon, where she began her interview technique: "I wanted to show students that human speech is not neat. I agree with Pinter: speech is a strategy to cover nakedness."

Fires in the Mirror is part of a series of one-woman shows she has done called "On the Road: A Search for American Character." She worked with director Christopher Ashley, but the final decisions are hers. "I'm not an impersonator. I don't have a photographic memory. I don't have a genius ear, like people who remember everything they hear. I work through voice rhythms, the impact of the words on my body." Smith is an ideal theater artist for the '90s, as America attempts to synthesize an increasingly diverse culture. "My whole project is about the acceptance of others," she says. Unflinchingly, she shows how difficult and necessary that acceptance is.

Source: J. Kroll, "A Woman for All Seasons: The Many Faces of Anna Deavere Smith," in *Newsweek*, Vol. 119, No. 22, June 1, 1992, p. 74.

SOURCES

Brustein, Robert, "Awards vs. Achievements," in *New Republic*, Vol. 207, No. 2, July 6, 1992, pp. 28–30.

Schechner, Richard, "Anna Deavere Smith: Acting as Incorporation," in *TDR: The Drama Review*, Vol. 37, No. 4, Winter 1993, pp. 63–64.

Smith, Anna Deavere, *Fires in the Mirror: Crown Heights, Brooklyn and Other Identities*, Dramatists Play Service, 1993.

"When Art Meets Journalism," in *Time*, Vol. 141, No. 18, May 3, 1993, p. 81.

FURTHER READING

"Brooklyn Highs," in *Entertainment Weekly*, No. 168, April 30, 1993, p. 44.
    The anonymous critic in this short review discusses the PBS television production of *Fires in the Mirror*.

Rayner, Richard, "Word of Mouth," in *Harper's Bazaar*, Vol. 126, No. 3376, April 1993, pp. 248–49.
    Rayner focuses on Smith's methodology in *Fires in the Mirror* and includes a profile of the artist.

Reinelt, Janelle, "Performing Race: Anna Deavere Smith's *Fires in the Mirror*," in *Modern Drama*, Vol. 39, No. 4, Winter 1996, pp. 609–17.
    Providing an analysis of the television production of Smith's play, Reinelt discusses Smith's performance and dramaturgical technique as well as the play's commentary on race relations.

Rich, F., "Diversities of America in One-Person Shows," in *New York Times*, Vol. 141, No. 48967, May 15, 1992, p. C1.
    Rich reviews *Fires in the Mirror* and Ron Vawter's *Roy Cohn/Jack Smith*, arguing that both shows are adept at revealing the racial tensions in the United States in the early 1990s.

Rugoff, Ralph, "One-Woman Chorus," in *Vogue*, Vol. 183, No. 4, April 1993, pp. 224–26.
    A profile of Smith that includes her thoughts about *Fires in the Mirror*, Rugoff's article praises the play and Smith's performance in it.

For Services Rendered

SOMERSET MAUGHAM

1932

When *For Services Rendered* opened at the Globe Theatre in London in 1932, Somerset Maugham had been heralded as the most successful playwright in England. Maugham was praised for his adept storytelling skills, which had entertained audiences for thirty years. This night, however, English audiences were not prepared for the anti-war focus of his new play, and, as a result, it closed after just seventy-eight performances.

Appreciation for the play has grown over the years since its first production. Now *For Services Rendered* is acclaimed as one of Maugham's best plays. The story, that so shocked early audiences, focuses on the devastating effects of World War I on an English family. As Maugham chronicles the damaged lives of each member of the Ardsley family and their friends, he presents a scathing indictment of the war and the governments that convince young men to sacrifice their lives in the name of glory.

AUTHOR BIOGRAPHY

William Somerset Maugham was born on January 25, 1874, in Paris, France. Maugham's father, Robert, worked for the British Embassy as a solicitor. After the deaths of both of his parents within two years of each other, the eleven year-old Maugham was sent to Kent, England, and raised by his uncle, a reverend in a local vicarage, and his wife. Maugham had a difficult time at King's School in

Canterbury due to a persistent stammer and his small stature, which made him painfully shy. In 1890, at sixteen, he began studying philosophy at the University of Heidelberg.

After returning to Kent a few years later, he started writing but decided to go into medicine to pay the bills. He trained for six years at St. Thomas's Hospital in London where he worked as a midwife for working-class mothers. After he earned his medical degree in 1897, he gave up the profession and turned to writing full-time, gaining confidence from his initial literary success. His first novel, *Liza of Lambeth*, which reflected his work as a midwife, was published that same year along with short stories that appeared in *Punch* and other journals. He continued writing after he moved to Paris but lived in poverty there until his literary reputation began to grow after the production of his first play, *Lady Frederick*, in 1907, and four other plays the following year.

After Oscar Wilde's infamous trial in 1895, Maugham became much more secretive about his own homosexuality. In 1915, he married Syrie Wellcome, an interior designer with whom he had a child.

During World War I, Maugham served with a Red Cross ambulance unit and as a medical officer. He later served with British Secret Service in Switzerland and Russia. During World War II, Maugham served with the British Ministry of Information in Paris. His play, *For Services Rendered*, was a scathing attack on the English government's treatment of war veterans. In 1916, he met Gerald Haxton, an American ambulance driver, and despite his marriage to Wellcome, the two became lovers and companions for the next thirty years. Maugham and Wellcome divorced in 1929.

After the war years, Maugham's overwhelming success as a playwright, novelist, and travel writer, which made him one of the world's richest authors, afforded him a lavish lifestyle. He entertained royalty and the wealthy in his villa in southeast France, once owned by Leopold II, and amassed a fortune in art. He died in Nice, France, in 1965.

PLOT SUMMARY

Act 1

The entire play takes place in the home of Leonard and Charlotte Ardsley, situated in a small country town outside of Canterbury, England. One

Somerset Maugham © Bettmann/Corbis

afternoon, Mrs. Ardsley takes tea with her son Sydney, who has become blind as a result of war injuries. She tells him that her daughter Ethel has arrived and that her husband, Howard, will pick her up later. The two discuss Howard's drinking problem and his relationship with Ethel.

Ethel arrives with Gwen, a family friend, whose pitying tone toward Sydney becomes quite annoying. Mrs. Ardsley's younger daughters, Lois and Eva, soon come in from playing tennis with Wilfred Cedar, Gwen's husband, and Collie Stratton, another family friend. As Eva leaves to get the maid, the others discuss the fact that Eva never got over losing her fiancé during the war. Gwen makes ignorant remarks about class in front of Ethel, who has married beneath her, and the others upbraid Gwen for it.

Wilfred decides to stay and play another game of tennis and talks Gwen into leaving him there, which she reluctantly agrees to do. Sydney tells the others how much he appreciates how well Eva takes care of him. Collie and Wilfred discuss Lois's limited marital prospects in the small town. Collie admits that he is having financial problems with his auto business and asks Wilfred for a loan, but Wilfred refuses.

After Wilfred leaves, Eva appears with tea and they discuss her care of Sydney. She tries to encourage Collie to find a wife, but he rebuffs her suggestion. Leonard arrives; he offers his sympathy and advice about Collie's financial problems. After the rest leave, Mrs. Ardsley discusses her medical problem with her brother, a doctor.

When they are alone, Wilfred tells Lois that he is "crazy about" her and suggests that she run off with him. Lois refuses his advances, insisting that he is old enough to be her father. Howard arrives and, after quickly assessing the situation, tells Wilfred to leave Lois alone. When Gwen appears, Wilfred becomes livid, calling her a fool for her jealousy and insisting that she leave immediately. After Howard falls into a drunken sleep, Ethel tries to defend him to Eva. Eva soon leaves to play chess with Sydney, a game she admittedly loathes.

Act 2

Eva gets increasingly agitated as she and Sydney argue while playing chess until finally, she throws all the pieces on the floor. Eva declares that she does not want to be his caretaker any longer and is sick of "being a drudge." Mrs. Ardsley tries to get Eva to sympathize with Sydney's situation, but Eva cannot, insisting that she has already given enough—the man that she loved. Eva fears that she will never have another opportunity for marriage. After she rushes out of the room in tears, Sydney tells his mother that he understands Eva's feelings and does not blame her for them.

Gwen arrives and tells Mrs. Ardsley that she thinks her husband is in love with Lois. Mrs. Ardsley advises her to ignore him and says that nothing will come of it. Lois soon appears wearing a pearl necklace that she claims is fake, but that Gwen suspects is real. Her mother tells Lois that she thinks she needs a rest at her aunt's for a week or two. Later, Lois confronts Wilfred about whether the pearls he gave her are real. When he admits that they are, Lois insists that she cannot accept them, but he soon changes her mind. He confesses his love again and asks her to run away with him.

Lois tells Ethel of Wilfred's proposal and Ethel tries to talk her sister out of it. Their conversation shifts to Ethel's relationship with Howard, who Lois says is "common." Ethel admits that she had a strong physical attraction for him when she met him and that she fell in love with him. Lois concludes that she is not as romantic as her sister. She tells Ethel that she will not run away with Wilfred but admits that "it's rather exciting to have the chance."

Later that afternoon, Ardsley informs Collie that Collie will most likely be sent to jail for the bad checks that he wrote on his overdrawn account. Collie complains that a naval hero should not be treated so poorly and asks Ardsley for his help. Ardsley insists that there is little that he can do.

After Ardsley leaves, Eva appears and begs Collie to let her help him by lending him money. Collie refuses, noting the impropriety of her offer. Eva admits her feelings toward him and suggests that they become engaged, which would make it easier for him to accept the money. When Collie rejects her, suggesting that some day she will find someone that she "really like[s]," Eva is humiliated. Collie apologizes and leaves.

When Lois later criticizes Howard's drinking, he admits that he likes "to have a good old laugh now and again," but that Ethel does not. Howard tells Lois that she appears to be "a bit of a devil" and asks for a kiss. Ignoring her protests, he kisses her, which makes her furious. He tries to convince her that she is "missing out" and invites her up to his farm. His obvious desire for her makes her pause, but Mrs. Ardsley's appearance breaks the tension. When Mrs. Ardsley tells her daughter that she has made arrangements for her to visit her aunt, Lois agrees.

Act 3

Later, Wilfred confronts Lois, begging her not to leave, but she refuses. He convinces her to keep the pearls and insists that he would do anything for her. The others come in and discuss Lois' trip when Ardsley bursts in and tells them that Collie has shot himself. Eva breaks down, blaming all of them for not trying to save him, and insists that she and Collie were engaged.

When Lois and Howard are left alone, Lois admits that she is attracted to him. Later Sydney expresses guilt over Collie's fate and blames the government for not taking care of the men who served in the war. When his father tries to defend the country, Sydney argues that men were sacrificed to the government's "vanity, their greed, and their stupidity" and that patriotism and glory are "bunk." Howard admits that he enjoyed the war since it was more exciting than his life now.

Mrs. Ardsley's doctor tells Mrs. Ardsley that she needs an operation or she will not live more than a few months. Realizing that she has cancer, Mrs. Ardsley refuses. Mrs. Ardsley concludes that the knowledge that she is going to die gives her "a funny sort of thrill" because she is now free.

Gwen appears and informs Mrs. Ardsley that Lois and Wilfred are running off to London. She begs Lois not to go, insisting that she will never give her husband a divorce. Lois later admits to Ethel that she does not love Wilfred, but she enjoys having power over him. Eva walks into the room, drugged, and announces that Collie is coming. In the final scene, Ardsley appears, telling his family how wonderful it is to have them all together and praises England "and all it stands for." The play closes with Eva singing "God save the King," "in a thin and cracked voice," which horrifies everyone.

CHARACTERS

Charlotte Ardsley

Charlotte is sympathetic and sensitive to her family's and friends' troubles. She understands that Esther married Howard because they were in love. Open and willing to accept change, she admits that she thought class divisions would ease after the war.

Charlotte's love for her husband has prompted her to shield him from harsh realities like her illness. She tries her best to protect her family, but is tired and so feels a giddy sense of freedom when she knows she will soon die.

Eva Ardsley

Eva has accepted her role as Sydney's caretaker and also helps run the house since her mother is in ill health. Sydney suggests that she likes being a martyr, claiming, "it's jam for Evie to have an invalid to look after." He insists that "Nature destined her to be a saint and it's damned lucky for her that I'm around to give her the opportunity of earning a heavenly crown."

Sydney, however, recognizes only one of his sister's motivations. Helping others does give her a purpose in life, but she increasingly resents the fact that she has no other options. She desperately wants a husband and children.

Leonard Ardsley

Leonard "always looks at the bright side of things," but only so that he does not have to get involved with painful truths. Mrs. Ardsley notes that "he can never see further than the end of his nose" and explains that she "always had to take care that he didn't trip over the obvious and hurt himself."

He is initially sympathetic to Collie's dilemma, but his limited sympathy does not prompt him to take any measures to help him out. He refuses to blame the government for the war or its consequences, excusing their neglect of men like Collie when he insists "the nation can't afford itself the luxury of supporting an army of officers it has no use for."

Lois Ardsley

Lois has become hard and selfish as a result of her limited prospects. Even though she does not love Wilfred, she is excited by the drama of running away with him. She never considers the suffering she will cause Gwen, or her sister, as she contemplates an affair with Howard. Her sisters' bleak lives frighten Lois and prompt her to think only of herself.

Sydney Ardsley

Sydney has adapted to his blindness with a combination of sardonic wit and sympathetic understanding of other's limitations. He uses his wit sometimes at his own expense, such as when he tells his mother that she must console herself by thinking that she has a hero for a son. The war, however, has embittered Sydney. He argues that he and others who served "have had our chance of making a good job of life snatched away from us."

Claiming a certain hardness, Sydney argues that suffering has not ennobled him. He cynically wonders what Eva would do without the family to wait on, suggesting that she wants to be made a saint. Yet, Sydney sympathizes with those around him. He is gracious when an annoying Gwen pities him, and he expresses sorrow when he learns of Collie's suicide. Recognizing that his disability is hard on others.

Ethel Bartlett

Ethel is a decent, proud woman. She holds onto romantic memories of how much she and Howard were in love when they first met. Her common sense forces her to recognize the tensions in her marriage, but she refuses to complain, insisting that she has done her best. Her selflessness prompts her to blame herself for breaking class rules, claiming that their marriage has been harder on Howard than on her.

Howard Bartlett

Howard drinks too much and tries to appear grander than he is, but his speech gives him away. He tells Wilfred that he was an officer and a gentleman and warns, "don't you forget it." Tired of being thought of as common in comparison to a

TOPICS FOR FURTHER STUDY

- Write a screenplay based on one act of the play. What problems would you face if you were to make a film version of the play?

- Research the English class structure in the years following World War I. How difficult was it to move from the lower to the upper classes? Consider economic as well as social factors.

- Investigate women's roles in England after the war. What kind of opportunities, if any, did they have outside the home?

- Investigate the English government's treatment of veterans after World War I. What kind of support did they offer them?

lady like Ethel, Howard tries to seduce Lois because she has "a bit of devil in her."

Gwen Cedar

Gwen is "desperately hanging on the remains of her youth," especially since she has a philandering husband. Trying too hard to ingratiate herself with others, she is annoyingly sympathetic to Sydney. She also lacks tact, as when she blurts out in front of Ethel, "it's always a mistake to marry out of one's class." She hovers over her husband and spies on him, desperate to do anything she can to prevent him from leaving her.

Wilfred Cedar

Wilfred is a selfish and cold-hearted man who thinks nothing of hurting or humiliating Gwen in front of her friends. He admits to Collie that he made a good deal of money in the market and now he's "going to live like a gentleman." Yet, when Collie asks to borrow money in order to keep from being sent to prison, Wilfred refuses, insisting, "I'm not made of money, you know. . . . I haven't got more than I can spend." He will soon pay a good deal of money for pearls, but only to satisfy his lust for Lois. When Lois asks what would become of Gwen if Wilfred left her, he responds, "Oh damn Gwen. I can only think of myself."

Collie Stratton

Collie commanded a destroyer for the British Navy during the war but has been unable to adequately support himself in the years after. He is an honest man who has no business sense. Although he writes bad checks, he believes that he will somehow get the money to pay them off. He admits, "I'd had it drummed into me for so many years that nothing is impossible in the British Navy. It was hard to give in while I still had some fight in me." His pride prevents him from accepting Eva's offer of money, and he is too decent to take advantage of her feelings toward him. He treats Eva kindly and gently as he refuses her.

THEMES

Hypocrisy of War

Maugham reveals the hypocrisy of governments that recruit young men to fight wars for the honor and glory of their country. Sydney explains how Englishmen initially believed that "every sacrifice was worth it." At the end of the war, they were convinced that those who died did not do so in vain. Men "who were broken and shattered . . . were buoyed up by the thought that if they'd given everything they'd given it in a great cause."

Yet, Sydney insists, these men were "the dupes of the incompetent fools who ruled the nations." They were, he concludes, "sacrificed to their vanity, their greed, and their stupidity." He worries that "they'll muddle us all into another war," and declares that if they do, he will go out into the streets and yell, "it's all bunk what they're saying to you, about honour and patriotism and glory, bunk, bunk, bunk." Maugham shows how these men have been abandoned by their government, and stripped of their glory, as they struggle to endure the physical and economic hardships as a result of the war. Sydney must endure his blindness and his total dependence on his family. After his celebrated service in the British navy, Collie has been left no options other than to try to make his small business succeed. When it fails, he sees no recourse for himself except suicide.

Class Consciousness

The rigid British class system in this era restricted the lives of the upper and lower classes. Men and women who married beneath their class brought shame to their families and tensions to their marriages. Gwen accurately captures the conventional attitude toward such arrangements when she notes, "It's always a mistake to marry out of one's own class. It's never a success." Ethel's marriage to the drunken, philandering Howard proves her point. When she married a tenant farmer, she embarrassed her family who have watched her "grow old and tired and hopeless." And her husband, who has grown tired of always looking up to his wife, now looks elsewhere for a bit of "fun."

Sexism

The rigid class system, coupled with an endemic sexism, severely limits the options for women in the play. Howard reflects the traditional attitude when he declares, "no place like home, and home's a woman's place." Eva is trapped in her home, relegated to the traditional role of caretaker as she devotes long hours attending to Sydney. Her only hope for escape, as is the case for all of the women in the play, is through marriage. When all of her avenues for escape are cut off after Collie's suicide, Eva's mind cracks. Ironically, sexist attitudes also ruin Collie when he refuses Eva's offer of help because he cannot accept money from a woman.

Lois is not forced into marriage in order to escape the limiting life in the country, yet the only other option available for her is to accept Wilfred's invitation to run off to London with him. Facing the reality of life for aging women, she agrees to this arrangement because she does not love Wilfred. If he leaves her for a younger woman, she will not be heartbroken.

Gwen's life will be destroyed when Lois runs off with Wilfred, for as she recognizes, she is "too old to be left alone." She, like Ethel, accepts her husband's philandering because she has no other choice. At fifty, Gwen is too old to find a new husband, and so she must do everything she can to try to hold on to him, including humiliating herself by begging assistance from others.

STYLE

Suspense

Maugham's plots follow the traditional characteristics of a well-made play, with a clear pattern of conflict, climax and resolution. Often his plots focus on secrets that are eventually revealed by the end of the play. Suspense is heightened as the audience waits for the secrets to be revealed. *For Services Rendered* follows this pattern. There are two main secrets in the plot: Mrs. Ardsley's cancer and Lois's relationships with both Wilfred Cedar and Howard Bartlett. While Mrs. Ardsley's secret does not produce much conflict in the play, Lois' does: the play ends with her decision to run off with Cedar and perhaps enter into a sexual relationship with Howard, her sister's husband, which will affect her sister, Cedar's wife Gwen, and the reputation of Lois's family. The other conflict in the play, which centers on the relationship between Eva and Collie, ends in tragedy when Collie kills himself and Eva loses her sanity.

Irony

Maugham employs irony in his characterization of the blind Sydney, who can "see" much more clearly than any of the other members of his family. He understands the sacrifices that Eva is making and does not blame her for her outbursts, and he alone knows that his mother is dying from cancer. Sydney also has a clear vision of the hypocrisy of his government when he insists that he and men like him "were the dupes of the incompetent fools who ruled the nations," that they were "sacrificed to their vanity, their greed, and their stupidity." Ironically, Sydney's father is blind to the reality of the horrors of war that surround him. He claims, "we none of us have anything very much to worry about" and not "very much to complain of," in front of his daughter, whose mind has been destroyed by the deaths of the two men she loved.

HISTORICAL CONTEXT

World War I

World War I was triggered by the assassination of Archduke Franz Ferdinand, the heir to the Austro-Hungarian empire, on June 28, 1914, in Sarajevo, Bosnia. The conflict started a month later when Austria-Hungary declared war on Serbia. Soon after, other European countries made their own declarations of war. Britain entered the war on August 4th after Germany began its invasion of France. The war between the allied powers (France, Russia, Britain and the United States) and the Central Powers (Germany and Austria-Hungary) raged until 1918. The number of total casualties is extraordinary, estimated at 10,000,000, of which approximately 750,000 were British.

After a short post-war period of economic prosperity, unemployment in England increased as returning soldiers looked for work. In 1921, the number of unemployed men increased to 2,000,000. That number rose to 3,000,000 by 1932.

COMPARE
&
CONTRAST

- **1930s:** After WWII, there is a response to the rise of totalitarian regimes in Germany, Italy, and Japan. Over two hundred countries band together to fight the militaristic expansion in Europe.

  Today: The United States and Britain, along with thirty-three other countries, invade Iraq in 2003. The initial motive for the invasion is the assumed threat of Iraq's weapons of mass destruction. Several coalition allies pull out of Iraq as weapons of mass destruction are not found.

- **1930s:** Britain follows America into the Depression, with approximately 3,000,000 unemployed in Britain by 1932.

  Today: Economic policies, like unemployment compensation, are in place in England. These policies are designed to prevent the country from falling into a severe economic depression, like that of the 1930s.

- **1930s:** The "New Woman" comes to describe women who challenge traditional notions of a woman's place, especially the roles of wife and mother. These challenges are seen as a threat to the fabric of the British family.

  Today: Women have the opportunity to work inside or outside of the home, or both. However, those who choose to have children and a career face difficult time-management choices balancing work and home schedules.

In the aftermath of World War I, British society went through a period of change. Traditional beliefs in God, country, and humanity were shaken as the British people faced the devastation of a war of this magnitude. The feelings of confusion and dislocation that resulted led to a questioning, and often a rejection, of conventional morality and beliefs.

World War II

The world experienced a decade of aggression in the 1930s that would culminate in World War II. This Second World War resulted from the rise of totalitarian regimes in Germany, Italy, and Japan. These militaristic regimes gained control as a result of the economic depression experienced by most of the world in the early 1930s, and from the conditions created by the peace settlements following World War I. The dictatorships established in each country encouraged expansion into neighboring countries. In Germany, Hitler strengthened the army during the 1930s. In 1936, Benito Mussolini's Italian troops took Ethiopia. From 1936–39, Spain was engaged in civil war involving Francisco Franco's fascist army, aided by Germany and Italy. In March 1938, Germany annexed Austria, and in March 1939, Germany occupied Czechoslovakia. Italy took Albania in April 1939. One week after Nazi Germany and the U.S.S.R. signed a Treaty of Nonaggression, on September 1, 1939, Germany invaded Poland and World War II began. On September 3, 1939, Britain and France declared war on Germany after a U-boat sank the British ship *Athenia* off the coast of Ireland. Another British ship, the *Courageous*, was sunk on September 17. All the members of the British Commonwealth, except Ireland, soon joined Britain and France in their declaration of war.

CRITICAL OVERVIEW

When *For Services Rendered* opened at the Globe Theatre in London in 1932, audiences were not prepared for its anti-war focus. As a result, the play closed after just 78 performances. As Ted Morgan argues in his biography on Maugham, the play is "an indictment of a whole nation. . . . The patriots and promise-makers, the apostles of a better world, were shown up as rogues and hypocrites."

Anthony Curtis, in his introduction to the play, writes that "the London critics damned it with

British soldiers of the East Lancashire Regiment in a trench during World War I © Hulton-Deutsch Collection/Corbis

qualified praise." He cites one such critic, Charles Morgan, writing anonymously in *The Times*, that "Mr. Maugham has given us an enthralling theatrical entertainment, if nothing more." Curtis notes that in *The Spectator*, Peter Fleming concluded that Maugham tries too hard to blame the war for all of the problems that the characters face. Fleming writes that,

> if the war decreed that Mrs. Ardsley should find post-war life a sad and silly business, no longer in the best of taste, it is not the war's fault that she must shortly leave it."

Other reviewers were much more harsh. Curtis quotes enraged novelist Cecil Roberts who ranted in his article, "Should Maugham Get Away With It?" for *The Daily Express*, "It is worse than a bad play. . . . It is a play of malevolent propaganda against those who live with courage and hope." Yet in response, Wimbledon tennis champion Bunny Austin wrote an eloquent defense of the play to the paper a few days later. Some reviewers, like Desmond MacCarthy in the *New Statesman* and John Pollock in the *Saturday Review* considered it to be his best play.

The play's reputation has increased since its first production. Curtis notes that its 1979 production by the Royal National Theatre was hailed by many in the press as Maugham's "theatrical masterpiece." He adds, "At this distance of time, the play appears as a microcosmic image of what Auden later described as 'a low dishonest decade.'" M. K. Naik, in his study of Maugham's work, finds "a greater mellowness; and the awareness of the graver issues of life" than in Maugham's previous work. Laurence Brander, in his guide to Maugham, insists that the play "was much too accurate a picture to be a success on the stage" and concludes, "It is a bitter picture of a macabre world which is realized in this very expert piece of writing."

CRITICISM

Wendy Perkins

Perkins is a professor of American and English literature and film. In this essay, Perkins focuses on the damaging effects of war and social class on the women in Maugham's play.

Ted Morgan argues, in his biography on Maugham, that *For Services Rendered* is "an indictment of a whole nation." He claims that

❝

THE SAVAGE IRONY
OF EVA'S DERANGED SONG AT THE
END OF THE PLAY OFFERS
A FITTING TESTAMENT TO THE
MEN AND WOMEN WHOSE LIVES
HAVE BEEN DESTROYED
BY THE FIRST WORLD WAR."

Somerset Maugham exposes "the patriots and promise-makers, the apostles of a better world" as "rogues and hypocrites." Maugham does this by showing the devastating effects of the war on an English family. Sydney Ardsley's heroic actions during World War I earned him the Military Cross but little else. Blinded in the war, Sydney is confined to his home and must depend on his family's kindness and care, since the government has turned its back on him and the other soldiers who bravely fought for their country. As Sydney notes, everything continues the way it had before the war, "except that we're all broke to the wide and a few hundred thousand fellows like me have had our chance of making a good job of life snatched away from us." Another fellow like him, Collie Stratton, is driven to suicide after his business fails and he sees no hope for the future.

The most dramatic effects of the war are seen on the men in the play, but Maugham also illustrates the damage done to women. Through his chronicle of the lives of the three Ardsley sisters and their friend Gwen, Maugham illustrates how the war, exacerbated by the rigid British class system, affected in more subtle, but no less destructive, ways the women who were left behind.

Eva Ardsley becomes the most tragic figure in the play. The thirty-nine year old woman is restless and haggard when she first appears. The combination of class and war has severely limited her chances for happiness. Eva has never gotten over the death of her fiancé, who was killed in the war. Her mother explains, "in a place like this she could hardly hope to. By the end of the war there were very few young men left. And girls were growing up all the time." In a culture that revered youth and beauty, Eva did not have much opportunity to find

a suitable husband, which was the goal for every woman in that era. Another man had been interested in her, but she rejected him because he was not of her class. Women like Eva were under pressure not only to marry, but to marry well.

Since she has no husband and no immediate prospects, Eva has accepted the role of her brother's caretaker, playing endless hours of chess with him, which she admittedly loathes. She concludes that looking after Sydney helped her to bear the loss of her fiancé. Yet she has not given up her dream of some day marrying, for society has convinced her that "it's a woman's province to have a home of her own and children to look after."

Eva has adopted the role of saint, since she had little opportunity for anything else, claiming that she is glad to do what she can "to make life a little easier" for Sydney. Sydney argues that Nature destined her for sainthood and decides "it's damned lucky for her that I'm around to give her the opportunity of earning a heavenly crown." Yet Sydney ignores the social pressures that have encouraged Eva to take on this role and that have left her no other options.

Eva is unable, however, to maintain her saintly demeanor as she recognizes the bleak future that lies ahead of her. During the chess game with Sydney, she fires back after Sydney criticizes her moves with, "good God, don't I spend my life looking ahead. And a damned cheerful prospect it is." Her frustration rises until she scatters the pieces on the floor and declares, "why should I be sacrificed all the time?" In her anger, Eva blames Sydney for her limited prospects, exclaiming "it's monstrous that he should try to prevent any one else from having a good time." Yet, it is not Sydney who is making Eva unhappy; the war and the rigid social mores that have determined her place have taken away her future.

Making one last attempt to secure herself a husband, Eva suggests to Collie that they marry, which would help him out of his financial difficulties. Ethel has encouraged the match, concluding, "even a marriage that isn't quite satisfactory is better than not being married at all." Collie rejects Eva, assuring her that some day she will find someone that she "really like[s]," and Eva is humiliated. Yet later, when her father tells her that Collie has killed himself, she passionately defends him, insisting that they were engaged. She reaches the point of hysteria when she claims that marrying Collie was her "only chance" and damns them all.

Ethel, the oldest daughter, has succeeded where her sister failed. She has married and has children, but her situation has not brought her happiness. The war has hurt her family financially, as the government has not lived up to its promise to support the country's tenant farmers. As a result, she and her husband work long hours in order to survive.

Ethel's marriage to a working-class man has brought shame to her family and resentment from her husband. Her mother admits, "When all that slaughter was going on it seemed so snobbish to object to a man because he was just a small tenant farmer." But Gwen's insensitive comment reflects more accurately the rigid attitudes of the British class system: "It's always a mistake to marry out of one's own class. It's never a success."

Ethel tries to convince everyone of her happiness, insisting that she has "nothing to complain of," but she reveals her true feelings when she breaks down as she watches her drunken husband sleep. She later admits that life as a tenant farmer's wife has been difficult and that sometimes his commonness upsets her. After acknowledging that it would have been better for Howard to marry in his own class, she reveals, "that's why I feel I must always have patience with him." Howard suggests the cause of his drinking when he concludes that Ethel is too good for him. He acknowledges that he is "only a common farmer . . . only . . . you don't always want to be looking up to your wife, do you?" As a result, he looks elsewhere to Lois, whom he considers more fun than his wife.

Gwen's suffering results from her husband's philandering. At fifty, she is "desperately hanging on to the remains of her youth," knowing that she is "too old to be left alone." In a frantic attempt to hold onto her husband, Gwen humiliates herself as she begs Mrs. Ardsley to persuade Lois not to run away with him. Mrs. Ardsley tries to comfort Gwen by telling her that "men of that age are often rather taken by bright young things" and suggests that "a sensible wife just shrugs her shoulders and laughs. Her safety is that the bright young things look upon her husband as an old fogey." Gwen, however, takes little comfort in her words, recognizing that her husband's wealth and her age put her in a vulnerable position. "I'm old and he's all I've got," she insists. "I'm too old to start fresh." Her only recourse is to threaten a scandal if Lois runs off with Wilfred.

Lois appears to have more prospects than her sisters because of her youth and beauty, but her choices are also limited and not very appealing. As Wilfred concludes, "girls nowadays who live in the country have to take what they can get." There are

WHAT DO I READ NEXT?

- *The Sun Also Rises* (1926), by Ernest Hemingway, focuses on a group of disillusioned Americans living in Paris after World War I.

- Virginia Woolf's *Mrs. Dalloway* (1925) focuses on the devastating effects of World War I on an Englishman.

- In his most famous work, *Of Human Bondage* (1915), Maugham incorporates autobiographical elements in his chronicle of a young man's lonely life.

- Nigel Viney collects compelling, artistic visions of war in his *Images of Wartime: British Art and Artists of World War I* (1992).

few options for a woman who cannot afford to live in the city. Lois admits that Wilfred is old enough to be her father, but she considers taking him up on his offer to run off with him since she sees no other way to get out. Recognizing the war's effects, she complains "the chances are that it'll go on like this till we're all weary old women." When Ethel tries to discourage her, she insists, "I'm getting on you know. . . . What have I got to look forward to exactly? Getting jumpy like Eva or making the best of a bad job like you?"

Lois considers Wilfred a safe prospect since she does not love him and therefore will not suffer if he eventually leaves her for a younger woman. Watching Ethel "grow old and tired and hopeless" has frightened her and prompted her to settle for Wilfred. She admits that she is going to leave with Wilfred because of what his money will bring her: "freedom and opportunity." As a result of her limited choices, Lois has become "hard and selfish."

By the end of the play, Lois prepares to run off with Wilfred and perhaps engage in an affair with Howard, which will further damage the lives of Ethel and Gwen. Eva has lost her sanity, evident in her announcement to the family that she and Collie are to be married. The savage irony of Eva's deranged song at the end of the play offers a fitting testament to the men and women whose lives have been destroyed by the First World War.

Source: Wendy Perkins, Critical Essay on *For Services Rendered*, in *Drama for Students*, Thomson Gale, 2006.

Richard A. Cordell

In the following essay, Cordell discusses Maugham's career as a playwright.

Maugham has never entertained or expressed solemn and highfalutin notions about the drama. By 1927 he had made up his mind that "a prose play is scarcely less ephemeral than a news sheet," and that anyone can learn playwriting if he has the "knack" (never defined). He felt strongly that unnecessary verbiage must be ruthlessly cut out of a play and that the shrewdness and quickwittedness of the playgoer must be assumed. His professed low opinion of the lasting quality of prose drama, except, he admits, for a few comedies that have haphazardly survived a century or two, is hard to share. It is inconceivable that *Caesar and Cleopatra*, *Hedda Gabler*, *The Wild Duck*, and *Rosmersholm* will not outlive all the poetic dramas of the late nineteenth century. *Man and Superman*, *Major Barbara*, *The Three Sisters*, *The Cherry Orchard*, *The Plough and the Stars*, *Saint Joan*, and *The Circle* will not be museum pieces for many years to come; not one play in verse written between 1900 and 1925 approaches them in merit. Maugham's attack on the drama of ideas, although amusing and not altogether unsound (Walter Kerr would agree with it thoroughly at this late date), is in part a defense of his own limitations and tastes, like Poe degrading the long poem and novel; it also results from his failure to admit that ideas are basic in his own plays: in a shrewd treatment of a corner of society such as *Our Betters*, or an intelligent dissection of human conduct and ethics as in *The Circle*. Moreover *For Services Rendered* and *Sheppey* are charged with ideas. Time has proved Maugham justified in his harsh estimate of such palely intellectual dramatists as Granville-Barker, but his cool entombment of Ibsen and Shaw seems recklessly premature.

After forty years of playwriting he grew tired of it and also realized that the public had little interest in the kind of play he liked to and could write. When he finished *Sheppey* he felt a sense of exaltation and freedom. The impact of the vigorous, free-wheeling American drama of the 1920's and 1930's was being felt abroad, and Maugham was perspicacious enough to see that both critics and playgoers were assessing with seriousness and respect the plays of Sidney Howard, Odets, Wilder, Sherwood, Lillian Hellman, and Kingsley. Then came the more subtle drama of the new French school, particularly that of Girandoux, Anouilh, Sartre, and Aymé. These new French plays were as popular in the London theatre as the American plays and aroused sharper, more respectful attention from the young British playwrights. Still later the grotesqueries of Beckett, Betti, and Ionesco and the roughneck plays of the Angry Young Men and Angry Young Women have also failed to create in him any desire to return to the theatre as a playwright.

Outside the theatre itself, however, Maugham has had a vast and attentive audience in the postwar years. On the wireless and television in Britain, and to a less extent in America and on the continent, his plays are frequently performed, the early comedies as well as the more serious late plays. Even *For Services Rendered*, relentless and hopeless as it is, was well received in an expert television production in 1959 and struck no London reviewer as dated. *The Letter*, *The Land of Promise*, and *The Sacred Flame* (which somehow escapes censorship) are established television favorites. Even such minor and otherwise forgotten plays as *The Camel's Back* and *Love in a Cottage* do well enough in the new medium.

In 1957 an indefatigable team of historians of the theatre, Raymond Mander and Joe Mitchener, made a reasonably complete pictorial record of Maugham's plays, as they have likewise done with the theatre of Shaw and Coward. It is valuable for reference, and the many photographs are most interesting. A staggering amount of industry went into assembling the data and pictures. They even brought to light an unperformed full-length play, *The Road Uphill*. Maugham thought that he had destroyed all copies of the manuscript, but he admitted that writing the play had not been a waste of time, for later he frugally used the theme in *The Razor's Edge*.

What place will there be for Maugham in the theatre of the future? Will he be forced to the library shelves along with Peele, Kyd, Greene, Dekker, Fielding, Scribe, Bulwer-Lytton, H. J. Byron, Rachel Crothers, Clyde Fitch, and hundreds of others who once filled the theatres? Will the time come when the public mood will respond to the diatribes of *For Services Rendered* (*Time* magazine in 1958 dismissed the equally bitter play *Paths of Glory* as "unfashionably anti-militaristic"), or find the trenchant satire of *Sheppey* sardonically amusing? Or is Maugham correct in prophesying that of all his plays only one or two of the high comedies will survive to please occasional audiences of the future? His own prediction is very modest: "I think that one or two of my comedies may retain for some time a kind of pale life, for they are written in the tradition of English comedy and on that account may find a place that began with the Restoration dramatists. It may be that they may secure me a line or two in the histories of the English theatre."

Source: Richard A. Cordell, "The Theatre of Somerset Maugham," in *Somerset Maugham*, Indiana University Press, 1965, pp. 208–11.

M. K. Naik

In the following essay, Naik discusses the last four plays of Maugham's career.

"For some years," says Maugham in the preface to the last volume of his collected plays, "I had in mind the four plays with which I proposed to finish my career as a practising dramatist. I was prepared to write them only on this account, for I did not think any of them was likely to succeed." These four plays are *The Sacred Flame* (1928), *The Bread-winner* (1930), *For Services Rendered* (1932), and *Sheppey* (1933). They, too, show the same features as Maugham's novels of the last phase: the realization that he is no longer young and therefore not "in the movement"; a greater mellowness; and the awareness of the graver issues of life.

The first feature is well substantiated in *The Breadwinner*, which has been described as "an inverted *Doll's House*." It portrays a middle-aged stockbroker who becomes bored with his job, his routine life, his snobbish wife, and self-centered children, and escapes for his "soul's sake" to travel "in Romance." Maugham's attitude toward the young in the play is significant. He shows them to be completely selfish and self-centered, narrow-minded and intolerant, and hard and brazenly cynical; in short, he views them through the suspecting eyes of one who has left his youth far behind. The cynicism of *The Breadwinner* is of a jaded and bored variety. This is what the middle-aged stockbroker thinks about the relationship between parent and child:

> Of course, when they are small, one's fond of one's children. One likes them as one likes puppies or kittens. They're dependent on you, and that's rather flattering. But almost before you know where you are they're young men and women with characters of their own. They are not part of you any more. They are strangers. Why should you care for them?

His wife, who coolly says what a lark it would be if he dies, leaving her free and rich, has no illusions about marriage. "Do you think women find marriage amusing?" she asks, "They have been bored stiff by it for a thousand generations. Half

the women I know are so bored by their husbands that they could scream at the sight of them."

And, lastly, this is what the young people in the play think about life: "After all, I did not ask to be brought into the world. He [i.e., father] did it entirely for his own amusement. He must be prepared to pay for it."

For Services Rendered is a ghastly picture of the aftermath of war, ending on a note of savage irony in Eva's hysterical cry, "God save our king." It shows the disillusionment of those of the younger generation who, in Siegfried Sassoon's words, "were destroyed by the War, though they escaped its shells." There is much pity in *For Services Rendered*, but it is the milk of human kindness turned sour. The reason is that there is a total blackout of the positive values in the play. Matthew Arnold rejected his own *Empedocles on Etna*, because he thought that it was not truly tragic since its suffering did not find a "vent in action." *For Services Rendered* fails by the same logic, though it is full of the seriousness of Maugham's last phase.

This note of seriousness is struck in *The Sacred Flame*, also, though here again Maugham missed the authentic tragical note. The play portrays a mother who calmly murders her invalid son, when she finds that the continuance of his life would only bring him dishonor and disillusionment. There is too much of the "detective yarn" in the play, with the secret of the murder being revealed only at the end and with the usual search for a motive and evidence comprising the body of the drama. There is, again, a lack of intensity in the play which prevents it from attaining the tragical level. An undercurrent of philosophy is, no doubt, discernable in some of the speeches of Mrs. Tabret, but, on the whole, there is too much of the "thriller" in the tone of *The Sacred Flame*. Once again, a theme of tragical proportions is handled in a very superficial manner.

The setting of his last play, *Sheppey*, is most unusual for Maugham. The hero is a barber's assistant who, winning an £8,000 prize in the sweepstakes, suddenly decides to spend it all on the poor, which naturally makes his relatives think that the sudden good fortune has unsettled his mind. Maugham says in his preface, "*Sheppey* does not set out to be a problem play; I should describe it as a sardonic comedy." The central situation in the play does, however, suggest a problem in ethics, viz., the conflict between materialism and the claims of the spirit. But considered even as a "sardonic comedy" pure and simple, *Sheppey* does not succeed.

There is no doubt some pungent irony in the scenes where Sheppey's daughter fervently prays to God that her father may be declared mad and when the learned doctor pronounces Sheppey to be a lunatic because, "a sane man is not going to give all his money away to the poor. A sane man takes money from the poor." The doctor adds that "philanthropy in general could always be ascribed to repressed homosexuality." Maugham also seems to take a special delight in exposing the snobbery, the self-importance, the cocksureness, and the selfishness of young Florrie and her fiancée, and with cynical glee he further points out how the underdogs, whom Sheppey is so eager to help and reform, ultimately prefer their old crooked ways to receiving charity.

Sheppey, as a whole, however, lacks power: first, because the sudden change in Sheppey in no way appears to be convincing and probable, and thus makes the whole play seem artificial; second, because the sarcasm of the play loses its edge since the struggle between Sheppey and his relatives is not made intense enough. Ibsen's *An Enemy of the People* has virtually the same theme: Dr. Stockmann, too, like Sheppey, goes against the herd and pays the price of his audacity. But Ibsen's play throbs with intense conflict, and the hero has the proper stature to make this conflict powerful. In Ibsen's play the result is tremendous irony, but in Maugham's, the result is pale insignificance. Once again, in *Sheppey*, Maugham has a theme bursting with great potentialities, but they go unrealized.

Source: M. K. Naik, "The Last Phase," in *W. Somerset Maugham*, University of Oklahoma Press, 1953, pp. 102–05.

SOURCES

Brander, Laurence, *Somerset Maugham: A Guide*, Oliver & Boyd, 1963.

Curtis, Anthony, "Introduction," in *W. Somerset Maugham: Plays: Two*, Methuen, 1999, pp. xiii–xxix.

Maugham, W. Somerset, *For Services Rendered: A Play in Three Acts*, Heinemann, 1932.

Morgan, Ted, *Maugham: A Biography*, Simon and Schuster, 1980.

Naik, M. K., *W. Somerset Maugham*, University of Oklahoma Press, 1966.

FURTHER READING

Cordell, Richard A., *Somerset Maugham: A Biographical and Critical Study*, Indiana University Press, 1961.
    Cordell presents insightful analyses of Maugham's work, including his plays.

Curtis, Anthony, *The Pattern of Maugham: A Critical Portrait*, Hamilton, 1974.
    Curtis concludes that Maugham's work is an accurate reflection of British society during the war years.

Loss, Archie K., *W. Somerset Maugham*, Ungar, 1987.
    Loss sheds light on the man and his work.

Sanders, Charles, "W. Somerset Maugham," in *Dictionary of Literary Biography*, Vol. 10, *Modern British Dramatists, 1900–1945*, edited by Stanley Weintraub, Gale Research, 1982, pp. 22–42.
    Sanders presents a comprehensive overview of Maugham and his plays.

Habitat

JUDITH THOMPSON
2001

Judith Thompson became one of Canada's leading contemporary playwrights when, after a series of negative reviews, her play *The Crackwalker* (1980) was recognized as a brilliant piece of cutting-edge theater. Bleak and affronting, about the lives of those marginalized and abandoned by society, the play set a standard for a career writing realistic drama with psychologically profound characters and a commentary on the key social issues in modern-day Canada.

Thompson's drama *Habitat*, which premiered on September 20, 2001 at the Bluma Appel Theatre in Toronto, also examines issues facing marginalized members of Canadian society. It focuses on the tribulations of a group home for troubled teenagers and the struggles of the home's manager to remain on a prosperous suburban street while the street's residents campaign to have the group home removed. Raine, whose mother has just died of cancer, grows and changes emotionally while she gets to know the man who runs the group home, one of its troubled wards, and an older woman who lives on the street. In addition to addressing themes of teenage anger and rebellion, the play explores the power and importance of the mother figure as well as what it really means to create a habitat of love and acceptance.

AUTHOR BIOGRAPHY

Thompson was born in Montreal on September 20, 1954, the daughter of W. R. Thompson, a geneticist

and the head of the psychology department at Queen's University, and Mary, who taught in the Queens Drama Department for many years. After attending Queen's University and graduating in 1976, Thompson enrolled in the National Theater School's acting program. Afterwards, Thompson worked as an actor for a year, but then gave up acting to pursue writing.

Thompson's first play, *The Crackwalker*, follows the doomed relationship of a mentally retarded woman and an emotionally unstable man. It caused a sensation when it was first produced in 1980 and was very highly regarded in Canada's theater scene. Thompson's second play, *White Biting Dog* (1984), was eagerly anticipated and went on to win Thopmson's first Governor's General Award for Drama. Thompson settled in Toronto and began a working relationship with the Tarragon Theater, where most of her plays have premiered.

Thompson's *I Am Yours*, about a struggle for custody of a baby, debuted in Toronto in 1987. Thompson wrote two further plays in the 1990s as well as a number of award-winning radio, television, and film scripts. *Perfect Pie* (2000) follows the unlikely friendship of two girls when they are reunited years after they were separated in a train accident. *Habitat* premiered in 2001. Since then, Thompson has continued to live and work in Canada, producing plays including *Capture Me* (2004), which is about the stalking and eventual murder of a teacher by an abusive husband whom she had left ten years before.

Judith Thompson is a full tenured professor at the University of Guelph in the School of English and Theatre Studies, where she has taught for 13 years.

PLOT SUMMARY

Act 1, Scenes 1–7

Habitat begins in a hospital room with Raine talking to her mother, Cath, who is too weak to speak because she is dying of cancer. Raine tells Cath she is going to take her bank card. Then Raine experiences a sort of trance in which she remembers when she almost died as a baby because Cath failed to bring her to the hospital soon enough. Cath then wakes up, but Raine leaves to meet her friends.

In the next scene, Lewis Chance introduces himself to the community in a high school auditorium, explaining that he is opening a group home

on the prosperous suburban street Mapleview Lanes that will be full of children that everyone has "failed." In scene 3, Janet breaks into her mother's house because Margaret will not answer the door, they have a fight, and Janet leaves.

Raine meets Margaret by accident in scene 4, while she is trying to find the group home. In scene 5, Raine meets Lewis, who tells her she is "home . . . at . . . last!" During these scenes it is revealed that Cath died shortly after Raine left her in the first scene, and Raine's father did not take her to live with him. In scene 6, Janet talks to her children about the group home and about how much she loves them.

Act 1, Scenes 8–21

In scene 8, Janet apologizes to Margaret, who is short with her and tells her to do something about the group home. Lewis tells Raine how much love he has for her, and Margaret speaks to a neighbor about the group home. Sparkle then describes to Raine how he broke into a house on Mapleview Lanes.

In the scenes that follow, Margaret shouts at someone from the group home from her back window, Lewis plays charades with Sparkle and Raine, Sparkle tells Raine that he killed his parents, and Lewis talks to his mother on the phone. Margaret meets Raine on a midnight walk in scene 16, and Margaret tells her that Lewis pockets most of the money he gets from the government for the group home. In scene 17, Sparkle tells Raine a story about his family and then reveals that he was lying.

Sparkle tells Lewis he thinks Lewis is sexy, and Lewis tells Sparkle he is fed up with him not caring about anything. Margaret complains to Janet in scene 20 that she is not doing anything to get rid of the group home, and in scene 21 Lewis finds Raine looking through his papers. He defends himself from her accusation that he is pocketing government money by telling her the story about how he failed to save his baby brother from dying even though he walked six miles to the hospital in the snow.

Act 2

In act 2, scene 1, Janet and Margaret visit Lewis to tell him of their concerns about the group home, but things turn very sour and Lewis tells Margaret to stick her petition up her arse. Lewis refuses to tell Janet whether any of the residents have criminal records, tears up the petition, and orders her to leave. In scene 2, Sparkle insults Raine while the two of them are smoking marijuana, and then Lewis talks to his mother about her medication and about his legal battle with the other residents of Mapleview Lanes.

Janet tells her husband it is her duty to protect the neighborhood. In scene 5, Sparkle tries to seduce Lewis. In scene 6, there is the subtle implication, which later becomes clear, that Lewis is having an affair with Sparkle. In scene 7, Raine and Sparkle tease Lewis lightheartedly until he explodes and tells them he is "BLEEDING TO DEATH."

Raine confronts Margaret in scene 8 about her role in getting rid of the group home, and when Margaret starts to change her mind, Janet tells her that it is too late to stop now. Raine starts cutting herself in scene 9, saying that she hates everyone and everything, while Sparkle walks away, and in scene 10 Sparkle describes how he does not care about anything. Lewis then comforts Raine, and Sparkle tells Margaret that she has broken his best friend's heart.

In scene 13, Raine tells the city council why they should let the group home stay and Janet denounces Lewis. Lewis then tells the council about all of his indiscretions, including his criminal record when he was young, and his affair with Sparkle. He tells Margaret to decide whether the group home should stay or go, and Margaret cannot bring herself to go against her friends. In scene 14, Janet explains how she no longer feels love for her children, and then Margaret tells Raine that she is sorry that she has a stinted will. Raine tells Lewis she hates him in scene 16, and then Raine and Sparkle burn down the group home. In the final scene, Raine speaks to her mother about what it is like not to be able to breathe.

CHARACTERS

Bethany

Bethany is Janet's daughter, whom Janet calls "Bethany Bright."

Cath

Raine's mother, Cath dies of cancer after the first scene. She is in her forties and Raine describes her as always yelling with a "sharp" voice. This, in addition to the fact that she failed to bring Raine to the hospital when Raine was deathly ill, suggests that Cath may have been an irresponsible mother. It is also possible, however, that Raine is taking out some anger at her mother when she describes her this way. Cath seems kind when she comments in the first scene that Raine is so pretty.

Lewis Chance

Lewis is an outspoken and caring man who runs the group home. He grew up in rural Herring Cove, New Brunswick, where he was inspired to work in social services after he walked six miles in the snow to bring his sick brother, William, to the hospital. Lewis's brother died, and Lewis felt that he had failed William, so he vowed to give his life to helping other children that have been failed by society. Lewis continues to have a very close connection to his mother and his family, as is clear from his phone conversations with his mother.

Lewis is charming and compelling, but has the tendency to become frustrated and then explode in anger. He is a gay man; at one point he has an affair with Sparkle, one of his wards. Lewis admits this, as well as the fact that he used some government money for his own purposes (although he paid it back), during the city council hearing that decides the fate of the group home. Lewis is devoted to social services and has a great deal of love for troubled teenagers, but after he loses the battle on Mapleview Lanes, there is the implication that he may be giving up, too exhausted to keep fighting. This is why Raine says she hates him.

William Chance

William is Lewis's brother, born when their mother was forty-seven. He dies in infancy, after Lewis walks six miles in the snow to bring him to the hospital.

Crystal

Crystal is Raine's friend, and Raine tells her mother that she expects to live with Crystal in a place called Cabbagetown.

Dad

Raine's father moves to Cornwall with his lover, Patrice, and does not take Raine with him. This is why Lewis calls him a "selfish [sh——t]." Raine says that when her father was young, neighbors used to throw rocks at his house because his family was Jewish.

Margaret Deacon

Margaret is a longtime resident of Mapleview Lanes who changes markedly as the play unfolds. In her opening scene, she is still so traumatized by her husband's death two years previously that she refuses to clean the house, answer the door, or talk to anyone. Seventy-four years old, Margaret has always been cruel to her daughter, Janet, and puts an enormous amount of pressure on Janet by degrading her and yelling at her.

Margaret's transformation begins when she accidentally meets Raine. She remains short-tempered with Janet throughout the play, but she begins to be much more organized and starts taking out her frustration and anger on the group home. Margaret and Raine have a peculiar friendship, but they become close quite quickly. Margaret begins to feel very guilty about trying to oust the group home from the street when she realizes how much it is hurting Raine. When Lewis asks her whether they should stay or go at the city council meeting, however, Margaret is too weak to say that they should stay.

Hamish

Hamish is Janet's little boy, who suggests that Janet is being racist when she explains to him why she is concerned about the group home.

Janet

Janet is Margaret's daughter, a lawyer who lives on Mapleview Lanes. She is married with two children and is defined in many ways by her relationship with her mother. Constantly trying to please Margaret, Janet engineers the effort to have the group home removed from the street because Margaret tells her to do so. Janet feels insecure around her mother and tells her during their important scene of act 1, scene 21, "You make me feel ... well, really, kind of invisible." Margaret brushes this off, but it is a crucial insight into how their relationship works.

After Janet's confrontation with Lewis, Lewis implies when speaking to his mother that he considers Janet his enemy. This is partly due to the fact that, while Lewis is overflowing with love and may even have too much love for his wards, Janet grows to feel no love for her children. This is Janet's major development in the play; she changes from feeling that God is blowing more and more adoration into her, like a balloon, to feeling that she does not like her children and is waiting in vain for love for them to pour down on her like a waterfall. Thompson implies that this has something to do with Janet's role in kicking out the group home, and something to do with Janet's troubled relationship with her own mother.

Michael

Michael is Janet's husband, to whom she frequently talks on the phone.

Patrice

Patrice is Dad's girlfriend, or possibly his second wife. Raine tells Cath that Dad is always groping Patrice, and that Patrice asked Raine whether she was prepared for Cath to die. After Cath dies, Patrice moves with Dad to Cornwall, Ontario, and leaves Raine to live in a group home.

Raine

The main character of the play, Raine is a sixteen-year-old girl forced to live in a group home after her mother dies and her father does not take her in. The parts of her childhood that are revealed in the play are somewhat traumatic, including when she almost died when she was a baby because her mother failed to bring her to the hospital soon enough. Raine tells her mother in the first scene that she has come to hate her voice because Cath always used to yell at her. Raine emphasizes throughout the play that she does not love her mother nor grieve her death.

As the play progresses, it becomes clear that this response to her mother's death may be, in part, a defense mechanism that Raine uses to pretend that she is fine. This may be why Raine attaches herself to Margaret—because she is in need of a mother figure and mourns Cath. As Raine gets to know Lewis and Sparkle at the group home, however, she begins to reveal her pain and attach herself to them. At first she does not trust Lewis, but by the end of act 1 she appears to need his love.

Raine suffers deeply from the events leading up to the closure of the group house. In act 2, scene 9, she cuts herself and exclaims how much she hates everyone. By the end of the play, however, Raine is able to focus this anger into a political awareness and a dedication to what she thinks is right. This is why Lewis tells her that "we need someone like you" to "Keep fightin the fight" for social justice, although Raine says that she hates Lewis in this scene because she feels that he is giving up on the fight for failed children. In her final monologue, Raine suggests that she has come to terms with her feelings for her mother and, in a sense, grown up.

Sparkle

Sparkle is a resident of the group home and one of the play's most enigmatic characters. A troubled teenager who has been involved in crime, he is gay and strongly attracted to Lewis. He says he is in a group home because he killed his parents, but he could be lying because he lies to Raine about the other elements of his past. In act 2, scene 10, he explains how he cares about certain basic needs but, as he says, he doesn't "CARE about anything" from world issues to the fate of the group home.

TOPICS FOR FURTHER STUDY

- Thompson is quite interested in the psychological theories of Sigmund Freud, and many of Freud's ideas are said to appear in Thompson's plays. Research some of the key theories of the famous Austrian psychoanalyst. What are the major ways Freud has influenced Western drama? How do Freud's ideas manifest themselves in *Habitat*? How do you think Freud would analyze the major characters of Thompson's play?

- *Habitat* exposes the plight of group homes struggling to survive in neighborhoods that do not want them there. Research the history of group homes in Canada and the United States. How have the Canadian and United States governments addressed social services for troubled teens? How have courts tended to deal with complaints against group homes? Find some key examples of group homes clashing with the communities around them. Discuss the implications of these cases.

- Which do you think are the most important and definitive scenes in *Habitat*, and why? Which are the key scenes in developing the major themes of the play, and why? Choose one of these scenes, cast its roles, rehearse it, and act it out. Then, discuss your performance. How were you able to express the important aspects of the scene, and what obstacles did you encounter? What did acting out the scene reveal about the themes and stylistic aspects of the play? Describe any insights into the play that were revealed by your performance.

- Thompson is an established Canadian playwright with a number of critically-acclaimed works. Read another of her plays, such as *The Crackwalker* (1980) or *Perfect Pie* (2000), and compare it to *Habitat*. Describe some common elements you see in Thompson's style and themes, and discuss what key issues continually reappear in her work. Discuss some of the key differences between the plays and between the characters. Does one play speak to you and move you more than another? Discuss why or why not.

Sparkle can be charming and funny, and he does manage to seduce Lewis, presumably in act 2, scene 6, when Lewis drags Sparkle into the office. It is not clear exactly what happened in Sparkle's history, but he has been in group homes for quite a while and likely has had some kind of traumatic past. He walks away when Raine is cutting herself, but then reveals in his final appearance of the play, when he insults Margaret and breaks things in her house, that he considers Raine his best friend and is extremely hurt that Margaret has broken Raine's heart.

THEMES

Acceptance, Love, and the Home

The central themes of *Habitat* relate to the concept of the title—a habitat where one feels accepted, loved, and at home. Much of the play deals with various characters' struggles to find an environment such as this, particularly the central plot of the group home that is under threat of expulsion from Mapleview Lanes. Sparkle has lived in group homes for years, and Raine is living in one for the first time, but both of them are in need of a supportive and loving habitat because they have been failed in the past.

Thompson's idea of a habitat is not as simple as a traditional family structure, however. As the events of the play reveal, it is no easy task to create an atmosphere of love and acceptance. The two homes on Mapleview Lanes that the audience is allowed to see in addition to the group home, for example, are quite dysfunctional and certainly seem less loving and accepting than Lewis's group home, since neither Margaret nor Janet consistently love or even like their children. Margaret is harsh and cold with her daughter, and Janet seems overflowing with love for her children at the beginning of the play, but by the end reveals that she does not even like them anymore.

Lewis, on the other hand, is overflowing with love, and may even show too much of it since he has been involved sexually with Sparkle. Thompson makes the audience wonder if this is actually so inappropriate and bad for Sparkle, however, since Lewis is probably the only person to really support Sparkle in all of his experiences in group homes. In fact, Thompson questions many conventional assumptions about what is important in a habitat, implying that love and acceptance are often found in situations that some might consider dysfunctional while the most problematic and unsupportive situations appear in traditional, "normal" homes.

Motherhood

Thompson returns frequently to the theme of mothers and motherhood in her play. The opening scene provides a compelling glimpse into Raine's relationship with her mother both at the time of Cath's death and during Raine's near-death experience as an infant. Throughout the play, Raine works through her relationship with her mother, reacts to her mother's death, and considers whether she loves Cath or blames and dislikes her. By the end of the play, Raine seems to have come to terms with her feelings towards Cath, stressing that it is impossible to escape one's mother, and suggesting that the mother is inseparable from the idea of the home.

Thompson tends to associate mothers with love, or a lack of love, and they are important in all of the major characters' lives except Sparkle's, which is perhaps why Sparkle is so troubled. Margaret plays a key role in how Raine grows and changes in her attitude towards her mother, and they may connect with each other, in part, because their actual mother-daughter relationships are both so dysfunctional. Margaret puts an enormous amount of pressure on her daughter Janet, but also ignores her, criticizes her, and fails to show any signs of love.

Teenage Rage

Raine and Sparkle are angry, rebellious teenagers, and Raine in particular feels a sense of injustice at what has happened to her in the past and is happening to her now. At first they take out this rage in different ways, partly because Sparkle does not "care" about any larger sense of political injustice while Raine becomes very politically aware. Sparkle robs a resident of Mapleview Lanes and becomes involved in a physical fight, while Raine cuts herself, and then voices her sense of injustice at the city council meeting. At the end of the play, however, they burn down the group home together, sharing a sense of rage at everyone and everything. Thompson may be suggesting that this anger and rebellion comes from a society that has failed teenagers in providing them with the acceptance, love, and home discussed above.

STYLE

Psychological Depth

Thompson—who is known for her interest in the work of psychoanalyst Sigmund Freud—is careful to imbue her characters with a sense of great psychological depth, partly by showing the audience incidents from her character's respective childhoods. Examples of how the characters' personalities are grounded in realistic psychological portraits are Lewis's childhood trauma with his brother, Janet's sense of inadequacy that stretches back to her childhood with Margaret, and Raine's process of working through her relationship with her mother, as well as her near-death experience as an infant. Even Sparkle, whose past remains unclear, seems to have a well-defined traumatic experience in his childhood that is the key to his angry and irresponsible personality.

Trances

In the first and last scenes of the play, Raine breaks out of the realistic, straightforward narrative and into two examples of what Thompson refers to as "trance[s]." In the first scene, despite the fact that she was probably too young to have any memory, Raine describes what it was like to fall off her mother's breast and stop breathing, while Cath interjects her memories of the situation. The implication is that Cath is not really speaking at all, but joining Raine in a sort of flashback. In the last scene, Raine does not seem to be in any specific time or place at all; she merely describes her emotional state, her feelings about motherhood and her mother Cath, and her sense that she is home. The dramatic technique of breaking out of the straightforward narrative is a useful tool for placing extra emphasis on the events in the trance. The characters seem to be coming out of the play and revealing something extremely important about themselves and their memories.

HISTORICAL CONTEXT

Contemporary Canada

Canada, a former British colony, is the second-largest country in the world, although much of its land is sparsely populated. Queen Elizabeth II of Great Britain is the official head of state, but Canada is a modern democracy whose liberal leader, Paul Martin, was returned to power in June of 2004. Most of Canada is English-speaking, but French is also an official language, and the French-speaking province of Quebec has a unique culture in which separatism is still a major issue.

Canada's political and social climate is strongly affected by its powerful southern neighbor, the United States. With one of the most extensive trade relationships in the world, the two countries have close economic ties, although the Canadian government has been concerned about United States environmental pollution near its borders and United States tariffs on Canadian timber. Canada also has a very distinct foreign policy from that of the United States; it did not support the United States-led war on Iraq in 2003, for example, and it does not support the United States trade embargo on Cuba.

Suburban life in English-speaking Canada near a city such as Toronto, which is just over an hour's drive from the United States border, has many similarities with suburban life in the United States. Most people own automobiles, crime rates are low, prosperity is the norm, and there is little racial or class diversity in comparison with urban areas, although Canada has a high immigration rate and a large immigrant population. Canada has higher taxes and more extensive social services than the United States, however, and government funding for something like a group home would likely be more accessible than in the United States.

Canada has a unique and flourishing dramatic scene, although theater in English-speaking Canada is quite distinct from the scene in Quebec. David Fennario, who is known for his portrayal of working-class life, is a prominent example of a contemporary Canadian playwright writing in English, as is Carol Bolt, who helped to develop an alternate theater scene in Toronto during the 1970s. Known for their mix of mysticism and social commentary, Bolt's plays, including *Red Emma* (1974), have received wide critical acclaim.

Perhaps the best-known of the playwrights who revitalized theater in Toronto in the 1970s, however, is David French. In addition to popularizing the

Mother and daughter arguing © Ariel Skelley/Corbis

brand of realism that characterizes Thompson's work, French was influential in working very closely with the director of his productions. The director with whom French collaborated most frequently was Bill Glassco, the founding director of Toronto's Tarragon Theater, and the practice of playwrights working closely with directors has continued through Thompson's long-standing relationship with the Tarragon.

CRITICAL OVERVIEW

Judith Thompson enjoys an excellent critical reputation in English-speaking Canada. Although it was widely criticized in its initial reviews, her first play *The Crackwalker* eventually brought her praise and notoriety in Canada. As her career progressed, Thompson's plays also began to be produced in the United States, where they have generally not been received as warmly as in Canada. In addition to her prominent career as a playwright, Thompson is a successful writer for film, television, and radio.

Habitat was moderately successful in Canada, receiving fairly positive reviews. In the United States, however, reviews were more mixed. In his review of the United States premiere of the play at the Epic Theater in New York, Ron Cohen writes in *Back Stage* that Thompson's "well-defined characters and sharply written dialogue—if sometimes a bit too heavy-handed—are permeated with her passion for the subject." Cohen then goes on to list some of the thematic and stylistic problems he finds in Thompson's script after commenting, "But she also stuffs her script with such a multitude of themes that it becomes increasingly difficult to fathom what she's really writing about." Neil Genzlinger also criticizes Thompson's script while praising the Epic Theater production of the play in his review in *The New York Times*. After briefly describing the plot and the actors, Genzlinger argues that "Ms. Thompson loses control of this promising premise in the play's second act" because she overwrites the background of the characters and because the teenagers' speeches sound "too savvy to be said by a real teenager."

CRITICISM

Scott Trudell

Trudell is an independent scholar with a bachelor's degree in English literature. In the following essay, Trudell explores the meaning of breathing and loss of breath in Habitat.

Perhaps Thompson's most important motif in *Habitat* is breathing. Throughout the play, she calls attention to the breathing patterns of her characters along with their abnormalities in breathing. Breathing provides a kind of rhythm for the play; it helps to define the mood and meaning of each scene and informs the audience when tension is building or decreasing. This is why the key crises of the play—Cath's inability to speak as she is dying, Lewis's brother's death, and Raine's recollection of her near-death experience as an infant—are defined by strained breathing, rapid breathing, or an inability to breathe at all.

In her introduction to the 2001 Playwrights Canada Press edition of *Habitat*, Iris Turcott writes about the first draft of the play, "Each character also had their own idiosyncratic obsessions with breathing which collectively articulated her thematic exploration of physical, psychic, and spiritual survival and how they are linked." Indeed, breathing is critical in developing not just the theme of survival but all of the themes in Thompson's play; it is a stylistic and thematic device at the heart

of the meaning of the work. *Habitat* is full of characters defined literally or figuratively by their interaction with air, whether they are suffocating, breathing easily, full of air like a balloon, or attempting to breathe life into others. Examining the ways in which Thompson invokes her motif of breathing ties together the meaning of each character's experience and suggests how the various thematic strands of the play are woven together.

The important first example of Thompson's motif is Cath's belabored breathing during act 1, scene 1. The stage directions not only read in the opening paragraph, "*We hear her struggling to breathe throughout the scene*"; Thompson refers to Cath's loss of breath seven additional times in the brief scene. Establishing the symbolic meaning of breathing, Thompson outlines two of the most important ways that breathing will be significant throughout the play. Raspy, labored breathing is almost the only noise Cath makes outside of her "trance," when she remembers Raine's infant trauma, and since it is clearly communicating so much about Cath's mindset, breathing is established as a basic and important kind of voice. Also, since her death is imminent, it is clear that Cath's "struggle" to breathe is a struggle to survive, which reinforces the basic idea that to breathe freely is to live fully and freely.

During Raine's trauma as an infant, when she fell off her mother's breast, Raine struggled desperately to breathe and then stopped breathing entirely. Thompson describes in detail this defining event in Raine's life and returns to it at the end of the play, stressing its importance to the central message of the work. Occurring on Sunday, the day of family gathering, the specific nature of the trauma is important to its thematic meaning. Associated ambiguously with both the loss of the mother's life-giving breast and the idea that Raine might "choke" on her mother's milk, the event is, in Raine's mind, similar to drowning; she cannot breathe in her dream and envisions herself far underwater. The experience is also connected to a loss of voice, since Raine cannot hear herself cry when she is given a breathing tube: "I cry and I cry with no voice no voice." Again, therefore, Thompson emphasizes that breathing is associated with voice and self-expression as well as with free, uninhibited life, as though the nurturing ideas of mother's milk and the family are in danger of stifling and suffocating a child.

Thompson's breathing symbolism continues to play an important role in the other key episodes of *Habitat*. For example, in the other main childhood trauma in the play, that of Lewis and his brother William, abnormal breathing, rasping, and a breathing tube create a sense of great foreboding. When Lewis says, "[William] was breathin way to fast, eh, I never heard such fast breathing, and there was this rasping every time he breathed," and when, like Raine, William is tightly held to the chest of his protector and nurturer, the audience begins to fear that William will die, since all of this is parallel to Raine's near-death experience. Thompson therefore uses breathing as a foreshadowing device associated with children who have not been properly nurtured and are in danger of death.

It is important to note, here and in the first scene, that free breathing is not a privilege of those who have been fed properly and held close. On the contrary, the children who suffer from abnormal breathing are being held closely to their protector's chests and, in Raine's case, actually overwhelmed and choked by the nurturing fluid of the mother's milk. Thompson's symbolism thus comes closer to the typical figurative connotation of breathing: that children need space to breathe, or independence and respect, in order to prosper. *Habitat* suggests that the children that society has failed are not always simply abandoned by society, but that they are often inhibited and stifled by their parents. Thus, Thompson associates symbolism of drowning, choking, and suffocation with the suffering children of the play.

The implication of Thompson's breathing symbolism is useful in unraveling the important subplot involving the mother-child relationships between Margaret, Janet, and Janet's children. Although Margaret's relationship with Janet, and Janet's relationships with Hamish and Bethany, are healthy and upright in the eyes of the neighborhood, they are actually much more troubled and dysfunctional than the relationships between Lewis and his wards. Margaret is vicious and dismissive to her daughter—to the point that Janet has developed an extreme inferiority complex, and Janet finds by the end of the play that she does not love or even like her children anymore. Thompson uses this subplot as a counterpoint, or a contrasting but parallel theme, to the children of the group home that have been "failed" by their parents and by society.

Janet, the central character in the Deacon family drama, is defined more than anything else by the following imagery, which is associated with her love for her children as well as her relationship to her mother:

> I just feel like I could explode, like a balloon that has more and more air every time I look at you it's like

> God is blowing more more adoration into me and I'm the balloon and there is just more and more adoration and I'm getting bigger and bigger and more and more see-through and one day, one day I am just going to—I'm a big balloon mother and if anyone in any way hurts my children, that's you two I will basically explode.

This ominous imagery is similar to Thompson's dramatizations of abnormal breathing and loss of breath in the sense that Janet's breath, or the air that she feels God is blowing into her, is locked inside her and ready to burst. It is also connected to Thompson's breathing symbolism in the sense that the mother and protector is fruitful and powerful, but also unsupportive and unloving, in the sense that Janet locks all of this love inside herself. She requires this love for herself because she lacks any nurturing love from her own mother. Because all Janet has known of a mother's love is Margaret's constant badgering and yelling, all of Janet's love for her own children is expressed in the form of scolding and criticizing.

Janet's balloon imagery is an important foreshadowing device for her eventual explosion, which she takes out on the group home and which leaves her barren of love for her children. By scolding her children and persecuting their neighbors, Janet reveals her misguided notions of how to protect and love them. Thompson implies with the balloon image that it is because Janet does not understand how to let her children breathe, and because she has not been loved and allowed to breathe by her own mother, that she is brought to this point.

For Thompson, letting one's children breathe is also a symbol for letting them develop a voice and a capacity for self-expression. Janet is so insecure and unable to express her emotions for her children mainly because her mother makes her feel

WHAT DO I READ NEXT?

- Thompson's first play, *Crackwalker* (1980), is an urban drama set in a slum in Kingston, Ontario. Famous for its fascinating bleakness, the play shows the failing relationship of a mentally impaired woman and a man who is not stable.

- In Douglas Coupland's compelling novel *Girlfriend in a Coma* (1998), a teenager from Vancouver falls into a coma and misses seventeen years of her life. When she wakes up, her boyfriend and friends have grown up, and she must attempt to deal with a rapidly changing world.

- *Leaving Home* (1972), by David French, is a play about a working-class family conflict in which two sons leave their father and their Newfoundland home. Critically acclaimed, it was extremely influential in the Canadian drama scene in the 1970s.

- Jeff Karabanow's *Being Young and Homeless: Understanding How Youth Enter and Exit Street Life* (2004), Vol. 30 of the Adolescent Cultures, School, and Society series, is an account of homelessness, public policy, poverty, and street life among adolescents.

---

invisible, never looks at her when she speaks to her, and never really cares what she says. Margaret has "failed" Janet because of this, just like the children from the group home have been "failed" because they were "screamed at for breathing, or using the bathroom, screamed at for breathing." Lewis repeats "screamed at for breathing" because it is so important to Thompson's central symbolism about letting a child grow and develop a voice.

Raine is Thompson's central example of a child learning to live freely and develop a voice, despite a society that has failed to nurture her, love her, and let her breathe. In fact, her near-death experience when she stopped breathing as an infant serves as a metaphor for the entire play. During this trauma, Raine chokes on the milk of a mother who yells at her but fails to support her, let her breathe, and notice when she is deathly ill. She must accept a breathing tube from the doctor and develop the ability to hear herself cry, or find her voice. Similarly, after her mother dies and cannot take care of her, Raine must accept the love and habitat of the group home in order to discover her emotions and find her voice as an adult. Breathing is Thompson's most important symbol for Raine's childhood flashback as well as for the present drama, since Raine is "*out of breath*" after she has cut herself and struggles, in her last monologue, to be "able to breathe," to "get enough air," to "pull it in" and fill her body. The last scene is

ambiguous whether Raine has been irreconcilably failed by society or whether she will be able to learn how to breathe on her own.

Source: Scott Trudell, Critical Essay on *Habitat*, in *Drama for Students*, Thomson Gale, 2006.

Curt Guyette

Guyette, a longtime journalist, graduated from the University of Pittsburgh with a degree in English. In this essay, Guyette examines how Thompson evokes compassion for characters that are tragically flawed.

Viewed on one level, Margaret Thompson's *Habitat* is an entirely contemporary piece. The controversy and conflict generated when a group home for wayward teens opens in an upscale residential neighborhood is a story that could currently be found in any metropolitan newspaper. But there is much more to this play than the simple exploration of a hot-button social issue. This is a compelling piece that lays bare the duality of human nature. People are flawed, often damaged by the vagaries of life itself, whether it be the actions of parents or the often cruel whims of fate. Despite this damage, they retain the ability to overcome hardship and, given the proper perspective, can come to view the shortcomings of others not with contempt but with true compassion. It is just such a worldview Thompson brings to this play.

In the real world, no one is either pure good or all bad; everyone is a mixture of both. Thompson showcases that basic quality with unflinching, sometimes brutal candor, creating characters with glaring, even hideous, faults. There are no traditional heroes in this play, no one of untarnished virtue fighting a battle of absolute good. Still, just as none of the players are heroes in the usual sense, neither are they true villains. Despite being burdened with all sorts of emotional baggage, they carry on with life as best they can.

When a group home for troubled teens is established in an exclusive residential area, the question arises as to whether it should be allowed to exist there. Certainly, the teens that have been sent there think so. They deserve lovely, tree-shaded streets and clean air and safe surroundings as much as anyone. But what about the people already living there, many of whom are elderly? Is it fair to them to be forced to sit and watch as their property values are driven down and their once tranquil neighborhood is disrupted by rowdy kids who party in their front yards and break into their homes? It is this ambiguity that gives the play its thought-provoking complexity.

This same complexity is used by Thompson to evoke intense compassion for a group of characters that are all severely flawed. She does so by revealing another aspect of the human condition—the psychological wounds that all people live with. Because everyone has suffered some emotional hurt in their lives, when these traumas are revealed, the audience can relate, and empathize.

Thompson's determination to reveal the ugly side of her characters is evident from the moment the curtain rises. As her mother lays dying of cancer, Raine is only concerned with her own shallow desires. She wants money to buy new jeans and perhaps a black dress to wear to her mother's funeral. She complains about her shoes and raises the issue of back allowance that is owed her. To be so heartless at such a time is almost unfathomable, but Raine does not give her selfishness a second thought.

Other characters appear equally unlikable as they are introduced. Lewis Chance, owner of the group home Raine is sent to following her mother's death, initially comes across as a glib conman. Making his pitch to the residents of Mapleview Lanes, he first plays on their emotions by exaggerating the plight of his wards describing them as the ones who were "raped every night, or used to make pornographic films just a few miles from your fine homes," and then attempting to close the deal by turning on the folksy manner of an innocent hick

"THE VOICE SHE IMAGINES IS NOT THE HARD-EDGED KNIFE SHE DESCRIBED AT THE PLAY'S BEGINNING BUT ONE OF UNDERSTANDING."

from the sticks, asking his new neighbors, "Are you comin' with? Are you—comin' with?"

Margaret and her daughter Janet also take the stage bathed in an unflattering light. Margaret angrily rebuffs her daughter's attempts to provide some assistance. Janet's sincere offer of help is met with hostility and cutting criticism as she is chastised and told to "go and give your poor lonely children some of your time you selfish twit." At that point, Janet screams at her mother, calling her "crazy" and "demented."

Perhaps most unappealing of all is the teenage boy named Sparkle. He lies. He torments Lewis, who is gay, by making repeated sexual advances knowing that Lewis would be in serious trouble if he is discovered engaging in such a relationship with one of his wards. As Sparkle first takes the stage, he brags that he likes Halloween because of the opportunities it offers for making mischief, to break windows and throw eggs and steal candy from smaller children. A short time later, Sparkle arrives at the group home in the middle of the night toting a bag of items he stole from a neighborhood home.

The harsh light these characters are initially shown in, however, grows softer as the play progresses. Their flaws remain exposed, but the sorrow and hurt underlying all the dysfunction is gradually exposed.

In a long monologue, Lewis Chance reveals how, as a young boy, he was forced to carry his gravely ill infant brother six miles though a blizzard to the hospital in what was ultimately a failed attempt to save the baby's life. Decades later, that failure continues to haunt him, and the guilt associated with it motivates him to try and save other children by providing them a home and giving them emotional support. He admits to having a criminal past but makes a convincing argument that having made mistakes as a teenager enables him to better help the troubled kids he has taken in.

Margaret confesses to Raine just how difficult it has been dealing with her husband's death, saying that she wakes every day feeling as if she had been "battered." Later, trying to explain why she failed to support the home, she describes how life had stunted her will, equating it to the way Chinese geisha girls once had their feet bound and crippled by men who were excited by the deformity. Despite what can be perceived as Margaret's moral failure, it is difficult to judge her harshly. She is old and wants to live out her few remaining years continuing to enjoy the friendship of people who have been her neighbors for decades.

Janet, an initial supporter of the home, reverses her position and, because of her skill as a lawyer, helps force its closure. Although she denies it is a factor, it is clear that she is largely motivated by a desire to gain her mother's approval. She literally begs Margaret to validate her actions and provide a single kind word: "Mum. Please look at me. I need you to look at me. I need you to say thank you." She is not evil, only weak and unable to cope with her mother's lack of affection and approval, which she desperately needs. For a time, the unmitigated love of her children filled the void, infusing her with joy. Just as she eventually sought the home's closure to please her mother, Janet also claimed to be protecting her children. As the play ends, she admits that the love those children once showered upon her had evaporated, leaving her to feel empty. They had stopped even seeing her. "Like my mother," Janet says. "They look through me now, like she does." She wants to be loved but all she receives is "contempt." How can the audience do anything but pity her?

Even Sparkle, who causes trouble throughout the play and is accused by Raine of not caring about anything except himself, is revealed in the end to be capable of compassion. Sparkle describes for Raine the emotionally draining experience of walking through those doors for the first time, saying it was as if "all the breath in me escaped, and I was a flat plastic beachball." Asked by Raine what happened after some time passed, he replies, "Well you're just not the same as you were, that's all. You're something different." When Sparkle confronts Margaret, telling her how much he despises her for betraying Raine, his anger is transformed into pain. Breaking down, he shows true emotion for the first time, deploring how the old woman has "broken my best friend's heart." As he says this, Sparkle falls to the ground, crying and clutching Margaret's ankles in despair. Even he, as bad as he is, is deserving of pity.

The play comes full circle at the end with Raine baring her soul to the ghost of her dead mother. Instead of the selfish, self-centered, uncaring brat on display in the opening scene, a girl who hated the sound of her mother's voice and was glad that cancer had rendered her speechless, Raine admits to how she has secretly longed for her mother's voice, even imagined her mother speaking to her and comforting her as she was in prison for burning down the group home after neighbors forced its closure. The voice she imagines is not the hard-edged knife she described at the play's beginning but one of understanding. In that understanding, she finds peace and solace.

Source: Curt Guyette, Critical Essay on *Habitat*, in *Drama for Students*, Thomson Gale, 2006.

SOURCES

Cohen, Ron, Review of *Habitat*, in *Back Stage*, Vol. 44, No. 29, July 18, 2003, p. 48.

Genzlinger, Neil, "Home for Wayward Teenagers Ruffles Pristine Feathers," in the *New York Times*, May 28, 2003, p. E3.

Thompson, Judith, *Habitat*, Playwrights Canada Press, 2001.

FURTHER READING

Conolly, L. W., ed., *Canadian Drama and the Critics*, Talonbooks, 1995.
Conolly compiles and edits a collection of the key critical reactions to the leading contemporary Canadian playwrights through 1994.

Grace, Sherrill, and Albert-Reiner Glaap, *Performing National Identities: International Perspectives on Contemporary Canadian Theatre*, Talonbooks, 2003.
Grace and Glaap offer a compilation of opinions on the Canadian drama scene during the late twentieth and early twenty-first centuries.

Gussow, Mel, "Theater: *Crackwalker*, Canadian Urban Drama," in the *New York Times*, April 8, 1987, p. C24.
Gussow's negative review of a New York production of Thompson's first play, *Crackwalker*, provides an insight into the American reaction to Thompson's early work.

Zimmerman, Cynthia D., "Judith Thompson," in *Playwriting Women: Female Voices in English Canada*, edited by Jean Paton, Simon & Pierre, 1994, pp. 176–209.
In Zimmerman's overview of Thompson's career through 1994, she provides a brief biography of Thompson as well as an analysis of the early plays and their relationship to contemporary Canadian theater.

I Hate Hamlet

PAUL RUDNICK

1991

As its title suggests, Paul Rudnick's 1991 play *I Hate Hamlet* deals with the question of just how relevant William Shakespeare's *Hamlet* is for modern audiences. The play centers around a young actor who has just earned fame and fortune on a television doctor show and is apprehensive about returning to New York to play Hamlet in the prestigious Shakespeare in Central Park festival. To add to his insecurities, his realtor has rented him an apartment once inhabited by John Barrymore, who many consider to have given one of the greatest performances of Hamlet in the twentieth century. A séance brings the ghost of John Barrymore back to the apartment where he once lived. Barrymore offers guidance to the young actor, who has to decide between the easy money that he could make with a new television series and the confidence to be gained by facing the world's most difficult acting challenge. Rudnick fills the play with laughs, as he lightly satirizes greedy realtors, vacuous Hollywood producers, pretentious but well-meaning actresses, and hard-drinking, womanizing actors.

I Hate Hamlet opened on Broadway on April 8, 1991, at the Walter Kerr theater. In its initial run, Nicol Williamson, playing the ghost of John Barrymore, immersed himself into his part, channeling the famous rogue with such fury that he once hurt another actor during an onstage duel, causing an understudy to step in for act 2. Since its initial run, the play has been a favorite for small theaters, enjoyed for its wit and its reflection on the actor's art in the modern, commercialized world.

Paul Rudnick   Photo by Frank Micelotta. Getty Images

AUTHOR BIOGRAPHY

Paul Rudnick was born in 1957 in Piscataway, New Jersey. He grew up in an unremarkable suburban milieu with both practical and artistic influences. His father was a physicist and his mother was involved with the *Partisan Review* and the Pennsylvania Ballet. Early on, he knew what he wanted to do with his life, writing in a grammar school essay that he wanted to be a playwright.

After graduation from high school, Rudnick studied drama at Yale University. After graduation he moved to New York City. He supported himself with miscellaneous jobs, including writing book jacket copy for novels and painting sets for the Julliard School of Drama. His first play, *Poor Little Lambs*, was produced in 1982; the off-Broadway production drew mixed critical responses, though the solid cast included several actors, such as Bronson Pinchot and Kevin Bacon, who went on to gain fame on TV and in movies. *I Hate Hamlet*, first produced in 1991, was the play that brought Rudnick national fame. In 1993 his play *Jeffrey*, about a gay man who lets his fear of the AIDS epidemic cripple his love life, successfully mixed the broad humor that had been common in Rudnick's previous plays with the sadness of the

epidemic's destructive toll on the gay community, boldly taking the risk of being misinterpreted as making light of a tragic situation. The play was successfully adapted to an independent film by Rudnick, who was also the movie's co-producer.

Rudnick continued to write plays, but he also wrote for Hollywood. One of his earliest disappointments was his script for the movie *Sister Act*: as Rudnick envisioned it, starring his idol, Bette Midler, it was to be a satire of *The Singing Nun* (a 1966 Debbie Reynolds vehicle), but the final version, starring Whoopie Goldberg, was so watered down that Rudnick took his name off of the film, and had himself billed as "Joseph Howard" instead. He did uncredited script revision for *The Addams Family* and its sequel, *Addams Family Values*. His script for the 1997 film *In & Out* was acclaimed, as was his script for 2004's remake of *The Stepford Wives*. He also wrote film scripts that were critical and financial failures, such as the Jacqueline Susann biography *Isn't She Great* and *Marci X*, a spoof featuring Lisa Kudrow as a rich white woman who embraces hip-hop culture.

In the 1980s, Rudnick published two novels, *Social Disease* and *I'll Take It*. He has had a long-running film review column in *Premier* magazine under the pseudonym Libby Gelman-Waxner. His most recent play, *Pride and Joy*, was produced for the TriBeCa Theater Festival in New York in 2004. Rudnick still lives in the apartment that John Barrymore once lived in, his inspiration for *I Hate Hamlet*.

PLOT SUMMARY

Act 1

I Hate Hamlet begins with Andrew Rally—a young actor who has just gained national fame for his part in a cancelled mediocre television program called "LA Medical"—moving into his new apartment in an imposing brownstone in New York City. The apartment is large and gothic, not the sort of place where Andrew imagines himself living, but his real estate agent, Felicia Dantine, explains that she rented it for him because legendary actor John Barrymore once lived there, and she assumed that Andrew would find the connection with Barrymore to be "a match." Felicia approves of Andrew's commercial success, but Andrew is embarrassed about it. They are soon joined by Deirdre McDavey, who has been Andrew's girlfriend since the days when he was a struggling New York actor, and Lillian Troy, Andrew's agent. Lillian has been in the apartment before, years ago, when she had an affair with Barrymore. She blithely asks Andrew if he has found her hairpins.

When Andrew announces that he has been offered the part of Hamlet, which was considered Barrymore's most artistic achievement as an actor, Deirdre suggests that they should try to contact the famed actor's spirit. Felicia says that she has psychic ability and has contacted her dead mother in the past. During the ensuing séance, Felicia talks to her mother, who recognizes Andrew Rally from "LA Medical," but Andrew is hesitant about soliciting acting advice from Barrymore because, he says, "I hate Hamlet." When he says this, thunder rises; a shadow of a handsome profile, which was Barrymore's trademark feature, is cast on the wall in a lightning flash, but only Andrew sees it.

The séance is called off and considered a failure, with Felicia explaining that they do not seem to have anything Barrymore would want, to lure him to them. Lillian and Felicia leave, but not before Lillian finds one of the hairpins she lost in the apartment decades earlier. Andrew tells Deirdre that he has been apprehensive about his ability to play Hamlet, saying that he is more comfortable with easy acting roles, such as his television work, but Deirdre is romantically attracted to the Shakespearean theater. She agrees to stay at the apartment that night, but refuses to have sex with Andrew, saving herself for marriage but rebuffing his proposal of marriage. Frustrated and feeling inadequate, Andrew phones Lillian, leaving a message for her to cancel his part in *Hamlet*. He picks up a bottle of champagne that Lillian brought in to celebrate Andrew's new home: when the cork pops, the ghost of John Barrymore materializes.

Barrymore announces that he is there to help Andrew with his performance as Hamlet, explaining that there is a theatrical tradition of actors playing the role calling on earlier actors for advice. He watched Andrew's modern interpretation of the part, and pronounces it horrible. His advice is to play Hamlet as "a young man, a college boy, at his sexual peak. Hamlet is pure hormone." Andrew relates his sexual frustration with Deirdre. When Deirdre enters in her nightgown, Barrymore continues to talk to Andrew, even though she cannot see him; Andrew talks back, and Deirdre assumes that he is pretending to be insane, as Hamlet did. He acts out lines from the play, with coaching from the ghost, and nearly seduces her when the doorbell rings.

MEDIA ADAPTATIONS

- John Barrymore was never filmed in the role of Hamlet, but Films for the Humanities & Sciences has released a two-cassette package of *The Great Hamlets*. The first tape has famous actors—Derek Bailey, Joseph Wishy, Trevor Nunn, Laurence Olivier, Ben Kingsley, and Maximilian Schell—commenting on the difficulties of the role, while the second cassette includes critic Trevor Nunn exploring the underlying dynamics of the play. This program was released in 1996.

Gary Peter Lefkowitz enters. A self-described "writer-producer-director," Gary tries to recruit Andrew for his next television project, disparaging theatrical acting as boring and pretentious. When Gary leaves, Barrymore tells Andrew that the money and fame he would get from the TV show are not worth what he would lose in glory. The more that Barrymore tries to convince Andrew that he could be a talented actor, the more Andrew resists, leading to a sword duel between the two. When he is injured, Andrew becomes strong and decisive, choosing to play Hamlet.

Act 2, Scene 1

Six weeks later, it is opening night of Andrew's performance of Hamlet in Central Park. Felicia and Deirdre discuss the change in Andrew, how serious he has become about acting, citing the influence of Barrymore's apartment, not realizing that Barrymore himself, unseen, stands nearby, mocking them. Deirdre explains that, because of her romantic ideals, she believes she will never meet the person that she really wants to marry. Gary enters, and expresses the opinion that there might be no way of knowing if Andrew is good or bad in his role because Shakespeare is so much more complex than television and movies.

Andrew enters, dressed as Hamlet and acting grandly, like Barrymore. When Gary and Felicia leave together, Deirdre is smitten with Andrew's new seriousness. She leaves, and Andrew and

Barrymore talk like comrades about the triumph that Andrew expects. Andrew asks for advice about how to act, and Barrymore recites for him Hamlet's advice to actors, from act 3, scene ii of Shakespeare's play. He tells Andrew that his fear of the role is to be expected, but Andrew points out that, after playing Hamlet, Barrymore went to Hollywood and made terrible movies to finance his drinking and womanizing. Barrymore defends himself, saying, "But before all that, in my prime—I faced the dragon. . . . I played Hamlet! Have you?"

While Andrew is off to the play, Barrymore and Lillian reminisce about their long-ago affair. Barrymore knows that once Andrew has played the role, Barrymore will have to leave the earth, but Lillian assures him that Andrew is old enough to face life on his own. The lights fall on this scene as Lillian and Barrymore begin to rekindle the passion they once had.

Act 2, Scene 2

At seven o'clock the next morning, Barrymore is asleep in a chair in front of the television when Andrew's commercial for a breakfast cereal comes on. Andrew comes home and admits, after Barrymore's prodding, that his performance was terrible. Gary comes in with the morning newspapers, which confirm that Andrew's performance was bad, and then Gary offers him three million dollars to act in the television series. Andrew turns the money down. Felicia enters and says goodbye, because she is leaving for Los Angeles with Gary. Deirdre, who has been asleep upstairs, comes down and relates a strange experience that she had the night before: after contemplating suicide, she stood on the roof of the apartment building and felt a breeze caress her neck like a hand. The next thing she knew, it was morning, and there was a rose on the pillow beside her, and her copy of *Romeo and Juliet* was open to a speech from Juliet. It is obvious that Barrymore's ghost has made love to her, but, unaware of that, she amorously invites Andrew upstairs with her. Instead of following her, Andrew turns to the ghost, angry that he has taken Deirdre's virginity, but is calmed. Andrew recalls for Barrymore the few lines in the performance when he felt that he had it right, and Barrymore tells him that one could expect no more.

Before leaving him, Barrymore asks Andrew to show how he bows. In preparing to do so, Andrew looks out and sees an audience, the theater audience, applauding. Barrymore takes center stage and makes a grand, overwrought show of bowing, then calling upon Andrew to do the same, as the curtain comes down.

CHARACTERS

John Barrymore

The character in this play is the ghost of John Barrymore, an actor who actually lived from 1882 to 1942. Starting in the early 1920s, Barrymore was a hit on the Broadway stage with his performances in Shakespearean dramas, starting with *Richard III* in 1920 and leading to his portrayal of Hamlet in 1921, which was hailed as one of the finest acting achievements of his generation. After *Hamlet*, Barrymore, who was as devoted to hard drinking and womanizing as he was to his craft, left the stage and moved to Hollywood to appear in a series of mediocre but well-paying movies.

In this play, the ghost of John Barrymore returns to the apartment that he once rented after he is called forth by a séance and lured with a bottle of champagne. He explains to Andrew Rally that his real reason for returning from the dead is to help Andrew prepare for his upcoming performance as Hamlet, because doing so is a tradition with former Hamlet players. When Andrew is hesitant about his ability to play the role, Barrymore does what he can to make Andrew perform, first comforting and reassuring him and then challenging him until, after they duel with swords, Andrew ends up feeling confident. Similarly, Barrymore gives confidence to Deirdre McDavey, Andrew's girlfriend, who has been hesitant to enter into a sexual relationship with him; when Barrymore makes love to her on the night of Andrew's Hamlet performance, Deirdre does not know what has happened, but she finds herself feeling ready to take her relationship with Andrew further.

When his performance as Hamlet is a failure, Andrew turns on Barrymore, pointing out the fact that, despite his brilliance as Hamlet, he wasted the rest of his life as a washed-up drunk who was willing to act in anything for money. Barrymore admits that is true, but says that it does not weaken his achievement in playing the most difficult role of all. The play ends with the ghost taking a grand bow to the audience, ostensibly to show Andrew how it is done, but obviously reveling in the attention.

Felicia Dantine

Felicia is the real estate agent described in the production notes as having "an almost carnal passion for Manhattan apartments." Although Andrew is hesitant about committing to life in a gloomy old apartment, Felicia is insistent, feeling that the apartment's historical connection to John Barrymore is relevant to Andrew's career as a television actor. While Andrew is ashamed of the television show and commercial that he has done, Felicia is an enthusiastic fan of his most crassly commercial work.

Near the end of the first act, Felicia plays a significant role in moving the plot along when she announces that she has studied spiritualism and has in fact made psychic contact with her dead mother. She is convinced by the other characters to use her ability to contact the spirit of John Barrymore. During the ensuing séance, she chats breezily with her mother, but once the connection is broken she is disappointed to find that she has not reached Barrymore. Although she does not know it, the audience has seen Barrymore's shadow and is aware that Felicia's power as a spiritualist is stronger than she herself suspects. He later materializes after she is gone.

In the second act, Felicia is on stage only briefly, passing through to announce that she is leaving with Gary for Los Angeles. The shallow artistic sensibility that she showed by announcing her enjoyment of the breakfast cereal commercial Andrew once did makes her an ideal companion for the shallow and unartistic Gary, and Felicia's interest in making money is suitably matched to his.

Gary Peter Lefkowitz

Gary is a fast-talking, superficial Hollywood writer-producer-director. He is one of the few people who is able to see the ghost of Barrymore, which is explained as being because he is so self-centered that it would not make any difference anyway, a claim borne out by the fact that Gary's only comment on Barrymore's Shakespeare costume is that it is "retro." In contrast to the opportunity to play Hamlet, Gary offers Andrew the chance to star in a television series, which sounds like a serious role as a teacher in an inner-city school, until Gary adds that the teacher is to have super powers at night. Like many people who work around artists but do not have artistic sensibilities, Gary occasionally feels that he should quit the superficial. When he is enthused about going to the *Hamlet* performance, he states, naively, "Maybe I should just chuck everything, leave LA, just produce, direct and write Shakespeare." Gary's cheesy artistic sensibilities reflect the tastes of mainstream America; Andrew has a difficult time resisting the money and fame that Gary offers, especially when the Hamlet performance goes poorly.

In the end, when Andrew has turned down the television show Gary is producing, Gary leaves for Hollywood with Felicia, the real estate agent, who has a similar, financially-driven world view.

Deirdre McDavey

Deirdre is the long-time girlfriend of Andrew Rally, the play's star. She met him in college, when they were both studying acting. While Andrew is not interested in acting in a Shakespeare play at first, the opportunity is a dream come true for Deirdre. She is described in the stage notes as "irresistibly appealing, a Valley girl imagining herself a Brontë heroine." For Deirdre, the life described in old romantic novels and plays is real life, and the life that she leads in twentieth-century New York is just a distraction: in this way, the romantic, artistic ghost who shows up is more appropriate to Deirdre's view of the world than to Andrew's. She aspires to play Ophelia, the female lead, opposite Andrew's Hamlet, and ends up cast as one of Ophelia's handmaids.

One of the defining characteristics of Deirdre is that, at the age of twenty-nine, she is a virgin. This is played for comedy, as it is opposed to the other characters' modern sensibilities. She explains her old-fashioned stance, that she does not want to have sex with anyone until she is married, but at the same time she refuses to marry Andrew.

On the night of Andrew's debut as Hamlet, Deirdre becomes so sad at the fact that his performance is being ignored—mosquitoes buzz around the actors, and a plane callously flies overhead—that she decides to drown herself in Central Park Lake, like Ophelia did in Hamlet. But she loses her nerve and goes back to the apartment. There, standing on the roof and looking at the moon, she feels a slight breeze at the back of her neck, one which she later describes as feeling like a hand caressing her. The next morning, she wakes up with a rose on her pillow: it is obvious to Andrew, and to the audience, that the ghost of John Barrymore has made love to her. Feeling herself at last ready for sex, she seductively invites Andrew up to the roof with her.

Andrew Rally

Andrew is the play's central character. He is an actor who studied drama in New York, and then quickly reached financial success in Hollywood as young Dr. Jim Corman, rookie surgeon, on the television program "LA Medical." He is most famous, though, for his role in a commercial for a breakfast cereal, "Trailbuster Nuggets," which is memorable because the commercial has a catchy jingle.

When the play opens, "LA Medical" has been cancelled, and Andrew has moved back to New York, where he has arranged to play Hamlet in a "Shakespeare in the Park" production. He contacted a real estate agent, Felicia, before leaving Los Angeles, and she rented an apartment for Andrew that the great actor John Barrymore once lived in. While Felicia seems to think that, being an actor, Andrew would want to be associated with Barrymore, the proximity to a man widely considered to be one of history's greatest interpreters of Hamlet adds to Andrew's sense of insecurity. In addition, Andrew is sexually frustrated: his girlfriend, Deirdre, refuses to have sex before she is married, but she will not marry him.

When the ghost of John Barrymore manifests itself, Andrew initially feels overwhelmed, and for good reason: Barrymore's reputation as an actor and as a ladies' man seems to overshadow anything that Andrew could hope to accomplish. At the end of the first act, though, the two actors duel: in the course of this fight, when Barrymore draws blood, Andrew's aggression grows, and he begins to feel that they are on equal footing and that he is ready to perform Hamlet.

In the second act, Andrew has taken on Barrymore's artistic intensity and his sense of importance. Around humans, it seems as if his change of personality is due to over-preparation. With the ghost, though, there is a bond of camaraderie, with the common element being that they are both performers of the role. When his self-confidence crumbles, just before it is time to leave for the theater for his first performance, Andrew is assured by Barrymore, but then Andrew turns against Barrymore and points out the ways in which the master actor's life was less than solid. Barrymore convinces Andrew that, despite his insecurity, playing Hamlet is something that he must do.

Andrew is harder on his performance than anyone else: his newspaper reviews are negative, but they do not call his performance terrible, as he does. Still, when offered a chance to leave the theater and make an impossibly huge sum of money on a frivolous television show, he turns it down, preferring to labor at his craft. In the end, Andrew and the ghost of John Barrymore have been drawn closer than ever.

Lillian Troy

Lillian is Andrew's agent. She is a very old woman and a chronic smoker. When she visits Andrew at the apartment that was once John Barrymore's, she explains that she has been there before, in the 1940s, when she and Barrymore had an affair. At the end of act I, scene 1, when everyone else has left, Barrymore's ghost is surprised to

find that Lillian can see him: as she explains, "I am very old. I see everything." With a little prodding, she makes Barrymore remember their affair in detail. When the curtain falls, they are laughing and about to make love again.

THEMES

Repression

Much of what is troubling Andrew Rally has to do with psychological repression of his desires. He feels sexually repressed because his long-time girlfriend, Deirdre, insists on retaining her virginity. Despite the fact that he feels it is ridiculous for people of their age to guard their chastity for old-fashioned, romantic notions, Andrew only slightly pressures Deirdre to change her mind. His respect for her does not change his desire. In addition to repressing his sexuality, Andrew also represses his urge to be a great actor because he is worried that he will not be up to the challenge of performing Hamlet. He spends the first act pretending that the life of a Hollywood star, performing in bad television programs and even worse commercials, is suitable for him.

Andrew's outlook changes under the tutelage of John Barrymore. In the sword fight that ends act 1, Andrew lets go of his inhibitions, and acts out of instinct. The blood that Barrymore draws from him symbolizes Andrew's true desires being set free. Barrymore proceeds, in act 2, to convince Andrew that he can become a great actor after all. Though his first attempt at playing Hamlet is a failure, Andrew does not abandon the theater, but instead devotes himself to his craft, turning away from the multi-million dollar television deal that Gary Peter Lefkowitz offers him. Barrymore also eases Andrew's sexual repression by romancing Deirdre without her knowing it: her flirtatious exit at the end of the play makes it clear that she will not turn away Andrew's sexual advances anymore.

Melancholy

Throughout the four centuries since the play was first performed, the character of Hamlet has been described as "the Melancholy Dane." Melancholia is the condition of being gloomy, pensive, heavy of heart, given to sudden outbreaks of anger. Andrew, in this play, displays the same kind of melancholy that afflicted Hamlet: he is frightened of the big changes in his life (in Hamlet's case, the presumed murder of his father, and in Andrew's

TOPICS FOR FURTHER STUDY

- Think of a famous dead person, from a field that interests you, whom you would not mind appearing to you as a ghost. Write a list of questions that you would ask. Also, write the responses that you believe this ghost would give.

- Andrew is a television actor who has a background in theater and is invited to play the prestigious role of Hamlet in a New York theater production. Choose a young actor on a television show that you like and research that person's acting background. Then, choose a role from one of Shakespeare's plays, or from another classic play. Explain why you think this actor could play that role well.

- John Barrymore's performance as Hamlet, though universally acclaimed, was never filmed, so modern audiences cannot see it. Research some other respected actor who worked in the theater before sound or film recording techniques. Report on why you think that reviewers of that person's time were so impressed with the actor.

- Most of John Barrymore's movies are considered forgettable; only one, *Twentieth Century* (1934), is considered a classic. Watch that movie and review it. In what ways would you consider Barrymore a great actor who should give advice and criticism to a successful television performer like Andrew Rally? In what ways do you think Barrymore has been overly praised?

---

case the daunting prospect of performing the most difficult acting role ever), and is frustrated in his love life. As a result, Andrew behaves increasingly like Hamlet did. He wanders around his apartment, which turns more and more dark and foreboding, talking to himself (or to the ghost that others cannot see), and, when with his girlfriend, recites the lines Hamlet spoke to Ophelia. To Andrew, feeling melancholy makes it easier to understand Hamlet and therefore easier to play the role. It also helps him take his own life seriously at a time that he has seen it become more and more ridiculous, with recent acting offers including consoling and kissing a puppet squirrel and playing a schoolteacher with super powers. If Hamlet's, and Andrew's, melancholy seems a bit too grim, it is just a reaction to the frivolousness of the lives that surround them.

Culture Clash

The opposing forces that pull at Andrew Rally in this play are represented by two influential main characters. First there is Deirdre, who worships things that represent the romantic ideal. Deirdre's identification with Shakespeare's romantic heroine Ophelia is so strong that she tends to forget that she is participating in a play: though she is only playing one

of Ophelia's handmaids, the director has had to stop her from taking Hamlet's dagger and killing herself when Ophelia is feeling suicidal. Deirdre is so estranged from the real world that she feels she could never marry a living person. "I've always wanted to be Joan of Arc or Juliet or Guinevere," she tells Felicia. "And I want to love someone like Hamlet or King Arthur or Socrates"—in other words, someone ideal, not real. A turning point comes for Deirdre when she is unable to drown herself like Ophelia did in the play, and she realizes that she must live in the real world.

A completely unromantic view of reality is represented in the play by the character of Gary Peter Lefkowitz, a show business insider with no sense of artistry or spirituality. Gary talks disparagingly about Andrew's plan to play Hamlet, focusing only on the low salary that Andrew will earn, with no sense at all of the artistic merit of what Andrew is trying to accomplish. It is because Gary is so oblivious to anything outside of his own cultural frame that he is able to see Barrymore's ghost: Gary has no idea of what he is seeing, so the experience makes no difference to him. Still, Gary does become slightly enthusiastic about artistic culture, and imagines himself being part of it, if only in a superficial way, when he imagines himself leaving Los Angeles to "produce, direct, and write Shakespeare," clearly not understanding what "Shakespeare" is. Though Gary's understanding is flawed, his curiosity is piqued.

It is Barrymore's ghost that unites the two cultures for Andrew. Like Deirdre, Barrymore understands artistry and spirituality, but he also shows, in the way that he wasted his later years making bad movies, womanizing and drinking, that he understands the materialistic point of view that Gary represents. Through Barrymore, Andrew learns balance.

STYLE

Monologue

In act 2, scene 1 of *I Hate Hamlet*, the play comes to a climax when Andrew asks John Barrymore for some definitive help in tackling what is considered the most difficult role for the stage, the lead in *Hamlet*. Rather than write an original response for Barrymore, Rudnick has him repeat the advice that Hamlet gave to actors in the play, using Shakespeare's words from 1601: "Speak the speech, I pray you, as I pronounce it to you," etc. Using this speech in this place works on several different levels. For one thing, it is a sampling from *Hamlet*, giving Barrymore a chance to show Andrew how to deliver a Shakespearean monologue. Also, this particular speech tells the listener to copy the speaker's inflections and mannerisms, which is exactly what Barrymore is asking Andrew to do. This speech is one of the most famous that has ever been written about the subject of acting: in reciting it, Barrymore affirms his faith in Shakespeare's relevance to modern actors like Andrew. Finally, in speaking to Andrew in Hamlet's words, Barrymore builds upon the bond that he and Andrew share: his purpose in coming back from the grave has been, from the very start, to pass the role down from one Hamlet actor to the next, and so it makes perfect sense that the most important interaction of their relationship should be in Hamlet's words.

Tone

Although there are serious issues of art and reality addressed in this play, it is essentially a comedy, built on clever situations and humorous characters and filled with witty dialog. Rudnick uses some big, obvious jokes, meant to gain big laughs from the whole audience, such as Andrew's telling

Deirdre "you're a twenty-nine-year-old virgin. And you tell everyone. I think fear of silliness is not the issue." Another example is when Barrymore, told that he was married to an actress, responds, "To an actress? Is that legal?" But Rudnick also peppers every page of the script with humorous asides and small, quick, subtle lines that audience members who are not paying much attention might miss. An example of this is when, during the séance, Deirdre refuses to believe that Felicia would never summon anyone from hell, and Felicia, in a dig at lawyers, responds, "Well, if I have a legal problem. . ." The same sly comic style shows itself when Barrymore, hearing Deirdre say that he lost his virginity at age fourteen to his stepmother, says, to no one in particular, "I'm a Freudian bonus coupon." Lines like these go beyond the story and the characters, communicating humor directly from the author to the audience, but they do not break the reality of the situation because the play is consistent in its humorous tone throughout.

HISTORICAL CONTEXT

Shakespeare in Central Park

The theater that Andrew gives his Shakespeare performance in is New York City's prestigious Shakespeare Festival, performed in Central Park each summer. The festival has come to be a landmark of New York's cultural identity. The Shakespeare Festival was the idea of director and producer Joseph Papp, who, in the mid-1950s, conceived of a theater that would make classical drama accessible for all citizens. In 1956, he started the Public Theater as a mobile venture, traveling on a used truck to the five boroughs of New York with his company's production of *Romeo and Juliet*. The following summer, the truck was rendered inoperable: Papp parked it in Central Park, near the Belvedere Castle, and collected donations from corporate sponsors in order to put on plays for free. He fought for support from the city government, holding to the idea that the shows ought to be free to the public. In 1960, Papp solicited funds from George T. Delacorte, head of Delacorte Publishing. Instead of simply donating a token sum, Delacorte put up $150,000 to build an outdoor theater for staging free shows. The resulting Delacorte Theater was built a short distance away from the Shakespeare Garden, which the city had built in 1916 to commemorate the three hundredth anniversary of Shakespeare's death. With easy access to Broadway talent and a mission to make theater accessible, Shakespeare in the Park grew to be one of the world's great venues for performing Shakespeare's works.

Today, the Public Theater (renamed the Joe Papp Public Theater in 1992) still holds performances in the Delacorte Theater throughout the summer. Best known for the Shakespeare in Central Park series, it also showcases works by other writers, both established and unknown. True to Papp's original scheme, performances are free to the public, though, due to the theater's worldwide fame, the wait for each day's tickets can exceed several hours.

Method Acting

In act 1, when Andrew is preparing to show the ghost of Barrymore his interpretation of the role of Hamlet, the stage directions say that, "he is being ultra-naturalistic, very Method." This refers to a specific acting style that became popular in the last half of the twentieth century, overtaking the sort of traditional Shakespearian acting that Barrymore favors. While traditional acting style entails grand, artificial gestures that do not resemble the ways that people really move and talk, Method actors try to reach within themselves to find the emotional truth of the character they are portraying. To achieve the most reality, they try to find experiences in their own lives that will let them relate to that emotional truth.

The term "Method" derives from the principles of Konstantin Stanislavski (1863–1938), a Russian actor and director who explored principles that would allow actors to give more realistic performances. Stanislavski's "System" became famous because of his influence as co-founder and principle director at the prestigious Moscow Art Theater, and for the school for young actors, "First Studio," which he founded in 1918. His theories spawned "The Method," which was the approach developed by the Group Theater in New York in the late 1930s.

Method acting was the principle technique taught at the Actors Studio, founded in 1947. Actors that came out of the Studio shocked the world with their powerful new style, which mimicked reality. While formal actors of previous generations spoke clearly and tried to project their voices, Method actors mumbled, sighed, and improvised lines; while traditional actors moved in grand, sweeping gestures, Method actors fumbled, scratched, and twitched. Sure of the reality that they are playing,

Method actors direct their attention toward the character, not the audience, and are therefore often mocked by actors trained to perform with the audience in mind.

CRITICAL OVERVIEW

Ever since its opening in April of 1991, theater critics have been uneasy about how to review Paul Rudnick's *I Hate Hamlet*. The division of critical opinion stems from the different expectations that different writers hold for a theatrical comedy. While most reviewers agree that the humor in this play works well, many question whether a play should not try to accomplish more than just providing jokes, a function that has been taken from Broadway comedies in recent decades by sitcoms on television.

Reviewing the play's original New York run, *Variety* critic Jeremy Gerard pegged it as "a spun-sugar confection yielding a moment's delight before disappearing into the ether." While recognizing that it "glitters with one-liners," Gerard expected it to close early, being the kind of "boulevard comedy" that had gone out of style in a theatrical world of escalating costs and ticket prices.

Gerald Weales, writing in *Commonweal* in June of 1991, a few months after the play's opening, began his review declaring surprise that the play was still running, dismissing it as "a foolishness." Sarcastically, Weales suggested that the play's ending, with Andrew Rally turning down a lucrative Hollywood contract to stay in New York and work in the theater, might have made for a funnier joke than most of the play's intended gag lines. "[G]iven the quality of much of the comedy in the play," he wrote, "it would have been a step ahead of dumb-Hollywood-director jokes, male-genitalia-in-tights jokes, cigarette-addicted agent jokes ... twenty-nine-year-old virgin jokes." In the end, Weales asked rhetorically, "Is it knee-slappers like that that define a Broadway play?"

A more balanced critical view came after the play had survived for four years. When it opened in Chicago, Lewis Lazare, writing for *Variety*, acknowledged that *I Hate Hamlet* is "lightweight" but entertaining, questioning whether its humor would be able to satisfy audiences without any other traditional theatrical strengths. Calling it a "slick but very thin piece of writing," Lazare praised it by noting that "Rudnick is almost as adept at crafting laugh lines as the master himself, Neil Simon." But,

Laurence Olivier in the 1948 film version of Hamlet © John Springer Collection/Corbis

he went on, the "play is done in by the unceasing barrage of clever quips that constantly draw attention to the fact that little else is happening onstage." It is quite possibly this very lightness that has made I Hate Hamlet a favorite of small community theaters, where audiences expect little more than an evening of entertainment.

CRITICISM

David Kelly

Kelly is an instructor of creative writing and literature. In this essay, Kelly examines the ways in which I Hate Hamlet *weakens its dramatic impact by being unclear about how important the Shakespearean tradition really is.*

Some people like Paul Rudnick's play *I Hate Hamlet* because it tries so hard to please its audiences, while others resent it for just the same reason. The play, a favorite of community theater and college productions, addresses serious issues about art and integrity, but it does not address them with much depth. With topics that range from high culture to television commercials, it has something for everyone, and little to offend anyone.

Critics have faulted Rudnick for taking such a superficial approach to his material, but it could just as well be said that the play is successful as a work of art, because it achieves exactly what it sets out to do. *I Hate Hamlet* aims to please, and loading it up with too much moral or sociological complexity would detract from its ability to do so. But being light does not mean the same thing as being free of content. As it stands, the play contains some clear contradictions. The question that arises is whether taking contradictory positions is a weakness or a strength of the play. Purists argue against taking contradictory positions in the same work, but the fact remains that an inconsistence stance can allow a writer to, at least potentially, be all things to all people.

The main thing about *I Hate Hamlet* is that it is a comedy. This means two things. The first is that the play must end on a happy note, with all of the problems solved, so that audiences can walk away from the theater focused on the good time they had, not on issues of greater importance. This is the comic tradition, though it is seldom enforced as powerfully and obviously as it is here. One would be hard put to find another play that practically forces audiences to applaud as a part of the script, as Rudnick does by having his two leads come out, face the audience, and bow, slowly and grandly.

The other ramification of being a comedy is that this is a play that wants laughs, and lots of them. It is a work where jokes, zingers, one-liners, witticisms and wise-cracks dominate over any other element. Rudnick is not afraid, or possibly not even unable, to have a character say something that would not be consistent with what they should be feeling if it means a chance to say something funny. Would the ghost of a Shakespearean actor, returned to earth to teach another actor to play Hamlet well, quip about how he would take the ridiculous television role that he has just seen the other actor turn down? Would the spirit of a dead mother respond to her daughter's psychic call only when she hears that "the rates have gone down?" Would any sexually frustrated lover complain that his girlfriend's desire to retain her virginity is like "show business for Mormons?" Unlikely as dialog like this would be in the real world, it is just the way people talk in the certain kind of light comedy that Rudnick has presented here. He can only be faulted for his jokes if they are inconsistent; as it is, however, the humor, far from intruding on the play, *is* the play. The rest—characters, situation, setting, action, and the other aspects—just serve to create a vehicle for delivering the jokes.

Some critics charge the play with a failure to be all that it should be, pointing out that its simple concept (ghost of Barrymore returns to help a struggling actor) and the action (modern actor learns to appreciate stagecraft) offer weak reasons for audiences to stay in their seats for two hours. Audiences, however, do not seem to mind. The jokes are frequent and clever enough to justify the night at the theater. To those seeking nothing more than amusement, the events and characterizations are only useful in that they make a play out of *I Hate Hamlet*; almost as good would be four or five comics, standing around on stage, trying to one-up one another. From an entertainment perspective, the trouble is not that the laughs get in the way of the play, but that the play gets in the way of the laughs.

But *I Hate Hamlet is* a play, after all. Regardless of how little audience members expect beyond mere entertainment, there are still dramatic elements that can heighten or flatten the experience. The first of these, of course, is a compelling lead character. In raising the ghost of John Barrymore, Rudnick has brought together elements that all— audiences, actors and writers—can appreciate. Rudnick's Barrymore is a charming rogue—a lover, a drunk, an artist. True to the actual career of John Barrymore, he is both a superb actor and a miserable failure. He has been through poverty and riches, critical success and the jeers that haunt a sellout. With all of these contradictions driving him, there is one fact that makes Barrymore such a prize role for any actor: he is noble.

That is, he is noble when the script calls on him to be. When the ghost of Barrymore focuses on what he has to offer to the living, following a tradition of Hamlet actors returning from the dead to pass the craft on to other actors, he has a sense of grandeur that one associates with the Shakespearean stage. He can duel with Andrew or seduce Deirdre, and audiences look up to him. He is otherworldly. The problem is that Rudnick is consistently on the lookout for ways in which the play can subvert expectations. For the sake of comic reversal, Barrymore is not always grand or even particularly supernatural. For example, having established him as one of the great artists of the stage, Rudnick seems unable to stop himself from showing Barrymore eating junk food and watching television, like any ill-bred slob, after having seduced the girlfriend of his protégé, which may or may not be a part of the lesson he brings to Andrew. It is not the witty dialog that causes this character's inconsistency: John Barrymore was a man of many aspects, but the play does not present

> " THE DISTINCTION BETWEEN PEOPLE WHO APPRECIATE SHAKESPEARE AND PEOPLE WHO APPRECIATE TELEVISION IS ONE OF THIS PLAY'S CENTRAL POINTS. WHERE THE PLAY DOES AUDIENCES A REAL DISSERVICE IS BY ASSUMING, WITHOUT PROVING, THAT THE SHAKESPEAREANS HAVE IT RIGHT."

him as a complex character, just as one who might be one thing or another at any given time.

Which is exactly the problem with the play's protagonist, Andrew Rally. Viewed simply, Andrew's problems are not at all difficult to understand. Professionally, he wants the wealth and fame that his television career offers him, but he also wants the self-esteem of playing Hamlet in Shakespeare in the Park. Personally, he wants to respect Deirdre's wishes, but his own wish is that she would not insist on saving herself for marriage. By the end of the play, both problems seem to be settled, but they really are not. Audiences leave the play feeling that Deirdre will give in to Andrew, but only because she has been sexually invigorated by the ghost of the great lover, Barrymore: Andrew can look forward to a love life with her, but not because they trust or understand each other any better. Also, in the end Andrew turns down a successful television career in favor of a struggling career on the stage. If this were clearly good for him, then this would indeed be a happy ending, but as it stands it is only an ending that *seems as if* it ought to be happy.

The play's seeming happy ending stems from the idea that Andrew will be a better man for devoting his life to understanding Hamlet. Rudnick makes this the preferred fate for Andrew by playing up the weakness of the alternative, acting in the ridiculous television series proposed to him by writer/director/producer Gary Peter Lefkowitz. Earlier, Andrew expressed his humiliation about

WHAT
DO I READ
NEXT?

- Audiences who watch *I Hate Hamlet* without being familiar with William Shakespeare's play *Hamlet* will not be able to fully appreciate the humor, nor the depth of the characters' emotions about Shakespeare's tortured character. Written some time around 1600, *Hamlet* is considered by many to be the author's greatest work.

- Paul Rudnick's first novel, *Social Disease*, was published in 1986 and has recently been reissued by St. Martin's Press. It is a humorous commentary on life in Manhattan in the 1980s.

- After *I Hate Hamlet*, Rudnick's most famous work for the theater is his play *Jeffrey* (1993). Like the earlier play, Rudnick infuses a serious situation—in this case, a gay man coming to grips with the devastation that AIDS is causing around him—with humor.

- Jason Miller, a Pulitzer Prize winning playwright (for *That Championship Season*) and actor (he had one of the leads in the movie *The Exorcist*) wrote, late in his life, a short, one-person play called *Barrymore's Ghost* (1998), which gives a serious approach to the conceit that is treated lightly by Rudnick. The play is available from Dramatist's Play Service.

- Of the many biographies written about Barrymore, the most important is Gene Fowler's *Good Night, Sweet Prince: The Life and Times of John Barrymore* (1981). Fowler knew Barrymore and covered his Broadway career for the *New York American*. The book, published soon after Barrymore's death in the forties, is currently available from Buccaneer Books.

---

acting in a television commercial that required him to converse with a puppet squirrel, then kiss it to make it feel better; presumably, the television series about a high school teacher with super powers would be at least humiliating to Andrew's professionalism. The moral of the play is that it is better to be poor with dignity than to be wealthy and self-loathing. This much is fine, assuming that a lifetime of playing Hamlet is a lifetime of dignity.

Obviously, there are people who feel that this is exactly the case. Some people live for art, and for some of those, there is no art greater than Shakespeare's. The distinction between people who appreciate Shakespeare and people who appreciate television is one of this play's central points. Where the play does audiences a real disservice is by assuming, without proving, that the Shakespeareans have it right.

This is a play constructed around wall-to-wall one-liners: in spite of the swords and tights, it has more in common with any situation comedy on television than it does with Shakespeare's comedies. It uses the over-earnest Elizabethan values for laughs, as Deirdre, in her gown and tennis shoes,

dreams of a more spiritual existence than her own. Even John Barrymore, the great interpreter of Shakespeare's greatest role, rises to interest in the role only infrequently, focusing most of the time on women, champagne, and even television. As he explains when Andrew questions him about the years of his life that he spent away from the stage, "I faced the dragon." Audiences might take comfort at the end by believing that Andrew is sacrificing himself for art, but in fact what the play truly values is not the process of playing Hamlet. The real point of *I Hate Hamlet* is that it is best to get one's artistic notions over and done with, so that one can go on with a real, Shakespeare-free life.

Of course, audiences seldom notice this contradiction. They leave the theater knowing that Andrew is going to walk away from the foolishness of television and is going to continue to perform Hamlet, which the characters in the play (and, no doubt, the English teachers they remember) have consistently said is a good thing. Audiences leave feeling that Andrew is triumphant in the end because of the grand bow that he takes; they know that he really deserves to take this bow because the ghost of the great thespian told him he deserves it. The play ends on an upbeat note, and few people except the most jaded critics notice that, despite all that is said about the redemptive powers of performing Shakespeare, the play itself does not seem to have much use for Hamlet, other than as a comic situation.

I Hate Hamlet is an effective comedy precisely because its values are held so loosely: Rudnick is free to set up situations and support positions that he can later knock apart, humoring audiences with the unexpected. The play gives free reign to the playwright's wit and does not let plot constraints hinder that wit. In the end, though, the play resolves the tension between the modern worldview and the view of the Shakespearean dramatist by conceding that classic drama is more artistically legitimate: this is a safe position to take, but it is not consistent with the rest of the play.

Source: David Kelly, Critical Essay on *I Hate Hamlet*, in *Drama for Students*, Thomson Gale, 2006.

Laura Carter

Carter is currently employed as a freelance writer. In this essay, Carter focuses on Rudnick's lighthearted contemporary comedy and it's ability to speak to the magic of Shakespeare's Hamlet.

In keeping with one of the major themes of Shakespeare's *Hamlet*, Paul Rudnick's *I Hate Hamlet* is a contrast between both old and new, the value of Shakespearean theater versus the instant gratification of television fame. Rudnick draws on historical figure John Barrymore for his inspiration, an actor captivated by the role of Shakespeare's prince. A sentimental, lighthearted social commentary, Rudnick's Hamlet is not a tragedy, does not seek to redeem or preach a heavy handed message. But it does illuminate the value of the genre to which it speaks. Says the playwright: "*I Hate Hamlet* celebrates the theater, in all its artifice and happy dementia. May the Barrymore panache rule all productions."

Rudnick's play introduces Andrew Rally, an unemployed actor who has previously enjoyed great celebrity status in his role as a physician on television. When Andrew is offered the lead in *Hamlet*, his girlfriend swoons, his broker cheers and his agent campaigns for Andrew to take the part. But Andrew does not share the same enthusiasm. When girlfriend Dierdre tells him he must accept the honorable challenge, he responds: "But why? Just because it's supposed to be this ultimate challenge? Because everyone's supposed to dream of playing *Hamlet*?" Dierdre, however, continues

> " FOR AS TACTLESS, AND
> AS TACKY AS HE IS, GARY IS
> PLUGGED IN, TURNED ON,
> AND TUNED IN TO THE
> ENTERTAINMENT DEMANDS OF
> POP CULTURE AND WHAT IT
> MEANS TO BE SUCCESSFUL."

to push through Andrew's protests, ignoring his objections based on his short lived studies in acting school and his ultimate decision to leave to become a hack actor on a primetime series.

Dierdre's insistence on his participation in "the most beautiful play ever written" becomes part of a clever banter exposing the potential flaw in Dierdre's thinking. Her description of the play is one of heavy despair, of tragedy, "It's about how awful life is, and how everything gets betrayed," declares Dierdre. "But then Hamlet tries to make things better. And he dies!" Andrew responds humorously, "Which tells us . . . .," questioning the play's redeeming value. To Andrew, playing what is historically identified as Shakespeare's most challenging character is not necessarily the boost his career needs, it's potentially career suicide. Modern television did not demand any real talent, claims Andrew, "I had the right twinkle, the demographic appeal."

With Andrew, and with Gary, Rudnick's work offers an illuminating contemporary perspective on Shakespearean theater. Gary can only respond to *Hamlet*, commenting, "Whoa, God, other centuries. Like, people who weren't me." He is Rudnick's pop culture icon. Obnoxious, at times calculating, he is not remiss in playfully admitting it. He is completely self-absorbed, and primarily motivated by his own self interest rather than by Andrew's happiness. Playing devil's advocate, Gary reduces the production of Shakespeare in Central Park to "algebra on stage," calling it "snack theater" or "Shakespeare for squirrels." He continues to plead with Andrew to come to his senses, to realize that purchasing fine art is intrinsically more valuable than trying to emulate it, painting a portrait of his young protégé as one doomed to basement productions of Chekov scheduled between AA meetings.

In this clever juxtaposition of ideas of what is really art versus contemporary entertainment, Gary dismantles or tears apart tradition by challenging the idea that *Hamlet*, by virtue of its sophistication, is a higher, more noble art form. For as tactless, and as tacky as he is, Gary is plugged in, turned on, and tuned in to the entertainment demands of pop culture and what it means to be successful. He identifies happiness with materialism, and truly believes he is not only acting in his best interests, but in Andrew's as well. And he exposes the follies of dreamers, like Dierdre, who, spurred by sentimentality, live in a world of high-flying ideals, completely out of touch with reality.

Barrymore is Gary's alter ego and an advocate for the arts. After hearing Andrew declare his dislike for *Hamlet*, Barrymore appears, his mission to reform his understudy, to convince him to embrace the role he so covets. Unlike Gary, Barrymore detests modern theater. In a conversation with Andrew, Barrymore likens the "introduction of truth" into modern theater to such artifice as "synthetic fibers" and the "GE Kitchen of Tomorrow." He sees Andrew at a crossroads, having to make the choice between a timeless role as Hamlet or television's slick marketing hype, asking "What will you be—artist, or lunchbox?" And Barrymore sees, as Andrew begins to eventually believe, that implicit in such a choice is a challenge, to truly follow one's passion, to accept more difficult acting parts and truly master one's craft, or to succumb to the materialistic, easy money that to Barrymore equates to a career on television. Gary, however, is more impressed with the enormous television contract, hoping that Andrew's interest in Hamlet is short lived.

Gary and Barrymore are archetypes, examples Rudnick employs to drive a discussion about the value of *Hamlet*, and by extension, of art. And both characters make somewhat reasonable, if not believable arguments for both sides, expressing their views or understood notions of what authentic art is, and further, what is politically correct in the art world. Barrymore fervently condemns modernity in any form. Gary celebrates it. While Barrymore looks to the past for his inspiration, Gary embraces the future, claiming that theater "doesn't make sense," that television is "progress," or "art perfected." The idea that in addition to commanding less of his attention, he can eat, talk and view commercials makes television all the more appealing. "It's distilled" entertainment, Gary claims, never demanding an unnecessary amount of his time and energy.

For all of Barrymore's protestations and endless pontification or preaching on the subject of television, the audience discovers the dead actor is not as virtuous as his views suggest. In Act 2, Scene 1, in the midst of Andrew's struggle with stage fright, Barrymore calls Andrew a "sniveling brat." Andrew responds, claiming, "After you played Hamlet, you left the theater!" Barrymore attempts to absolve himself, putting Andrew even more on the offensive. It is during this scene the audience learns that Barrymore left for Hollywood, purchased a mansion in Beverly Hills, and made movie after movie, "most of them garbage," according to Andrew.

But, Barrymore admits that movies ruined him, made him a hopeless, unemployable drunk and eventually left him unable to perform. Admittedly, before his departure for Hollywood fame and fortune, his face "five stories high and six zeroes wide," Barrymore found more personal satisfaction in playing the role of Hamlet. In his estimation, during his acting stint as Hamlet, he was in his prime professionally, having "faced the dragon." Says Barrymore, "I accepted a role so insanely complex, so fantastic and impossible, that any attempt is only that—an attempt!"

What gives Barrymore great credibility is that he stood at the crossroads of Andrew's life, was given a chance at fame and fortune, or the opportunity to remain a Shakespearean actor playing what is considered to be the noblest of roles, and chose to forsake his talents for the instant gratification Hollywood has to offer. When it comes to Andrew, however, his motive is seemingly as self-serving as Gary's, the audience discovers in a conversation with Lillian. He admits that getting Andrew to accept the role of Hamlet was the sole purpose of his return. Barrymore claims he wanted Andrew to learn from his "sorry excuse for a life." And, he admits that although he was offered every conceivable opportunity, "Andrew is my last vain hope. My cosmic lunge at redemption."

Rudnick's play is in part about Barrymore's legacy. By most historical accounts, one would be hard-pressed to label him a Shakespearean actor. According to Gene Fowler, in *Good Night Sweet Prince*, Barrymore was enthralled with the role of Hamlet, "possessed. . . . A voice clearly had challenged him from across three centuries. . . . He would climb the highest of the magic mountains, the last great peak he was to scale in the fabulous domain of the theatre." (bard.org) Critics have been apt to point out that Barrymore, as any actor finding himself in any great role, identified with the Prince of Denmark in an intensely personal way. According to Fowler, the actor himself "declared the Prince to be 'the easiest role he ever played.'" (bard.org)

The play is also driven by strong Shakespearean undercurrents, leading one critic from Utah's Shakespearean Festival to comment that Rudnick's work "is a comedy and a very funny one," yet "under the surface laughter there is a strong *Hamlet* current that carries us along in the same way it carries Andrew Rally and in the same way it carried John Barrymore." (bard.org) The play resonates with the audience as the Prince of Denmark's character has been historically throughout the world, leading critics the likes of Harold Bloom to conclude, "No other single character in the plays, not even Falstaff or Cleopatra, matches Hamlet's infinite reverberations. The phenomenon of Hamlet, the prince without the play, is unsurpassed in the West's imaginative literature." (bard.org)

Fundamentally, Hamlet has fascinated the literary world for centuries as a Prince whose good intentions led to his ultimate failure. And throughout the centuries, the character, according to some, has come to personify humanity's most perplexing problems and dearest hopes. As did a long line of actors before him, Barrymore included, Andrew comes to identify with the character of Hamlet on many levels. Hamlet in the beginning is a challenge, a chance for Andrew to prove himself, but in the end, Andrew internalizes the role. Andrew took on the role with the intention of winning Dierdre's affections and sending Barrymore back to the afterlife, yet by the play's end the character Hamlet manages to reach right down to the very core of his being, changing his life.

Sifting through Dierdre's, Barrymore's and Gary's arguments, one is hard pressed to make a decision concerning Andrew's future as an entertainer. If Andrew is a mediocre actor, should he dare consider passing up a three-million-dollar contract with a major television network to suffer the embarrassment of playing Hamlet? Or will he eventually conquer the role, as Barrymore once did, and finally conquer his own private demons?

What Paul Rudnick's *I Hate Hamlet* does so well is to illuminate the schism between classic and contemporary; old and new; art and progress to provide a humorous glimpse into the life, the drama and the glory of the theater. It leaves the audience to ponder age old questions and unresolved arguments about the legitimacy of art in contemporary life. Ultimately, though, Rudnick's work is sentimental. It resonates with a desire all beings feel, that is, to reach

for a dream and connect with it on the deepest level possible. For Andrew that dream is the stage, to meet and conquer the role of Hamlet, the greatest acting challenge of his career. Andrew is not alone. For many actors, the role of Hamlet goes beyond art for art's sake, it is the final vista, the ultimate challenge, the apex of their careers. It captures that one moment, that glimmer of hope, of supreme accomplishment that most of us continue to strive for, whether or not we have "8,000 lines to go."

Source: Laura Carter, Critical Essay on *I Hate Hamlet*, in *Drama for Students*, Thomson Gale, 2006.

David Remy

Remy is a freelance writer in Warrington, Florida. In the following essay, Remy examines the ways in which Rudnick's play comments upon popular culture.

As a play, *I Hate Hamlet* is a comedy, a melodrama, a send-up of tradition and grandeur, a contrast between high and low culture, yet as a commentary on many of the ideas that pervade contemporary popular culture, it remains a biting satire. From the opening scene, there exists a juxtaposition between the characters' expectations and their methods for realizing them, a dichotomy that makes for amusing, playful entertainment. Often, it seems that willpower alone is enough to communicate with the dead or transform the career of a TV actor into that of a theatrical star, but, alas, this is not so. To be fair, Rudnick satirizes not only the aspirations of his protagonist but those of the other characters as well. By exposing his characters' ideas about education, fame, and art, Rudnick creates a picture of a contemporary society that is influenced more by popular culture than it is by tradition and the eternal verities it represents.

In *I Hate Hamlet*, education is viewed as a means to an end rather than something worth pursuing to enrich one's life. Because society advances at an ever accelerating pace, an education now develops over the short-term, and any information that falls beyond the focus of an individual's immediate goals is discarded as useless or antiquated. In other words, an education should help one solve a particular problem, and it should do nothing more or nothing less than that. Solutions should be found easily so that one is able to devote one's time to more leisurely pursuits. For example, when Felicia, the real estate broker, fails to reconcile her feelings for her departed mother through counseling, she takes a course entitled "Spiritual Transcommunication: Beyond The Physical Sphere." Felicia becomes a

> WITHIN A CONTEXT OF POPULAR CULTURE, FAME, RUDNICK SUGGESTS, BESTOWS NOTORIETY AT THE SAME TIME IT MAKES ALL ACHIEVEMENTS EQUAL."

medium practically overnight, avoiding a long apprenticeship that might interfere with her more urgent need of contacting her mother. As a result of having taken the course, Felicia enjoys a better relationship with her mother, whom she talks to regularly in the hereafter as though they were chatting over the telephone. Furthermore, even though Andrew expresses doubt about contacting the dead, he is willing to go along with the séance if contacting the famous actor John Barrymore will help him perform the role of Hamlet. Andrew would rather take a shortcut than study the performances of those who have played the venerable role before him.

Although his formal dramatic training (a mere two years) has left him ill-prepared for playing the role of Hamlet, Andrew believes, quite naïvely, that he can prepare for this role in much the same manner that he did for the episodes of *LA Medical* and the cereal commercial that made him famous. When the TV show is canceled, Andrew, acting on "a whim," decides to try his luck in New York City, the home of the American theatre. He assumes that all he needs to do to match his previous success is "[t]ake some classes, maybe do a new play, ease back in," as though such a challenge as performing *Hamlet* could be done in a paint-by-numbers fashion. In a popular culture where willpower ("attitude") and a penchant for self-promotion can carry one far, Andrew, in an ironic commentary upon both his profession and the times in which he lives, mistakenly believes that every acting assignment demands the same amount of preparation, whether it requires him to perform as a pitchman for a breakfast cereal or to assume the mantle worn by Barrymore and the august line of actors that preceded him in performing the role of Hamlet. However, by the time Andrew leaves for his opening-night performance, he understands that common sense favors a more traditional approach

toward learning the part. "Instant actor! Just add Shakespeare! . . . I don't think it works that way!" he says, filled with a sense of horror worse than any case of opening-night jitters could ever produce.

Fame is yet another aspect of popular culture that Rudnick satirizes at length within the play. Fame is a commonplace occurrence, something that is sought after and achieved by many through different means, though the context for one's fame may not always be flattering. Andrew feels the exhilaration fame brings when he sees his face on the cover of *TV Guide* at the supermarket checkout line, "right next to the gum." Nevertheless, he remains flushed with excitement, as though he celebrates his Bar Mitzvah whenever his associates and the adoring public smile back at him. "That's what California is," Andrew says, "it's one big hug—it's Aunt Sophie without the pinch." The medium of television broadcasts Andrew's image far and wide, making him recognizable and, therefore, famous. Within a context of popular culture, fame, Rudnick suggests, bestows notoriety at the same time it makes all achievements equal. For example, Andrew is known as much for a commercial in which he acts alongside a talking chipmunk as he is for playing the role of Jim Corman, "rookie surgeon," on *LA Medical*. When Felicia meets Andrew at the Barrymore apartment, one of the first things she does is remark upon how much she enjoys watching him act on television, his show and the Trailburst Nuggets commercial receiving equal merit even though she cannot quite seem to recall the product he advertises. With his show now canceled, Andrew's fame, such as it is, comes down to his singing a few bars of a jingle to remind her.

In this way, fame, which the playwright suggests is fleeting and achieved all too easily, distinguishes itself from glory, which, as embodied by the ghost of John Barrymore, is far more enduring. Fame can last for as long as one thirty-second commercial or for the length of an entire broadcast season, perhaps longer if the show goes into syndication. Fame is regarded as superficial because one does not necessarily have to possess talent in order to be famous—at one point Barrymore refers to Andrew as a "hack"—and yet popular culture considers fame to be something worthy of attaining. Although Andrew may claim that he is "not that superficial" for being motivated more by fame than by money when he is offered the series *Night School*, he unwittingly undermines his artistic integrity when he remarks upon how many people will see the show "even if it's a bomb." As Barrymore observes, fame may make Andrew "admired, lusted after," but at the same time he will acquire "all the attributes of a well-marketed detergent." Fame and its attendant celebrity cannot compare with glory, which endures above and beyond such trappings as better pay, "beachfront property," and "body-guards," for glory is attained when an actor establishes a rapport with his or her audience and holds it spellbound, as Barrymore did many times throughout his long and illustrious career on stage and as Andrew does briefly when he recites his soliloquy. The moment becomes memorable because it is unique and cannot be reproduced *ad nauseum* as it can on film. Glory, at least the kind that performing the role of Hamlet can bestow upon an actor, transcends the ages.

While Rudnick espouses glory as the actor's supreme reward, a legacy that is handed down from one generation of actors to the next, glory's essential component, art, does not fare nearly as well in a society that values commerce and forms of entertainment designed for mass consumption. Art, when it is appreciated at all, is regarded as a money-making venture, a business proposition guaranteed to secure lasting value. "You don't do art," Gary says when Andrew announces his decision to play Hamlet. "You buy it." Rudnick provides an ironic commentary on drama in contemporary society when Gary confuses a live performance of Shakespeare in the park with *Hallmark Hall of Fame*, sentimental made-for-TV dramas that are sponsored by a popular greeting-card company. The connection between the dramas and their sponsor is so indelible that commerce and entertainment have become synonymous with each other. Furthermore, Gary embodies the pervading belief among his colleagues in the entertainment industry that a conscious decision to create art, such as the decision Andrew has made to perform *Hamlet*, diminishes an actor's "star power," his value as a commodity on the market. Thus, Gary warns Andrew that the Hollywood bigwigs will think he's "washed up" if he plays the Danish prince. Andrew has a reputation to consider; he should think twice before donning tights. To choose art over commercial value (and the potential to increase that value many times over) is tantamount, in Gary's opinion, to committing professional suicide.

Perhaps as a result of the entertainment industry's view of art, Andrew, in trying to perform his role with a dependable degree of accuracy and confidence, approaches the role of Hamlet with something akin to scientific investigation. Indeed, his preoccupation with concepts like "preparation," "substitution," "internalizing the role," and "finding

an emotional through-line"—all aspects of the modern acting technique known as The Method—strikes Barrymore as "utterly appalling," for he, like the actors and actresses of his era, honed his craft during countless performances of the classics. One developed a role over time, learning the nuances that revealed themselves with each reading and performance of the play. Moreover, Barrymore discounts Andrew's ideas about "communication," which the veteran actor refers to as "[t]hat absolute assassin of romance." In sharp contrast to popular opinion, Barrymore dismisses modern acting technique as nonsense, inferring that performing the role of Hamlet cannot be reduced to an elaborate series of formulae. Rather, the role gives the actor "an opportunity to shine," to express in language and in deed the eternal verities of the heart, for this is how the role of Hamlet must be played, with passion and a generosity of spirit that knows no bounds.

Rudnick's *I Hate Hamlet* satirizes the ideas and opinions that serve too often as intellectual guideposts in popular culture, particularly as they influence the entertainment industry's view on art. However, the ghostly figure of John Barrymore reminds both the audience and the reader that, though these ideas and opinions may come and go, there will always be a need for the enduring art of Shakespeare.

Source: David Remy, Critical Essay on *I Hate Hamlet*, in *Drama for Students*, Thomson Gale, 2006.

SOURCES

Gerard, Jeremy, Review of *I Hate Hamlet*, in *Variety*, April 15, 1991 pp. 209–10.

"*I Hate Hamlet*: Tragedy Becomes Comedy," *Utah Shakespearean Festival*, February 16, 2004, www.bard.org.

Lazare, Lewis, Review of *I Hate Hamlet*, in *Variety*, December 11–17, 1995, p. 97.

Rudnick, Paul, *I Hate Hamlet*, Dramatists Play Service, 1992.

Weales, Gerald, "To Hate or Not to Hate," in *Commonweal*, Vol. 118, Issue 11, June 1, 1991, pp. 373–74.

FURTHER READING

Hoffman, Carol Stein, *The Barrymores: Hollywood's First Family*, University Press of Kentucky, 2001.
   Barrymore was only slightly better known in his time than his sister Ethel and brother Lionel. Each

generation of the family seems as much cursed as blessed. Hoffman worked closely with John Drew Barrymore (the son of John and father of Drew Barrymore) for almost a quarter of a decade in compiling this portrait that spans from Elizabethan England to the *Charlie's Angels* movie franchise.

Mills, John A., *Hamlet on Stage: The Great Tradition*, Greenwood Press, 1985.
Mills's analysis includes a fairly thorough retrospective of the ways in which the role of Hamlet has been interpreted over the past four centuries, giving details of how each actor has individualized the role.

Morrison, Michael A., *John Barrymore, Shakespearean Actor*, Cambridge Studies in American Theatre and Drama series, Vol. 10, Cambridge University Press, 1997.
Morrison reconstructs those few years in the early 1920s when Barrymore redefined the art of interpreting Shakespeare for Broadway with his keen portrayals. His analysis goes beyond biography.

Scofield, Martin, *The Ghosts of Hamlet: The Play and Modern Writers*, Cambridge University Press, 1980.
Scofield examines the meaning of ghosts, in particular the one in Shakespeare's play, and how the interpretations have changed over the years.

Imaginary Friends

NORA EPHRON

2002

Lillian Hellman and Mary McCarthy had been feuding ever since they met at a writer's conference at Sarah Lawrence College in 1948. In 1980, McCarthy delivered the cruelest blow when she declared in a television interview with Dick Cavett that "every word [Lillian Hellman] writes is a lie, including 'and' and 'the.'" This comment prompted Hellman, who was watching the interview, to bring a slander suit against McCarthy. Nora Ephron's play, *Imaginary Friends*, which opened on Broadway on September 29, 2002, focuses on this lawsuit and the feuding that lead up to it.

Their bickering stemmed from, as Ephron notes in her introduction to the play, "McCarthy's love of the truth—which she turned into a religion—and ... Hellman's way with a story, which she turned into a pathology." In *Imaginary Friends*, Ephron imagines a final meeting between the two women, in Hell, as they assess their lives and their antagonistic relationship through a series of razor-sharp verbal attacks on each other. Lisa D. Horowitz, in her review of the play for *Variety*, writes that Ephron's Hellman and McCarthy "prove, quite entertainingly, that they are each other's own special hell."

AUTHOR BIOGRAPHY

Nora Ephron was born on the Upper West Side of Manhattan on May 19, 1941 to Henry and Phoebe

Nora Ephron Photo by Matthew Peyton. Getty Images

Ephron, prominent screenwriters of such classic films as *Daddy Long Legs*, *Desk Set*, and *Carousel*. The family moved to Beverly Hills when Nora was three years old, thus exposing her to Hollywood and setting the scene for her career in screenwriting. Ephron was raised in a family that valued verbal jousting. In an article from *Vanity Fair*, Nora's sister commented that their nightly dinner table resembled the Algonquin Round Table. Ephron's finely honed verbal skills became one of the most popular characteristics of her written work.

Ephron graduated from Wellesley College in 1962 with a degree in journalism. She used this degree to get work as an assignment reporter for *The New York Post* and as an essayist for *Esquire* and *New York* magazines. During this time, she authored three books, *Scribble, Scribble*, *Crazy Salad*, and *Wallflower at the Orgy*, that were filled with her observations of human relationships. In 1983, Ephron wrote the bestselling novel *Heartburn*, a satire of her failed marriage to Watergate journalist Carl Bernstein. *Heartburn* was later made into a film starring Meryl Streep and Jack Nicholson and won Ephron her first Academy Award Nomination.

Ephron began writing screenplays as a way to support herself and her two sons, Jacob and Max, after her divorce. Her first screenplay *Silkwood*

(1983) won an Academy Award Nomination for best original screenplay. In 1987, she married Nicholas Pileggi, journalist and screenwriter of *Goodfellas* and *Casino*. In 1989, *When Harry Met Sally*, Epron's most popular screenplay, was awarded an Academy Award for Best Script. In 1993, *Sleepless in Seattle* was released, which won Ephron another Academy Award for best script. Ephron also co-authored screenplays for the films *Michael*, *Mixed Nuts* and *You've Got Mail*.

As Ephron observed her parents and friends' screenwriting careers, which were effectively over by the time they turned 50, she decided to get involved in writing plays and directing films. Ephron began her directing career in 1992 with *This Is My Life* and her playwriting career with *Imaginary Friends*. Ephron is an active member of the Writers Guild of America, the Authors Guild, the Directors Guild of America, and the Academy of Motion Picture Arts and Sciences.

PLOT SUMMARY

Act 1

The play opens on a bare stage where two women, Lillian Hellman and Mary McCarthy, are smoking. They try to recall if they had ever met, but soon admit that they were both at Sarah Lawrence College in 1948, when the two were invited to a writers' conference there. McCarthy remembers being incensed at what she considered Hellman's lies about the Spanish civil war. She interrupted and corrected Hellman, and the two began to argue.

Hellman shifts the focus to her speech to the House Un-American Activities Committee in 1952. She recalls how she refused to identify communists by insisting, "I cannot and will not cut my conscience to fit this year's fashions," her most famous quote. The two women then bicker over details of Hellman's past and discuss other female writers. They conclude that no one reads either of them anymore.

Their conversation turns back to their personal feud, which culminated in Hellman bringing a slander suit against McCarthy for declaring in a television interview with Dick Cavett that Hellman likens their situation to a story about two U-boats who engage in battle.

The next scene jumps to Hellman's childhood in New Orleans. Hellman plays herself as a child and reminisces about her happy experiences grow-ing up. When she sees her father in a passionate embrace with Fizzy, a young neighbor, she falls out of the tree she had been climbing. Her nurse Sophronia comforts her and extracts a promise that she will tell no one about her father's indiscretion.

The scene changes to Minneapolis, where McCarthy and her siblings moved after her parents died. McCarthy recalls that no one actually ever told them the truth about her parents' death. They were sent to live with a great-aunt and her new hus-band, Uncle Myers, who physically abused her.

The action shifts to a nightclub in New York, where Hellman and McCarthy, both in their late twenties, sit drinking at the bar. In brief phrases, each begins to recant the details of her history up to that point, revealing that their lives have been remark-ably similar. They begin to argue when Hellman in-sists that she had sex with Philip Rahv, McCarthy's lover. They each admit wanting one thing the other had, McCarthy has beauty and Hellman has wealth.

Hellman tries to compensate for her lack of beauty with the fact of her relationship with the writer Dashiell Hammett, which she romanticizes in glowing detail. McCarthy insists Hellman's vi-sion of him is a figment of her imagination, de-claring, "He was just a story." Hellman counters with the fact that Hammett gave her a true report about two schoolgirls in Scotland who accused their teachers of engaging in a lesbian relationship. She turned this story into her first play, *The Chil-dren's Hour*, which became very successful. Hell-man admits that she liked the shocking nature of the play because it gained her public attention.

Literary critic and scholar Edmund Wilson comes in the bar and sits next to McCarthy, who discusses her reasons for marrying him and their subsequent stormy relationship. Philip Rahv enters when McCarthy admits that she was in love with him when she married Wilson. McCarthy and Rahv spar over class issues. After a prolonged argument, McCarthy insists that they were "incredibly happy."

McCarthy's reasons for marrying Wilson are not clear. McCarthy tells Hellman that it is odd that the two women "might never have become real writers" if they had not had relationships with older men. The two compliment each other's work. They then begin discussing their differing political posi-tions and their activities during the cold war years, including Hellman's famous statement to the House Un-American Activities Committee.

The scene then shifts back to their meeting at Sarah Lawrence. They try to get the details straight but can agree on little. McCarthy accuses Hellman of lying about writer John Dos Passos' political ac-tivities. They continue to bicker about what hap-pened and then wonder if they could have ever been friends. The first act ends with the appearance of Muriel Gardiner.

Act 2

The two women carry their dolls on stage and sing a song about imaginary friends to them. The scene then depicts a moment in McCarthy's past when she was beaten by her uncle. Hellman hears her screams, breaks down the door and rescues her. The two women then climb up Hellman's fig tree and hide. When Hellman announces that she has saved McCarthy, the latter gets angry, insisting that Hellman is always "trying to take over." Mary then falls out of the tree.

Two characters, Fact and Fiction, appear and sing. The scene then shifts to 1963 after the two women have become famous authors. They discuss their careers as they verbally jab at each other. Af-ter Hellman notes that she remained in the public eye while McCarthy's star faded, she becomes sur-rounded by interviewers asking about her child-hood and especially about her story "Julia," which was made into a successful film. Hellman becomes upset when remembering the story, which she says was based on her relationship with a woman who was working for the anti-Nazi movement during World War II.

One of the reporters talks with McCarthy, telling her all the famous stories about Hellman. McCarthy starts to rehash all of the encounters the two of them have had, and includes her comment to Dick Cavett, which is all recorded by the interviewer.

The scene shifts to New York, where McCarthy is talking to her college friend Abby Kaiser about her upcoming interview with Dick Cavett. They dis-cuss whether or not McCarthy should use the line about Hellman being a liar that she had told to a French reporter. The two plan how she can casually insert the line so it will appear spontaneous.

In the next scene, Hellman watches McCarthy's interview with Cavett, which soon cuts to McCarthy being served with a summons. Then the action re-turns to New Orleans, where Hellman and McCarthy sit in the fig tree, staging Hellman's memories of her father's affair with Fizzy. When Mary takes over the scene, she has Fizzy criticize Hellman. The two women begin to fight and fall out of the tree.

In the final scene, the two women are older, looking back on the trial, noting how much publicity it got. Some of the figures involved, including lawyers and reporters, make brief appearances. McCarthy's lawyer tries to get her to retract or soften her statement about Hellman, but she refuses.

Mary calls Muriel Gardiner, a psychoanalyst, to the witness stand, who suggests that she is the real Julia that Hellman wrote about in *Pentimento*. Hellman will not admit that Julia was based on Gardiner, but claims that it does not matter one way or the other since both women became famous as a result.

Speaking as a psychoanalyst, Gardiner begins to analyze the character of each of the two women. She determines that the lies told to Mary about her parents caused her to make "a religion out of the truth," which turned into her "blind spot." Hellman, she argues, was traumatized by seeing her father's infidelities and being told to lie about them. As a result, Hellman spent her life "telling lies and expecting to be applauded for it."

After Gardiner leaves, the two women discount her analyses and admit that the trial never took place. They argue about the motive for the lawsuit and its ultimate effect on the reputation of each. After each tries to viciously belittle the other, they attempt to leave but realize that they are "stuck together forever." They end their time on stage with a reiteration of their essential difference: McCarthy believes in the truth while Hellman believes in the story.

CHARACTERS

Muriel Gardiner

Muriel Gardiner, a psychoanalyst, is called to the imaginary witness stand in the play and suggests that she is the real Julia that Hellman wrote about in *Pentimento*. Muriel serves two purposes in the play: to support McCarthy's point that Hellman's story about her relationship with Julia is fabricated, and to psychoanalyze McCarthy and Hellman.

Dashiell Hammett

Dashiell Hammett was McCarthy's long-time companion and, she claims, lover. He appears as one of his characters, "Nick," in the film he wrote, *The Thin Man*, speaks a few lines, and then falls off a barstool, obviously drunk. By having him speak dialogue from the film, Ephron suggests that McCarthy may be right in her claim that Hellman had fabricated her account of her relationship with him.

Lillian Hellman

Ephron explains Hellman's devotion to fabrication through an examination of her past, concluding that Hellman was traumatized by seeing her father's infidelities and being told to lie about them. As a result, Gardiner insists, she spent her life "telling lies and expecting to be applauded for it." She does have a great penchant for self-promotion as she demonstrates with her stories about "Julia" and her relationship with Dashiell Hammett. At one point, during a discussion with McCarthy about top women writers, Hellman admits that she had included Jean Stafford only to make herself "seem open-minded." When a scene from McCarthy's childhood appears, in which she is being beaten by her uncle, Hellman comes to the rescue, saving her and so becoming, as she notes, the heroine of McCarthy's story. McCarthy complains that Hellman is always trying to "take over."

Hellman continually tries to heighten the drama of events even as she acknowledges that her memory is faulty. After agreeing, for example, that she told lies to the Sarah Lawrence audience, she tries to recreate the scene by putting on the bracelets that McCarthy insists she was wearing.

Although Mary McCarthy's vicious attack against Lillian Hellman's credibility was the impetus for Hellman's suit against her, which becomes the main subject of the play, Hellman appears to be nastier and more unrelenting in her jabs at McCarthy. Hellman had a reputation for cruelty, which is tempered here a bit by her wit, but still causes her to lash out repeatedly at McCarthy. Hellman obviously feels quite competitive with her foe, and perhaps her acknowledged desire to be better-looking adds fuel to her attacks, since McCarthy is an attractive woman.

Abby Kaiser

Abby Kaiser is McCarthy's college friend. Kaiser is sympathetic when McCarthy declares that her latest book is not selling well and the two women think of ways to help promote it. Abby supports McCarthy's decision to use the same line about Hellman that she told the Paris reporter, and the two discuss how to make it seem spontaneous.

Mary McCarthy

Ephron determines that McCarthy was also significantly shaped by the events of her childhood. Gardner insists that the lies told to Mary about her parents caused her to make "a religion out of the truth," which turned into her "blind spot." This blind spot caused her to overlook the consequences of her words, as she did in her famous remark about

Hellman to Dick Cavett. Family, friends, and ex-lovers all tried to sue her after the publication of her essays and "fiction."

McCarthy experiences this blind spot, however, with the details of her own life as well. After an especially combative scene with her lover, Philip Rahv, McCarthy concludes, "we were incredibly happy." While she insists that she is a "a fanatic Trotskyite," she acknowledges that she became one "almost by chance," and her discussions with Rahv and Hellman suggest that she does not have strong political convictions.

As she tries to explain why she married Edmund Wilson while she was in love with Rahv, McCarthy insists that she did not pursue him, that it just happened. Hellman points out her indecisiveness about her politics and marriage when she inquires, "what decisions in your life did you actually make?"

McCarthy also had a penchant for self-promotion as she notes that the shocking nature of her story, "The Man in the Brooks Brothers Suit," would gain her publicity. This trait became more evident as her popularity began to fade. Her remark to Cavett was spurred by her desire to promote a book that was earning her little recognition, and she eventually admits that the public feuding between the two women helped their careers.

Paris Reporter

McCarthy first declared that "every word [Hellman] writes is a lie, including 'and' and 'the,'" while speaking to a reporter. When the reporter spends most of the interview praising Hellman and the film *Julia* and has little to say about McCarthy, the latter gets angry and tries to discredit Hellman.

Philip Rahv

Philip Rahv was the editor of the *Partisan Review*, a highly-respected literary journal. He and McCarthy were lovers, and Hellman claims that she slept with him as well. He appears in one scene where he bickers with McCarthy about politics and ethnicity. McCarthy notes that he was "intense" and that they "waged class struggle[s] every day." He obviously feels he has the superior intellect and criticizes her for her "bourgeois" habits and tastes.

THEMES

Ambition

Both women were extremely ambitious, which Ephron suggests was a necessary trait in the middle part of the twentieth century, when not many female authors were celebrated, let alone recognized. Both did become successful authors, but as Hellman acknowledges, they "might never have become real writers if it weren't for these two older men who came into [their] lives at almost the same moment." Hellman suggests that this was the motive for McCarthy's agreeing to marry Edmund Wilson, when she seemed to be in love with Philip Rahv.

Hellman and McCarthy understood the power of the media and used it to keep themselves in the public eye. Both women made names for themselves with their publication of shocking stories: Hellman's *The Children's Hour* and McCarthy's "The Man in the Brooks Brothers Suit." They also admit that they played up their fight for the infamy it would afford them.

In a rare moment of truth, they each confess to wanting one thing the other had, Hellman wants McCarthy's beauty and McCarthy wants Hellman's wealth. This desire was one of the impetuses for their fierce competition.

Competition

At one point McCarthy insists, "it's just too easy to say that the reason women fight with each other is because they're jealous," but jealousy was one of the factors in their ongoing battle. A more important factor, though, was their ambition. There was not a lot of room for female authors during this period, and each wanted to be considered the best.

The two women compete in every scene, over artistic success, men, and public attention. Hellman starts the battle, as McCarthy notes that she was teaching at Sarah Lawrence when Hellman came to speak by pointing out that she never "had" to teach. Hellman remembers the students never taking their eyes off of her as she told such wonderful stories. After she insists that McCarthy came to her lecture to pick a fight, she ratchets up the competition when she inquires whether it was because she slept with Rahv or if it was that McCarthy was jealous of her.

McCarthy retaliates in response to Hellman's complaint that McCarthy was always writing "mean things" about her, by admitting "I didn't write much about you." Hellman later is on the attack when she remembers watching McCarthy's interview with Cavett and declares "I was completely happy at seeing how badly you'd aged." When the two women discuss their political positions during the forties and fifties, Hellman insists that

TOPICS FOR FURTHER STUDY

- View the film *Julia*, which depicts Hellman's relationship with Dashiell Hammett. Do you see any parallels between Ephron's Hellman and Hellman as she is depicted in the film?

- Read Ephron's *Scribble, Scribble* and apply what she says about writing in the book to this play.

- Do a biographical study of either Hellman or McCarthy and determine whether Ephron's depiction of the two women is realistic.

- Research the terms Trotskyite and Stalinist and determine whether the play suggests that the women were true followers of these movements. Check out biographical details to see if they support Ephron's characterizations of the women in this regard.

McCarthy is jealous because she and other communist sympathizers became heroes during the House Un-American Activities Committee hearings in 1952.

Their fiercest jabs are thrown when they discuss each other's work. Hellman notes that McCarthy's best-seller *The Group* was "viciously reviewed" by some of her "closest friends." McCarthy counters with her declaration that Hellman was "washed up as a playwright" and so turned to memoirs. Hellman returns by declaring that no one reads McCarthy's essays on war. At one point, they grudgingly admit that they liked each other's work, but McCarthy immediately qualifies her statement that Hellman's plays "were so well made" by claiming, "too well made, really—there was way too much of the gun over the mantel in the first act being fired at the end of the play."

Ultimately, though, they acknowledge the theatrical nature of their competition. When they identify themselves as enemies, and Hellman quotes Goethe—"you must choose your enemies well," she suggests their competition has benefited both of them.

STYLE

Past and Present

Ephron constantly juxtaposes present, when Hellman and McCarthy are reviewing their lives in Hell, with past, which focuses on the two women's memories. This structure helps illustrate and reinforce Ephron's focus on the tension between truth and fiction. As each character remembers details of her past, the other inevitably joins in, exclaiming, "that never happened," which is usually confirmed by both. An example of this occurs when Hellman is discussing Julia's story, which was made into a film, and which she claims was based on her own life. When Jane Fonda as Hellman in *Julia* throws her typewriter out of the window, Hellman admits that it never happened. In other scenes, Ephron has each woman editing and staging the other's memories.

Music

Ephron places songs between scenes to enhance and comment on the action of the play. Sometimes she has an ensemble, used as a traditional chorus, as in the first act when Hellman is reminiscing about her childhood. The ensemble sings "The Fig Tree Rag" to heighten the fictional nature of Hellman's memories. In the second act, Ephron introduces two male characters, Frankie Fact and Dick Fiction, who sing about their "act." They admit that they "tend to tangle" at times, just as the main characters do, but their main point is that "fact may in fact be fiction" and "sometimes, in fact, there's fiction too."

HISTORICAL CONTEXT

Fascism

Fascism is a totalitarian system of government that directs the state to take absolute control of the lives of its people. The term was first used by supporters of Benito Mussolini, Italy's dictator from 1922, until his capture and execution during World War II. Other countries that have established fascistic regimes include Francisco Franco's Spain and Adolph Hitler's Germany.

Fascism emerged as a counter-force to the egalitarianism of socialism and democracy, which frightened many conservative Europeans at the end of the nineteenth century and the beginning of the twentieth century. They feared that the lower classes would take power away from the middle

COMPARE
&
CONTRAST

- **1940s:** World War II comes about in response to the rise of totalitarian regimes in Germany, Italy, and Japan. Over two hundred countries band together to fight their militaristic expansion in Europe.

- **Today:** The United States, along with thirty-four other countries, invade Iraq in 2003. The initial motive for the invasion was the assumed threat of Iraq's weapons of mass destruction.

- **1940s:** The USSR emerges as a superpower.

Today: The communist system in the U.S.S.R. collapses in 1991, along with the Republic a few months later. Russia becomes increasingly more rigid under the rule of Vladimir Putin in 1999.

- **1940s:** During the years of World War II, a strong underground movement emerges that helps stop Nazi aggression through sneak attacks, sabotage, and espionage.

Today: Insurgents in Iraq, made up of Iraqi civilians and terrorist groups, carry out similar attacks against occupational forces.

---

and upper classes. These conservatives also feared the chaos and general anarchy that inevitably ensue after political revolutions. Fascists played on these concerns, appealing to the people's nationalistic sentiments and promising a return to law and order and Christian morality.

The doctrine of fascism includes the glorification of the state and the complete subordination of the people to it. The state creates its own absolute law. A second principle, that of survival of the fittest, is borrowed from Social Darwinism and applied to the state. Fascists use this as a justification for aggressive imperialism, claiming that weaker countries will inevitably fall to more powerful ones. This elitist dogma extends to the fascist concept of an authoritarian leader, a superman with superior moral and intellectual powers—borrowed from the theories of philosopher Friedrich Nietzsche. This super leader would unite his people and carry on the vision of the totalitarian state.

World War II

The world experienced a decade of aggression in the 1930s that would culminate in World War II. This Second World War resulted from the rise of totalitarian regimes in Germany, Italy, and Japan. These militaristic regimes gained control as a result of the Great Depression experienced by most of the world in the early 1930s, and from the conditions created by the peace settlements following

World War I. The dictatorships established in each country encouraged expansion into neighboring countries. In Germany, Hitler strengthened the army during the 1930s. In 1936, Benito Mussolini's Italian troops took Ethiopia. From 1936-39, Spain was engaged in civil war involving Francisco Franco's fascist army, aided by Germany and Italy. In March 1938, Germany annexed Austria and in March 1939, Germany occupied Czechoslovakia. Italy took Albania in April 1939. One week after Nazi Germany and the Union of Soviet Socialist Republics (USSR) signed the Treaty of Nonaggression, on September 1, 1939, Germany invaded Poland and World War II began. On September 3, 1939, Britain and France declared war on Germany after a U-boat sank the British ship *Athenia* off the coast of Ireland. Another British ship, the *Courageous*, was sunk on September 17. All the members of the British Commonwealth, except Ireland, soon joined Britain and France in their declaration of war.

The Anti-Nazi Underground Movement

During World War II an underground movement emerged in Western Europe organized by the Allies to undermine the German war machine. In France, Norway, Denmark, Holland, Belgium, Italy, and Greece, Allies created fighting forces trained in guerrilla warfare, and supported them through airdrops and radio communications from

Mary McCarthy   © Bettmann/Corbis

London. These resistance forces, led, for the most part, by American and British-trained officers, conducted industrial sabotage, espionage, and sneak attacks against the enemy, made and distributed propaganda, and organized escape routes for Allied prisoners of war. These activities contributed to the defeat of Germany and the end of World War II.

The Cold War

Soon after World War II, when Russian leader Joseph Stalin set up satellite communist states in Eastern Europe and Asia, the "Cold War" began, so-called because no actual fighting took place. The Cold War ushered in a new age of warfare and fear triggered by several circumstances: the United States's and the USSR's emergence as superpowers; each country's ability to use the atomic bomb; the communist expansion and the United States's determination to check it. Each side amassed stockpiles of nuclear weapons that could not only annihilate each country, but also the rest of world. Both sides declared the other the enemy and redoubled their commitment to fight for their own ideology and political and economic dominance.

As China fell to the Communists in 1949, Russia crushed the Hungarian revolution in 1956, and the United States adopted the role of world policeman, the Cold War accelerated. In 1950, the United

States resolved to help South Korea repel Communist forces in North Korea. By 1953, 33,629 American soldiers had been killed in the Korean War.

The Cold War induced anxiety among Americans, who feared both annihilation by Russians and the spread of communism at home. Americans were encouraged to stereotype all Russians as barbarians and atheists who were plotting to overthrow the US government and brainwash its citizens. The fear that communism would spread to the US led to suspicion and paranoia, and many suspected communists or communist sympathizers saw their lives ruined. This "Red Scare" was heightened by the indictments of ex-government official Alger Hiss (1950) and Julius and Ethel Rosenberg (1951) for passing defense secrets to the Russians. Soon, the United States would be engaged in a determined and often hysterical witch hunt for communists, led by Senator Joe McCarthy and the House of Representatives's Un-American Activities Committee (HUAC). (In 1954, McCarthy was censured by the Senate for his unethical behavior during the Committee sessions.) By the time of McCarthy's death in 1957, almost six million Americans had been investigated by government agencies because of their suspected Communist sympathies, yet only a few had been indicted.

CRITICAL OVERVIEW

When *Imaginary Friends* opened on Broadway on September 29, 2002, it received both positive and negative reviews. *Time* magazine's Richard Zoglin complains that the play has "two acts full of distractions and gimmicks" and claims, "what this play needs is Roger Rewrite." Yet Lisa D. Horowitz in her review for *Variety* praises Ephron's focus and structure. She comments, "Nora Ephron's Lillian Hellman . . . and Mary McCarthy . . . prove, quite entertainingly, that they are each other's own special hell." Horowitz adds that when Ephron mixes "fact with fiction in a way that would no doubt infuriate both of her protagonists, Ephron sticks to the broad outlines of the truth while adding drama and conflict to a static situation." She applauds Ephron's use of real people, which helps "[ground] events in reality." Commenting on Ephron's inclusion of music, Horowitz determines that "the device works, adding depth and helping to avoid the monotony inherent in what is essentially a talky two-hander."

Other reviews were mixed. John Lahr, in his review for *The New Yorker*, calls the play "gleeful" and writes that it "glitters with professionalism but to almost no point." He notes McCarthy's devotion to truth and Hellman's to story and comments, "in *Imaginary Friends*, sad to say, we get neither." Most reviewers praised the subject of the play, echoing Horowitz's assessment that "Ephron makes it clear she thinks these are writers worth reading, and worth writing about. . . . [S]he makes them pertinent to contemporary [audiences] as well."

CRITICISM

Wendy Perkins

Perkins is a professor of American and English literature and film. In this essay, Perkins examines the theme of fact verses fiction in relation to art in Ephron's play.

In his article on *Imaginary Friends* for *The Nation*, David Kaufman asserts that the play captures our attention because of the compelling questions it raises concerning "truth versus mendacity, fact versus fiction." He writes that the argument Lillian Hellman and Mary McCarthy have over these questions points to what he calls "one of the more troubling developments of the twentieth century," intensified in the twenty-first: "the culture's growing tendency to conflate fact with fiction, both diluting and polluting our reality."

Ephron's exploration of fact versus fiction in the play focuses attention not on the ways culture dilutes and pollutes reality, but on the complexities inherent in the artist's attempt to express reality. In her presentation of the often acerbic, always humorous confrontations between Hellman and McCarthy, Ephron illustrates the intricate relationship between art and experience.

Both women grapple in the play with the question of fact and fiction in art, but Hellman does so in a more obvious way. McCarthy's declaration to Dick Cavett that "every word [Hellman] writes is a lie, including 'and' and 'the,' " was, of course, a gross exaggeration, but it did have more than a note of truth to it. Hellman's most famous "lie" was her claim that "Julia" in her memoir, *Pentimento*, who, she wrote, helped fund the anti-Nazi movement during World War II, was based on her own experience. As Hellman's slander suit against McCarthy gained publicity, the identity of the real Julia—psychoanalyst Muriel Gardiner—surfaced. Subsequent study of Hellman's memoirs found other major and minor discrepancies.

MCCARTHY'S DECLARATION TO DICK CAVETT THAT 'EVERY WORD [HELLMAN] WRITES IS A LIE, INCLUDING 'AND' AND 'THE,' WAS, OF COURSE, A GROSS EXAGGERATION, BUT IT DID HAVE MORE THAN A NOTE OF TRUTH TO IT."

In *Imaginary Friends*, Ephron's focus on McCarthy's statement, and Hellman's subsequent suit against her, illuminates the ways that fact and fiction can be intermingled in art. Ephron suggests that the work of art cannot be separated from the artist. Readers would assume a non-fiction work like Hellman's *Pentimento*, which promises to provide an accurate recording of the details of the author's life, to be objective. Yet, New Historicist scholars insist that it is impossible to create a truly objective history, that even works called non-fiction are fictional constructs, as the author relies on memory or someone else's accounts of the past. The author's careful arrangement of what are considered to be facts into a history or biography completes the artist's vision of reality. Through her characterization of the two women, Ephron argues that each author brings her own subjective vision to her experience and that vision forms the basis of her art.

Ephron posits, through Muriel Gardiner's psychoanalysis of the two women, that Hellman's penchant for fabrication resulted from childhood incidents. Hellman, she argues, was traumatized by seeing her father's infidelity and being told to lie about it. As a result, she spent her life "telling lies and expecting to be applauded for it." As a scene from the film is played on stage, Hellman admits to McCarthy that some of the details of her story about Julia were fabricated. She alludes to the fictional nature of her memory when, after Jane Fonda as Hellman in *Julia* throws a typewriter out the window, Hellman declares, "that never happened."

Ephron illustrates the impact her father's infidelity had in a scene where Hellman remembers her childhood. Initially, her memories are quite theatrical.

WHAT
DO I READ
NEXT?

- Ephron's novel *Heartburn* (1983) chronicles the dissolution of her marriage to reporter Carl Bernstein. She later adapted the novel for the screen.

- Lillian Hellman's *Pentimento* (1973) is an autobiographical work that includes a story about a woman named Julia, a friend of Hellman's who worked for the underground during World War II.

- *Anne Frank: The Diary of a Young Girl*, published in English in 1952, chronicles the courageous life of its author, a gifted Jewish teenager, after she and her family went into hiding in Nazi-occupied Amsterdam. Anne later died in a German concentration camp.

- *Agents for Escape: Inside the French Resistance, 1939–1945* (1996) is a firsthand account of a member of the French Resistance, Andre Rougeyron. He helped downed Allied pilots return to England through an underground network of people. He was later captured and sent to the concentration camp at Buchenwald.

- Mary McCarthy's *The Group* (1963) traces the careers and relationships of a group of Vassar women from the time of their graduation until seven years later. This witty satire of American society in the 1930s follows the eight women as they struggle to live up to their ideals amid the general duplicity that surrounds them.

- McCarthy's *A Charmed Life* (1955) examines a collection of people who are defined by their historical moment.

She claims, "I was the sweetest-smelling baby in New Orleans," and comments to the audience, "you probably heard that about me." She tells romanticized stories of her relationships with the "wildly glamorous" children in the neighborhood. However, when Hellman sees her father embrace Fizzy, a young neighbor, she falls out of the tree. The adult Hellman picks her up and discovers that she is a doll, a fiction like her memories. The real Hellman tells of her promise to her nanny, Sophronia, to keep the truth about her father a secret.

Hellman's story about Julia could have also reflected her relationship with her mother, Julia Hellman. John MacNicholas, in his article on Hellman in the *Dictionary of Literary Biography*, Vol. 7, notes that while she and her mother had opposite personalities, Hellman's ties to her mother were quite strong and became a focus of some of her work.

Ephron suggests that Hellman's desire for self-promotion was another impetus for the creation of Julia. Insisting that she was friends with the true Julia, and that she smuggled money to her and so made a significant contribution to anti-Nazi activities during World War II, made the story Hellman told all the more compelling and more marketable.

When Muriel Gardiner speculates that she is the real Julia, Hellman refuses to agree but claims that it does not matter one way or the other since the two became famous as a result. Both Hellman and McCarthy acknowledge how difficult it was for women to become successful writers during their careers. The two women express a brief, ironic note of camaraderie on this point when they agree that they were invited to speak at Sarah Lawrence because they were token female writers.

McCarthy also accuses Hellman of lying about her relationship with Dashiell Hammett, whom the latter wrote about in her memoirs. Ephron implies that Hellman tried to compensate for her lack of beauty with a romanticized vision of her relationship with him when Hammett makes occasional appearances as Nick in the play, a character he wrote for the film *The Thin Man*. Hellman insists that he modeled Nick's wife Nora after her. McCarthy, however, argues that none of it happened and tells Hellman that her romantic vision of him is a "figment of [her] imagination. He was just a story."

While McCarthy continually insists throughout the play that she always tells the truth, she often undercuts herself. Gardiner reinforces this contradiction when she insists that the lies told to Mary about her parents caused her to make "a religion out of the truth," which turned into her "blind spot." This blind spot ironically causes her to fictionalize her memories. At one point, when McCarthy and Hellman are reminiscing about the past, McCarthy becomes quite theatrical in her declaration "we all lead our lives more or less in vain." When she adds that she is "trying to be brave" as she looks back on her past, Hellman responds with a note of reality when she insists that the two had great fun while they were writing, "drinking and flirting" and that they feuded "just so people would know who we were."

In a memory of her childhood, McCarthy creates a vivid picture of her life with her aunt and abusive uncle, but paints a romantic figure of her father. She tells Hellman a story that shows her father's heroism, but later admits it never happened.

McCarthy's truth, like Hellman's fiction, often becomes self-serving. She recalls a conversation with her friend about an interviewer in Paris who, she says, kept going on "all about dashing Lillian Hellman and frumpy me." Her remark about Hellman's lies first appeared in that interview, most likely as a counter to the reporter's praise about her nemesis. As she talks to her friend about her upcoming appearance on the Dick Cavett show, the two discuss how she can casually insert the line so it will appear spontaneous. These incidents suggest that McCarthy's fiction, which she claims is based on personal experience, is, like Hellman's memoirs, an intricate combination of fabrication and truth.

In the second act, Ephron inserts a song sung by two characters, Fact and Fiction, who address the complexities of the creative act. Together they sing, "when we do our number / it's something of an art / and now and then they even say; it's tough to tell us apart." In *Imaginary Friends*, Ephron illustrates, through the confrontations between her sharp-tongued combatants, that it is often difficult to separate truth from fiction in the process of artistic creation.

Source: Wendy Perkins, Critical Essay on *Imaginary Friends*, in *Drama for Students*, Thomson Gale, 2006.

Laura Carter

Carter is currently employed as a freelance writer. In this essay, Carter considers Ephron's discussion on the value of truth versus fiction.

The nature of truth in Nora Ephron's drama *Imaginary Friends* is illusive. The play is based on the real life feud of two of the most colorful literati

> " WHAT HAS TRANSPIRED BETWEEN THE TWO WRITERS SIMPLY IS WHAT IT IS. DESPITE A FEW EXISTENTIAL MOMENTS, THERE WILL BE NO GRAND RECONCILIATIONS, NO NEW LEVEL OF SELF-AWARENESS, NO FINAL RESOLUTION, JUST TWO BITTER WOMEN WHO CAN AGREE TO DISAGREE."

of the twentieth century, Mary McCarthy and Lillian Hellman. In creating this fictional confrontation, Ephron shuttles the audience through the drama of both Mary and Lillian's personal lives. The work takes the audience from their childhood experiences to Sarah Lawrence College, where their rivalry began and beyond, in an attempt to make sense of a lifetime of contempt led by two writers. The fantastic conceit that forms the basis for the work, a moment in the afterlife where both Mary and Lillian meet to reopen old wounds, amplifies the unrealistic expectations inherent in such a reunion. Ultimately, the play does little to resolve their differences; rather, it questions whether the truth is indeed better, or stranger, than fiction.

Mary and Lillian spent time in Minneapolis, ran in the same intellectual circles, and enjoyed healthy writing careers; yet, they never met and managed to become obsessed with each other's respective careers. In Ephron's production, the lives of both Mary and Lillian unfold accordingly. Their childhood stories begin as parallel plot lines whose pivotal moments come in subsequent accounts during the play. As a small child, Lillian observes her father's affair and is instructed by an overprotective nurse to lie, then tells her not to "go through life making trouble for people." Mary reveals that she was orphaned at a young age, forced to live with an abusive uncle who saw her as spoiled and undeserving, claiming, "No one told us our parents were dead. No one ever told us."

The stories are retold by both women several times during the play, each time a bit more revealing until eventually, the temptation of both writers to edit each other's work takes hold. In act 2, scene 1, Mary again recounts the moment of her childhood when her uncle punishes her for allegedly taking a small butterfly tin from her brother. As the scene progresses, a cheerful Lillian skips towards the house. Hearing Mary scream, she bangs on the door before going inside to retrieve Uncle Myers, flinging him out the door. Says Mary to Lillian, "Hey, wait a minute. It was my uncle, and my house—and my story. And now you're the queen of it." Realizing that in Lillian's account they are now hiding in a fig tree, Mary exclaims, "There are no fig trees in Minneapolis."

In act 2, scene 6, a new account of Lillian's experience is retold by Mary. It begins with Mary chastising Lillian for telling her that the scene is "very Tennessee Williams" and that despite the hot day, Lillian should "lose the fan." After repeated criticism from Mary, Lillian exclaims, "I give up. You write the scene." Mary does indeed write it and, instead of coming to Lillian's rescue, she takes the opportunity to embellish on the affair between her father and Fizzy, injecting great romance and passion, before adding a few less than favorable comments about her rival into the hurtful dialogue. Mary takes her digs at Lillian using dialogue. In Mary's version of the story, Lillian's father characterizes his daughter as "that nosy child of mine." His lover asserts, "She spies on me when I'm getting dressed, and she tells lies, too, Max, she tells lies all the time, everything she says is a lie." A furious Lillian responds, leading the two in a round of childish insults, before both fall from a fictional fig tree.

Ephron's clever interweaving of both Mary and Lillian's stories serves an important purpose. Each childhood story is told in a repetitive fashion, eventually uniting both characters. By sharing intimate details of their own lives, the assumption naturally would be that each writer would forge an emotional bond, bringing them closer together. To have both writers rewrite the script of their lives also seems to be an excellent means of reconciliation. Both Mary and Lillian's insights may lead to a better understanding of one another's contributions to their longstanding battle. Ephron takes a different path, allowing her characters to drive the outcome of their afterlife reunion. Having these two writers rework the events of their lives, sometimes working with input from one another, sometimes turning over their story completely, reveals how bias works to further personal agendas. For example, Mary is offered the chance to rewrite Lillian's

childhood tale, but instead of defending Lillian, she uses the opportunity to take a few digs at her in an extremely vulnerable moment.

Both women retell each other's stories the way they see fit, which leads the audience to the conclusion that the truth about their relationship is largely subjective. Ephron may take license with the dialogue, but the events driving it are real, a product of careful research. In her introduction, the playwright concedes that when she met Lillian, she was initially under her spell, before revealing that the "fabulous stories she entertained her friends with" were, in fact, "stories." But she also came to understand in Mary "an intellectual and a star in a world that had a pathological distrust not just of commercial success but also of stars." Lillian was that star. Nor does she side with either character. Concludes Ephron, "How could you take sides after all? They were both wrong. And at the same time, they were both right."

Ultimately Ephron's reconstruction of history heightens the dance between Mary and Lillian, and the audience discovers that where there is passion there is fire. In scene 7, a fictional brush with Muriel Gardiner, psychoanalyst and model for Lillian's "Julia," forms the climax for the play. Mary and Lillian create a courtroom scenario, calling Gardiner to the stand, where she eventually analyzes the character of both writers. The two commiserate after Gardiner's grand exit, then argue the reason for their union in the afterlife. The fight crescendos as the two exchange comments, sling insults at each other, then in a moment of burning hatred, grab each other and kiss.

This dramatic gesture serves as the climax to the play, leading to a moment of personal reflection with each opponent pondering what has led up to their eternal union. To Lillian, all of this pondering leads her to conclude, "I'm just a story. So are you. The question is, who gets to tell it?" Mary, however, insists that the truth and the story are interdependent upon one another. This is betrayed in a demand directed toward Lillian: "Don't tell me there's no such thing as the truth. I don't believe that." In Lillian's world, however, artistic license trumps the truth. She bases her stories on the lives of others rather than her own, which in her estimation, makes for a more exciting story. For Mary, the integrity of a tale is only as sound as the facts supporting it.

The comment from Gardiner forming the basis for the play's conclusion informs the entire work—that the truth is indeed relative, a construct often based on the individual perspective rather than group conscience. Ephron, in her characterization of both Mary and Lillian, hits both characters with insights the audience may have, at this point in the work, concluded on their own. Gardiner looks to both writers, insisting she "has something to tell." To Mary, she says, "Someone once told you a lie, a terrible lie, so you made a religion out of the truth." She sees this event as a blind spot for Mary, claiming that "you never understood how subjective and elusive and abstract the truth is—you simply thought that if you could prove someone was telling a lie, you'd won." To Lillian, she offers,

> You, on the other hand, witnessed a traumatic version of a primal scene, and then you were persuaded to lie about it. So you spent your life telling lies and expecting to be applauded for it.

Ephron frames the climax around a much anticipated speech that could very well resolve the tension between Mary and Lillian. In this instance, self-knowledge could lead to self-empowerment, alleviating the need to stand on false principal and self-righteous indignation. In this existential moment, rather than digest and embrace Gardiner's accurate analysis, both writers choose to turn away from it, dismissing the assessment as little more than "A perfect example of the limits of Freudian analysis." Instead, it launches them into a new round of finger-pointing. Lillian claims to have sued Mary to shorten her life, and Mary counters with "And I'm glad I outlived you."

In Ephron's attempts to make sense out of the scenario, the playwright thoroughly explores key moments of each character's life, sometimes bringing them together, sometimes pulling them apart, sifting through both Mary and Lillian's history to make sense of a lifetime spent on intense hatred, with no resolution. What has transpired between the two writers simply is what it is. Despite a few existential moments, there will be no grand reconciliations, no new level of self-awareness, no final resolution, just two bitter women who can agree to disagree. Ephron concludes that this was the only logical outcome, sharing that she "could perhaps end up with something that was not the truth, and not the story, but something else, to begin with, a play."

A strong human component surfaces in Ephron's nonsensical fight. Her work is more than mere sentimental recollection; it raises questions concerning the fine line that can be drawn between fact and fiction and, consequently, that getting to the truth of any matter is, at times, challenging if not impossible. Her character study reaches to the very depths of human experience, of the curiosity

Lillian Hellman   © Oscar White/Corbis

everyone shares about the dynamics of human interaction and the nature of relationships. It seeks not to draw any direct moral conclusions about either writer but to emphasize that there is no likely conclusion to the story, no resolution to the conflict between these two creative divas.

Nora Ephron's *Imaginary Friends* is more than an amusing play about a fictitious reunion that never occurred. Depictions of both Hellman and McCarthy support the idea that human beings are all limited, only as receptive to being taught as they are teachable. In a more contemporary world driven by self-help, therapy and psychotropic medication, there simply are no certainties in the realm of human experience. The meaning of truth, the nature of fame, and the value of integrity are all relative in Ephron's world. Happiness is relative. And of their ever being any resolution to the McCarthy versus Hellman battle—it depends on who is writing the story.

Source: Laura Carter, Critical Essay on *Imaginary Friends*, in *Drama for Students*, Thomson Gale, 2006.

David Kaufman

In the following review, Kaufman describes Ephron's play in light of its being her first.

The public feud between Mary McCarthy and Lillian Hellman continues to warrant our attention

> BUT EVEN IF THE COMIC-BOOK TONE SEEMS, AT FIRST, TO TRIVIALIZE HELLMAN AND MCCARTHY, IT ULTIMATELY BRINGS THEM DOWN TO A HUMAN SCALE, WHERE THEIR FOIBLES ARE WRIT LARGE, ENABLING US TO SEE THAT ON ONE LEVEL THEIR WAR REALLY STEMMED FROM THE CLASH OF TWO OUTSIZED PERSONALITIES VYING FOR PUBLIC ATTENTION."

long after its two vehement opponents have left the stage. To be sure, the nature of their dispute transcended the specific questions it raised regarding Hellman's misrepresentation of her past. Truth versus mendacity, fact versus fiction, call it what you will—at the heart of their argument was one of the more troubling developments of the twentieth century, which has only intensified as we've moved into the twenty-first: the culture's growing tendency to conflate fact with fiction, both diluting and polluting our reality.

In retrospect, the war between the Jewish leftist Hellman and the Catholic liberal McCarthy seems to have been inevitable. Hellman was a playwright and memoirist who clearly believed in a writer's artistic license to embroider. Though McCarthy based some of her novels on her own life, she was a stickler—and ultimately a crusader—for the truth.

What might be viewed as their lifelong rivalry culminated in 1980, when McCarthy famously said of Hellman during a TV interview with Dick Cavett: "Every word she writes is a lie, including 'and' and 'the.'" In spite of Hellman's bringing a $2.25 million lawsuit against her, McCarthy has been vindicated over the years, as we've come to learn that the plaintiff indeed lied about any number of things in her ostensibly autobiographical trilogy: *An Unfinished Woman, Pentimento* and *Scoundrel Time.*

While the hyperbolic thrust of McCarthy's remark would probably have proven indefensible in a court of law, Hellman's charges never made it to trial—not until now, that is, via the playful and bitchy imagination of Nora Ephron. In *Imaginary Friends,* her new "play with music" at the Ethel Barrymore Theatre, Ephron has these grande dames of American letters confront each other in a handsome and stylish red set in hell, where they bicker over everything, from how often they actually met to how the play that contains them should be staged. (When a relatively sedate McCarthy asks if there really has to be music, the more flamboyant Hellman says, "Why not? We have musicians.")

It's both sad and ironic to realize that while Hellman's own plays are produced with less and less frequency, *Imaginary Friends* is at least the third play to feature her as a main character, following William Luce's *Lillian* and Peter Feibleman's *Cakewalk.* (Neil Simon has written a fourth, *Rose and Walsh,* based on Hellman's relationship with Dashiell Hammett; it is to begin previews in Los Angeles at the end of this month.) But then, as Robert Brustein wrote in his tribute to Hellman shortly after her death in 1984, "It may be that her life, with its strong alliances, combative courage, and abrupt domestic scenes, will eventually be considered her greatest theater." And in a witty defense of his subject's tendency to dissemble, biographer Carl Rollyson also emphasized Hellman's sense of theatricality when he claimed, "She suspended her own sense of disbelief."

Ephron herself is no stranger to the blurring of fact and fiction, having based her novel *Heartburn* on her marriage to Carl Bernstein, which she subsequently adapted for a Mike Nichols film of the same name. She is best known as a writer for the screen (in addition to *Heartburn,* she wrote the screenplays for *Silkwood* and *When Harry Met Sally . . .*) as well as film director (*Sleepless in Seattle* and *You've Got Mail*). In view of her uneven script for *Imaginary Friends,* it comes as no surprise to read in the program that this is her first play.

Without really having anything new to say about either Hellman or McCarthy, Ephron has found a highly unusual way for saying it, via comic routines, music-hall numbers and old-fashioned vaudeville shtick. Her cartoony approach may seem inappropriately matched to such hardcore intellectuals, and it's bound to offend literary purists. But even if the comic-book tone seems, at first, to trivialize Hellman and McCarthy, it ultimately brings them down to a human scale, where their foibles are writ large, enabling us to see that on one level their war really stemmed from the clash of two outsized personalities vying for public attention.

Besides, given her frequent lunges for the limelight, Hellman in particular began to resemble something of a clown—albeit an outspoken one—in her later years. Consider what is doubtless the most familiar, lingering image of her: donning a fur coat for a ubiquitous Blackglama ad that coyly asked, "What becomes a legend most?" (How, one wonders, did Hellman ever reconcile that ad with her famous remark for the House Un-American Activities Committee: "I cannot and will not cut my conscience to fit this year's fashions"?)

When we first meet "Lillian" in *Imaginary Friends*, she assumes that same imperious Blackglama pose, with an extended hand elegantly displaying a cigarette. The play opens with her asking "Mary" if they ever met, and her being told that they had, "once or twice." It quickly backs up to visit Hellman's childhood in New Orleans, and then McCarthy's in Seattle and Minneapolis, where we view pivotal developments that Ephron suggests prompted the first to become a lifelong liar and the second a consistent seeker of truth.

The narrative proceeds to jump around in time and place as we meet the various men in their respective lives, and observe their initial confrontation at a writers' conference at Sarah Lawrence College in 1948, when McCarthy felt Hellman misrepresented the Spanish Civil War to some students. As it closes the first of two acts, the scene is actually—and quite humorously—played out twice, to accommodate their different memories of what transpired. The play climaxes with Ephron's invented trial, during which Muriel Gardiner takes the stand to say that she was the real one who helped smuggle money to fight the fascists during World War II, as opposed to Hellman, who stole her story for the "Julia" portion of *Pentimento* and made it her own.

The one constant throughout the play is Hellman's and McCarthy's seething anger at each other. ("I ruined your third act," says Mary. "I was your third act," rejoins Lillian.) But in her attempt to appeal to the widest possible Broadway audience, Ephron tends to oversimplify some of the rather complex issues she was compelled to cover. What follows is a typical exchange:

> Mary: I was the palest of pinkos. . . . I became a Trotskyite almost by chance.
>
> Lillian: No one here even knows what a Trotskyite is anymore.

> Mary: No one here knows what a Stalinist is, either. She was a Stalinist. Tell them what you believed.
>
> Lillian: The Stalinists believed that a certain amount of bad stuff was part of any revolution, and that it would eventually stop.
>
> Mary: And the Trotskyites believed that bad stuff was bad stuff and would lead to more bad stuff.

Such didactic catechism would quickly become tiresome if not for the wonderful delivery skills of Swoosie Kurtz and Cherry Jones. The offbeat comedian Kurtz portrays a brazenly haughty Hellman, and the patrician Jones plays a softer and more confident McCarthy. Though neither is giving what might be deemed an exact impersonation, each manages to evoke both the mannerisms and the vocal inflections of their real models with winning results. Though he only has time to present brief caricatures of his real-life counterparts, Harry Groener is equally effective playing everyone from Edmund Wilson and Dashiell Hammett to Philip Rahv and Stephen Spender. The production is also blessed with a first-rate ensemble of eight dancers and singers.

Although Ephron's scenario is overladen with cinematic jump-cuts and transitions, they are smoothly accomplished by Jack O'Brien's smart, staccato direction, which accentuates the theatricality of the enterprise. The evening is also nicely kept in motion by Marvin Hamlisch's tuneful, pastiche score and by Craig Carnelia's lyrics, which veer from being sophisticated and witty to pedestrian. As the tap-dancing, anthropomorphized "Frankie Fact" and "Dick Fiction" sing, with straw hats and canes, no less: "And since you're comfortable with which is which/Some performances we pull a switcheroo/Fact may in fact be Fiction/Out of his jurisdiction/Sometimes in fact there's fiction too."

Source: David Kaufman, Review of *Unfinished Women*, in *Nation*, Vol. 276, No. 3, January 27, 2003, p. 32.

SOURCES

Ephron, Nora, "Introduction," in *Imaginary Friends*, Vintage Books, 2002, pp. xi–xv.

Horowitz, Lisa D., Review of *Imaginary Friends*, in *Variety*, Vol. 388, No. 8, October 7, 2002, p. 32.

Kaufman, David, "Unfinished Women," in the *Nation*, Vol. 276, No. 3, January 27, 2003, p. 32.

Lahr, John, "Killing for Company," in the *New Yorker*, Vol. 78, No. 40, December 23, 2002, p. 163.

Zoglin, Richard, "Catfight! Broadway Resurrects a Famed Literary Spat," in *Time*, Vol. 160, No. 26, December 23, 2002.

FURTHER READING

Ephron, Nora, *Scribble, Scribble: Notes on the Media*, Knopf, 1978.
    Ephron collected here her hysterical columns and articles previously published in magazines like *Esquire* and *New York*.

Gelderman, Carol, ed., *Conversations with Mary McCarthy*, University Press of Mississippi, 1991.
    McCarthy discusses her life and work in a series of interviews.

Griffin, Alice, and Geraldine Thorsten, *Understanding Lillian Hellman*, Understanding Contemporary American Literature series, University of South Carolina Press, 1999.
    Griffin and Thorsten place Hellman's work into a historical context.

Grumbach, Doris, *The Company She Kept: A Revealing Portrait of Mary McCarthy*, Coward-McCann, 1967.
    Grumbach presents an intriguing account of McCarthy's life and relationships.

Hellman, Lillian, *Conversations with Lillian Hellman*, edited by Jackson Bryer, Literary Conversations series, University Press of Mississippi, 1986.
    Hellman sheds light on her writing process and the themes of her plays.

Podhoretz, Norman, *Ex-Friends: Falling Out with Allen Ginsberg, Lionel & Diana Trilling, Lillian Hellman, Hannah Arendt, and Norman Mailer*, Free Press, 1999.
    Podhoretz presents entertaining and insightful snapshots of Hellman's life and those of her contemporaries in the literary scene.

Rollyson, Carl, *Lillian Hellman: Her Legend and Her Legacy*, St. Martin's Press, 1998.
    In an examination of newly-discovered diaries, letters, and interviews, Rollyson offers insight into Hellman's life and work.

The Laramie Project

MOISÉS KAUFMAN
2000

Research for the *The Laramie Project*, Moisés Kaufman's internationally successful play, began one month after a horrific crime occurred in the city of Laramie, Wyoming. Members of Kaufman's theatrical group, Tectonic Theater Project, volunteered to travel with their director from New York City to the wide-open ranges of the West in order to gather in-person interviews from Laramie's populace. The idea was to capture the emotions, reflections, and reactions of the people who were most closely related to the crime—a brutal beating and subsequent death of a young college student. Was this a hate crime? Or was it a random, senseless assault and robbery? No matter which, Kaufman's objective was to learn through the town folks' raw responses how the issues of homosexuality, religion, class, economics, education, and non-traditional lifestyles were reflected through this crime. How did this crime define the culture, not just of this Western town, but of the entire United States?

In 1998, Matthew Shepard, a twenty-one-year-old gay student registered at the University of Wyoming, was tied to a cattle fence, beaten about the head, robbed, and left to die on a bitterly cold night in October. Eighteen hours later, he was accidentally discovered by a biker, who had trouble believing that the figure he saw attached to the fence was human. Police and ambulances were dispatched, and Shepard was taken to a local hospital; but this was all done to no avail. Shepard was beyond recovery. He never regained

Moisés Kaufman Photo by George De Sota. Getty Images

consciousness and died several days later due to his head injuries. Two local young men were charged with the crime.

The play is based on over 400 interviews with about 100 Laramie residents, as well as journal entries from the members of Tectonic Theater Project and Kaufman, as they reflect on their own reactions to the crime and to the interviews they carried out. It is structured as if it were a documentary as it attempts to re-enact the events that occurred on that fateful night.

The play opened at the Denver Theater Center in March 2000 and two months later moved to Union Square Theater in New York, where it ran for five months. Later, HBO, working with the Sundance Theater Lab, turned the play into a film, which Kaufman also directed. It was presented as the opening-night film at the 2002 Sundance Film Festival, with Robert Redford, the founder of Sundance, making a special appearance to introduce the movie. For his work, Kaufman received two Emmy Award nominations for director and writer of the film.

AUTHOR BIOGRAPHY

Moisés Kaufman is an award-winning director and playwright, whose plays have engrossed audiences around the world. He is also the founder and artistic director of the New York-based Tectonic Theater Project, the group that traveled to Wyoming with Kaufman to help research the play *The Laramie Project* (2000).

Kaufman was born and raised in Caracas, Venezuela. He attended a business school for a while but soon grew bored with that subject and joined a local dramatic group, Thespis. At the age of twenty-three, Kaufman decided he wanted to become a director. It was around this same time, writes Don Shewey for *American Theatre*, that Kaufman also came "to grips with his homosexuality" and decided to move to New York. While in the States, Kaufman continued to study his dramatic art at New York University.

Kaufman's homeland, however, has not forgotten him. Venezuela demonstrated its pride for its native son by presenting a retrospective of his work at the Consulate General of Venezuela in 1993. In 1999, Venezuela once again honored him with the Artist of the Year Award, presented by the Casa del Artista.

Kaufman's adopted home, the United States, has also celebrated Kaufman's creative genius by bestowing him with several prestigious awards. He won the Joe A. Callaway Award as writer and director of *Gross Indecency: The Three Trials of Oscar Wilde*, a play that ran for over 600 performances in New York City alone. First published in 1997, the play went on to win many other prizes, including the Lucille Lortel Award, the Outer Critics Circle Award, the Garland Award, and the GLAAD Media Award. This play, which explores what Victorian men and women thought about such topics as homosexuality, class, religion, and the British monarchy, also won the Lambda Book Award when the play was published as a book in 1998. It was the money made from the production of *Gross Indecency* that would finance Kaufman's subsequent and also extremely successful venture, *The Laramie Project*.

Kaufman directed the 2004 Pulitzer Prize and Tony Award-winning play *I Am My Own Wife*, a story about a German transvestite. In addition to his roles as director and writer, Kaufman has taught the art of direction at the 42nd Street Collective in New York. As of 2005, he was working on an original piece called *33 Variations*, a story inspired by Beethovan's *Diabelli Variations*.

PLOT SUMMARY

Act 1

The Laramie Project begins with what is titled, "Moment." It is in this brief section (which is repeated throughout the play) that the members of Tectonic Theater Project read entries from the journals they have kept during the process of interviewing the people of Laramie. This repeated section also affords special characters a chance to deliver longer monologues than those given in the rest of the play, which is set up as interviews. After an opening comment by the narrator, one of Laramie's long-time residents provides a bit of personal history about living in Laramie. Through this narration, the audience also gains some insights into the history of the town. Other people join in: some are newcomers to the town; others have lived in Laramie for a long time. All of them provide background information on what it is like, in general, to be involved in the culture of the town. This sets up the atmosphere of the play. It gives the audience an idea of what life was like before the murder of Matt Shepard.

The tension of the plays turns when Jedadiah Schultz begins to talk. This is the first time that there is an allusion to the fact that something seriously wrong has happened to Laramie—that the town has changed. Jedadiah begins with the statement: "It's hard to talk about Laramie now." Then he continues: "If you would have asked me before, I would have told you Laramie is a beautiful town." Things have obviously changed.

Another "Moment" is provided. In this one, Rebecca Hilliker, a college professor, offers her opinions of the students. They are different from ones she has taught before in other towns, in other states. They speak their mind. They have strong opinions, which Hilliker likes because this creates a "dynamic in education." The "Moment" next changes focus, returning to the thoughts of Jedadiah, who relates the story of how he won a scholarship to the University by performing a scene from the play about homosexuality, *Angels in America*. He concludes by stating that his parents were opposed to his doing this and did not show up for his performance. His statements begin to demonstrate the chasm in the community between those who are open-minded about homosexuality and those who are not.

The play returns to the interview format, with several more community members giving their views of the town. They provide more history, such

- *The Laramie Project* was adapted as a film by HBO in 2001. It stared Christina Ricci, Steve Buscemi, Peter Fonda, Janeane Garofalo, Dylan Baker, Amy Madigan, and many others.

as the presence and influence of the railroads. Marge Murray discusses the class distinction that she feels between those who are educated and those who are not. But overall, Marge believes that the general sentiment of the people is "live and let live." However, when Marge is told that what she is saying will eventually end up in a play, she decides that she had better not tell the interviewer everything that she knows.

In the next "Moment," Andy Paris, a member of Tectonic Theater Project, reveals that they have finally come across someone who really knew Matthew Shepard. This person is Doc O'Connor, a limousine driver who befriended Shepard. Doc provides a description of Shepard, depicting him as a slightly built young man, who was not afraid of speaking his mind. The next few people who are interviewed continue with a description of Shepard. They talk about how friendly he was despite his initial shyness.

Doc reappears, and he provides more background information about the people of Laramie, stating that Shepard was by far not the only gay person in town. Most gay people of the town will not make this information public, Doc believes, but that does not mean that they do not exist. Doc also believes that the overall belief that underlies the community is that of "live and let live."

Next, the interviews switch to a variety of religious opinions. A Baptist minister appears; his message from the pulpit is that the Bible does not condone homosexuality. A representative of the Mormon Church reinforces this statement. A member of the Unitarian Church speaks next; this person is open-minded about homosexuality. Then a young Muslim woman is interviewed. She talks about how difficult she found it to wear a scarf, a symbol of her religion's prescribed modesty. She believes that people in the community challenged her right to wear it.

The scene changes to that of the Fireside Bar, the last place that Shepard was seen alive. The owner and the bartender are interviewed. Matt Galloway, the bartender, relates what happened in the bar on the night that Shepard was killed. It was in the bar that the accused murderers, Aaron McKinney and Russell Henderson, go over to Shepard, talk to him, and later leave with him.

In the next section there is a discussion about McKinney and Henderson. Residents give their opinions about the young men, most of them talking about how nice the two boys are. Henderson, they say, was an Eagle Scout. McKinney was a "good kid."

The last section of the first act provides the description of how Aaron Kreifels finds Shepard after he was beaten and left for dead. There is also a statement from Reggie Fluty, the first police officer on the scene and from Dr. Cantway, the emergency room doctor who treats Shepard upon his arrival at the hospital.

Act 2

Act 2 begins with an account of how the media arrived in Laramie after the news story about Shepard was released. There are also comments from the people of Laramie about how they responded to the media, as well as how they responded to the news. There is disbelief, anger, and fear. At the arraignment, most of the people who witnessed it broke down in tears. There are discussions that question how such a thing could have happened in Laramie.

Interspersed between various interviews are medical updates on the physical condition of Shepard, who had fallen into a coma. Meanwhile, both McKinney and Henderson plead not guilty to the charges. Citizens reflect on how they might have prevented this from happening. The bartender, Matt Galloway, believes he should have stepped in and stopped Shepard from driving away with McKinney and Henderson, sensing that the two young men were looking for trouble.

Reggie Fluty tells her story about finding Shepard. She also relates the fear she has of having contacted AIDS from having handled Shepard's bloody body without gloves. She must go through a series of tests to see if she is infected.

Jedadiah reflects on Shepard's beating and questions his minister's belief that it is wrong to be a homosexual. Several other residents keep hammering

home their concepts that homosexuality is against God's wishes. There is a vigil, organized by the Catholic priest. But none of the other ministers will attend. During the homecoming parade, a large group of Laramie residents come together, marching behind a banner for Shepard. As the parade winds around town, the group keeps growing in size.

There is another medical update. Shepard has died.

Act 3

A funeral is arranged for Shepard. It is held in the Catholic Church. Not attending is Reverend Fred Phelps, who makes a statement that even God has hate. And the Reverend believes it is his job to preach God's hate. "WE [sic] love that attribute of God, and we're going to preach it. Because God's hatred is pure." The Reverend adds: "If God doesn't hate fags, why does he put 'em in hell?"

This causes a reaction in Romaine Patterson; she organizes a group of friends who decide to dress up as angels after they hear that the Reverend is coming to Laramie for Henderson's trial. "There'll be ten to twenty of us that are angels— and what we're gonna do is we're gonna encircle Phelps . . . and because of our big wings—we are gonna com-plete-ly block him."

There is the jury selection scene and then a scene in which Henderson changes his plea from not guilty to guilty. Henderson makes a statement that he is sorry. The judge, however, does not believe Henderson is truly remorseful and sentences him to life in prison. A year later, McKinney is put on trial. During the trial, a tape of his confession is heard. The details of the beating are related. The jury finds him guilty of felony murder, which means he could have been given the death sentence. Shepard's father, however, asks that he be given life in prison instead.

> I would like nothing better than to see you die, Mr. McKinney. However, this is the time to begin the healing process. To show mercy to someone who refused to show any mercy. Mr. McKinney, I am going to grant you life, as hard as it is for me to do so, because of Matthew.

CHARACTERS

Sherry Aanenson

Sherry is Russell Henderson's (one of the men convicted of Matt Shepard's death) landlord. She found Russell to be "so sweet."

Baptist Minister

The Baptist Minister (who does not want his name used) believes that it is stated in the Bible that homosexuality is wrong.

Stephen Belber

Stephen is one of the members of Tectonic Theater Project who traveled to Laramie, conducted interviews, helped to write the play, and played himself, as well as several other characters in the play.

Dr. Cantway

Dr. Cantway is an emergency room doctor at Ivinson Memorial Hospital in Laramie. He helps try to save Matt Shepard's life. He describes Matt's injuries as looking as if he had been in an accident in a car going "eighty miles an hour."

Catherine Connolly

Catherine is a professor at the University of Wyoming in Laramie and she considers herself to be the "first 'out' lesbian or gay faculty member on campus." She feels fear grip her after the death of Matt Shepard and is afraid to walk down the street.

Rob DeBree

Rob is a detective sergeant for the Albany County Sheriff's Department in Laramie. He is the chief investigator of Matt Shepard's murder.

Philip Dubois

Philip is the president of the University of Wyoming. He is a relative newcomer to Wyoming but prefers it to big-city life. He used to feel that Laramie was a safe place to raise children.

Tiffany Edwards

Tiffany is a local Laramie reporter. She describes the outside media that descend on Laramie after the news of Matt Shepard's death is broadcast as "predators."

Reggie Fluty

Reggie is the policewoman who responds to the 911 call and has to be tested for HIV after attempting to save Matt Shepard's life. She is the first police official on the scene.

Leigh Fondakowski

Leigh is a member of Tectonic Theater Project who traveled to Laramie to conduct interviews. She is a character in the play but does not play herself or any other characters.

Matt Galloway

Matt was the bartender at the Fireside bar. He was also a student at the University of Wyoming. He witnessed Matt Shepard leaving with Russell Henderson and Aaron McKinney on the night of the murder. He later regretted not having done something to prevent the events that happened later that night. He disbelieves that Shepard would have approached these two men as some other people believed.

Jim Geringer

Jim is the governor of Wyoming. He makes a statement against the "heinous crime," but falls short of calling it a hate crime. He is challenged by a reporter who asks him why he has not pushed for hate crime legislation.

Amanda Gronich

Amanda is a member of Tectonic Theater Project who went to Laramie and conducted interviews. She plays herself and several other characters in the play.

Russell Henderson

Russell is twenty-one years old when he offers Matt Shepard a ride home, then beats and robs him and leaves him to die. He later changes his plea from not guilt to guilty of the crime and is sentenced to life in prison.

Rebecca Hilliker

Rebecca is the head of the theater department at the University of Wyoming. She has recently moved to Wyoming and found the people there to be generally nice to one another. She states that she likes the fact that her students are such "free thinkers," unlike other students she has had. "You may not like their opinions," she says, "but they are honest."

Sergeant Hing

Hing is a detective at the Laramie Police Department and third generation resident. He offers a history of Laramie in the beginning of the play.

Sherry Johnson

Sherry was an administrative assistant at the University of Wyoming. She is a bit disheartened by the news coverage that the death of Matt Shepard has received, while the death of a Laramie policeman receives no attention at all.

Aaron Kreifels

Aaron is a student at the University of Wyoming. He was riding his bike the night Matt Shepard was murdered. He found Matt tied to the fence and called an ambulance. He felt that God had wanted him to find Matt and that is why he took a different route on his bike.

Doug Laws

Doug is the leader of the Mormon Church in Laramie. He believes that the word of God proclaims that "a family is defined as one woman and one man and children."

Aaron McKinney

Aaron is one of the young men who offered to drive Matt Shepard home on the night he was murdered. He is put on trial and found guilty.

Bill McKinney

Bill is the father of Aaron McKinney. He makes the statement that if this had been a murder of a heterosexual man, "this never would have made the national news." He is concerned that his son will be proven guilty before he even gets a trial.

Matt Mickelson

Matt is the owner of the Fireside Bar, the place where Matt Shepard was last seen. He offers some history of the place.

Marge Murray

Marge is mother to Reggie Fluty. She was very worried about the possibility of Reggie contacting AIDS from Matt Shepard after Reggie administered medical services to him. Marge has lived in Laramie all her life and knows just about everyone. She offers a cultural history of the place, but when she finds out that all this information might be used in a play, she decides not to tell her interviewers all that she knows.

Doc O'Connor

Doc was a limousine driver and had driven Matt Shepard to Colorado on occasion. He is from the East Coast, originally, but has lived in Wyoming for quite some time. He offers his reflections on the type of people who live in Laramie. He says that he liked Matt Shepard " 'cause he was straightforward."

Andy Paris

Andy was a member of Tectonic Theater Project who went to Laramie to conduct interviews and to help write the play. Andy plays himself as well as several other characters in the play.

Romaine Patterson

Romaine is a close friend of Matt Shepard's. She says she used to call him "Choo-choo." What she remembers most of him is his "beaming smile." He was friendly with everyone, she says. At his funeral, she and a group of her friends dress up in angel costumes in order to block the Fred Phelps' group of protestors.

Jon Peacock

Jon, a professor of political science, was Matt Shepard's academic advisor at the University of Wyoming. He helped Matt open up when he first came to Laramie. Matt wanted to work on issues of human rights, Jon states. And when Matt figured this out, he was excited by it.

Reverend Fred Phelps

Fred is a minister in Laramie. He is extremely anti-gay and comes to the funeral with a group of people to protest. He is concerned that everyone is making "Matthew Shepard into a poster boy for the gay lifestyle."

Greg Pierotti

Greg is a member of Tectonic Theater Project who went to Laramie to collect interviews and help with the writing of the play. Greg plays himself as well as several other characters in the play.

Barbara Pitts

Barbara is a member of Tectonic Theater Project who went to Laramie to collect interviews and help with the writing of the play. She played herself as well as several other characters in the play. She records the words of a sign she sees upon entering Laramie. It reads: "Hate is not a Laramie value."

Father Roger Schmit

Roger is a very outspoken Catholic priest in Laramie. He sets up a vigil as Matt lies dying in the hospital. He is disappointed when other ministers in the town will not become involved.

Jedadiah Schultz

Jedadiah is a student at the University of Wyoming. He used to love Laramie, but after Matt Shepard's death, he's afraid that everyone in the world will look at Laramie as another Waco—a place of a violent crime. Jedadiah won a scholarship to the University based on a performance he did, a scene from the play *Angels in America*, which deals with homosexuality. His parents refused to come to see the play. Later, despite his minister's statements that homosexuality is wrong, Jedadiah comes to his own conclusions.

Dennis Shepard

Dennis is the father of Matt Shepard. He makes a very emotional statement at the trial of Henderson, stating that he would not seek the death penalty.

Lucy Thompson

Lucy was Russell Henderson's grandmother. She makes a plea for his life at his trial.

Harry Woods

Harry is an older man who lives in the heart of Laramie. He offers the information that he is a homosexual and he secretly celebrates the addition of hundreds of people who join the homecoming parade in honor of Matt Shepard.

THEMES

Prejudice

The theme of prejudice is an undercurrent in *The Laramie Project*. Whether it is a prejudice caused by class, education, economics, religion, or sexual preference, when one person rigidly believes in one side of a concept and cannot perceive the other side and more importantly, will not tolerate someone else accepting another side, prejudice rears its head. In this play, the town must deal with its prejudice. Some of the people in the play represent the extreme edges of prejudice, such as the Reverend Fred Phelps, who believes so deeply that homosexuality is wrong that he preaches that God, himself, has hate. Other people, such as the parents of Jedadiah Schultz, who refuse to go to Jedadiah's tryout for a scholarship because their son is acting out a scene that involved homosexuality, have prejudice that is less strident. They miss the opportunity to share in their son's important moment. But this prejudice, at least in this one act, causes no physical harm to their son. Whether the accused murderers of Matthew Shepard were prejudiced against homosexuals or just used that as an attempt to excuse their murderous actions is not clear. In other words, the question remains, did they beat Matthew so severely because they did not like homosexuals or would they have done the same to any other student whom they might have robbed that night?

Marge Murray talks briefly about a prejudice that is possibly based on a combination of class, education, and economics. There are those without an education who work minimum-wage jobs and those who work at the university, she says, splitting the town into two different groups. She insinuates that one part of the population looks down on the other, which is where prejudice begins.

After the murder of Matthew Shepard, some members of the gay community in Laramie fear for their lives because they are concerned that other straight people in town might want to do the same to them. Their fears are based not only on the prejudice people might hold against the gay members of town but also on the prejudice that some of the gay community might hold against the townspeople. Yes, there was a murder that might have been a hate crime. But the fear that someone in the straight community might commit a similar crime is in some ways another form of prejudice. The stereotyping of a macho cowboy is just as much a prejudice as that of a stereotyping of a gay person.

Hate Crimes

There is a discussion in part of this play about why the murder of Matthew Shepard received so much media attention. After all, the statement goes, there was a policeman who was killed during the same period, and no one paid much attention to it. Aaron McKinney's father also makes the statement that if Matthew Shepard had been a heterosexual, not as much would have been made of the crime. So what is the difference? Why was Shepard's murder so heinous? For some reason, a random murder, such as one that might occur during a robbery, seems less sensational. Whereas a crime committed out of hate seems more pointed. Is it the attitude behind the crime that arouses so much attention? Currently there is a national debate going on as courts attempt to define hate crimes. Are the definitions to include crimes committed against disabled people, people of color, or of different nationalites? What about crimes against people of a different sexual orientation? And how does one prove that the crime was a hate crime? There are no conclusions made in this play. The facts are presented. The interpretation of the facts is left for the audience to think about. Was Shepard's death the result of a hate crime? The facts, as well as the media attention, seem to say yes. Or was it a random crime with no premeditation or specific hate? The truth may never be known.

Conflict

Conflict drives a dramatic work, and this play has a lot of it. There is the obvious conflict between those who live a gay lifestyle and those who live a straight lifestyle. There is also the conflict between the various religions and their interpretations of the

TOPICS FOR FURTHER STUDY

- Find an organization that supports gay rights in your community. Gather information about this group and prepare a paper that covers such issues as current legislation, the challenges that face homosexuals in your community, the history of homosexuals as a group, and common political goals of homosexuals.

- Matthew Shepard was majoring in political science at the University of Wyoming at the time of his death. He was interested in the issue of human rights. Choose a specific country and research that country's human rights' issues. What legislation has been passed? What is the history of the fight for human rights in that country? What are some of that country's major organizations that focus on human rights?

- Research hate crimes in the world. First, what is the definition of a hate crime? How do hate crimes differ from other types of crimes? What are the statistics of hate crimes in each country? Which countries have laws that specifically address hate crimes? Since the passing of legislation in each country, have the incidents of hate crimes decreased?

- Read Tony Kushner's *Angels in America.* Try to figure out which scene in that play might have been used by Jedadiah Schultz for his competition for a scholarship to the University of Wyoming. Memorize the scene and perform it in front of your class.

- Pretend to be the defense attorney for Aaron McKinney. Prepare the closing remarks that you would present to the jury in an attempt to save his life. Find some reason that McKinney should live, and build an emotional plea that might sway some of the jurors.

Bible or their spiritual value systems. There is also the conflict between parents and children, especially in the case of Jedadiah Schultz and his parents, who do not want him associating with anything that has to do with homosexuality. But there are also internal conflicts, such as those expressed by Jedadiah. He wants to believe that his parents and his minister are right. But he senses that something is wrong with their beliefs against homosexuality. So Jedadiah struggles within himself, trying to come to terms with the conflict between the basic tenets of the adults in his life and his own experiences.

Another emotional conflict revolves around the death penalty. Is it justified to kill someone who has killed another? Should the accused murderers be given death sentences? The most poignant conflict is the one that occurs in the mind of Dennis Shepard, the father of Matthew. He admits that he would like to see McKinney receive the death penalty for having murdered his son. But he concludes that Matthew would not want that. So Dennis Shepard has an internal conflict, much like Jedadiah, and finally concludes that he will defer to what he believes his son would have called for—an end to violence.

STYLE

Docudrama

The docudrama is a fact-based representation of real events. Unlike other forms of drama, the docudrama tries to represent the truth of an event that really happened. To think of it in another way, you might say that a docudrama is a nonfiction play.

The Laramie Project is a docudrama. It was written as if it were an actual documentary. Moisés Kaufman took his group, Tectonic Theater Project, to Laramie, Wyoming, to gather interviews concerning the murder of Matthew Shepard. This was a real event, and the interviews were given by real citizens of Laramie, where the murder occurred. The point of the play was to present the reactions of the people of Laramie to this horrendous crime. Kaufman believed that a reflection of this event by the people involved would provide a vehicle for discussion about homosexuality and hate crimes around the world. In order to present the information that he and his troupe had gathered as closely as possible to the truth, Kaufman created the illusion of reality by formatting his play, not as a fictional story, but rather as a re-enactment of those interviews. The fictional part, or artistic part, of the play was in how Kaufman pulled all this information together and made it tell a story. There were few props in the play, and only a handful of actors to play the multiple roles. The material was grouped according to themes that were used to build up the tension in the play. In a few cases, some of the Laramie residents asked that their names not be used, but overall, real names were used. And much of the dialogue came from the recorded interviews.

Structural Patterns

The format of the play followed a regular pattern, broken down into three different shapes. The first shape was called a "Moment." These were interspersed throughout the play and provided the audience with a more focused look at specific parts of the drama. Often, the Moments were reflections by Tectonic Theater Project members as they thought about their reactions to being in Laramie and having to face the comments and emotions of Laramie residents. At other times, the Moment sections were used to explore the reactions and emotions of specific residents in order to give the audience a deeper appreciation of some of the people's fears or beliefs.

In between the Moments sections, the play used short segments of interviews. Sometimes a person's comments would be interrupted by the comments of someone else, who either agreed or disagreed with them, offering the audience a balanced approach to the reactions to the murder. The interview segments were loosely structured to provide a sort of timeline to the events that lead up to the crime, as well as to those that took place afterwards. The interviews were also used to provide background information on the town of Laramie and the culture of the people who lived there.

The third portion of the pattern were direct announcements or speeches that were longer than the comments offered in interviews. For example, there are announcement made by the medical staff at the hospital where Matthew Shepard fought for his life. There were statements from the press, supposedly taken from actual news accounts. There was also the speech that Matthew's father presented in the courtroom.

Contrast and Juxtaposition

The snippets of conversations that were held between the members of Tectonic Theater Project and the residents of Laramie are arranged in such a way in the presentation of the play that the audience feels the emotions of the people who felt them. In order to do this, Kaufman has placed actual statements in positions of contrast or juxtaposition— either against one another or complimenting one another. For example, in one section of the play there are a series of comments offered by various religious leaders of the town. Some of these leaders are very much against homosexuality, while others have more open minds concerning this lifestyle. While one interviewee speaks of Biblical passages that provide the right to hate homosexuals, another religious person denies this, offering a counter-interpretation. Another example is provided when the interviews focus on the accused murderers. The people of Laramie cannot understand how two of their children could have committed such an awful crime. In order to present the emotions they are feeling, or to further enhance these emotions, Kaufman offers the audience not only a discussion of the crime and its hideous details, not only the scene in which it is noted that Matthew's face was washed in his tears, not only the transcript of McKinney's confession of the crime, but also comments by people who remember what a sweet child McKinney was.

Another example is the various comments by people of the town who claim that the overall atmosphere of the people was a "live and let live" attitude. There are claims made that most people do not mind that one person or another might be a homosexual. It is nobody's business but their own. But in contrast to that opinion are the comments offered by gay members of the community, who express their fear for their own lives.

HISTORICAL CONTEXT

Gay Rights

The Society for Human Rights, established in Chicago in 1924, was the first organization in the United States that promoted the rights of people who classified themselves as homosexuals. But it would take almost thirty more years before a national gay rights group would be founded. That came in the establishment of the Mattachine Society, headed by Harry Hay, whom many people consider the father of the gay rights movement. Five years later, in 1956, a group devoted completely to women, the Daughters of Bilitis, was created to bring together a focused movement specifically for lesbians. But it was during the 1960s, a time when the attention of the nation was focused on civil rights for African Americans and for women, that the movement for gay rights truly gained momentum. One particular incident, called the Stonewall Riots, which occurred at a New York gay bar when customers resisted arrest, ignited the gay rights movement in the United States. This night in 1969 would go down in history as the first time gay people fought back. As the news of the resisted arrests spread, the movement for gay rights became more determined and people began to demand civil and social rights for homosexuals.

Homosexual acts were illegal in the United States until 1962, when Illinois became the first state to decriminalize homosexual acts in the privacy of one's own home. By the end of the twentieth century most states had repealed these laws that prohibited homosexual acts. Those states that continued to enforce laws against homosexual acts were made invalid by a Supreme Court ruling in 2003 in the case *Lawrence* v. *Texas*, which invalidated the criminal prohibition of homosexual acts.

In the twenty-first century, the fight for gay rights is focused on civil unions and the right for same-sex marriage. Although this is a contentious issue in the United States, several European countries and several provinces in Canada do recognize same-sex marriage.

Matthew Shepard

Matthew Shepard was born in Casper, Wyoming, in 1976. He attended college first at Catawba and Casper Colleges before transferring to the University of Wyoming in Laramie, where he was majoring in political science. On the night of October 6, 1998, Matthew left the Fireside Bar in Laramie with Aaron McKinney and Russell Henderson. Eighteen hours later, Matthew was found alive but unconscious, tied to a cattle fence outside of Laramie. After being taken to the Poudre Valley Hospital in Fort Collins, it was determined that he suffered from a skull fracture that extended from the back of his head to the front of his right ear. He also had several deep lacerations on his face, neck, and head. The medical team decided that his injuries were too severe to operate. Matthew never regained consciousness and died on October 12, at 12:53 a.m.

McKinney and Henderson were apprehended shortly after the beating. The bloody gun that had been used to pistol-whip Matthew was found, as well as Matthew's shoes and credit card. McKinney's and Henderson's girlfriends supplied false alibis for the two suspected murderers.

Henderson pleaded guilty of the crime on April 5, 1999, and agreed to testify against McKinney in a plea bargain for his life. In exchange for his testimony, Henderson received two consecutive life sentences with no chance for parole. McKinney was tried and found guilty. After Matthew Shepard's father made a statement against the death penalty, McKinney was given two consecutive life sentences without chance of parole.

Wyoming

Ancient tribes lived in Wyoming at least 12,000 years ago. Remnants of this old culture can still be seen at places like Medicine Wheel, outside of Lovell. More modern tribes, like the Sioux, Shoshone, and Cheyenne were cultivating the land when the first white explorer, John Colter, arrived in 1807. Fur trappers soon followed and included such legendary names as Kit Carson and Jedediah Smith. When gold was discovered in California, more and more settlers drove their wagon trains through Wyoming, creating a need for re-stocking stations and military forts. Fort Laramie was one of the most important military installations in Wyoming. More people streamed through the state, and many of them decided to settle there, creating some of the first cattle ranches, where huge herds of buffalo once roamed.

Wyoming is known as the Equity State, being one of the first states in the Union to recognize the rights of women. In 1869, Wyoming was the first government in the world to give the right to vote to women. One year later, Ester Hobart Morris became the first woman appointed as a justice of the peace. In 1924, Nellie Tayloe Ross was elected the first female governor in the United States.

Laramie, named for the trapper Jacques LaRamee, was first established by the confluence of a small settlement building around a military fort (Fort Buford) and a later need by the railroad, which was being built across the West, for a place to maintain the trains. Two things that made Laramie a good site were the abundance of fresh water, the Laramie River, and a nearby forest of trees in the Medicine Bow Mountains. But by the end of the nineteenth century, two more additions to the town—the University of Wyoming and the

Memorial message for Matthew Shepard written on a rock at the site of his attack   © Adam Mastoon/Corbis

Wyoming Territorial Prison, provided economic stability. The finding of gold and silver in the mountains at the turn of the century was also a welcomed boost.

Today, Laramie is a small town of less than 30,000 residents that enjoys relatively mild weather, a low cost of living, and below-national-average unemployment. The town sits in the southeastern corner of the state on Interstate 80, about forty miles northwest of Cheyenne. The town is more than a mile high and is surrounded by national forests. The Laramie River runs through the town. It is interesting to note that many websites for the town make reference to Matthew Shepard.

CRITICAL OVERVIEW

The Laramie Project is often praised, as it was in the publication *American Theatre* by Don Shewey, as "a powerful and evocative work of art." The emotions that were exposed upon the actual murder of Matthew Shepard may have focused the world's attention on the town of Laramie, but Kaufman's play, as Shewey pointed out, provides not only the town of Laramie but the world "an opportunity . . . to talk about things that are on its

mind." As M. S. Mason, writing for the *Christian Science Monitor* explained: "The arts can shed light on social problems, but rarely does a region like this one have so much need for clarity and thoughtful response to its recent history." *The Laramie Project*, according to Mason, helps people "put hate crimes in perspective." Mason concludes that Kaufman's play offers "a genuine optimism about human goodness" and a "recognition that evil is not beyond remedy, if we as a society are ready to renounce hate."

Writing for *Time Magazine*, which named *The Laramie Project* one of the top ten plays of the year, Richard Zoglin stated that Kaufman and his troupe were more than capable in expressing "the work's passion and power." Adding to the praise was Victor Gluck, writing for *Back Stage*, who referred to the play as "the most ambitious and powerful new American play of the past year." By the end of his review, Gluck described the play as a "disturbing, haunting theatre experience."

Not all reviews were positive. For instance, the *New Republic*'s Robert Brustein concluded that *The Laramie Project* had "its moments, but the piece lacks a powerful protagonist." The play focused too much on the reaction of the townspeople, Brustein found, and too little on who Matthew Shepard and his killers were. "We leave the theater knowing as little about them as when we first arrived," Brustein wrote. Then he added: "Instead of penetrating character, the play prefers to argue for legislation, as if special laws could somehow change the way people behave." Elizabeth Pochoda, for the *Nation* had similar comments. "Laramie," she wrote, "is a town with a terrible crime, but no terrible truths come to light here." Then she adds: "This beautifully staged canvassing of its citizens is well paced and absorbing but not ultimately affecting." Pochoda continued that the play does not go deep enough into the information. She believed the play should have provided more details about what was not already known. She found herself, as she watched the play, wondering what the members of the troupe "didn't find."

On the other side of the issue, Ed Kaufman, writing for the *Hollywood Reporter*, found the play to be "a stunning and thought-provoking piece of theater." This reviewer then suggested that the writer and director of this play had asked the question: "'Is theater a medium that can contribute to the national dialogue on current events?'" And that the answer to this question "is yes, especially when art and life come together so wonderfully well."

When the play was published in book form, three publications offered reviews. Jack Helbig, writing for the *Booklist*, found that the play "has moments of astonishing power." Meanwhile, Emily Lloyd, writing in *School Library Journal*, referred to *The Laramie Project* as a "remarkable play" and "a thoughtful and moving theatrical tour de force." And finally, Howard Miller, for the *Library Journal* stated: "This true story of hate, fear, hope, and courage touched and changed many lives and will do so for everyone who reads or watches a performance of this theatrical masterpiece."

CRITICISM

Joyce Hart

Hart is a freelance writer and author of several books. In this essay, Hart examines Kaufman's docudrama to discover how the playwright created theatrical drama in a work that is almost nonfiction.

Moisés Kaufman's *The Laramie Project* is most often referred to as a docudrama, a play that is largely based on real facts. To this point, the play is all but a work of nonfiction. But despite the fact that the basic elements of the play are based

on actual events with their own inherent drama, Kaufman's talents as a playwright were used to enhance the emotional impact of the events and thus create an atmosphere that ultimately stirred his audience more than just the reading of the actual events might have caused. The question is then, how did he do this? How did he formulate the play in such a way that he made the events come alive not with just the details but with all the complexities that surrounded the crime? How did he piece together not only the central events of Matthew Shepard's murder, but also the information that he and the members of Tectonic Theater Project gathered? How did Kaufman arrange his material so that people who came to see the play were stirred to the point of wanting to ask more questions of themselves, of their community, and of their society as a whole? In other words, how did Kaufman turn real events into a work of creative theatrical drama?

Most of these questions can be answered in a very simple way. The overall tool that Kaufman uses to create drama is contrast. But what is less obvious is how he uses this tool. To begin this exploration, one needs to go no further than the beginning of the first act. It is here that readers can witness how the playwright pits one thought against another, as he dives into the interviews and arranges the sentences of each interviewee so that one stands either in partial or complete contradiction with the other. For example, several townspeople offer background information about what life, under normal circumstances, is like in Wyoming. "You have an opportunity to be happy in your life here," states Rebecca Hilliker, a professor at the University of Wyoming, where Matthew Shepard attended classes. The setting that Hilliker describes is in stark contrast to the circumstances that are about to be discussed, of course.

But it is through contradictions such as this that Kaufman plays with the emotions of his audience. Another example occurs when Kaufman offers the statement of Philip Dubois, president of the same university. Dubois describes how safe he feels living in Wyoming. In contrast to what he would do if he lived in a large city, in Laramie Dubois allows his children to play unsupervised outside at night. "My kids play out at night till eleven and I don't think twice about it," Dubois says. This statement resonates with the audience, which is already aware that Shepard was killed at night, possibly in a similar location in which Dubois's children might have played. It is in this way that Kaufman sprays a mist of emotional colors throughout his play, teasing his audience first in one direction, than jerking them abruptly to the other edge of the spectrum.

Even though the general consensus of the interviewees at the beginning of the play is that of peace and the belief that Wyoming is a nice place to live, Kaufman weaves through these positive comments statements that hint otherwise. Another example is the comment of Doc O'Connor, a relatively new arrival to Wyoming. Although O'Connor agrees that Wyoming is a great place to live, he adds a sinister touch to his statement. "They say the Wyoming wind'll drive a man insane," he says. By including O'Connor's statement, Kaufman throws out yet another hint of the macabre acts that are later recorded—the brutal and irrational beating of Shepard. O'Connor's comment thus becomes a type of foreshadowing of the murder or at least a warning that crazy things have previously occurred in Wyoming. It is in this way that the audience—which at first was being lulled into believing in an idyllic environment and is shown a virtual-Wyoming, where everyone is happy and where the "live and let live" attitude of the state's residents allows a seemingly unusual sense of freedom—is suddenly (and quite subtly) reminded that something dreadful is lurking in the background. Let the audience beware, Kaufman is suggesting. All is not perpetual goodness in this so-called paradise.

So although Kaufman appears to be delivering just the facts of the case, he is cleverly manipulating the information. He could easily claim that he is only re-iterating the statements of the people he interviewed. And this is partially true. But by craftily layering one person's sentence upon another person's, Kaufman orchestrates the overall effect just as inventively as a composer who connects one note to another to build a musical work that creates a symphony that stirs the emotions. Yes, Kaufman raises a lot of questions that he leaves for his audience to answer for themselves. However, the questions that arise are the questions that Kaufman wants the audience to take home with them.

Another example of how Kaufman uses contrast to provide drama is shown with the presentation of the crime scene, which he does in several different ways. Each time the audience is taken there, the emotional reaction is purposefully deepened. The first mention of the field where Shepard was killed takes place in the beginning of the play. Sergeant Hing is talking about the Wyoming landscape and about how he took some reporters to the murder scene. Hing speaks about the area where Shepard was beaten as being a beautiful place. On

> " PAY ATTENTION TO THIS, THE PLAYWRIGHT SEEMS TO BE YELLING. THIS IS IMPORTANT, AND I AM NOT GOING TO LET YOU GO WITHOUT FEELING THE INCREDIBLE AND UNFORGETTABLE DRAMA OF IT ALL."

the day he took the reporters there, Hing recounts that the sky was blue and the mountains had a dusting of snow on them. The area, Hing states, is a popular place with bikers and joggers. Upon hearing this, one reporter asks: "Who in the hell would want to run out here?" To which Hing confides that he thought this woman was "missing the point." Hing felt that the media was stupid because they could not turn around and see the beauty of the land. "They were just—nothing but the story," Hing explains.

In other words, Hing has all but erased the memory of the murder that occurred at that place. He was in love with the land and, no matter what had happened there on that specific spot of land, all he saw was the beauty of the surrounding landscape. The reporters, however, were living in a completely different world. They had, of course, come to cover the story, but more than that, they felt the ghost of the murder around them when they stood on that spot. They could not be there and not have their minds cluttered by the thoughts of despair and death as Shepard lay dying there after the beating. These reporters, most of whom had come from outside of Wyoming, looked at the crime scene with eyes focused on only one thing—the brutal murder of a young student. For Hing, Shepard's murder might be one of many he has had to investigate, and he might be questioning why the Shepard case had gained such national attention. And Kaufman, through Hing, might want his audience to ask the same question. Why was Shepard's death more relevant than hundreds of other murders that had taken place that year? Why had the crime become so momentous it had caused a media frenzy? Whatever the reason for Kaufman's

WHAT DO I READ NEXT?

- *Angels in America: A Gay Fantasia on National Themes*, first produced in 1993, a Pulitzer Prize and Tony Award–winning play written by Tony Kushner and mentioned in *The Laramie Project*, was a play described as profoundly moving and yet also funny. It deals with the lives of people who must confront their own homosexuality or that of someone close to them. Tragedy and comedy are mixed just as magic realism and stark reality are. It is political and private. It is a criticism of the Reagan years and its denial of the AIDS epidemic, as well as a meditation of what it means to know that one is dying.

- The Obie Award–winning play *I Am My Own Wife* was written by Doug Wright, directed by Moisés Kaufman, and produced in 2003. It is a one-man show about the German transvestite, Charlotte von Mahlsdorf, an antique collector living in Nazi Germany. This play's major theme is that of survivor living in a very oppressive society.

- *Gross Indecency: The Three Trials of Oscar Wilde* (1997) is Kaufman's other outstanding play. It recounts the trials of Oscar Wilde, a playwright who was sentenced to ten years of hard labor for having made love to another man. In this play, Kaufman explores how Victorian homophobia in politics, culture, and law severely punished the brilliant and witty author.

- The works of Oscar Wilde, one of the most famous playwrights and authors of the nineteenth century, have been collected in *Complete Works of Oscar Wilde: Stories, Plays, Poems, and Essays* (1989). Some of his most important pieces include *The Picture of Dorian Gray* (1890), *Salome* (1893), and *An Ideal Husband* (1899). His writing is often compared to that of Shakespeare for its cleverness and wit.

---

use of these contrasting visions, the results pull the audience into the play. And Kaufman knows that the more an audience invests, the more emotionally involved the audience will become in his play.

As act 1 closes, Kaufman takes the audience back to the crime scene. It begins with one of Kaufman's "moments," which has the subtitle "The Fence." Stephen Mead Johnson introduces this section by telling the audience how this area has become a place of pilgrimage. Johnson's depiction of the area drastically differs from the previous one given by Hing. "It is so stark and so empty and you can't help but think of Matthew out there for eighteen hours in nearly freezing temperatures," Johnson says. Then he relates Shepard's experience to the suffering of Christ on the cross by quoting from the Bible "God, my God, why have you forsaken me." This is the first real reference to Shepard's pain. Previously, the accounts of his death are mentioned merely in an unemotional way. A few details are provided but there is nothing mentioned

of the pain. A young man was killed, is all the audience is really told up until this scene. After Johnson's reference to the suffering that Shepard must have experienced, a member of Tectonic Theater Projects intensifies this moment by offering his own personal reactions to having visited the crime scene. "I broke down the minute I touched it [the fence]." Now the audience not only has a visual image of the fence, they also have a sense of having touched it. And in doing so, the audience is touched in return.

The first act closes with commentary from people who were there on the night of the crime. First there is Aaron Kreifels, the young man who found Shepard. Next is a report from Officer Reggie Fluty, the first police officer on the scene. And the third person interjected into this part of the play is Dr. Cantway, the physician on duty at the emergency room where Shepard was taken. All the bloody details are provided by these three people. And through them, Kaufman provides the audience

Peace vigil for Matthew Shepard © Liss Steve/Corbis Sygma

with an in-your-face reproduction of that night. From three different points of view, the audience sees Shepard's bloody body through the experience of the young boy who found him and called for help. Then Fluty describes the scene in a very clinical manner, noting such things as the position of his body and the way Shepard was tied to the fence. And the doctor, despite all the wounds he has seen in the past, describes the horror of discovering the unimaginable destruction caused by one human upon another.

This is not going to be an easy play to sit through, the audience must be thinking at this point. Kaufman is not going to allow anyone in the audience to passively watch and listen as the story encapsulated in the play unfolds. Kaufman has masterfully crafted this work of art, slowly wrapping his fingers around each person's heart and squeezing it. Pay attention to this, the playwright seems to be yelling. This is important, and I am not going to let you go without feeling the incredible and unforgettable drama of it all.

Source: Joyce Hart, Critical Essay on *The Laramie Project*, in *Drama for Students*, Thomson Gale, 2006.

Robert Brustein

In the following review, Brustein describes the documentary-like nature of Kaufman's play.

The Laramie Project now playing at the Union Square Theatre in New York, is the joint product of the director-playwright Moises Kaufman and a group of eight lively actors who call themselves the Tectonic Theatre Project (TTP). "Tectonic" refers to deformations in the earth's crust, and *The Laramie Project* suggests that these deformities are often caused by humans. It is a play about the murder of Matthew Shepard, a gay Wyoming student who was beaten by two particularly brutal hoodlums who virtually crucified him against a wire fence. (Terence McNally would have done better to have made the crucified Shepard, instead of the crucified Jesus, into the gay hero of *Corpus Christi*.)

Some years ago, the same collaborative team gave us *Gross Indecency*, about the three trials of Oscar Wilde on charges of sodomy and pederasty. It is apparent that the tectonic deformations perceived by Mr. Kaufman and TTP are often related to the treatment of homosexuals in a homophobic society. This is an important theme for dramatic investigation. It is also a theme that is getting somewhat overworked. It must seem callous to apply artistic standards to the presentation of atrocities such as the Matthew Shepard case. But it is Kaufman who has made this terrible event into a matter of art; and when you make polices into art, then politics must be prepared to meet an aesthetic

> "INSTEAD OF PENETRATING CHARACTER, THE PLAY PREFERS TO ARGUE FOR LEGISLATION, AS IF SPECIAL LAWS COULD SOMEHOW CHANGE THE WAY PEOPLE BEHAVE."

standard. Kaufman and TTP succeeded in drawing an engrossing evening of theater out of the unjust treatment of the homosexual Oscar Wilde in *Gross Indecency*, partly because the hero was such a brilliant man. *The Laramie Project* also has its moments, but the piece lacks a powerful protagonist.

Actually, the problem with *The Laramie Project* is that it has too many protagonists. It is less concerned with the murder of young Shepard than with the way the local residents reacted to the public notoriety that they received as a result of the crime. It starts from the very sensible notion that when a particularly heinous event occurs, then the entire area is often perceived as sharing in the guilt of the perpetrators. Reporters refer to "Columbine" and "Watts," for example, as a shorthand method of identifying disturbances; but in employing such generic language they manage to implicate everyone in town. As one of the Laramie townspeople ruefully remarks, "We've become Waco—Jasper—a noun."

Apparently inspired by the method of Anna Deveare Smith—conducting interviews that serve as material for an enacted scenario—*The Laramie Project* is much more a documentary than a play. Like Smith going to Crown Heights or South Central, Kaufman and his Tectonic actors went to Laramie to meet with the citizens and to ask each of them in turn, "What was your response when this happened to Matthew Shepard?" Over two years and six visits, they interviewed about 200 people, most of them only too eager to rescue the reputation of their town from infamy. More than sixty of these characters are represented on stage by the eight actors, who also sometimes play themselves. This is a very generous representation. By the end of the evening, we feel that we have met a fair sampling of Laramie residents. The problem is

we cannot tell them apart very well, or even remember their names.

On a bare stage, backed with a brick wall against which "Journal Entries" are projected, and dressed with five tables and eight chairs, the actors represent a police chief, a university theater head, a woman rancher, a limo driver, a university president, a lesbian waitress, a lesbian faculty member, a Muslim feminist, a student defying his family by performing in *Angels in America*, and any number of friendly people just sitting around and mulling over how this sort of thing could have happened in their neighborhood. Some critics have pointed out resemblances between the town of Laramie and *Our Town*. Indeed, people even show up at Shepard's funeral carrying black umbrellas. But considering what happened to Shepard, this *Our Town* is at times closer in spirit to Kenneth Tynan's satire of it—that typical American village where they lynch blacks, spit on Jews, and punch out the lights of gays between visits to the drugstore for vanilla sodas.

This is not to say that the people interviewed by the TTP actors are in way evil or malign. Quite the contrary. Virtually all of them, including the governor of Wyoming, testify to having been "sickened" by the murder. "We don't grow children like that here," says another, adding, "But it's pretty clear we do grow children like that here." Laramie's attitude towards gay people, says another, "is live and let live." One clergyman affirms that he does not condone that kind of violence—or, as he feels compelled to add, "that kind of lifestyle." Although this particular murder was motivated by hatred of gays, one woman notes, Matthew was neither a saint nor a martyr. If the victim had been a policeman, would the newspapers have shown the same interest?

Still, most of them—except for a few anti-gay fanatics, one of whom carries a placard reading "God hates fags"—are tolerant of homosexuals. A hundred people march on behalf of Matthew Shepard wearing yellow armbands. Others wave placards reading "Peace and Love." And although one angry lesbian demands the death penalty for Matthew's killers, his father asks clemency for them, and they get it: life imprisonment. The citizens of Laramie, in short, are more likely than not to show a benevolent face. And so are the well-scrubbed actors who play them. (Even the cigarettes they smoke are environment-friendly, being unlit.) Sitting on stage watching each other perform, their expressions alternating between piety and sanctimony, these actors work very hard to avoid the chief danger of this kind of presentation, a tone of self-congratulation.

One can almost sense the director leaping up to squash the impulse towards condescension, not always successfully. With a few exceptions, notably Mercedes Herrero as a tough-minded policewoman worrying about contracting AIDS after cleaning away the blood of the HIV-positive Shepard, the performers are too often unspeakably awed by the inspirational way they are playing their characters; they seem forever on the verge of moving themselves to tears. In a filmed documentary, it is easy to respond to the simplicity of average people. In stage impersonations, that simplicity too easily falls into folksiness. *The Laramie Project* brings up unintended questions about the relationship of the stage to reality, and the responsibility of actors to the actual people whom they are trying to impersonate.

And this brings us to the main problem with the enterprise. Although the play is inspired by one of the worst hate crimes in recent American history, it draws back before the fact of human evil. For all the references to the killers, Russell A. Hendemon and Aaron J. McKinney, by friends, family members, prosecutors and police officers, we leave the theater knowing as little about them as when we first arrived. (We also learn very little about Matthew Shepard.) What kind of people could snuff out the life of a human being because he was perceived to come onto them in a bar? What does that tell us about the nature of the human heart?

Instead of penetrating character, the play prefers to argue for legislation, as if special laws could somehow change the way people behave. But passing more laws will not eradicate racial, religious, or sexual hatred. It may just drive it underground to fester in uglier forms. A priest in the play says it sows the seeds of violence to say "fag" or "dyke." But it is a real question whether laundering the language—elsewhere known as "freedom from speech"—would lower the incidence of violence. The crime for which Henderson and McKinney were apprehended, tried, and convicted was not violating speech codes but murder, for which there are already plenty of laws on the books.

Upon reflection, *The Laramie Project* may be more important as a purgative than as a performance, for it succeeds best as a rite of exorcism for a lot of troubled people, as a kind of dramatized encounter group for the entire town. One resident may insist that "hate is not a Laramie value," but as another replies that "we need to admit we live in a country where shit like this happens."

The play also manages to make an argument for the normality of being gay, foreseeing a time when people will consider homosexuality neither right nor wrong, but simply a fact of biology. This is devoutly to be wished, for reasons moral, political, personal, and aesthetic. Such a condition might very well help to eliminate gaybashing. It might also help restore the theater to its original purpose—which is not to confirm liberal audiences in what they already believe, but to uncover the veiled mysteries of the human heart. And such a dispensation might permit our artists once more to explore the nature of sexuality rather than the issue of sexual preference, which is a condition of the whole of humanity and not just its wounded and divided parts.

Source: Robert Brustein, "On Theater: The Staged Documentary," in *New Republic*, Vol. 222, No. 25, June 19, 2000, pp. 29–30.

SOURCES

Brustein, Robert, "The Staged Documentary," in the *New Republic*, Vol. 222, No. 25, June 19, 2000, pp. 29–30.

Gluck, Victor, Review of *The Laramie Project*, in *Back Stage*, Vol. 41, No. 22, June 2–8, 2000, p. 56.

Helbig, Jack, Review of *The Laramie Project*, in the *Booklist*, Vol. 98, No. 1, September 1, 2001, pp. 43–44.

Kaufman, Ed, Review of *The Laramie Project*, in *Hollywood Reporter*, Vol. 373, June 11–17, 2002, p. 22.

Kaufman, Moisés, and the members of Tectonic Theater Project, *The Laramie Project*, Vintage Books, 2001.

Lloyd, Emily, "*The Laramie Project*: A Play," in *School Library Journal*, Vol. 47, No. 11, November 2001, p. 194.

Mason, M. S., "*Laramie Project* Connects Stage to Social Ills," in the *Christian Science Monitor*, March 31, 2000, p. 19.

Miller, Howard, Review of *The Laramie Project: A Play*, in *Library Journal*, Vol. 126, No. 14, September 1, 2001, p. 179.

Pochoda, Elizabeth, "The Talk in Laramie," in the *Nation*, Vol. 270, No. 24, June 19, 2000, pp. 33–34.

Shewey, Don, "Town in a Mirror," in *American Theatre*, Vol. 17, No. 5, May–June 2000, pp. 14–22.

Zoglin, Richard, "Voices from Laramie," in *Time*, Vol. 155, No. 19, May 8, 2000, p. 86.

FURTHER READING

Clum, John M., *Acting Gay*, Columbia University Press, 1992. Clum examines twentieth-century American and British plays that involve gay men, including those by Noel Coward, Arthur Miller, Tennessee Williams, Edward Albee, Harold Pinter, and Peter Shaffer.

Helminiak, Daniel A., *What the Bible Really Says about Homosexuality*, Alamo Square Press, 1994.

>   Helminiak is a Catholic priest who has carefully studied the Bible in search of passages that relate to homosexuality. This book is based on his interpretations of his studies as well as other scholarly research, which conclude that the Bible does not condemn homosexuality.

Loffreda, Beth, *Losing Matt Shepard*, Columbia University Press, 2000.

>   Loffreda arrived at the University of Wyoming after the murder of Matt Shepard. But as advisor of the campus Lesbian Gay Bisexual Transgender Association, she has both an insider's and an outsider's view on how Shepard's death affected, and still affects, the Laramie community.

O'Connor, Sean, *Straight Acting: Popular Gay Drama from Wilde to Rattigan*, Cassell, 1998.

>   O'Connor examines the role and influence of Oscar Wilde's plays and lifestyle on playwrights that were to follow him, taking the reader from the late nineteenth-century drama productions to those of the 1960s.

Perry, Barbara, *In the Name of Hate: Understanding Hate Crimes*, Routledge, 2001.

>   Perry not only provides an historical account of hate crimes but offers her evaluation that hate crimes are symptomatic not just of hate, but also of inequalities within a culture and fear of differences.

Swigonski, Mary E., *From Hate Crimes to Human Rights: A Tribute to Matthew Shepard*, Haworth Social Work Practice Press, 2001.

>   Swigonski and other academics illuminate the road from hate crimes to legislation that may one day provide some sense of justice to the victims.

Machinal

SOPHIE TREADWELL

1928

Machinal was first produced in 1928. It premiered on Broadway with Clark Gable cast as the lover, Dick Roe. It was a critical success and ran for 91 performances. In 1931, the drama premiered in London to some mixed reviews, mostly because of the sexual and violent nature of the play. However, *Machinal*'s greatest success came in Russia at Moscow's Kamerny Theatre, after which the play toured throughout the Russian provinces. Later, in 1954, the play was even produced for television.

The play's title means "automatic" or "mechanical" in French. Sophie Treadwell wrote the play based loosely on the murder trial of Ruth Snyder and her lover, Judd Gray, who together murdered Snyder's husband. Convicted of murdering her husband, Snyder later received the electric chair. Out of this event came the powerful, demanding drama, *Machinal*.

A woman's role during this era in history is confined and regimented to wife, mother, housekeeper, and sexual partner. Love is considered unnecessary, and thus many women are trapped in their dependant status, living a hellish life in a loveless marriage. The relationship between Helen Jones and her husband, George H. Jones, is no different. However, when a man intercedes and Helen is given a momentary glimpse of passion, her life is forever changed. She sees how society confines her, how her husband unconsciously dominates her every decision, and she feels that there is no escape. With a feeling of hopelessness, Helen commits an egregious crime, murdering her

Sophie Treadwell   © Bettmann/Corbis

husband to free herself from the constraints of society and, ironically, to save her husband from the pain of a divorce. This heavy play is a powerful expressionistic drama about women's forced financial dependency upon men during the 1920s and their trapped existence in a male-dominated, oppressive wasteland.

AUTHOR BIOGRAPHY

Sophie Treadwell, an early-twentieth century expressionistic playwright, is one of the United States's most under-recognized female writers of fiction, drama and journalism. Although a productive writer, Treadwell's greatest achievement may be attributed to what she did to advance women's exposure in an oppressive, male-dominated world.

Treadwell was born on October 3, 1885 in Stockton, California. She was born to her father, Alfred Treadwell, a lawyer, city prosecutor, justice of the peace, and judge, and her mother, Nettie Treadwell. Their marriage was troubled and the two separated in the early 1890s. Although separated, Nettie never completely freed herself from her husband with a divorce. The economic and emotional impact of Nettie's inability to divorce Alfred

troubled Treadwell for all her life and greatly influenced both her writing and views of marriage and society.

Regardless of Treadwell's family life, she was an excellent student and she enrolled at the University of California-Berkeley in 1902. Four years later she received her Bachelor of Letters in French.

After graduating from UC-Berkeley, Treadwell moved about teaching and trying her hand at professional theater in Los Angeles. Nothing much took hold and, in 1908, Treadwell left Los Angeles for San Francisco in order to care for her ailing mother, who was in ill health. In 1914, she was given her big break when the *San Francisco Bulletin's* editor asked her to go undercover as a homeless prostitute to see what type of charitable help was available. The result was outstanding, creating an 18-part serial which was entitled "An Outcast at the Christian Door," and inspiring the play *Sympathy*. Aside from the impact the serial had on Treadwell's writing, it also rocketed her to the forefront of female journalists. She was sent on assignment to Europe to cover World War I, making her the first female war correspondent.

Upon her return to the United States, Treadwell began work as a journalist at the *New York Tribune*. There, Treadwell established herself nationally as a journalist with her adept and eye-opening coverage of Mexico and Mexican-American relations. One of her greatest journalistic feats was an expansive, exclusive profile of the legendary bandit, Pancho Villa. Treadwell was the only interviewer from the United States who was granted access to Villa. The two-day interview helped her complete her journalistic coup and served as the inspiration for the play *Gringo* (which appeared in 1922) and the novel *Lusita* (published in 1931).

However, there may still be one piece of nonfiction that had even a greater effect on Treadwell. In 1927, she attended the murder trial of Ruth Snyder and Judd Gray. Ruth Snyder and her lover, Gray, plotted and killed Snyder's husband. The two were convicted and sentence to die in the electric chair. From this event sprung forth *Machinal*, Treadwell's greatest dramatic success, which was produced for the first time in 1928. Beyond the success of the play, Treadwell's characters and her sympathy for the murderess caused a stir, quietly creating a rift between conservative, disciplinarian men and a new rank of feminists.

Although her works were progressive, enlightening and revealing, Treadwell was still under the heel of a male-dominated world. Nonetheless, she persevered, pushing forward, writing countless plays, continuing with her journalism and her struggle for her place, not only amongst the ranks of women, but all humans, until her death on February 20, 1970.

PLOT SUMMARY

Episodes 1–4

The first episode takes place within the George H. Jones Company office. A young woman (later revealed to be Helen Jones) is late for work, and her coworkers chide her, telling her she may lose her job. She is a frantic woman, crushed by society. She is often late because she cannot stand the stifling crowds of the subway. This serves as a metaphor for how she feels about society in general. In the office, it becomes apparent that George H. Jones, a kind, flabby-handed, slovenly man, has asked Helen to marry him. She does not know how to answer. Helen wants nothing more than to be free of her terrible job, but the answer is a loveless marriage to an unattractive, unappealing man.

Helen returns home to discuss the proposal with her mother. At first her mother does not understand why Helen feels that she must get married. Helen even says, "All women get married, don't they?" However, as soon as Helen's mother discovers that the man is wealthy, she changes her tune, telling her daughter to marry him straightaway. Helen tries to explain that she does not love George, and her mother responds, "Love!—What does that amount to! Will it clothe you? Will it feed you? Will it pay the bills?" The two women argue, and a major theme of the play is expressed: the role of marriage and a woman's dependant status on her husband's wealth in the 1920s.

In episode three, it is clear that Helen and George have wed. They are on their honeymoon. George is not a bad person and, for the right woman, could even be an excellent husband, but he is very preoccupied with money. He does not mistreat his wife, but he also does not see her as an equal. In their hotel bedroom, George tries to seduce Helen. He is not rude or forceful, but he does express his desires, and Helen finds it impossible to resist. She has already succumbed to her role as a wife; the next logical step is to become her husband's sexual partner. Helen tearfully complies, laden with self-disgust.

At least nine months later, Helen is in a hospital having just given birth to a newborn girl. She is disgusted and depressed, feeling that the position

MEDIA ADAPTATIONS

- A television adaptation of *Machinal* was produced and aired in the United States in 1954.

she finds herself in (being a wife and mother) was pressed upon her by society. When the nurse asks if she wants her baby, Helen shakes her head. When George enters the room, Helen begins to gag, as if repulsed by her husband. It is only when the doctor insists that the nurse put the baby to Helen's breast that she screams, "No!" Only after everyone leaves does Helen begin to speak. In a long, rambling diatribe, Helen remembers her dog, Vixen, giving birth and how the puppies drowned in blood. Helen seems to be hoping for death and crying out that she will not submit any more.

Episodes 5–7

In a bar, two men are waiting for two women to arrive. The two men are Harry Smith and Dick Roe. Harry Smith is waiting to meet a girl from the George H. Jones Company, referred to in the play as Telephone Girl. According to Smith, Telephone Girl is bringing a friend that she plans to introduce to Dick Roe. Eventually, the two women arrive. Telephone Girl's friend is Helen Jones. Introductions are made and small talk ensues. Quickly, Telephone Girl and Harry Smith reveal that they are leaving to consummate their ongoing affair. Helen and Roe are left to talk with one another. Roe reveals that he once killed two men while traveling in Mexico. According to Roe, he was taken captive and while he was being detained, he filled a glass bottle with small stones, creating a club. At the right moment, Roe clubbed his captors to death. Roe's stories and exciting life entrap Helen.

In the next scene, Roe and Helen have obviously shared intimate time together. She is smitten and, for the first time in the play, talkative and excited about life. She contemplates their lives together and even sings for Roe. Eventually, she realizes that she must hurry, dress, and return to her husband. Before she leaves, she asks Roe if she can have a lily blooming in a bowl of small stones and water that sits on his windowsill. Roe agrees and Helen departs with her memento.

Back with her husband, Helen is traumatized. Both read the newspaper, and George is unchanged, rambling about sales, money, interest, and business. Helen is making comments that foreshadow suicide, murder, and divorce. However, George notices nothing. The phone rings and from the way George is talking, he is doing business and things are going well. Intermittently, as George and Helen exchange small talk, the phone rings several more times, all of the calls are related to George's business. This scene is full of heavy foreshadowing, of Helen and of George's death, drowning, suicide, and murder. George finally notices that Helen seems upset and he suggests that they take a vacation to relax.

Episodes 8–9

Episode 8 opens in a courtroom. Helen is on trial for the murder of her husband. Treadwell uses this scene to comment on the media, having one reporter obviously in favor of Helen and the other staunchly opposed. During the trial, it is revealed that Helen and George lived together for six years without a single quarrel and have had only one child, a five year-old girl. The lawyer for the prosecution asks if Helen murdered her husband, revealing that someone killed George H. Jones by smashing his head with a bottle full of small stones. Helen professes her innocence, claiming that she saw two men looming over her husband's side of the bed. The two men then smashed her husband's head and fled the room. The lawyer for the prosecution then reveals he has a signed affidavit from Richard (Dick) Roe, Helen's lover. The statement explains that Roe and Helen had intimate relations and that he had told Helen about how he killed two men with a bottle full of small stones. Before the lawyer for the prosecution can even finish reading the letter, Helen confesses to the murder. She claims that she murdered her husband because she wanted "to be free." The judge asks why she did not simply divorce her husband and, ironically, she responds, "Oh I couldn't do that!! I couldn't hurt him like that!"

In the final episode, Helen is with a priest, and she is being given her last rites. A condemned man is singing a Negro spiritual. Soon, barbers arrive to shave a portion of Helen's head in preparation for the electric chair. Helen fights them off, but the barbers prevail. In a last gasp, she screams, "Submit! Submit! Is nothing mine?" and asks the priest if she will ever find peace, if she will ever be free. Her mother arrives, and they embrace for the last time. At last, Helen is lead to the electric chair where the two reporters are awaiting her execution. In a final statement, Helen cries out her final words, "Somebody! Somebod—" but is cut short by the electric chair. In the end, Treadwell ties up her metaphor of society as a machine. Helen was caught within the machine but refused to work as part of it and, as a result, was brought to her destruction.

CHARACTERS

Adding Clerk

Adding Clerk is an unnamed male character who, in the first episode, helps emphasize and embellish the noises of the office with his audible number counting and the sound of his adding machine. Sound and noise is an important element in Treadwell's play, creating background and atmosphere.

Doctor

In episode four Helen gives birth to her firstborn. The doctor comes into the room and the nurse explains that Helen does not want her baby and appears weak because she gags when her husband enters. The doctor insists that Helen breastfeed; she refuses and asks to be left alone. The doctor is confused and perturbed by her behavior.

Filing Clerk

Filing Clerk is an unnamed, younger male character who, in the first episode, helps emphasize and embellish the noises of the office with his audible enunciation of letters as he files. Sound and noise is an important element in Treadwell's play, creating background and atmosphere.

First Reporter

In episode eight, Helen is in the courtroom on trial for the murder of her husband, George H. Jones. The First Reporter is one of the many members of the press in the crowded courtroom. As he takes notes, First Reporter reads them aloud. His comments are positive regarding Helen, her behavior, movements, character and emotions. First Reporter's comments are the polar opposite of Second Reporter's anti-Helen commentary, exemplifying the subjectivity of the media.

Helen's Mother

Helen's mother acts a guidebook for the society that Helen wishes to escape. Helen's mother constantly reminds her daughter that it is more important to get married before she is too old and that it is most important to marry a man that can provide financial stability. The old woman explains that love will never pay the bills, clothe you, or put food on the table. She tells Helen that love is not real. Life is real, things like clothes, food, a bed to sleep in, etc., and that the rest is in your head. She pressures Helen to forget about things like love, and marry George because he has money, is a decent man, and can care for both. Helen and her mother. Helen's mother is the voice that is the opposition to Helen's feelings. Helen's mother is convincing and powerful. It could be reasoned that Helen's mother's pressure is the catalyst that forces Helen into marriage, motherhood, and, eventually, murder.

George H. Jones

George H. Jones is the owner of George H. Jones Company. He employs the Adding Clerk, Filing Clerk, Stenographer, Telephone Girl and Helen Jones. He is a fat, slovenly man, but he is harmless. His hands are large and flabby; they disgust Helen. George is more dedicated to work than anything else and it shows because his business is successful. Although George's company is successful, he has never been married. He takes a special interest in Helen and decides to ask his office worker to take his hand in marriage. Reluctantly, Helen accepts, mostly because of the prodding of her mother. Helen becomes Mrs. Jones for the sake of monetary stability. She feels no love for George and, in fact, is repulsed by everything about the man. George is patient and, in a way, loving towards his new bride. He is not forceful with his sexual advances and he is eager to support both Helen and her mother. George plans to give both women a nice, comfortable life, he is willing to be faithful and compassionate, and he yearns to start a family. In many ways, George has the potential to be a good, loving husband. Soon after their marriage, Helen gives birth to their firstborn. George is excited to be a father and support his family. He is a good provider, but Helen constantly feels trapped by her husband, child, mother and life. Eventually, Helen murders George to free herself from her constraints. Ironically, she evens see murder as a better option than divorce for George because Helen does not want to *hurt* him by ending their marriage. This belief is both sad and insane. Helen believes divorce would do more damage to George than ending his life.

Helen Jones

Helen Jones is frequently referred to as "Young Woman" throughout the play. In the beginning, Helen is an employee of the George H. Jones Company. Soon she finds herself married to George and the mother of a newborn child. Helen's mother exercises a decisive amount of control over her daughter's decision-making process, pressuring her daughter to accept George's marriage proposal. Helen is a disturbed woman. She is crushed by societal norms and can find no way to escape what she sees as extremely tethering social dogmas. Helen is quiet and introspective. She seems fearful of the world, but only in that it is full of stifling pressures. She does not want to feel forced into caring for her mother; she does not want to discard the possibility of love for the reassurance of stability; she does not want to stifle sexual desire in exchange for living in a faithful, loveless marriage. Helen desires a progressive, modern feminist sense of freedom that she cannot find in her world and her life. Throughout the course of the play she succumbs to each social pressure that she is so repulsed by—marriage, financial stability, motherhood, and passionless sex—only to give herself momentary relief through an affair with Dick Roe. Their relationship is brief, but does at least give Helen a taste of a life that she felt was unattainable. Unfortunately, with Roe's departure Helen spirals into a ridiculous, dead-end choice, murdering her husband to free herself and save George from the *pain* of divorce. Of course, Helen escapes nothing and winds up in prison, on trial and eventually is executed for murdering her husband.

Judge

In episode eight, Helen is in the courtroom on trial for the murder of her husband, George H. Jones. The Judge is presiding over the courtroom and her trial.

Lawyer for the Defense

In episode eight, Helen is in the courtroom on trial for the murder of her husband, George H. Jones. The Lawyer for the Defense is defending her against the allegations.

Lawyer for the Prosecution

In episode eight, Helen is in the courtroom on trial for the murder of her husband, George H. Jones. The Lawyer for the Prosecution is prosecuting her on the charges of murder in the first degree.

Nurse

In episode four Helen gives birth to her firstborn. The nurse is in her room trying to help the new mother become accustomed to her child.

Helen refuses her baby, gags when her husband enters the room, and is wholly repulsed by the world. The nurse is confused by Helen's actions and calls on the doctor for assistance.

Priest

In the final episode, moments before Helen is taken to the electric chair, Helen converses with the Priest. Mostly, she talks at the Priest as he reads her last rites. Helen divulges many of her feelings in the final episode of the play. She is extremely emotional about her forced submission into work, marriage, sex, and motherhood. The Priest is calm, collected and regimented. He gives Helen her last rites and then her head is shaved and she is led to her death in the electric chair.

Dick Roe

Dick Roe is sitting with Harry Smith in the bar during episode five. The men are waiting for Telephone Girl and Helen Jones. Telephone Girl and Smith are in the midst of an extended affair. Roe and Helen have never met, but Telephone Girl and Smith have brought the two together with the intention of a relationship beyond friendship. Helen is reluctant, as she is married and has a child, but is lifeless and dying inside because of her existence. Roe is a handsome, exciting man. He is a traveler and has adventurous stories to tell. Once, he explains to Helen, while traveling in Mexico he was kidnapped and held hostage. He had to murder his two captors and did so by slowly filling a glass bottle with tiny pebbles, creating a heavy, blunt clubbing object. Roe smashed the two men about the head, crushing their skulls and killing them both. During their affair, Helen is completely smitten with Roe and his lifestyle. After one of their trysts, Helen takes a lily in a bowl full of tiny rocks from Roe's apartment. In a strange twist, Roe's story and the bowl are the impetus to Helen's plot to murder her husband. Roe returns to Mexico and gives a written deposition that is the most damning evidence against Helen. He explains how Helen took the lily and how he told her about his daring escape from his captors. Helen's husband met a fate similar to Roe's captors and the rocks from the lily bowl were used as part of the murder weapon. Ultimately, Roe's testimony leads to Helen's murder conviction.

Second Reporter

In episode eight, Helen is in the courtroom on trial for the murder of her husband, George H. Jones. The Second Reporter is one of the many members of the press in the crowded courtroom. As he takes notes, Second Reporter reads them aloud. His comments are negative regarding Helen, her behavior, movements, character and emotions. Second Reporter's comments are the polar opposite of First Reporter's pro-Helen commentary, exemplifying the subjectivity of the media.

Harry Smith

Harry Smith is sitting with Dick Roe in the bar during episode five. Smith is planning to introduce Roe to his mistress's friend, Helen Jones. When Helen and Telephone Girl—Smith's mistress—arrive at the bar, the four individuals introduce each other and exchange brief dialogue. Following this, Telephone Girl and Smith depart together, leaving Roe and Helen alone together.

Stenographer

Stenographer is an unnamed, faded, drying female character who, in the first episode, helps emphasize and embellish the noises of the office as she audibly recites portions of stale, business letters. Sound and noise is an important element in Treadwell's play, creating background and atmosphere.

Telephone Girl

Telephone Girl is an unnamed, cheap, amorous female character who, in the first episode, helps emphasize and embellish the noises of the office as she repeats dry, office telephone greetings. Telephone Girl reappears in episode five, where she introduces Helen Jones to Dick Roe. Helen and Telephone Girl arrive at the bar with plans to meet Roe and his friend, Harry Smith. It is clear that Telephone Girl is having an affair with Smith and, eventually, the two depart together, leaving Jones and Roe alone together in the bar. This is the catalyst for Helen and Roe's affair.

THEMES

Expressionism

Expressionism is the leading theme in *Machinal*. Expressionism is a theory in art, drama, or writing that seeks to depict the subjective emotions and responses that objects and events arouse in the artist, dramatist or writer. Before exploring expressionism in *Machinal*, the term "subjective" must first be understood. To depict a subjective emotion or response, Treadwell would have to

TOPICS FOR FURTHER STUDY

- Expressionism is most frequently used to describe a movement in art; however, it is also used to describe movements in drama and fiction. Examine another expressionistic work, whether it be in art or in fiction. Compare and contrast this work with Treadwell's *Machinal*. How does the use of expressionism change from one art form to another? Does the sex of the artist, author or playwright influence the use of expressionism in their work?

- Read the book *A Giacometti Portrait* by James Lord. Using what you know about expressionism, decide whether or not Giacometti is an expressionistic artist. Why or why not? Once you decide, apply your criteria to James Lord. Is Lord an expressionist? Why or why not?

- Treadwell uses the Snyder-Gray murder trial as the catalyst for her expressionistic drama. Select a moment from the past, historical or personal, and create your own short expressionistic piece. Remember, your focus should not be on realism, but on the creation of a story and landscape that best conveys your subjective emotional response to the moment.

- Beneath the shroud of expressionism, Treadwell clearly reveals her emotions about feminism and early twentieth-century male-dominated society. *Machinal* is a story about a woman trapped in a male-driven, social machine. Compare and contrast Helen's entrapment with that of Charlotte Perkins Gilman's main character in her story, "The Yellow Wallpaper." Can you think of any other works of drama or fiction where men or women are trapped, in a symbolic or realistic way, by the dictates of society?

---

perfectly convey her personal feeling. Philosophically, it is impossible to convey a subjective emotion or response because it is inherent to each individual; it is a matter of personal taste. Hence, Treadwell cannot convey her subjective feeling to anyone because once someone else experiences her attempt to convey her emotion or response, it necessarily becomes the other person's subjective interpretation of her emotion or response. This is a difficult concept to grasp, but it is crucial to understanding expressionism.

Artistically, expressionism exists in a remarkable way. In attempts to convey their emotions, painters and dramatists did works that depicted raw and powerfully emotional states of mind. Treadwell was considered an expressionist because she abandoned the traditional structure of plays and delivered her plotlines through unique, fresh techniques. She used real events, like the Snyder-Gray murder trial and her interviews with Pancho Villa, to pour her own raw emotion into the creation of an unconventional drama. This movement is often considered decadent because it is, by its very nature, one individual's tunnel-vision interpretation of the world.

Returning to *Machinal* as the expressionistic example, Treadwell takes her subjective emotional response to the Sndyer-Gray murder trial and depicts it to the world through her play. The trial obviously stirs feelings of despair and hopelessness in Treadwell for all the women trapped in the societal norm of loveless, hellish marriages. Her emotive response to Snyder is not one of repulsion for committing a heinous act, but one of sadness for a woman left with no escape from the strangling grasp of a male-dominated society. To further accentuate her emotion, Treadwell turns away from traditionally structured theatre, constructing a nine-episode play that mimics the nine-month gestation that women must endure when they are pregnant. This is why Treadwell, and especially *Machinal*, are considered examples of American expressionistic drama.

Society as a Machine

In the play, society as a machine creates a metaphoric theme. Throughout *Machinal*, Helen struggles against society. Through Treadwell's use of sound and repeated dialogue, each phase of Helen's life is punctuated by repetition, noise, and an unseen, daunting force that pushes her along. Whether it is the opening scene in the office with the human voices creating an "office machine" or the noises of the world invading her hospital visit, Helen cannot escape society. Even though she does not want to submit, she is pushed forward, forced to carry out each of her roles in the machine—first as a secretary, then as a wife, then as a sexual partner, then as a mother—even though she hates each of her positions along the way and she continually feels pressured into submission. With this, Helen never finds a way to escape the clutches of the machine. In the end, when she tries to free herself by murdering her husband, she makes her first stand and she steps outside of her role as assigned by the machine. Almost immediately, she is devoured by society. The machine grinds her up and disposes of her once she refuses to fulfill her role. At the end of the play as Helen sits in the electric chair awaiting her death, the first reporter asks, "Suppose the machine shouldn't work!" and the second reporter responds, "It'll work!—It always works!" These statements in the final moments complete the play's metaphor. Anyone who steps outside the bounds of society will meet their end at the hands of its ever-grinding gears.

Hopelessness and Despair

Hopelessness and despair are the primary emotional themes that run through *Machinal*. Helen rarely experiences anything but these two feelings. Before George H. Jones asks her to marry him, she is trapped working in an office. When George proposes to her, she sees a relief from her horrible life in the office, only to replace it with another living hell: a loveless marriage. Succumbing to the pressures of society and her mother, Helen finds herself married, living a hopeless, desperate life. Her next role sends her spiraling into despair, as she must fulfill the prophecy of wife to become sexual partner and subsequently, mother. Given only a momentary glimmer of happiness through her affair with Dick Roe, Helen is cast down even deeper when her short-term lover leaves. Her final effort to escape her hopelessness and despair is the murder of her husband. To add insult to injury, her lover essentially convicts her with his written affidavit, leaving Helen completely hopeless and desperate. These emotions permeate all of Helen's life and serve as the driving theme that taunts her to escape her role in society.

STYLE

The Tragic Heroine

Although the plot of *Machinal* would seem to make Helen Jones a villain, her role is quite the contrary. She is clearly intended to be a tragic heroine. The play is written with heated anger. Helen Jones and all other women are doomed to wander the dead wasteland of a male-dominated society. Remember, this is an expressionistic play and its intent is to convey emotion and feeling, not realism. Hence, to read this play from the point of view of realism is to, of course, damn Helen to death by the electric chair and label her a villain. However, through the eyes of expressionism, Helen becomes a heroine, struggling against male oppression for all of womankind. Helen does not murder her husband because she is evil; she is left with no other choice. At the point of the murder it appears that it may be necessary for certain wives in certain circumstances to murder their husbands. With her last, failed attempt to free herself from the clutches of a male-dominated society, Helen becomes a tragic heroine.

Episodes

Structure is a crucial element in all forms of expressionism; Treadwell's *Machinal* is no different. In the play, Treadwell abandons the traditional dramatic structure of acts and scenes for nine episodes. Each episode is aptly titled to fit the setting or mood and the number is intended to reflect each month of the nine months of pregnancy.

With each passing episode, the title is the framework around which Treadwell constructs her commentary of a woman's role in a male-dominated society. In "Episode I To Business," *Machinal* opens in the office of the George H. Jones Company. The scene is bustling with office workers and a cacophony of office noises. Although it is an office, the dialogue is focused on Helen and her prospective marriage to George H. Jones. Treadwell calls the episode "To Business," but the conversation is nothing of the sort. This title is more indicative of Treadwell telling the audience what she plans to reveal than what actually happens in the episode. Through the title of her first episode and the nine-episode construction of *Machinal*, Treadwell is announcing her intention to comment on the male-dominated society of the 1920s. The episodes that follow are all aptly named—At Home, Honeymoon, Maternal, Prohibited, Intimate, Domestic, The Law, and, lastly, A Machine. The ninth and final episode not only echoes the nine months

COMPARE
&
CONTRAST

- **1920s:** Amelia Earhardt is the first woman to fly across the Atlantic Ocean.

  Today: Women of all ethnicities train as commercial, military, and private pilots, flying all over the world for companies, governments, and individuals.

- **1920s:** The first scheduled television broadcast airs in New York City.

  Today: Countless television programs air constantly through cable and satellite connections. Programs air in numerous languages from a vast number of networks, stretching far and wide across the entire globe.

- **1920s:** Black Friday occurs, spiraling the world into an economic crisis.

  Today: The world economy exists on a precarious balance that could easily be disrupted with war, shortages, or unemployment.

- **1920s:** Lenin, Hitler, and Mussolini all begin their rise to power in their respective countries, a precursor to World War II.

  Today: With heavy political unrest around the world, the United States is in the middle of a controversial war taking place in Iraq.

---

of gestation and a woman's place as a mother, it also comments on the finality of woman's place in society. The title—A Machine—directly refers to Helen's date with the electric chair.

However, Treadwell is commenting on something much deeper. With the nine episodes ending with "A Machine," Treadwell is highlighting a woman's role as nothing more than a cog in the male-dominated social machine. The play is nine episodes, just as a gestation is nine months; the ninth episode is "A Machine," just as a woman's role in society is to produce children—to be *a machine* within the male-dominated patriarchal social construct. Treadwell is surprisingly effective with her dramatic structure. *Machinal* is powerful and thought-provoking, even when viewed from afar with a unique breakdown of the general dramatic structure.

HISTORICAL CONTEXT

The Snyder-Gray Murder Trial

During the spring of 1927, Treadwell attended the notorious trial of Ruth Snyder and her lover, Judd Gray. Although she did not officially cover the trial as a reporter, her time spent in the courtroom served as the catalyst for *Machinal*. Snyder was a seemingly harmless housewife from Long Island, and her lover was portrayed as a dim-witted accomplice. Most notably, the trial attracted an amazing public interest and was fueled by hundreds of reporters that where assigned to cover the trial. Every day there was something new about the Snyder-Gray trial in the newspapers. The media frenzy did not cease until the defendants were finally executed by the electric chair in January, 1928. With her execution, Snyder became the first woman executed in New York State in the twentieth century.

Albert Snyder, Ruth's husband, was found beaten, drugged with chloroform, and strangled in his bed on March 20, 1927. When the police arrived, Ruth was bound and gagged outside their daughter's room. She told police that a tall man grabbed her, and she had fainted. Ruth told police that she remained unconscious for at least five hours. Police were suspicious when they found Ruth's jewelry under a mattress. The house appeared to be ransacked, but it seemed strange that the thief would have left the jewelry. Secondly, when Ruth came to, she did not inquire about her husband. This also caused the police to wonder about Ruth's role in the murder and the supposed burglary. The police questioned Ruth for nearly

Ruth Snyder © Bettmann/Corbis

twenty hours, and she finally confessed that she and her lover, Gray, had beaten her husband to death. Later, Ruth would change her story, stating that although she participated, Gray masterminded the entire murder.

The two were placed on trial for the murder of Albert Snyder, and the crime captured the minds of the American people. In addition to the 180 reporters assigned to the case, some 1,500 people attended the trial every day. Although Treadwell was not assigned to the cover the trial, she was a spectator as often as possible. For the first time in history, microphones and speakers were set up so everyone in the courtroom could hear the testimonies. Sadly for Ruth, her jury of peers was composed of all men, and many female reporters and thinkers of the day believed she never stood a chance. Not surprisingly, they were right. The prosecution and even Gray's defense attorney, tried to use the all-male jury to their advantage. The prosecution told the jury that Snyder killed her husband to escape an unhappy marriage, not an abusive one. With this statement, the prosecutor sealed Snyder's fate by instilling fear in each male juror, who had to begin to wonder if other wives were capable of the same crime. The jury was quick to convict and condemn Ruth Snyder to death in the electric chair.

CRITICAL OVERVIEW

Although Treadwell was a prolific playwright and an outstanding journalist, there is still little information written about her life or plays. It is remarkable that a woman who has had successful runs of her plays on Broadway and internationally, plus had wide success as a journalist, has not received greater attention. As a journalist, Treadwell infiltrated prostitution in San Francisco, posing as a homeless prostitute to expose the lack of charitable help available to homeless women. During World War I, Treadwell was on assignment in Europe, making her one of the first female foreign war correspondents in American history. Her greatest journalistic success may have come from her two-day interview with the Mexican revolutionary bandit, Pancho Villa. Treadwell was the only American journalist granted access to Villa at his Mexican hideout.

Critically, *Machinal* was a smash success, having long runs on Broadway, in London and throughout Russia. It also catapulted Treadwell to the forefront of expressionism, making her one of the first female, American dramatists to write in the genre. Barbara L. Bywaters solidifies Treadwell's place in expressionism by comparing her to the genre's most renowned visual artist, Edvard Munch. Bywaters states her essay, "Marriage, Madness, and Murder in Sophie Treadwell's *Machinal*," in *Modern American Drama: The Female Canon*:

> Combining expressionistic techniques, such as repetitive dialogue, audio effects, numerous short scenes, and the distortion of inner and outer reality, Treadwell creates, with the evocative disorientation of an Edvard Munch, the picture of an ordinary young woman driven by desperation to murder.

Although Treadwell is most often seen as an expressionist, her plays unearth prejudices and inequalities. It is fair to say that *Machinal* is a statement against a male-dominated, oppressive society; the play is trying to expose a regimented social machine that confines and defines women not by their natures, but by their husbands. However, as most critics agree, Treadwell delivers her interpretations of society through an expressionist's palate, creating suggestive, raw, emotional dramatic landscapes for her characters and plotlines.

CRITICISM

Anthony Martinelli

Martinelli is a Seattle-based freelance writer and editor. In this essay, Martinelli examines how the patriarchal machine of the 1920s stifled Helen Jones, and the women's movement writ large, by forcing Helen into roles created by a male-dominated, oppressive social structure.

The Women's Suffrage movement finally delivered to women the right to vote on August 26, 1920, when Henry Burns cast the deciding vote that made Tennessee the thirty-sixth, and final, state to ratify the Nineteenth Amendment to the United States Constitution. Although this was a landmark movement in the Women's Movement, the struggle for equality certainly did not end then. Women continued to be subjected to sexual discrimination, both professionally and personally. Sophie Treadwell wrote *Machinal* in the wake of the ratification of the Nineteenth Amendment, understanding and foreshadowing the uphill struggle women still faced in the United States.

Machinal in particular spoke to the countless women forced to enter loveless marriages in order to survive in a world in which jobs were scarce for men and non-existent for women. During the years prior to and immediately following the Great Depression, women were forced into roles created by a male-dominated, oppressive social structure. Some women were lucky enough to find mutually loving relationships. Other women were willing to submit to their roles in exchange for financial stability. However, as is the case with Helen Jones, the tragic heroine of Treadwell's *Machinal*, some women could not tolerate the lives that the patriarchal machine demanded of them. The patriarchal machine is the social construction of the first half of the twentieth century. During these decades, men dominated and operated this machine with their vast, pervasive control of economics, politics, and expression. Only rare, extraordinary women were able to shake free of this machine, making advances in the Women's Movement.

Interestingly, though, Treadwell's protagonist is not an example of the *extraordinary woman* of the Suffrage Movement or the later Women's Liberation Movement. Instead, Treadwell challenges the patriarchal machine with not a unique, outspoken activist, but "an ordinary young woman, any woman." Although Helen progresses within the system, changing roles from secretary-to-wife, wife-to-sexual partner, and sexual partner-to-mother, Treadwell does not let her "any woman" silently age into obscurity. Helen challenges the patriarchal machine with her madness and, ultimately, the murder of her husband. This deliberate decision to challenge a male-dominated society with an *any*

 YET, TREADWELL DOES NOT STOP WITH HELEN'S SIMPLE DEFEAT AT THE HANDS OF THE MACHINE; INSTEAD SHE FORGES FURTHER AHEAD, EXPOSING HELEN'S INSANITY AND MAKING THE AUDIENCE CRINGE WITH SHAME AND REPULSION AT THE SOCIAL CONSTRUCT THEY WILLINGLY LIVE WITHIN."

woman dramatically empowers Treadwell's message, instilling fear into men and their formidable machine, that all women—not a select few—can dramatically impact, change and destroy their husband's lives.

In the beginning of *Machinal*, Treadwell depicts the first role of the patriarchal machine that Helen must fill. Helen works as a secretary in the office of George H. Jones. During this first episode, Helen and George have not wed and Helen feels that her work is stifling. Treadwell effectively creates a living, office-like machine in the first episode through her use of repetitious sounds, noises and voices. The office, although inhabited by humans, moves and sounds like a machine. At the helm is, of course, a man: George H. Jones. In the first episode, Treadwell makes it clear that George has asked for Helen's hand in marriage. However, the young woman is confused by the proposition because she does not love her boss. Her mother, on the other hand, cannot understand Helen's problem with marrying for financial stability. When Helen states that she wants to marry for love, her mother responds, "Love!—what does that amount to! Will it clothe you? Will it feed you? Will it pay the bills?" With this statement, Helen's mother reveals the conundrum presented before Helen in the first episodes: her only escape from the hell that is her stifling job, is to step directly into the claustrophobia of a loveless, passionless marriage. Although Helen may change roles, she does not escape the patriarchal machine. She would still be controlled by the male-dominated society. As

WHAT DO I READ NEXT?

- *The Yellow Wallpaper*, written by Charlotte Perkins Gilman and first published in 1899, is a classic, haunting story about a trapped woman's mental disintegration, due largely to the oppressiveness of the society she lived in.

- *Plays* (1987), by Susan Glaspell, is a collection of plays by the early twentieth-century female playwright and winner of the Pulitzer Prize for Drama in 1931. Her plays are unique, and she is known for her refusal to create stereotypical female characters.

- *Gringo* (1922), by Sophie Treadwell, is a play that depicts and highlights the stereotypical prejudices that Mexicans and Americans have felt about each other.

- *Elmer Rice: Three Plays* (1965) is a collection from a man often held in high regard as an influential playwright. He is often noted for bringing German expressionism into American theatre.

Barbara L. Bywaters writes in *Modern American Drama: The Female Canon*,

> Helen would be free of economic pressures if she marries her employer; on the other hand, she would be subordinate in every sense, legally, physically, emotionally, and economically, to a man she does not love or respect.

Sadly, Helen is propelled forward, under the prodding of her mother and the pressure of the machine, and marries George, submitting to her second role in society: wife.

The natural procession from marriage is, of course, into sex. However, in the case of Helen entering into a loveless marriage, the prospect of sexual intercourse with George is not only unpleasant, it is terrifying. In episode four, Helen and George are on their honeymoon. George, although not physically forceful, does pressure Helen into sexual intercourse telling her, "you got to relax little girl," offering to help her take off her clothes, and

remarking, "Say, what you got under there?" as he pinches her thigh. The end of this episode, with George successfully pressuring Helen into sex, paints a vile, unpleasant picture of what Helen becomes the moment she submits to her role as George's sexual partner. The patriarchal machine first pressures Helen out of her financial instability to become a married, financially stable wife. Then, as it is considered natural for a husband and wife to engage in sexual intercourse, Helen is again pressured into sexual intercourse. This forced coitus is terrifying on two despicable levels. First of all, if the progression is traced, Helen ends up sleeping with George not out of love or for pleasure, but simply because it means her continued financial stability. Essentially, her sexual intercourse with George is a drawn-out form of prostitution. As if this were not enough, the forcible pressures of the patriarchal machine that propel a wife forward into her role as sexual partner clearly results in a form of rape. A rape occurs when sexual intercourse is carried out against a person's will. Helen has no desire to engage in sexual intercourse with George and, although he does not physically force her into sex, the will and power of the patriarchal machine symbolically holds Helen in her place as her husband's sexual partner.

Following the honeymoon, Treadwell jumps directly into Helen's next role as mother. In what the patriarchal machine would generally consider a woman's final role, Treadwell uses this end as a means to see into Helen's madness. In the hospital, after giving birth to her daughter, Helen is at the apex of her own claustrophobia. She can barely speak, only shaking her head "no" when the doctor and nurse ask if she would like to breastfeed her baby. Helen is so repulsed by the finality of her life as a mother that she gags at the sight of her husband and finally screams to be left alone. At the end of this scene, Helen gives one of her long, disjointed diatribes in which she begs for death, questions God, and foreshadows the murder of her husband. These reoccurring monologues give a glimpse into Helen's mind as she struggles against the machine and, ultimately, fails, repeatedly submitting to the pressures and roles that she is forced to fulfill. As Jerry Dickey states of Treadwell in his essay, "The 'Real Lives' of Sophie Treadwell," in *Speaking the Other Self: American Women Writers*, "While creating works that depict women as subjects of drama, Treadwell cannot yet envision them completely empowered or victorious, but she refuses to allow her audiences to feel comfortable with their defeat." Helen is quite blatantly the subject of *Machinal* and she is not empowered because she still submits to the forces of the machine. Yet, Treadwell does not stop with Helen's simple defeat at the hands of the machine; instead she forges further ahead, exposing Helen's insanity and making the audience cringe with shame and repulsion at the social construct they willingly live within.

With the fate of her life seemingly confined to her final role as mother, Helen begins a restless, manic pursuit for an escape. In episodes five and six, Helen is introduced to a man, Dick Roe, who quickly becomes her lover. Roe represents Helen's lost freedom and deceased hopes. He is good looking, well traveled and adventurous. However, Helen mistakes their brief, passionate tryst for true love and when Roe leaves, ending the affair, Helen is devastated. With his departure, Helen sees that she has once again submitted to the powers of the patriarchal machine. Where she thought she had found release, she had simply committed another submissive act: becoming Roe's lover. She believed Roe would save her from her role in the loveless hell that was her life as wife, sexual partner and mother, only to be used for sexual pleasure and tossed back into the machine without a second glance.

In the final episodes of *Machinal*, Helen the *any woman* challenges the patriarchal system with one, last attempt to subvert the patriarchal machine. She decides that her only escape from the machine that has sentenced her to motherhood is to murder her husband. With George's death, the ties that bind her to the patriarchal machine would be undone, leaving her free for the first time in her life. She would still have financial stability, but she would no longer be bound to the roles she forcibly accepted to originally secure her financial footing. Her final decision to murder George also secures her own insanity. Yet, it is as if Treadwell is asking, who would not go insane? Helen has withstood incredible physical and psychological restrictions; she was forced to remain in perpetually claustrophobic environments and endure countless rapes. Helen was never allowed the opportunity to explore her dreams, fulfill her hopes, or understand her own identity. She lived a perpetually stifled, restricted, confined and tortured life. However, as the play demands to expose, this is the life that every woman, *any woman* is expected to live. Thus, if *any woman* could be driven to the point of murder to challenge the patriarchal machine and free herself from its oppressive, male-dominated structure, then every ordinary man, *any man*, should fear, if not expect,

a similar response. Treadwell finishes her play hoping to instill fear in the machine that "any ordinary young woman, any woman" could be willing, able and dedicated enough to struggle, fight, and possibly murder to escape oppression. With *Machinal*, Treadwell seems to be trying to telegraph this message to a younger generation, hoping that anything, even fear, will help stop the machine and free women from its roles, confines, and inequalities.

Source: Anthony Martinelli, Critical Essay on *Machinal*, in *Drama for Students*, Thomson Gale, 2006.

Kornelia Tancheva

In the following essay, Tancheva explores the reasons behind the initial mainstream success of Machinal.

Writing about Sophie Treadwell, one of the early feminist playwrights in the American theatre, is not an easy task. For all her prolific work over a span of sixty years, the critical attention she has received is not overwhelming. Despite Treadwell's relative unpopularity with scholars today, however, those few (feminist) critics who actually know her work and consider it worthy of critical attention never fail to praise it lavishly, especially as far as her expressionistic play *Machinal* is concerned.

Machinal premiered at the Plymouth Theatre in New York on 7 September 1928 and ran for ninety-one performances. It tells the fragmented life story of Helen Jones, a young woman who is first seen working in an inhumanely stifling office dominated by the presence of machines; she is desperately and unsuccessfully trying to escape an environment that reduces everyone else to a mere extension of a machine. For the lack of a better alternative, she almost forces herself into believing that marriage to her leering, repulsive boss would constitute the easiest escape route out of misery and drudgery into some financial security for herself and her mother. After all, this is the way of the world ("All women get married, don't they?"). A kaleidoscopic texture presents a string of scenes designed to illustrate the stages of her life: the honeymoon, with her husband's smug complacency and her animal-like terror; the unwanted motherhood, with the doctor's spiteful indifference and her piercing pain; the prohibited quest for pleasure in the speakeasy with little scenes of seduction, desertion, punishment, resignation, and some (imaginary) hope for human understanding between the Young Woman and the Man; the

" IT IS PRECISELY THIS TEXTUAL UNCERTAINTY IN THE REPRESENTATION OF MALE-FEMALE RELATIONS AND THE INSTITUTION OF MARRIAGE, WITH ALL THE ENTAILING ISSUES OF ECONOMIC, ROMANTIC, OR SEXUAL REFERENCES, THAT MUST HAVE PLAYED A VITAL PART IN ENSURING THE SUCCESS OF *MACHINAL.*"

intimacy of the Lover's bedroom, suggesting a faint possibility for happiness, yet overwhelmingly haunted by the Lover's "Quien sabe?"; the insufferably suffocating domestic scene, with the failure to communicate on any level whatsoever; the courtroom, with the law machine effectively at work, objective and inhuman, administering justice to all, that is, a death sentence for Helen Jones who murdered her husband; and finally, the machine that never fails, the nothingness of the electric chair, cutting off the Young Woman's final plea for somebody out there.

In the light of *Machinal*'s later appreciation and appropriation within a feminist discourse of women's resistance, it is intriguing to note that the original production was successful both with mainstream (Broadway) audiences and mainstream (New York) critics. To explain this curious development, a number of possibilities present themselves. First, one can assume that mainstream audiences' and critics' sensibilities of the 1920s and modern feminist interpretations curiously converge at some point. Second, *Machinal*'s popular success in the 1920s and its feminist interpretations today may be taken as an illustration of diachronic cultural relativism and the impossibility of fixed meaning; that is, the mainstream endorsement in the past and the antimainstream appropriation in the present are purely coincidental and have no bearing on any "textual evidence." Since the latter

possibility can serve only to preclude discussion, this chapter examines the former at greater length.

As arbitrary as historical parallels might be, it is not inconceivable that distinct historical periods share common if not identical concerns and consequently that intellectual climates overlap at various points. Such parallels between the 1920s' socially acceptable and condoned semiotization of gender and our present-day feminist debates on the construction of gender, however, seem somewhat unwarranted. For one, there is the difference of positioning within the larger cultural context, that is, a difference of "mainstream" versus "marginal." What is more, there is also a profound conceptual clash. An exhaustive consideration of the 1920s in terms of pro- and antifeminist issues and discourses will greatly overstep the limited boundaries of this essay, so this chapter will only point to a few characteristic trends that are clearly at variance with a post-1960s feminist cultural milieu.

After the decades of the women's suffrage movement culminated in the adoption of the Nineteenth Amendment in 1920, there was a swing back of the pendulum: the battle had been won and a respite was due. Whether or not the backlash was anything more than representational is certainly open to debate, yet as far as culturally produced images went, a clear metamorphosis of the challenging figure of the New Woman into the neurotic housewife had been effectively accomplished. A reconfiguration of women's place in society was begun that had to somehow reconcile traditional ideas of the private sphere with the very public political stand of the earlier decades, advocated by a radical feminist movement. One of the channels through which this was accomplished was the popular discourse on marriage, which sought to present it as the venue of *true* equality and independence. On the one hand, the idea of the *companionate marriage* was reinforced. On the other, the discourse on marriage was successfully intertwined with the one on technological progress and mechanization of household labor which allowed for an increase of women's leisure time and thus represented marriage as a desirable goal for young women. If that was the mainstream cultural attitude—largely antiwoman by feminist standards—then *Machinal*'s mainstream success cannot be considered tangential to its modern feminist stature.

Now, since mainstream success in the 1920s can hardly be reconciled with a strong subversive feminist message, it might be argued that *Machinal* has no bearing on contemporary feminist concerns and was only later reinterpreted along such lines. Unfortunately (or maybe fortunately), the complacency of this claim is instantly exposed when Treadwell's own involvement in the earlier stages of the women's movement (she not only espoused feminist ideas, but took an active part in the women's suffrage marches as well), or her introductory notes to the play, insisting that it is an Everywoman's story are taken into account. Granted this is external evidence, granted authorial intentions no longer count, there still remains the uneasiness of reconciling such a conflict. The claim collapses entirely, however, when the play itself is explored as much as possible on its own terms. It is so strongly immersed in the discussion of gender roles and gender interaction as to render such a claim virtually void.

If none of these possibilities will sufficiently stand on its own, then a third explanation must be sought. On the basis of the critical reviews that appeared after the original production of *Machinal* (unfortunately no audience surveys are available), we can reasonably assume that its success was due to the choice of the interpretative framework within which it was inserted. The interpretative choices made by the critics attempting to come to terms with what might be seen as a potentially very unsettling and upsetting text that appeared to subvert the very foundations of the culture that produced it reveal the mechanisms of reconfiguration *Machinal* was subjected to. The ultimate result was its unproblematic inclusion in a more traditional (i.e., already conventionalized) horizon of expectations.

The first line of critical interpretation that contributed most to toning down whatever subversion could be perceived in *Machinal* was the critics' preoccupation with the theatrical realization of the production and its importance within the work of Arthur Hopkins, the director, and Robert E. Jones, the set designer. Much of the praise was lavished on Hopkins, Jones, and the leading actors, Zita Johann (the Young Woman), George Stillwell (the Husband), and Clark Gable (the Lover). Even some of the headlines suggested the focus of attention: "Zita Johann Gets Ovation in 'Machinal'," "*Machinal*, a Tragedy in Fine Stage Clothing, with Sudden Glory for Zita Johann," "Elaborate Drama and New Lighting Seen at Plymouth." Hopkins's production was alternatively immensely skillful, unfailingly effective, superintelligent; Jones's suggestive backgrounds were vividly alive and splendidly lighted, illuminated by his fine imagination and his superb taste; Zita Johann's performance was superb, thrilling, warm, honest, heartbreaking, true, vivid, the most sensational aspect of the evening, conveying simplicity, power, delicacy, and understanding that "charms, thrills, and impresses"; her voice was singularly beautiful; the other members of the cast were admirable, excellent, splendidly competent. This list can go on forever.

Second, and closely related to the first, there was a unanimous concentration on the style of the piece as one of its greatest achievements, which allowed for its comparative positioning within the already established expressionism on the American stage. Treadwell's style inspired such great approval for its unsurpassed beauty and splendor that superlatives were typical: "There is a fine fluency in the writing of the scenes. Miss Treadwell has stripped them down to bare bones of drama, and flung them across the play in a swift staccato movement, which gives it *unique power and terrific momentum*" (emphasis added). Even those critics who were not particularly happy with the drama itself made sure to comment positively on the production: "The evening is primarily Mr. Jones's, secondarily Miss Johann's, Mr. Hopkins's, then Miss Treadwell's," insisted David Carb in *Vogue;* or found a single redeeming quality in the rhythm or the setting, as did Gilbert Seldes in the *Dial.*

Third, there emerged an exclusive concern with the antimechanization message of the play facilitating its unproblematic incorporation within the register of another universal discourse, that on technological progress and its effect on human interaction. The play's interpretation as a powerful representation of antimechanization and dehumanization obscures all other interpretative possibilities: "probably it is the story of Ruth Snyder; which doesn't matter, since beyond that 'Machinal' is the piteous, terror-laden tale of human revolt against the engine"; "'Machinal' is less murder play than . . . study of character," the character of the Young Woman, who only asks for "rest and peace, clean air, quiet, freedom from the endless pressure of bodies, pity and understanding," but can never find them in this "shrill and clattering metropolis to which the French title refers"; it displays a "treacherous chorus of machinery," the "breathless pace of a woman fleeing from one treadmill to another, the din of machines always in her ears, the iron rain of noise beating her down until she dies at last in the embrace of a grim machine of wires and wailing agony." The Young Woman is a "human fly caught in the web of the spider, Life, thwarted and frustrated at every turn, squelched by the insuperable Will of the Great Machine," a "child and victim of the Machine Age . . . fed into the greedy maw of the machine."

A typical interpretation in which the discourse on mechanization was privileged at the expense of that on gender interrelations is to be found in the *New York Sun* review: "It is no one man who hacks out the destiny of . . . Mrs. Jones. It is the Machine Age, and the Machine Age's wanton son, the City."

Finally, the Young Woman and her actions were particularized by stressing the "real-life" basis of the play, that is, the Snyder-Gray murder case trial. The link between the play and the Snyder-Gray case was explicit in the reviews in *Women's Wear Daily* ("definite memories of a recent infamous New York murder case"), the *New York Sun* ("seized upon the Snyder-Gray case," "founded on an all too recent and painful actuality"), the *New York Evening Journal* ("Snyder Case Suggested in a Magnificent Tragedy"), and the *New York American* ("Drama Founded on Ruth Snyder's Life Is Not for Morose"), among others. One reviewer referred to Helen Jones as "Mrs. Snyder's dramatic alias," another saw the play as "obviously founded on the life story of Ruth Snyder" and its end paralleling "the end of Ruth Snyder's mean, pitiful life," while yet another even recounted some rumors that Zita Johann's costume was identical to the one worn by Mrs. Snyder at her trial.

To summarize the reviews of the original 1928 production of *Machinal,* one finds that most of them were exclusively concerned with matters of style, complimenting Treadwell for the unemotional yet convincing rendering of the story of a sensational murder that did not drown it in the maudlin idiom of melodrama as well as with the superb staging of the piece. Those of the reviews that went beyond these concerns dearly conceptualized it as partaking of a serious public debate, that on the disadvantages and advantages of a mechanized civilization. Yet its relevance to "feminist" anxieties was totally silenced, and in no way did the interpretation envision a construction of a female subjectivity either in the characters or in the audience. Despite some individual differences, the overall trend among critics was to avoid interpreting *Machinal* as referring to a broader social context determined and defined by patriarchal structures; rather, they construed it as a representation of an individual woman's predicament in a society in which the agents and venues of oppression did not discriminate on the basis of gender. The parallel with the Snyder-Gray case was used to obscure a potentially dangerous possibility, that is, that Helen Jones was indeed Every-woman in the contemporary context. Instead, by alluding to an all too familiar murder trial, sensationalized by the press, the critical interpretations particularized and disciplined the play. (On another level, of course this also allowed for the inclusion of *Machinal* within the host of murder plays popular at the time.) At least one significant difference was glossed over, namely, that in the actual case, both the woman and her lover were convicted and executed for the murder of the husband, while in the play Treadwell chose to have the Lover instrumental in convicting the Young Woman. (He sends an affidavit supplying the murder motive from Mexico, where he is at the time.)

In other words, the argument in this chapter is that *Machinal* was successfully interpreted within a mainstream cultural discourse precisely because it was universalized along the first three lines, and particularized along the fourth.

The concern hereafter will be a possible explanation for such a development beside the obvious ideological assumptions of the critics and the overall cultural and intellectual climate in which the play appeared where certain discourses were both available and popularly familiar. This chapter attempts to show that *Machinal*'s relatively unimpeded inclusion within the discourse of technological progress at the expense of a "feminist" one was facilitated, among other things, by its ambiguity as far as an indictment of the "patriarchal" institution of marriage was concerned. In other words, an analysis of the structure of the play, the speech patterns, and the resolution of the conflict can destabilize its appropriation by a consistent feminist critique, for it clearly leaves open the possibility for a *companionate marriage,* that is, a marriage of mutual love and understanding which Helen Jones did not obtain but could possibly have succeeded in obtaining—a view that a middle-class mainstream audience could easily endorse and identify with. The argument could be made that her ending up on the electric chair was as much her fault and bad luck as it might have been the fault of a socially construed practice.

In the first place, she started with the "wrong" premises, she married exclusively for financial security and provision, knowingly entering into a physically and romantically repulsive union. Since other characters are also aware of the choices available to the Young Woman or their possible repercussions, her decision can also be interpreted as being of her own making and not entirely the result of social pressure. The choice of interpreting Helen as bringing disaster onto herself is left open for an audience immersed in the discourse of the *companionate marriage* and the openly admitted significance of sexual compatibility for a privately and publicly successful marriage.

The scenes that further enhance a perception of the "false" premises on which Helen Jones married and, hence, could never succeed in convincing herself that she could learn to reconcile the conflicting longings for financial security and romantic love are the ones with the Lover. The explanation that he has of what is wrong with Helen is: "1ST MAN. You just haven't met the right guy—that's all—a girl like you—you got to meet the right guy," suggesting that, if it had been somebody else, it might have been different— "Quien sabe?"

In other words, given the proper conditions, would it not be possible to transpose the Young Woman's inadaptability from a representative to an idiosyncratic level? Is she any woman, as Treadwell maintains in her notes, or is her character an isolated case study, that is, is there something wrong with the synchronic conceptualization of the institution of marriage, as many of the scenes will seem to argue, or is it a particular marriage arrangement that did not work out? Should one wonder at the critics' insistence on the Snyder-Gray connection, then, instead of recognizing a pattern of particularization launched by the ambiguous stand within the text itself?

The Lover is certainly not "the right guy" for the Young Woman, as the conflict resolution demonstrates. Let us go one step further, however, and see what interpretative possibilities are delineated in their brief encounter through a comparative analysis of the Young Woman's speech patterns. In the office scene, she is as caught in the mechanical pattern of linguistic and behavioral repetition as her co-workers, but in contrast to them she is not able to make the logical connections between the stretches of words that they seem to blurt out almost involuntarily. They repeat and shorten their phrases for reasons of clarity and efficiency, but never fail to hold on to a link of contiguity, while the Young Woman's speech pattern is broken to the point where it does not exhibit any trace of logical consistency. Instead, it hinges on similarity and allusion.

The similarity/contiguity distinction becomes all the more relevant when considered in terms of artistic versus scientific/technological conceptualization. Contiguity is usually associated with progress logically pursued and attained by metonymically coping with reality, attempting to describe a part, or an effect, and infer the whole, or the cause. Similarity, on the other hand, metaphorically transcends the human ability to master reality logically for it strives at a totality of explanation and retreats into itself when baffled by its own frailty.

Probably the first and only time when the Young Woman is able to contiguously describe a situation, instead of metaphorically allude to it, is in episode 6, "Intimate." When she is with her Lover, her sentences are complete and even the actual metaphors are explicated. Similarly, the only instance of a possible logical planning of her life comes, curiously enough, again in the scenes with the Lover. Curiously, since, in a way, she conforms to contiguity and machine-like precision when she is supposed to be escaping the mundane logic of everyday existence. Why should the Lover, of all characters, include Helen Jones in the abhorrent reality of mechanization and dehumanization? (The instance discussed here is merely preliminary to his ultimate betrayal, to be sure.) Is it not because he is not "the right guy" within the acceptable social behavior and mores of the times? Maybe. "Quien sabe?"

It is precisely this textual uncertainty in the representation of male-female relations and the institution of marriage, with all the entailing issues of economic, romantic, or sexual references, that must have played a vital part in ensuring the success of *Machinal.* Whether, however, the play's ambiguous stance and its deep entanglement in the contradictory ideas of women's place in society were deliberately ignored or genuinely not recognized at the time of its production is not to be settled from our historical distance and anachronistic perspective.

Source: Kornelia Tancheva, "Sophie Treadwell's Play *Machinal*: Strategies of Reception and Interpretation," in *Experimenters, Rebels, and Disparate Voices: The Theatre of the 1920s Celebrates American Diversity*, edited by Arthur Gewirtz and James J. Kolb, Praeger, 2003, pp. 101–07.

Jennifer Jones

In the following essay, Jones examines how Treadwell uses Machinal *to explore Ruth Snyder's mind and the story left out of her court proceedings.*

On March 20, 1927, Albert Snyder was found murdered in his bed, beaten on the head with a blunt

> SHE SETS FORTH HER
> ARGUMENT IN A DRAMA, NOT TO
> PROVE SNYDER'S INNOCENCE, BUT
> TO ASK IF PERHAPS THERE IS
> ANOTHER WAY OF LOOKING AT
> THE CASE, ONE THAT THE ALL-
> MALE JURY AND PREDOMINANTLY
> MALE PRESS CORPS DID NOT
> UNDERSTAND."

object, chloroformed, and strangled with a piece of picture wire. When the police arrived, his wife, Ruth, was discovered outside their daughter's room, bound and gagged. She told police she had been attacked by a tall Italian man, and claimed to have fainted when he grabbed her, remaining unconscious for over five hours. The small house had been ransacked, drawers were emptied, and Ruth's jewelry stolen. Police became suspicious when the "stolen" jewelry was found under Ruth's mattress, and when she neglected to ask after her husband they felt sure she was involved in the murder. When told he was dead, they said the tears she shed were "suspiciously few." After nearly twenty hours of questioning, Ruth Snyder confessed that, with her lover, Judd Gray, she had beaten her husband to death with a sash weight while her nine-year-old daughter slept in the next room. Later she would change her story to say that it was Gray who had masterminded the murder and that she had been unable to stop him.

Ultimately both Ruth and Gray were convicted of murder and executed at Sing Sing on January 12, 1928. Eight months after Ruth Snyder died in the electric chair, Sophie Treadwell's play *Machinal*, directed by Arthur Hopkins, and designed by Robert Edmund Jones, opened at the Plymouth Theatre in New York City. Increasingly, scholars and directors are "rediscovering" this play, and many consider it to be one of America's finest expressionist dramas. Most of the original reviewers in 1928 wrote that *Machinal* was only loosely based on the Ruth Snyder case, and this position has been quoted and accepted by contemporary scholarship.

However, a close examination of that trial and the unprecedented coverage it received lead me to believe that Ruth Snyder was never far from Sophie Treadwell's mind as she wrote *Machinal*.

In a last-minute attempt to save Ruth's life, her attorneys had asked that an alienist (psychiatrist) be brought in to testify on her behalf. Hoping to save their client, the lawyers wanted to examine Ruth's mind in light of modern science. The Governor denied the request. It is possible to look at *Machinal* as Treadwell's attempt to examine Ruth's mind in the light of modern drama, ironically, giving her an appropriately theatrical life-after-death. I believe *Machinal* is the testimony, disallowed by the court of law, that Treadwell wished to introduce into the court of public opinion. She sets forth her argument in a drama, not to prove Snyder's innocence, but to ask if perhaps there is another way of looking at the case, one that the all-male jury and predominantly male press corps did not understand. But in order to appreciate Treadwell's defense of Ruth, it is first necessary to contextualize the actual trial.

Albert Snyder's murder had captured the imagination of the public and created a media event of astonishing proportions. Over 1500 people attended the Snyder trial and 180 reporters were assigned to the case. Treadwell, an experienced journalist, was not officially covering the trial, but she was a spectator in the courtroom. For the first time in history, microphones and speakers were set up in a courtroom so that everyone could hear the testimony. One had to have a ticket to be admitted, and scalpers were ready, as always, to make a quick buck, selling tickets for fifty dollars apiece. The second day Ruth took the stand, the *New York Times* described the spectators in the courtroom as "a typical Broadway audience, sophisticated and cynical." In attendance were playwright Willard Mack; philosopher Will Durant; W.E. Woodward; Ben Hecht; Fannie Hurst; and Nora Bayes. Spectators were as interested in the stars as in the trial, and the tabloids solicited celebrity opinions for their columns. David Belasco, who came every day and sat in a front row seat, wrote:

> Poor unfortunate woman—drawn into this mess as she embarked on what she thought was to be the great romance of her life! I have looked at her with much sympathy.

Peggy Hopkins Joyce was less kind:

> And so I say there is no excuse for Ruth Snyder. Maybe if I knew the woman intimately I could find something that would explain her kissing her lover and sash-weighting her husband to death almost

simultaneously. But looking at her in court where she is on exhibition as a sort of blue-ribbon defendant and where she is supposed to be trying to impress a jury with her innocence, I shudder. *How did she get that way?* (my italics)

Newspapers capitalized on the huge market for this sordid courtroom drama. By May 5, 1927 (according to the *Evening Post*) "Approximately 1,500,000 words about the Snyder story" had been "filed on press wires." The *New York Times* ran an article on the trial almost every day from the morning of the murder to the night of the execution. For those who could not attend, the newspapers, in column after column, recreated the trial in phenomenal detail: reprinting the testimony, reporting everything Snyder and Gray said or did, reviewing their performances on the stand, and keeping a running commentary on the "audience's" reaction.

The characters in this courtroom drama were easily recognizable—The Wife, The Lover, The Cuckold—and journalists became stage managers, arranging the narrative, casting the characters, and manipulating audience response to this stock scenario. When Gray testified that he and Ruth had planned to kill Albert Snyder two weeks earlier but had gotten "cold feet," the *New York Times* reporter wrote:

> There was a general, noisy sigh of relief throughout the courtroom over this good news. Carried away by the dramatic interest of the story, the hearers forgot themselves and enjoyed the illusion of a happy ending for a fraction of a second. Then a few lines later the confession launched into a description of the reconstruction of the plot and its execution on March 20.

The lawyers were apparently given to theatrics, and they too became characters in the media drama. Describing the cross-examination of Gray by Snyder's attorney, the *New York Times* reporter wrote:

> Mr. Hazelton denounced Gray, he reinforced his rhetoric with pantomime. He gave a sort of dramatic reading of the part which he claimed Gray played in the case. Swaggering about in the first place as the spruce lady-killer which he pictured Gray to be, he snapped into an imitation of Gray on the murder night. The lawyer distorted his face, bent himself over like a hunchback, thrust forth his chin, stuck out his arms, moved his hands about with all fingers vibrating at a terrific rate and scurried to and fro in front of the jury.

The language of the theatre was constantly invoked to describe the trial. Damon Runyon wrote:

> This remains the best show in town, if I may say so, as I shouldn't. Business couldn't be better. In fact, there is some talk of sending out a No. 2 company and 8,000,000 different blondes are being considered for the leading female role. No one has yet been picked for Henry Judd Gray's part but that will be easy. Almost any citizen will do, with a little rehearsal.

When Ruth first learned that her jury would be all men, she said, "I'm sorry. I believe that women would understand this case better than men." Ruth was right to be worried about her credibility in the eyes of the twelve men chosen to judge her. The jury and the press seemed to excuse Gray's part in the murder by casting him as the weak-willed, impressionable sap. His attorney's opening statement made it clear who the villain was in this murder story:

> He was dominated by a cold, heartless, calculating mastermind and master will. He was a helpless mendicant of a designing, deadly, conscienceless abnormal woman, a human serpent, a human fiend in the guise of a woman. He was in the web, in the abyss; he was dominated, he was commanded, he was driven by this malicious character. He became inveigled and was drawn into this hopeless chasm, when reason was gone, when mind was gone, when manhood was gone and when his mind was absolutely weakened by lust and by passion and by abnormal relations.

Despite his lawyers' efforts, Gray was found guilty, and on May 13, 1927 both he and Ruth were sentenced to die in the electric chair. After the verdict one juror told the *New York Times* reporter: "There was little doubt in any of our minds as to what the verdict would be. We all knew that Mrs. Snyder was lying. . . . We all believed every word that Gray said."

The execution proved to be as dramatic as the trial; rumors that Snyder's attorneys were planning to resuscitate Ruth after her death created a riot in the streets of New York. Thousands lined up to watch the prisoners brought to the death house at Sing Sing. The few women reporters covering the trial were barred from witnessing the execution, and most waited outside the prison gates with the mob. Ishbel Ross, in her book *Ladies of the Press,* describes the scene outside Sing Sing on the night Ruth Snyder was electrocuted.

> On the night that Ruth Snyder died, Miss McCarthy, who was then on the *Journal,* was one of the newspaper women who waited outside the prison while a huge crowd made shocking whoopee at the gates. It might have been a carnival instead of an execution. There was a screaming mob of more than 2000. There were cars with licenses from five different states. Boys in raccoon coats with bottles of gin in their pockets sat in parked roadsters. . . . Vendors sold hot dogs and popcorn . . .

> The most seasoned reporters were startled by the antics of this ghoulish crowd. Brick Terrett . . . came out after it was over. He had seen Ruth die in the chair.

"Julia, for God's sake take a walk with me," he said to Miss McCarthy. "Talk to me about anything. My God, she looked so little."

Another man who had come out with him from witnessing the same scene vomited on the spot.

The ultimate act in this media drama took place when a reporter from the *Daily News,* managing to sneak a camera into the execution chamber by strapping it to his leg, took a picture of Ruth Snyder at the moment of her death. In the end, the trial was transformed into a spectacular production, worthy of Belasco himself. The day after Snyder and Gray were executed, the *New York World* headline read: "SNYDER TRAGEDY IN PROSAIC SETTING: Dramatic Police Work Got Speedy Confessions From Wife and her Lover—Trial a Jazzy Affair." A *New York Times* editorial said simply—"The End of the Show."

Although public opinion ran strongly against Ruth Snyder, several newspapers ran editorials claiming that the trial had been unable to determine the real "truth" of the murder. One journalist for the *New York Evening Post,* echoing Peggy Joyce Hopkins, asked:

How then does Mrs. Snyder differ from those other dissatisfied wives with heavily insured husbands? Or from the subtle women who meet men without their husbands' knowledge? We do not know the answers to these questions, and will perhaps never know them. The law does not try to find out; it deals only with events and with the superficial motives leading to them. So here is the real mystery in the Snyder case. It is the profound mystery of personality. The mystery of impulses.

It is the mystery "of personality and impulse" that Treadwell explores in *Machinal,* using an expressionistic style to freely enter the subconscious mind of her subject and convey the part of Ruth's story that was not heard at the trial. Treadwell looks beyond the "events and superficial motives" that were revealed in the courtroom and questions the court's assumptions of cause and effect, asking if there might not be a more complex psychological reality involved in this case.

In *Machinal,* surface details differ, often substantially, from the Ruth Snyder story; this led most reviewers to write that the play was only loosely based on the Snyder case. But, just as an expressionist painting reveals the inner, rather than outer, life of its subject, so *Machinal* explores the subtext of the trial whose surface details were so well known to Treadwell's audience. Treadwell begins the play with what some have seen as a disclaimer of the connection to Ruth Snyder. "THE PLOT is the story of a woman who murders her husband— an ordinary young woman, any woman." Rather than distancing the play from the real-life trial, this statement articulates the subliminal fear that made Ruth Snyder so threatening and so interesting. In an analysis of the case, written for law students in 1938, John Kobler explains the fascination Ruth Snyder had for the average citizen.

Psychotic freaks who go in for fancy dismemberment and other baroque horrors may momentarily titillate the old gentleman in carpet slippers, but when Mrs Jones next door laces her husband's chowder with weed killer that same old gentleman is jounced off his perch. The thing is too near home, too understandable. Subconsciously he identifies himself with poor Jones. He may even view his own consort in fresh perspective—and wonder a little.

The prosecuting attorney proved that Ruth killed her husband to get out of an unhappy marriage, but how was the Snyder marriage different from thousands of other unhappy marriages? The trial couldn't explain what made this particular unhappy wife kill her husband, and so, subliminally, all wives became suspect. Ruth's very ordinariness was her danger.

Throughout the script Treadwell makes subtle allusions to the media's portrayal of the real Ruth Snyder. In her character description, Treadwell says of the Young Woman, "*The confusion of her own inner thoughts, emotions, desires, dreams cuts her off from any actual adjustment to the routine of work*"; the tabloids made much of the fact that Ruth constantly read "Love Magazines" and lived in the dream world of a romance novel. Treadwell also describes the Young Woman as "*constantly arranging her hair over her ears.*" Ruth was very concerned with her appearance, and a great newspaper debate raged over whether she should be allowed to have cosmetics in prison. She requested that a hairdresser dye her hair before she was executed, but the warden denied her request. Determined, she washed her own hair before she died. Reporters noted that in a final "womanly gesture" she smoothed her hair before the executioner put the mask on her face. This moment, complete with the reporter's commentary, is recreated in the final scene of *Machinal.*

Other events in the play allude to specific testimony at the trial. In the opening episode, the Young Woman repeats several times that she felt as though she was going to faint on the subway. Ruth's attorney claimed that she had fainted when Gray attacked her husband, and had been unable to prevent the murder. The defense spent considerable time establishing that Ruth was a woman prone to fainting. Ruth also fainted in her prison cell several times.

Still, many of *Machinal*'s plot details do correspond directly to Ruth's life, and they serve to connect Treadwell's narrative to the actual trial. In *Machinal,* the Young Woman, like Ruth Snyder, is an office worker who marries her much older boss. She doesn't love him but she welcomes the security that his money would provide. Ruth admitted that financial considerations played a large part in her decision to wed Snyder, eleven years her senior; she said, "I think the diamond had as much as anything to do with my consenting to marry him. I wouldn't have given that ring up for anything after once [sic] I had it on my hand."

Treadwell spends considerable time establishing the unhappiness of the Young Woman's marriage. This is in contrast to the real trial, where the defense attorney, attempting to portray Ruth as a good wife, shied away from the unpleasant facts of this marriage, which seemed doomed from the start. Ruth Snyder had fallen ill on the day of her wedding and after the ceremony refused to leave with her husband. On their wedding night, Albert Snyder went home alone while Ruth stayed with her mother. Treadwell interprets that night in the third episode of *Machinal,* entitled "The Honeymoon." While happy couples dance below her, the Young Woman, repulsed by her husband on their wedding night, cowers by the bed, calling for her mother.

In Gray's testimony he described a conversation he had with Ruth at their second meeting.

> She said she had never really known what sexual pleasures were with her husband. I sympathized with her, as I recall, that it was too bad, as I felt that was probably one of the greatest reasons for her unhappiness. She told me that when he came over into bed with her that to her it was so disgusting and degrading that she felt like killing him.

The experience of having one's body used by a man one does not love was probably not one that the male jury could sympathize with or understand. Ruth's attorneys never used this line of reasoning in her defense, but in *Machinal,* Treadwell makes the Young Woman's sexual degradation a central part of her testimony against the system that convicted Ruth Snyder.

Ruth's extra-marital affair was perhaps the most damning evidence against her. At first, the romantic stage lover Richard Roe, an adventurer who travels to exotic places, seems a far cry from Judd Gray, the corset salesman from Syracuse. But to Ruth Snyder, whose husband kept her close at home, Gray's life as a traveling salesman represented freedom and adventure. In the court testimony she says that accompanying Gray on a ten-day sales trip across New York state was the happiest time of her life. If we look not at the outward details but at the internal desires of an unhappy woman, we can see Roe and his exotic travels as a romanticized version of Judd Gray, the traveling salesman.

There was substantial evidence that Albert Snyder beat his wife and his child on several occasions. The couple quarrelled often and Ruth testified that her husband had recently bought a gun and that he had threatened to shoot her. Ruth's attorney, trying to portray her as the model wife, did not bring up this line of questioning, but in his testimony, Judd Gray described another conversation with Ruth—remember he is testifying *against her.*

> She said she could not live with him any longer . . . I asked her if she really felt in her own mind that he would kill her. She said that he was liable to do anything. At that particular time she complained bitterly about his treatment towards their youngster. She said that he had slapped her on that particular day, and almost knocked her down. I asked her if that was usual. She said that he had slapped her many times and that that particular time she felt as though she could kill him.

Ruth's own attorney never remarked on Albert Snyder's violence towards his wife and child, and it was one of the few parts of the testimony never reported by the press. In light of these circumstances, Episode Six in *Machinal,* entitled "Intimate," a scene in which the Young Woman discovers love for the first time after years in an unhappy marriage, resonates with compassion rather than judgement. Treadwell shows the Young Woman, who has never experienced love or pleasure at the hands of her husband, in a moment of supreme happiness as sexual passion is finally awakened. She emphasizes the importance of this scene by returning to a naturalistic style of dialogue, asserting that this "illicit" love is more natural and necessary than the degrading sexual manipulation of the woman's marriage. Treadwell's stage directions for this scene are telling: *"her dressing [is] a personification, an idealization of a woman clothing herself. All her gestures must be unconscious, innocent, relaxed, sure and full of natural grace."* The public condemned Ruth for her sexual relationship with a man who was not her husband, and in their eyes she was a fallen woman. But Treadwell uses the affair and the awakening of sexual passion to bring the Young Woman, finally, into the fullness of her womanhood. Treadwell defends Ruth's infidelity by reversing the court's assumption that a woman's duty is to her husband and asserting that she has a more important duty to herself.

Of course, the most dramatic difference between *Machinal* and the Snyder trial comes in the actual trial scene. Treadwell makes the Young Woman, alone, responsible for the murder of her husband. Her lover, aside from giving her the idea (by telling her how he once killed a man by hitting him on the head with a bottle full of stones), had nothing to do with the husband's death. But again, Treadwell is not looking at the surface details of the trial, but at its subtext. It was always Ruth Snyder's trial—she was the focus of the media, she was perceived as the master mind behind the murder, she was given the blame for corrupting the innocent Gray. Although Gray inflicted the fatal blows to Albert Snyder's head, it was Ruth Snyder who bore the blame for the act. In *Machinal,* it is a letter from her lover (safely ensconced in Mexico) that convicts the Young Woman; without that testimony she might have gone free. By having the Young Woman's lover convict her, Treadwell portrayed the political reality of Ruth's trial. It was the testimony of Gray, her co-defendant, that ultimately convicted Ruth. There were no witnesses to the murder, and it came down to his word against hers. In his summation, Ruth's attorney said:

> Now I am going to remark at the outset, in no uncertain terms, that you gentlemen might now understand, that *this is a case of Henry Judd Gray and the people of the state of New York against Ruth Snyder, and nothing else.* She is sandwiched in between two prosecutors and you know it, and the district attorney need only sit idly by and watch the condemnation of this woman by this co-defendant.

Despite the many connections to the trial, there is one moment in *Machinal* in which Treadwell sharply diverges from Snyder's story. When Ruth was strapped into the electric chair, her last words were, "Father forgive them." Treadwell is not willing to have her Young Woman forgive so easily. As she is being led to the electric chair she pleads to see her daughter, crying, "Wait! Wait! Tell her! Wait! Just a minute more! There's so much I want to tell her—Wait—"

"I'm sorry," Ruth Snyder had said. "I believe women would understand this case better than men." *Machinal*, a woman's story, told by another woman, premiered on Broadway only eight months after the "Broadway crowd" had seen Ruth Snyder condemned to die. Overall, the play was a critical success, but the reviewers rarely saw how masterfully

Treadwell had woven the Snyder trial into her narrative. Their inability to look beyond the surface differences of plot prevented them from appreciating Treadwell's defense of Ruth Snyder and her inherent questioning of the male perspective in the trial. Atkinson of the *New York Times* wrote:

> In superficial details the story resembles the Snyder and Gray murder case. But Sophie Treadwell, who is Mrs. W.O. McGeehan in private life, has in no sense capitalized a sensational murder trial in her strangely moving, shadowy drama. Rather she has written a tragedy of submission.

It is interesting that Atkinson, who felt the need to define Treadwell in terms of her marital status by assigning her husband's name as her true identity, could not see a tragedy of submission in Ruth Snyder's story.

Robert Littell, in his review for *Theatre Arts Monthly,* also fails to see any significant connection between Treadwell's drama and the Snyder case.

> Sophie Treadwell was one of the newspaper women who witnessed the trial of Ruth Snyder and Judd Grey [sic]. This brutal, inhuman murder, one of the ugliest on record, gave her the starting point for *Machinal,* but only the starting point. Having seen the two monsters, and the motives which led them to kill Snyder, she forgets their story and their characters and asks herself, How is it possible for a sensitive woman of deep feelings to be so oppressed by life and by her husband that she kills him?

Littell categorically dismisses the idea that Ruth Snyder might have feelings or sensitivities, and disallows the possibility that she may have been oppressed by life or brutalized by her husband. The need to keep Ruth an aberration is strong for these reviewers. Ironically, Littell ends up being so sympathetic to Treadwell's Young Woman that he says, "I cannot help feeling that [Miss Treadwell] would have been artistically more successful if she had stopped short of the end."

No doubt Ruth would have preferred that as well.

Source: Jennifer Jones, "In Defense of the Woman: Sophie Treadwell's *Machinal*," in *Modern Drama*, Vol. XXXVII, No. 3, Fall 1994, pp. 485–93.

Barbara L. Bywaters

In the following essay, Bywaters places Machinal *and its message of "female insurrection" within the context of feminist discourse and social protest of the twentieth century.*

> don't touch me—please—no—can't—must—...
> I want to rest—no rest—earn ... all girls—most
> girls—married

Let me alone—I've submitted to enough . . . Vixen
   crawled off
under bed—eight—there were eight—a woman
   crawled off
under the bed . . . one two three four . . . I'll not
submit any more—

I put him out of the way—yes . . . To be free . . .

When I did what I did I was free! . . . my child . . .
Let her live! Live! Tell her—

Sophie Treadwell's *Machinal* transmits a terse, telegraphic message: the institution of marriage is a breeding ground for anger, desperation, and violence. This 1928 expressionist drama imparts the story of an ordinary young woman's marriage to her employer and the societal and psychological pressures that lead her ultimately to murder him. Trivialized by theater critic Robert Brustein in 1960 as "one of those banal tabloid stories . . . about how a sensitive dish of cream is curdled in the age of the machine," Treadwell's slighted work often has been characterized as a derivative drama of social criticism targeted at the effects of mechanization on the individual. Treadwell's social protest, however, reaches beyond the machine age of the twentieth century. Augmenting a female tradition of literature that dissects the restrictive institution of marriage and its effects on women, *Machinal* stands as an early twentieth-century piece of subversive drama, conveying the message that female insurrection can lead to "one moment of freedom" before the patriarchal "machinery" crushes the revolt.

Born in Stockton, California, in 1885, Treadwell belongs to a group of early modern American women writers who flourished in what Elaine Showalter has labeled "feminism's awkward age." A respected journalist, actress, playwright, as well as producer and director of her own work when necessary, Treadwell could pose as a prototype for the independent and adventuresome "New Woman" of the early twentieth century. Graduating from the University of California at Berkeley in 1906, Treadwell, like many women writers in the first half of the century, began her writing career in journalism, working as a staff writer for the *San Francisco Bulletin,* where she covered as well as participated in the marches for women's suffrage. After her marriage to journalist William O'Connell McGeehan, she moved to the New York *Herald Tribune,* which sent her to Europe as a war correspondent during World War I. Alternating between journalism and playwriting, Treadwell had her first professional production in 1922 with the drama *Gringo,* influenced by her exclusive interview with the Mexican revolutionary Pancho Villa

PERHAPS INSTEAD OF BEING MISREAD OR MISINTERPRETED BY MALE CRITICS, *MACHINAL* HAS BEEN COMPREHENDED ALL TOO WELL. SILENCED FOR DECADES BY THE LITERARY 'MACHINE,' SOPHIE TREADWELL STILL HAS A MESSAGE TO TELEGRAPH TO HER 'DAUGHTERS.'"

a year earlier. Although Treadwell wrote thirty full-length plays before her death in 1970, only seven were performed on Broadway, and of this handful, only *Machinal* and *Hope for a Harvest* (1941) were ever published. Performed in European theaters and produced for television in 1960, *Machinal* remains Treadwell's only commercial success, and yet it also has been largely overlooked in traditional drama surveys by critics.

Although an analysis of Treadwell's dramatic canon reveals a broad spectrum of dramatic forms ranging from light comedy to melodrama to social criticism, it is her longstanding "partisanship of feminism" that marks the majority of her works. Plays such as *Oh Nightingale* (1925), a conventional comedy about an aspiring actress in New York City; *Lone Valley* (1933), a melodrama of a reformed prostitute; and *Hope for a Harvest,* a realistic drama of a woman's attempt to restore her family's farm, all feature female protagonists who struggle for autonomy (albeit not always successfully) in a male-dominated society. Perhaps the strongest declaration of Treadwell's commitment to feminist concerns is her play *Rights,* an unpublished biographical drama of Mary Wollstonecraft, the eighteenth-century author of the seminal feminist work *A Vindication of the Rights of Woman.* Copyrighted in 1921 but never produced, *Rights* frames Wollstonecraft's bid for personal freedom against the broader struggle of the French Revolution. Criticized as didactic and unfocused, *Rights* nevertheless capsulizes some feminist issues that receive powerful, searing dramatization in

Machinal seven years later, particularly the role of women in the institution of marriage. The bold, vibrant character of Wollstonecraft in *Rights,* who lashes out, "I am opposed to marriage. . . . I will not submit to an institution I wish to see abolished," stands behind the docile wife portrayed in *Machinal.*

Like *Rights, Machinal* (French for "mechanical") voices Treadwell's feminism with a particular vehemency and radicalism that is softened in many of her other plays. Combining expressionistic techniques, such as repetitive dialogue, audio effects, numerous short scenes, and the distortion of inner and outer reality, Treadwell creates, with the evocative disorientation of an Edvard Munch, the picture of an ordinary young woman driven by desperation to murder. Using her newspaper writing experiences, Treadwell based her play in part on the celebrated 1927 murder trial of Ruth Snyder and Judd Gray, two lovers convicted of killing Mrs. Snyder's husband. With this sensational crime as her foundation, Treadwell builds the story of a young woman forced by economic and societal pressures to marry her employer. Trapped in a loveless marriage, the young woman drifts into an extramarital affair with a handsome adventurer. After her lover's return to Mexico, the woman's sense of confinement and anguish overwhelm her and lead her to murder her husband by striking him over the head with a bottle of stones, a method related to her by the lover. The young woman is convicted of murder when her lover informs the police of their affair in an effort to keep himself from punishment. The play ends with the execution of the young woman.

Coming eight years after the extension of the franchise to women in 1920, *Machinal* occupies an unusual place in early twentieth-century drama by women. Although a number of theatrical works by women from 1910 to 1920 focused on women characters and feminist themes, by the late 1920s the figure of the independent, daring "New Woman" who challenged the traditional roles for women had been subdued. The "New Woman" who declared in Jesse Lynch Williams's 1918 hit play, *Why Marry?* had by as early as 1925 metamorphosed into the neurotic housewife of George Kelly's critically acclaimed *Craig's Wife,* who sought not just independence but "control over the man [she] married." In this respect, the portrayal of women in the dramatic productions of the 1920s and 1930s mirrored the changes in women's roles in the social and economic structures of the time. After the crucial success of achieving the vote in 1920, the feminist movement began to wane, partly because of

the conservative backlash prompted by the economic and social turmoil of the late 1920s and early 1930s. A decline in women's enrollment in colleges and in their participation in the work force and professional fields all contributed to an increasing return to traditional domestic roles for women after 1920. Within this more conservative context in both society and the theater, Treadwell's drama of the restrictive nature of traditional marriage for women indeed stands alone as an "isolated expression[ ] of 'feminist' theatre."

Focusing on the social and psychological restrictions imposed on women in a male-dominated society, *Machinal* features not a "New Woman" of extraordinary talents and determination, but an "Every Woman," one who is neither politically motivated nor ambitious or creative. Opening with the simple statement, "The plot is the story of a woman who murders her husband—an ordinary young woman, any woman", Treadwell begins to construct her "strategy of resistance" against the patriarchal system. Emphasizing the average rather than the special woman, Treadwell implies that it is not the extraordinary "New Woman" of the suffrage movement that the patriarchal system has to fear but rather the outwardly docile, ordinary woman who can be transformed by the social pressures of the patriarchy to act. This accent on the ordinary constitutes the radical in Treadwell's work.

Divided into nine episodes, *Machinal* opens with a business scene, replete with office workers and cacophonous office machinery, but the topic of the office conversation centers less on business accounts than marriage. Almost like an Austen novel, the characters speculate on whether the female protagonist, Helen (referred to throughout the play as the "Young Woman" to emphasize her anonymity), will marry the boss, George Jones: "Will she have him? . . . will he have her?" Early in the play, this juxtaposition of business with marriage establishes Treadwell's concentration on the economic basis of marriage. On one hand, Helen would be free of economic pressures if she marries her employer; on the other hand, she would be subordinate in every sense, legally, physically, emotionally, and economically, to a man she does not love or respect. Neither alternative—a life of work or marriage—meets her personal needs.

Helen recognizes that the dilemma posed by the two alternatives is compounded by the social pressure to conform to marriage: "all girls—most girls—married." This emphasis on traditional domestic roles for women accompanied the political and social conservatism of the late 1920s and 1930s. After the early successes of the women's movement in the first decade of the century, many women again began to view marriage as their only option. As Jane F. Bonin stresses in her analysis of prize-winning American plays, many major plays of the 1920s and 1930s, especially those by male playwrights, reinforced the belief that marriage was a necessary goal in a young woman's life:

> Again and again, these plays insist that marriage, to any man and under any conditions, is better than none. Especially during the twenties and early thirties, a period when many women were questioning whether a life exclusively preoccupied with home and family was necessary or desirable, the important plays seemed to assume that salvation for women could be found only in marriage, even an unhappy one.

In the expressionistic, telegraphic style that characterizes *Machinal*, Helen's disjointed monologue at the end of the first episode summarizes this social and psychological conflict confronting the average, young working woman in the early twentieth century:

> Mrs. George H. Jones—money—no work—no worry—free!—rest—sleep till nine—sleep till ten—sleep till noon—now you take a good rest this morning—don't get up till you want to—thank you—oh thank you—oh don't—please don't touch me—I want to rest—no rest—earn—got to earn—married—earn—no—yes—earn—all girls—most girls—ma—pa—ma—all women—most women—I can't—must—maybe— must—somebody—something—ma—pa—ma—can I, ma? Tell me, ma—something—somebody.

Helen's vague but desperate need for "something—somebody" to tell her how to resolve the conflicts she faces in a male-dominated society resurface throughout the play.

Helen's cry for "somebody" to rescue her from a life of work or marriage merges in episode 2 with her dreams of romance, of "somebody young—and—and attractive—with wavy hair." While at dinner with her mother in their shabby apartment, Helen tries to express her inner turmoil about love and marriage. But Helen's mother, hardened and worn by the rigors of work and an unhappy marriage herself, scoffs at her daughter's romantic idealism, "Love!—what does that amount to! Will it clothe you? Will it feed you? Will it pay the bills?" She exposes with brutal pragmatism the economic basis of the traditional marriage, which often negates romantic love. In this way, Helen's mother is a poorer, less frivolous Mrs. Bennet, but underneath her motivations are the same as Austen's characters'. They both know that for the impecunious

young woman, marriage, even a flawed one, is preferable to being alone in a male-dominated society. The absence of Helen's father (he is never mentioned in the play) and her mother's financial dependence on her daughter illustrate in this episode how the traditional marriage can fail to provide the woman with economic or emotional support. Because her mother's financial welfare plays a part in Helen's decision to marry Mr. Jones, it symbolizes how the burden of the marriage devolves on to the next generation of young women trapped in the system.

The metaphor of marriage for women as confinement or imprisonment is introduced in the first two opening scenes and reinforced throughout the play. Using psychosomatic disorders such as claustrophobia and anorexia, which feminist critics Sandra M. Gilbert and Susan Gubar have interpreted as expressions of escape in women's writing, Treadwell conveys her female protagonist's inability to cope with the social pressures placed on women. In the first episode, Helen experiences a "stifling" feeling in the subway that makes her repeatedly late for work, an unconscious avoidance of Mr. Jones's attentions. This sense of claustrophobia or suffocation returns in the discussion of marriage with her mother in episode 2. Here, not only does Helen have difficulty breathing; she is unable to swallow her meal. These psychological reactions reappear at key moments in the play whenever Helen feels especially threatened by the inexorable pressures of the marriage.

If Helen's need to escape the confines of marriage is represented by the "stifling" and "gagging" she experiences, her rebellion against male-dominated society can be read in her "madness," which results in the murder of her husband near the end of the play. Gilbert and Gubar's first volume in their critique of modernist works, *The War of the Words,* describes the madwoman figure of nineteenth-century women's texts who escapes from the attic to take center stage in a number of works by twentieth-century women writers. Linked with militant feminism and violence against the patriarchy, Gilbert and Gubar's madwoman embodies female anger and anxiety over male dominance and, most importantly, the power to resist the formidable pressure to conform to male-prescribed roles. Helen, identified at the outset of the play as an ordinary woman, seems to incorporate little of the madwoman-rebel figure. But her resistance to marriage and, later in the play, to maternity, causes her to be labeled as "crazy" and "neurotic" by those about her. Helen's act of murder, however, injects a mad-like dimension to her behavior that most strongly links her to the rebel figure.

Repeatedly chastised by her mother in the second episode as "crazy" for her refusal to marry Mr. Jones, Helen ultimately displays a level of repressed anger and despair that clashes with her earlier passivity. Marriage is again the catalyst. Throughout episode 2, Helen searches for an escape from marriage to love. Resigning herself to marriage at one point in the scene, Helen dully concedes, "And I suppose I got to marry somebody—all girls do." But as the inevitability of her marriage to Jones looms larger, her feelings of claustrophobia intensify: "it's like I'm all tight inside." Her mother's unsympathetic response, "You're crazy," in the face of her desperation causes Helen to explode in violent anger: "Ma—if you tell me that again I'll kill you! I'll kill you!" This uncharacteristic response is difficult to reconcile with the passivity and tractability that Helen displays throughout the earlier part of the scene. The almost monster-like quality to Helen's explosion indicates another side, a "mad double" that many women writers have used to allow their "proper" heroines to express the violent acts of rebellion they dare not express otherwise. Although Helen Jones is not given a "mad double" in the play, there is some indication in both this scene and in the murder scene of a "darker side" that lurks within her, foreshadowing the murder of her husband that follows.

Episode 2 closes with Helen's numb capitulation to marriage, leading to the honeymoon scene of episode 3. Staging a harsh, unromantic honeymoon night in a tawdry hotel room with jazz music from the dance casino next door intruding in the background, Treadwell again connects economics to marriage in this scene in a way that sharply exposes the traditional patriarchal marriage. Jones's obsession with money, "Twelve bucks a day! They know how to soak you in these pleasure resorts," is coupled with his crass, sexual humor, "Say, what you got under there?" Helen, unprepared for the sexual realities of the night and repelled by a man she does not love, is seized with claustrophobic reactions and ends the scene weeping in terror. Despite the criticism of Freudian scholar W. David Sievers, who has characterized Helen as a "sexually baffled" woman with an unnatural fear of sex communicated by her mother's own sexual frigidity, Helen can more accurately be interpreted as a young woman who feels pressured by the "rules" of the traditional marriage to be intimate with a man against her will.

Here Treadwell charges that the basis of the patriarchal marriage, an exchange of intimacy for economic security, is tantamount to prostitution. The tone of Jones's comment on the cost of the hotel room, "Twelve bucks! Well—we'll get our money's worth out of it all right," seems more appropriate for the brothel than the honeymoon suite. At the conclusion of the episode, Helen pleads for her mother, for "somebody," to save her, but the throbbing rhythm of the jazz music overpowers her cries as the scene blacks out. Criticized in 1931 as "revolting" in British reviews of the play, the honeymoon episode depicts the sexual relationship between husband and wife with a degree of verisimilitude that was considered too "true to life" for public presentation. Treadwell's portrayal of marital intimacy is "revolting" in this episode in a way that the critics failed to realize. Helen's plea for "somebody" to help her suggests the possibility of a rescue, a revolution against a tradition that requires a woman to submit to a kind of "legalized rape" that is truly "revolting."

Following a natural progression, episode 4 opens in a maternity ward of a major hospital. Here Treadwell presents one of the most critical portraits of motherhood in modern literature. The claustrophobic set design—one room closed in by a corridor, the window view blocked by the construction of a tall, phallus-like building—and the jarring audio effects of the riveting machine that permeate and overpower the dialogue characterize the sacred institution of motherhood, creating a truly radical vision of what western society considers woman's primary function, maternity. The scene opens with the nurse making her rounds. She tries to engage Helen in routine conversation, "No pain? . . . Such, a sweet baby you have, too. . . . Aren't you glad it's a girl? Your milk hasn't come yet—has it?", all questions to which Helen signals "no" in a counter rhythm of negation against the nurse's trite observations on motherhood and the sound of the riveting machine in the background. Helen's responses to motherhood, as an Every Woman figure, are particularly telling. Her refusal to communicate, only gesturing "no," and her inability to eat as she gags on her food both imply a rejection of motherhood. Helen's power to choose what she does with her life, however, is limited. Pressured and pressed into the "machinery" of the patriarchal marriage in the opening scenes and forced by her coarse husband in the honeymoon episode, Helen becomes solidly "riveted" into the system by giving birth. Her severe reaction, the repeated negation of "self," tragically emphasizes her total subsumption by the institution. Treadwell illustrates the totality of Helen's subjection by stressing the lack of control she has over even her own body in this scene.

Helen confronts three male guardians of patriarchy in the maternity ward who claim authority over her. First her husband visits, exhorting her to just "brace up," and "face things." He minimizes the pain of her pregnancy and assumes a measure of authority over the birth process itself, "Everybody's got to brace up and face things! That's what makes the world go round. I know all you've been through but—Oh, yes I do! I know all about it!" Despite his overbearing assertions, Jones understands as little about Helen's experience of childbirth as he did of her distress on their honeymoon night. Helen reacts to this statement with a "violent gesture" of negation and then withdrawal. It is when Jones states with male arrogance, "Having a baby's natural! Perfectly natural thing—" that Helen gags and emphatically gestures for her husband to leave. This is the potent truth that Helen tries to reject throughout the maternity episode: as a woman she has little control over her fate; she is bound to reproduction.

Helen's lack of power is underscored by the male doctor's entrance immediately after the exit of her husband. The doctor usurps jurisdiction over her body in a very literal way. He immediately commands, "Put the child to breast," although she has no milk and refuses to breast-feed. Then, when informed of Helen's nausea, the doctor ignores the protests of both Helen and the nurse and prescribes food for her anyway in a kind of forced feeding. Helen's reaction is one of desperation and despair, and her response to the doctor is simply, "Let me alone." This cry for autonomy then forms the theme of her closing interior monologue. In a stream-of-consciousness flow, Helen remembers the pregnancy of a pet dog of her childhood. The string of associations that follow link the woman to dog as breeding animals in an inescapable bond of biological determinism. In melding the past with present, Helen even expresses a death wish for her own child.

> I won't submit to any more—crawl off—crawl off in the dark—Vixen crawled under the bed—way back in the corner under the bed—they were all drowned— puppies don't go to heaven—heaven—golden stairs— long stairs . . . all the children coming down—coming down to be born—dead going up—children coming down—going up—

As the dog and the woman fuse in a form of reproductive destiny, the paternal authority reaches its zenith when the earthly patriarch, Helen's husband, merges with the ultimate patriarchal authority, God the Father,

> What kind of hair has God? no matter—it doesn't matter—everybody loves God—they've got to—got to—got to love God—God is love—even if he's bad they got to love him—even if he's got fat hands— fat hands—

Helen objects that "God never had [a baby]"; Mary was the one who gave birth. "God's on a high throne," and Mary's place is "in a manger—the lowly manger." Clearly the position and the power, God on top and Mary underneath, is with the male. Helen's recognition and indictment of a male society based on biology is underscored with her final lines of the scene, "I'll not submit any more— I'll not submit—I'll not submit—." But as the sound of the riveting machine overpowers her final cry, it is already too late for this ordinary young woman to escape.

Instead of the ardent figure of the newly bound prisoner, episode 5 depicts a Helen Jones whose despondency and restlessness ("I want to keep moving") lead her to an encounter in a bar with a stranger and a subsequent affair. Treadwell's skillful use of setting and the interplay of background dialogues in this scene, significantly entitled "Prohibited," reveals the illusion of escape from marital restrictions that the extramarital affair appears to offer. In addition, Treadwell stresses the subversive side of the intimate encounter that places it outside the boundaries of the legal and sanctioned union of marriage and labels it as an "outlaw" relationship. Helen's initial meeting with her lover occurs in a darkened bar with the mechanical tunes from an electric piano and exchanges between a series of other couples in the bar counterpointed against the main dialogue. One such conversation between a man and woman centers on the possible abortion of her child, which she reluctantly agrees to after being reminded harshly by her lover that she will lose her job if she keeps the child. Again, Treadwell emphasizes that economics and biology play a central role in male-female relationships even outside of marriage.

Against this bleak backdrop, Treadwell stages Helen's love affair. Played by Clark Gable in the original production, the man Helen falls in love with fulfills all the requirements of the romantic lead: he is an experienced lover ("They all fall for you") with "coarse wavy hair" and an adventurer from Mexico who tells stories of his daring escapades, "I got the two birds that guarded me drunk one night, and then I filled the empty bottle with small stones—and let 'em have it!" Trapped in a marriage that provides no emotional or physical fulfillment, Helen yields easily to a man with a handsome face and quick tongue who represents to her a form of outlaw freedom. During their intimate encounter in a dismal basement room in episode 6, Helen experiences a fleeting moment of release and fantasizes a romantic escape with her lover in a series of childhood associations that combine romance with the fairy tales and nursery rhymes told to children: "And the dish ran away with the spoon—I never thought that had any sense before—now I get it." But like marriage and motherhood, romance in a patriarchal society offers neither happiness nor freedom, but an illusion or a momentary feeling of being "on top of the world," "purified." Helen is merely one of many women for her lover—"Jeez, honey, all women look like angels to me" and these few illicit hours have brought her no closer to the freedom she craves—"I'll never get—below the Rio Grande—I'll never get out of here." This grim realization that as a woman she must play out the submissive role determined for her leads Helen from one subversive act, an illicit affair, to the ultimate subversive act of killing her husband—a bid for self-liberation that results simultaneously in self-destruction.

The place of action for Helen's violence is again domestic. Episode 7 portrays a typical evening conversation between Jones and Helen that focuses on his business deals and the news from the daily newspaper. The mechanical and repetitive quality of the exchanges on business illustrates the absence of any real communication between them and the emptiness of their union. Treadwell's integration of newspaper material into the dialogue, however, exposes the true schism between not just this particular married couple but between the male perception of what is significant, "newsworthy," and the conflicting female view of reality. In the opening exchange, both Jones and Helen "read" their own versions of what constitutes the "news," the record of the times:

Husband: Record production.

Young Woman: Girl turns on gas.

Husband: Sale hits a million—

Young Woman: Woman leaves all for love—

Husband: Market trend steady—

Young Woman: Young wife disappears—

Husband: Owns a life interest—

Helen "reads" a woman's story of anguish and escape while her husband sees only economic prosperity. As the scene progresses, Helen interprets a more radical version of the female story, "Prisoner escapes—lifer breaks jail—shoots way to freedom,"

and finally, "Woman finds husband dead." The possibility of freedom through revolution in these lines indicates the presence of an emerging subversive female consciousness that undermines the male version of what is "real" and which, if acted upon, would threaten the male-dominated social structure. As the weight of her role as wife and mother intensifies, Helen feels "stifled" and "drowned," painfully conscious of her confinement. The background music and internal voices escalate at the conclusion of the scene, and as the possibility of freedom possesses Helen, the "mad double," the agent of rebellion, takes control of her actions. In the middle of night, when the moon is full, she fills a bottle with stones and strikes at her husband in his sleep.

Judged and punished by "The Law" in episodes 8 and 9 for the murder of her husband, Helen completes her metamorphosis from a passive young woman who succumbs to economic and social pressures at the beginning of the play to the militant rebel of the final scenes. Helen's initial description of the killers indicates how far she has moved beyond passivity to actor. Helen tells the prosecutor that she was awakened by hearing "somebody—something—in the room." These two words, "somebody—something," which have formulated her "motif of yearning" in the marriage and honeymoon scenes, are reiterated here with telling significance. Her repetition of the words "somebody," "something" to describe who killed her husband link her violent act with rescue or liberation. In these earlier episodes, the rescuer is vague, an indeterminate pronoun—Helen is the one who is acted upon. But when she identifies her husband's killer as "something," " somebody," "a big dark looking man," on one level she is describing herself because she is the killer. The "somebody," "something," that rescues her from the prison of marriage is this time within herself, something big and dark from within.

Machinal ends with the same kind of understated rebellion that marks Treadwell's first lines. Although Helen confesses her crime, there is no act of contrition and submission as in episode 2 when she begs for her mother's forgiveness and obediently agrees to marry Mr. Jones. Instead, in the final scene before her death, Helen declares to the priest that her only free moment on earth was when she killed her husband: "When I did what I did I was free!" This lack of penitence, almost to the point of exaltation, must be punished by death. Moments before the execution, her mother enters for a final goodbye, and Helen's exclamation, "But she's never known me—never known me—ever—," changes to reconciliation, and her last entreaty is for her own daughter,

> Wait! Mother, my child; my little strange child! I never knew her! She'll never know me! Let her live, Mother. Let her live! Live! Tell her—

Generation to generation of women seem alienated, "never known" to one another, each new mother raising her daughter to conform to her expected role in a male-dominated social structure. Helen's plea to communicate to her daughter the realities that Helen has discovered, to "Tell her—," holds the hope of change, of solidarity among generations of women, but this message is cut off abruptly, left uncompleted as Helen is forced to the electric chair. Given the subversive possibilities, that Helen Jones is "any woman, any ordinary woman" who murders her husband, it is imperative that the machine works at the end of *Machinal:* "It'll work!—It always works!" Otherwise, Helen Jones might be able to pass the message on to her daughter that "somebody," "something," this emerging female consciousness, can help her live.

Sophie Treadwell belongs to the coterie of early modern women playwrights who portrayed with relentless honesty women's struggle for autonomy against a patriarchal system. Concentrating on women's issues and employing the male-dominated mode of drama, feminist playwrights such as Treadwell have threatened to subvert the traditional theater by seeking their own powerful public voice. Their efforts until now have condemned them to a literary anonymity of unpublished works and hasty critiques such as that suffered by Treadwell. The contributions of Sophie Treadwell and women dramatists like her merit reassessment. The story in *Machinal* of one ordinary woman's attempt to strike back at a repressive institution needs to be communicated. Perhaps instead of being misread or misinterpreted by male critics, *Machinal* has been comprehended all too well. Silenced for decades by the literary "machine," Sophie Treadwell still has a message to telegraph to her "daughters."

Source: Barbara L. Bywaters, "Marriage, Madness, and Murder in Sophie Treadwell's *Machinal*," in *Modern American Drama: The Female Canon*, edited by June Schlueter, Associated University Presses, 1990, pp. 97–110.

SOURCES

Bywaters, Barbara L., "Marriage, Madness, and Murder in Sophie Treadwell's *Machinal*," in *Modern American Drama: The Female Canon*, edited by June Schlueter, Associated University Presses, 1990, pp. 97–110.

Dickey, Jerry, "The 'Real Lives' of Sophie Treadwell: Expressionism and the Feminist Aesthetic in *Machinal* and *For Saxophone*," in *Speaking the Other Self: American Women Writers*, edited by Jeanne Campbell Reesman, University of Georgia Press, 1997, pp. 176–84.

Tancheva, Kornelia, "Sophie Treadwell's Play *Machinal*: Strategies of Reception and Interpretation," in *Experimenters, Rebels, and Disparate Voices: The Theatre of the 1920s Celebrates American Diversity*, edited by Arthur Gewirtz and James J. Kolb, Praeger, 2003.

Treadwell, Sophie, *Machinal*, Nick Hern Books, 1993, pp. xi, 16, 17, 23, 24, 75, 79, 82, 83.

FURTHER READING

Dickey, Jerry, *Sophie Treadwell: A Research and Production Sourcebook*, Greenwood Press, 1997.
> This book chronicles the achievements of Sophie Treadwell, including a career and biographical overview, detailed plot summaries of her plays, criticism, and an annotated bibliography.

Jones, Jennifer, "In Defense of the Woman: Sophie Treadwell's *Machinal*," in *Modern Drama*, Vol. XXXVII, No. 3, Fall 1994.
> Jones highlights the similarities between *Machinal* and the Snyder-Gray murder trial of 1927.

Kuhns, David F., *German Expressionist Theatre: The Actor and the Stage*, Cambridge University Press, 1997.
> Kuhns traces the powerfully stylized, anti-realistic methods of symbolic acting on the German Expressionist stage from 1916 to 1921.

Styan, J. L., *Modern Drama in Theory and Practice*, Vol. 3, *Expressionism and Epic Theatre*, Cambridge University Press, 1981.
> This book traces expressionism from German through American playwrights, including Eugene O'Neill, Thornton Wilder, and Sean O'Casey.

Off the Map

JOAN ACKERMANN

1994

Off the Map was first published in 1994. It has been produced throughout the United States and has won a fair amount of critical acclaim. Most notably, *Off the Map* caught the eye of intelligent, independent film director, Campbell Scott. Scott, who has a propensity for moving stories from the stage to the screen, fell in love with Ackermann's drama. The movie premiered at the 2003 Sundance Film Festival. Although it did not win awards, the film had a short national run and received complimentary reviews.

The play's title comes from the location where the Groden family lives in northern New Mexico. The family is so far removed from any sense of conventional society that they live almost completely *off the map*. With *Off the Map*, Ackermann constructs a memory play in which Adult Bo Groden reflects back upon one summer of her childhood. During this summer, Young Bo, an eleven-year old girl, lives with her mother and father, Arlene and Charley. Other than Charley's friend, George, the family has little contact with the outside world. During this summer, Charley falls into a deep depression that challenges the Groden family. An unlikely visitor, William Gibbs, arrives at their doorstep to collect on back taxes. Gibbs is also suffering from depression and quickly develops a distant, unspoken bond with Charley. Strangely, Gibbs falls in love with the Grodens and their lifestyle, never returning to his life *on the map*. Beyond the sad, funny, and heartwarming moments, the Groden family and Gibbs share during

the summer's struggle with individual demons and depression, Ackermann is also able to use the memory play to question the differing freedoms Bo experiences both as a young girl and an adult banker.

AUTHOR BIOGRAPHY

Joan Ackermann, a contemporary American playwright, is one of the freshest voices in modern theater, so much so that one of her most recent plays has already been filmed and released as a major motion picture. *Off the Map* has won acclaim not only on stage, but also as a Campbell Scott-directed film. The movie starred Joan Allen and Sam Elliott, was screened in competition at the 2003 Sundance Film Festival, and then received a limited release around the country in 2004.

Ackermann is also the co-founder and Artistic Director of Mixed Company theatre in Great Barrington, Massachusetts. The company has been in existence for 23 years. Ackermann is a prolific playwright and, in addition to *Off the Map*, her many works include *Zara Spook and Other Lures* (1990), *Bed and Breakfast*, *Rescuing Greenland*, and *Isabella: a Young Physician's Primer on the Perils of Love*. *Isabella: a Young Physician's Primer on the Perils of Love* is a musical for which Ackermann wrote the music and lyrics. Ackermann's plays have been produced by a host of prestigious houses, such as Vineyard Theatre, Circle Rep, and the Atlantic Theatre Company.

Biographical information about Ackermann is elusive at best. However, her writing precedes her, and her writing repertoire is impressively extensive and diverse. In addition to her stage and film work, she has written and produced for television. She is also a special contributor to *Sports Illustrated*, and she freelances for *The Atlantic*, *Audubon*, *GQ*, and *New York Magazine*.

PLOT SUMMARY

Act 1, Scenes 1–6

The play opens with the narrator, Adult Bo Groden. She introduces us to herself as an eleven-year old child living *off the map* in northern New Mexico. Young Bo is a sassy, intelligent, determined young girl. She is creative, often writing letters to large companies, complaining about products and demanding free samples. Charley, her

MEDIA ADAPTATIONS

- *Off the Map* was adapted as a film by Campbell Scott, starring Sam Elliott at and Joan Allen. It premiered at the Sundance Film Festival in January 2003 and experienced a short run in theaters. It was re-released in U.S. theaters in March 2005.

father, is experiencing an oppressive bout with depression. The man is always crying, not sobbing: tears are constantly draining from his eyes. Arlene, her mother, is a strong, stable woman who is able to support the family through Charley's debilitating depression. Adult Bo also introduces us to Charley's friend, George, a large, quiet man with a deep dedication to the Grodens.

Young Bo quickly expresses her desire to leave her life off the map. She plans to achieve her goal by applying for an American Express credit card so she can, "buy a one-way ticket out of this hell hole." Although the Grodens rarely receive mail outside of Bo's free samples, they receive a letter stating that they are being audited. Arlene finds the prospect amusing because the family makes less than five thousand dollars a year.

Charley's depression is taking a toll on Arlene, Bo and George. Everyone wants to help him and he wants to help himself, but they are at a loss. Charley has given way to endorsing physical pain, willingly pulling his own diseased tooth. He relishes the discomfort because at least the pain allows him to feel something. Arlene finally asks George to go to town and visit a psychiatrist. She knows the doctor will not give George medicine for Charley, so she asks him to pretend he has depression. George agrees to go see the psychiatrist because he is willing to do anything to help his friend.

A few days after George visits the psychiatrist, George and Bo go fishing. During their outing, Bo asks George a lot of questions about banking, account numbers, and social security numbers, foreshadowing Bo's application for an American Express credit card. George reads her questions as curiosity and answers all of Bo's questions.

During their discussion, George also talks about visiting the psychiatrist and that he must return for several more counseling sessions before the doctor will prescribe any medications.

Bo continues her dedication to writing companies, demanding freebies. She writes Hostess stating that the Twinkie samples they sent "contained what I can only describe as a rodent part. Internal organ or foot, I'm not sure." Bo's letter to Hostess confirms her sassy, sneaky sensibilities and supports the view of her as a young, creative con artist.

Act 1, Scenes 7–15

In scene seven, William Gibbs, the IRS agent sent to audit the Grodens, arrives at their home. The family lives so far off the map that Gibbs arrives on foot. He has parked his car many miles away and has trekked through the desert to find their home. Upon his arrival, he spots Arlene gardening in the nude. Startled, Gibbs screams and turns his back out of respect. However, Arlene is unabashed with her nakedness. With his back turned, Gibbs explains that he is an IRS agent sent to audit the Grodens and Arlene invites him inside.

Once inside, Bo is upset that her mother is naked and demands that Arlene put on some clothes. The young girl introduces herself to Gibbs as "Cecilia-Rose," claiming that she is just around to help out Charley and Arlene. Gibbs reveals that he's been stung by bees and he begins to feel very weak. He falls into a terrible fever and is left weak and delirious on the family's couch for three days.

During his days on the couch, Charley wakes Gibbs once to give the man water and ask if he has ever been depressed. Gibbs answers, "I've never not been depressed," explaining that he has felt emotionally damaged his entire life. Gibbs tells Charley that his depression started when he was six years old and had returned from school to discover that his mother had committed suicide.

Arlene uses herbs to help ease Gibbs' pain. The man struggles with his allergic reaction, but recovers. Just as Gibbs recovers, Bo receives her credit card from American Express. She keeps it a secret. Although Gibbs has recovered from the stings, Charley is still battling depression. He almost feels worse knowing that Gibbs has depression because he feels that Gibbs has a good reason. The hardest aspect of Charley's depression is his inability to isolate a cause.

Charley leaves a painful pebble in his shoe, again showing the man's endorsement of physical pain to offset his depression. Gibbs shows no

indication that he will be leaving soon. He has fallen in love with Arlene and has unearthed a passion for art.

Act 2, Scenes 1–5

Act 2 opens with Arlene trying to convince Charley to take an anti-depressant. George successfully feigned depression and was prescribed the drug. Per Arlene's wishes, George passed the pills on to Charley. Reluctantly, Charley swallows the pill and cracks a giant, fake smile. It is revealed that five weeks have passed since Gibbs' arrival. The man is still staying with the Grodens and he has completed a thirty-one foot watercolor of the ocean's horizon. In addition, it has been settled that the Grodens owe the IRS $1,260.00 in back taxes and penalties.

Adult Bo reads a letter that her younger self wrote to an advice column. The letter reveals that Young Bo is frightened that her father's depression might be contagious and that it may lead to his suicide. During this scene a rifle shot rings out, alarming Bo and Arlene. Gibbs staggers in, covered with blood. The tension is broken when Charley arrives announcing they had shot a bear. Not being a hunter, Gibbs is noticeably shaken. Arlene is also disturbed, both out of fear that her husband had killed himself, and because her young daughter is concerned with and affected by her father's depression. On the other hand, Bo is excited that her letter has been published.

Charley is very agitated and he blames the drugs. George arrives nicely dressed because he is going on a date with a woman named Consuela. Charley wants to wrestle with George because he is searching for some sort of painful release from his depression and his manic reaction to the drugs. George resists, stating that he is meeting someone. Charley throws two glasses of beer on his friend, trying to incite him. Finally, George explodes, but instead of hurting Charley, he simply pins his friend to ground, holding him there until he stops struggling. Once exhausted, Charley relaxes and thanks his friend.

Act 2, Scenes 6–10

The scene opens on Charley's birthday. Bo is upset because George is not in attendance. He has moved to Mexico with Consuela. Bo is devastated. Arlene tries to explain that life is about changes. Eventually, Bo reveals that she has purchased a sailboat for her father with her American Express credit card. Everyone is surprised and no one seems upset. In fact, everyone is amazed and flabbergasted that Bo was able to acquire a credit card. They are nervous about paying for the boat, but for the first time all summer, Charley shows a flash of excitement. In a symbolic transition during this emotional turning point—Charley is showing a glimmer of hope for recovery—it is revealed that Arlene's favorite coyote has been killed. Although Bo killed the coyote, for reasons beyond rationality, Arlene never confronts her daughter. Bo and Arlene bury the coyote together the next day, symbolically laying to rest the weight of the summer.

That night, Gibbs and Charley discuss depression and, more importantly, their individuality. In a shared moment, Gibbs begins to sob, expressing his envy of Charley. Gibbs explains that he sees Charley's life, with his loving wife and daughter, as perfect. With Gibbs's emotional release, Charley's perpetual crying ceases. The two begin their recovery from depression.

Charley is showing dramatic signs of improvement. He has stopped taking the drugs, as they only caused him more mental trauma. Gibbs has moved into a bus on the Groden's property and paints constantly. Arlene is concerned with the American Express bill and the money owed to the IRS, however she is happy because her husband is recovering. For the first time in the play, Charley expresses passion for his wife, admiring her leg. In the end, Charley has recovered; Bo has been able to break away from living off the map, attending a public school; and Arlene has even re-entered society, playing catcher on a softball team. Gibbs continues to paint and live with the Grodens.

With the closing memories, Adult Bo recollects back to Gibbs's mysterious death. He was found lying on his back, arms outstretched, with a sketchbook in one hand and a crayon in the other. He seemed at peace, as he had finally achieved freedom through art. More importantly, he escaped his depression and discovered his individuality. Adult Bo also states that Gibbs became a famous artist posthumously and was able to give back to the Grodens after his death. Although the family felt no debt was owed, a collector purchased Gibbs's thirty-one foot painting of the ocean's horizon for $9,000—enough to pay off the IRS, the American Express bill, and fit Bo with a set of braces. Adult Bo remembers the painting, thinking that it symbolized life with "the ocean as the past, the sky as the future, and the present as that thin precarious line where both meet, precarious because as we stand there it curves under foot. Ever changing."

CHARACTERS

George

George is Charley Groden's best friend and is also considered part of the Groden family by Arlene and Bo. He is a large, strong, quiet man with a charming demeanor. He is an important friend to Bo, especially during her father's terrible and unexpected bout with depression. George is often mistaken for being dull or unintelligent, when in actuality he is a deep thinker. In the early stages of Charley's depression, George gives Arlene a watercolor set and asks her to give it to Charley. George is trying to help motivate his best friend in any way possible. However, George's demeanor does not allow him to express emotion and, thus, he asks Arlene to deliver the paints without mentioning that they are a gift. George's dedication to the Grodens is clear. When Arlene asks George to take Bo fishing because Bo has also been depressed, he does not hesitate. His fraternal love for Charley is highlighted in two major instances. First, George willingly goes to a psychiatrist and pretends to have depression—even going as far as a series of counseling sessions—to receive an anti-depressant prescription to pass on to Charley. Later, charged with his attempts to combat depression, Charley tries to antagonize George and make the large man hurt him. George resists Charley's prodding, wrestles him to the ground, and restrains Charley until he calms down. Although he is a man of few words, George has a deep love for the Grodens and is a vital support mechanism for their family.

William Gibbs

William Gibbs is an outsider and IRS agent assigned to audit the Grodens. He arrives at their home on foot. The Grodens live far *off the map* in New Mexico, making access to their home difficult. When Gibbs arrives, he is immediately struck by Arlene because she is gardening in the nude. The woman is unabashed and does not flinch or cover up. Immediately, Gibbs is smitten. Oddly, he quickly falls dramatically ill from an allergic reaction to bee stings and is left in the care of the Grodens. The IRS agent spends three days sweating with the fever on the couch. During this time, Gibbs and Charley exchange a few moments of sparse dialogue. Charley talks openly with Gibbs about his depression. Gibbs offsets Charley's bout with depression stating, "I've never not been depressed." These exchanges make Gibbs a crucial character in *Off the Map*.

Not only does Gibbs's character create a reference point for Charley's own depression, it is also echoes Ackermann's quiet support for clinical psychology. Charley needs Gibbs, someone outside of his family and his life, to discuss his mental problems. Following Gibbs's recovery from the bee stings, he continues to reside with the Grodens. He takes up painting and becomes close to Arlene and Bo. Bo is intensely interested in Gibbs because he is from the outside world that she is so motivated to explore. Yet, Gibbs continues to remain slightly distant from Charley. There is no tension between the men and, in fact, they share some of the play's most dramatic dialogue. It appears that, although Charley does not want to see a psychiatrist, he is interested in and benefits from his counselor-like relationship with Gibbs. Gibbs feels no obligation to this role in Charley's life because he may be unaware of the impact. However, the IRS agent does feel uncomfortable because of his love for Arlene.

Eventually, Gibbs begins using Charley's watercolors and develops an incredible love of painting. He creates spectacular pieces, many of which are paintings and sketches of Arlene in the nude. She does not pose for Gibbs, but a crisp memory of her naked body is obviously burned into his mind, once again supporting his deep, intense love for Arlene. His newfound love of art pulls Gibbs from his own depression. Thus, George's gift has its desired effect, just not on the intended recipient. In his transition out of depression, Gibbs sobs one evening to Charley, telling him that he, Charley, has a perfect and enviable life with Bo and Arlene. Gibbs's tears mark the end of his depression and prove to be the catalyst for Charley's recovery. Gibbs continues living with or near the Grodens until his untimely, mysterious death in the desert. He is found on his back, arms outstretched with a sketchbook and a blue pastel crayon. Immediately following his death, his paintings become very popular on the retail market, generating a much needed revenue boost for the Grodens.

Arlene Groden

Arlene Groden is a free-spirited, compassionate, powerful woman, wife of Charley, and mother to Bo. Arlene is the strongest, most spirited character of the play. She becomes a citadel for the family, for George and for Gibbs. She is earthy, attractive and carefree. An incredible example is her naked gardening. Even when spied by a complete stranger—Gibbs—Arlene is not taken aback. She approaches the man, invites him into their home and even remains mostly unclothed until her daughter prompts her to get dressed. However, Arlene proceeds with these actions in an acceptable manner.

She addresses Gibbs in a courteous, friendly manner, as if she were clothed. She is unashamed and refuses to be controlled by societal norms, hence her willing decision to live off the map.

Arlene is a dedicated mother and wife, constantly aware of her daughter's and husband's feelings. When she realizes that Charley may not pull himself out of his depression, Arlene creates a plan, sending George to the psychiatrist to get a prescription for anti-depressants. Unfortunately, the plan fails and the pills have a negative effect on Charley. Still, Arlene's dedication and constant work to help her husband is impressive. As Charley slips farther and farther into depression, leaving Arlene with more and more responsibilities, Arlene is still a focused mother and compassionate wife. Although she is stretched to nearly the end of her means, Arlene is able to give to her daughter, attend to her feelings, and help her cope with her father's illness. This is an amazing feat. Not only can Arlene help her husband with depression, she can support the entire family and tirelessly give to her daughter. It is no wonder that Gibbs falls in love with Arlene. It is trite to assume that his infatuation is centered on seeing the woman naked. Even though she has a beautiful body, it is her enigmatic, loving character that draws Gibbs into the Groden family and causes him to stay with them until his death. It is quite clear that the family would have crumbled and fallen into an amazing despair if it were not for Arlene's impressive fortitude.

Adult Bo Groden

Adult Bo Groden narrates the play. She is a filter through which descriptions of characters flow. Adult Bo is a bank manager in Salt Lake City, Utah, and dresses the conservative part. Her language is florid. She adds descriptions of characters that are not always accurate, but they offer an opinionated view of what happened during the summer of her father's depression. Adult Bo states, "I look to that summer for answers to great mysteries. Of deep love. And loss." The Adult Bo dialogue does two things: first, it leads us into scenes, setting a mood and providing background information that adds increased depth, clarity and meaning to sequences; and second, Adult Bo's life, language and attitude that she has developed living *on the map* in society emphasizes the life the Grodens lived *off the map* outside of society. Some of Adult Bo's comments seem critical of her upbringing, but she still relies on and recollects back to her days in New Mexico when she contemplates life's mysteries. It seems as though Adult Bo is torn between her current life in society and her childhood outside of it. She waffles emotionally on the benefits and ills of both lifestyles. The theme of a lost childhood constantly repeats itself in all types of writing, whether it be plays, fiction or poetry, and Adult Bo is the manifestation of this theme.

Young Bo Groden

Young Bo is the fiery, outspoken eleven year-old daughter of Charley and Arlene. Where her adult counterpart waffles on the benefits of a lifestyle removed from society, Young Bo desires nothing more than an escape from her life *off the map*. The young girl has a vibrant imagination. In one scene, she plays with imaginary dogs. Although she does not attend a traditional school, her mother, father, George, and Gibbs all take on different roles in contributing to her education. Nonetheless, Bo's energies are intensely directed at the outside world. She writes outlandish letters to companies, claiming faults in their products with the intent of receiving free samples. Bo also has a Mexican pen pal in prison named Carlos Martinez. She is immediately drawn to Gibbs, an outsider, whom she bombards with a constant stream of questions. Bo wants to escape her life, though she is not miserable. She simply wants more and her mind is constantly searching and exploring. Her desires developed her crafty and sneaky sensibilities. Nonetheless, her frustration with her isolated lifestyle is often exposed through her actions. When Gibbs arrives, she decides to change her name to Cecilia-Rose. She claims that she does not live there and that she's simply helping out Charley and Arlene. These are all clear signs of her attempts to separate herself from her life. The apex of Bo's resolute attempts to integrate society and escape her solitary, peaceful life comes with her purchase of a boat for her father. Through crafty means, Bo applies and receives an American Express credit card. With her card she purchases a five-thousand-dollar boat to be delivered to the Grodens. Although her action is guileful, her intention is good. She planned on giving the boat to her father to help with his depression. Oddly, the Grodens find her actions impressive and, although they do not know how they'll pay for Bo's purchase, Charley shows excitement for the first time during the summer. Young Bo's tribulation with her life helps construct a mysterious summer that, as revealed by Adult Bo, continues to affect her as she ages.

Charley Groden

Charley Groden is a Korean-War veteran, husband to Arlene, and father to Bo. He has limited dialogue during the play, but he is central to the plot. The play takes place during a summer when Charley is struggling with a severe case of depression. Before his depression set in, Charley was the backbone of the family. He is strong, vibrant man who is skilled in many trades and is normally characterized by his energetic, efficient nature. He teaches his daughter important lessons, both constructive and emotive. However, during this summer, and the duration of the play, he has lost any tendency towards his manic pursuits and is wallowing in a deep depression. Throughout the play it is clear that Charley understands his own condition. He realizes that his body and mind are lifeless. He lacks any emotional feeling whatsoever and although he never sobs, his eyes frequently leak tears. The only sensation he can feel is pain and he embraces it on several occasions. For example, Charley pulls his own decaying tooth; he leaves a painful pebble in his shoe; and even tries to antagonize his large, strong friend, George, into a fistfight, relishing the pain of each moment. Everyone is affected by Charley's depression.

Bo has little understanding of why her father is suddenly so distant from her. They used to share many moments together, hiking through the woods and scavenging at the dump. George, a peaceful, quiet man, often relied heavily on Charley to maintain conversation and to be a good friend and companion. Charley's depression has left George frustrated and worried. Arlene has stepped up to the challenge and is coping with Charley's illness with dedication. She has taken on as much of Charley's responsibilities as possible, but relies heavily on Gibbs and George to help with Bo. In addition, the depression has extinguished Charley's sex drive and, although her love never wanes, Arlene struggles with the absence of physical contact. Charley is saved from his depression by a series of events. Gibbs's crying and discussion of his own personal depression, and envy of Charley's life and family, helps to pull Charley from his own despair. Plus, Bo's creative, sneaky purchase of a boat piques Charley's interest and ignites his first energetic dedication to a project in a long time. With these two catalysts, Charley begins to pull out of his deep depression, returning to his friends, his daughter and his wife.

THEMES

Fortitude and Frailty

These antonyms create an important thematic struggle in *Off the Map*, most remarkably in

TOPICS FOR FURTHER STUDY

- *Off the Map* is focused on Adult Bo's recollection back to a pivotal summer in her life. Think back to an event in your childhood that you believe still affects your life and write a short one-act play about how the event has shaped your life today.

- Depression has a large impact on the plot and the characters in *Off the Map*. Think of three plays, or works of fiction, where an illness has been at the forefront of the story and compare them to *Off the Map*. Are the illnesses in the works you selected mental or physical? How are the illnesses different from, or similar to, depression as seen in *Off the Map*?

- *Off the Map* has been produced as a motion picture. Pick one other play that you know has also been turned into a motion picture, then read the play, watch the film and compare the movie to the play. How do they differ? How are they similar? Does the movie follow the script of the play or even the plot?

- The Grodens live off the map, removed from society. In addition to drawing a comparison with Ralph Waldo Emerson, the Grodens may have similarities to Henry David Thoreau. Drawing from Thoreau's book, *Walden*, what connections can be made between Thoreau and the Grodens? Between Thoreau and Gibbs? If there is no correlation, explain the differences.

Charley Groden. However, this theme is also applicable to the Groden family and their decision to live off the map. Charley Groden is a large, powerful man. He is able-bodied and intelligent. Charley is responsible for constructing, fixing and building up the Groden's home. Yet, during the summer of this play, Charley has become amazingly frail. His mind has been clouded with a thick, dark fog that has rendered him useless. The only remainder of his fortitude is his ability to withstand pain and, as if to remind himself of what he used to be, Charley welcomingly embraces a diseased tooth, a painful stone in his shoe, and a physical altercation with a friend. The Grodens live in a constant awareness of their balance between fortitude and frailty. Although they are courageous and have proven they have the fortitude to withstand nature, they are also much more vulnerable than if they were living in society. In a strange paradox, living outside of society makes you stronger than living within society, yet living outside of society leaves you more susceptible. The Grodens tread a fine line. They live outside of society and they live well. Their child is educated, their home is warm, they eat well and they love each other. However, as expressed through Charley's illness, the Grodens are

exceptionally vulnerable to an outside debacle. Without steady income, regular medical or dental care, access to public schools, or a sizeable support mechanism, the Grodens could easily slip from isolated, peaceful fortitude to desperate, longing frailty. This balance helps create tension in *Off the Map* and, more importantly, it plays a key role in developing Charley and Arlene.

Depression

Both Charley Groden and William Gibbs suffer from depression. They both feel sad. Charley is prone to long periods of inaction, difficulty thinking, and feelings of dejection. Gibbs feels similar, but with a special emphasis on hopelessness. Charley is constantly leaking tears from his eyes, while Gibbs hasn't cried in ages. However, aside from these clinical symptoms that set the mood of the play, depression also plays a thematic role. These two men and their separate struggles against a common demon create the primary plot and conflict of *Off the Map*. Charley lives off the map and struggles with depression. Gibbs lives on the map and also struggles with depression. With this, both men begin to realize that their problems are internalized. There is not something outside of either man responsible for their depression; they must look within themselves to discover what is causing their illness. When both men see their opposites in each other—Charley off the map, Gibbs on the map—but recognize that they share a common ailment, it becomes clear that they must resolve their issues by turning inward. It is as if they suddenly understand that their circumstance is not responsible for their illness. No longer does either man feel the need to search outside of himself for a cause or cure for their depression. Each individual's recognition of the other's battle with depression helps free them both from their external constraints, allowing them both to look inward to their psychological well-being. With this, Ackermann makes a statement about depression, its effect on others, and the importance of expressing and sharing feelings.

Upsetting Harmony and Coming-of-Age

The crescendo of Bo Groden's life may very well be the summer setting of *Off the Map*. For many kids, coming-of-age is tied to upsetting some sort of harmony in the world. A youth begins to grow up through subversive, disobedient actions. More often than not a child truly comes of age by upsetting the harmony of their life as it is predetermined by their family. Of course, this is not usually a permanent or damaging action; it can be as simple as having a pen pal in prison or illegally acquiring an American Express card. Regardless of the particular action, the crux of coming-of-age through upsetting harmony rests completely on a young person turning against what is convention in order to go out on his or her own. During this summer, Bo successfully comes of age. It is no wonder that her adult self looks "to that summer for answers to great mysteries." This summer changed Bo's life. Her actions sent her on her own path, back into society, one that she followed throughout the course of her life. Looking back, the change that upsets the harmony is always somewhat in question, considering such a big decision was made at such a young age.

STYLE

Memory and Mood

The prevailing feeling of the play is love. Throughout the summer of Charley's depression, love keeps the family and friends bound closely together. Regardless of Charley's outbursts—fighting with George—or Bo's revolt against her

mother—killing the coyote—the characters love for one another never wavers. Often, when love is the prevailing mood, its development is cheap and shabby. Ackermann conquers this with a realistic portrayal that is emphasized with Adult Bo's memory of her family and friends. Although she lends insights into characters and scenes, at the heart of Adult Bo's desire to recollect this summer is her memory of the love that held everyone together. Without the keen development of love as mood and the touching recollection of Adult Bo's memories, Ackermann's play would have felt like an incomplete melodrama. Instead, it is a remarkable portrayal of a love shared between family and friends.

Monologues

Adult Bo steps in at various times during *Off the Map* to give the audience her spin on the scene and characters. Adult Bo lives on the map in Salt Lake City, Utah and works as a banker. Her language and dress are formal. This is directly juxtaposed with Young Bo and her family living off the map in northern New Mexico. The Grodens are not uneducated or unintelligent, but they are very informal in language and dress—in Arlene's case, she dresses informally when she's actually clothed. The diametric tones are intentional. Not only do they separate Adult Bo's life from her youth, it also helps to emphasize the family's separation from society. The stark difference between Adult Bo in Utah and Young Bo in New Mexico is drastic, just as the Groden family's way of life was drastically different from the social norm.

HISTORICAL CONTEXT

Social Effects of the Vietnam War

Off the Map takes place in the present and, mainly, the early 1970s. During the late 1960s and early 1970s, the United States of America was fighting the Vietnam War. In the wake of John F. Kennedy's assassination, President Lyndon B. Johnson decided to take offensive action against the North Vietnamese. This launched what would prove to be a gruesome, tiresome and poorly organized war against the North Vietnamese. In the years that followed, Johnson increased the number of young Americans sent to battle in Vietnam. As the number of troops drafted increased, so did the number of protesters back in the States. United hippies emerged in full force. They were seen as outsiders, rejecting the mores of established

Isolated building in Lincoln, New Mexico © Reinhard Eisele/Corbis

society. In general, hippies were longhaired, anti-war advocates, who followed the teachings of Gandhi and Dr. Martin Luther King, Jr. They were advocates of non-violent protest and, being that they were primarily Caucasians, the hippies were propelled to the forefront of the national media. Soon, people were burning draft cards, marching on Washington, and some even immolated themselves in protest. The movement against the Vietnam War was impressive. Thousands of people were arrested—even famous individuals like Muhammad Ali—for refusing to be drafted.

The Vietnam War stirred a great sense of racial and social unrest in the United States. The bulk of the troops drafted were poor or minorities, or both. Most people who legally escaped the draft were in college. This was an elite group, comprised most of wealthy Caucasians. With a large number of Caucasians escaping the draft, the military turned towards African-Americans. This discrepancy fueled racial injustice, as the Civil Rights Movement was gaining power behind the great Dr. Martin Luther King, Jr. Many African-Americans found it difficult to go fight for a country that did not respect, honor, or dignify them. In many parts of the Southern United States, African-Americans were still denied the right to vote and, thus, it seemed

like there was little reason to go to Vietnam to fight communism and install democracy, when it did not seem to be working at home. All of these problems led to the enormous anti-war movement of the 1960s and early 1970s.

However, these movements against the government were not the only anti-social responses of this generation. In addition to the highly publicized Civil Rights Movement and the hippies of the Anti-War Movement, many people disappeared from the United States's radar screen all together. There was a massive exodus of people leaving the United States for Canada or other foreign countries. Plus, still more simply disappeared *off the map*, as in Ackermann's play.

In what can only be a testimony to understanding war, Charley—a Korean War Veteran—and his wife Arlene started their family in a shack in the outer edges of uninhabited northern New Mexico. With an amazing capacity for empathy, they felt so moved by the times that they desired to escape what was becoming an unpalatable, violent society. In an attempt to save themselves and their daughter from the hate, unrest and prejudice of the world, the Grodens simply uprooted themselves and disappeared. Although they were eventually discovered by Gibbs, the family was still significantly off the map and, thus, they lived a hard, but more peaceful life outside of the luxury, decadence and instability of the social norm.

CRITICAL OVERVIEW

Ackermann's play *Off the Map* was originally published in 1994 when it was selected as one of seven plays included in the collection *Women Playwrights: The Best Plays of 1994*. This collection's playwrights were not as ethnically diverse as other anthologies and no criteria was given for the selection or inclusion of these works. Nonetheless, Ackermann's inclusion is note-worthy. Other fresh voices of the collection include Lynne Alvarez, Marlane Meyer, Theresa Rebeck, Jacquelyn Reingold, Paula Vogel, and Allison Eve Zell.

Dramatic criticism and reviews for *Off the Map* are elusive at best. Very little has been written or is easily unearthed about the play. However, there are a handful of short, critical reviews circulating throughout the Internet. In general, this criticism praises *Off the Map* and the play is frequently described as accessible, but poetic. Most frequently, critics write about the mood of the play, the expression of the family's love, about struggle and survival. Although critics generally touch on the emotional side of Ackermann's play, there is little written about the deeper message behind the family's survival, one that challenges contemporary views of society, personal freedom, and individuality.

Off the Map continues to be produced throughout the United States at both the collegiate and professional level. The play is considered accessible and underwent a rebirth when the independent film director Campbell Scott turned Ackermann's play into a movie. The movie premiered at the 2003 Sundance Film Festival, to excellent reviews. Although the movie did not win any awards, it received a remarkable response behind the support of a well-known director, Scott, and well-known film stars Sam Elliot and Joan Allen.

CRITICISM

Anthony Martinelli

Martinelli is a Seattle-based freelance writer and editor. In this essay, Martinelli examines how the characters in Off the Map *struggle with depression and desires in pursuit of self-reliance.*

> OUTSIDE OF SOCIETY, GIBBS AND CHARLEY ARE FREE TO HELP ONE ANOTHER, TO COMFORT AND CONSOLE EACH OTHER IN WHAT CAN ONLY BE DESCRIBED AS A MUTUAL SELF-RELIANCE."

In *Off the Map*, Joan Ackermann paints a picture of the Groden family living outside of society in northern New Mexico. With limited contact from friends and no contact with the outside world, except for sparse mail delivery, the Grodens have created a life that is sheltered, productive and amicable. Yet, during the summer of the play, Charley Groden, the father to Bo Groden and husband to Arlene Groden, slips into a deep depression. He is distant and full of sadness. Soon thereafter, an IRS agent, William Gibbs, arrives to collect back taxes. Gibbs also suffers from terrible depression. Both men struggle with a common ailment, only in very different ways. The last character involved in a focused struggle is Bo Groden. The eleven-year-old girl is determined to escape her parents' lifestyle for a life in society. All three characters successfully change their lives, pulling themselves from depression or changing their position in society, resulting in what Ralph Waldo Emerson would call self-reliance.

Before Emerson's values can be applied to the success of each individual, their unique struggle must be examined. To begin with, Charley is typically a strong, powerful man with great abilities and outstanding composure. Although his wife is an amazing, steadfast individual, she benefits greatly from his talents and love. During the summer of the play, however, Charley has fallen dreadfully ill with depression. He has no passion for his wife, nor life, nor interest in their daughter. He cannot complete simple tasks and lives a life heavy with dejection, with tears constantly leaking from his eyes. Charley is most devastated by his inability to pinpoint a reason for his depression, stating, "I don't even remember how I got here." His new friend, Gibbs, originally claims that his own depression was from

WHAT DO I READ NEXT?

- *The Batting Cage* (1999), a play by Joan Ackermann, tells the story of two estranged sisters who make unlikely journeys as the try to regain their control of their lives after the death of their dearly loved third sister.

- *Marcus is Walking* (1999), a play by Joan Ackermann, examines, in eleven short, offbeat vignettes, the emotional landscape people navigate while they travel in their cars.

- *How I Learned to Drive* (1997), a play by Paula Vogel, examines the destructive and incestuous relationship between Li'l Bit and her uncle. It is written with frank language and straightforward honesty that creates a remarkably candid view of a dysfunctional family.

- *The Waverly Gallery* (2000), a play by Kenneth Lonergan, is a potently impressive and frequently hilarious story about the last years of a fiery, talkative grandmother's battle with Alzheimer's disease.

---

a moment when he "came home from school and [his] mother had hung herself." This is what Charley is searching for, something outside of himself that can be a catalyst for his depression. With jealous Charley replies, "You put me to shame . . . a good reason like that." For Charley, his depression should be something he can fix, like an old car. There should be a concrete problem that needs to be corrected or, at least, an event that can be pointed to as a cause for the damage. Unfortunately, depression is rarely an easy, quick fix.

Secondly, Gibbs steps into the Grodens' life as a stranger delivering bad news. He arrives on foot at the Grodens' property to collect back taxes. Living *off the map*, the Grodens had not filed tax forms in five years and, although they live poor and outside of society, the IRS does not see them as being exempt from filing tax forms. When Gibbs arrives, he has been stung by bees, and he falls ill with a terrible allergic reaction. Gibbs is forced to spend three days sweating with fever on the Grodens' couch. During this time, Charley interrupts Gibbs late in the evenings to bring him water, but, more importantly, to question him about depression. The two men discover that they both suffer from a common ailment and neither man can identify a potential cure. To Charley's dismay, Gibbs has been suffering from depression his whole life. Gibbs states, "I've never not been depressed." Gibbs is extremely isolated by his depression. Although he lives within society, he moves frequently and is rarely pleased. He has nothing of value or love in his life and, thus, is devoid of nearly any emotion. Unlike Charley, Gibbs never cries. In a strange way, Gibbs living in society restricts him, making him less free to express emotion than Charley, who is living outside of society. One man is a spigot of tears, while the other is bone dry.

With Gibbs and Charley, Ackerman makes an interesting statement about depression, society, and self-reliance. Both men suffer from a common affliction, both men share different symptoms, and neither Gibbs nor Charley seem to make any progress against their disease on their own. Although Gibbs and Charley must overcome their depressions on their own, each man achieves their mental health through observing the other. In what is easily defined as the turning point in both men's struggle against depression, Adult Bo recounts a conversation between Gibbs and Charley. Gibbs tries to express his admiration and envy of Charley and his family. He expresses his gratitude for being allowed to stay with the Grodens and, for the first time in his life, enjoy living and exploring art. Sharing his feelings with Charley brings Gibbs to tears for the first time in twenty years. Adult Bo recollects,

> as the valve opened in William Gibbs . . . releasing a torrent of tears, it seems the same valve continued turning in my father all the way to the off position, shutting off that steady leak that had streaked his face and our lives for more than half a year.

In this instant, Ackermann has linked Gibbs and Charley's different, independent battles with depression. Gibbs, through Charley and his family, becomes aware of how he used to live his life on the map; he realizes that his new life *off the map* has enabled him, for the first time, to be true to himself and to express his feelings. Charley, through Gibbs's words of admiration and understanding, is reintroduced to the spectacular life he lives with his family *off the map*. Adult Bo finishes with wise words stating, "In comforting others do we comfort ourselves."

Adult Bo's final statement is a perfect segue into Ralph Waldo Emerson and a better understanding of self-reliance. It would seem as though Gibbs and Charley relied on each other to defeat their depression. However, a sharper analysis reveals that Gibbs and Charley were incapable of helping themselves until they could help each other, something that is quite impossible within society. As Emerson states in his essay, "Self-Reliance,"

> Society everywhere is in conspiracy against the manhood of every one of its members. . . . The virtue in most request is conformity. Self-reliance is its aversion. It loves not realities and creators, but names and customs.

With Emerson's words in mind, Ackermann's play takes on entirely new meaning. Quietly, Ackermann comments on society and the "conspiracy against manhood" with Adult Bo's remarks that the two men helped cure themselves by comforting each other. Outside of society, Gibbs and Charley are free to help one another, to comfort and console each other in what can only be described as a mutual self-reliance. In yet another twist, it would appear that Ackermann is making her opinion known about pharmaceutical drugs and the cure for depression. At one point, Charley takes an antidepressant to help with his condition. The drug does nothing positive. In fact, it incites Charley to attack his friend, George. These drugs are a chemical demand for Charley's conformity. Without their position outside of society, Ackermann would claim, neither man would have successfully overcome their depression.

However, as the play draws to an end, Adult Bo's recollection of Gibbs's painting of an ocean's horizon alludes to something positive within society; a glimmer of hope. Emerson writes, "We first share the life by which things exist and afterwards see them as appearances in nature and forget that we have shared their cause." It is fair to state that nature, for Emerson, is all things outside of the individual. His statement, in its dedication, asks that humankind not forget our role in society and its impact on nature. It is the forgetting that causes the damage. Adult Bo, living on the map in society, may be Ackermann's glimmer of hope because she does look back on her life outside of society, questioning her differing lives. If Adult Bo remembers and dissects her different lives, then there is hope for humankind. In the closing moments of the play, Adult Bo describes Gibbs's painting, stating that she views "the ocean as the past, the sky as the future, and the present as that thin precarious line where both meet, precarious because as we stand there it curves under foot. Ever changing." This is how Adult Bo feels about her past and her shared cause, living both *off the map* and *on the map*. Adult Bo has not forgotten her past and she understands that each moment in the present means that life is ever changing and, thus, so is her impact on the world.

Although Ackermann is quietly critical of society, she does leave us with hope. The Grodens are a strong, functional family, even through Charley's depression. They are accepting, reasonable people, opening their arms to friends and strangers. And although Ackermann may not say much about the positive aspects of society, her creation of Adult Bo leaves a great deal of hope. If society was made up of nothing but the likes of Adult Bo, then there is a good chance that Emerson would be happy to live in such a place. As Emerson writes, "Nothing can bring you peace but yourself." Oddly, living within a society where such mass self-reliance was endorsed would mean that everywhere would have to be *off the map*, raising the question of whether such a society could ever exist. Hence, as Emerson and Ackermann would concur, life must be a struggle for self-reliance; where it can truly be achieved is yet another question.

Source: Anthony Martinelli, Critical Essay on *Off the Map*, in *Drama for Students*, Thomson Gale, 2006.

SOURCES

Ackermann, Joan, *Off the Map*, Dramatists Play Service, 1999, pp. 7, 8, 14, 23, 24, 46, 49.

Emerson, Ralph Waldo, "Self-Reliance," in *Selected Essays, Lectures, and Poems*, Bantam Books, 1990, pp. 151, 158, 171.

FURTHER READING

Earley, Michael, and Philippa Keil, eds., *The Modern Monologue: Women*, Routledge, 1993.
    This book is an exciting selection of speeches drawn from important plays of the twentieth century. The monologues in this book are all written for women characters and they provide an excellent sampling of a wide array of styles.

Ensler, Eve, *The Vagina Monologues: The V-Day Edition*, Villard, 2000.
    This play is a direct, hilarious celebration of female sexuality. However, it delivers a powerful message.

This edition celebrates the grassroots movement, inspired by this play, to stop violence against women.

Falk, John, *Hello to All That: A Memoir of War, Zoloft, and Peace*, Henry Holt, 2005.
This book is a bizarre, heartbreaking, and sometimes hilarious memoir of a war correspondent and his continuous struggle against chronic depression.

Storr, Anthony, *Solitude: A Return to the Self*, Ballantine Books, 1989.
Storr uses history's greatest artists and minds—Goya, Kafka, Trollope, Kant and others—linking the capacity to be alone with self-discovery and becoming aware of one's deepest feelings.

Topdog/Underdog

SUZAN-LORI PARKS

2001

Like the title suggests, *Topdog/Underdog* (published in 2001) is a play about competition, reversals, and mirror images that reflect the true self. The idea that became *Topdog/Underdog* can be found in one of Parks's earlier plays, *The America Play* (1995), which features a gravedigger named the Foundling Father whose obsession with Abraham Lincoln leads him to find work in a sideshow. Like Link in *Topdog/Underdog*, the Foundling Father applies whiteface, models several different types of fake beards, and sits in a chair awaiting visitors who pay to assassinate "Abraham Lincoln" with a cap gun. Though the Foundling Father and Link hold the same job, any similarities between these two protagonists end there. Regardless, Parks's fascination with history, especially personal history, and the ways in which illusion can reveal identity makes for riveting drama.

Topdog/Underdog tells the story of two brothers, Lincoln and Booth, who, abandoned by first one parent and then the other, have had to depend upon each other for survival since they were teenagers. Now in their thirties, the brothers struggle to make a new life, one that will lead them out of poverty. Lincoln, a master of the con game three-card monte, has abandoned a life of crime for a more respectable job impersonating Abraham Lincoln at an arcade. Booth, on the other hand, earns his living as a petty thief, one who wishes to emulate his older brother's success by learning how to "throw the cards." Throughout the play, the brothers compete against each other, vying for

Suzan-Lori Parks Photo by Scott Gries. Getty Images

control. At any given moment, one may yield power over the other, only to relinquish it in the next. Hence, *Topdog/Underdog* reveals a topsy-turvy world in which Lincoln and Booth live, a chaotic world that is as dangerous as it is illusory.

AUTHOR BIOGRAPHY

Suzan-Lori Parks, the daughter of an Army colonel, was born in Fort Knox, Kentucky, in 1964. As a member of a military family, Parks moved often, first to west Texas and then to Germany, where she settled during her teenage years. While attending German schools, Parks began to write short stories. When she returned to the United States, Parks attended Mount Holyoke College, where she studied creative writing with the novelist James Baldwin. Baldwin was the first to encourage her development as a playwright, for at the time Parks had the habit of acting out the characters' parts when she read her short stories in class. Her first play, *The Sinner's Place*, was produced in 1984 in Amherst, Massachusetts. While at Mount Holyoke, Parks was a member of the Phi Beta Kappa honor society and graduated cum laude with a Bachelor of Arts degree in 1985.

She also studied at the Yale University School of Drama.

After college, Parks traveled to London to write plays and study acting. Her second play, *Betting on the Dust Commander*, was produced in 1987, followed by *Imperceptible Mutabilities in the Third Kingdom*, which won a 1989 Obie Award for Best Off-Broadway play of the year. Parks's fifth play, *The Death of the Last Black Man in the Whole Entire World* (1990), continued to explore the issues of racism and sexism that have been hallmarks of her work from her earliest days as a playwright. These plays, like the others that followed, defy the conventions of the modern theatre as they address social issues like slavery, gender roles, and poverty. Parks won her second Obie for *Venus* (first produced in 1996), a dramatic account of how, in 1810, a Khoi-San woman was brought from South Africa to England to serve as a sideshow attraction. Parks's greatest critical acclaim to date arrived with the production of *Topdog/Underdog*, a play that she began writing in 1999 and that was produced Off Broadway at the Joseph Papp Public theater in 2001 under the direction of George C. Wolfe. The play, the first of Parks's to appear on Broadway, debuted in April 2002 at the Ambassador Theater and, shortly thereafter, won the 2002 Pulitzer Prize for drama, thereby making Parks the first African-American woman to receive that award.

Parks has received numerous awards and honors throughout her career, among them a National Endowment for the Arts grant, a Rockefeller Foundation grant, the Whiting Writers' Award, a Kennedy Center Fund for New American Plays, and the PEN-Laura Pels Award for Excellence in Playwriting. In addition to the aforementioned Obie awards and Pulitzer Prize for drama, Parks has been awarded a Guggenheim fellowship and the prestigious MacArthur Foundation fellowship, also commonly known as the "genius grant."

Since 2000, Parks has directed the Audrey Skirball Kirn's Theater Projects writing program at the California Institute of the Arts. Her first novel, *Getting Mother's Body*, was published in 2003 to favorable reviews. Parks has written two screenplays: *Anemone Me* (1990) and *Girl 6* (1996). The film version of *Girl 6* was directed by Spike Lee. Parks is writing a stage musical about the Harlem Globetrotters entitled *Hoopz*, in addition to adapting Toni Morrison's novel *Paradise* for a film to be produced by Oprah Winfrey.

PLOT SUMMARY

Scene 1

The play opens on a Thursday evening in a boardinghouse room with Booth practicing his three-card monte routine over a board supported by two milk crates. He practices his patter, imagining that he has won a large sum of money. Lincoln, wearing a frock coat, top hat, and fake beard, sneaks up behind his brother, who whirls and pulls a gun.

Booth tells Lincoln to take off his disguise because he fears Lincoln's getup will scare Grace, with whom Booth has a date the next day. Booth claims that Grace is in love with him, and that no man can love her the way he can. Booth then shows Lincoln a "diamond-esque" ring he plans to give Grace. The ring is stolen, but it is smaller than the one he gave her when they were together two years before; therefore, Booth, by giving his beloved a smaller ring, decreases the chance that she will give the ring back because she cannot remove it once it has been placed upon her finger.

Booth insists that Lincoln remove his costume. He does not understand why his brother does not leave the costume at work, but Link says that he is afraid someone might steal it.

Lincoln then relates a story about how a "little rich kid" asked him for an autograph while riding the bus home for work. Link decides to charge the kid ten dollars for the favor, but the kid only has a twenty-dollar bill. Lincoln, in the guise of Honest Abe, promises to bring the kid his change the next time they meet on the bus, but Lincoln buys a round of drinks at Lucky's instead.

Lincoln questions Booth about his card setup. Booth, wanting to create a new persona for himself, informs Lincoln that he is thinking about changing his name. Lincoln suggests an African name like "Shango," which would be an easy name for everyone to say and would not, in Lincoln's opinion, "obstruct . . . employment possibilities."

Lincoln has brought Chinese food home for dinner, and the brothers begin converting the card setup into a dinner table, which prompts a discussion about their present living arrangement. Lincoln points out the room's shortcomings, such as the absence of a toilet or a sink, but Booth does not see anything wrong with the amenities (or lack thereof).

Lincoln goes to get the food and finds a playing card on the floor. He places the card on the table and asks Booth if he has been playing cards. Booth says he has been playing solitaire rather than

MEDIA ADAPTATIONS

admit that he has been practicing his three-card monte routine unsuccessfully.

The brothers argue over who will eat what. Lincoln relents and gives Booth the "skrimps." Curious, Lincoln brings up the subject of solitaire again, and Booth suggests that they play a hand of poker or rummy when they have finished eating. Lincoln reminds Booth that he will not touch the cards, but Booth insists that it would be "[j]ust for fun." Lincoln remains adamant, but Booth presses the issue, wanting to know whether Lincoln would break his vow if they played for money.

Lincoln says that Booth has no money because he, Lincoln, is the one who brings home the paycheck. Booth claims to have an "inheritance," but Lincoln says that Booth might as well have nothing because he never plans to spend the money he has. Booth responds by saying that Lincoln "blew" his inheritance.

The conversation abates and returns to the subject of food. The brothers compare their fortune cookie messages. Booth finishes eating and begins practicing his three-card monte routine again. His movements remain awkward and clumsy, and Lincoln tries his best to ignore him. Lincoln, however, cannot refrain from making comments about Booth's patter. Finally, Lincoln tells Booth that if he wants to throw the cards properly, he must practice the routine in smaller sections.

Booth suggests that they work as a team, but Lincoln changes the subject by saying he will clean up after the meal. Booth then announces that from then on he wants to be called "3-Card." Booth says that everyone calls him that; according to him, Grace especially likes the name. Lincoln thinks that both the name and his brother are "too much." "Im making a point," Booth says. "Point made, 3-Card. Point made," replies Lincoln.

Booth again raises the idea of the brothers working as a team. He has visions of making easy money, but Lincoln reminds him that there is more to making money at three-card monte than finding a mark. Booth goads Lincoln into accepting his proposition by reminding him that their success would attract women. Lincoln questions Booth's relationship with Grace, which does not seem all that secure. Booth appeals to Lincoln's sense of vanity by reminding him that at one time he was the best three-card dealer in the city. Lincoln, however, states that he does not touch the cards anymore.

Booth tries another tack by calling his brother names and by reminding him of how he, Booth, discovered their mother packing her things to leave. Booth tells Lincoln that their mother asked him to look out for his older brother, which brings the conversation around again to how, in Booth's view, he is trying to create an "economic opportunity" while Lincoln sits around and does nothing. Booth concludes his harangue by shouting, "YOU STANDING IN MY WAY, LINK!"

Lincoln apologizes, saying that he would prefer to do "honest work." Booth chides Lincoln about his costume and how he must impersonate "some crackerass white man," but Lincoln says that visitors to the arcade are not misled. "When people know the real deal it aint a hustle," he says.

Booth twists Lincoln's words and says that the card game would be the real deal. Booth implies that Lincoln's working at the arcade transcends his role of The Great Emancipator to embody slavery. Essentially, Booth says that his brother has enslaved himself to the owners of the arcade, who controls his destiny. Lincoln warns Booth not to push him; his anger is rising.

Booth informs Lincoln that he will have to leave because their living arrangement was intended to be temporary. Lincoln agrees to leave without complaint and then plays a blues tune on the guitar. The song is sad and mournful, its theme one of abandonment and displacement. Booth likes the song, which Lincoln composed while at work.

Lincoln tells Booth about how they got their names. Their father was drunk when he told Lincoln that he named his sons Booth and Lincoln because "It was his idea of a joke."

Scene 2

The scene opens with Booth dressed like he is about to go on an Arctic expedition and checking to see if Lincoln is home. As he undresses, he reveals layers of clothing that he has stolen. He lays one suit on Lincoln's easy chair and another on his own bed. He sets two glasses and a bottle of whiskey on top of the stacked milk crates. Booth sits in a chair pretending to read a magazine when Lincoln walks in.

Lincoln enters the room to the sound of improvised fanfare. Booth knows that today, Friday, is payday, and the brothers, referring to each other as "Ma" and "Pa," begin to celebrate their prosperity. Lincoln pours two glasses of whiskey, and Booth begins counting the money Lincoln has brought home. Lincoln tells him to budget the money because he wants to know how much is available for the week. Booth, indignant that Lincoln has failed to notice the suit he stole for him, says that Lincoln would not notice his ex-wife Cookie if she was in bed. The jibe makes Lincoln wistful, but then his mood brightens when he sees the blue suit lying on the chair.

Booth brags about how he "boosted" the suits and other items of clothing from a department store. "I stole and I stole generously," he tells his brother. "Just cause I aint good as you at cards dont mean I cant do nothing."

Lincoln compliments Booth on his haul and then delivers a speech about how clothes do not make the man. "All day long I wear that getup. But that dont make me who I am," he says. He is reminded of how their father's clothes would hang in the closet, whereupon Booth, resentful about how their father spent more time and money on his mistresses than on his children, tells Lincoln that he took their father's clothes outside and burned them. Lincoln, on the other hand, is preoccupied with his job security and how he would leave the job when the time came. He concludes by sounding a refrain about his true identity: "Fake beard. Top hat. Dont make me into no Lincoln. I was Lincoln on my own before any of that."

After the brothers finish dressing and modeling their clothes for each other, Booth tells Lincoln that he looks like he did when he was with Cookie. Booth also thinks about how his new suit will impress Grace. Lincoln thinks that they should switch ties, and so they do. Both are pleased with the results.

Lincoln asks Booth to do the budget. He calculates how much they will need to pay the utilities, some of which, like the phone, they do not actually use. Booth wants to pay their bill so service will be restored and they can call their lady friends. Booth has it all worked out that having a phone will transform him into a ladies man, but Lincoln, depressed and dejected, does not believe that a woman would ever call him. Booth chastises Lincoln for not having any knowledge or confidence when it comes to women. Booth resumes calculating the budget, allowing money for alcohol and meals.

Lincoln tells Booth that there is talk of cutbacks at the arcade. Since Lincoln has been working there for only eight months, he would most likely be one of the first employees to be let go. "Dont sweat it man, we'll find something else," Booth replies, acknowledging that their fates are entwined together. Lincoln says that he likes his job because he can sit there all day and let his mind "travel." It is what he calls "easy work."

Sometimes Lincoln thinks about women, but most of the time he lets his mind "go quiet" as he composes songs, makes plans, and sits there trying to forget about the past. He invites Booth to come down again, but Booth says that once was enough. He asks if the Best Customer came in today, as he does most days, and Lincoln says, "He shot Honest Abe, yeah." They discuss some of the things the Best Customer whispers into Honest Abe's ear, and Booth concludes that the Best Customer is "one *deep* black brother."

Booth also concludes that Lincoln's job is bizarre. Lincoln says it is a living, but Booth challenges him by saying that he is not really living at all. "Im alive aint I?" Lincoln retorts. He then tells about how Lonny's death made him give up the cards for a secure, less dangerous, job. Lincoln likes his work at the arcade, but he cannot let go of his fear that he might lose his job and be forced to seek employment again. Booth, in an effort to cheer his brother up and perhaps win him over to the idea that they should work together as a team, reminds Lincoln that he was once lucky with the cards, but Lincoln dismisses the notion that anything but skill is involved in throwing the cards.

When Lincoln once again expresses his fear about losing his job, Booth tells him that he has to "jazz up" his act if he wants to attract more customers and keep his job. He gives his brother some pointers on how to make his performance more dramatic. However, when Lincoln asks Booth to help

him practice, Booth tells him he does not have time because he must get ready for his date with Grace. Claiming that it is the "biggest night" of his life, Booth asks Lincoln for a small loan.

Lincoln gives Booth a five-dollar bill. Booth, perhaps feeling guilty about abandoning his brother, suggests that they rehearse when he gets back from his date. Lincoln agrees, and Booth leaves.

Alone, Lincoln undresses and hangs his clothes neatly over a chair. Leaving his feet bare, he dons his work uniform, securing the top hat beneath his chin with an elastic band. His outfit is complete except for the white makeup. Lincoln pretends to get shot, falls down, and writhes on the floor. He gets up and is about to practice his moves again when he decides to pour himself a large glass of whiskey. The scene ends with Lincoln sitting in the easy chair drinking.

Scene 3

The scene opens much later that Friday evening, with Lincoln asleep in the recliner, which has been extended to its full horizontal position. He wakes suddenly, hung-over and wearing his costume. Booth enters, swaggering and slamming the door in an attempt to wake his brother, but Lincoln does not react, so Booth slams the door again. Lincoln wakes up, still bleary-eyed. Booth walks around him, strutting like a rooster, to make sure Lincoln sees him.

Lincoln asks if Booth has hurt himself, but Booth replies that he has had "an evening to remember." Lincoln says that Booth looks like he has hurt himself, but all he can talk about is how Grace wants him back. According to Booth, she has "wiped her hand" over her past so that she can say they have never been apart. She has forgiven him for his mistakes. Lincoln asks about their date, and Booth begins to divulge details of his sexual conquest. He interrupts his story because, he says, he does not want to make his brother jealous. Booth provides more details of the evening's encounter, but even so he feels guilty about making his brother feel bad. Lincoln prompts his brother to tell him more, and Booth obliges, saying that Grace was so sweet his teeth hurt. After more hesitation, Booth reveals intimate details of his sexual relations with Grace, each detail becoming more salacious and vivid.

The conversation revolves around the use of condoms, which Lincoln says he never had to do because he was married. Booth says that Grace will not let him go without one next time; she will be real strict about that. Lincoln, in a gesture of manly bravado, tells Booth that he will find a way to avoid using one. "You put yr foot down and she'll melt," he says.

Lincoln keeps drinking while Booth is in his bedroom, playing with the condoms. From the other side of the screen that divides the room, Booth tells Lincoln how Grace is not like all the other girls he has been with because she attends cosmetology school and has plans for the future. When Booth tells Lincoln about Grace's expertise as a cosmetologist, Lincoln cracks a joke, saying that it is too bad Booth is not a woman. Booth asks him to repeat what he said, but Lincoln changes his tone, saying that Booth could have his hair and nails done for free.

Booth continues to sing Grace's praises. Their breakup two years ago happened because, he says, he had a "little employment difficulty," and she needed time to think. Lincoln observes that that time is over, and Booth agrees.

Lincoln asks what Booth is doing. He may have been trying on a condom, but he says that he is resting because Grace left him exhausted. Lincoln asks Booth if he would like some "medsin"—a drink of whiskey—but Booth says no. Lincoln tells Booth to help him practice his moves, but Booth asks if they can practice tomorrow. Lincoln remains persistent, saying that he has been dressed up and waiting for Booth to help him. Lincoln's tone becomes urgent when he confesses his fear of being replaced by a wax dummy.

At first Booth is surprised to hear this, and Lincoln concedes that the idea may be nothing more than talk. He presses Booth again, reminding him that he loaned him five bucks so Booth could entertain Grace properly. Booth replies that he is tired, which prompts Lincoln to respond that Booth did not have sex with Grace earlier that evening; Booth made up that story to save face. Booth says that Lincoln is jealous. Lincoln counters by saying that the only sex Booth has is when he rustles the pages of his girlie magazines. Booth defends himself by saying that he is a passionate man who needs "sexual release." He justifies his frequent masturbation by saying that if he did not he would be out spending money and committing crimes to satisfy his passionate nature. Angry, Booth attacks Lincoln by denigrating his manhood. He tells Lincoln that his wife Cookie left him because he was impotent. Booth extends his role of topdog by saying, "I gave it to Grace good tonight. So goodnight." Lincoln says goodnight.

Lincoln sits in his chair while Booth lies in bed. After awhile, Booth checks on his brother to see if he is asleep, but Lincoln keeps an eye out for him. Lincoln breaks the silence by telling Booth that he does not need him to hustle a game of three-card monte. Booth says that he had planned to do it that way. Lincoln offers to contact his old crew, but Booth insists that he can assemble one of his own. "I don't need yr crew. Buncha has-beens. I can get my own crew," he says. Lincoln ignores Booth, telling him that back in the day he and his crew would pull in seven thousand dollars a week. Booth, however, remains stubborn until Lincoln, appealing to his brother's vanity, paints a verbal picture of Booth taking wads of cash off of tourists at the Mexican border. Booth slowly warms to the idea of Lincoln setting him up as a dealer.

Lincoln reminds Booth that he would have to have a gun for protection, but Booth says he already has one. Lincoln refers to Booth's piece as a "pop gun." He says that Booth would have to have a gun that matched his skill as a hustler, some "upper echelon heat." Booth will not listen to what his brother says because Lincoln has been away from the game for too long, six or seven years. Lincoln says he knows about guns because he works around them every day at the arcade. Booth wants to know what kinds of guns they have at the arcade, but Lincoln reminds him that Booth has been there and seen them before. Lincoln describes the guns as "Shiny deadly metal each with their own deadly personality."

Booth begins to think about what he could steal if he did visit the arcade. Lincoln tries to tell him that it would not be worth the trouble of stealing a gun because they all shoot blanks, to which Booth makes a reference to Lincoln doing the same thing sexually. Booth asks Lincoln if he ever wonders if one of the visitors will come in with a real gun, but Lincoln says he has no enemies, not even his ex-wife Cookie. Booth wonders about the Best Customer, but Lincoln dismisses the thought, saying he "cant be worrying about the actions of miscellaneous strangers."

Booth asks Lincoln if he knows anything about the people who visit the arcade, but Lincoln says he does not see a thing because he is in character, and Honest Abe is supposed to be staring straight ahead, looking at a play. Besides, Lincoln says, the arcade is kept dark "To keep thuh illusion of thuh whole thing," though occasionally he can see an inverted image in the metal casing of the fuse box in front of him. That is where he sees the "assassins." Lincoln then describes how he anticipates each assassin's arrival and how the tourist can know he is alive when the gun's cold metal touches his skin. Lincoln describes how he slumps, closes his eyes, and falls, repeating this routine with each paying customer that comes through the turnstile. He describes the many types of people who want to shoot Honest Abe. At the end of his speech, Lincoln says, "I do my best for them. And now they talking bout replacing me with uh wax dummy."

Booth suggests that Lincoln remind his boss about all the things he can do that a wax dummy cannot. Booth thinks that Lincoln would get his point across if he added more "spicy s—" to his routine. When Lincoln asks him how, Booth tells him that, for one thing, he should scream when he is shot. Booth takes charge, assuming the role of his namesake. Lincoln practices a scream, but Booth thinks he should add some cursing, so Lincoln lets fly with a string of profanity. Lincoln, however, does not think the screaming and cursing will go over too well, so Booth suggests that he try rolling on the floor. After Lincoln tries, Booth says that he should wiggle and scream. Booth then suggests that Lincoln hold his head. "And look at me! I am the assassin! *I am Booth!!*," he says. "Come on man this is life and death! Go all out!"

Lincoln goes all out. Booth says that they should end the rehearsal there because things were beginning to look "too real or something." Lincoln says that the owners of the arcade do not want his performance to look too real because it will scare the customers. That would get him fired for sure. Lincoln accuses Booth of trying to get him fired, but Booth says he was just trying to help. Lincoln says that people are "funny" about how they want history re-enacted. "They like it to unfold the way they folded it up. Neatly like a book. Not raggedy and bloody and screaming." Again, he accuses Booth of trying to get him fired. Lincoln says it is not easy for him to play the role, but somehow he makes it look easy. The fact that he and Honest Abe have the same name helped him get hired. "Its a sit down job. With benefits," he says. Lincoln does not want to get fired because then he will not get a good reference.

Booth tells Lincoln that they could "hustle the cards together" if he got fired. Lincoln says he would not remember what to do, it has been so long since he was in the game. Booth reassures him and says goodnight. Lincoln disagrees and says goodnight before stretching out in his recliner. Booth stands over him, waiting for Lincoln to change his mind, but he is already fast asleep. Booth covers Lincoln with a blanket, turns out the lights, and

locates one of his girlie magazines under the bed before the lights fade and the scene ends.

Scene 4

The scene opens just before dawn on Saturday. Lincoln awakens and looks around the room. Booth is fast asleep. Lincoln complains about the lack of running water as he stumbles around the room looking for something to use as a urinal. Finally, he finds a plastic cup and uses it, stowing it out of sight once he is finished. Then, he grabs his Lincoln getup and tries to remove it, tearing it. He removes his clothes until he is wearing nothing but his T-shirt and shorts.

Lincoln talks about how he hates falling asleep in his costume. He is worried that he will have to pay for the beard now that he has ripped it. He imagines what the bosses will say when they see the beard, and he visualizes strangling his boss as a form of retribution for being fired. He contemplates the irony of having a sit down job with benefits and being at another's mercy when he once was the best three-card monte dealer anyone had ever seen. He looks back over his career and reminds himself that it is best to quit while you are ahead. But he did not do that. He threw the cards one time too many, and Lonny got shot.

Lincoln consoles himself with the thought that he found a good job once he left the street. He convinces himself that he will find another good job when the arcade finally lets him go. He will not have to return to hustling. "Theres more to Link than that. More to me than some cheap hustle. More to life than cheating some idiot out of his paycheck or his life savings."

Lincoln thinks about Lonny and how the two worked so well together. He remembers how they took a couple for hundreds, even thousands, of dollars. "We took them for everything they had and everything they ever wanted to have," he says. He justifies hustling people who are greedy, but then he remembers what happened to Lonny and why he swore off the cards even though he was good at them.

Lincoln then experiences a moment of realization and picks up a pack of cards, choosing three from the deck. He stands over the three-card monte setup and begins going over his moves, slowly at first but then gathering speed. Unlike Booth's routine, Lincoln's is "deft, dangerous, electric." Lincoln puts himself through the paces, refining his patter. Lincoln speaks in a low voice, but Booth awakens and listens to his brother as he moves two red cards and one spade around and around on the table. Lincoln's confidence builds with each hand he deals until, finally, he beats the mark. Lincoln puts the cards down and moves away from the table. He sits down on the edge of his chair, unable to take his eyes off the cards.

Scene 5

The scene opens on a Wednesday night, with Booth sitting in his new suit. The three-card monte setup is nowhere to be seen. In its place is a table and chairs; the table has been set for a romantic evening for two, including champagne glasses and candles. The apartment looks much cleaner than it did before; new curtains cover the windows. Booth sits at the table, checking to make sure everything is perfect.

Booth curses because he finds one of his girlie magazines poking out from beneath his bed. He kicks it back under the bed and pulls down the spread to conceal his collection. Nervous, Booth checks the champagne and the food. He tells himself not to worry, that Grace will arrive soon. Still restless, he checks the mattress for springiness and lays two dressing gowns marked "His" and "Hers" across the foot of the bed. He can still see the girlie magazines sticking out from beneath the bed, so he removes his pants and crawls under the bed to stow the magazines away safely.

Lincoln comes in, wearing his frock coat and carrying the rest of his costume in a plastic bag, but Booth, half dressed, mistakenly believes that Grace has arrived. He tries to keep his brother from coming in. Lincoln asks if he is interrupting anything, saying that he can go if Booth is "in thuh middle of it," meaning a sexual encounter with Grace. Booth tells him that the room is "off limits" tonight, but Lincoln insists that he could stay and sit there quietly composing songs just like he did whenever their parents had sex in the two-room apartment they shared with the boys. Booth insists that his brother find someplace else to stay and asks if he intends to spend the night with friends. Booth waits for Lincoln to leave, but Lincoln refuses to go.

Lincoln tells Booth that he lost his job at the arcade. He did everything correctly, but the owners had already purchased a wax dummy to take his place. Lincoln was so stunned by the news that he walked out wearing his costume. He believes that the owners will take him back if he tells them he is willing to take a pay cut, but Booth tells him that he should not. "Yr free. Don't go crawling back. Yr free at last! You can do anything you want." Lincoln, however, quickly understands that Booth wants him to return to hustling.

Booth tries to get Lincoln to go because Grace is expected at any moment, but Lincoln just plops into his easy chair without budging. He says he will leave when Grace arrives. Booth again insists that his brother leave. Lincoln asks what time Grace is coming, and Booth tells him that she is already late, although she could arrive momentarily. Lincoln asks what time she was supposed to be there, and Booth says that she was supposed to arrive at eight o'clock. Lincoln points out that it is after two in the morning—she is very late. Lincoln does not want to embarrass his brother, so he tells him that Booth can cover him with a blanket and pretend that he is alone when Grace arrives. Lincoln's tired and needs to sit down after walking all day, but he will go once Grace gets there.

Booth asks for Lincoln's opinion of the table setting. Lincoln approves. Things look so nice that for a moment he thought that Booth had gone and spent his inheritance. Booth tells him that he boosted the china, silver, and crystal. "Every bit of it." By now Booth is impatient, so Lincoln tells him that Grace will arrive shortly. "Dont sweat it," he says. Booth sits down at the table and tries to relax. "How come I got a hand for boosting and I dont got a hand for throwing cards?" he asks Lincoln.

Lincoln tells Booth to look out the window. He promises to leave when Grace arrives, and Booth says that maybe his brother has "jinxed" the evening already by showing up. Booth quickly changes his mind, however. "Shes just a little late. You aint jinxed nothing," he says. Booth then sits by the window, watching for Grace on the street. Meanwhile, Lincoln sits in the recliner and sips from a whiskey bottle. He rummages around until he finds a worn photo album, which he peruses.

Looking at a photograph, Lincoln asks Booth if he remembers a house they lived in when Lincoln was eight and Booth was five. Lincoln calls it the "best [f——ing] house in the world." Booth tells him to stop going down "memory lane" because, if he does not, he will spoil the mood Booth has tried so hard to create. Booth does not want any of his brother's "raggedy collections" to interfere with his romantic plans. Lincoln ignores his brother's wishes and continues to reminisce. Booth tries to dispel Lincoln's notion that the times they spent in that house were idyllic. Ironically, Booth resists the romance of looking back upon his childhood years.

Lincoln reminds Booth of a prank they pulled on their father when he backed his car out of the driveway. The car's tires went flat because the boys had placed a row of nails behind them. Lincoln takes pride in the fact that neither one of them gave themselves away. Booth admires his brother for staying so cool under pressure. After a pause, he asks Lincoln for the time. It is after three in the morning, so Lincoln suggests that Booth call Grace because something might have happened. When Lincoln observes that Booth looks sad, Booth shrugs it off, searching for a word to describe his mood. "Cool," suggests Lincoln. "Yeah. Cool," replies Booth, who comes over and pours himself a big glass of whiskey. He continues looking out the window, this time with a drink in his hand.

Booth asks if Lincoln received any severance pay. Lincoln says he blew a week's pay on nothing in particular. He just felt good spending money like he did when he was hustling and making lots of cash. He was his own man then, and he did not have to worry about being replaced by a wax dummy. "I was thuh [sh——t] and they was my fools," Lincoln says. "Back in the thuh day."

Lincoln asks Booth why he thinks their parents left them. Booth says he does not think about it that much, but Lincoln thinks that their parents left because they did not like them. "I think there was something out there that they liked more than they liked us and for years they was struggling against moving towards that more liked something," he says. To Lincoln's mind, each parent had something to struggle against. When the family moved from a nasty apartment into a house, the struggle became worse for their parents because they each could not live up to their individual expectations of what domestic life should be.

Booth agrees that the idea of a normal family life was too much for their parents. First their mother left, then, two years later, their father did. "Like thuh whole family mortgage bills going to work thing was just too much," says Booth. "I seen how it cracked them up and I aint going there." Upset by Grace's failure to arrive on time, Booth relates his parents' experience to his own by saying that, regardless of Grace's wishes, he will not wear a "rubber" (condom) the next time they are together.

Lincoln remarks that their mother told him he should not marry. Booth says that she told him the same thing, which leads Lincoln to observe that both of their parents gave them $500 before they "cut out." Booth says that he will do the same thing when he has kids.

Leaving their kids money and cutting out was the one thing Booth says that their parents could agree upon. Lincoln does not understand at first, but then he sees Booth's point when they compare stories about how each of the brothers received $500 from their parents. Lincoln imagines that his parents have begun a new life, one that includes two boys different from them. Both the whiskey bottle and glasses are empty, so Booth pops the cork on the champagne bottle.

Booth tells Lincoln that he did not mind his parents leaving because he knew that he still had his brother to rely on. They were better off on their own than they would have been had they been under the protection of some child welfare agency. "It was you and me against thuh world, Link," Booth says. "It could be like that again."

Lincoln reminds Booth that throwing the cards is not as easy as it looks. The perspective Booth had when he was on the sidelines is much different than that of the customer. Booth demonstrates his understanding of the game by explaining Lonny's role as the stickman. The brothers discuss the various roles each of the crew plays, and Lincoln says that Booth stands a chance of being successful if he learns a few basic moves, which Lincoln is willing to demonstrate. Lincoln tells Booth to set up the cards, and, "in a flash," Booth clears the romantic dinner setting and replaces it with the three-card monte setup.

Lincoln begins by telling Booth that the deuce of spades is the one to watch. Booth prefers to work with the deuce of hearts, but spades are okay. Lincoln reviews the roles the crew members play, and Booth agrees to be the lookout. He is ready, he says, because he is already carrying a gun. Lincoln cannot understand why Booth would always carry a gun, even on a date, but Booth says that you never know when you might need to use it. Lincoln asks for the gun, which Booth hands over. Lincoln says that there is no point in having a lookout if there are not any cops, so Booth says he will be the stickman instead. Lincoln says that Booth does not have the experience to be a stickman, so he can be the sideman.

Lincoln begins the lesson by saying, "First thing you learn is what is. Next thing you learn is what aint. You don't know what is you don't know what aint, you don't know [sh——t]." Booth understands. Booth gets defensive when he sees Lincoln sizing him up. He cannot understand why Lincoln would want to size up someone who is on his team, but Lincoln explains that everyone, including his crew, is part of the crowd, and the dealer always has to size up the crowd before he begins the hustle.

After sizing up the imaginary crowd, Lincoln decides that he does not want to play. Booth calls him on it, but Lincoln explains that not wanting to play is just part of the dealer's attitude. This is what lures the mark in because the mark thinks that he can beat the dealer. Booth asks if Lincoln is sizing him up again. Lincoln explains that there are two parts to throwing the cards, both of which are "fairly complicated." Lincoln says that Booth has to work on what he is doing with his mouth and what he is doing with his hands because both count. Lincoln continues to explain how the mark sets himself up to be taken.

Lincoln reminds Booth to look at his eyes, not his hands. He says it is important that Booth not think too much about throwing the cards. Lincoln is trying to get Booth to immerse himself totally in throwing the cards. "Dont think about nothing," Lincoln says. "Just look into my eyes. Focus." Booth responds literally by saying that Lincoln's eyes are red, and he asks if his brother has been crying. Lincoln loses his patience, but he proceeds with the demonstration anyway by having Booth point to the deuce of spades. When Booth asks if he has pointed to the right one, Lincoln tells him to point with confidence. Lincoln flips the card over, and it is indeed the deuce of spades. Lincoln is "slightly crestfallen" because Booth has beaten him.

Booth begins to celebrate. "Make room for 3-Card! Here comes thuh champ!" he cries. Lincoln tells him not to get too excited. He should focus. Lincoln tells Booth to listen when he adds the "second element" of words.

Lincoln goes into a long and convoluted patter that lures the mark in and confuses him. At the end of Lincoln's monologue, he asks Booth to pick again. He does, and once again Booth picks the deuce of spades. Confident, Booth begins to challenge his brother's ability, but Lincoln remains determined to teach his brother a lesson by beating him at cards. Lincoln decides to make Booth back up his words with actions by switching roles and having him be the dealer. Lincoln reminds Booth that a light touch is necessary, but Booth moves the cards around awkwardly. His speech is not too good either. Soon, Lincoln bursts out laughing. Booth puts on his coat and places his gun inside one of the pockets.

Lincoln criticizes Booth's patter. If he does not smooth it out, he will get locked up every time. Lincoln recalls a time when they had $800 on the line and Booth misunderstood Link's signals, causing the mark to win. Lincoln says that everything turned out okay because they won the money back, but, really, a light touch is what Booth needs if he

wants to throw the cards successfully. Lincoln tells Booth that he should touch the cards as though he were touching Grace's skin.

Lincoln holds up a watch, and Booth lets out a burst of anger when he sees how late it is and that he has been stood up. Booth immediately thinks that Grace is out with another man, but Lincoln, still willing to give Grace the benefit of a doubt, thinks that maybe something has happened to her. Booth says that the only thing that has happened is that she has made him look like a "chump." "I aint her chump. I aint nobodys chump," he says.

Lincoln offers to go to the payphone on the corner, but Booth cuts him off, saying that, unlike his brother, he is a man of action. "Thuh world puts its foot in yr face and you dont move... But Im my own man, Link. I aint you." Booth leaves the room, slamming the door behind him. "You got that right," Lincoln says, picking up the cards, moving them around faster and faster.

Scene 6

The scene opens on a Thursday night. The room appears empty, as though no one is home. Lincoln enters drunk; he leaves the door slightly open. As he does in an earlier scene, he imitates the sound of fanfare as he enters the room. He calls Booth's name and pulls out a large wad of cash once he's sure no one is home. He secures the money with an elastic band and puts it into his pocket. He sits down in his chair and takes the money out again, counting it quickly like he did when he was on the street.

Lincoln begins a monologue in which he celebrates finding himself again. He's just returned from Lucky's, where everyone saw the old Link again. Not only does Lincoln still possess his skill with cards but the women have started coming around again now that he shows flashes of the old success. "Who thuh man?" he asks. "Link. Thats right," he answers. Lincoln is full of drink and bravado, making fun of the tourists he's swindled out of money.

Just then Booth comes out from behind the dressing screen that separates the room. He stands at the door without making a sound. Meanwhile, Lincoln continues talking about his conquest and how he's not a has-been anymore. Booth closes the door, which prompts another spell.

Lincoln asks Booth if he's had another "evening to remember," and Booth says he has, though perhaps he wouldn't have used those words to describe it. Lincoln begins to tell Booth about his own "memorable evening" when Booth announces that he has some news to tell. Lincoln tells him to go first. After some hesitation, Booth says that Grace got down on her knees and asked him to marry her. Lincoln cannot believe it, and neither can Booth. "Amazing Grace!" he says. Booth then offers an explanation for why Grace did not show up the other night. He says he made a mistake by getting the days switched. She was not out with another man; she was at home watching television.

Booth continues his story, saying that Grace wants to get married immediately. She wants to have a baby; she wants to have *his* baby. Seeing the downcast look on Lincoln's face, Booth tells him not to worry: they'll name their baby boy after him.

A short spell ensues, and Booth asks Lincoln what news he has to tell. At first Lincoln does not want to say anything, so Booth asks him if the news about Grace is "good news." Then Booth shifts the topic to the bad news; that is, Grace plans on their living together as man and wife, so Lincoln will have to move. "No sweat," says Lincoln. Booth is apologetic, but he assuages his guilt by saying that it was "a temporary situation anyhow." Lincoln finds a suitcase and begins packing his belongings.

Booth cannot believe that Lincoln would take the bad news so easily, especially after he just lost his job and does not have any friends who will put him up. Furthermore, Booth cannot believe that Lincoln would be willing to leave him that quickly. Lincoln thanks Booth for his generosity. He tells Booth that he will not have a hard time finding another place to live because he already has another job working as a security guard. Lincoln continues packing his things and picks up the whiskey bottle. Booth tells him to take the "med-sin" with him; he will not need it because he has Grace's love to keep him warm.

Lincoln asks if Booth plans to find a job or let Grace support him. "I got plans," Booth says, though he does not reveal what they are. Lincoln warns Booth that he will lose Grace if he is not able to support himself. She will not like working hard, only to find that he was just lying around doing nothing. Booth responds by saying that Grace accepts him for who he is. Lincoln backs off, saying that he was just offering some advice, though it appears that Booth is doing fine on his own.

A long spell ensues, and Booth says he never understood why their father never took any of his things with him when he left. Lincoln says it was because their father was drunk. Booth cannot understand why their father would leave his clothes,

and Lincoln points out that he did worse than that: he left his two sons behind. He tells Booth to stop worrying about the past. "I mean, you aint gonna figure it out by thinking about it. Just call it one of thuh great unsolved mysteries of existence," Lincoln says.

Booth announces that their mother had a man on the side. Lincoln counters by telling Booth that their father had many mistresses, one of whom let Lincoln into her bed once his father was finished having sex.

A short spell ensues, and Lincoln takes his getup out of the closet. He is not sure if he should take it with him. Booth tells Lincoln that he will miss seeing him coming home in costume; he wishes he had a picture of Honest Abe for the album. Lincoln agrees to put on the costume if Booth gets the camera. Why not? They have nothing to lose. Booth searches the apartment and finds the camera while Lincoln applies makeup that more closely resembles war paint than it does whiteface.

Lincoln tells Booth that he did not get fired because he was not any good; he was fired because the owners had to cut back on expenditures. Lincoln reiterates that getting fired had nothing to do with his performance. Booth agrees and tells him to smile for the camera, but Lincoln points out that Honest Abe never smiled. Booth says that Lincoln should smile because he has got a new job and having a "good day." Lincoln protests, but Booth takes his picture anyway.

Lincoln suggests that they take a picture of them together, but Booth declines, saying that he would prefer to save the film for the wedding. Lincoln says that the job at the arcade was not so bad after all; he just "outgrew" it. He tells Booth that he would be glad to put a word in for him when business picks up again, but Booth says that he cannot pretend to be someone else all day. Lincoln says that he was not pretending because he was composing songs and thinking about women, including his ex-wife. Booth then recalls an episode where Cookie went looking for Lincoln but could not find him because he was out drinking at Lucky's. When she came to Booth's apartment and did not find Lincoln there, she seduced Booth because, he says, Lincoln was impotent and could not satisfy such a passionate woman. Booth was so taken with Cookie that he promised to marry her if she would leave Lincoln, but he changed his mind.

Lincoln says that he does not think about his ex-wife anymore. Booth observes that Lincoln does not "go back" because he cannot. "No matter what you do you cant get back to being who you was.

Best you can do is just pretend to be yr old self," Booth says. Lincoln thinks that is nonsense, and soon the brothers argue over Booth's plans to earn a living by throwing the cards. Lincoln does not believe Booth can make it; Booth responds by saying that Lincoln is scared. Lincoln tells him to get out of the way: he is leaving. Booth blocks the way. He says Lincoln's scared of him because he picked the deuce of spades twice correctly. Lincoln accepts Booth's challenge by ordering him to set up the cards.

Booth sets up the board and the milk crates. Lincoln throws the cards. After a display of his skill, Lincoln asks Booth to pick the deuce of spades. Booth points to a card, which is the deuce of spades. "Who thuh man?!" asks Booth. Meanwhile, Lincoln looks at the other two cards as though he is unsure what went wrong. Booth continues taunting Lincoln, until he concedes that Booth has beaten him. "You thuh man, man," Lincoln concedes. Booth wants more, however, and he becomes angry when he realizes that Lincoln has been throwing out on the street earlier that day. Lincoln tells Booth that he was going to tell him, but he did not say anything because he still hasn't regained his old form. Booth knows that Lincoln has been putting him on, so he insists that this time Lincoln throw the cards for real.

Booth starts to get down on himself, but Lincoln reminds him that the "essential elements" of the street and the crowd are missing. Booth says that cash would make it real, so he suggests that Lincoln put down some of the money he won earlier that day. A short spell ensues, and Booth taunts Lincoln, asking him if he is afraid of losing to a chump. Lincoln puts his wad of money ($500) down on the table as a bet. Booth looks it over and gives his brother permission to begin the next round.

Booth stops Lincoln before he can get going because he, Booth, does not believe that Lincoln is "going full out." Lincoln says that he was just warming up. Besides, he put his money down, and that makes it real. Booth says that in order for things to be real he has to match the bet. Lincoln does not think Booth has any money because he hasn't held a job in years. Lincoln wonders if maybe Booth has been putting aside some money from the budget for himself, but Booth proudly declares that he has money of his own. The two brothers size each other up before Booth disappears. He returns with a nylon stocking containing money. A spell ensues.

Booth tells Lincoln how he discovered their mother's "Thursday man." He tells about the time he overheard their mother asking her man for some money because "thered been some kind of problem

some kind of mistake had been made some kind of mistake that needed cleaning up." Booth alludes to his mother having an abortion. Her man refused to give her any money, so she had to face the problem by herself. Booth does not know if she kept the baby or "got rid of it," but he remains certain that she knew he was going to walk in on her because, before she left, she had $500 to give him in a nylon stocking. Booth places the nylon stocking on the table to match Lincoln's bet.

"Now its real," Booth says, but Lincoln does not want his brother to bet his money. Booth orders Lincoln to throw the cards, but he says he does not want to play. Booth yells at him to throw the cards, and Lincoln begins his patter. Again, Lincoln asks Booth to pick the deuce of spades. Lincoln reminds him that this time it is for real, so he had better choose the right card. "You pick wrong Im in yr wad and I keep mines," Lincoln says. "I pick right I got yr [sh——t]," replies Booth.

Lincoln asks if Booth thinks they are really brothers; Booth says he does. A long spell ensues, and Lincoln asks Booth to find the deuce. Booth quickly points out a card. Before he turns the card over, Lincoln asks Booth if he is sure that is the one. The brothers stare at each other, and then Lincoln turns over the card Booth picked. Booth breaks away to see that he has chosen the wrong card. It is the deuce of hearts.

Lincoln collects the money and wishes Booth better luck next time. He begins to ridicule Booth, saying he has two left hands. Lincoln backs off, however, saying that cards aren't everything. After all, Booth has Grace. Booth does not respond, so Lincoln asks him if something is wrong. Booth says nothing's wrong, so Lincoln begins to boast a bit. Dejected, Booth admits that his brother still has the moves. Lincoln chuckles, though he is quick to tell Booth that he is not laughing at him. The game is too complicated, he says, perhaps amazed at how quickly he has regained his old form. Lincoln then sits down in the easy chair and starts untying the knot at the top of the nylon stocking.

Lincoln comments that their mother tied the knot tightly, which prompts Booth to admit that he has never opened the stocking. Lincoln cannot believe that his brother was never tempted to spend the $500 the stocking contains. Booth says he has been saving the money. He asks Lincoln not to open the stocking, but Lincoln wants to see what's inside. Booth angrily tells him that they don't need to open it because they already know what's inside. Lincoln calls Booth a "chump" because there could be more than $500 in there—or there could be nothing. Booth begs Lincoln not to open it, and a spell ensues.

Lincoln cannot untie the knot. Again, he tells Booth that he is not laughing at him; he is just laughing. Lincoln asks his brother how he knew his mother was for real when she gave him the money. How did he know she was not "jiving" him? Lincoln, now the topdog, continues to taunt Booth about how he was in too big of a hurry to learn the cards correctly. The first move separates the player from the played, says Lincoln. "And thuh first move is to know that there aint no winning." The only time you win is when the man lets you, Lincoln says. He mocks how Booth thought he was a winner. Lincoln let him win. He played him.

Humiliated, Booth screams "[F—k] you!" several times, each time growing in intensity and anger. Lincoln ignores him, however, and pulls a knife out of his boot so he can cut the knot, chuckling all the while. Booth joins in the laughter as Lincoln holds the knife high, ready to cut the stocking. He tells Booth to turn his head because he may not want to look. Booth turns away slightly as they continue laughing. Lincoln lowers the knife to cut the stocking.

Out of nowhere, Booth makes a confession. "I popped her," he says. "Grace. I popped her." He said he popped her because she said he had nothing going for him. He showed her what he had going on by popping her two, maybe three, times. Booth says Grace is not dead, but Lincoln gets him to admit that she is indeed dead. Lincoln says he will give Booth back the stocking. Booth says he cannot take being condescended to anymore. He just could not take any more of that "little bro [sh——t]." Booth says that he is 3-Card now; he is not Booth anymore. Lincoln once again says that he will give Booth back his money, but Booth grows even more angry, asking "Who thuh man now, huh? Who thuh man now?!" Lincoln tells Booth to take the money, but Booth says he will not be needing it. He tells Lincoln that he should open the stocking because he won the money, but Lincoln refuses. Booth orders him to open the stocking, and a spell ensues shortly thereafter.

Booth grabs Lincoln from behind as he lowers the knife to cut the stocking. Like the assassins in the arcade, Booth pulls out his gun and places it against the left side of Lincoln's neck. "Dont," Lincoln tells him, but Booth pulls the trigger and Lincoln slumps out of his chair onto the floor. Booth paces the floor, the gun smoking in his hand.

Booth begins a final monologue in which he rails against his brother for taking his inheritance.

Lincoln had his own inheritance, and he blew it. Booth says that Lincoln will not be needing the money anymore, so he might as well take it. The money was his inheritance, one which he had been saving ever since he received it. Lincoln should not have taken it because it was still his; their mother had given it to Booth, not Lincoln. Booth practices his patter again, thinking about how he will match his brother's fame as a dealer. He bends down to pick up the money and crumples to the floor. Booth sits beside Lincoln's body, holding him close. He sobs and lets out a wail to end the play.

CHARACTERS

Best Customer

The Best Customer is a "miscellaneous stranger" who visits the arcade daily to shoot Honest Abe. The Best Customer "[s]hoots on the left whispers on the right." Link is unsure whether the Best Customer, a black male, knows that Link is also a "brother." The Best Customer utters cryptic messages that possess a quasi-metaphysical quality. He goes so far as to whisper a message in Honest Abe's ear after he has been shot. Link does not think much of the Best Customer, though, ironically, he acknowledges that the Best Customer "makes the day interesting." Booth, on the other hand, regards him as "one *deep* black brother."

Booth

Booth is Link's younger brother, who aspires to become a master of the three-card monte. He rents the room the brothers share, although he does not hold down a job. Instead, he earns his living as a petty thief. Booth tries to get Link to show him how to throw the cards, but Link refuses, which infuriates Booth. Booth believes that if he knew how to throw the cards, he could earn lots of money with which he could win Grace's heart. Booth calls himself "3-Card" to bolster his confidence. However, Grace plays games with him and thus keeps him uncertain about their future. The frustration Booth feels as a result of these personal relationships finds an outlet through the girlie magazines he peruses constantly and through violence, which forever separates the symbiotic bond that binds the brothers together.

Cookie

Cookie is Link's wife from whom he is now divorced. One night, she comes over to Booth's apartment looking for Link, who is out drinking, but ends up having sexual relations with his brother, who promises to marry her if she leaves Link. She justifies her actions because Link is sexually impotent, which contradicts his portrayal of himself as a ladies man.

Grace

Grace is Booth's girlfriend. She attends cosmetology school, thus differentiating her from the "fly-by-night gals" Booth saw before her. Grace is ambitious and career-oriented, yet she also knows how to have fun. Booth describes her as "Wild. Goodlooking." According to him, Grace is so sweet she makes his teeth hurt. She was with Booth for two years before they broke up. She needed time to think, and he had what he refers to euphemistically as a "little employment difficulty." Booth tries to woo her back with gifts and empty promises like the ones he made to Cookie. She is supposed to come over to the apartment for a romantic dinner Booth has arranged, but she never appears. Booth reacts to being stood up by shooting her dead.

Honest Abe

Honest Abe is the name Lincoln uses to refer to himself when he is in character, including the time when a kid riding on the bus asks him for an autograph. Link, seeing that the kid comes from a rich family, charges him ten dollars for the autograph. When the kid hands Link a twenty-dollar bill, Link promises to meet him on the bus the next day to give him his change. Instead, he spends the entire twenty dollars buying drinks at Lucky's.

The Ladies

The Ladies are unidentified women whom Pops conducts affairs with on the sly. He brings Link along as an alibi, but sometimes Pops would let Link watch him make love, "like it was this big deal this great thing he was letting me witness," says Link. One of the ladies liked Link and took him to bed once Pops fell asleep, thus initiating Link further into the world of adult sexuality.

Lincoln

Lincoln is Booth's older brother, who impersonates Abraham Lincoln—Honest Abe—at an arcade. Before he took the job at the arcade, Lincoln was a master of the three-card monte, but he stopped hustling tourists and other passersby when his stickman, Lonny, got shot. Ever since Cookie left Lincoln, he has shared a room in a boarding house with his brother Booth. Lincoln once thought of himself

as a ladies man, much as Booth does throughout the play, although Lincoln understands that his philandering contributed to the demise of his marriage. He is grateful to have a job with "benefits" that allows him to sit down and think his private thoughts all day. Lincoln's concerns about the security of his job cause him to fall into despair, especially when he learns that he has been replaced by a wax dummy. He briefly entertains the thought of throwing the cards again when he sees that he has lost none of his technique. At play's end, Lincoln's display of talent and his mocking tone cause Booth to shoot him in a pique of anger and jealousy.

Link

See Lincoln.

Lonny

Lonny was Link's "stickman" when he was master of the three-card monte. The stickman is the member of the crew who looks like another member of the crowd but knows every aspect of the game in progress. One day, Link is throwing the cards, and the next day he discovers that Lonny has been shot dead. Lonny's death serves as a warning to Link to stop living such a dangerous life hustling people on the street.

Lucky

Lucky is the proprietor of the eponymous bar Link frequents whenever he has a little cash to spare. Lucky has a dog he keeps behind the bar.

Mom

Mom was the first of the brothers' parents to leave. She left two years before her husband did. Before she leaves, she gives Booth a nylon stocking filled with five hundred-dollar bills. Until the time of her departure, she had a lover who visited the house regularly on Thursdays. For this reason, Booth refers to him as his mother's "Thursday man." Booth once overheard his mother and her Thursday Man discussing a problem, which was most probably an unwanted pregnancy. How she resolved this problem remains unclear, though her asking her Thursday Man for money suggests that she intended to have an abortion.

Pops

Pops names his sons Lincoln and Booth as a joke. He leaves the house two years after Mom deserted him and the boys. Pops visits his mistress at the same time Mom sees her Thursday Man. Before he leaves the boys to start a new life, Pops gives Link ten fifty-dollar bills wrapped in a hand-kerchief and tells him not to mention a word about the money to anybody, "especially that Booth."

3-Card

See Booth

Thursday Man

The Thursday Man is Mom's lover, who vis-its her at the house every Thursday. Booth knows about his visits, but he does not say anything to anyone about them.

THEMES

History

The play is imbued with a strong sense of his-tory, though it is of a more personal nature than the type of history associated with textbooks. Through-out *Topdog/Underdog*, the brothers reveal parts of their past that have shaped their present circum-stances. For example, Lonny's death influenced Lincoln's decision to stop dealing three-card monte. When Booth shows Lincoln the ring he boosted, he reveals a past relationship with Grace that has been nothing short of disappointing. Sim-ilarly, during an outburst of anger, Booth reveals the reasons why he slept with Lincoln's wife Cookie. Moreover, the one item that the brothers have salvaged from their days as a family is a "raggedy" photo album. It contains a link to a past that, though turbulent, still held hopes and dreams for the future.

Identity

Identity is an important theme within the play. Although Lincoln may share the name of The Great Emancipator, he knows who he is before he ever donned his costume. "I was Lincoln on my own be-fore any of that," he says. This knowledge allows Lincoln to wear his costume home on the bus with-out confusion about his identity. In fact, Lincoln is able to swindle the "little rich kid" out of twenty dollars because he knows he no longer plays the role of Honest Abe once he leaves the arcade. The Lincoln who rides the bus is free to hustle at will.

Booth, on the other hand, possesses a more complicated view of himself. He is forever imag-ining himself to be someone else, whether that someone else is a ladies man, a respectable hus-band, or a master three-card monte dealer like his brother. Booth even goes so far as to invent a name

for himself to solidify his new identity: "3-Card." So fragile is his sense of identity that he will allow no one—not even Grace—to call him by his given name. He insists upon being called "3-Card" or nothing else. When he loses the final game of cards to Lincoln and tells him that he shot Grace, Booth begins to exact his revenge when he announces, "That Booth [sh——t] is over. 3-Cards thuh man now—"Only by assuming his new identity in full can 3-Card (Booth) commit the unpardonable act of fratricide.

Illusion

Illusion is at the very heart of the three-card monte hustle. Not only must the dealer be a mas-ter of sleight-of-hand, but he, with the help of his crew, creates confusion to beat his mark. The crew deflects the mark's attention so that he loses track of reality (i.e., the card's location). Furthermore, by pretending not to want to throw the cards, the dealer creates the illusion that he is an unwilling partici-pant. Knowing what is real and what is not is the key to winning a hand of three-card monte. As Lincoln tells Booth, "First thing you learn is what is. Next thing you learn is what aint. You dont know what is you dont know what aint, you don't know [sh——t]."

The theme of illusion is best demonstrated within the play through the "getup" Lincoln wears when he portrays Honest Abe at the arcade. The illusion is made even more incredible when one considers that a black man must wear whiteface to perform the role. According to Lincoln, the arcade is kept dark to "keep thuh illusion of thuh whole thing" going. Even so, he can see the inverted im-ages of his assailants in a dented fuse box before him. The inverted images distort reality even fur-ther, and it is not until Lincoln feels the cool metal of the gun against his neck that the assassin knows that he is alive and that he can now be shot dead.

Perhaps the most chilling illusion in the play is the one Booth has about his mother's intentions. He holds onto the nylon stocking because it is his inheritance; it is the last vestige he possesses of the relationship he had with his mother, even if that re-lationship was based on deceit and complicity in concealing the presence of her "Thursday man." That complicity is compounded by the fact that she may have had an abortion. Moreover, there is doubt as to whether the stocking actually contains the $500 Booth says it does. Booth casts aside any il-lusions he has about his mother, however, when he bets his inheritance against Lincoln's talent at three-card monte.

TOPICS FOR FURTHER STUDY

- Write a short monologue from the perspective of a member of Lincoln's crew. How does this crew member view the mark and the dealer? What are his observations? What role does he play in the hustle? Is it necessary for him to watch the cards at all times?

- Research the history of blackface in America. What are its origins? Who were some of its more famous practitioners? Are aspects of blackface visible in today's entertainment media?

- Make a list of famous figures and the people who assassinated them. In some cases, the assassin, such as John Wilkes Booth, garners as much notoriety as the person they murdered. Why is this so?

- Consider the way in which the set design influences the audience's perception of the drama unfolding onstage. How would the audience's perception of the relationship between Lincoln and Booth change if the play were set on a large stage as compared to a small, confining space?

- Cookie, Grace, and Mom are mentioned in the play but never appear on stage. They are also absent from the lives of the play's two protagonists. How does the absence of women in *Topdog/Underdog* illuminate the brothers' emotional, sexual, and social condition?

- Identify the ways in which history plays a role in the play. Is this sense of history broadly defined, or is it limited to a more personal interaction among characters? Discuss your conclusions.

Sibling Rivalry

The theme of sibling rivalry is as old as the biblical story of Cain and Abel, and in *Topdog/Underdog* Parks uses a variation of that familiar tale to highlight the "mix of loving bonds and jealousies" that bind Lincoln and Booth together in a symbiotic relationship. As the title of the play suggests, the two brothers compete to see who will have the upper hand. When one succeeds, he is quick to ask, "Who thuh man?" Booth constantly measures his ability to throw the cards against that of his brother, a former master of three-card monte. Even though Booth has a talent for "boosting" things, he remains discontent because he cannot best his brother at cards. This dynamic of sibling rivalry contributes to the dramatic tension that makes the play's final scene so memorable, for, without the constant struggle for power that marks Lincoln and Booth's relationship, the audience would witness just another card game.

Sex and Death

Sex and death are inextricably tied within this play. From the outset, Booth's gun is seen as a symbol of what critic Margaret B. Wilkerson describes as his "sexual potency," one that may be more fiction than fact. He carries the gun with him always, loaded and at the ready, which is how he views himself with regard to women; he is constantly on the prowl for sexual adventure. Furthermore, Booth comments about how the shooters at the arcade fire blanks, which leads him to taunt Lincoln about the sexual impotence that cost him his marriage to Cookie. The theme of sex and death again presents itself when Booth helps Lincoln rehearse his dying so that he will be able to deliver a better performance and keep his job. Booth tells Lincoln to scream when he dies, but then Booth admonishes him for sounding too much like he is having sex.

Sex is a force for destruction when Ma asks her Thursday Man for some money to help with a problem. He refuses, and Ma is left to take care of her pregnancy on her own. It is not known whether she kept the child or aborted it, but sex, a life-giving force, can also lead to death. Moreover, Ma and Pa's sexual peccadilloes, extended over the course of several years, eventually lead to the death of their family. The most dramatic reference to sex and death in the play, however, occurs when Booth announces that he "popped" Grace. The word *popped* has sexual connotations, but here Booth uses it to refer to his having shot Grace, because she would not grant him her sexual favors.

STYLE

Naturalism

Topdog/Underdog is less fantastic than some of Parks's other plays. Though the set design evokes social realism, the play is naturalistic in the sense that Lincoln and Booth respond to the environmental forces, such as poverty, that shape their lives externally, as well as to the private desires and ambitions that exert an equal, if not greater, force psychically. The brothers are subject to deterministic sociological and economic forces that lead them to contemplate a life of petty crime. Furthermore, Booth's frank discussions of his sexual needs indicates that strong biological instincts also inform his decisions. Fear and the need for escape, whether through drink or through sex, are other primal forces at work in the play. Though characters in naturalistic works of drama or fiction are occasionally viewed as victims of fate, Parks makes no moral judgments about her characters. She remains objective in the presentation of her material, leaving it to the audience to decide whether life should be viewed pessimistically or optimistically.

Humor

Parks often uses humor to underscore the tragedy of a particular situation as it offsets the dire circumstances the play's protagonists live in. Moreover, humor serves to leaven the pathos of the situation, particularly when one of the protagonists appears to struggle against a sense of inertia that has plagued him throughout his life. For example, Booth's attempts to win Grace's heart after their two-year separation is placed in a comical light when he tells Lincoln that he has boosted a "diamond-esque" ring that is slightly too small for her. Booth did this on purpose so that, once the ring is on her finger, she will not be able to give it back to him the way she did two years before. Booth thinks he is "smooth" to avoid rejection this way, but this humorous scene underscores the way Booth is, as Lincoln says, always "scheming and dreaming."

Booth's desperation would be tragic if his plan to win Grace weren't so funny.

Humor is also used within the play to juxtapose comedy with moments of vivid realization. For example, when Booth returns from the department wearing layer upon layer of clothes he has stolen, the visual effect is comical because the audience realizes that his ability to steal matches his audacity. "I stole and I stole generously," Booth says. When Lincoln tries on his new suit and says that clothes don't make the man, he reverses a truism: the fact that he can wear a fake beard and hat does not make him a great man. "I was Lincoln on my own before any of that," he says. Ironically, Lincoln seems less beaten down, less despairing, once he dons the new suit. Another example of how comedy highlights moments of clarity occurs during the scene where the brothers rehearse Lincoln's dying. The scene is uproariously comical even though Lincoln's future employment may be at stake.

Language

Booth and Lincoln both speak a street language that is raw with power and filled with poetry. Their speech is also marked by profanity that assaults the very essence of the person it is directed against. By eliminating the use of apostrophes in contractions, Parks, following the example of the great Irish playwright George Bernard Shaw, creates a language on the printed page that is immediate and unpolished, yet it contains a quality of verisimilitude that reflects her characters' true natures. They are uneducated but streetwise, and the phonetic spellings indicate this lack of sophistication. In addition, the play's dialogue is alone a delight to read and hear. The brothers use words like weapons to undermine each other's confidence, creating a verbal assault that is at times hypnotic and at others menacing.

Stage Directions

In the Author's Notes to the play, Parks includes a short guide to interpreting her "slightly unconventional theatrical elements." Among these are spells and rests. Spells are indicated by the repetition of character names and possess something of an "architectural look." No dialogue is spoken during a spell. Rather, they are designed to aid the characters in revealing "their pure true simple state." Parks leaves any additional interpretation open to the director. Rests, on the other hand, reflect something akin to a musical rest, in that the actor is permitted time to pause, take a breath, or make a transition.

Mos Def and Jeffrey Wright in a 2002 production of Topdog/Underdog Michal Daniel/Reuters/Landov

HISTORICAL CONTEXT

The Assassination of President Abraham Lincoln

As the American Civil War was drawing to a close, President Abraham Lincoln and his wife, Mary Todd Lincoln, attended a performance of *Our American Cousin*, a musical comedy, at Ford's Theatre in Washington, D.C. While Lincoln sat in his box seat in the balcony, John Wilkes Booth, an actor and rebel sympathizer from Maryland, sneaked into the president's box and fired one shot at point-blank range from his Deringer, shouting, "*Sic simper tyrannis!*" ("Thus always to tyrants"). Some reports have Booth adding, "The South is avenged!" Booth leaped to the stage below, limping to an exit and escaping on his horse. Lincoln lay mortally wounded and was carried across the street, where he entered a coma until he died the next morning, on April 15, 1865. Booth received medical attention while on the run, but was fatally shot when he was discovered hiding in a Virginia barn.

Blackface

Blackface minstrelsy was among the most popular forms of live entertainment in America during the years preceding the Civil War. Minstrel shows featured white entertainers who wore blackface to imitate the mannerisms and speech of Southern slaves or slaves who had been freed in the North. Many minstrel routines included singing and dancing that bordered on caricature. The entertainer Al Jolson brought this tradition to the silver screen in the film entitled *The Jazz Singer*, which was the first motion picture to feature sound. In *Topdog/Underdog*, Parks stands the blackface tradition on its head by having Lincoln, a black man, apply whiteface to imitate the very man who was responsible for freeing blacks from slavery.

CRITICAL OVERVIEW

Les Gutman, reviewing the original Off-Broadway production for the Internet theater magazine *CurtainUp*, observes that, "with *Topdog/Underdog*, [Suzan-Lori Parks] has taken a giant step toward fulfilling the promise with which she was labeled." He finds the narrative "linear and quite straightforward" compared to some of Parks's earlier plays, which have been regarded by critics and audiences alike as rather "meditative and inaccessible." Gutman views *Topdog/Underdog* as the culmination of a talent that is equal to the playwright's ambition. "Parks aims for the sky but succeeds mightily in bringing her subject right into the cross hairs. Kudos all around," he concludes. Elizabeth Pochoda, writing for *The Nation*, remains impressed by the "visceral" impact of the play's flowing language that complements the "swift, inevitable momentum" of the play's direction. "Parks writes dialogue so vigorous and beautiful and hilarious you'd almost think these men were free," she observes.

Not all critics, however, were as impressed with the play's language. Citing dialogue that seems "too diffuse" and an ending that seems "a contrivance" because the audience garners little understanding of the effect family history has had on the brothers' emotional lives, Charles Isherwood, writing in *Variety*, regards *Topdog/Underdog* as a disappointment. He concludes that, although there is a "vaudevillian energy and style to some of the livelier physical set pieces," Parks "may be a playwright who is less comfortable in the real world than in the fantastical one of her imagination." Robert Brustein, writing for *The New Republic*, expounds further upon this static quality, referring to the play as "essentially actionless." Indeed, if there is a common complaint among critics, it concerns what Elyse Sommer calls "that all too inevitable ending." While *Newsweek* critic Marc Peyser concedes that the brothers' relationship possesses a "deadly dynamic," one that projects an "epic feel," a timeless, biblical quality generated in large part by Parks's "linguistic panache," he believes that Parks's fascination with the dramatic potential of street language ultimately does the play and its audience a disservice. "If 'Topdog' has a flaw," Peyser notes, "it may be that Parks flaunts her comic and verbal dexterity at the expense of building to her fatal climax."

CRITICISM

David Remy

Remy is a freelance writer in Warrington, Florida. In this essay, Remy considers the ways in which Parks's use of historical references and figures belies a more compelling sense of personal history within the play.

Topdog/Underdog is a play rich in historical overtones, yet these should not be confused with events that shaped the course of American social and political development during the years after the Civil War. Although the Lincoln assassination

> THE REPETITIVE ACT OF ASSASSINATION THAT OCCURS WHEN EACH TOURIST REDEEMS A TICKET SYMBOLIZES THE STATIC QUALITY OF LINK'S LIFE, WHICH HAS BECOME INCREASINGLY MORIBUND SINCE HE ACCEPTED A 'SIT DOWN JOB ... [W]ITH BENEFITS.'"

exerts a pervading influence on how the audience reacts to developments within *Topdog/Underdog*, the assassination itself is nothing more than an augury of the play's ending. Historical fact serves as a backdrop for theater—nothing more—and the events that occur onstage result from a knowledge of family history that is repressed rather than acknowledged openly. Therefore, the historical figures of Lincoln and Booth should not be identified too strongly with the brothers who bear the same names. Rather than recreate a scene from history on stage, a scene which is remembered more for a single act of vengeance than for the events that preceded it, Parks chooses to focus instead on the dramatic possibilities inherent in a shared personal history, one which the brothers Lincoln and Booth bring to a denouement marked by violence and desperation equal to that of historical events.

Parks draws upon her audience's knowledge of history to establish an immediate conflict between her characters, for the play is a series of reversals wherein power is shared alternately by each of the protagonists. Most everyone who has received a grade-school education is familiar with the attack at Ford's Theatre that forever bound the name of President Abraham Lincoln to that of his assailant John Wilkes Booth, but the relationship of victim and murderer, and the social issues that led to the assassination, should not be perceived as a template for understanding events as they develop between the brothers in *Topdog/Underdog*. The audience would be wise to remember that the brothers were named Lincoln and Booth by their father as a joke, one which is perpetrated upon anyone who interprets the parallels between historical fact and fiction too closely. A more appropriate analogy for the brothers' relationship would be that between the biblical characters Cain and Abel, but then Parks is much too subtle a dramatist to resort to overt comparisons.

If there is a connection between the play's characters and recorded history, it is a symbolic, tangential one. In spite of Lincoln's name, an association with The Great Emancipator that is made even more ironic when Link wears a top hat, fake beard, and whiteface, Link's job impersonating the president at the arcade emphasizes the precarious state of Link's employment rather than his holding a position of power. On the contrary, Link remains at the mercy of his employers, who eventually replace him with a wax dummy. The repetitive act of assassination that occurs when each tourist redeems a ticket symbolizes the static quality of Link's life, which has become increasingly moribund since he accepted a "sit down job . . . [w]ith benefits." Although Link has made a conscious effort to abandon the dangerous street life he knew when he was master of the three-card monte, this change forces him to yield to a form of inertia that ultimately breaks his spirit. Link's job as an unsuspecting victim of assassination symbolizes his having become a victim of socioeconomic forces that render him helpless—a stationary target, in effect, which is something he never would have become had he continued earning his livelihood on the street.

Rather than dwell excessively on the historical reverberations of her characters, Parks focuses instead on their shared personal history to dramatize an often ambiguous, and ultimately violent, sibling rivalry. In verbal exchanges that move from banter to accusation at a moment's notice, pieces of family history loom large before the brothers and the audience, revealing allegiances that place Link and Booth in the roles of antagonists. For example, in scene 5, when the brothers discuss the circumstances that led to their parents' departures, Booth observes, "They didnt leave together. That makes it different." Booth and Link then assume that, despite the indifference between their parents, they had an "agreement," by which they would each give a son five hundred dollars and then leave. "Theyd been scheming together all along," Booth says. "They left separately but they was in agreement." The brothers' suspicions of a plot against them are ignited further when each reveals to the other that he was sworn to secrecy when he received money from his parent, and this revelation leads the brothers, now temporarily united, to speculate that perhaps their parents abandoned them to start a new family, one that would not include them.

The knowledge of this suppressed history breeds resentment—and, ultimately, violence—as feelings of abandonment and questions about the brothers' respective paternities arise. Even though the brothers have had to depend upon each other to survive, this fact, like the example of false domesticity their parents set before them years ago, does not mean that they must honor their responsibilities to each other indefinitely. Booth is already envious of his brother's ability to throw the cards, and his envy intensifies once he fails to convince Link to return to his old ways. "How come I got a hand for boosting and I dont got a hand for throwing cards?" he wonders. Booth mistakenly believes that his life would improve if his brother showed him how to master the three-card monte, for then he would be able to win Grace's heart and have plenty of cash with which to entertain her. Booth seeks more than knowledge from Link; he seeks freedom. When Booth fails to obtain the object of his desire, he becomes more frustrated and angry, his resentment building to a dangerous level: "Here I am trying to earn a living and you standing in my way. YOU STANDING IN MY WAY, LINK!" Booth's frustration with his girlfriend and with his brother increases his desperation as it reveals a historical pattern, contributing to what appears to be an impulsive act in the play's final scene.

Furthermore, Booth's feelings of frustration are exacerbated by the brothers' mutual dependency, a form of symbiosis that is governed by Booth's jealousy and impotent rage, and which keeps the brothers locked tightly within each other's orbit. As the brothers begin to question their paternity and the reasons why their parents abandoned them, Booth struggles to find freedom while Link sinks slowly into despair. The pain Booth felt when his mother walked out on them has never left him, as represented by his refusal to spend his "inheritance," for he seems to still hold out hope that one day she will return. Thus, Booth, like his brother Link, remains unable to break free from the hold of personal history. However, Booth reaches a point where he is willing to do whatever is necessary to change the repetitive pattern of failure his life has taken. In a deluded vision of marital bliss, Booth tells Link to leave (the room is rented in Booth's name), even though Booth fears abandonment and the thought of living his life alone. When Booth's plans again collapse, he chooses to face failure the only way he knows how—through an act of violence. Just as Booth refuses to give Grace the opportunity to dump him for another man by shooting her, so, too, does he prevent Link from mocking him further by

WHAT DO I READ NEXT?

- The plays of Suzan-Lori Parks have been noted especially for their reworking of history to provide audiences with political and social commentary that is relevant to today's society. *The Death of the Last Black Man in the Whole Entire World* (1990) creates a new view of history that debunks many of the racial stereotypes about blacks that Parks uses to tell her story. Featuring characters with names like Black Man with Watermelon, Black Woman with Fried Drumstick, Lots of Grease and Lots of Pork, and Yes and Greens Black-Eyed Peas Cornbread, *The Death of the Last Black Man in the Whole Entire World* depicts a mythos of archetypal proportions. In the play, Parks transforms black vernacular English into a form of poetry that pays homage to the past as it brings history firmly into the present.

- Ntozake Shange's *for colored girls who have considered suicide/when the rainbow is enuf* (1975) is a group of twenty poems about the power of black women to overcome pain and hopelessness. As each actor recites her poem, she gestures and moves her body in accompaniment to the emotions she expresses while the rest of the ensemble stands silent and motionless. The group then chants and moves as one in response to the actor's poem. This form of call and response creates a unifying bond among the women on stage, an energy that extends to the audience as well.

- Sam Shepard's play *True West* (1980) combines humor and pathos to explore the meaning of identity within a dysfunctional family, particularly as identity relates to the idea of the American frontier and the mythological freedom it represents. In the play, which is set outside of Los Angeles, two brothers, Austin, a successful Hollywood screenwriter, and Lee, a burglar, house-sit for their mother while she is away on vacation in Alaska. During the time they spend together, the two brothers fight, drink excessively, and nearly destroy the house as they compete to get their screenplays produced. *True West* addresses the ways in which a materialistic society fosters lawlessness and the desire to obtain freedom, even if that sense of freedom remains ever-elusive.

- Through images and associations that range from the surreal to the absurd, Adrienne Kennedy's plays embody a modernist sensibility as they employ avant-garde techniques to address issues of gender, race, and identity within contemporary African-American society. Kennedy's anti-realist approach toward playwriting and stagecraft, such as that found in the one-act plays *Funnyhouse of a Negro* (1970) and *The Owl Answers* (1968) mixed genres and narrative techniques at a time when other playwrights were beginning to explore the dramatic possibilities of juxtaposed styles. Her characters so deeply reflected the institutionalized racism of the day that they appeared to have internalized society's mores.

- British playwright Caryl Churchill combines text, dance, and music with historical themes to depict the erotic and political desires of characters, mostly women, who, because of the sociological forces that oppress them, are unable to realize their strongest ambitions. Churchill, a playwright with a sense of humor that at times borders on the macabre, has experimented with various genres and narrative styles to convey her artistic vision. In plays like *Top Girls* (1982) and *Cloud Nine* (1983), Churchill favors an episodic approach toward narrative rather than relying upon intricate plot structures to advance the story. As a result, scenes are loosely connected and build upon one another to form a pattern that emphasizes the play's development rather than its climax.

Topdog/Underdog *playbill*   Performing Arts Books, N.Y.C.

pulling the trigger in a scene that transforms his father's joke into a tragic prophecy.

By revealing a family history that Booth and Link reluctantly acknowledge but do not fully understand, one which binds them inexorably toward a violent end, Parks emphasizes the drama of lives that are no less tragic than those of historical figures. The end result is a play rich with associations that simultaneously challenge and satisfy the audience's expectations, creating two brothers who continue to live on in memory.

Source: David Remy, Critical Essay on *Topdog/Underdog*, in *Drama for Students*, Thomson Gale, 2006.

Catherine Dybiec Holm

Holm is a short story and novel author, and a freelance writer. In this essay, Holm looks at how the brothers in this play prey on each other's insecurities in a tailspin toward tragedy.

Topdog/Underdog is a play about the tension and the contrast between two brothers. Each brother struggles with his own demons. Booth feels inferior to Lincoln. Lincoln is trying to live a respectable life, with a real job. Each brother preys on the other brother's shortcomings, propelling this

play toward its volatile conclusion. Booth seems to be meaner to Lincoln than Lincoln is to Booth, but Lincoln also has his dark side. Parks shows not only how each brother preys on the other, but also how each character is tormented by his own insecurities.

Booth is introduced first, and Parks immediately establishes him as an unsavory, frustrated character. Booth reveals an edgy meanness as he practices his con game, alone in his room. While he sweet-talks and cajoles an imaginary mark ("you aint no clown"), Booth lets his meanness come out after the imaginary transaction, in the privacy of his room.

> Sucker! Fool! . . . I bet yr daddy heard how stupid you was. . . . I bet yr mama seen you when you comed out and she walked away from you. . . . Ha Ha Ha! And 3-Card, once again, wins all thuh money!!

Booth's mean-spirited outlash directs the reader to wonder what Booth is so angry about. It sets the reader up for further revelations about Booth. Booth knows that throwing the cards does not come as naturally to him as it does to Lincoln. This effectively sets the reader up for the volatile last part of the play, where Lincoln laughs at Booth and Booth shoots Lincoln. Booth wants nothing more than the ease of making lots of money with the con game and making it as easily as Lincoln once did. Booth is upset that Lincoln will not throw the cards and pesters him relentlessly.

Booth is also effectively revealed as a person who deceives himself. There are plenty of examples of this throughout the play. This portrays Booth as a character whose word cannot be trusted. Booth is continually backtracking on what he says, after Lincoln points out discrepancies.

> Booth: You could afford to get laid! Grace would be all over me again.
>
> Lincoln: I though you said she was all over you.
>
> Booth: She is she is. Im seeing her tomorrow.

Booth repeats "she is" and Parks runs the words together. The reader can almost hear Booth trying to convince himself, as well as Lincoln, that Grace really does want him.

Booth's insecurities are heightened when it comes to women, as shown when he continues to bend the truth about Grace. Booth says, "Shes in love with me again but she dont know it yet. . . . I got her this ring today. Diamond. Well, diamondesque, but it looks just as good as the real thing." The reader clearly understands that Booth is continually trying to con himself and his brother.

If Lincoln was a meaner character, he could torment Booth regarding Grace. But Lincoln is usually gentle with Booth in these situations, even when Grace never shows up and the brothers wait all night long. Lincoln does not hesitate, however, to give it to Booth on another occasion, when Booth claims he had sex with Grace.

> Lincoln: You didnt get s—t tonight. You laying over there . . . waiting for me to go back to sleep or black out so I wont hear you rustling thuh pages of yr . . . book.

Booth also knows how to hit Lincoln where it hurts. He continually reminds Lincoln that Lincoln is degrading himself by dressing up in whiteface to get "shot" everyday in a reenactment of Abraham Lincoln's assassination. Even though Lincoln tries to find some redemption in his job ("People know the real deal. When people know the real deal it aint a hustle"), Booth tells him that he "aint living."

The terrible irony at the end of the play is that Lincoln's "assassination" comes true, at the hands of his brother. The symbolism of Abe Lincoln's assassination is chillingly apparent. Lincoln's arcade job may well represent another kind of symbolism, the suggestion of a man slowly dying a little every day, having to do a degrading, low paying job and impersonate a white man. The man that talks to Lincoln at the arcade alludes to this when he says, "Does thuh show stop when no ones watching or does the show go on?"

All of Booth's actions are driven by his rampant insecurities. He is the younger brother. He does not have a real job nor does he have the ability to con people like his brother. Because of his inferiority complex, Booth is caught between trying to impress his brother by shoplifting fancy clothes or by one-upping him by reminding Lincoln that he slept with Lincoln's wife.

Booth is manipulative and works this skill effectively on his brother. At one point, Booth angrily shouts at Lincoln, accusing him of denying Booth success since Lincoln will not teach Booth about the cards.

> Booth: Here I am interested in an economic opportunity, willing to work hard, willing to take risks and . . . all you can tell me is how you dont do no more what I be wanting to do. Here I am trying to earn a living and you standing in my way, YOU STANDING IN MY WAY, LINK!

Booth's manipulation is effective. Lincoln appears to buy into Booth's accusation, and it helps lead Lincoln toward his downfall.

It is to Parks's credit that the play sustains such tension and energy. Parks pulls this off by showing the reader what shaped these brothers into the

> "LINCOLN'S ARCADE JOB MAY WELL REPRESENT ANOTHER KIND OF SYMBOLISM, THE SUGGESTION OF A MAN SLOWLY DYING A LITTLE EVERY DAY, HAVING TO DO A DEGRADING, LOW PAYING JOB AND IMPERSONATE A WHITE MAN."

men they are today. The reader learns that the world has not been good to these men: their parents left them when they were boys; their parents had lovers on the side; and, no one had much money. Because of this past, Lincoln and Booth have had to do whatever is necessary to survive. Because Parks reveals to the reader what kind of circumstances these boys grew up in, the reader is able to understand and possibly sympathize with the characters' actions.

Lincoln is a different character than Booth in many ways. While Booth cut school nearly every day, Lincoln only missed it in an emergency, such as when their mother walked out on them. Lincoln had been married. Lincoln also stopped playing the cards, even though it made him more money than the arcade job. In every respect, Lincoln has made more of an effort at leading a respectable life. However, Booth knows how to zero in on the insecurities that plague Lincoln. Lincoln could not sustain a marriage, is working a dead-end job, and cannot get a woman. It is Lincoln's awareness and frustration with his insecurities, along with Booth's constant nagging, that drive Lincoln back to throwing the cards.

The reader knows intuitively that things are going to begin spiraling downward in this play, once Lincoln picks up the cards. Parks has foreshadowed this effectively with Lincoln's almost irrational fear of even touching the cards, earlier in the play. Like the recovering alcoholic who can never take another drink, the reader senses the dangerous tension and attraction between Lincoln and the cards. When Booth rips the fancy tablecloth from the makeshift table and reveals the seedy card table underneath, it is a fitting metaphor for Lincoln's life. Lincoln tried to live a respectable life and hold a real job. But underneath the respectable veneer, Lincoln still has the

Jeffrey Wright, director George C. Wolfe, Suzan-Lori Parks, and Mos Def during curtain call at the opening night of Topdog/Underdog *at the Ambassador Theater in New York City, April 7, 2002*

Getty Images

heart of a con artist. It is Lincoln's and Booth's fascination with the cards, their ability to prey on each other, and their struggles with their own demons that drive these brothers on a path to tragedy.

Source: Catherine Dybiec Holm, Critical Essay on *Topdog/ Underdog*, in *Drama for Students*, Thomson Gale, 2006.

Carol Ullmann

Ullmann is a freelance writer and editor. In the following essay, Ullmann examines Parks's use of foreshadowing in her play.

In her Pulitzer-Prize winning play *Topdog/ Underdog*, Parks uses the literary device of foreshadowing in telling the story of the relationship between two brothers. The foreshadowing of Lincoln's death by his brother Booth's hand has many layers, from the obvious to the more personal and subtle. By the end of the play, Parks leaves the reader wondering whether Lincoln's death was inevitable, no matter what choice either brother made.

On the broadest, most obvious level, the "joke" of the brothers' names, Lincoln and Booth—after President Abraham Lincoln and his assassin John Wilkes Booth—foreshadows Lincoln's death by

his brother Booth at the end of the play. To reinforce the historical connection, the brothers have as their first names what the historical figures used as surnames. There would have been little dramatic impact if they had been named Abraham and John.

Abraham Lincoln was the 16th president of the United States and a crucial figure in bringing an end to legalized slavery in America. The Civil War (1861–1865) began in response to his controversial election because he was so staunchly opposed to slavery in America's new territories. The end of legalized slavery (beginning with the Emancipation Proclamation of 1863 and culminating with the Thirteenth Amendment to the Constitution in 1865) had a profound impact on the thousands of Africans and their American-born children who were discriminated against based solely on the color of their skin. The fact that the brothers in *Topdog/ Underdog* are black Americans is both ironic and indicative of their difficult struggle to overcome their impoverished situation. One could also interpret their tough financial position as a way in which *de facto* discrimination continues to exist in the United States today. Their poverty is an additional overarching foreshadowing of an unhappy ending.

John Wilkes Booth presents an even more interesting comparison as a namesake for the character Booth in *Topdog/Underdog*. John Wilkes Booth was a popular professional actor but still less successful than his older brother, Edwin, who was widely considered the greatest Shakespearean actor of nineteenth-century America. John Wilkes Booth resented his brother's greater fame. He also deeply believed in slavery and conspired with others to abduct President Lincoln. When he heard news that General Lee had surrendered at the Appomattox Court House in Virginia in April 1865, he resolved to assassinate President Lincoln and his Cabinet. Although John Wilkes Booth was successful in assassinating the president, he was captured twelve days later by soldiers and mortally shot after refusing to turn himself in.

The similarity between John Wilkes Booth and the character Booth of *Topdog/Underdog* is exhibited early on in the play by Booth's emulation of Lincoln in three-card monte; Booth wants to play the same game as his brother but has never been as good. His jealousy is obvious to the observer and reader. At the end of the play, Booth lies and says that he and his on-and-off girlfriend Grace are going to get married. This declaration could be interpreted as another way for Booth to show his brother that he is the topdog since Lincoln's marriage has failed. Booth even claims to have had sex with Lincoln's ex-wife Cookie.

Booth attempts to leave behind his past identity as the underdog, the younger, less capable and successful brother, by renaming himself 3-Card after the shell game three-card monte. Booth sees himself making a successful career hustling people for money, as well as obliquely claiming precedence over his brother Lincoln, who used to be a very good three-card monte hustler. Lincoln goes along with the name change and eventually lets Booth practice his card hustling on him. Booth appears to be improving and even over-taking his brother in skill, but Lincoln is still more practiced than Booth at card handling. After leading Booth and the reader on for the whole play that he was losing his touch, in the last crucial card throw, Lincoln wins his brother Booth's inheritance money. It is a classic shell game ploy. The foreshadowing of Lincoln's win is subtle. He is talked about throughout the play as having once been the best three-card monte hustler; however he keeps losing to Booth and even appears distraught. He is so good at the game that he cannot stop himself from taking in his own blood relation.

LINCOLN: And thuh first move is to know that there aint no winning. It may look like you got a chance

> " WHEN LINCOLN LOSES HIS JOB, THE READER MIGHT BE TEMPTED TO THINK THAT HE WILL BE DRAWN AWAY FROM WHAT SEEMS TO BE AN INEVITABLE DEATH. BUT LINCOLN IS MOVING IN A CLOSED CIRCLE."

but the only time you pick right is when thuh man lets you. And when its thuh real deal, when its thuh real f—g deal, bro, and thuh moneys on thuh line, thats when thuh man wont want you picking right. He will want you picking wrong so he will make you pick wrong. Wrong wrong wrong. Ooooh, you thought you was finally happening, didn't you? You thought yr ship had come in or some s—t, huh? Thought you was uh Player. But I played you, bro.

Lincoln's first career, hustling people for money, was a financial success but personal disaster. Lincoln made a lot of money, but the death of his partner Lonny made him turn his back on hustling: "I knew I was next, so I quit. I saved my life." His current job as an Abraham Lincoln impersonator at an arcade, however, foreshadows an untimely end even more strongly. Not only is he named for and impersonating a president who has been assassinated, but his job is specifically to recreate President Lincoln's assassination:

LINCOLN: This is sit down, you know, easy work. I just gotta sit there all day. Folks come in kill phony Honest Abe with the phony pistol. I can sit there and let my mind travel.

When Lincoln loses his job, the reader might be tempted to think that he will be drawn away from what seems to be an inevitable death. But Lincoln is moving in a closed circle. He is drawn back into hustling by his brother Booth's recent interest (and perhaps insistence that Lincoln has lost his touch with the cards), a need for cash so that he can get his feet under him and move out of his brother's apartment, and probably also a need to feel good about himself by winning at something. Unfortunately, three-card monte foreshadows death for Lincoln as well. In scene 4, just before throwing the cards again for the first time, he says, "Link is just here hustling hisself."

In the opening scene of the play, Lincoln surprises his brother Booth when he walks in the door.

Booth's reaction is to draw his gun. This foreshadows and bookends the closing of the play when Booth draws his gun in anger against Lincoln and shoots and kills him.

In this scene, the brothers are having Chinese food for dinner. The fortunes they open foreshadow events to follow:

LINCOLN: Whats yr fortune?

BOOTH: "Waste not want not." Whats yrs?

LINCOLN: "Your luck will change!"

Booth's fortune is an oblique warning against killing his girlfriend and brother. These are relationships that are irreplaceable. Their abandonment by their parents, especially their mother, has been hard on Booth, the younger brother. In the play, he does not appear to have anyone close to him other than Lincoln and Grace, the two people he eventually kills.

Lincoln's fortune is a warning that the honest path he has been arduously following will soon take a turn. Fortunes are often ambiguous and easy to manipulate into an interpretation that pleases the recipient. In this case, although honest work can be unpleasant, it is the safest route for Lincoln to pursue—he should be wary of his luck changing.

Another example of foreshadowing in the first scene happens when Booth threatens to shoot anyone who does not call him by the name 3-Card. Lincoln goes along with this for most of the play but slips up twice near the end, once in scene 5 and once in scene 6. One could also interpret Grace's death at Booth's hand as a result of her refusal to accept Booth's new guise as an up-and-coming three-card monte hustler, although this all happened off-stage and readers only have Booth's version of events to go on.

A strong example of foreshadowing in the first scene is when Lincoln sings the song he made up in his head while at work. The song has a classic blues rhythm and encapsulates his sad life, talking about how his parents have left him, he has no money, no home, his "best girl" has thrown him out, and his "favorite horse" (Lonny) has been ground into meat. In the final lines of the song, Lincoln foreshadows his own death, building as well upon the fortune he got at dinner:

My luck was bad but now it turned to worse
Dont call me up a doctor, just call me up a hearse.

In scene 3, Booth and Lincoln talk about Lincoln's job. Booth is fascinated that his brother has no problem letting people shoot at him all day long. "You ever wonder if someones gonna come in there

with a real gun? A real gun with real slugs? Someone with uh axe tuh grind or something?" This line of questioning is ironic and foreshadowing of Booth's passionate and possibly pre-meditated assault on his brother at the end of the play. Booth, as an underdog who wants to be topdog, has a lifelong axe to grind with his older brother.

A stronger element of foreshadowing in this scene occurs when Booth urges Lincoln to practice having a more dramatic death in order to impress his boss and keep his job. In his excitement, he yells, "And look at me! I am the assassin! *I am Booth!*! Come on man this is life and death!" Here Booth is directly identifying himself with John Wilkes Booth while he urges his brother to perform a more dramatic interpretation of President Lincoln's death throes. The comment that this performance is "life and death" is more true than either brother realizes. Lincoln does not return to the deadly game of three-card monte until after he loses his job at the arcade.

In scene 5, returning home after losing his job, Lincoln slips up and calls his brother by his old name, Booth, rather than Booth's adopted new name of 3-Card. Stage directions do not indicate that Booth notices but this still reinforces the foreshadowing from the first scene of the play when Booth declared that he would shoot anyone who didn't call him 3-Card. Lincoln slips again at the beginning of scene 6, although he and the reader are not immediately aware that Booth is in the scene.

Many clues in *Topdog/Underdog* foreshadow Booth killing his brother Lincoln. With so much stacked against them, including history (the Civil War, after all, has been described as the only American war that pitted brothers against brothers), poverty, gambling, and a dysfunctional family, could Lincoln's death by his brother's hand have been avoided? Perhaps if Lincoln had stayed away from three-card monte, then Lincoln may have survived. Then again, as the topdog and older brother, Lincoln—or just the idea of Lincoln, who was older, more successful, more confident, more comfortable with himself—may have been too much for Booth to live up to.

Source: Carol Ullmann, Critical Essay on *Topdog/Underdog*, in *Drama for Students*, Thomson Gale, 2006.

SOURCES

Brustein, Robert, "On Theater—A Homeboy Godot," in the *New Republic*, May 13, 2002, p. 25.

Fanger, Iris, "Pulitzer Prize Winner Shakes Off Labels," in the *Christian Science Monitor*, April 12, 2002, p. 19.

Garrett, Shawn-Marie, "The Possession of Suzan-Lori Parks," in *American Theatre*, Vol. 17, No. 8, October 2000, p. 22.

Gutman, Les, Review of Original Off-Broadway Production of *Topdog/Underdog*, in *CurtainUp*, http://www.curtainup.com/topdog.html (accessed November 24, 2004).

Isherwood, Charles, Review of *Topdog/Underdog*, in *Variety*, Vol. 383, No. 11, August 6, 2001, p. 25.

Newsmakers, "Suzan-Lori Parks, 1st Black Woman to Win Pulitzer for a Drama," in *Jet*, Vol. 101, No. 19, April 29, 2002, p. 25.

Parks, Suzan-Lori, *Topdog/Underdog*, Theatre Communications Group, 2001.

Peyser, Marc, "*Topdog* on Broadway," in *Newsweek*, April 22, 2002, p. 64.

Pochoda, Elizabeth, "I See Thuh Black Card . . .," in the *Nation*, Vol. 274, No. 20, May 27, 2002, p. 36.

Sommer, Elyse, "*Topdog/Underdog* Moves to Broadway," in *CurtainUp*, http://www.curtainup.com/topdog.html (accessed November 24, 2004).

Wilkerson, Margaret B., "2001–2002 Best Play: *Topdog/Underdog*," in *The Best Plays of 2001–2002*, edited by Jeffrey Eric Jenkins, Limelight Editions, 2003.

Wilmer, S. E., "Restaging the Nation: The Work of Suzan-Lori Parks," in *Modern Drama*, Vol. 43, No. 3, Fall 2000, p. 442.

FURTHER READING

Elam, Harry J., Jr., and Robert Alexander, eds., *The Fire This Time: African-American Plays for the 21st Century*, Theatre Communications Group, 2004.
Taking their title from a collection of essays made famous by James Baldwin, Elam and Alexander have compiled an anthology of African-American plays that reflects a broad continuum of artistic styles and voices, from August Wilson to Kamilah Forbes and Hip-Hop Junction. Suzan-Lori Parks's *In the Blood*, a play about a homeless black woman and her children, is included.

Fornes, Maria Irene, *Plays: Mud, The Danube, The Conduct of Life, Sarita*, PAJ Publications, 1986.
The Cuban-American playwright Maria Irene Fornes, whose plays often engage audiences in unconventional ways, such as incorporating language instruction tapes and marionettes into a production, has been an important influence on the American theatre since the 1960s. Fornes avoids ideological constructs when composing her plays, focusing instead on the needs of her characters. Forness's avant-garde plays, stark and often lyrical, revolve around characters who search for meaning in their lives in the face of psychological tyranny.

Mahone, Sydné, *Moon Marked and Touched by Sun: Plays by African-American Women*, Theatre Communications Group, 1994.
Among the playwrights included in this anthology are Adrienne Kennedy, Thulani Davis, Kia Corthron, and Suzan-Lori Parks. Mahone emphasizes the shift that has occurred in black women's consciousness, one that has contributed significantly to the elimination of racial and sexual oppression within society. In her introductions to each work, Mahone includes in-depth interviews that illuminate the playwrights' perspectives on the role of the artist within a commercial theatre.

Smith, Anna Deavere, *Fires in the Mirror*, Anchor Books, 1993.
Based on interviews with people who witnessed New York City's 1991 Crown Heights racial riots, *Fires in the Mirror* presents, through a series of monologues, a wide variety of characters and insights that cast light on the racial attitudes dividing a city. By juxtaposing her characters' personalities, Anna Deavere Smith captures basic human truths in an artistic blend of theatre, journalism, and social commentary.

Glossary of Literary Terms

A

Abstract: Used as a noun, the term refers to a short summary or outline of a longer work. As an adjective applied to writing or literary works, abstract refers to words or phrases that name things not knowable through the five senses. Examples of abstracts include the *Cliffs Notes* summaries of major literary works. Examples of abstract terms or concepts include "idea," "guilt" "honesty," and "loyalty."

Absurd, Theater of the: See *Theater of the Absurd*

Absurdism: See *Theater of the Absurd*

Act: A major section of a play. Acts are divided into varying numbers of shorter scenes. From ancient times to the nineteenth century plays were generally constructed of five acts, but modern works typically consist of one, two, or three acts. Examples of five-act plays include the works of Sophocles and Shakespeare, while the plays of Arthur Miller commonly have a three-act structure.

Acto: A one-act Chicano theater piece developed out of collective improvisation. *Actos* were performed by members of Luis Valdez's Teatro Campesino in California during the mid-1960s.

Aestheticism: A literary and artistic movement of the nineteenth century. Followers of the movement believed that art should not be mixed with social, political, or moral teaching. The statement "art for art's sake" is a good summary of aestheticism. The movement had its roots in France, but it gained widespread importance in England in the last half of the nineteenth century, where it helped change the Victorian practice of including moral lessons in literature. Oscar Wilde is one of the best-known "aesthetes" of the late nineteenth century.

Age of Johnson: The period in English literature between 1750 and 1798, named after the most prominent literary figure of the age, Samuel Johnson. Works written during this time are noted for their emphasis on "sensibility," or emotional quality. These works formed a transition between the rational works of the Age of Reason, or Neoclassical period, and the emphasis on individual feelings and responses of the Romantic period. Significant writers during the Age of Johnson included the novelists Ann Radcliffe and Henry Mackenzie, dramatists Richard Sheridan and Oliver Goldsmith, and poets William Collins and Thomas Gray. Also known as Age of Sensibility

Age of Reason: See *Neoclassicism*

Age of Sensibility: See *Age of Johnson*

Alexandrine Meter: See *Meter*

Allegory: A narrative technique in which characters representing things or abstract ideas are used to convey a message or teach a lesson. Allegory is typically used to teach moral, ethical, or religious lessons but is sometimes used for satiric or political purposes. Examples of allegorical works include Edmund Spenser's *The Faerie Queene* and John Bunyan's *The Pilgrim's Progress.*

Allusion: A reference to a familiar literary or historical person or event, used to make an idea more easily understood. For example, describing someone as a "Romeo" makes an allusion to William Shakespeare's famous young lover in *Romeo and Juliet.*

Amerind Literature: The writing and oral traditions of Native Americans. Native American literature was originally passed on by word of mouth, so it consisted largely of stories and events that were easily memorized. Amerind prose is often rhythmic like poetry because it was recited to the beat of a ceremonial drum. Examples of Amerind literature include the autobiographical *Black Elk Speaks,* the works of N. Scott Momaday, James Welch, and Craig Lee Strete, and the poetry of Luci Tapahonso.

Analogy: A comparison of two things made to explain something unfamiliar through its similarities to something familiar, or to prove one point based on the acceptedness of another. Similes and metaphors are types of analogies. Analogies often take the form of an extended simile, as in William Blake's aphorism: "As the caterpillar chooses the fairest leaves to lay her eggs on, so the priest lays his curse on the fairest joys."

Angry Young Men: A group of British writers of the 1950s whose work expressed bitterness and disillusionment with society. Common to their work is an anti-hero who rebels against a corrupt social order and strives for personal integrity. The term has been used to describe Kingsley Amis, John Osborne, Colin Wilson, John Wain, and others.

Antagonist: The major character in a narrative or drama who works against the hero or protagonist. An example of an evil antagonist is Richard Lovelace in Samuel Richardson's *Clarissa,* while a virtuous antagonist is Macduff in William Shakespeare's *Macbeth.*

Anthropomorphism: The presentation of animals or objects in human shape or with human characteristics. The term is derived from the Greek word for "human form." The fables of Aesop, the animated films of Walt Disney, and Richard Adams's *Watership Down* feature anthropomorphic characters.

Anti-hero: A central character in a work of literature who lacks traditional heroic qualities such as courage, physical prowess, and fortitude. Anti-heros typically distrust conventional values and are unable to commit themselves to any ideals. They generally feel helpless in a world over which they have no control. Anti-heroes usually accept, and often celebrate, their positions as social outcasts. A well-known anti-hero is Yossarian in Joseph Heller's novel *Catch-22.*

Antimasque: See *Masque*

Antithesis: The antithesis of something is its direct opposite. In literature, the use of antithesis as a figure of speech results in two statements that show a contrast through the balancing of two opposite ideas. Technically, it is the second portion of the statement that is defined as the "antithesis"; the first portion is the "thesis." An example of antithesis is found in the following portion of Abraham Lincoln's "Gettysburg Address"; notice the opposition between the verbs "remember" and "forget" and the phrases "what we say" and "what they did": "The world will little note nor long remember what we say here, but it can never forget what they did here."

Apocrypha: Writings tentatively attributed to an author but not proven or universally accepted to be their works. The term was originally applied to certain books of the Bible that were not considered inspired and so were not included in the "sacred canon." Geoffrey Chaucer, William Shakespeare, Thomas Kyd, Thomas Middleton, and John Marston all have apocrypha. Apocryphal books of the Bible include the Old Testament's Book of Enoch and New Testament's Gospel of Peter.

Apollonian and Dionysian: The two impulses believed to guide authors of dramatic tragedy. The Apollonian impulse is named after Apollo, the Greek god of light and beauty and the symbol of intellectual order. The Dionysian impulse is named after Dionysus, the Greek god of wine and the symbol of the unrestrained forces of nature. The Apollonian impulse is to create a rational, harmonious world, while the Dionysian is to express the irrational forces of personality. Friedrich Nietzche uses these terms in *The Birth of Tragedy* to designate contrasting elements in Greek tragedy.

Apostrophe: A statement, question, or request addressed to an inanimate object or concept or to a nonexistent or absent person. Requests for inspiration from the muses in poetry are examples of apostrophe, as is Marc Antony's address to Caesar's corpse in William Shakespeare's *Julius Caesar:* "O, pardon me, thou bleeding piece of earth, That I am meek and gentle with these butchers! . . . Woe to the hand that shed this costly blood! . . ."

Archetype: The word archetype is commonly used to describe an original pattern or model from which all other things of the same kind are made. This term was introduced to literary criticism from the psychology of Carl Jung. It expresses Jung's theory that behind every person's "unconscious," or repressed memories of the past, lies the "collective unconscious" of the human race: memories of the countless typical experiences of our ancestors. These memories are said to prompt illogical associations that trigger powerful emotions in the reader. Often, the emotional process is primitive, even primordial. Archetypes are the literary images that grow out of the "collective unconscious." They appear in literature as incidents and plots that repeat basic patterns of life. They may also appear as stereotyped characters. Examples of literary archetypes include themes such as birth and death and characters such as the Earth Mother.

Argument: The argument of a work is the author's subject matter or principal idea. Examples of defined "argument" portions of works include John Milton's *Arguments* to each of the books of *Paradise Lost* and the "Argument" to Robert Herrick's *Hesperides.*

Aristotelian Criticism: Specifically, the method of evaluating and analyzing tragedy formulated by the Greek philosopher Aristotle in his *Poetics.* More generally, the term indicates any form of criticism that follows Aristotle's views. Aristotelian criticism focuses on the form and logical structure of a work, apart from its historical or social context, in contrast to "Platonic Criticism," which stresses the usefulness of art. Adherents of New Criticism including John Crowe Ransom and Cleanth Brooks utilize and value the basic ideas of Aristotelian criticism for textual analysis.

Art for Art's Sake: See *Aestheticism*

Aside: A comment made by a stage performer that is intended to be heard by the audience but supposedly not by other characters. Eugene O'Neill's *Strange Interlude* is an extended use of the aside in modern theater.

Audience: The people for whom a piece of literature is written. Authors usually write with a certain audience in mind, for example, children, members of a religious or ethnic group, or colleagues in a professional field. The term "audience" also applies to the people who gather to see or hear any performance, including plays, poetry readings, speeches, and concerts. Jane Austen's parody of the gothic novel, *Northanger Abbey,* was originally intended for (and also pokes fun at) an audience of young and avid female gothic novel readers.

Avant-garde: A French term meaning "vanguard." It is used in literary criticism to describe new writing that rejects traditional approaches to literature in favor of innovations in style or content. Twentieth-century examples of the literary *avant-garde* include the Black Mountain School of poets, the Bloomsbury Group, and the Beat Movement.

B

Ballad: A short poem that tells a simple story and has a repeated refrain. Ballads were originally intended to be sung. Early ballads, known as folk ballads, were passed down through generations, so their authors are often unknown. Later ballads composed by known authors are called literary ballads. An example of an anonymous folk ballad is "Edward," which dates from the Middle Ages. Samuel Taylor Coleridge's "The Rime of the Ancient Mariner" and John Keats's "La Belle Dame sans Merci" are examples of literary ballads.

Baroque: A term used in literary criticism to describe literature that is complex or ornate in style or diction. Baroque works typically express tension, anxiety, and violent emotion. The term "Baroque Age" designates a period in Western European literature beginning in the late sixteenth century and ending about one hundred years later. Works of this period often mirror the qualities of works more generally associated with the label "baroque" and sometimes feature elaborate conceits. Examples of Baroque works include John Lyly's *Euphues: The Anatomy of Wit,* Luis de Gongora's *Soledads,* and William Shakespeare's *As You Like It.*

Baroque Age: See *Baroque*

Baroque Period: See *Baroque*

Beat Generation: See *Beat Movement*

Beat Movement: A period featuring a group of American poets and novelists of the 1950s and 1960s—including Jack Kerouac, Allen Ginsberg, Gregory Corso, William S. Burroughs, and Lawrence Ferlinghetti—who rejected established social and literary values. Using such techniques as stream of consciousness writing and jazz-influenced free verse and focusing on unusual or abnormal states of mind—generated by religious ecstasy or the use of drugs—the Beat writers aimed to create works that were unconventional in both form and subject matter. Kerouac's *On the Road* is perhaps the best-known example of a Beat Generation novel, and Ginsberg's *Howl* is a famous collection of Beat poetry.

Black Aesthetic Movement: A period of artistic and literary development among African Americans in the 1960s and early 1970s. This was the first major African-American artistic movement since the Harlem Renaissance and was closely paralleled by the civil rights and black power movements. The black aesthetic writers attempted to produce works of art that would be meaningful to the black masses. Key figures in black aesthetics included one of its founders, poet and playwright

Amiri Baraka, formerly known as LeRoi Jones; poet and essayist Haki R. Madhubuti, formerly Don L. Lee; poet and playwright Sonia Sanchez; and dramatist Ed Bullins. Works representative of the Black Aesthetic Movement include Amiri Baraka's play *Dutchman,* a 1964 Obie award-winner; *Black Fire: An Anthology of Afro-American Writing,* edited by Baraka and playwright Larry Neal and published in 1968; and Sonia Sanchez's poetry collection *We a BaddDDD People,* published in 1970. Also known as Black Arts Movement.

Black Arts Movement: See *Black Aesthetic Movement*

Black Comedy: See *Black Humor*

Black Humor: Writing that places grotesque elements side by side with humorous ones in an attempt to shock the reader, forcing him or her to laugh at the horrifying reality of a disordered world. Joseph Heller's novel *Catch-22* is considered a superb example of the use of black humor. Other well-known authors who use black humor include Kurt Vonnegut, Edward Albee, Eugene Ionesco, and Harold Pinter. Also known as Black Comedy.

Blank Verse: Loosely, any unrhymed poetry, but more generally, unrhymed iambic pentameter verse (composed of lines of five two-syllable feet with the first syllable accented, the second unaccented). Blank verse has been used by poets since the Renaissance for its flexibility and its graceful, dignified tone. John Milton's *Paradise Lost* is in blank verse, as are most of William Shakespeare's plays.

Bloomsbury Group: A group of English writers, artists, and intellectuals who held informal artistic and philosophical discussions in Bloomsbury, a district of London, from around 1907 to the early 1930s. The Bloomsbury Group held no uniform philosophical beliefs but did commonly express an aversion to moral prudery and a desire for greater social tolerance. At various times the circle included Virginia Woolf, E. M. Forster, Clive Bell, Lytton Strachey, and John Maynard Keynes.

Bon Mot: A French term meaning "good word." A *bon mot* is a witty remark or clever observation. Charles Lamb and Oscar Wilde are celebrated for their witty *bon mots.* Two examples by Oscar Wilde stand out: (1) "All women become their mothers. That is their tragedy. No man does. That's his." (2) "A man cannot be too careful in the choice of his enemies."

Breath Verse: See *Projective Verse*

Burlesque: Any literary work that uses exaggeration to make its subject appear ridiculous, either by treating a trivial subject with profound seriousness or by treating a dignified subject frivolously. The word "burlesque" may also be used as an adjective, as in "burlesque show," to mean "striptease act." Examples of literary burlesque include the comedies of Aristophanes, Miguel de Cervantes's *Don Quixote,*, Samuel Butler's poem "Hudibras," and John Gay's play *The Beggar's Opera.*

C

Cadence: The natural rhythm of language caused by the alternation of accented and unaccented syllables. Much modern poetry—notably free verse—deliberately manipulates cadence to create complex rhythmic effects. James Macpherson's "Ossian poems" are richly cadenced, as is the poetry of the Symbolists, Walt Whitman, and Amy Lowell.

Caesura: A pause in a line of poetry, usually occurring near the middle. It typically corresponds to a break in the natural rhythm or sense of the line but is sometimes shifted to create special meanings or rhythmic effects. The opening line of Edgar Allan Poe's "The Raven" contains a caesura following "dreary": "Once upon a midnight dreary, while I pondered weak and weary. . . ."

Canzone: A short Italian or Provencal lyric poem, commonly about love and often set to music. The *canzone* has no set form but typically contains five or six stanzas made up of seven to twenty lines of eleven syllables each. A shorter, five- to ten-line "envoy," or concluding stanza, completes the poem. Masters of the *canzone* form include Petrarch, Dante Alighieri, Torquato Tasso, and Guido Cavalcanti.

Carpe Diem: A Latin term meaning "seize the day." This is a traditional theme of poetry, especially lyrics. A *carpe diem* poem advises the reader or the person it addresses to live for today and enjoy the pleasures of the moment. Two celebrated *carpe diem* poems are Andrew Marvell's "To His Coy Mistress" and Robert Herrick's poem beginning "Gather ye rosebuds while ye may. . . ."

Catharsis: The release or purging of unwanted emotions—specifically fear and pity—brought about by exposure to art. The term was first used by the Greek philosopher Aristotle in his *Poetics* to refer to the desired effect of tragedy on spectators. A famous example of catharsis is realized in Sophocles' *Oedipus Rex,* when Oedipus discovers that his wife, Jacosta, is his own mother and that the stranger he killed on the road was his own father.

Celtic Renaissance: A period of Irish literary and cultural history at the end of the nineteenth century. Followers of the movement aimed to create a romantic vision of Celtic myth and legend. The most significant works of the Celtic Renaissance typically present a dreamy, unreal world, usually in reaction against the reality of contemporary problems. William Butler Yeats's *The Wanderings of Oisin* is among the most significant works of the Celtic Renaissance. Also known as Celtic Twilight.

Celtic Twilight: See *Celtic Renaissance*

Character: Broadly speaking, a person in a literary work. The actions of characters are what constitute the plot of a story, novel, or poem. There are numerous types of characters, ranging from simple, stereotypical figures to intricate, multifaceted ones. In the techniques of anthropomorphism and personification, animals—and even places or things—can assume aspects of character. "Characterization" is the process by which an author creates vivid, believable characters in a work of art. This may be done in a variety of ways, including (1) direct description of the character by the narrator; (2) the direct presentation of the speech, thoughts, or actions of the character; and (3) the responses of other characters to the character. The term "character" also refers to a form originated by the ancient Greek writer Theophrastus that later became popular in the seventeenth and eighteenth centuries. It is a short essay or sketch of a person who prominently displays a specific attribute or quality, such as miserliness or ambition. Notable characters in literature include Oedipus Rex, Don Quixote de la Mancha, Macbeth, Candide, Hester Prynne, Ebenezer Scrooge, Huckleberry Finn, Jay Gatsby, Scarlett O'Hara, James Bond, and Kunta Kinte.

Characterization: See *Character*

Chorus: In ancient Greek drama, a group of actors who commented on and interpreted the unfolding action on the stage. Initially the chorus was a major component of the presentation, but over time it became less significant, with its numbers reduced and its role eventually limited to commentary between acts. By the sixteenth century the chorus—if employed at all—was typically a single person who provided a prologue and an epilogue and occasionally appeared between acts to introduce or underscore an important event. The chorus in William Shakespeare's *Henry V* functions in this way. Modern dramas rarely feature a chorus, but T. S. Eliot's *Murder in the Cathedral* and Arthur Miller's *A View from the Bridge* are notable exceptions. The Stage Manager in Thornton Wilder's *Our Town* performs a role similar to that of the chorus.

Chronicle: A record of events presented in chronological order. Although the scope and level of detail provided varies greatly among the chronicles surviving from ancient times, some, such as the *Anglo-Saxon Chronicle,* feature vivid descriptions and a lively recounting of events. During the Elizabethan Age, many dramas—appropriately called "chronicle plays"—were based on material from chronicles. Many of William Shakespeare's dramas of English history as well as Christopher Marlowe's *Edward II* are based in part on Raphael Holinshead's *Chronicles of England, Scotland, and Ireland.*

Classical: In its strictest definition in literary criticism, classicism refers to works of ancient Greek or Roman literature. The term may also be used to describe a literary work of recognized importance (a "classic") from any time period or literature that exhibits the traits of classicism. Classical authors from ancient Greek and Roman times include Juvenal and Homer. Examples of later works and authors now described as classical include French literature of the seventeenth century, Western novels of the nineteenth century, and American fiction of the mid-nineteenth century such as that written by James Fenimore Cooper and Mark Twain.

Classicism: A term used in literary criticism to describe critical doctrines that have their roots in ancient Greek and Roman literature, philosophy, and art. Works associated with classicism typically exhibit restraint on the part of the author, unity of design and purpose, clarity, simplicity, logical organization, and respect for tradition. Examples of literary classicism include Cicero's prose, the dramas of Pierre Corneille and Jean Racine, the poetry of John Dryden and Alexander Pope, and the writings of J. W. von Goethe, G. E. Lessing, and T. S. Eliot.

Climax: The turning point in a narrative, the moment when the conflict is at its most intense. Typically, the structure of stories, novels, and plays is one of rising action, in which tension builds to the climax, followed by falling action, in which tension lessens as the story moves to its conclusion. The climax in James Fenimore Cooper's *The Last of the Mohicans* occurs when Magua and his captive Cora are pursued to the edge of a cliff by Uncas. Magua kills Uncas but is subsequently killed by Hawkeye.

Colloquialism: A word, phrase, or form of pronunciation that is acceptable in casual conversation but not in formal, written communication. It is considered more acceptable than slang. An example of colloquialism can be found in Rudyard Kipling's *Barrack-room Ballads:* When 'Omer smote 'is bloomin' lyre He'd 'eard men sing by land and sea;

An' what he thought 'e might require 'E went an'
took—the same as me!

Comedy: One of two major types of drama, the
other being tragedy. Its aim is to amuse, and it typically ends happily. Comedy assumes many forms,
such as farce and burlesque, and uses a variety of
techniques, from parody to satire. In a restricted
sense the term comedy refers only to dramatic pre-
sentations, but in general usage it is commonly applied to nondramatic works as well. Examples of
comedies range from the plays of Aristophanes,
Terrence, and Plautus, Dante Alighieri's *The Divine Comedy,* Francois Rabelais's *Pantagruel* and
Gargantua, and some of Geoffrey Chaucer's tales
and William Shakespeare's plays to Noel Coward's
play *Private Lives* and James Thurber's short story
"The Secret Life of Walter Mitty."

Comedy of Manners: A play about the manners and
conventions of an aristocratic, highly sophisticated
society. The characters are usually types rather than
individualized personalities, and plot is less important than atmosphere. Such plays were an important
aspect of late seventeenth-century English comedy.
The comedy of manners was revived in the eighteenth century by Oliver Goldsmith and Richard
Brinsley Sheridan, enjoyed a second revival in the
late nineteenth century, and has endured into the
twentieth century. Examples of comedies of manners
include William Congreve's *The Way of the World*
in the late seventeenth century, Oliver Goldsmith's
She Stoops to Conquer and Richard Brinsley Sheridan's *The School for Scandal* in the eighteenth
century, Oscar Wilde's *The Importance of Being
Earnest* in the nineteenth century, and W. Somerset Maugham's *The Circle* in the twentieth century.

Comic Relief: The use of humor to lighten the
mood of a serious or tragic story, especially in
plays. The technique is very common in Elizabethan works, and can be an integral part of the
plot or simply a brief event designed to break the
tension of the scene. The Gravediggers' scene in
William Shakespeare's *Hamlet* is a frequently cited
example of comic relief.

Commedia dell'arte: An Italian term meaning
"the comedy of guilds" or "the comedy of professional actors." This form of dramatic comedy was
popular in Italy during the sixteenth century. Actors were assigned stock roles (such as Pulcinella,
the stupid servant, or Pantalone, the old merchant)
and given a basic plot to follow, but all dialogue
was improvised. The roles were rigidly typed and
the plots were formulaic, usually revolving around
young lovers who thwarted their elders and attained

wealth and happiness. A rigid convention of the
commedia dell'arte is the periodic intrusion of Harlequin, who interrupts the play with low buffoon-
ery. Peppino de Filippo's *Metamorphoses of a
Wandering Minstrel* gave modern audiences an
idea of what *commedia dell'arte* may have been
like. Various scenarios for *commedia dell'arte*
were compiled in Petraccone's *La commedia del-
l'arte, storia, technica, scenari,* published in 1927.

Complaint: A lyric poem, popular in the Renaissance, in which the speaker expresses sorrow about
his or her condition. Typically, the speaker's sadness is caused by an unresponsive lover, but some
complaints cite other sources of unhappiness, such
as poverty or fate. A commonly cited example is "A
Complaint by Night of the Lover Not Beloved" by
Henry Howard, Earl of Surrey. Thomas Sackville's
"Complaint of Henry, Duke of Buckingham" traces
the duke's unhappiness to his ruthless ambition.

Conceit: A clever and fanciful metaphor, usually expressed through elaborate and extended comparison,
that presents a striking parallel between two seemingly dissimilar things—for example, elaborately
comparing a beautiful woman to an object like a garden or the sun. The conceit was a popular device
throughout the Elizabethan Age and Baroque Age
and was the principal technique of the seventeenth-
century English metaphysical poets. This usage of
the word conceit is unrelated to the best-known definition of conceit as an arrogant attitude or behavior. The conceit figures prominently in the works of
John Donne, Emily Dickinson, and T. S. Eliot.

Concrete: Concrete is the opposite of abstract, and
refers to a thing that actually exists or a description that allows the reader to experience an object
or concept with the senses. Henry David Thoreau's
Walden contains much concrete description of nature and wildlife.

Concrete Poetry: Poetry in which visual elements
play a large part in the poetic effect. Punctuation
marks, letters, or words are arranged on a page to
form a visual design: a cross, for example, or a
bumblebee. Max Bill and Eugene Gomringer were
among the early practitioners of concrete poetry;
Haroldo de Campos and Augusto de Campos are
among contemporary authors of concrete poetry.

Confessional Poetry: A form of poetry in which
the poet reveals very personal, intimate, sometimes
shocking information about himself or herself. Anne
Sexton, Sylvia Plath, Robert Lowell, and John
Berryman wrote poetry in the confessional vein.

Conflict: The conflict in a work of fiction is the
issue to be resolved in the story. It usually occurs

between two characters, the protagonist and the antagonist, or between the protagonist and society or the protagonist and himself or herself. Conflict in Theodore Dreiser's novel *Sister Carrie* comes as a result of urban society, while Jack London's short story "To Build a Fire" concerns the protagonist's battle against the cold and himself.

Connotation: The impression that a word gives beyond its defined meaning. Connotations may be universally understood or may be significant only to a certain group. Both "horse" and "steed" denote the same animal, but "steed" has a different connotation, deriving from the chivalrous or romantic narratives in which the word was once often used.

Consonance: Consonance occurs in poetry when words appearing at the ends of two or more verses have similar final consonant sounds but have final vowel sounds that differ, as with "stuff" and "off." Consonance is found in "The curfew tolls the knells of parting day" from Thomas Grey's "An Elegy Written in a Country Church Yard." Also known as Half Rhyme or Slant Rhyme.

Convention: Any widely accepted literary device, style, or form. A soliloquy, in which a character reveals to the audience his or her private thoughts, is an example of a dramatic convention.

Corrido: A Mexican ballad. Examples of *corridos* include "Muerte del afamado Bilito," "La voz de mi conciencia," "Lucio Perez," "La juida," and "Los presos."

Couplet: Two lines of poetry with the same rhyme and meter, often expressing a complete and self-contained thought. The following couplet is from Alexander Pope's "Elegy to the Memory of an Unfortunate Lady": 'Tis Use alone that sanctifies Expense, And Splendour borrows all her rays from Sense.

Criticism: The systematic study and evaluation of literary works, usually based on a specific method or set of principles. An important part of literary studies since ancient times, the practice of criticism has given rise to numerous theories, methods, and "schools," sometimes producing conflicting, even contradictory, interpretations of literature in general as well as of individual works. Even such basic issues as what constitutes a poem or a novel have been the subject of much criticism over the centuries. Seminal texts of literary criticism include Plato's *Republic*, Aristotle's *Poetics*, Sir Philip Sidney's *The Defence of Poesie*, John Dryden's *Of Dramatic Poesie*, and William Wordsworth's "Preface" to the second edition of his *Lyrical Ballads*. Contemporary schools of criticism include deconstruction, feminist, psychoanalytic, poststructuralist, new historicist, postcolonialist, and reader-response.

D

Dactyl: See *Foot*

Dadaism: A protest movement in art and literature founded by Tristan Tzara in 1916. Followers of the movement expressed their outrage at the destruction brought about by World War I by revolting against numerous forms of social convention. The Dadaists presented works marked by calculated madness and flamboyant nonsense. They stressed total freedom of expression, commonly through primitive displays of emotion and illogical, often senseless, poetry. The movement ended shortly after the war, when it was replaced by surrealism. Proponents of Dadaism include Andre Breton, Louis Aragon, Philippe Soupault, and Paul Eluard.

Decadent: See *Decadents*

Decadents: The followers of a nineteenth-century literary movement that had its beginnings in French aestheticism. Decadent literature displays a fascination with perverse and morbid states; a search for novelty and sensation—the "new thrill"; a preoccupation with mysticism; and a belief in the senselessness of human existence. The movement is closely associated with the doctrine Art for Art's Sake. The term "decadence" is sometimes used to denote a decline in the quality of art or literature following a period of greatness. Major French decadents are Charles Baudelaire and Arthur Rimbaud. English decadents include Oscar Wilde, Ernest Dowson, and Frank Harris.

Deconstruction: A method of literary criticism developed by Jacques Derrida and characterized by multiple conflicting interpretations of a given work. Deconstructionists consider the impact of the language of a work and suggest that the true meaning of the work is not necessarily the meaning that the author intended. Jacques Derrida's *De la grammatologie* is the seminal text on deconstructive strategies; among American practitioners of this method of criticism are Paul de Man and J. Hillis Miller.

Deduction: The process of reaching a conclusion through reasoning from general premises to a specific premise. An example of deduction is present in the following syllogism: Premise: All mammals are animals. Premise: All whales are mammals. Conclusion: Therefore, all whales are animals.

Denotation: The definition of a word, apart from the impressions or feelings it creates in the reader. The word "apartheid" denotes a political and economic policy of segregation by race, but its connotations— oppression, slavery, inequality—are numerous.

Denouement: A French word meaning "the un- knotting." In literary criticism, it denotes the reso- lution of conflict in fiction or drama. The *denouement* follows the climax and provides an outcome to the primary plot situation as well as an explanation of secondary plot complications. The *denouement* often involves a character's recogni- tion of his or her state of mind or moral condition. A well-known example of *denouement* is the last scene of the play *As You Like It* by William Shake- speare, in which couples are married, an evildoer repents, the identities of two disguised characters are revealed, and a ruler is restored to power. Also known as Falling Action.

Description: Descriptive writing is intended to al- low a reader to picture the scene or setting in which the action of a story takes place. The form this de- scription takes often evokes an intended emotional response—a dark, spooky graveyard will evoke fear, and a peaceful, sunny meadow will evoke calmness. An example of a descriptive story is Edgar Allan Poe's *Landor's Cottage,* which offers a detailed depiction of a New York country estate.

Detective Story: A narrative about the solution of a mystery or the identification of a criminal. The conventions of the detective story include the de- tective's scrupulous use of logic in solving the mys- tery; incompetent or ineffectual police; a suspect who appears guilty at first but is later proved inno- cent; and the detective's friend or confidant—often the narrator—whose slowness in interpreting clues emphasizes by contrast the detective's brilliance. Edgar Allan Poe's "Murders in the Rue Morgue" is commonly regarded as the earliest example of this type of story. With this work, Poe established many of the conventions of the detective story genre, which are still in practice. Other practitioners of this vast and extremely popular genre include Arthur Co- nan Doyle, Dashiell Hammett, and Agatha Christie.

Deus ex machina: A Latin term meaning "god out of a machine." In Greek drama, a god was often lowered onto the stage by a mechanism of some kind to rescue the hero or untangle the plot. By ex- tension, the term refers to any artificial device or coincidence used to bring about a convenient and simple solution to a plot. This is a common device in melodramas and includes such fortunate cir- cumstances as the sudden receipt of a legacy to save the family farm or a last-minute stay of execution. The *deus ex machina* invariably rewards the virtu- ous and punishes evildoers. Examples of *deus ex*

machina include King Louis XIV in Jean-Baptiste Moliere's *Tartuffe* and Queen Victoria in *The Pi- rates of Penzance* by William Gilbert and Arthur Sullivan. Bertolt Brecht parodies the abuse of such devices in the conclusion of his *Threepenny Opera.*

Dialogue: In its widest sense, dialogue is simply conversation between people in a literary work; in its most restricted sense, it refers specifically to the speech of characters in a drama. As a specific lit- erary genre, a "dialogue" is a composition in which characters debate an issue or idea. The Greek philosopher Plato frequently expounded his theo- ries in the form of dialogues.

Diction: The selection and arrangement of words in a literary work. Either or both may vary de- pending on the desired effect. There are four gen- eral types of diction: "formal," used in scholarly or lofty writing; "informal," used in relaxed but edu- cated conversation; "colloquial," used in everyday speech; and "slang," containing newly coined words and other terms not accepted in formal usage.

Didactic: A term used to describe works of litera- ture that aim to teach some moral, religious, polit- ical, or practical lesson. Although didactic elements are often found in artistically pleasing works, the term "didactic" usually refers to literature in which the message is more important than the form. The term may also be used to criticize a work that the critic finds "overly didactic," that is, heavy-handed in its delivery of a lesson. Examples of didactic lit- erature include John Bunyan's *Pilgrim's Progress,* Alexander Pope's *Essay on Criticism,* Jean-Jacques Rousseau's *Emile,* and Elizabeth Inchbald's *Sim- ple Story.*

Dimeter: See *Meter*

Dionysian: See *Apollonian and Dionysian*

Discordia concurs: A Latin phrase meaning "dis- cord in harmony." The term was coined by the eighteenth-century English writer Samuel Johnson to describe "a combination of dissimilar images or discovery of occult resemblances in things appar- ently unlike." Johnson created the expression by re- versing a phrase by the Latin poet Horace. The metaphysical poetry of John Donne, Richard Crashaw, Abraham Cowley, George Herbert, and Edward Taylor among others, contains many ex- amples of *discordia concurs*. In Donne's "A Vale- diction: Forbidding Mourning," the poet compares the union of himself with his lover to a draftsman's compass: If they be two, they are two so, As stiff twin compasses are two: Thy soul, the fixed foot, makes no show To move, but doth, if the other do; And though it in the center sit, Yet when the other far doth roam, It leans, and hearkens after it, And grows erect, as that comes home.

Dissonance: A combination of harsh or jarring sounds, especially in poetry. Although such combinations may be accidental, poets sometimes intentionally make them to achieve particular effects. Dissonance is also sometimes used to refer to close but not identical rhymes. When this is the case, the word functions as a synonym for consonance. Robert Browning, Gerard Manley Hopkins, and many other poets have made deliberate use of dissonance.

Doppelganger: A literary technique by which a character is duplicated (usually in the form of an alter ego, though sometimes as a ghostly counterpart) or divided into two distinct, usually opposite personalities. The use of this character device is widespread in nineteenth- and twentieth-century literature, and indicates a growing awareness among authors that the "self" is really a composite of many "selves." A well-known story containing a *doppelganger* character is Robert Louis Stevenson's *Dr. Jekyll and Mr. Hyde,* which dramatizes an internal struggle between good and evil. Also known as The Double.

Double Entendre: A corruption of a French phrase meaning "double meaning." The term is used to indicate a word or phrase that is deliberately ambiguous, especially when one of the meanings is risque or improper. An example of a *double entendre* is the Elizabethan usage of the verb "die," which refers both to death and to orgasm.

Double, The: See *Doppelganger*

Draft: Any preliminary version of a written work. An author may write dozens of drafts which are revised to form the final work, or he or she may write only one, with few or no revisions. Dorothy Parker's observation that "I can't write five words but that I change seven" humorously indicates the purpose of the draft.

Drama: In its widest sense, a drama is any work designed to be presented by actors on a stage. Similarly, "drama" denotes a broad literary genre that includes a variety of forms, from pageant and spectacle to tragedy and comedy, as well as countless types and subtypes. More commonly in modern usage, however, a drama is a work that treats serious subjects and themes but does not aim at the grandeur of tragedy. This use of the term originated with the eighteenth-century French writer Denis Diderot, who used the word *drame* to designate his plays about middle-class life; thus "drama" typically features characters of a less exalted stature than those of tragedy. Examples of classical dramas include Menander's comedy *Dyscolus* and Sophocles' tragedy *Oedipus Rex.* Contemporary dramas include Eugene O'Neill's *The Iceman Cometh,* Lillian Hellman's *Little Foxes,* and August Wilson's *Ma Rainey's Black Bottom.*

Dramatic Irony: Occurs when the audience of a play or the reader of a work of literature knows something that a character in the work itself does not know. The irony is in the contrast between the intended meaning of the statements or actions of a character and the additional information understood by the audience. A celebrated example of dramatic irony is in Act V of William Shakespeare's *Romeo and Juliet,* where two young lovers meet their end as a result of a tragic misunderstanding. Here, the audience has full knowledge that Juliet's apparent "death" is merely temporary; she will regain her senses when the mysterious "sleeping potion" she has taken wears off. But Romeo, mistaking Juliet's drug-induced trance for true death, kills himself in grief. Upon awakening, Juliet discovers Romeo's corpse and, in despair, slays herself.

Dramatic Monologue: See *Monologue*

Dramatic Poetry: Any lyric work that employs elements of drama such as dialogue, conflict, or characterization, but excluding works that are intended for stage presentation. A monologue is a form of dramatic poetry.

Dramatis Personae: The characters in a work of literature, particularly a drama. The list of characters printed before the main text of a play or in the program is the *dramatis personae.*

Dream Allegory: See *Dream Vision*

Dream Vision: A literary convention, chiefly of the Middle Ages. In a dream vision a story is presented as a literal dream of the narrator. This device was commonly used to teach moral and religious lessons. Important works of this type are *The Divine Comedy* by Dante Alighieri, *Piers Plowman* by William Langland, and *The Pilgrim's Progress* by John Bunyan. Also known as Dream Allegory.

Dystopia: An imaginary place in a work of fiction where the characters lead dehumanized, fearful lives. Jack London's *The Iron Heel,* Yevgeny Zamyatin's *My,* Aldous Huxley's *Brave New World,* George Orwell's *Nineteen Eighty-four,* and Margaret Atwood's *Handmaid's Tale* portray versions of dystopia.

E

Eclogue: In classical literature, a poem featuring rural themes and structured as a dialogue among shepherds. Eclogues often took specific poetic forms, such as elegies or love poems. Some were written as the soliloquy of a shepherd. In later centuries, "eclogue" came to refer to any poem that was in the pastoral tradition or that had a dialogue or monologue structure. A classical example of an eclogue is Virgil's *Eclogues,* also known as *Bucolics.* Giovanni Boccaccio, Edmund Spenser, Andrew Marvell, Jonathan Swift, and Louis MacNeice also wrote eclogues.

Edwardian: Describes cultural conventions identified with the period of the reign of Edward VII of England (1901–1910). Writers of the Edwardian Age typically displayed a strong reaction against the propriety and conservatism of the Victorian Age. Their work often exhibits distrust of authority in religion, politics, and art and expresses strong doubts about the soundness of conventional values. Writers of this era include George Bernard Shaw, H. G. Wells, and Joseph Conrad.

Edwardian Age: See *Edwardian*

Electra Complex: A daughter's amorous obsession with her father. The term Electra complex comes from the plays of Euripides and Sophocles entitled *Electra,* in which the character Electra drives her brother Orestes to kill their mother and her lover in revenge for the murder of their father.

Elegy: A lyric poem that laments the death of a person or the eventual death of all people. In a conventional elegy, set in a classical world, the poet and subject are spoken of as shepherds. In modern criticism, the word elegy is often used to refer to a poem that is melancholy or mournfully contemplative. John Milton's "Lycidas" and Percy Bysshe Shelley's "Adonais" are two examples of this form.

Elizabethan Age: A period of great economic growth, religious controversy, and nationalism closely associated with the reign of Elizabeth I of England (1558–1603). The Elizabethan Age is considered a part of the general renaissance—that is, the flowering of arts and literature—that took place in Europe during the fourteenth through sixteenth centuries. The era is considered the golden age of English literature. The most important dramas in English and a great deal of lyric poetry were produced during this period, and modern English criticism began around this time. The notable authors of the period—Philip Sidney, Edmund Spenser, Christopher Marlowe, William Shakespeare, Ben Jonson, Francis Bacon, and John Donne—are among the best in all of English literature.

Elizabethan Drama: English comic and tragic plays produced during the Renaissance, or more narrowly, those plays written during the last years of and few years after Queen Elizabeth's reign. William Shakespeare is considered an Elizabethan dramatist in the broader sense, although most of his work was produced during the reign of James I. Examples of Elizabethan comedies include John Lyly's *The Woman in the Moone,* Thomas Dekker's *The Roaring Girl, or, Moll Cut Purse,* and William Shakespeare's *Twelfth Night.* Examples of Elizabethan tragedies include William Shakespeare's *Antony and Cleopatra,* Thomas Kyd's *The Spanish Tragedy,* and John Webster's *The Tragedy of the Duchess of Malfi.*

Empathy: A sense of shared experience, including emotional and physical feelings, with someone or something other than oneself. Empathy is often used to describe the response of a reader to a literary character. An example of an empathic passage is William Shakespeare's description in his narrative poem *Venus and Adonis* of: the snail, whose tender horns being hit, Shrinks backward in his shelly cave with pain. Readers of Gerard Manley Hopkins's *The Windhover* may experience some of the physical sensations evoked in the description of the movement of the falcon.

English Sonnet: See *Sonnet*

Enjambment: The running over of the sense and structure of a line of verse or a couplet into the following verse or couplet. Andrew Marvell's "To His Coy Mistress" is structured as a series of enjambments, as in lines 11–12: "My vegetable love should grow/Vaster than empires and more slow."

Enlightenment, The: An eighteenth-century philosophical movement. It began in France but had a wide impact throughout Europe and America. Thinkers of the Enlightenment valued reason and believed that both the individual and society could achieve a state of perfection. Corresponding to this essentially humanist vision was a resistance to religious authority. Important figures of the Enlightenment were Denis Diderot and Voltaire in France, Edward Gibbon and David Hume in England, and Thomas Paine and Thomas Jefferson in the United States.

Epic: A long narrative poem about the adventures of a hero of great historic or legendary importance. The setting is vast and the action is often given cosmic significance through the intervention of supernatural forces such as gods, angels, or demons. Epics are typically written in a classical style of grand simplicity with elaborate metaphors and allusions that enhance the symbolic importance of a hero's adventures. Some well-known epics are Homer's *Iliad* and *Odyssey,* Virgil's *Aeneid,* and John Milton's *Paradise Lost.*

Epic Simile: See *Homeric Simile*

Epic Theater: A theory of theatrical presentation developed by twentieth-century German playwright Bertolt Brecht. Brecht created a type of drama that the audience could view with complete detachment. He used what he termed "alienation effects" to create an emotional distance between the audience and the action on stage. Among these effects are: short, self-contained scenes that keep the play from building to a cathartic climax; songs that comment on the action; and techniques of acting that prevent the actor from developing an emotional identity with his role. Besides the plays of Bertolt Brecht, other plays that utilize epic theater conventions include those of Georg Buchner, Frank Wedekind, Erwin Piscator, and Leopold Jessner.

Epigram: A saying that makes the speaker's point quickly and concisely. Samuel Taylor Coleridge wrote an epigram that neatly sums up the form: What is an Epigram? A Dwarfish whole, Its body brevity, and wit its soul.

Epilogue: A concluding statement or section of a literary work. In dramas, particularly those of the seventeenth and eighteenth centuries, the epilogue is a closing speech, often in verse, delivered by an actor at the end of a play and spoken directly to the audience. A famous epilogue is Puck's speech at the end of William Shakespeare's *A Midsummer Night's Dream.*

Epiphany: A sudden revelation of truth inspired by a seemingly trivial incident. The term was widely used by James Joyce in his critical writings, and the stories in Joyce's *Dubliners* are commonly called "epiphanies."

Episode: An incident that forms part of a story and is significantly related to it. Episodes may be either self-contained narratives or events that depend on a larger context for their sense and importance. Examples of episodes include the founding of Wilmington, Delaware in Charles Reade's *The Disinherited Heir* and the individual events comprising the picaresque novels and medieval romances.

Episodic Plot: See *Plot*

Epitaph: An inscription on a tomb or tombstone, or a verse written on the occasion of a person's death. Epitaphs may be serious or humorous. Dorothy Parker's epitaph reads, "I told you I was sick."

Epithalamion: A song or poem written to honor and commemorate a marriage ceremony. Famous examples include Edmund Spenser's "Epithalamion" and e. e. cummings's "Epithalamion." Also spelled Epithalamium.

Epithalamium: See *Epithalamion*

Epithet: A word or phrase, often disparaging or abusive, that expresses a character trait of someone or something. "The Napoleon of crime" is an epithet applied to Professor Moriarty, arch-rival of Sherlock Holmes in Arthur Conan Doyle's series of detective stories.

Exempla: See *Exemplum*

Exemplum: A tale with a moral message. This form of literary sermonizing flourished during the Middle Ages, when *exempla* appeared in collections known as "example-books." The works of Geoffrey Chaucer are full of *exempla.*

Existentialism: A predominantly twentieth-century philosophy concerned with the nature and perception of human existence. There are two major strains of existentialist thought: atheistic and Christian. Followers of atheistic existentialism believe that the individual is alone in a godless universe and that the basic human condition is one of suffering and loneliness. Nevertheless, because there are no fixed values, individuals can create their own characters—indeed, they can shape themselves—through the exercise of free will. The atheistic strain culminates in and is popularly associated with the works of Jean-Paul Sartre. The Christian existentialists, on the other hand, believe that only in God may people find freedom from life's anguish. The two strains hold certain beliefs in common: that existence cannot be fully understood or described through empirical effort; that anguish is a universal element of life; that individuals must bear responsibility for their actions; and that there is no common standard of behavior or perception for religious and ethical matters. Existentialist thought figures prominently in the works of such authors as Eugene Ionesco, Franz Kafka, Fyodor Dostoyevsky, Simone de Beauvoir, Samuel Beckett, and Albert Camus.

Expatriates: See *Expatriatism*

Expatriatism: The practice of leaving one's country to live for an extended period in another country. Literary expatriates include English poets Percy Bysshe Shelley and John Keats in Italy, Polish novelist Joseph Conrad in England, American writers Richard Wright, James Baldwin, Gertrude Stein, and Ernest Hemingway in France, and Trinidadian author Neil Bissondath in Canada.

Exposition: Writing intended to explain the nature of an idea, thing, or theme. Expository writing is often combined with description, narration, or argument. In dramatic writing, the exposition is the introductory material which presents the characters, setting, and tone of the play. An example of dramatic exposition occurs in many nineteenth-century drawing-room comedies in which the butler and the maid open the play with relevant talk about their master and mistress; in composition, exposition relays factual information, as in encyclopedia entries.

Expressionism: An indistinct literary term, originally used to describe an early twentieth-century school of German painting. The term applies to almost any mode of unconventional, highly subjective writing that distorts reality in some way. Advocates of Expressionism include dramatists George Kaiser, Ernst Toller, Luigi Pirandello, Federico Garcia Lorca, Eugene O'Neill, and Elmer Rice; poets George Heym, Ernst Stadler, August Stramm, Gottfried Benn, and Georg Trakl; and novelists Franz Kafka and James Joyce.

Extended Monologue: See *Monologue*

F

Fable: A prose or verse narrative intended to convey a moral. Animals or inanimate objects with human characteristics often serve as characters in fables. A famous fable is Aesop's "The Tortoise and the Hare."

Fairy Tales: Short narratives featuring mythical beings such as fairies, elves, and sprites. These tales originally belonged to the folklore of a particular nation or region, such as those collected in Germany by Jacob and Wilhelm Grimm. Two other celebrated writers of fairy tales arc Hans Christian Andersen and Rudyard Kipling.

Falling Action: See *Denouement*

Fantasy: A literary form related to mythology and folklore. Fantasy literature is typically set in non-existent realms and features supernatural beings. Notable examples of fantasy literature are *The Lord of the Rings* by J. R. R. Tolkien and the Gormenghast trilogy by Mervyn Peake.

Farce: A type of comedy characterized by broad humor, outlandish incidents, and often vulgar subject matter. Much of the "comedy" in film and television could more accurately be described as farce.

Feet: See *Foot*

Feminine Rhyme: See *Rhyme*

Femme fatale: A French phrase with the literal translation "fatal woman." A *femme fatale* is a sensuous, alluring woman who often leads men into danger or trouble. A classic example of the *femme fatale* is the nameless character in Billy Wilder's

The Seven Year Itch, portrayed by Marilyn Monroe in the film adaptation.

Fiction: Any story that is the product of imagination rather than a documentation of fact. characters and events in such narratives may be based in real life but their ultimate form and configuration is a creation of the author. Geoffrey Chaucer's *The Canterbury Tales,* Laurence Sterne's *Tristram Shandy,* and Margaret Mitchell's *Gone with the Wind* are examples of fiction.

Figurative Language: A technique in writing in which the author temporarily interrupts the order, construction, or meaning of the writing for a particular effect. This interruption takes the form of one or more figures of speech such as hyperbole, irony, or simile. Figurative language is the opposite of literal language, in which every word is truthful, accurate, and free of exaggeration or embellishment. Examples of figurative language are tropes such as metaphor and rhetorical figures such as apostrophe.

Figures of Speech: Writing that differs from customary conventions for construction, meaning, order, or significance for the purpose of a special meaning or effect. There are two major types of figures of speech: rhetorical figures, which do not make changes in the meaning of the words, and tropes, which do. Types of figures of speech include simile, hyperbole, alliteration, and pun, among many others.

Fin de siecle: A French term meaning "end of the century." The term is used to denote the last decade of the nineteenth century, a transition period when writers and other artists abandoned old conventions and looked for new techniques and objectives. Two writers commonly associated with the *fin de siecle* mindset are Oscar Wilde and George Bernard Shaw.

First Person: See *Point of View*

Flashback: A device used in literature to present action that occurred before the beginning of the story. Flashbacks are often introduced as the dreams or recollections of one or more characters. Flashback techniques are often used in films, where they are typically set off by a gradual changing of one picture to another.

Foil: A character in a work of literature whose physical or psychological qualities contrast strongly with, and therefore highlight, the corresponding qualities of another character. In his Sherlock Holmes stories, Arthur Conan Doyle portrayed Dr. Watson as a man of normal habits and intelligence, making him a foil for the eccentric and wonderfully perceptive Sherlock Holmes.

Folk Ballad: See *Ballad*

Folklore: Traditions and myths preserved in a culture or group of people. Typically, these are passed on by word of mouth in various forms—such as legends, songs, and proverbs—or preserved in customs and ceremonies. This term was first used by W. J. Thoms in 1846. Sir James Frazer's *The Golden Bough* is the record of English folklore; myths about the frontier and the Old South exemplify American folklore.

Folktale: A story originating in oral tradition. Folktales fall into a variety of categories, including legends, ghost stories, fairy tales, fables, and anecdotes based on historical figures and events. Examples of folktales include Giambattista Basile's *The Pentamerone,* which contains the tales of Puss in Boots, Rapunzel, Cinderella, and Beauty and the Beast, and Joel Chandler Harris's Uncle Remus stories, which represent transplanted African folktales and American tales about the characters Mike Fink, Johnny Appleseed, Paul Bunyan, and Pecos Bill.

Foot: The smallest unit of rhythm in a line of poetry. In English-language poetry, a foot is typically one accented syllable combined with one or two unaccented syllables. There are many different types of feet. When the accent is on the second syllable of a two syllable word (con-*tort*), the foot is an "iamb"; the reverse accentual pattern (*tor*-ture) is a "trochee." Other feet that commonly occur in poetry in English are "anapest", two unaccented syllables followed by an accented syllable as in inter-*cept*, and "dactyl", an accented syllable followed by two unaccented syllables as in *su*-i-cide.

Foreshadowing: A device used in literature to create expectation or to set up an explanation of later developments. In Charles Dickens's *Great Expectations,* the graveyard encounter at the beginning of the novel between Pip and the escaped convict Magwitch foreshadows the baleful atmosphere and events that comprise much of the narrative.

Form: The pattern or construction of a work which identifies its genre and distinguishes it from other genres. Examples of forms include the different genres, such as the lyric form or the short story form, and various patterns for poetry, such as the verse form or the stanza form.

Formalism: In literary criticism, the belief that literature should follow prescribed rules of construction, such as those that govern the sonnet form. Examples of formalism are found in the work of the New Critics and structuralists.

Fourteener Meter: See *Meter*

Free Verse: Poetry that lacks regular metrical and rhyme patterns but that tries to capture the cadences of everyday speech. The form allows a poet to exploit a variety of rhythmical effects within a single poem. Free-verse techniques have been widely used in the twentieth century by such writers as Ezra Pound, T. S. Eliot, Carl Sandburg, and William Carlos Williams. Also known as *Vers libre.*

Futurism: A flamboyant literary and artistic movement that developed in France, Italy, and Russia from 1908 through the 1920s. Futurist theater and poetry abandoned traditional literary forms. In their place, followers of the movement attempted to achieve total freedom of expression through bizarre imagery and deformed or newly invented words. The Futurists were self-consciously modern artists who attempted to incorporate the appearances and sounds of modern life into their work. Futurist writers include Filippo Tommaso Marinetti, Wyndham Lewis, Guillaume Apollinaire, Velimir Khlebnikov, and Vladimir Mayakovsky.

G

Genre: A category of literary work. In critical theory, genre may refer to both the content of a given work—tragedy, comedy, pastoral—and to its form, such as poetry, novel, or drama. This term also refers to types of popular literature, as in the genres of science fiction or the detective story.

Genteel Tradition: A term coined by critic George Santayana to describe the literary practice of certain late nineteenth-century American writers, especially New Englanders. Followers of the Genteel Tradition emphasized conventionality in social, religious, moral, and literary standards. Some of the best-known writers of the Genteel Tradition are R. H. Stoddard and Bayard Taylor.

Gilded Age: A period in American history during the 1870s characterized by political corruption and materialism. A number of important novels of social and political criticism were written during this time. Examples of Gilded Age literature include Henry Adams's *Democracy* and F. Marion Crawford's *An American Politician.*

Gothic: See *Gothicism*

Gothicism: In literary criticism, works characterized by a taste for the medieval or morbidly attractive. A gothic novel prominently features elements of horror, the supernatural, gloom, and violence: clanking chains, terror, charnel houses, ghosts, medieval castles, and mysteriously slamming doors.

The term "gothic novel" is also applied to novels that lack elements of the traditional Gothic setting but that create a similar atmosphere of terror or dread. Mary Shelley's *Frankenstein* is perhaps the best-known English work of this kind.

Gothic Novel: See *Gothicism*

Great Chain of Being: The belief that all things and creatures in nature are organized in a hierarchy from inanimate objects at the bottom to God at the top. This system of belief was popular in the seventeenth and eighteenth centuries. A summary of the concept of the great chain of being can be found in the first epistle of Alexander Pope's *An Essay on Man,* and more recently in Arthur O. Lovejoy's *The Great Chain of Being: A Study of the History of an Idea.*

Grotesque: In literary criticism, the subject matter of a work or a style of expression characterized by exaggeration, deformity, freakishness, and disorder. The grotesque often includes an element of comic absurdity. Early examples of literary grotesque include Francois Rabelais's *Pantagruel* and *Gargantua* and Thomas Nashe's *The Unfortunate Traveller,* while more recent examples can be found in the works of Edgar Allan Poe, Evelyn Waugh, Eudora Welty, Flannery O'Connor, Eugene Ionesco, Gunter Grass, Thomas Mann, Mervyn Peake, and Joseph Heller, among many others.

H

Haiku: The shortest form of Japanese poetry, constructed in three lines of five, seven, and five syllables respectively. The message of a *haiku* poem usually centers on some aspect of spirituality and provokes an emotional response in the reader. Early masters of *haiku* include Basho, Buson, Kobayashi Issa, and Masaoka Shiki. English writers of *haiku* include the Imagists, notably Ezra Pound, H. D., Amy Lowell, Carl Sandburg, and William Carlos Williams. Also known as *Hokku.*

Half Rhyme: See *Consonance*

Hamartia: In tragedy, the event or act that leads to the hero's or heroine's downfall. This term is often incorrectly used as a synonym for tragic flaw. In Richard Wright's *Native Son,* the act that seals Bigger Thomas's fate is his first impulsive murder.

Harlem Renaissance: The Harlem Renaissance of the 1920s is generally considered the first significant movement of black writers and artists in the United States. During this period, new and established black writers published more fiction and poetry than ever before, the first influential black literary journals were established, and black authors and artists received their first widespread recognition and serious critical appraisal. Among the major writers associated with this period are Claude McKay, Jean Toomer, Countee Cullen, Langston Hughes, Arna Bontemps, Nella Larsen, and Zora Neale Hurston. Works representative of the Harlem Renaissance include Arna Bontemps's poems "The Return" and "Golgotha Is a Mountain," Claude McKay's novel *Home to Harlem,* Nella Larsen's novel *Passing,* Langston Hughes's poem "The Negro Speaks of Rivers," and the journals *Crisis* and *Opportunity,* both founded during this period. Also known as Negro Renaissance and New Negro Movement.

Harlequin: A stock character of the *commedia dell'arte* who occasionally interrupted the action with silly antics. Harlequin first appeared on the English stage in John Day's *The Travailes of the Three English Brothers.* The San Francisco Mime Troupe is one of the few modern groups to adapt Harlequin to the needs of contemporary satire.

Hellenism: Imitation of ancient Greek thought or styles. Also, an approach to life that focuses on the growth and development of the intellect. "Hellenism" is sometimes used to refer to the belief that reason can be applied to examine all human experience. A cogent discussion of Hellenism can be found in Matthew Arnold's *Culture and Anarchy.*

Heptameter: See *Meter*

Hero/Heroine: The principal sympathetic character (male or female) in a literary work. Heroes and heroines typically exhibit admirable traits: idealism, courage, and integrity, for example. Famous heroes and heroines include Pip in Charles Dickens's *Great Expectations,* the anonymous narrator in Ralph Ellison's *Invisible Man,* and Sethe in Toni Morrison's *Beloved.*

Heroic Couplet: A rhyming couplet written in iambic pentameter (a verse with five iambic feet). The following lines by Alexander Pope are an example: "Truth guards the Poet, sanctifies the line,/ And makes Immortal, Verse as mean as mine."

Heroic Line: The meter and length of a line of verse in epic or heroic poetry. This varies by language and time period. For example, in English poetry, the heroic line is iambic pentameter (a verse with five iambic feet); in French, the alexandrine (a verse with six iambic feet); in classical literature, dactylic hexameter (a verse with six dactylic feet).

Heroine: See *Hero/Heroine*

Hexameter: See *Meter*

Historical Criticism: The study of a work based on its impact on the world of the time period in which it was written. Examples of postmodern historical criticism can be found in the work of Michel Foucault, Hayden White, Stephen Greenblatt, and Jonathan Goldberg.

Hokku: See *Haiku*

Holocaust: See *Holocaust Literature*

Holocaust Literature: Literature influenced by or written about the Holocaust of World War II. Such literature includes true stories of survival in concentration camps, escape, and life after the war, as well as fictional works and poetry. Representative works of Holocaust literature include Saul Bellow's *Mr. Sammler's Planet,* Anne Frank's *The Diary of a Young Girl,* Jerzy Kosinski's *The Painted Bird,* Arthur Miller's *Incident at Vichy,* Czeslaw Milosz's *Collected Poems,* William Styron's *Sophie's Choice,* and Art Spiegelman's *Maus.*

Homeric Simile: An elaborate, detailed comparison written as a simile many lines in length. An example of an epic simile from John Milton's *Paradise Lost* follows: Angel Forms, who lay entranced Thick as autumnal leaves that strow the brooks In Vallombrosa, where the Etrurian shades High over-arched embower; or scattered sedge Afloat, when with fierce winds Orion armed Hath vexed the Red-Sea coast, whose waves o'erthrew Busiris and his Memphian chivalry, While with perfidious hatred they pursued The sojourners of Goshen, who beheld From the safe shore their floating carcasses And broken chariot-wheels. Also known as Epic Simile.

Horatian Satire: See *Satire*

Humanism: A philosophy that places faith in the dignity of humankind and rejects the medieval perception of the individual as a weak, fallen creature. "Humanists" typically believe in the perfectibility of human nature and view reason and education as the means to that end. Humanist thought is represented in the works of Marsilio Ficino, Ludovico Castelvetro, Edmund Spenser, John Milton, Dean John Colet, Desiderius Erasmus, John Dryden, Alexander Pope, Matthew Arnold, and Irving Babbitt.

Humors: Mentions of the humors refer to the ancient Greek theory that a person's health and personality were determined by the balance of four basic fluids in the body: blood, phlegm, yellow bile, and black bile. A dominance of any fluid would cause extremes in behavior. An excess of blood created a sanguine person who was joyful, aggressive, and passionate; a phlegmatic person was shy, fearful, and sluggish; too much yellow bile led to a choleric temperament characterized by impatience, anger, bitterness, and stubbornness; and excessive black bile created melancholy, a state of laziness, gluttony, and lack of motivation. Literary treatment of the humors is exemplified by several characters in Ben Jonson's plays *Every Man in His Humour* and *Every Man out of His Humour.* Also spelled Humours.

Humours: See *Humors*

Hyperbole: In literary criticism, deliberate exaggeration used to achieve an effect. In William Shakespeare's *Macbeth,* Lady Macbeth hyperbolizes when she says, "All the perfumes of Arabia could not sweeten this little hand."

I

Iamb: See *Foot*

Idiom: A word construction or verbal expression closely associated with a given language. For example, in colloquial English the construction "how come" can be used instead of "why" to introduce a question. Similarly, "a piece of cake" is sometimes used to describe a task that is easily done.

Image: A concrete representation of an object or sensory experience. Typically, such a representation helps evoke the feelings associated with the object or experience itself. Images are either "literal" or "figurative." Literal images are especially concrete and involve little or no extension of the obvious meaning of the words used to express them. Figurative images do not follow the literal meaning of the words exactly. Images in literature are usually visual, but the term "image" can also refer to the representation of any sensory experience. In his poem "The Shepherd's Hour," Paul Verlaine presents the following image: "The Moon is red through horizon's fog;/ In a dancing mist the hazy meadow sleeps." The first line is broadly literal, while the second line involves turns of meaning associated with dancing and sleeping.

Imagery: The array of images in a literary work. Also, figurative language. William Butler Yeats's "The Second Coming" offers a powerful image of encroaching anarchy: Turning and turning in the widening gyre The falcon cannot hear the falconer; Things fall apart. . . .

Imagism: An English and American poetry movement that flourished between 1908 and 1917. The Imagists used precise, clearly presented images in their works. They also used common, everyday speech and aimed for conciseness, concrete imagery, and the creation of new rhythms. Participants in the Imagist movement included Ezra Pound, H. D. (Hilda Doolittle), and Amy Lowell, among others.

In medias res: A Latin term meaning "in the middle of things." It refers to the technique of beginning a story at its midpoint and then using various flashback devices to reveal previous action. This technique originated in such epics as Virgil's *Aeneid.*

Induction: The process of reaching a conclusion by reasoning from specific premises to form a general premise. Also, an introductory portion of a work of literature, especially a play. Geoffrey Chaucer's "Prologue" to the *Canterbury Tales,* Thomas Sackville's "Induction" to *The Mirror of Magistrates,* and the opening scene in William Shakespeare's *The Taming of the Shrew* are examples of inductions to literary works.

Intentional Fallacy: The belief that judgments of a literary work based solely on an author's stated or implied intentions are false and misleading. Critics who believe in the concept of the intentional fallacy typically argue that the work itself is sufficient matter for interpretation, even though they may concede that an author's statement of purpose can be useful. Analysis of William Wordsworth's *Lyrical Ballads* based on the observations about poetry he makes in his "Preface" to the second edition of that work is an example of the intentional fallacy.

Interior Monologue: A narrative technique in which characters' thoughts are revealed in a way that appears to be uncontrolled by the author. The interior monologue typically aims to reveal the inner self of a character. It portrays emotional experiences as they occur at both a conscious and unconscious level. images are often used to represent sensations or emotions. One of the best-known interior monologues in English is the Molly Bloom section at the close of James Joyce's *Ulysses.* The interior monologue is also common in the works of Virginia Woolf.

Internal Rhyme: Rhyme that occurs within a single line of verse. An example is in the opening line of Edgar Allan Poe's "The Raven": "Once upon a midnight dreary, while I pondered weak and weary." Here, "dreary" and "weary" make an internal rhyme.

Irish Literary Renaissance: A late nineteenth- and early twentieth-century movement in Irish literature. Members of the movement aimed to reduce the influence of British culture in Ireland and create an Irish national literature. William Butler Yeats, George Moore, and Sean O'Casey are three of the best-known figures of the movement.

Irony: In literary criticism, the effect of language in which the intended meaning is the opposite of what is stated. The title of Jonathan Swift's "A Modest Proposal" is ironic because what Swift proposes in this essay is cannibalism—hardly "modest."

Italian Sonnet: See *Sonnet*

J

Jacobean Age: The period of the reign of James I of England (1603–1625). The early literature of this period reflected the worldview of the Elizabethan Age, but a darker, more cynical attitude steadily grew in the art and literature of the Jacobean Age. This was an important time for English drama and poetry. Milestones include William Shakespeare's tragedies, tragi-comedies, and sonnets; Ben Jonson's various dramas; and John Donne's metaphysical poetry.

Jargon: Language that is used or understood only by a select group of people. Jargon may refer to terminology used in a certain profession, such as computer jargon, or it may refer to any nonsensical language that is not understood by most people. Literary examples of jargon are Francois Villon's *Ballades en jargon,* which is composed in the secret language of the *coquillards,* and Anthony Burgess's *A Clockwork Orange,* narrated in the fictional characters' language of "Nadsat."

Juvenalian Satire: See *Satire*

K

Knickerbocker Group: A somewhat indistinct group of New York writers of the first half of the nineteenth century. Members of the group were linked only by location and a common theme: New York life. Two famous members of the Knickerbocker Group were Washington Irving and William Cullen Bryant. The group's name derives from Irving's *Knickerbocker's History of New York.*

L

Lais: See *Lay*

Lay: A song or simple narrative poem. The form originated in medieval France. Early French *lais* were often based on the Celtic legends and other tales sung by Breton minstrels—thus the name of the "Breton lay." In fourteenth-century England, the term "lay" was used to describe short narratives written in imitation of the Breton lays. The most notable of these is Geoffrey Chaucer's "The Minstrel's Tale."

Leitmotiv: See *Motif*

Literal Language: An author uses literal language when he or she writes without exaggerating or embellishing the subject matter and without any tools of figurative language. To say "He ran very quickly down the street" is to use literal language, whereas to say "He ran like a hare down the street" would be using figurative language.

Literary Ballad: See *Ballad*

Literature: Literature is broadly defined as any written or spoken material, but the term most often refers to creative works. Literature includes poetry, drama, fiction, and many kinds of nonfiction writing, as well as oral, dramatic, and broadcast compositions not necessarily preserved in a written format, such as films and television programs.

Lost Generation: A term first used by Gertrude Stein to describe the post-World War I generation of American writers: men and women haunted by a sense of betrayal and emptiness brought about by the destructiveness of the war. The term is commonly applied to Hart Crane, Ernest Hemingway, F. Scott Fitzgerald, and others.

Lyric Poetry: A poem expressing the subjective feelings and personal emotions of the poet. Such poetry is melodic, since it was originally accompanied by a lyre in recitals. Most Western poetry in the twentieth century may be classified as lyrical. Examples of lyric poetry include A. E. Housman's elegy "To an Athlete Dying Young," the odes of Pindar and Horace, Thomas Gray and William Collins, the sonnets of Sir Thomas Wyatt and Sir Philip Sidney, Elizabeth Barrett Browning and Rainer Maria Rilke, and a host of other forms in the poetry of William Blake and Christina Rossetti, among many others.

M

Mannerism: Exaggerated, artificial adherence to a literary manner or style. Also, a popular style of the visual arts of late sixteenth-century Europe that was marked by elongation of the human form and by intentional spatial distortion. Literary works that are self-consciously high-toned and artistic are often said to be "mannered." Authors of such works include Henry James and Gertrude Stein.

Masculine Rhyme: See *Rhyme*

Masque: A lavish and elaborate form of entertainment, often performed in royal courts, that emphasizes song, dance, and costumery. The Renaissance form of the masque grew out of the spectacles of masked figures common in medieval England and Europe. The masque reached its peak of popularity and development in seventeenth-century England, during the reigns of James I and, especially, of Charles I. Ben Jonson, the most significant masque writer, also created the "anti-masque," which incorporates elements of humor and the grotesque into the traditional masque and achieved greater dramatic quality. Masque-like interludes appear in Edmund Spenser's *The Faerie Queene* and in William Shakespeare's *The Tempest.* One of the best-known English masques is John Milton's *Comus.*

Measure: The foot, verse, or time sequence used in a literary work, especially a poem. Measure is often used somewhat incorrectly as a synonym for meter.

Melodrama: A play in which the typical plot is a conflict between characters who personify extreme good and evil. Melodramas usually end happily and emphasize sensationalism. Other literary forms that use the same techniques are often labeled "melodramatic." The term was formerly used to describe a combination of drama and music; as such, it was synonymous with "opera." Augustin Daly's *Under the Gaslight* and Dion Boucicault's *The Octoroon, The Colleen Bawn,* and *The Poor of New York* are examples of melodramas. The most popular media for twentieth-century melodramas are motion pictures and television.

Metaphor: A figure of speech that expresses an idea through the image of another object. Metaphors suggest the essence of the first object by identifying it with certain qualities of the second object. An example is "But soft, what light through yonder window breaks?/ It is the east, and Juliet is the sun" in William Shakespeare's *Romeo and Juliet.* Here, Juliet, the first object, is identified with qualities of the second object, the sun.

Metaphysical Conceit: See *Conceit*

Metaphysical Poetry: The body of poetry produced by a group of seventeenth-century English writers called the "Metaphysical Poets." The group includes John Donne and Andrew Marvell. The Metaphysical Poets made use of everyday speech, intellectual analysis, and unique imagery. They aimed to portray the ordinary conflicts and contradictions of life. Their poems often took the form of an argument, and many of them emphasize physical and religious love as well as the fleeting nature of life. Elaborate conceits are typical in metaphysical poetry. Marvell's "To His Coy Mistress" is a well-known example of a metaphysical poem.

Metaphysical Poets: See *Metaphysical Poetry*

Meter: In literary criticism, the repetition of sound patterns that creates a rhythm in poetry. The patterns are based on the number of syllables and the presence and absence of accents. The unit of rhythm in a line is called a foot. Types of meter are classified according to the number of feet in a line. These are the standard English lines: Monometer, one foot; Dimeter, two feet; Trimeter, three feet; Tetrameter, four feet; Pentameter, five feet; Hexameter, six feet (also called the Alexandrine); Heptameter, seven feet (also called the "Fourteener" when the feet are iambic). The most common English meter is the iambic pentameter, in which each line contains ten syllables, or five iambic feet, which individually are composed of an unstressed syllable followed by an accented syllable. Both of the following lines from Alfred, Lord Tennyson's "Ulysses" are written in iambic pentameter: Made weak by time and fate, but strong in will To strive, to seek, to find, and not to yield.

Mise en scene: The costumes, scenery, and other properties of a drama. Herbert Beerbohm Tree was renowned for the elaborate *mises en scene* of his lavish Shakespearean productions at His Majesty's Theatre between 1897 and 1915.

Modernism: Modern literary practices. Also, the principles of a literary school that lasted from roughly the beginning of the twentieth century until the end of World War II. Modernism is defined by its rejection of the literary conventions of the nineteenth century and by its opposition to conventional morality, taste, traditions, and economic values. Many writers are associated with the concepts of Modernism, including Albert Camus, Marcel Proust, D. H. Lawrence, W. H. Auden, Ernest Hemingway, William Faulkner, William Butler Yeats, Thomas Mann, Tennessee Williams, Eugene O'Neill, and James Joyce.

Monologue: A composition, written or oral, by a single individual. More specifically, a speech given by a single individual in a drama or other public entertainment. It has no set length, although it is usually several or more lines long. An example of an "extended monologue"—that is, a monologue of great length and seriousness—occurs in the one-act, one-character play *The Stronger* by August Strindberg.

Monometer: See *Meter*

Mood: The prevailing emotions of a work or of the author in his or her creation of the work. The mood of a work is not always what might be expected based on its subject matter. The poem "Dover Beach" by Matthew Arnold offers examples of two different moods originating from the same experience: watching the ocean at night. The mood of the first three lines—The sea is calm tonight The tide is full, the moon lies fair Upon the straights. . . . is in sharp contrast to the mood of the last three lines—And we are here as on a darkling plain Swept with confused alarms of struggle and flight, Where ignorant armies clash by night.

Motif: A theme, character type, image, metaphor, or other verbal element that recurs throughout a single work of literature or occurs in a number of different works over a period of time. For example, the various manifestations of the color white in Herman Melville's *Moby Dick* is a "specific" *motif,* while the trials of star-crossed lovers is a "conventional" *motif* from the literature of all periods. Also known as *Motiv* or *Leitmotiv.*

Motiv: See *Motif*

Muckrakers: An early twentieth-century group of American writers. Typically, their works exposed the wrongdoings of big business and government in the United States. Upton Sinclair's *The Jungle* exemplifies the muckraking novel.

Muses: Nine Greek mythological goddesses, the daughters of Zeus and Mnemosyne (Memory). Each muse patronized a specific area of the liberal arts and sciences. Calliope presided over epic poetry, Clio over history, Erato over love poetry, Euterpe over music or lyric poetry, Melpomene over tragedy, Polyhymnia over hymns to the gods, Terpsichore over dance, Thalia over comedy, and Urania over astronomy. Poets and writers traditionally made appeals to the Muses for inspiration in their work. John Milton invokes the aid of a muse at the beginning of the first book of his *Paradise Lost:* Of Man's First disobedience, and the Fruit of the Forbidden Tree, whose mortal taste Brought Death into the World, and all our woe, With loss of Eden, till one greater Man Restore us, and regain the blissful Seat, Sing Heav'nly Muse, that on the secret top of Oreb, or of Sinai, didst inspire That Shepherd, who first taught the chosen Seed, In the Beginning how the Heav'ns and Earth Rose out of Chaos. . . .

Mystery: See *Suspense*

Myth: An anonymous tale emerging from the traditional beliefs of a culture or social unit. Myths use supernatural explanations for natural phenomena. They may also explain cosmic issues like creation and death. Collections of myths, known as mythologies, are common to all cultures and nations, but the best-known myths belong to the Norse, Roman, and Greek mythologies. A famous myth is the story of Arachne, an arrogant young girl who challenged a goddess, Athena, to a weaving contest; when the girl won, Athena was enraged and turned Arachne into a spider, thus explaining the existence of spiders.

N

Narration: The telling of a series of events, real or invented. A narration may be either a simple narrative, in which the events are recounted chronologically, or a narrative with a plot, in which the account is given in a style reflecting the author's artistic concept of the story. Narration is sometimes used as a synonym for "storyline." The recounting of scary stories around a campfire is a form of narration.

Narrative: A verse or prose accounting of an event or sequence of events, real or invented. The term is also used as an adjective in the sense "method of narration." For example, in literary criticism, the expression "narrative technique" usually refers to the way the author structures and presents his or her story. Narratives range from the shortest accounts of events, as in Julius Caesar's remark, "I came, I saw, I conquered," to the longest historical or biographical works, as in Edward Gibbon's *The Decline and Fall of the Roman Empire,* as well as diaries, travelogues, novels, ballads, epics, short stories, and other fictional forms.

Narrative Poetry: A nondramatic poem in which the author tells a story. Such poems may be of any length or level of complexity. Epics such as *Beowulf* and ballads are forms of narrative poetry.

Narrator: The teller of a story. The narrator may be the author or a character in the story through whom the author speaks. Huckleberry Finn is the narrator of Mark Twain's *The Adventures of Huckleberry Finn.*

Naturalism: A literary movement of the late nineteenth and early twentieth centuries. The movement's major theorist, French novelist Emile Zola, envisioned a type of fiction that would examine human life with the objectivity of scientific inquiry. The Naturalists typically viewed human beings as either the products of "biological determinism," ruled by hereditary instincts and engaged in an endless struggle for survival, or as the products of "socioeconomic determinism," ruled by social and economic forces beyond their control. In their works, the Naturalists generally ignored the highest levels of society and focused on degradation: poverty, alcoholism, prostitution, insanity, and disease. Naturalism influenced authors throughout the world, including Henrik Ibsen and Thomas Hardy. In the United States, in particular, Naturalism had a profound impact. Among the authors who embraced its principles are Theodore Dreiser, Eugene O'Neill, Stephen Crane, Jack London, and Frank Norris.

Negritude: A literary movement based on the concept of a shared cultural bond on the part of black Africans, wherever they may be in the world. It traces its origins to the former French colonies of Africa and the Caribbean. Negritude poets, novelists, and essayists generally stress four points in their writings: One, black alienation from traditional African culture can lead to feelings of inferiority. Two, European colonialism and Western education should be resisted. Three, black Africans should seek to affirm and define their own identity. Four, African culture can and should be reclaimed. Many Negritude writers also claim that blacks can make unique contributions to the world, based on a heightened appreciation of nature, rhythm, and human emotions—aspects of life they say are not so highly valued in the materialistic and rationalistic West. Examples of Negritude literature include the poetry of both Senegalese Leopold Senghor in *Hosties noires* and Martiniquais Aime-Fernand Cesaire in *Return to My Native Land.*

Negro Renaissance: See *Harlem Renaissance*

Neoclassical Period: See *Neoclassicism*

Neoclassicism: In literary criticism, this term refers to the revival of the attitudes and styles of expression of classical literature. It is generally used to describe a period in European history beginning in the late seventeenth century and lasting until about 1800. In its purest form, Neoclassicism marked a return to order, proportion, restraint, logic, accuracy, and decorum. In England, where Neoclassicism perhaps was most popular, it reflected the influence of seventeenth-century French writers, especially dramatists. Neoclassical writers typically reacted against the intensity and enthusiasm of the Renaissance period. They wrote works that appealed to the intellect, using elevated language and classical literary forms such as satire and the ode. Neoclassical works were often governed by the classical goal of instruction. English neoclassicists included Alexander Pope, Jonathan Swift, Joseph Addison, Sir Richard Steele, John Gay, and Matthew Prior; French neoclassicists included Pierre Corneille and Jean-Baptiste Moliere. Also known as Age of Reason.

Neoclassicists: See *Neoclassicism*

New Criticism: A movement in literary criticism, dating from the late 1920s, that stressed close textual analysis in the interpretation of works of literature.

The New Critics saw little merit in historical and biographical analysis. Rather, they aimed to examine the text alone, free from the question of how external events—biographical or otherwise—may have helped shape it. This predominantly American school was named "New Criticism" by one of its practitioners, John Crowe Ransom. Other important New Critics included Allen Tate, R. P. Blackmur, Robert Penn Warren, and Cleanth Brooks.

New Negro Movement: See *Harlem Renaissance*

Noble Savage: The idea that primitive man is noble and good but becomes evil and corrupted as he becomes civilized. The concept of the noble savage originated in the Renaissance period but is more closely identified with such later writers as Jean-Jacques Rousseau and Aphra Behn. First described in John Dryden's play *The Conquest of Granada,* the noble savage is portrayed by the various Native Americans in James Fenimore Cooper's "Leatherstocking Tales," by Queequeg, Daggoo, and Tashtego in Herman Melville's *Moby Dick,* and by John the Savage in Aldous Huxley's *Brave New World.*

O

Objective Correlative: An outward set of objects, a situation, or a chain of events corresponding to an inward experience and evoking this experience in the reader. The term frequently appears in modern criticism in discussions of authors' intended effects on the emotional responses of readers. This term was originally used by T. S. Eliot in his 1919 essay "Hamlet."

Objectivity: A quality in writing characterized by the absence of the author's opinion or feeling about the subject matter. Objectivity is an important factor in criticism. The novels of Henry James and, to a certain extent, the poems of John Larkin demonstrate objectivity, and it is central to John Keats's concept of "negative capability." Critical and journalistic writing usually are or attempt to be objective.

Occasional Verse: poetry written on the occasion of a significant historical or personal event. *Vers de societe* is sometimes called occasional verse although it is of a less serious nature. Famous examples of occasional verse include Andrew Marvell's "Horatian Ode upon Cromwell's Return from England," Walt Whitman's "When Lilacs Last in the Dooryard Bloom'd"—written upon the death of Abraham Lincoln—and Edmund Spenser's commemoration of his wedding, "Epithalamion."

Octave: A poem or stanza composed of eight lines. The term octave most often represents the first eight lines of a Petrarchan sonnet. An example of an octave is taken from a translation of a Petrarchan sonnet by Sir Thomas Wyatt: The pillar perisht is whereto I leant, The strongest stay of mine unquiet mind; The like of it no man again can find, From East to West Still seeking though he went. To mind unhap! for hap away hath rent Of all my joy the very bark and rind; And I, alas, by chance am thus assigned Daily to mourn till death do it relent.

Ode: Name given to an extended lyric poem characterized by exalted emotion and dignified style. An ode usually concerns a single, serious theme. Most odes, but not all, are addressed to an object or individual. Odes are distinguished from other lyric poetic forms by their complex rhythmic and stanzaic patterns. An example of this form is John Keats's "Ode to a Nightingale."

Oedipus Complex: A son's amorous obsession with his mother. The phrase is derived from the story of the ancient Theban hero Oedipus, who unknowingly killed his father and married his mother. Literary occurrences of the Oedipus complex include Andre Gide's *Oedipe* and Jean Cocteau's *La Machine infernale,* as well as the most famous, Sophocles' *Oedipus Rex.*

Omniscience: See *Point of View*

Onomatopoeia: The use of words whose sounds express or suggest their meaning. In its simplest sense, onomatopoeia may be represented by words that mimic the sounds they denote such as "hiss" or "meow." At a more subtle level, the pattern and rhythm of sounds and rhymes of a line or poem may be onomatopoeic. A celebrated example of onomatopoeia is the repetition of the word "bells" in Edgar Allan Poe's poem "The Bells."

Opera: A type of stage performance, usually a drama, in which the dialogue is sung. Classic examples of opera include Giuseppi Verdi's *La traviata,* Giacomo Puccini's *La Boheme,* and Richard Wagner's *Tristan und Isolde.* Major twentieth-century contributors to the form include Richard Strauss and Alban Berg.

Operetta: A usually romantic comic opera. John Gay's *The Beggar's Opera,* Richard Sheridan's *The Duenna,* and numerous works by William Gilbert and Arthur Sullivan are examples of operettas.

Oral Tradition: See *Oral Transmission*

Oral Transmission: A process by which songs, ballads, folklore, and other material are transmitted by word of mouth. The tradition of oral transmission predates the written record systems of literate society. Oral transmission preserves material sometimes over generations, although often with variations. Memory plays a large part in the recitation and preservation of orally transmitted material. Breton lays, French *fabliaux,* national epics (including the Anglo-Saxon *Beowulf,* the Spanish *El Cid,* and the Finnish *Kalevala*), Native American myths and legends, and African folktales told by plantation slaves are examples of orally transmitted literature.

Oration: Formal speaking intended to motivate the listeners to some action or feeling. Such public speaking was much more common before the development of timely printed communication such as newspapers. Famous examples of oration include Abraham Lincoln's "Gettysburg Address" and Dr. Martin Luther King Jr.'s "I Have a Dream" speech.

Ottava Rima: An eight-line stanza of poetry composed in iambic pentameter (a five-foot line in which each foot consists of an unaccented syllable followed by an accented syllable), following the abababcc rhyme scheme. This form has been prominently used by such important English writers as Lord Byron, Henry Wadsworth Longfellow, and W. B. Yeats.

Oxymoron: A phrase combining two contradictory terms. Oxymorons may be intentional or unintentional. The following speech from William Shakespeare's *Romeo and Juliet* uses several oxymorons: Why, then, O brawling love! O loving hate! O anything, of nothing first create! O heavy lightness! serious vanity! Mis-shapen chaos of well-seeming forms! Feather of lead, bright smoke, cold fire, sick health! This love feel I, that feel no love in this.

P

Pantheism: The idea that all things are both a manifestation or revelation of God and a part of God at the same time. Pantheism was a common attitude in the early societies of Egypt, India, and Greece—the term derives from the Greek *pan* meaning "all" and *theos* meaning "deity." It later became a significant part of the Christian faith. William Wordsworth and Ralph Waldo Emerson are among the many writers who have expressed the pantheistic attitude in their works.

Parable: A story intended to teach a moral lesson or answer an ethical question. In the West, the best examples of parables are those of Jesus Christ in the New Testament, notably "The Prodigal Son," but parables also are used in Sufism, rabbinic literature, Hasidism, and Zen Buddhism.

Paradox: A statement that appears illogical or contradictory at first, but may actually point to an underlying truth. "Less is more" is an example of a paradox. Literary examples include Francis Bacon's statement, "The most corrected copies are commonly the least correct," and "All animals are equal, but some animals are more equal than others" from George Orwell's *Animal Farm.*

Parallelism: A method of comparison of two ideas in which each is developed in the same grammatical structure. Ralph Waldo Emerson's "Civilization" contains this example of parallelism: Raphael paints wisdom; Handel sings it, Phidias carves it, Shakespeare writes it, Wren builds it, Columbus sails it, Luther preaches it, Washington arms it, Watt mechanizes it.

Parnassianism: A mid nineteenth-century movement in French literature. Followers of the movement stressed adherence to well-defined artistic forms as a reaction against the often chaotic expression of the artist's ego that dominated the work of the Romantics. The Parnassians also rejected the moral, ethical, and social themes exhibited in the works of French Romantics such as Victor Hugo. The aesthetic doctrines of the Parnassians strongly influenced the later symbolist and decadent movements. Members of the Parnassian school include Leconte de Lisle, Sully Prudhomme, Albert Glatigny, Francois Coppee, and Theodore de Banville.

Parody: In literary criticism, this term refers to an imitation of a serious literary work or the signature style of a particular author in a ridiculous manner. A typical parody adopts the style of the original and applies it to an inappropriate subject for humorous effect. Parody is a form of satire and could be considered the literary equivalent of a caricature or cartoon. Henry Fielding's *Shamela* is a parody of Samuel Richardson's *Pamela.*

Pastoral: A term derived from the Latin word "pastor," meaning shepherd. A pastoral is a literary composition on a rural theme. The conventions of the pastoral were originated by the third-century Greek poet Theocritus, who wrote about the experiences, love affairs, and pastimes of Sicilian shepherds. In a pastoral, characters and language of a courtly nature are often placed in a simple setting. The term pastoral is also used to classify dramas, elegies, and lyrics that exhibit the use of country settings and shepherd characters. Percy Bysshe Shelley's "Adonais" and John Milton's "Lycidas" are two famous examples of pastorals.

Pastorela: The Spanish name for the shepherds play, a folk drama reenacted during the Christmas season. Examples of *pastorelas* include Gomez Manrique's *Representacion del nacimiento* and the dramas of Lucas Fernandez and Juan del Encina.

Pathetic Fallacy: A term coined by English critic John Ruskin to identify writing that falsely endows nonhuman things with human intentions and feelings, such as "angry clouds" and "sad trees." The pathetic fallacy is a required convention in the classical poetic form of the pastoral elegy, and it is used in the modern poetry of T. S. Eliot, Ezra Pound, and the Imagists. Also known as Poetic Fallacy.

Pelado: Literally the "skinned one" or shirtless one, he was the stock underdog, sharp-witted picaresque character of Mexican vaudeville and tent shows. The *pelado* is found in such works as Don Catarino's *Los effectos de la crisis* and *Regreso a mi tierra*.

Pen Name: See *Pseudonym*

Pentameter: See *Meter*

Persona: A Latin term meaning "mask." *Personae* are the characters in a fictional work of literature. The *persona* generally functions as a mask through which the author tells a story in a voice other than his or her own. A *persona* is usually either a character in a story who acts as a narrator or an "implied author," a voice created by the author to act as the narrator for himself or herself. *Personae* include the narrator of Geoffrey Chaucer's *Canterbury Tales* and Marlow in Joseph Conrad's *Heart of Darkness*.

Personae: See *Persona*

Personal Point of View: See *Point of View*

Personification: A figure of speech that gives human qualities to abstract ideas, animals, and inanimate objects. William Shakespeare used personification in *Romeo and Juliet* in the lines "Arise, fair sun,/ and kill the envious moon,/ Who is already sick and pale with grief." Here, the moon is portrayed as being envious, sick, and pale with grief—all markedly human qualities. Also known as *Prosopopoeia*.

Petrarchan Sonnet: See *Sonnet*

Phenomenology: A method of literary criticism based on the belief that things have no existence outside of human consciousness or awareness. Proponents of this theory believe that art is a process that takes place in the mind of the observer as he or she contemplates an object rather than a quality of the object itself. Among phenomenological critics are Edmund Husserl, George Poulet, Marcel Raymond, and Roman Ingarden.

Picaresque Novel: Episodic fiction depicting the adventures of a roguish central character ("picaro" is Spanish for "rogue"). The picaresque hero is commonly a low-born but clever individual who wanders into and out of various affairs of love, danger, and farcical intrigue. These involvements may take place at all social levels and typically present a humorous and wide-ranging satire of a given society. Prominent examples of the picaresque novel are *Don Quixote* by Miguel de Cervantes, *Tom Jones* by Henry Fielding, and *Moll Flanders* by Daniel Defoe.

Plagiarism: Claiming another person's written material as one's own. Plagiarism can take the form of direct, word-for-word copying or the theft of the substance or idea of the work. A student who copies an encyclopedia entry and turns it in as a report for school is guilty of plagiarism.

Platonic Criticism: A form of criticism that stresses an artistic work's usefulness as an agent of social engineering rather than any quality or value of the work itself. Platonic criticism takes as its starting point the ancient Greek philosopher Plato's comments on art in his *Republic*.

Platonism: The embracing of the doctrines of the philosopher Plato, popular among the poets of the Renaissance and the Romantic period. Platonism is more flexible than Aristotelian Criticism and places more emphasis on the supernatural and unknown aspects of life. Platonism is expressed in the love poetry of the Renaissance, the fourth book of Baldassare Castiglione's *The Book of the Courtier,* and the poetry of William Blake, William Wordsworth, Percy Bysshe Shelley, Friedrich Holderlin, William Butler Yeats, and Wallace Stevens.

Play: See *Drama*

Plot: In literary criticism, this term refers to the pattern of events in a narrative or drama. In its simplest sense, the plot guides the author in composing the work and helps the reader follow the work. Typically, plots exhibit causality and unity and have a beginning, a middle, and an end. Sometimes, however, a plot may consist of a series of disconnected events, in which case it is known as an "episodic plot." In his *Aspects of the Novel,* E. M. Forster distinguishes between a story, defined as a "narrative of events arranged in their time-sequence," and plot, which organizes the events to a "sense of causality." This definition closely mirrors Aristotle's discussion of plot in his *Poetics*.

Poem: In its broadest sense, a composition utilizing rhyme, meter, concrete detail, and expressive language to create a literary experience with emotional and aesthetic appeal. Typical poems include sonnets, odes, elegies, *haiku,* ballads, and free verse.

Poet: An author who writes poetry or verse. The term is also used to refer to an artist or writer who has an exceptional gift for expression, imagination, and energy in the making of art in any form. Well-known poets include Horace, Basho, Sir Philip Sidney, Sir Edmund Spenser, John Donne, Andrew Marvell, Alexander Pope, Jonathan Swift, George Gordon, Lord Byron, John Keats, Christina Rossetti, W. H. Auden, Stevie Smith, and Sylvia Plath.

Poetic Fallacy: See *Pathetic Fallacy*

Poetic Justice: An outcome in a literary work, not necessarily a poem, in which the good are rewarded and the evil are punished, especially in ways that particularly fit their virtues or crimes. For example, a murderer may himself be murdered, or a thief will find himself penniless.

Poetic License: Distortions of fact and literary convention made by a writer—not always a poet—for the sake of the effect gained. Poetic license is closely related to the concept of "artistic freedom." An author exercises poetic license by saying that a pile of money "reaches as high as a mountain" when the pile is actually only a foot or two high.

Poetics: This term has two closely related meanings. It denotes (1) an aesthetic theory in literary criticism about the essence of poetry or (2) rules prescribing the proper methods, content, style, or diction of poetry. The term poetics may also refer to theories about literature in general, not just poetry.

Poetry: In its broadest sense, writing that aims to present ideas and evoke an emotional experience in the reader through the use of meter, imagery, connotative and concrete words, and a carefully constructed structure based on rhythmic patterns. Poetry typically relies on words and expressions that have several layers of meaning. It also makes use of the effects of regular rhythm on the ear and may make a strong appeal to the senses through the use of imagery. Edgar Allan Poe's "Annabel Lee" and Walt Whitman's *Leaves of Grass* are famous examples of poetry.

Point of View: The narrative perspective from which a literary work is presented to the reader. There are four traditional points of view. The "third person omniscient" gives the reader a "godlike" perspective, unrestricted by time or place, from which to see actions and look into the minds of characters. This allows the author to comment openly on characters and events in the work. The "third person" point of view presents the events of the story from outside of any single character's perception, much like the omniscient point of view, but the reader must understand the action as it takes place and without any special insight into characters' minds or motivations. The "first person" or "personal" point of view relates events as they are perceived by a single character. The main character "tells" the story and may offer opinions about the action and characters which differ from those of the author. Much less common than omniscient, third person, and first person is the "second person" point of view, wherein the author tells the story as if it is happening to the reader. James Thurber employs the omniscient point of view in his short story "The Secret Life of Walter Mitty." Ernest Hemingway's "A Clean, Well-Lighted Place" is a short story told from the third person point of view. Mark Twain's novel *Huck Finn* is presented from the first person viewpoint. Jay McInerney's *Bright Lights, Big City* is an example of a novel which uses the second person point of view.

Polemic: A work in which the author takes a stand on a controversial subject, such as abortion or religion. Such works are often extremely argumentative or provocative. Classic examples of polemics include John Milton's *Aeropagitica* and Thomas Paine's *The American Crisis.*

Pornography: Writing intended to provoke feelings of lust in the reader. Such works are often condemned by critics and teachers, but those which can be shown to have literary value are viewed less harshly. Literary works that have been described as pornographic include Ovid's *The Art of Love,* Margaret of Angouleme's *Heptameron,* John Cleland's *Memoirs of a Woman of Pleasure; or, the Life of Fanny Hill,* the anonymous *My Secret Life,* D. H. Lawrence's *Lady Chatterley's Lover,* and Vladimir Nabokov's *Lolita.*

Post-Aesthetic Movement: An artistic response made by African Americans to the black aesthetic movement of the 1960s and early '70s. Writers since that time have adopted a somewhat different tone in their work, with less emphasis placed on the disparity between black and white in the United States. In the words of post-aesthetic authors such as Toni Morrison, John Edgar Wideman, and Kristin Hunter, African Americans are portrayed as looking inward for answers to their own questions, rather than always looking to the outside world. Two well-known examples of works produced as part of the post-aesthetic movement are the Pulitzer Prize-winning novels *The Color Purple* by Alice Walker and *Beloved* by Toni Morrison.

Postmodernism: Writing from the 1960s forward characterized by experimentation and continuing to apply some of the fundamentals of modernism, which included existentialism and alienation. Postmodernists have gone a step further in the rejection of tradition begun with the modernists by also rejecting traditional forms, preferring the anti-novel over the novel and the anti-hero over the hero. Postmodern writers include Alain Robbe-Grillet, Thomas Pynchon, Margaret Drabble, John Fowles, Adolfo Bioy-Casares, and Gabriel Garcia Marquez.

Pre-Raphaelites: A circle of writers and artists in mid nineteenth-century England. Valuing the pre-Renaissance artistic qualities of religious symbolism, lavish pictorialism, and natural sensuousness, the Pre-Raphaelites cultivated a sense of mystery and melancholy that influenced later writers associated with the Symbolist and Decadent movements. The major members of the group include Dante Gabriel Rossetti, Christina Rossetti, Algernon Swinburne, and Walter Pater.

Primitivism: The belief that primitive peoples were nobler and less flawed than civilized peoples because they had not been subjected to the tainting influence of society. Examples of literature espousing primitivism include Aphra Behn's *Oroonoko: Or, The History of the Royal Slave,* Jean-Jacques Rousseau's *Julie ou la Nouvelle Heloise,* Oliver Goldsmith's *The Deserted Village,* the poems of Robert Burns, Herman Melville's stories *Typee, Omoo,* and *Mardi,* many poems of William Butler Yeats and Robert Frost, and William Golding's novel *Lord of the Flies.*

Projective Verse: A form of free verse in which the poet's breathing pattern determines the lines of the poem. Poets who advocate projective verse are against all formal structures in writing, including meter and form. Besides its creators, Robert Creeley, Robert Duncan, and Charles Olson, two other well-known projective verse poets are Denise Levertov and LeRoi Jones (Amiri Baraka). Also known as Breath Verse.

Prologue: An introductory section of a literary work. It often contains information establishing the situation of the characters or presents information about the setting, time period, or action. In drama, the prologue is spoken by a chorus or by one of the principal characters. In the "General Prologue" of *The Canterbury Tales,* Geoffrey Chaucer describes the main characters and establishes the setting and purpose of the work.

Prose: A literary medium that attempts to mirror the language of everyday speech. It is distinguished from poetry by its use of unmetered, unrhymed language consisting of logically related sentences. Prose is usually grouped into paragraphs that form a cohesive whole such as an essay or a novel. Recognized masters of English prose writing include Sir Thomas Malory, William Caxton, Raphael Holinshed, Joseph Addison, Mark Twain, and Ernest Hemingway.

Prosopopoeia: See *Personification*

Protagonist: The central character of a story who serves as a focus for its themes and incidents and as the principal rationale for its development. The protagonist is sometimes referred to in discussions of modern literature as the hero or anti-hero. Well-known protagonists are Hamlet in William Shakespeare's *Hamlet* and Jay Gatsby in F. Scott Fitzgerald's *The Great Gatsby.*

Protest Fiction: Protest fiction has as its primary purpose the protesting of some social injustice, such as racism or discrimination. One example of protest fiction is a series of five novels by Chester Himes, beginning in 1945 with *If He Hollers Let Him Go* and ending in 1955 with *The Primitive.* These works depict the destructive effects of race and gender stereotyping in the context of interracial relationships. Another African American author whose works often revolve around themes of social protest is John Oliver Killens. James Baldwin's essay "Everybody's Protest Novel" generated controversy by attacking the authors of protest fiction.

Proverb: A brief, sage saying that expresses a truth about life in a striking manner. "They are not all cooks who carry long knives" is an example of a proverb.

Pseudonym: A name assumed by a writer, most often intended to prevent his or her identification as the author of a work. Two or more authors may work together under one pseudonym, or an author may use a different name for each genre he or she publishes in. Some publishing companies maintain "house pseudonyms," under which any number of authors may write installations in a series. Some authors also choose a pseudonym over their real names the way an actor may use a stage name. Examples of pseudonyms (with the author's real name in parentheses) include Voltaire (Francois-Marie Arouet), Novalis (Friedrich von Hardenberg), Currer Bell (Charlotte Bronte), Ellis Bell (Emily Bronte), George Eliot (Maryann Evans), Honorio Bustos Donmecq (Adolfo Bioy-Casares and Jorge Luis Borges), and Richard Bachman (Stephen King).

Pun: A play on words that have similar sounds but different meanings. A serious example of the pun is from John Donne's "A Hymne to God the Father": Sweare by thyself, that at my death thy sonne Shall shine as he shines now, and hereto fore; And, having done that, Thou haste done; I fear no more.

Pure Poetry: poetry written without instructional intent or moral purpose that aims only to please a reader by its imagery or musical flow. The term pure poetry is used as the antonym of the term "didacticism." The poetry of Edgar Allan Poe, Stephane Mallarme, Paul Verlaine, Paul Valery, Juan Ramoz Jimenez, and Jorge Guillen offer examples of pure poetry.

Q

Quatrain: A four-line stanza of a poem or an entire poem consisting of four lines. The following quatrain is from Robert Herrick's "To Live Merrily, and to Trust to Good Verses": Round, round, the root do's run; And being ravisht thus, Come, I will drink a Tun To my *Propertius.*

R

Raisonneur: A character in a drama who functions as a spokesperson for the dramatist's views. The *raisonneur* typically observes the play without becoming central to its action. *Raisonneurs* were very common in plays of the nineteenth century.

Realism: A nineteenth-century European literary movement that sought to portray familiar characters, situations, and settings in a realistic manner. This was done primarily by using an objective narrative point of view and through the buildup of accurate detail. The standard for success of any realistic work depends on how faithfully it transfers common experience into fictional forms. The realistic method may be altered or extended, as in stream of consciousness writing, to record highly subjective experience. Seminal authors in the tradition of Realism include Honore de Balzac, Gustave Flaubert, and Henry James.

Refrain: A phrase repeated at intervals throughout a poem. A refrain may appear at the end of each stanza or at less regular intervals. It may be altered slightly at each appearance. Some refrains are nonsense expressions—as with "Nevermore" in Edgar Allan Poe's "The Raven"—that seem to take on a different significance with each use.

Renaissance: The period in European history that marked the end of the Middle Ages. It began in Italy in the late fourteenth century. In broad terms, it is usually seen as spanning the fourteenth, fifteenth, and sixteenth centuries, although it did not reach Great Britain, for example, until the 1480s or so. The Renaissance saw an awakening in almost every sphere of human activity, especially science, philosophy, and the arts. The period is best defined by the emergence of a general philosophy that emphasized the importance of the intellect, the individual, and world affairs. It contrasts strongly with the medieval worldview, characterized by the dominant concerns of faith, the social collective, and spiritual salvation. Prominent writers during the Renaissance include Niccolo Machiavelli and Baldassare Castiglione in Italy, Miguel de Cervantes and Lope de Vega in Spain, Jean Froissart and Francois Rabelais in France, Sir Thomas More and Sir Philip Sidney in England, and Desiderius Erasmus in Holland.

Repartee: Conversation featuring snappy retorts and witticisms. Masters of *repartee* include Sydney Smith, Charles Lamb, and Oscar Wilde. An example is recorded in the meeting of "Beau" Nash and John Wesley: Nash said, "I never make way for a fool," to which Wesley responded, "Don't you? I always do," and stepped aside.

Resolution: The portion of a story following the climax, in which the conflict is resolved. The resolution of Jane Austen's *Northanger Abbey* is neatly summed up in the following sentence: "Henry and Catherine were married, the bells rang and every body smiled."

Restoration: See *Restoration Age*

Restoration Age: A period in English literature beginning with the crowning of Charles II in 1660 and running to about 1700. The era, which was characterized by a reaction against Puritanism, was the first great age of the comedy of manners. The finest literature of the era is typically witty and urbane, and often lewd. Prominent Restoration Age writers include William Congreve, Samuel Pepys, John Dryden, and John Milton.

Revenge Tragedy: A dramatic form popular during the Elizabethan Age, in which the protagonist, directed by the ghost of his murdered father or son, inflicts retaliation upon a powerful villain. Notable features of the revenge tragedy include violence, bizarre criminal acts, intrigue, insanity, a hesitant protagonist, and the use of soliloquy. Thomas Kyd's *Spanish Tragedy* is the first example of revenge tragedy in English, and William Shakespeare's *Hamlet* is perhaps the best. Extreme examples of revenge tragedy, such as John Webster's *The Duchess of Malfi,* are labeled "tragedies of blood." Also known as Tragedy of Blood.

Revista: The Spanish term for a vaudeville musical revue. Examples of *revistas* include Antonio Guzman Aguilera's *Mexico para los mexicanos,* Daniel Vanegas's *Maldito jazz,* and Don Catarino's *Whiskey, morfina y marihuana* and *El desterrado.*

Rhetoric: In literary criticism, this term denotes the art of ethical persuasion. In its strictest sense, rhetoric adheres to various principles developed since classical times for arranging facts and ideas in a clear, persuasive, appealing manner. The term is also used to refer to effective prose in general and theories of or methods for composing effective prose. Classical examples of rhetorics include *The Rhetoric of Aristotle,* Quintillian's *Institutio Oratoria,* and Cicero's *Ad Herennium.*

Rhetorical Question: A question intended to provoke thought, but not an expressed answer, in the reader. It is most commonly used in oratory and other persuasive genres. The following lines from Thomas Gray's "Elegy Written in a Country Churchyard" ask rhetorical questions: Can storied urn or animated bust Back to its mansion call the fleeting breath? Can Honour's voice provoke the silent dust, Or Flattery soothe the dull cold ear of Death?

Rhyme: When used as a noun in literary criticism, this term generally refers to a poem in which words sound identical or very similar and appear in parallel positions in two or more lines. Rhymes are classified into different types according to where they fall in a line or stanza or according to the degree of similarity they exhibit in their spellings and sounds. Some major types of rhyme are "masculine" rhyme, "feminine" rhyme, and "triple" rhyme. In a masculine rhyme, the rhyming sound falls in a single accented syllable, as with "heat" and "eat." Feminine rhyme is a rhyme of two syllables, one stressed and one unstressed, as with "merry" and "tarry." Triple rhyme matches the sound of the accented syllable and the two unaccented syllables that follow: "narrative" and "declarative." Robert Browning alternates feminine and masculine rhymes in his "Soliloquy of the Spanish Cloister": Gr-r-r—there go, my heart's abhorrence! Water your damned flower-pots, do! If hate killed men, Brother Lawrence, God's blood, would not mine kill you! What? Your myrtle-bush wants trimming? Oh, that rose has prior claims—Needs its leaden vase filled brimming? Hell dry you up with flames! Triple rhymes can be found in Thomas Hood's "Bridge of Sighs," George Gordon Byron's satirical verse, and Ogden Nash's comic poems.

Rhyme Royal: A stanza of seven lines composed in iambic pentameter and rhymed *ababbcc.* The name is said to be a tribute to King James I of Scotland, who made much use of the form in his poetry. Examples of rhyme royal include Geoffrey Chaucer's *The Parlement of Foules,* William Shakespeare's *The Rape of Lucrece,* William Morris's *The Early Paradise,* and John Masefield's *The Widow in the Bye Street.*

Rhyme Scheme: See *Rhyme*

Rhythm: A regular pattern of sound, time intervals, or events occurring in writing, most often and most discernably in poetry. Regular, reliable rhythm is known to be soothing to humans, while interrupted, unpredictable, or rapidly changing rhythm is disturbing. These effects are known to authors, who use them to produce a desired reaction in the reader. An example of a form of irregular rhythm is sprung rhythm poetry; quantitative verse, on the other hand, is very regular in its rhythm.

Rising Action: The part of a drama where the plot becomes increasingly complicated. Rising action leads up to the climax, or turning point, of a drama. The final "chase scene" of an action film is generally the rising action which culminates in the film's climax.

Rococo: A style of European architecture that flourished in the eighteenth century, especially in France. The most notable features of *rococo* are its extensive use of ornamentation and its themes of lightness, gaiety, and intimacy. In literary criticism, the term is often used disparagingly to refer to a decadent or over-ornamental style. Alexander Pope's "The Rape of the Lock" is an example of literary *rococo.*

Roman a clef: A French phrase meaning "novel with a key." It refers to a narrative in which real persons are portrayed under fictitious names. Jack Kerouac, for example, portrayed various real-life beat generation figures under fictitious names in his *On the Road.*

Romance: A broad term, usually denoting a narrative with exotic, exaggerated, often idealized characters, scenes, and themes. Nathaniel Hawthorne called his *The House of the Seven Gables* and *The Marble Faun* romances in order to distinguish them from clearly realistic works.

Romantic Age: See *Romanticism*

Romanticism: This term has two widely accepted meanings. In historical criticism, it refers to a European intellectual and artistic movement of the late eighteenth and early nineteenth centuries that sought greater freedom of personal expression than that allowed by the strict rules of literary form and logic of the eighteenth-century neoclassicists. The Romantics preferred emotional and imaginative expression to rational analysis. They considered the individual to be at the center of all experience and so placed him or her at the center of their art. The Romantics believed that the creative imagination reveals nobler truths— unique feelings and attitudes—than those that could be discovered by logic or by scientific examination.

Both the natural world and the state of childhood were important sources for revelations of "eternal truths." "Romanticism" is also used as a general term to refer to a type of sensibility found in all periods of literary history and usually considered to be in opposition to the principles of classicism. In this sense, Romanticism signifies any work or philosophy in which the exotic or dreamlike figure strongly, or that is devoted to individualistic expression, self-analysis, or a pursuit of a higher realm of knowledge than can be discovered by human reason. Prominent Romantics include Jean-Jacques Rousseau, William Wordsworth, John Keats, Lord Byron, and Johann Wolfgang von Goethe.

Romantics: See *Romanticism*

Russian Symbolism: A Russian poetic movement, derived from French symbolism, that flourished between 1894 and 1910. While some Russian Symbolists continued in the French tradition, stressing aestheticism and the importance of suggestion above didactic intent, others saw their craft as a form of mystical worship, and themselves as mediators between the supernatural and the mundane. Russian symbolists include Aleksandr Blok, Vyacheslav Ivanovich Ivanov, Fyodor Sologub, Andrey Bely, Nikolay Gumilyov, and Vladimir Sergeyevich Solovyov.

S

Satire: A work that uses ridicule, humor, and wit to criticize and provoke change in human nature and institutions. There are two major types of satire: "formal" or "direct" satire speaks directly to the reader or to a character in the work; "indirect" satire relies upon the ridiculous behavior of its characters to make its point. Formal satire is further divided into two manners: the "Horatian," which ridicules gently, and the "Juvenalian," which derides its subjects harshly and bitterly. Voltaire's novella *Candide* is an indirect satire. Jonathan Swift's essay "A Modest Proposal" is a Juvenalian satire.

Scansion: The analysis or "scanning" of a poem to determine its meter and often its rhyme scheme. The most common system of scansion uses accents (slanted lines drawn above syllables) to show stressed syllables, breves (curved lines drawn above syllables) to show unstressed syllables, and vertical lines to separate each foot. In the first line of John Keats's *Endymion*, "A thing of beauty is a joy forever:" the word "thing," the first syllable of "beauty," the word "joy," and the second syllable of "forever" are stressed, while the words "A" and "of," the second syllable of "beauty," the word "a,"

and the first and third syllables of "forever" are unstressed. In the second line: "Its loveliness increases; it will never" a pair of vertical lines separate the foot ending with "increases" and the one beginning with "it."

Scene: A subdivision of an act of a drama, consisting of continuous action taking place at a single time and in a single location. The beginnings and endings of scenes may be indicated by clearing the stage of actors and props or by the entrances and exits of important characters. The first act of William Shakespeare's *Winter's Tale* is comprised of two scenes.

Science Fiction: A type of narrative about or based upon real or imagined scientific theories and technology. Science fiction is often peopled with alien creatures and set on other planets or in different dimensions. Karel Capek's *R.U.R.* is a major work of science fiction.

Second Person: See *Point of View*

Semiotics: The study of how literary forms and conventions affect the meaning of language. Semioticians include Ferdinand de Saussure, Charles Sanders Pierce, Claude Levi-Strauss, Jacques Lacan, Michel Foucault, Jacques Derrida, Roland Barthes, and Julia Kristeva.

Sestet: Any six-line poem or stanza. Examples of the sestet include the last six lines of the Petrarchan sonnet form, the stanza form of Robert Burns's "A Poet's Welcome to his love-begotten Daughter," and the sestina form in W. H. Auden's "Paysage Moralise."

Setting: The time, place, and culture in which the action of a narrative takes place. The elements of setting may include geographic location, characters' physical and mental environments, prevailing cultural attitudes, or the historical time in which the action takes place. Examples of settings include the romanticized Scotland in Sir Walter Scott's "Waverley" novels, the French provincial setting in Gustave Flaubert's *Madame Bovary,* the fictional Wessex country of Thomas Hardy's novels, and the small towns of southern Ontario in Alice Munro's short stories.

Shakespearean Sonnet: See *Sonnet*

Signifying Monkey: A popular trickster figure in black folklore, with hundreds of tales about this character documented since the 19th century. Henry Louis Gates Jr. examines the history of the signifying monkey in *The Signifying Monkey: Towards a Theory of Afro-American Literary Criticism,* published in 1988.

Simile: A comparison, usually using "like" or "as", of two essentially dissimilar things, as in "coffee as cold as ice" or "He sounded like a broken record." The title of Ernest Hemingway's "Hills Like White Elephants" contains a simile.

Slang: A type of informal verbal communication that is generally unacceptable for formal writing. Slang words and phrases are often colorful exaggerations used to emphasize the speaker's point; they may also be shortened versions of an often-used word or phrase. Examples of American slang from the 1990s include "yuppie" (an acronym for Young Urban Professional), "awesome" (for "excellent"), wired (for "nervous" or "excited"), and "chill out" (for relax).

Slant Rhyme: See *Consonance*

Slave Narrative: Autobiographical accounts of American slave life as told by escaped slaves. These works first appeared during the abolition movement of the 1830s through the 1850s. Olaudah Equiano's *The Interesting Narrative of Olaudah Equiano, or Gustavus Vassa, The African* and Harriet Ann Jacobs's *Incidents in the Life of a Slave Girl* are examples of the slave narrative.

Social Realism: See *Socialist Realism*

Socialist Realism: The Socialist Realism school of literary theory was proposed by Maxim Gorky and established as a dogma by the first Soviet Congress of Writers. It demanded adherence to a communist worldview in works of literature. Its doctrines required an objective viewpoint comprehensible to the working classes and themes of social struggle featuring strong proletarian heroes. A successful work of socialist realism is Nikolay Ostrovsky's *Kak zakalyalas stal (How the Steel Was Tempered)*. Also known as Social Realism.

Soliloquy: A monologue in a drama used to give the audience information and to develop the speaker's character. It is typically a projection of the speaker's innermost thoughts. Usually delivered while the speaker is alone on stage, a soliloquy is intended to present an illusion of unspoken reflection. A celebrated soliloquy is Hamlet's "To be or not to be" speech in William Shakespeare's *Hamlet*.

Sonnet: A fourteen-line poem, usually composed in iambic pentameter, employing one of several rhyme schemes. There are three major types of sonnets, upon which all other variations of the form are based: the "Petrarchan" or "Italian" sonnet, the "Shakespearean" or "English" sonnet, and the "Spenserian" sonnet. A Petrarchan sonnet consists of an octave rhymed *abbaabba* and a "sestet" rhymed either *cdecde, cdccdc,* or *cdedce.* The octave poses a question or problem, relates a narrative, or puts forth a proposition; the sestet presents a solution to the problem, comments upon the narrative, or applies the proposition put forth in the octave. The Shakespearean sonnet is divided into three quatrains and a couplet rhymed *abab cdcd efef gg.* The couplet provides an epigrammatic comment on the narrative or problem put forth in the quatrains. The Spenserian sonnet uses three quatrains and a couplet like the Shakespearean, but links their three rhyme schemes in this way: *abab bcbc cdcd ee.* The Spenserian sonnet develops its theme in two parts like the Petrarchan, its final six lines resolving a problem, analyzing a narrative, or applying a proposition put forth in its first eight lines. Examples of sonnets can be found in Petrarch's *Canzoniere,* Edmund Spenser's *Amoretti,* Elizabeth Barrett Browning's *Sonnets from the Portuguese,* Rainer Maria Rilke's *Sonnets to Orpheus,* and Adrienne Rich's poem "The Insusceptibles."

Spenserian Sonnet: See *Sonnet*

Spenserian Stanza: A nine-line stanza having eight verses in iambic pentameter, its ninth verse in iambic hexameter, and the rhyme scheme ababbcbcc. This stanza form was first used by Edmund Spenser in his allegorical poem *The Faerie Queene.*

Spondee: In poetry meter, a foot consisting of two long or stressed syllables occurring together. This form is quite rare in English verse, and is usually composed of two monosyllabic words. The first foot in the following line from Robert Burns's "Green Grow the Rashes" is an example of a spondee: Green grow the rashes, O

Sprung Rhythm: Versification using a specific number of accented syllables per line but disregarding the number of unaccented syllables that fall in each line, producing an irregular rhythm in the poem. Gerard Manley Hopkins, who coined the term "sprung rhythm," is the most notable practitioner of this technique.

Stanza: A subdivision of a poem consisting of lines grouped together, often in recurring patterns of rhyme, line length, and meter. Stanzas may also serve as units of thought in a poem much like paragraphs in prose. Examples of stanza forms include the quatrain, *terza rima, ottava rima,* Spenserian, and the so-called *In Memoriam* stanza from Alfred, Lord Tennyson's poem by that title. The following is an example of the latter form: Love is and was my lord and king, And in his presence I attend To hear the tidings of my friend, Which every hour his couriers bring.

Stereotype: A stereotype was originally the name for a duplication made during the printing process; this led to its modern definition as a person or thing that is (or is assumed to be) the same as all others of its type. Common stereotypical characters include the absent-minded professor, the nagging wife, the troublemaking teenager, and the kind-hearted grandmother.

Stream of Consciousness: A narrative technique for rendering the inward experience of a character. This technique is designed to give the impression of an ever-changing series of thoughts, emotions, images, and memories in the spontaneous and seemingly illogical order that they occur in life. The textbook example of stream of consciousness is the last section of James Joyce's *Ulysses.*

Structuralism: A twentieth-century movement in literary criticism that examines how literary texts arrive at their meanings, rather than the meanings themselves. There are two major types of structuralist analysis: one examines the way patterns of linguistic structures unify a specific text and emphasize certain elements of that text, and the other interprets the way literary forms and conventions affect the meaning of language itself. Prominent structuralists include Michel Foucault, Roman Jakobson, and Roland Barthes.

Structure: The form taken by a piece of literature. The structure may be made obvious for ease of understanding, as in nonfiction works, or may obscured for artistic purposes, as in some poetry or seemingly "unstructured" prose. Examples of common literary structures include the plot of a narrative, the acts and scenes of a drama, and such poetic forms as the Shakespearean sonnet and the Pindaric ode.

Sturm und Drang: A German term meaning "storm and stress." It refers to a German literary movement of the 1770s and 1780s that reacted against the order and rationalism of the enlightenment, focusing instead on the intense experience of extraordinary individuals. Highly romantic, works of this movement, such as Johann Wolfgang von Goethe's *Gotz von Berlichingen,* are typified by realism, rebelliousness, and intense emotionalism.

Style: A writer's distinctive manner of arranging words to suit his or her ideas and purpose in writing. The unique imprint of the author's personality upon his or her writing, style is the product of an author's way of arranging ideas and his or her use of diction, different sentence structures, rhythm, figures of speech, rhetorical principles, and other elements of composition. Styles may be classified according to period (Metaphysical, Augustan, Geor-

gian), individual authors (Chaucerian, Miltonic, Jamesian), level (grand, middle, low, plain), or language (scientific, expository, poetic, journalistic).

Subject: The person, event, or theme at the center of a work of literature. A work may have one or more subjects of each type, with shorter works tending to have fewer and longer works tending to have more. The subjects of James Baldwin's novel *Go Tell It on the Mountain* include the themes of father-son relationships, religious conversion, black life, and sexuality. The subjects of Anne Frank's *Diary of a Young Girl* include Anne and her family members as well as World War II, the Holocaust, and the themes of war, isolation, injustice, and racism.

Subjectivity: Writing that expresses the author's personal feelings about his subject, and which may or may not include factual information about the subject. Subjectivity is demonstrated in James Joyce's *Portrait of the Artist as a Young Man,* Samuel Butler's *The Way of All Flesh,* and Thomas Wolfe's *Look Homeward, Angel.*

Subplot: A secondary story in a narrative. A subplot may serve as a motivating or complicating force for the main plot of the work, or it may provide emphasis for, or relief from, the main plot. The conflict between the Capulets and the Montagues in William Shakespeare's *Romeo and Juliet* is an example of a subplot.

Surrealism: A term introduced to criticism by Guillaume Apollinaire and later adopted by Andre Breton. It refers to a French literary and artistic movement founded in the 1920s. The Surrealists sought to express unconscious thoughts and feelings in their works. The best-known technique used for achieving this aim was automatic writing—transcriptions of spontaneous outpourings from the unconscious. The Surrealists proposed to unify the contrary levels of conscious and unconscious, dream and reality, objectivity and subjectivity into a new level of "super-realism." Surrealism can be found in the poetry of Paul Eluard, Pierre Reverdy, and Louis Aragon, among others.

Suspense: A literary device in which the author maintains the audience's attention through the buildup of events, the outcome of which will soon be revealed. Suspense in William Shakespeare's *Hamlet* is sustained throughout by the question of whether or not the Prince will achieve what he has been instructed to do and of what he intends to do.

Syllogism: A method of presenting a logical argument. In its most basic form, the syllogism consists of a major premise, a minor premise, and a conclusion. An example of a syllogism is: Major premise:

When it snows, the streets get wet. Minor premise: It is snowing. Conclusion: The streets are wet.

Symbol: Something that suggests or stands for something else without losing its original identity. In literature, symbols combine their literal meaning with the suggestion of an abstract concept. Literary symbols are of two types: those that carry complex associations of meaning no matter what their contexts, and those that derive their suggestive meaning from their functions in specific literary works. Examples of symbols are sunshine suggesting happiness, rain suggesting sorrow, and storm clouds suggesting despair.

Symbolism: This term has two widely accepted meanings. In historical criticism, it denotes an early modernist literary movement initiated in France during the nineteenth century that reacted against the prevailing standards of realism. Writers in this movement aimed to evoke, indirectly and symbolically, an order of being beyond the material world of the five senses. Poetic expression of personal emotion figured strongly in the movement, typically by means of a private set of symbols uniquely identifiable with the individual poet. The principal aim of the Symbolists was to express in words the highly complex feelings that grew out of everyday contact with the world. In a broader sense, the term "symbolism" refers to the use of one object to represent another. Early members of the Symbolist movement included the French authors Charles Baudelaire and Arthur Rimbaud; William Butler Yeats, James Joyce, and T. S. Eliot were influenced as the movement moved to Ireland, England, and the United States. Examples of the concept of symbolism include a flag that stands for a nation or movement, or an empty cupboard used to suggest hopelessness, poverty, and despair.

Symbolist: See *Symbolism*

Symbolist Movement: See *Symbolism*

Sympathetic Fallacy: See *Affective Fallacy*

T

Tale: A story told by a narrator with a simple plot and little character development. Tales are usually relatively short and often carry a simple message. Examples of tales can be found in the work of Rudyard Kipling, Somerset Maugham, Saki, Anton Chekhov, Guy de Maupassant, and Armistead Maupin.

Tall Tale: A humorous tale told in a straightforward, credible tone but relating absolutely impossible events or feats of the characters. Such tales were commonly told of frontier adventures during the settlement of the west in the United States. Tall tales have been spun around such legendary heroes as Mike Fink, Paul Bunyan, Davy Crockett, Johnny Appleseed, and Captain Stormalong as well as the real-life William F. Cody and Annie Oakley. Literary use of tall tales can be found in Washington Irving's *History of New York,* Mark Twain's *Life on the Mississippi,* and in the German R. F. Raspe's *Baron Munchausen's Narratives of His Marvellous Travels and Campaigns in Russia.*

Tanka: A form of Japanese poetry similar to *haiku.* A *tanka* is five lines long, with the lines containing five, seven, five, seven, and seven syllables respectively. Skilled *tanka* authors include Ishikawa Takuboku, Masaoka Shiki, Amy Lowell, and Adelaide Crapsey.

Teatro Grottesco: See *Theater of the Grotesque*

Terza Rima: A three-line stanza form in poetry in which the rhymes are made on the last word of each line in the following manner: the first and third lines of the first stanza, then the second line of the first stanza and the first and third lines of the second stanza, and so on with the middle line of any stanza rhyming with the first and third lines of the following stanza. An example of *terza rima* is Percy Bysshe Shelley's "The Triumph of Love": As in that trance of wondrous thought I lay This was the tenour of my waking dream. Methought I sate beside a public way Thick strewn with summer dust, and a great stream Of people there was hurrying to and fro Numerous as gnats upon the evening gleam, . . .

Tetrameter: See *Meter*

Textual Criticism: A branch of literary criticism that seeks to establish the authoritative text of a literary work. Textual critics typically compare all known manuscripts or printings of a single work in order to assess the meanings of differences and revisions. This procedure allows them to arrive at a definitive version that (supposedly) corresponds to the author's original intention. Textual criticism was applied during the Renaissance to salvage the classical texts of Greece and Rome, and modern works have been studied, for instance, to undo deliberate correction or censorship, as in the case of novels by Stephen Crane and Theodore Dreiser.

Theater of Cruelty: Term used to denote a group of theatrical techniques designed to eliminate the psychological and emotional distance between actors and audience. This concept, introduced in the 1930s in France, was intended to inspire a more intense theatrical experience than conventional theater allowed. The "cruelty" of this dramatic theory signified not sadism but heightened actor/audience involvement in the dramatic event. The theater of cruelty was theorized by Antonin Artaud in his *Le Theatre et son double* (*The Theatre and Its Double*), and also appears in the work of Jerzy Grotowski, Jean Genet, Jean Vilar, and Arthur Adamov, among others.

Theater of the Absurd: A post-World War II dramatic trend characterized by radical theatrical innovations. In works influenced by the Theater of the absurd, nontraditional, sometimes grotesque characterizations, plots, and stage sets reveal a meaningless universe in which human values are irrelevant. Existentialist themes of estrangement, absurdity, and futility link many of the works of this movement. The principal writers of the Theater of the Absurd are Samuel Beckett, Eugene Ionesco, Jean Genet, and Harold Pinter.

Theater of the Grotesque: An Italian theatrical movement characterized by plays written around the ironic and macabre aspects of daily life in the World War I era. Theater of the Grotesque was named after the play *The Mask and the Face* by Luigi Chiarelli, which was described as "a grotesque in three acts." The movement influenced the work of Italian dramatist Luigi Pirandello, author of *Right You Are, If You Think You Are.* Also known as *Teatro Grottesco*.

Theme: The main point of a work of literature. The term is used interchangeably with thesis. The theme of William Shakespeare's *Othello*—jealousy—is a common one.

Thesis: A thesis is both an essay and the point argued in the essay. Thesis novels and thesis plays share the quality of containing a thesis which is supported through the action of the story. A master's thesis and a doctoral dissertation are two theses required of graduate students.

Thesis Play: See *Thesis*

Three Unities: See *Unities*

Tone: The author's attitude toward his or her audience may be deduced from the tone of the work. A formal tone may create distance or convey politeness, while an informal tone may encourage a friendly, intimate, or intrusive feeling in the reader. The author's attitude toward his or her subject matter may also be deduced from the tone of the words he or she uses in discussing it. The tone of John F. Kennedy's speech which included the appeal to "ask not what your country can do for you" was intended to instill feelings of camaraderie and national pride in listeners.

Tragedy: A drama in prose or poetry about a noble, courageous hero of excellent character who, because of some tragic character flaw or *hamartia*, brings ruin upon him- or herself. Tragedy treats its subjects in a dignified and serious manner, using poetic language to help evoke pity and fear and bring about catharsis, a purging of these emotions. The tragic form was practiced extensively by the ancient Greeks. In the Middle Ages, when classical works were virtually unknown, tragedy came to denote any works about the fall of persons from exalted to low conditions due to any reason: fate, vice, weakness, etc. According to the classical definition of tragedy, such works present the "pathetic"—that which evokes pity—rather than the tragic. The classical form of tragedy was revived in the sixteenth century; it flourished especially on the Elizabethan stage. In modern times, dramatists have attempted to adapt the form to the needs of modern society by drawing their heroes from the ranks of ordinary men and women and defining the nobility of these heroes in terms of spirit rather than exalted social standing. The greatest classical example of tragedy is Sophocles' *Oedipus Rex*. The "pathetic" derivation is exemplified in "The Monk's Tale" in Geoffrey Chaucer's *Canterbury Tales*. Notable works produced during the sixteenth century revival include William Shakespeare's *Hamlet, Othello,* and *King Lear*. Modern dramatists working in the tragic tradition include Henrik Ibsen, Arthur Miller, and Eugene O'Neill.

Tragedy of Blood: See *Revenge Tragedy*

Tragic Flaw: In a tragedy, the quality within the hero or heroine which leads to his or her downfall. Examples of the tragic flaw include Othello's jealousy and Hamlet's indecisiveness, although most great tragedies defy such simple interpretation.

Transcendentalism: An American philosophical and religious movement, based in New England from around 1835 until the Civil War. Transcendentalism was a form of American romanticism that had its roots abroad in the works of Thomas Carlyle, Samuel Coleridge, and Johann Wolfgang von Goethe. The Transcendentalists stressed the importance of intuition and subjective experience in communication with God. They rejected religious dogma and texts in favor of mysticism and scientific naturalism. They pursued truths that lie beyond the "colorless" realms perceived by reason and the senses and were active social reformers in public education, women's rights, and the abolition of slavery. Prominent members of the group include Ralph Waldo Emerson and Henry David Thoreau.

Trickster: A character or figure common in Native American and African literature who uses his ingenuity to defeat enemies and escape difficult situations. Tricksters are most often animals, such as the spider, hare, or coyote, although they may take the form of humans as well. Examples of trickster tales include Thomas King's *A Coyote Columbus Story,* Ashley F. Bryan's *The Dancing Granny* and Ishmael Reed's *The Last Days of Louisiana Red.*

Trimeter: See *Meter*

Triple Rhyme: See *Rhyme*

Trochee: See *Foot*

U

Understatement: See *Irony*

Unities: Strict rules of dramatic structure, formulated by Italian and French critics of the Renaissance and based loosely on the principles of drama discussed by Aristotle in his *Poetics.* Foremost among these rules were the three unities of action, time, and place that compelled a dramatist to: (1) construct a single plot with a beginning, middle, and end that details the causal relationships of action and character; (2) restrict the action to the events of a single day; and (3) limit the scene to a single place or city. The unities were observed faithfully by continental European writers until the Romantic Age, but they were never regularly observed in English drama. Modern dramatists are typically more concerned with a unity of impression or emotional effect than with any of the classical unities. The unities are observed in Pierre Corneille's tragedy *Polyeuctes* and Jean-Baptiste Racine's *Phedre.* Also known as Three Unities.

Urban Realism: A branch of realist writing that attempts to accurately reflect the often harsh facts of modern urban existence. Some works by Stephen Crane, Theodore Dreiser, Charles Dickens, Fyodor Dostoyevsky, Emile Zola, Abraham Cahan, and Henry Fuller feature urban realism. Modern examples include Claude Brown's *Manchild in the Promised Land* and Ron Milner's *What the Wine Sellers Buy.*

Utopia: A fictional perfect place, such as "paradise" or "heaven." Early literary utopias were included in Plato's *Republic* and Sir Thomas More's *Utopia,* while more modern utopias can be found in Samuel Butler's *Erewhon,* Theodor Herzka's *A Visit to Freeland,* and H. G. Wells' *A Modern Utopia.*

Utopian: See *Utopia*

Utopianism: See *Utopia*

V

Verisimilitude: Literally, the appearance of truth. In literary criticism, the term refers to aspects of a work of literature that seem true to the reader. Verisimilitude is achieved in the work of Honore de Balzac, Gustave Flaubert, and Henry James, among other late nineteenth-century realist writers.

Vers de societe: See *Occasional Verse*

Vers libre: See *Free Verse*

Verse: A line of metered language, a line of a poem, or any work written in verse. The following line of verse is from the epic poem *Don Juan* by Lord Byron: "My way is to begin with the beginning."

Versification: The writing of verse. Versification may also refer to the meter, rhyme, and other mechanical components of a poem. Composition of a "Roses are red, violets are blue" poem to suit an occasion is a common form of versification practiced by students.

Victorian: Refers broadly to the reign of Queen Victoria of England (1837–1901) and to anything with qualities typical of that era. For example, the qualities of smug narrowmindedness, bourgeois materialism, faith in social progress, and priggish morality are often considered Victorian. This stereotype is contradicted by such dramatic intellectual developments as the theories of Charles Darwin, Karl Marx, and Sigmund Freud (which stirred strong debates in England) and the critical attitudes of serious Victorian writers like Charles Dickens and George Eliot. In literature, the Victorian Period was the great age of the English novel, and the latter part of the era saw the rise of movements such as decadence and symbolism. Works of Victorian literature include the poetry of Robert Browning and Alfred, Lord Tennyson, the criticism of Matthew Arnold and John Ruskin, and the novels of Emily Bronte, William Makepeace Thackeray, and Thomas Hardy. Also known as Victorian Age and Victorian Period.

Victorian Age: See *Victorian*

Victorian Period: See *Victorian*

W

Weltanschauung: A German term referring to a person's worldview or philosophy. Examples of *weltanschauung* include Thomas Hardy's view of the human being as the victim of fate, destiny, or impersonal forces and circumstances, and the disillusioned and laconic cynicism expressed by such poets of the 1930s as W. H. Auden, Sir Stephen Spender, and Sir William Empson.

Weltschmerz: A German term meaning "world pain." It describes a sense of anguish about the nature of existence, usually associated with a melancholy, pessimistic attitude. *Weltschmerz* was expressed in England by George Gordon, Lord Byron in his *Manfred* and *Childe Harold's Pilgrimage,* in France by Viscount de Chateaubriand, Alfred de Vigny, and Alfred de Musset, in Russia by Aleksandr Pushkin and Mikhail Lermontov, in Poland by Juliusz Slowacki, and in America by Nathaniel Hawthorne.

Z

Zarzuela: A type of Spanish operetta. Writers of *zarzuelas* include Lope de Vega and Pedro Calderon.

Zeitgeist: A German term meaning "spirit of the time." It refers to the moral and intellectual trends of a given era. Examples of *zeitgeist* include the preoccupation with the more morbid aspects of dying and death in some Jacobean literature, especially in the works of dramatists Cyril Tourneur and John Webster, and the decadence of the French Symbolists.

Cumulative Author/Title Index

Cumulative
Nationality/Ethnicity Index

Gale, Zona
Miss Lulu Bett: V17
Gardner, Herb
I'm Not Rappaport: V18
A Thousand Clowns: V20
Gerstenberg, Alice
Overtones: V17
Gibson, William
The Miracle Worker: V2
Gilroy, Frank D.
The Subject Was Roses: V17
Glaspell, Susan
Trifles: V8
The Verge: V18
Goldman, James
The Lion in Winter: V20
Goodrich, Frances
The Diary of Anne Frank: V15
Guare, John
The House of Blue Leaves: V8
Six Degrees of Separation: V13
Hackett, Albert
The Diary of Anne Frank: V15
Hammerstein, Oscar II
The King and I: V1
Hanff, Helene
84, Charing Cross Road: V17
Hansberry, Lorraine
A Raisin in the Sun: V2
Hart, Moss
Once in a Lifetime: V10
You Can't Take It with You: V1
Hayes, Joseph
The Desperate Hours: V20
Hecht, Ben
The Front Page: V9
Heggen, Thomas
Mister Roberts: V20
Hellman, Lillian
The Children's Hour: V3
The Little Foxes: V1
Watch on the Rhine: V14
Henley, Beth
Crimes of the Heart: V2
The Miss Firecracker Contest: V21
Hughes, Langston
Mulatto: V18
Hurston, Zora Neale
Mule Bone: V6
Hwang, David Henry
M. Butterfly: V11
The Sound of a Voice: V18
Iizuka, Naomi
36 Views: V21
Inge, William
Bus Stop: V8
Come Back, Little Sheba: V3
Picnic: V5
Kaufman, George S.
Once in a Lifetime: V10
You Can't Take It with You: V1
Kesselring, Joseph
Arsenic and Old Lace: V20

Kingsley, Sidney
Detective Story: V19
Men in White: V14
Kopit, Arthur
Oh Dad, Poor Dad, Mamma's Hung You in the Closet and I'm Feelin' So Sad: V7
Y2K: V14
Kramm, Joseph
The Shrike: V15
Kushner, Tony
Angels in America: V5
Lawrence, Jerome
Inherit the Wind: V2
The Night Thoreau Spent in Jail: V16
Lee, Robert E.
Inherit the Wind: V2
The Night Thoreau Spent in Jail: V16
Leight, Warren
Side Man: V19
Lindsay, Howard
State of the Union: V19
Luce, Clare Boothe
The Women: V19
MacArthur, Charles
The Front Page: V9
MacLeish, Archibald
J. B.: V15
Mamet, David
American Buffalo: V3
Glengarry Glen Ross: V2
A Life in the Theatre: V12
Reunion: V15
Speed-the-Plow: V6
Margulies, Donald
Dinner with Friends: V13
Martin, Steve
WASP: V19
McCullers, Carson
The Member of the Wedding: V5
The Square Root of Wonderful: V18
McNally, Terrence
Love! Valour! Compassion!: V19
Master Class: V16
Medoff, Mark
Children of a Lesser God: V4
Miller, Arthur
All My Sons: V8
The Crucible: V3
Death of a Salesman: V1
Miller, Jason
That Championship Season: V12
Norman, Marsha
'night, Mother: V2
O'Neill, Eugene
Anna Christie: V12
Beyond the Horizon: V16
The Emperor Jones: V6
The Great God Brown: V11
The Hairy Ape: V4
The Iceman Cometh: V5

Long Day's Journey into Night: V2
Mourning Becomes Electra: V9
Strange Interlude: V20
Odets, Clifford
Golden Boy: V17
Rocket to the Moon: V20
Waiting for Lefty: V3
Parks, Suzan-Lori
Topdog/Underdog: V22
Patrick, John
The Teahouse of the August Moon: V13
Pomerance, Bernard
The Elephant Man: V9
Rabe, David
The Basic Training of Pavlo Hummel: V3 Sticks and Bones: V13 Streamers: V8
Rebeck, Theresa
Spike Heels: V11
Rice, Elmer
Street Scene: V12
Rodgers, Richard
The King and I: V1
Rudnick, Paul
I Hate Hamlet: V22
Sackler, Howard
The Great White Hope: V15
Saroyan, William
The Time of Your Life: V17
Schary, Dore
Sunrise at Campobello: V17
Schenkkan, Robert
The Kentucky Cycle: V10
Shange, Ntozake
for colored girls who have con-sidered suicide/when the rain-bow is enuf: V2
Shepard, Sam
Buried Child: V6
Curse of the Starving Class: V14
Fool for Love: V7
True West: V3
Sherman, Martin
Bent: V20
Sherwood, Robert E.
Abe Lincoln in Illinois: V11
Idiot's Delight: V15
The Petrified Forest: V17
Shue, Larry
The Foreigner: V7
Simon, Neil
Biloxi Blues: V12
Brighton Beach Memoirs: V6
Lost in Yonkers: V18
The Odd Couple: V2
Smith, Anna Deavere
Fires in the Mirror: V22
Twilight: Los Angeles, 1992: V2
Stein, Joseph
Fiddler on the Roof: V7
Terry, Megan
Calm Down Mother: V18

Middleton, Thomas
  The Changeling: V22
  A Chaste Maid in Cheapside:
    V18
Nicholson, William
  Shadowlands: V11
Orton, Joe
  Entertaining Mr. Sloane: V3
  What the Butler Saw: V6
Osborne, John
  Look Back in Anger: V4
  Luther: V19
Pinter, Harold
  The Birthday Party: V5
  The Caretaker: V7
  The Homecoming: V3
  Mountain Language: V14
Rattigan, Terence
  The Browning Version: V8
Rice, Tim
  Jesus Christ Superstar: V7
Shaffer, Anthony
  Sleuth: V13
Shaffer, Peter
  Amadeus: V13
  Equus: V5
Shakespeare, William
  Othello: V20
  Romeo and Juliet: V21
Stoppard, Tom
  Arcadia: V5
  Dogg's Hamlet, Cahoot's Macbeth: V16
  Indian Ink: V11
  The Real Thing: V8
  Rosencrantz and Guildenstern Are Dead: V2
  Travesties: V13
Webber, Andrew Lloyd
  Jesus Christ Superstar: V7
Webster, John
  The Duchess of Malfi: V17
  The White Devil: V19
Wheeler, Hugh
  Sweeney Todd: The Demon Barber of Fleet Street: V19

French

Anouilh, Jean
  Antigone: V9
  Becket, or the Honor of God: V19
  Ring Around the Moon: V10
Artaud, Antonin
  The Cenci: V22
Beckett, Samuel
  Endgame: V18
  Krapp's Last Tape: V7
  Waiting for Godot: V2
Corneille, Pierre
  Le Cid: V21
de Beaumarchais, Pierre-Augustin
  The Barber of Seville: V16

The Marriage of Figaro: V14
Duras, Marguerite
  India Song: V21
Genet, Jean
  The Balcony: V10
Jarry, Alfred
  Ubu Roi: V8
Molière
  The Imaginary Invalid: V20
  The Misanthrope: V13
  Tartuffe: V18
Reza, Yasmina
  Art: V19
Rostand, Edmond
  Cyrano de Bergerac: V1
Sartre, Jean-Paul
  No Exit: V5

German

Brecht, Bertolt
  The Good Person of Szechwan: V9
  Mother Courage and Her Children: V5
  The Threepenny Opera: V4
Weiss, Peter
  Marat/Sade: V3

Greek

Aeschylus
  Prometheus Bound: V5
  Seven Against Thebes: V10
Aristophanes
  Lysistrata: V10
Euripides
  The Bacchae: V6
  Iphigenia in Taurus: V4
  Medea: V1
Sophocles
  Ajax: V8
  Antigone: V1
  Electra: V4
  Oedipus Rex: V1

Hispanic

Cruz, Nilo
  Anna in the Tropics: V21
Valdez, Luis
  Zoot Suit: V5

Indochinese

Duras, Marguerite
  India Song: V21

Irish

Beckett, Samuel
  Endgame: V18
  Krapp's Last Tape: V7
  Waiting for Godot: V2

Behan, Brendan
  The Hostage: V7
Friel, Brian
  Dancing at Lughnasa: V11
Leonard, Hugh
  Da: V13
O'Casey, Sean
  Red Roses for Me: V19
Shaw, George Bernard
  Arms and the Man: V22
  Major Barbara: V3
  Man and Superman: V6
  Mrs. Warren's Profession: V19
  Pygmalion: V1
  Saint Joan: V11
Sheridan, Richard Brinsley
  The Critic: V14
  The Rivals: V15
  School for Scandal: V4
Synge, J. M.
  The Playboy of the Western World: V18
Wilde, Oscar
  An Ideal Husband: V21
  The Importance of Being Earnest: V4
  Lady Windermere's Fan: V9
  Salome: V8

Italian

Ginzburg, Natalia
  The Advertisement: V14
Pirandello, Luigi
  Right You Are, If You Think You Are: V9
  Six Characters in Search of an Author: V4

Japanese

Abe, Kobo
  The Man Who Turned into a Stick: V14
Iizuka, Naomi
  36 Views: V21

Jewish

Gardner, Herb
  A Thousand Clowns: V20
Mamet, David
  Reunion: V15
Odets, Clifford
  Rocket to the Moon: V20
Sherman, Martin
  Bent: V20
Simon, Neil
  Lost in Yonkers: V18
Uhry, Alfred
  The Last Night of Ballyhoo: V15

Subject/Theme Index

Topdog/Underdog: 273, 275–276, 278, 289

Cruelty

The Cenci: 66, 68, 71–76

Fires in the Mirror: 138–139, 142–143, 145–147, 149

Machinal: 251–253, 255–258

Topdog/Underdog: 291–292, 294

Culture Clash

I Hate Hamlet: 185

Cynicism

Arms and the Man: 13, 15–16, 19–21

For Services Rendered: 165–166

D

Dadaism

The Cenci: 73

Death

The Cenci: 68, 74

The Changeling: 80–82, 84, 88, 90–91, 97–99, 101, 103–105

Copenhagen: 109, 112, 114–115

Fires in the Mirror: 139, 145, 151–152

Habitat: 167–169, 172, 174–176

The Laramie Project: 213–214, 216, 219–220, 222, 225–226, 228

Machinal: 233–234, 238, 240, 245–246, 248–250, 252–253, 257–258

Topdog/Underdog: 277, 279, 285, 287–290, 296–298

Depression

Off the Map: 266

Depression and Melancholy

I Hate Hamlet: 184–185

Machinal: 250–251

Off the Map: 260–263, 266–267, 269–271

Description

The Laramie Project: 215–216

Despair

Machinal: 231, 237–238

Dialogue

Arms and the Man: 14–15

Copenhagen: 114–122, 126–129

Imaginary Friends: 208

Machinal: 238, 240, 254, 256–258

Topdog/Underdog: 289, 291

Divorce

The Changeling: 98

Machinal: 232, 234

Drama

Arms and the Man: 1, 9–10, 14–15, 17–19, 24–27

The Belle's Stratagem: 39–40, 44–46, 51, 60

The Cenci: 66, 71–75, 77

The Changeling: 79, 86–88, 91–96, 98, 100–101, 103–104

Copenhagen: 126–128, 130

Fires in the Mirror: 150–151

For Services Rendered: 164–165

Habitat: 167, 173–174

I Hate Hamlet: 179, 181–182, 184, 186–193

The Laramie Project: 213–215, 220–221, 223–227

Machinal: 231–232, 236–237, 240, 243, 245–246, 248–250, 252–254, 259

Topdog/Underdog: 273, 289–290

Dreams and Visions

Arms and the Man: 18–20, 22–24

E

Emotions

Arms and the Man: 3, 9, 19

The Belle's Stratagem: 37

The Changeling: 84

Copenhagen: 126, 130

Fires in the Mirror: 143–145, 151–152

Habitat: 167, 172, 175–178

I Hate Hamlet: 187

Imaginary Friends: 208

The Laramie Project: 213, 220–221, 223–226

Machinal: 236–238, 240, 242, 254–255, 257

Off the Map: 262–263, 269–270

Topdog/Underdog: 291

Envy

The Belle's Stratagem: 29, 31, 37

Eternity

I Hate Hamlet: 193, 195

Europe

Arms and the Man: 8, 14, 16–17

The Belle's Stratagem: 29, 31–32, 38–39, 44–46, 50, 61–65

The Cenci: 73–74

The Changeling: 79–80, 86–87

Copenhagen: 107–110, 112–115, 117–120, 123, 127–128, 130–135

For Services Rendered: 154–157, 159–160

Imaginary Friends: 199, 202–204

Machinal: 231, 240

Evil

The Belle's Stratagem: 44, 49, 54, 59

The Cenci: 68, 72–73, 75

The Changeling: 81, 89, 91, 100, 102, 104–106

Copenhagen: 133–135

The Laramie Project: 219, 223

Machinal: 249

Execution

Machinal: 249–250

Expressionism

Machinal: 232, 236–238, 240, 248, 250, 253–255

F

Family Life

The Belle's Stratagem: 46, 48

Farm and Rural Life

Copenhagen: 133–134

Fate

Copenhagen: 113

Fate and Chance

Arms and the Man: 18, 21–23

The Belle's Stratagem: 52, 55–57, 60

The Cenci: 68, 72

The Changeling: 103–106

Copenhagen: 107, 110–115, 126–132

Topdog/Underdog: 275–276, 281, 284, 289, 291, 296–298

Fear and Terror

Arms and the Man: 19–20, 22–23

The Changeling: 103–106

The Laramie Project: 215–216, 219, 221, 224

Machinal: 254–256

Topdog/Underdog: 275, 277–278, 280–281, 283–284, 289

Femininity

The Belle's Stratagem: 47–48

Feminism

The Belle's Stratagem: 29, 37–38, 40

Machinal: 243–246, 253–255, 259

Feminism and Identity

The Belle's Stratagem: 37

Film

I Hate Hamlet: 181–182, 186

The Laramie Project: 214

Off the Map: 260, 269

Foreshadowing

Topdog/Underdog: 296–298

Fortitude and Frailty

Off the Map: 265

Freedom

Machinal: 253, 258

Friendship

Copenhagen: 111

G

Gender Roles

Machinal: 245

Ghost

The Changeling: 104–105

I Hate Hamlet: 179, 181–182, 185–190

God

The Cenci: 76–77

The Laramie Project: 216, 219

Machinal: 257

Greed

For Services Rendered: 156, 158–159

Guilt
The Changeling: 103, 105–106
The Laramie Project: 216, 222
Topdog/Underdog: 277, 283, 287

H

Happiness and Gaiety
The Belle's Stratagem: 50, 52, 57, 61–64
Hate Crimes
The Laramie Project: 219
Hatred
Arms and the Man: 3, 6–8, 10, 13, 14, 16
The Belle's Stratagem: 31, 37, 53–57, 61–63
The Changeling: 91–93, 95–96, 102–105
The Laramie Project: 213, 216, 219, 221, 223–224, 228–229
Heaven
Copenhagen: 109–110, 113
Heroism
Arms and the Man: 2, 5–9, 13–14, 16, 18–23
The Belle's Stratagem: 37–38, 40, 50–55, 57–62, 64
Copenhagen: 120–122
Machinal: 238
Historical Periods
Machinal: 244
History
Copenhagen: 107, 109, 115–116, 119–125, 131–135
Fires in the Mirror: 143–144
Imaginary Friends: 199
Topdog/Underdog: 287, 291–292, 294
Homelessness
The Belle's Stratagem: 44–46, 48
Homosexuality
The Laramie Project: 213, 215–216, 219–222, 227–229
Honor
The Belle's Stratagem: 53, 55–56, 58, 60, 62, 64
Copenhagen: 133–135
Hope
Arms and the Man: 24, 26–27
Off the Map: 271
Hopelessness and Despair
Machinal: 238
Humility
The Belle's Stratagem: 45–46, 48, 50–53, 57–59
The Changeling: 103–105
Humor
Arms and the Man: 1, 5, 7, 9, 10, 17–19, 21–22, 24–25, 27
The Belle's Stratagem: 42, 48, 50–52, 57–61, 63
The Changeling: 79, 85, 88, 102

I Hate Hamlet: 186–189, 191
Imaginary Friends: 210–211
Topdog/Underdog: 276, 278, 280, 289, 291
Hypocrisy of War
For Services Rendered: 158

I

Idealism
Arms and the Man: 1, 7, 9, 25–26, 28
Idealism Versus Realism
Arms and the Man: 7
Identity
Fires in the Mirror: 144
Topdog/Underdog: 287
Ignorance
The Belle's Stratagem: 52–53, 61–63
The Changeling: 93
Copenhagen: 133
Topdog/Underdog: 289
Illusion
Topdog/Underdog: 287
Imagery and Symbolism
Copenhagen: 109–110, 113, 116
Habitat: 174–176
Machinal: 233–234, 238
Off the Map: 263
Topdog/Underdog: 291–292
Imagination
Topdog/Underdog: 276–277, 280, 283–284, 287, 291
Insanity
The Belle's Stratagem: 32, 37
The Changeling: 79–81, 84, 86–88
Machinal: 241–243
Insecurity
Topdog/Underdog: 294–295
Inter-Community Relations
Fires in the Mirror: 143
Irony
Arms and the Man: 15–16, 21, 23
The Changeling: 84, 86, 96, 98–99, 101–105
For Services Rendered: 165–166

J

Jealousy
The Belle's Stratagem: 37
Judaism
The Belle's Stratagem: 42–44, 49–50
Copenhagen: 107, 109, 113–114
Fires in the Mirror: 137–139, 143, 145, 147–148, 151–153

K

Killers and Killing
The Cenci: 68, 72

The Changeling: 84, 86, 90, 103, 105
Fires in the Mirror: 137, 139, 145
The Laramie Project: 216, 219–220, 224–226, 228–229
Machinal: 233–234, 240, 249–252, 256, 258
Topdog/Underdog: 290, 297–298
Kindness
Arms and the Man: 17–18, 20, 22–24
The Belle's Stratagem: 53, 57, 59
Machinal: 250, 252
Knowledge
Copenhagen: 109–110, 112, 121–124, 126–128, 130–132, 134
Machinal: 247

L

Landscape
The Laramie Project: 222–223
Law and Order
The Cenci: 68, 71, 74
The Changeling: 98, 100–103
Fires in the Mirror: 139, 143, 145
The Laramie Project: 213, 216, 219, 221–222, 224, 228–229
Machinal: 234, 238–240, 248–252, 254, 256–258
Limitations and Opportunities
For Services Rendered: 162–163
Love and Passion
Arms and the Man: 1, 3–4, 6–7, 13–17, 19–24, 26–28
The Belle's Stratagem: 29, 31–32, 36–42, 44, 46, 48–50, 52–64
The Changeling: 79–82, 84–87, 91–96, 98–106
For Services Rendered: 156–157, 159
Habitat: 167–169, 171–172, 174–176
I Hate Hamlet: 181–182, 184–185, 188–190
Imaginary Friends: 197, 199, 201
Machinal: 231, 233–234, 238–252, 254–258
Off the Map: 260, 262–263, 266–267, 269
Topdog/Underdog: 275–276, 278, 283, 288
Loyalty
The Belle's Stratagem: 31, 36, 38
Copenhagen: 132–133
Fires in the Mirror: 150–151

M

Marriage
The Belle's Stratagem: 29, 31–32, 36–37, 40–41, 50–52, 54, 56–64